The *Encyclopédie*

Madame de Pompadour *by La Tour, with a volume of the* Encyclopédie *in the background*

# The *Encyclopédie*

## John Lough

*Professor of French in the*
*University of Durham*

Longman

LONGMAN GROUP LIMITED
London
Associated companies, branches and representatives throughout the world

First published 1971

ISBN 0 582 31377 5


Printed in Great Britain by William Clowes & Sons, Limited,
London, Beccles and Colchester

# Preface

Since there are no doubt several ways of writing a general work on the *Encyclopédie* which would be of interest to students of eighteenth-century French thought, it may be useful to state at the outset the principles on which this attempt to fill a well-known gap is based. Such readers will expect to find an account of the origins of the work, of the long struggle for its publication, and of those who contributed or subscribed to it. These topics are dealt with first in three fairly short chapters. What they will mainly seek, however, is an examination of the place of the work in the thought of the age; this is accordingly the subject of the six longer chapters which follow. The first of these examines the question as to how far the *Encyclopédie* was intended as a work of reference and how far as a vehicle for propaganda for the ideas of the *philosophes*. Contemporary critics of the work have a chapter to themselves; to understand the meaning of its underlying ideas it is essential to see how it appeared to men of that age. Hostile as most of these reactions were, they none the less help to make clearer the significance of the *Encyclopédie*. Finally there comes a group of four substantial chapters—the longest in the book—which are given up to a study of the ideas on philosophy, religion, politics and society which are to be found in the *Encyclopédie*.

In planning these four key chapters a choice had to be made between offering a fairly general discussion of the ideas in question and attempting to offer the reader, by means of a substantial amount of quotation, a firsthand view of the outlook of the contributors. If after considerable hesitation the second path was chosen, it was primarily because, given the enormous size of the

*Encyclopédie*, years of study of its pages are necessary before one can extract from it (often from the most unlikely places) the true views of Diderot and his more radical contributors. To quotations from a great number of articles from the *Encyclopédie* are added further quotations from the writings of contemporary critics. There is again good reason for adopting this method of exposition; if the reader is to understand the true meaning of many of the articles *in their eighteenth-century context*, it is often necessary to let them see how Diderot's contemporaries interpreted them. Only thus can the clash of ideas which took place as its successive volumes made their appearance in the 1750s and 1760s be made to stand out.

The difficulties of producing a book of this kind have become more and more obvious to the writer with the passing of the years since he first embarked upon it. Among all manner of practical difficulties that of selecting and arranging the material has proved one of the most troublesome. The greatest of all is one which might have been foreseen from the start: that to write a good book on an encyclopedia one needs an encyclopedic knowledge. The lack of it has certainly proved a serious handicap.

However, over thirty years' acquaintance with the *Encyclopédie* and a detailed examination of a fair number of the problems which a study of its pages throws up may perhaps be held to compensate in some measure for this deficiency. In embarking on such an enterprise one can also draw upon the numerous publications on the subject which have appeared in many countries since 1945. Here my greatest debt is to the writing of my Montpellier colleague, Professor Jacques Proust. Our researches, carried on for a long time in complete independence, have not always led us to the same conclusions; but I have derived from his books and articles on the *Encyclopédie* more than I can say.

*Durham*                                                              J.L.
*July 1969*

# Contents

# Illustrations

# Abbreviations

| | |
|---|---|
| *AL* | *Année littéraire*, Paris, 1754–90. |
| AT | Diderot, *Œuvres complètes*, ed. J. Assézat and M. Tourneux, Paris, 1875–77, 20 vols. |
| Best. | Voltaire, *Correspondence*, ed. Theodore Besterman, Geneva, 1953–66, 107 vols. |
| *Corr. litt.* | F. M. Grimm, ed., *Correspondance littéraire, philosophique et critique*, ed. M. Tourneux, Paris, 1877–82, 16 vols. |
| *Essays* | J. Lough, *Essays on the Encyclopédie of Diderot and d'Alembert*, Oxford University Press, 1968. |
| Gordon and Torrey | D. H. Gordon and N. L. Torrey, *The Censoring of Diderot's Encyclopédie and the Re-established Text*, New York, 1947. |
| Leigh | J. J. Rousseau, *Correspondance complète*, ed. R. A. Leigh, Geneva, 1965– (in course of publication). |
| May | L. P. May, 'Documents nouveaux sur l'*Encyclopédie*. L'histoire et les sources de l'*Encyclopédie*, d'après le registre de délibérations et de comptes des éditeurs, et un mémoire inédit', *Revue de Synthèse*, 1938. |
| *PL* | A. Chaumeix, *Préjugés légitimes contre L'Encyclopédie et Essai de réfutation de cet ouvrage*, Brussels-Paris, 1758–59, 8 vols. |
| *RV* | *La Religion vengée ou Réfutation des auteurs impies*, Paris, 1757–63. |

Roth                          Diderot, *Correspondance*, ed. G. Roth,
                              Paris, 1955– (in course of publication).

*References to the 'Encyclopédie'*
The titles of articles in the *Encyclopédie* are given in small capitals;
those preceded by an asterisk (e.g. *DROIT NATUREL) were furnished
by Diderot in his capacity as editor. References are given by
volume, page and column, thus [II.364a]; for the article
*ENCYCLOPÉDIE, which is foliated, not paginated, the recto or
verso is indicated, e.g. [V.66r/a]. Volume numbers of other works
cited are given in small roman numerals, in round brackets when
in text, e.g. (iv.26).

# Chapter 1

# Origins

The dust of the controversy stirred up by the appearance of the *Encyclopédie* between 1751 and 1772 in seventeen folio volumes of text and eleven of plates has not altogether settled even after two centuries. To assess its originality in the narrow technical sense by placing it among similar works of reference produced in the Europe of its day is no easy task as it involves comparisons with a variety of works in several different languages. Even more complex is the problem of assessing the place of so vast a compilation in the history of the French Enlightenment and its influence in France and abroad.

Its very bulk has been and remains a great obstacle to serious study of the *Encyclopédie*. A close reading of its large, double-columned pages continues to offer surprises, since passages reflecting the outlook of the Enlightenment are hidden away in the most unlikely places; and it is not easy to grasp in its entirety a work which by its very nature covers almost every conceivable topic from grammar to gardening, mathematics to cookery, theology to physics, medicine to technology, and which hops from one field to another according to the accidents of alphabetical order. In the past studies of this bulky work have often been based on an amazingly small selection of articles which were made to bear the weight of sweeping generalizations about both the significance and the influence of the whole enterprise.

In recent decades the work of scholars drawn from a variety of countries has brought us considerably nearer to a proper understanding of the *Encyclopédie* both as a work of reference and as a vehicle for the outlook of the Enlightenment. It is at last becoming possible to see the work in perspective against the background of its age and to assess the part which it played in the battle of ideas which preceded the French Revolution and at the same time to know in considerable detail what its contributors, famous or obscure, poured forth in tens of thousands of articles, signed or unsigned. A work of synthesis could still be held to be premature in the sense that the *Encyclopédie* is far from having yielded up all the secrets of its composition and publication; fresh discoveries will no doubt compel us to modify our ideas about its contents and their significance. None the less, thanks to an international effort by scholars in recent decades, it is unlikely that what is now known of the work and its history will be seriously modified by future research.

## Earlier reference works

Diderot's article *ENCYCLOPÉDIE begins with the etymology of the word and then goes on to define the aim of such a work:

Ce mot signifie *enchaînement de connaissances*; il est composé de la pré-position grecque ἐν, *en*, et des substantifs χύχλος, *cercle*, et παιδεῖα, *connaissance*.

En effet, le but d'une *Encyclopédie* est de rassembler les connaissances éparses sur la surface de la terre, d'en exposer le système général aux hommes avec qui nous vivons, et de le transmettre aux hommes qui viendront après nous, afin que les travaux des siècles passés n'aient pas été des travaux inutiles pour les siècles qui succéderont, que nos neveux, devenant plus instruits, deviennent en même temps plus vertueux et plus heureux, et que nous ne mourions pas sans avoir bien mérité du genre humain.

How original was the production of such a large scale work of reference in the middle of the eighteenth century? One may, of course, trace back to ancient Greece and China the history of the encyclopedia in its more primitive forms.[1] Of more immediate concern to the student of the *Encyclopédie* is to know what comparable works were available in the 1740s when the enterprise started up. The prospectus published by Diderot in 1750 casts some light on this question; what he offered potential subscribers was an

[1] See R. Collison, *Encyclopaedias: their history throughout the ages*, London, 1964.

encyclopedia or dictionary of arts and sciences 'recueilli des meilleurs auteurs et particulièrement des dictionnaires anglais de Chambers, d'Harris, de Dyche, etc.' At the very outset the debt of the *Encyclopédie* to these English works of reference was thus freely acknowledged.

It is, however, difficult to see that the *Encyclopédie* can have owed much to Thomas Dyche's posthumous work (completed by William Pardon), *A New General English Dictionary*, which first appeared in 1735 and had reached a third edition by 1740; it consists of one modest octavo volume, noticeably smaller than the *Concise Oxford Dictionary*. John Harris's *Lexicon Technicum; or an Universal English Dictionary of Arts and Sciences* was a much more substantial work. Its two folio volumes were published between 1704 and 1710; a fifth edition was published posthumously in 1736. By far the most important of the works mentioned by Diderot in his prospectus was Ephraim Chambers's *Cyclopaedia or an Universal Dictionary of Arts and Sciences* which was first published in 1728 in two large folio volumes, illustrated with a certain number of plates. It was this work which really gave the impetus for the production of Diderot's *Encyclopédie* since, to begin with, the plan had been to publish an enlarged translation of it. By 1741 Chambers's *Cyclopaedia* had reached a fourth edition; and after his death in 1740 a *Supplement* in two folio volumes was produced by other hands and finally appeared in 1753—in time to be purchased by the publishers of the *Encyclopédie* and to be drawn on occasionally by various contributors to the volumes which appeared after that date.

Even if the encyclopedia for which Diderot solicited subscriptions in 1750 had been confined to the promised ten volumes, including two of plates, it would still have been on a vastly greater scale than any of these English works. What is more, France too had a number of reference works of this smaller size on which an editor or contributor could draw. Indeed a writer like Chambers obviously made use of French as well as English sources as he made perfectly plain when he wrote in his preface:

I come like an heir to a large patrimony, gradually raised by the industry and endeavours of a long race of ancestors. What the French and Italian academies, the Abbé Furetière, the editors of Trévoux, Savary, Chauvin, Harris, Wolfius and others have done, has been subservient to my purpose.

The end of the seventeenth century had seen the appearance of a number of substantial French dictionaries. Antoine Furetière's *Dictionnaire universel* had appeared posthumously in three folio volumes in 1690, four years before the much more narrowly conceived *Dictionnaire* produced by the French Academy from which he had been expelled on a charge of plagiarism. In 1694 there also appeared the two folio volumes of Thomas Corneille's *Dictionnaire des arts et des sciences* which was intended as a supplement to the Academy's dictionary. Both these works were frequently reprinted in the following century. To the same decade belong the two folio volumes of Pierre Bayle's *Dictionnaire historique et critique* which were to weigh down many library shelves for the next century and more. Earlier still, in 1674, there had appeared the first edition of another famous work of reference, Louis Moreri's *Le Grand dictionnaire historique, ou le mélange curieux de l'histoire sainte et profane*. Beginning as a one volume folio work, it reached its eighth edition in 1698; by its eighteenth edition, published in 1740, it had been enlarged to eight folio volumes.

Another standard work of reference in eighteenth-century France was the so-called *Dictionnaire de Trévoux* (the opening words of its full title were *Dictionnaire universel français et latin . . .*). This Jesuit production, which first appeared in 1704, reached its sixth edition, in seven folio volumes, in 1752. Despite the attempts of some scholars to throw doubt on the story, there is no question that the Jesuits were seriously alarmed by the threat to their work which the *Encyclopédie* presented, and would dearly have liked to take over the whole enterprise when it ran into trouble with the authorities early in its career.

Reference works of the encyclopedia type were thus not lacking in France in the middle of the eighteenth century when Diderot and d'Alembert launched their enterprise. Yet even leaving aside for the moment the very different spirit which infused their undertaking, it is obvious that at that date neither England nor France had yet seen a reference work on so vast a scale. The first edition of the *Encyclopaedia Britannica* was not produced until some years after the complete text of the *Encyclopédie* had been published. It appeared in sixpenny parts between 1768 and 1771. Not only did its editors acknowledge their debt to what they called 'Le Grand Encyclopédie'; the first edition of the work was very modest in scale, consisting of only three quarto volumes. While the second edition (1777–84) had swollen to ten quarto volumes and the third (1788–97) to twenty, it was not until the publication of *The Cyclopaedia or Universal Dictionary of Arts, Sciences and Literature* of Abraham Rees which appeared in forty-five quarto volumes between 1802 and 1820 that a work on such a scale as the *Encyclopédie* made its appearance on this side of the Channel.

It is curious, however, that most studies of the *Encyclopédie* pay little or no attention to a massive German reference work which appeared complete in sixty-four folio volumes just before the first volume of the rival French work came from the press. This was the *Grosses vollständiges Universal-Lexicon aller Wissenschaften und Künste*, published in Halle and Leipzig by a bookseller named Johann Heinrich Zedler between 1732 and 1750. This massive work was further extended by the publication of a supplement which overlapped with the appearance of the *Encyclopédie* itself, as four volumes covering A–CAQ were brought out between 1752 and 1754. Whether or not the *Encyclopédie* owes anything to this vast work, completed before its first volume saw the light of day, still remains to be investigated. Even if the fact that very few of the contributors to the French work knew German makes any significant debt appear unlikely,[1] the existence of this large work ought not to be left entirely out of account when we consider the place of the *Encyclopédie* among the reference works available in eighteenth-century Europe.

An interest in science and, above all, in technology was widespread in Western Europe by the 1740s and the idea of a large new reference work bringing together information on these and other forms of knowledge was very much in the air. In 1737 the Jacobite writer, Andrew Michael Ramsay, delivered to a masonic lodge in Paris a speech in which there occurs the well-known passage:

Ainsi l'ordre exige de chacun de vous de contribuer par sa protection, par sa libéralité ou par son travail à un vaste ouvrage auquel nulle académie et nulle université ne peuvent suffire, parce que, toutes les sociétés parti-

---

[1] Because of his German birth Baron d'Holbach was the contributor most likely to have made use of Zedler in the large number of articles which he wrote for the *Encyclopédie*; but he does not seem to have had a copy of the *Universal-Lexicon* among the German books in his library. In the article *ENCYCLOPÉDIE [V.645r/b], in speaking of a possible second edition, Diderot writes: 'Ce serait un oubli inexcusable que de ne pas se procurer la grande *Encyclopédie allemande* . . .'

culières étant composées d'un très petit nombre d'hommes, leur travail
ne peut pas embrasser un objet aussi immense.

Tous les grands maîtres en Allemagne, en Angleterre, en Italie et par
toute l'Europe exhortent tous les savants et tous les artistes de la con-
fraternité de s'unir pour fournir les matériaux d'un dictionnaire universel
de tous les arts libéraux et de toutes les sciences utiles, la théologie et la
politique seules exceptées. On a déjà commencé l'ouvrage à Londres,
mais par la réunion de nos confrères on pourra le porter à sa perfection en
peu d'années. On y expliquera non seulement le mot technique et son
étymologie, mais on donnera encore l'histoire de la science et de l'art, ses
grands principes et la manière d'y travailler. De cette façon on réunira les
lumières de toutes les nations dans un seul ouvrage qui sera comme un
magasin général et une bibliothèque universelle de ce qu'il y a de beau, de
grand, de lumineux, de solide et d'utile dans toutes les sciences naturelles
et dans tous les arts nobles. Cet ouvrage augmentera dans chaque siècle
selon l'augmentation des lumières, répandra une noble émulation avec le
goût des belles-lettres et des beaux-arts dans toute l'Europe.[1]

Not only was the text of this speech rapidly printed and several
times republished, but it was also sent in advance to Cardinal
Fleury, who was then virtually the prime minister of France. Four
years later Ramsay had developed his plan a little further; he told a
German visitor that, reckoning that there were 3,000 freemasons in
Europe, this and other projects could be adequately financed if they
each subscribed 10 louis (roughly equivalent to £10 *in English
money of the time*). He also aimed to publish the work in French.[2]

Much time has been wasted in attempting to draw from this
speech the inference that from the very beginning the *Encyclopédie*
was a masonic enterprise. For all sorts of reasons this appears to be
an extremely improbable hypothesis, if only because neither the
publishers nor the editors nor any significant number of the contributors can be shown to have been freemasons.[3] Nor did Ramsay's project coincide completely with that of Diderot and
d'Alembert; they certainly excluded neither theology nor politics
from their encyclopedia. But taken for what it is—as evidence of
the way in which men's minds were prepared for a large undertaking of this kind (and one which incidentally was being carried

---

[1] The text of this speech was first published in *Lettres de M. de Voltaire, avec plusieurs pièces de différents auteurs*, The
Hague, 1738, pp. 60–2.
[2] See A. F. Büsching, *Beiträge zu der Lebensgeschichte denkwürdiger Personen*, Halle, 1783–86, 6 vols, iii, 328.
[3] See Dr R. Shackleton, 'The *Encyclopédie* and Freemasonry' in *The Age of Enlightenment. Studies presented to
Theodore Besterman*, Edinburgh, 1967, pp. 223–37.

out after a fashion by Zedler and his associates at that very moment)
—the document is an interesting one.

Ramsay's reference to the start which had been made in London
on this task was presumably to Chambers's *Cyclopaedia*. The success of this work appears to have attracted the attention of various
continental publishers. When the first volume of the *Encyclopédie*
appeared in 1751, the Dutch publisher Néaulme claimed that as
soon as Chambers was published, he had had the idea of producing
a French version of it in a revised and enlarged form.[1] Indeed a
writer in the *Gentleman's Magazine* in 1785[2] claimed that, during a
stay which Chambers made in Paris shortly before his death in
1740, 'he received an intimation that if he would publish a new
edition there and dedicate it to Louis the Fifteenth, he would be
liberally rewarded'. However, it was only in 1745, seventeen years
after the appearance of the first edition of the *Cyclopaedia*, that a
prospectus appeared in Paris for a work in five folio volumes
entitled *Encyclopédie, ou Dictionnaire universel des arts et des sciences,
. . . traduit de l'anglais d'Ephraïm Chambers . . .*[3]

## Le Breton, Mills and Sellius

The title-page of this prospectus bore the imprint of the printer
and publisher, André François Le Breton, who for the best part of
thirty years was to have the principal share in this commercial
venture. According to his account of the matter[4] the idea of a
translation was first laid before him in January 1745 by a certain
Gottfried Sell (or Sellius) from Dantzig who claimed to be acting
in association with an Englishman named John Mills, 'homme
riche et opulent', who would pay for the printing of the work as
well as revising the translation. Le Breton seems to have found
nothing odd in the idea of what d'Alembert was later to describe
sarcastically as 'la traduction française de Chambers entreprise par
un *Anglais* aidé d'un *Allemand*'.[5]

---

[1] F. Venturi, 'Le Origini dell'Enciclopedia in Inghilterra', *Itinerari*, 1954, p. 201.
[2] September, p. 672. The same periodical also printed three letters written by Chambers during his stay in France in 1738–39, April 1787 (pp. 314–17) and May (pp. 381–2).
[3] The title-page is reproduced in Gordon and Torrey, *The Censoring of Diderot's Encyclopédie and the Re-established Text* (plate facing p. 10).
[4] *Mémoire pour André-François Le Breton, Libraire et imprimeur ordinaire du Roi . . . contre le sieur Jean Mills, se disant gentilhomme anglais,* Paris, 1745 (Bibliothèque Nationale, 4° Fm.18251), p. 2.
[5] *Encyclopédie,* III, v.

Of these two men Sellius was the older and by far the better known.[1] Born probably in 1704, he had studied at the universities of Marburg and Leyden, where in 1730 he was awarded the degree of doctor of laws. From there he moved to Utrecht, where he is said to have married a wealthy heiress and to have acquired a handsome library, a collection of pictures and a physics laboratory. In 1733 he published a book in elegant Latin on the teredo which was ravaging the ships and dykes of Holland, and in the same year he was elected a fellow of the Royal Society. He was also made a member of the Imperial Academy of the *Naturae Curiosorum*. In 1735 he returned to Germany where he was appointed to a chair of law at Göttingen. However, after a year he moved to another chair at Halle where he also acquired the title of 'königlicher Hofrat'. There he counted among his assiduous students the young Winckelmann whose *Geschichte der Kunst des Altertums* he was to translate into French some thirty years later. Even before he moved to Halle he was apparently in a bad way financially; he was compelled to sell his library (there is a copy of the catalogue, dated 'Leipzig, 1737' in the British Museum) and finally to flee from his creditors. His financial difficulties caused strange rumours to circulate about him; many years later (in 1755) his great admirer, Winckelmann, picked up a rumour that he had been hanged for forging bills of exchange.

By this date Sellius, however, had been in France for over a decade. Down to his death in 1767 he was to translate into French a considerable number of works, sometimes in collaboration, from a variety of tongues—English and Dutch as well as German. The sad end of this curious figure was recorded in Bachaumont's *Mémoires secrets* in July 1767: '*Sellius*, ce savant en *us*, connu par de très grands ouvrages et par sa vaste érudition, mais surtout par le premier projet qu'il apporta en France en 1743 de l'*Encyclopédie*, vient de mourir à Charenton misérable et fol.'[2] The verdict of a contemporary on his translations is none too favourable: '. . . Quoiqu'il sût assez bien notre langue, il traduisait sans se gêner, à course de plume, se montrant plus attentif à rendre la lettre de son

---

[1] For fuller details on the early history of the *Encyclopédie* see my article 'Le Breton, Mills et Sellius', *Dix-huitième Siècle*, 1969, 277–97.

[2] *Mémoires secrets pour servir à l'histoire de la République des Lettres en France de 1762 jusqu'à nos jours*, London, 1777–89, 36 vols, iii, 198.

auteur ou le génie de sa langue qu'à le faire bien parler français, ce qui le rendait obscur.'[1] Though a man of undoubted gifts and wide interests (the current edition of the *Encyclopaedia Britannica* records the fact that he was the first person to show that the teredo is a bivalve mollusc) he had a decidedly odd career and was never what one could describe as a first-class translator.

Less is known about the other partner in the original enterprise, John Mills, a younger man who was to achieve a modest reputation as a writer on agriculture in the 1760s. From the fact that in 1786 he gave his age as nearly seventy we may deduce that he was about a dozen years younger than Sellius and was twenty-nine or thirty in 1745. He would appear to have spent a considerable part of his early life in France, though he was not born there. In 1741 he was in London and had plans for going to Jamaica, but 'having met with something more advantageous which engages me to stay in England', he gave up the idea.[2] In 1743 we find him back in Paris; indeed, if he can be identified with the 'Jean Mills, gentil-homme anglais' whose child was baptized on 27 April 1742, he must have returned there even sooner (a second child was born to the same John Mills and his French wife in May 1743). He seems to have left Paris soon after 1745, but he only really emerges from the shadows between 1762 and 1776 when he translated from French or Latin or else himself compiled a series of works on agriculture. The best known of these was *A New and Complete System of Practical Husbandry,* the five volumes of which appeared between 1762 and 1765. These writings earn for him a modest place in books on eighteenth-century writers on agriculture.[3] In 1766 he was elected to the fellowship of the Royal Society—some thirty years after his one time associate, Sellius—one of his sponsors being Benjamin Franklin. He was also made a member of the Mannheim Academy of Sciences and of the Royal Societies of Agriculture of Paris and Rouen. The date of his death is not known.

An agreement was made between Le Breton and the two translators. Le Breton was to take out in his own name a *privilège*—a licence to print and publish the work—a necessary formality under the Ancien Régime. The *privilège*, dated 25 February 1745,

---

[1] Meusnier de Querlon, quoted in the article on Sellius in the *Biographie Michaud*.
[2] Venturi, *Itinerari*, 1954, p. 202.
[3] See G. E. Fussell, *More Old English Farming Books from Tull to the Board of Agriculture*, London, 1950, pp. 47–50.

was sealed on 26 March and duly registered on 13 April.[1] The
prospectus was summarized at some length in the *Journal des
Savants*,[2] but praise was heaped on Mills by the Jesuit *Journal de
Trévoux*.[3] The *Mercure*[4] devoted yet more space to the enterprise
and even inserted the following paragraph on the English
translator:

A l'égard de la traduction elle est l'ouvrage de M. Mills, savant anglais qui
a été élevé en France, & à qui les deux langues sont devenues maternelles.
Il s'est associé dans son travail plusieurs personnes savantes et zélées pour
l'avancement des lettres. C'est le même M. Mills qui, non content des
soins qu'il s'est donnés pour cet ouvrage, a généreusement consacré sa
fortune à soutenir les frais considérables de cette entreprise et qui est seul
propriétaire du privilège. (p. 87)

Two letters of Mills, written in May and June 1745 to the Rev.
Thomas Birch, a historian who became a secretary of the Royal
Society and who was later to be one of Mills's sponsors, also give a
glowing account of the enterprise. Though they contain no mention of either Sellius or Le Breton, Mills claims that he is being
assisted 'by several Academicians, and by most of the Learned here,
as M. de Réaumur, l'abbé Pluche, M. de Jussieu, M. Nicole,
M. d'Alembert, M. de Fouchy, Secretary of the Royal Academy of
Sciences, and many others'.[5] How far this account of the situation
can be accepted as accurate it is not easy to say. It is disquieting to
find in two consecutive sentences of the same letter the statement
that, once the *privilège* had been obtained, 'I . . . immediately set to
work' and 'I have a very great part of it translated'. Moreover,
when he had fallen out with Le Breton, he even declared that he
had been working on the enterprise for two years 'sans discon-
tinuation et avec succès'. What is more, one French contemporary,
otherwise favourably disposed towards him, declares bluntly: 'Il
savait médiocrement notre langue', a serious drawback, particularly when he was translating from English into French.

The breach between Mills and Le Breton finally came on 7
August. Mills's version of the affair is contained in a document
entitled *Sommaire pour le sieur Jean Mills, gentilhomme anglais,*

[1] Bibliothèque Nationale, Ms. Fr. 21958, p. 374.     [2] March 1745, pp. 185–7.
[3] May 1745, pp. 934–9.     [4] June 1745, Ière partie, pp. 83–107.
[5] Venturi, *Itinerari*, 1954, pp. 217–18.

*contre le sieur Le Breton, libraire-imprimeur à Paris.*[1] This relates how on 7 August he wrote to Le Breton asking for some of the money received from the subscriptions in return for what he had already expended on the translation. It is then alleged that Le Breton called at his flat several times on that day and finally about 9 o'clock in the evening, when Mills was on his own, he came and made a scene: 'Le sieur Le Breton, transporté de colère, se répandit en emportements et violences; et non content des termes injurieux qu'il proféra contre le sieur Mills, il lui porta un coup de poing dans l'estomac, et deux coups de canne sur la tête, dont il fut terrassé.' To these charges of assault and battery Le Breton retorted in his *Mémoire* that he had acted purely in self-defence when Mills had drawn his sword.

In his reply Le Breton commented sarcastically on the puff which Mills had had inserted in the *Mercure*:

Le titre de *savant* dont Mills se décore, ne lui est pas acquis; il n'est âgé que de 29 à 30 ans; sa fonction à Paris est d'être *un des commis* de M. le Chevalier Lambert, banquier.[2] Le traité qu'il a fait avec Sellius, prouve qu'il n'était pas chargé de la traduction, qu'elle n'était pas même commencée le 17 février 1745, et qu'il lui était libre de ne travailler qu'autant que ses occupations lui permettraient; que les personnes savantes et zélées pour l'avancement des lettres étaient toutes réunies en la personne de Sellius; et on verra par ce qui sera dit dans un instant qu'il n'a point consacré sa fortune à soutenir des frais considérables, mais qu'il en voulait et aux souscripteurs et à la fortune du sieur Le Breton.

. . . La traduction faite par Sellius de la préface et des quatre articles de l'ouvrage de Chambers qui devaient entrer dans le *Prospectus*, fut trouvée si défectueuse quant à la traduction et si peu correcte quant à la diction française, de l'aveu même de Mills, qu'il fut arrêté entre lui et le sieur Le Breton qu'ils auraient recours à d'autres traducteurs pour le corps de l'ouvrage. C'était là cependant une occasion favorable au sieur Mills de faire paraître sa science en donnant un échantillon de la traduction à laquelle il travaillait depuis deux ans, comme il a la hardiesse de l'avancer dans son mémoire. (pp. 5–6)

It was certainly an odd situation.

---

[1] Neither the Bibliothèque Nationale nor the Archives Nationales can produce a copy of this document; it was reproduced—whether accurately or in its entirety we do not know—in an appendix to the *Mémoire pour Pierre-Joseph François Luneau de Boisjermain, Souscripteur de l'Encyclopédie*, Paris, 1771, pp. 8–9.

[2] Jean François Lambert, later naturalized (see H. Lüthy, *La Banque protestante en France de la Révocation de l'Édit de Nantes à la Révolution*, Paris, 1959–61, 2 vols, ii, 320).

Indeed, Le Breton alleges, Mills did not even have a copy of Chambers available: ' Le sieur Mills a promis d'abord de faire venir d'Angleterre deux exemplaires du dictionnaire de Chambers; il n'a point tenu parole. Ces deux exemplaires ne sont pas encore arrivés, et il a fallu emprunter à Paris deux exemplaires pour commencer la traduction' (p. 4). Without wearying the reader with a recital of all the technical detail about agreements and financial transactions with which Le Breton's *Mémoire* is filled, it is sufficient to quote the text of the pressing letter which Mills wrote to him on 7 August:

Quand la fortune en veut à quelqu'un, on serait quitte à trop bon marché, si on n'avait qu'un seul malheur à essuyer. Elle n'a jamais eu de pareils ménagements pour moi, car de tout côté elle me maltraite. Voici, me direz-vous, un début bien sérieux; je l'avoue, il répond au sujet de ma lettre. Je ne puis, Monsieur, me passer ce matin de cinquante louis d'or[1] pour une affaire pressante et de conséquence pour moi. Je n'ai pas voulu vous les demander hier, croyant les trouver chez des personnes qui me doivent; mais je cours inutilement depuis six heures au matin, sans être plus avancé que quand je suis sorti de chez moi. Ainsi je suis obligé d'envoyer cette lettre que M. Renaud, mon secrétaire, vous remettra, comptant que vous ne ferez pas difficulté de m'envoyer par lui un sac de 1200 liv. dont il vous donnera quittance pour moi que je tiendrai bonne et valable; et vous en tiendrai compte sur les 1000 liv. que j'ai payées à M. Sellius pour travailler au Chambers et les 300 et tant de livres que j'ai déboursées suivant le compte que je vous ai donné; vous avez entre vos mains les quittances de M. Sellius.[2] Vous me ferez, monsieur, un grand plaisir en m'envoyant cet argent par le porteur; et même si vous y ajoutiez trois ou quatre cents livres de plus, je vous en serais très obligé, car il faut que je paie avant midi les 1200 liv. et je resterai sans argent si vous n'avez la bonté d'y remédier, en quoi vous ne risquez rien, ayant plus de traduction faite que la valeur de ce surplus que je vous demande. L'un et l'autre me sont indispensablement nécessaires, mais je ne vous aurais demandé à cette heure ni l'un ni l'autre si j'avais pu trouver de l'argent ailleurs. J'attends de vous, monsieur, cette preuve de l'amitié que vous m'avez si souvent promise, et vous assure qu'il n'y en a pas de plus parfaite que celle que vous porte sincèrement, monsieur, votre très humble et très obéissant serviteur. *Signé*, Mills. (pp. 11–12)

This document blatantly contradicts Mills's claim that he had

---

[1] Some £50 in English money of that time.
[2] Le Breton alleges that both these sums were for fictitious payments.

devoted his fortune to producing a translation of Chambers. It is curious that similar 'hard luck stories' fill two letters, written some forty years later, in 1783 and 1786, and preserved today in the Archives of the Royal Society. By the time he wrote the second he was fifteen years in arrears with his subscription and the Society was threatening him with a debtors' prison. One gets the impression that Le Breton's account of his relations with Mills and Sellius is broadly correct and that they were a pair of impecunious adventurers.

According to Le Breton[1] the Chancellor, d'Aguesseau, within whose province all matters concerning the book trade lay, personally examined the *privilège* and the various agreements between him and the two 'translators'. The result was an *arrêt du Conseil*, issued on 28 August from Mélin in the Austrian Netherlands where Louis XV was with his victorious armies, cancelling the *privilège* registered in Le Breton's name on 13 April. Le Breton was evidently now determined to proceed with the project on his own account, though before applying to the Chancellor for a new *privilège*, he thought it advisable to share the risks of the undertaking with other publishers. On 18 October he signed an agreement with Briasson, Durand and David whereby he kept a half share in the enterprise, while the others were each partners for one-sixth. This agreement is to be found in the miraculously preserved fragment of the papers of this publishing venture, the so-called *Journal A,* which was discovered in the Archives Nationales in 1938 by Monsieur Louis Philippe May.[2] It makes clear that what was intended was not simply a translation of Chambers, but a revised and enlarged work. It is noteworthy that Harris's *Lexicon technicum* is also mentioned in the title of the publishers' *Livre des délibérations* which opens with the text of their agreement.

On 14 November it was further agreed that Le Breton would undertake the printing of the work. The number of copies was fixed at 1625 (75 of them with wide margins); this figure shows that at this stage the publishers took a relatively cautious view of the prospects of the work. They were to end, as we shall see, by printing more than twice that number.

[1] *Mémoire*, p. 19.
[2] Archives Nationales U 1051. See L. P. May, 'Histoire et sources de l'*Encyclopédie*', *Revue de Synthèse*, 1938. A copy of the agreement slightly different from the text in the *Journal A*, is to be found in the Bibliothèque Nationale (Nouvelles acquisitions françaises 3347, ff. 196–8).

The next step was to obtain a new *privilège*. To enable this to be taken out the *arrêt du Conseil* of 28 August had been annulled on the same day as the agreement between Le Breton and his partners had been signed.[1] On 21 January 1746 Le Breton was granted a fresh *privilège* (registered on 8 February)[2] in which the word *Encyclopédie*, which was not used in the earlier licence, makes its appearance, and on 31 January he duly ceded half of it to his three partners.

The accounts preserved in the *Journal A* show some signs of activity even before the end of 1745. The second item in the expenditure section concerns a payment of 105 livres to d'Alembert on 17 December and the fourth, dated the 31st, shows that he received another 84 livres. Although his connection with the *Encyclopédie* was to be both less close and less long than that of Diderot who does not make his first appearance in the accounts until the following February, d'Alembert would seem to have been more actively engaged at this very early stage. Two figures from the past, Mills and Sellius, make an appearance in the opening pages of the accounts. The fifth item on the expenditure side, dated 14 January 1746, runs as follows:

> Payé à M. Miltz pour les ms. rachetés      600 l.
>
> Deux carrosses pour aller chez led. Miltz     5 l.
>
> A un dîner et plusieurs carrosses          33 l.

Whether Mills was invited to the dinner—and Sellius too—is not stated. Sellius's name actually occurs (for a payment of 400 livres) in the very first item of expenditure, in December 1745, and he continued to receive payments, amounting to another 300 livres in all, down to 21 May of the following year. As so often this fascinating document is tantalizingly brief and leaves a great deal to the reader's imagination.

## The search for a new editor

The third payment listed in December 1745 went to the Abbé de Gua de Malves, an eccentric character who for a time held a chair

---

[1] Bibliothèque Nationale, Ms. Fr. 21958, f.103.

[2] Bibliothèque Nationale, Ms. Fr. 21958, pp. 471–2. For reasons which are obscure Le Breton took out yet another *privilège* on 26 April 1748 (*ibid.*, pp. 828–9); there seems nothing new in this document which contains no reference to the licence granted in 1746.

of philosophy at the Collège de France and was both a member of the Academy of Sciences and a fellow of the Royal Society. On 27 June of the following year he signed an agreement with the publishers by which he undertook to act as editor of the *Encyclopédie*.[1] The agreement contains a curious clause which shows that the publishers were well aware of the financial chaos in which their editor lived; it is stipulated that while he is free to assign to others the payments due to him as the work progressed, the publishers would honour such assignations only if the appropriate manuscripts and plates had been handed over to them. Another clause shows that already at this date d'Alembert and Diderot were playing a considerable part in the undertaking. It reads: 'Que s'il se trouve dans le total de la traduction des articles qui au jugement de MM. d'Alembert et Diderot aient besoin d'être traduits de nouveau, les dits libraires seront chargés de les faire retraduire.' The Abbé's editorship was not to last much more than a year; his agreement was cancelled on 3 August 1747.

When he died in 1786 at the age of seventy-four he was the subject of an *éloge* by Condorcet at the Academy of Sciences. In this it was claimed that the Abbé changed the whole conception of the work:

Ce n'était plus une simple traduction augmentée, c'était un ouvrage nouveau, entrepris sur un plan plus vaste. Au lieu d'un dictionnaire élémentaire des parties des sciences les plus répandues, les plus usuelles, ouvrage utile en lui-même et qui nous manque, M. l'abbé de Gua entreprit de réunir dans un dépôt commun tout ce qui formait alors l'ensemble de nos connaissances.[2]

As Condorcet was a mere toddler when the Abbé was supposed to be editing the *Encyclopédie*, it would be unwise to accept this panegyrist's claim. Since we know so little about the early stages of the whole undertaking it is impossible to say whether the transformation of the work was due to the Abbé or to Diderot and d'Alembert.

Although payments to a variety of contributors continued to be made before and after the Abbé's departure, the *Encyclopédie* was without an editor between the cancelling of his agreement on 3 August 1747 and the appointment of his successors on 16 October. Unfortunately we do not possess the text of the new contract.

---

[1] See L. P. May, 'Documents nouveaux . . .', pp. 18–20.      [2] *Œuvres*, Paris, 1847–49, 12 vols, iii, 248.

Briasson simply records in *Journal A* on 19 October: 'Ce jour la compagnie assemblée a reconnu avoir traité le 16 du courant avec MM. d'Alembert et Diderot pour remplacer en qualité d'éditeurs M. l'Abbé de Gua . . .'

'Diderot. Toujours suivi de d'Alembert' noted Flaubert in his *Dictionnaire des idées reçues.* Yet if here the publishers follow an unusual order, the preponderant part which Diderot was expected to play is made quite clear by the payments offered to the two editors: 3,000 l. to d'Alembert as against 7,200 to Diderot. Time was to show that it was on Diderot that the main burden of the whole undertaking was to fall. It was not indeed until twenty-five years later, when he was a man of nearly sixty, that he was at last to secure release from it.

## Chapter 2

# The struggle for publication

### Diderot and d'Alembert

Of the two young editors who were appointed by Le Breton and his partners in 1747 d'Alembert was by far the better known. By the age of thirty he had already made a name for himself as a mathematician with his *Traité de dynamique*, published four years earlier, and in 1747 he brought out a second important work, his *Réflexions sur les causes générales des vents*. He was already a member of the Académie des Sciences and, despite his connections with the *Encyclopédie*, he was to be elected to the Académie Française in 1754. No such honours ever came the way of the principal editor; although four years older than d'Alembert at the time of his appointment, Diderot was still virtually unknown except, because of his dangerous thoughts, to his *curé* and the police. His career as a man of letters had begun with the hackwork of translation. It was no doubt his part in the French translation of Robert James's *Medicinal Dictionary*, published between 1746 and 1748 by Briasson, David and Durand, which had brought him into the parallel enterprise of an enlarged Chambers's *Cyclopaedia*. All he had so far published—anonymously—was a free translation of Shaftesbury's *Inquiry concerning Virtue and Merit* under the title of *Essai sur le mérite et la vertu* (1745) and his first independent work, the short, but explosive *Pensées Philosophiques* (1746).

The publishers' accounts for the period between October 1747 and June 1751 when the first volume of the *Encyclopédie* at last came out are much fuller and more detailed than those for later years. From them we can gain some idea of the work done in this period to prepare for the publication of the volumes of both text and plates, although the information they contain is at times enigmatic and in any case concerns only the small minority of contributors who actually received payment for their articles. In July 1749, just as things seemed to be going smoothly, the principal editor was hauled off by *lettre de cachet* to the royal prison of Vincennes, an event reflected in the publishers' accounts by the following entry: 'Pour frais de carrosse tant le matin que l'après-dîner pour solliciter pour M. Diderot, le 24e juillet 7 [livres] 7 [sous].'[1] The publication of the *Lettre sur les Aveugles* in the previous month was too much for the authorities who had had their eye on Diderot ever since the *Pensées Philosophiques* had been burnt by the hangman three years earlier.

The publishers were to spend a good deal more of their money both on trips to Vincennes and on visits to ministers and other high personages in the period between 24 July and 3 November which Diderot spent in prison. On the day of Diderot's arrest the publishers sent to the Comte d'Argenson, the minister responsible for Paris, to whom the work was eventually to be dedicated, a letter begging for his release as essential to the progress of the whole enterprise:

Nous prenons la liberté de nous mettre sous la protection de Votre Grandeur et de lui représenter les malheurs auxquels nous expose la détention de M. Diderot, conduit ce matin à Vincennes par ordre du Roi. C'est un homme de lettres d'un mérite et d'une probité reconnus ; nous l'avons chargé depuis près de cinq ans de l'édition d'un *Dictionnaire universel des sciences, des arts et métiers.* Cet ouvrage, qui nous coûtera au moins deux cent cinquante mille livres et pour lequel nous avons déjà avancé près de quatre-vingt mille livres, était sur le point d'être annoncé au public. La détention de M. Diderot, le seul homme de lettres que nous connaissions capable d'une aussi vaste entreprise et qui possède seul la clef de toute cette opération, peut entraîner notre ruine.[2]

If after a month Diderot was no longer confined in the keep at Vincennes, but was allowed the run of the whole château, work on the *Encyclopédie* was still held up, as d'Alembert explained on 19 September in a letter to Formey, one of the contributors:

La détention de M. Diderot est devenue beaucoup plus douce ; cependant elle dure encore et l'*Encyclopédie* est suspendue. Je n'ai jamais prétendu me

---

[1] May, p. 52.        [2] Bibliothèque de l'Arsenal, Archives de la Bastille 11671, f. 8.

mêler que de ce qui regarde la partie de mathématiques et d'astronomie physique ; je ne suis en état de faire que cela, et je ne prétends pas d'ailleurs me condamner pour six ans à l'ennui de 7 à 8 in-folio. Je compte que, dès que M. Diderot sera libre (et ce sera bientôt selon toutes les apparences) on travaillera au prospectus, et qu'on ne sera pas longtemps sans mettre sous presse.[1]

This account of the future progress of the work was to prove too optimistic. Not only was Diderot not released until early in November, but the distribution of the prospectus of the *Encyclopédie* did not begin until October of the following year.

## The ' Prospectus' and the publication of the first volume

The prospectus actually bears the date ' 1751 ' on the title-page. The business side of the undertaking was explained as follows:

*Conditions proposées aux souscripteurs*
Ce dictionnaire sera imprimé sur le même papier et avec les mêmes caractères que le présent projet. Il aura dix volumes in-folio, dont huit de matière, de deux cent quarante feuilles chacun ; et six cents planches en taille-douce, avec leur explication, qui formeront les tomes IX et X.

On ne sera admis à souscrire que jusqu'au premier mai 1751 ; et l'on payera en souscrivant . . . . . . . . . . . . . . . . . . . . . . . . . . . . . . . . . . . . . . . . . 60 liv.

| | | |
|---|---|---|
| En juin 1751 . . . . . . . . . . . . . . . . . | le premier volume | 36 liv. |
| En décembre suivant . . . . . . . . . . | le second volume | 24 |
| En juin 1752 . . . . . . . . . . . . . . . . . | le troisième volume | 24 |
| En décembre suivant . . . . . . . . . . | le quatrième volume | 24 |
| En juin 1753 . . . . . . . . . . . . . . . . . | le cinquième volume | 24 |
| En décembre suivant . . . . . . . . . . | le sixième volume | 24 |
| En juin 1754 . . . . . . . . . . . . . . . . . | le septième volume | 24 |
| En décembre suivant . . . . . . . . . . | le huitième volume, avec les six cents planches en taille-douce qui formeront les tomes IX et X | 40 |

Total . . . 280 liv.

Les souscripteurs sont priés de retirer les volumes à mesure qu'ils paraîtront, et tout l'ouvrage un an après la livraison du dernier volume. A

[1] J. H. S. Formey, *Souvenirs d'un Citoyen*, Berlin, 1789, 2 vols, ii, 365–6.

faute de quoi, ils perdront les avances qu'ils auront faites; c'est une clause
expresse des conditions proposées.

Ceux qui n'auront pas souscrit, payeront les volumes à raison de vingt-
cinq livres chacun en feuille, et les six cents planches à raison de deux cent
soixante-douze livres; ce qui formera une somme de . . . . . . . 372 livres.
☞ Dans le cas où la matière de cet ouvrage produirait un volume de
plus, les souscripteurs payeront ce volume sept livres de moins que ceux
qui n'auront pas souscrit.

This last sentence did up to a point prepare the subscribers for a
rather larger work than was originally announced; but it entirely
failed to warn them that in the end there were to be seventeen
volumes of text and eleven of plates, costing not 280 livres, but 980.
Far from the work being completed by the end of 1754, Diderot
was not to get the last two volumes of plates off his hands until 1772.

The text of the prospectus, for which he was responsible, began
with a whopping lie: 'L'ouvrage que nous annonçons, n'est plus
un ouvrage à faire. Le manuscrit et les dessins en sont complets.'
Articles for the last ten volumes of text, which were not ready for
publication until the end of 1765, were still being composed well
over a decade later, and the expansion of the plates from two
volumes to eleven meant that in the end work on them continued
for another twenty years or so. The growth in the size of the work
and consequently in its cost was to give rise to a lengthy lawsuit
which caused a great deal of trouble both to the editor and to those
of the publishers who survived to see the end of the whole
undertaking.[1]

Diderot's text, which was eventually incorporated in the *Discours
préliminaire* at the head of the first volume of the *Encyclopédie*, made
in general a good impression. Subscriptions came in at a good rate,
and, in accordance with the timetable set out in the prospectus, the
first volume of text was published at the end of June 1751.
D'Alembert's *Discours préliminaire* made a considerable impact. At
their meeting on 3 July the publishers recorded that over 1,400
subscriptions had been received and it was decided to raise the
printing of the work to 2,050 copies, plus twenty-five with wide
margins.[2]

---

[1] Durand died in 1763 and David (l'aîné) in 1770.
[2] May, p. 25.

## The crisis of 1752

The second volume appeared only slightly behind the original schedule; although, like the first, it bears the date '1751', it did not come out in December as planned, but was not published until well into January 1752. The enemies of the work now united their efforts and seemed for a moment to have triumphed. On 7 February an *arrêt du Conseil* was issued from Versailles banning the first two volumes.

Sa Majesté [it began] a reconnu que dans ces deux volumes on a affecté d'insérer plusieurs maximes tendantes à détruire l'autorité royale, à établir l'esprit d'indépendance et de révolte et, sous des termes obscurs et équivoques, à élever les fondements de l'erreur, de la corruption des mœurs, de l'irréligion et de l'incrédulité. Sa Majesté, toujours attentive à ce qui touche l'ordre public et l'honneur de la religion, a jugé à propos d'interposer son autorité pour arrêter les suites que pourraient avoir des maximes si pernicieuses répandues dans cet ouvrage.

Yet not only was the publication of this *Arrêt du conseil* not followed by the arrest of the guilty editors; the *privilège* of the work was not even withdrawn. The two volumes so far published, and already distributed to subscribers, were merely 'suppressed':

Fait très expresses inhibitions et défenses à tous imprimeurs, libraires et autres de réimprimer ou faire réimprimer lesdits deux volumes; comme aussi de vendre, débiter ou autrement distribuer les exemplaires imprimés qui leur restent, à peine de mille livres d'amende, et de telle autre peine qu'il appartiendra, même en ce qui concerne les imprimeurs et libraires, à peine de déchéance et de privation de la maîtrise.

In the end this thunderbolt proved a sad disappointment to the enemies of the *Encyclopédie*. Far from putting paid to the whole enterprise as they had hoped, it remained a dead letter. All that happened was that the appearance of the third volume was somewhat delayed.

From the first d'Alembert had taken up a haughty attitude and had refused to continue as editor. He then laid down stringent conditions for resuming work, demanding an apology from the *Journal des Savants* for accusing him of propagating irreligious views in his *Discours préliminaire* and a ban on any further mention of the *Encyclopédie* in the Jesuit organ, the *Journal de Trévoux*. Towards the government and its *Arrêt du conseil* he took up an equally firm attitude, laying down the condition that

le conseil du Roi qui a traité les encylopédistes comme des cartouchiens, donnera un arrêt qui réhabilitera l'*Encyclopédie* avec éloge, lèvera la suppression des deux premiers volumes, moyennant quelques cartons dont les auteurs conviendront, et ordonnera la continuation de l'ouvrage.[1]

If the government did not go quite as far as that, d'Alembert could none the less write on 10 July:

L'affaire de l'*Encyclopédie* est arrangée. J'ai consenti, après avoir résisté pendant six mois, à donner ma partie mathématique, à condition que je ne me mêlerais point du reste,[2] que j'aurais satisfaction entière sur le *Journal des Savants*, et liberté entière pour ce que je voudrais dire, ou du moins un censeur tel qu'il me plaira. J'ai cru devoir faire enfin céder mon ressentiment à l'empressement du public qui me venge bien de la petite tracasserie qu'on a voulu nous faire.[3]

His patience, however, was not to survive the test imposed on it by a second crisis in the fortunes of the *Encyclopédie* at the end of 1757.

After this delay the third volume made its appearance in October 1753. The success of the work meant that the printing of this volume had been raised to 3,125 copies, and an additional 1,100 copies of the first two volumes had also been printed. In February 1754 the publishers agreed to print another 1,100 copies of the first three volumes, and it was decided that from the fourth volume onwards 4,225 copies of the work should be printed.[4] The succeeding volumes, down to VII, appeared at almost exactly twelve-month intervals—IV in October 1754, V in November 1755, VI in October 1756 and VII in November 1757.

## The second crisis, 1757–1759

All sorts of causes combined to produce a crisis in the history of the enterprise when the seventh volume came from the press. Its enemies were getting more and more restive and their attacks, in

---

[1] Letter to Formey of 24 May 1752, in Formey, *Souvenirs d'un Citoyen*, ii, 47–9.
[2] In practice, in Vols III–VII he was very far from confining himself to his own specialist field.
[3] Formey, *Souvenirs d'un Citoyen*, ii, 49.        [4] May, p. 27.

periodicals, books and pamphlets, were increasing in number and violence when this volume appeared towards the end of 1757. The attempt made by Damiens on the life of Louis XV in January of that year had led to the promulgation of a draconian law against subversive writings:

Tous ceux qui seront convaincus d'avoir composé, fait composer et imprimer des écrits tendant à attaquer la religion, à émouvir les esprits, à donner atteinte à notre autorité et à troubler l'ordre et la tranquillité de nos États, seront punis de mort.

D'Alembert's article GENÈVE was only one of those in Vol. VII which gave offence to the orthodox, but the uproar which followed filled him with disgust. On 1 January 1758 he wrote to one of the contributors:

L'*Encyclopédie*, Monsieur, est très sensible à vos bontés, mais selon les apparences elle ne sera plus guère en état d'en profiter. Je viens de déclarer à M. de Malesherbes et aux libraires que j'y renonce absolument, et je crois que mon collègue est dans les mêmes dispositions. Vous approuverez notre conduite, Monsieur, quand vous saurez le déchaînement des dévots et de la cour contre cet ouvrage, contre lequel ils ne peuvent cependant rien articuler de raisonnable. On nous inonde de satires et de brochures, qui ne seraient rien si elles se bornaient au pur littéraire, mais ces brochures se permettent les personnalités les plus odieuses et les plus infâmes, notamment contre moi, et ce qu'il y a de plus odieux encore, c'est qu'elles sont protégées et appuyées par ceux qui devraient en punir les auteurs, et qu'elles se vendent publiquement et avec faveur chez tous les libraires et à tous les spectacles. Ce n'est pas tout: un maraud de Jésuite nommé Chapelain a eu l'insolence de prêcher le jour de Noël contre nous devant le Roi, sans réclamation de la part de personne. Enfin, ce qu'il y a de pis, c'est que tandis qu'on accorde toute licence de parler et d'écrire contre nous, on veut exercer contre l'*Encyclopédie* une inquisition intolérable en nous donnant pour censeurs ce qu'il y a de plus capelan et de plus absurde dans la Sorbonne. Il n'est pas possible, Monsieur, de tenir à tout cela; il faut laisser là l'*Encyclopédie*, et c'est le parti que j'ai pris.[1]

D'Alembert's defection came as a heavy blow to the publishers. In November 1757, just before the seventh volume came out, they had broken it to the subscribers that the work was to be both larger

[1] Y. Laissus, 'Une lettre inédite de d'Alembert', *Revue d'Histoire des sciences et de leurs applications*, 1954, pp. 1–2.

and more expensive than had been laid down in the original prospectus. An *Avis aux souscripteurs de l'Encyclopédie* pointed out that the interest taken in the work by many writers who had not at first been contributors inevitably meant an increase in the number of volumes. While it was not yet possible to state exactly how many volumes of text there would be, the number of plates would be raised from 600 to 1,000 and from two volumes to four. The furious attacks on the work and d'Alembert's refusal to continue with his share of it led them to publish, in March 1758, an appeal to the public—the *Mémoire des Libraires associés à l'Encyclopédie sur les motifs de la suspension actuelle de cet ouvrage*—in which they made use of a wide variety of arguments to urge that the work should continue. They particularly stressed the economic importance for France of so large an undertaking with its considerable export market and appealed to d'Alembert to help to complete the whole work.

From the safety of Lausanne Voltaire, in addition to bombarding Diderot with demands for the return of certain articles which he had written for the *Encyclopédie*, kept on exhorting him to follow d'Alembert's example. Diderot took his time to answer. On 19 February he at last replied:

Abandonner l'ouvrage, c'est tourner le dos sur la brèche et faire ce que désirent les coquins qui nous persécutent. Si vous saviez avec quelle joie ils ont appris la désertion de d'Alembert, et toutes les manœuvres qu'ils emploient pour l'empêcher de revenir! . . .

Que faire donc? Ce qui convient à des gens de courage: mépriser nos ennemis, les poursuivre, et profiter, comme nous l'avons fait, de l'imbécillité de nos censeurs. Faut-il que, pour deux misérables brochures, nous oubliions ce que nous devons à nous-mêmes et au public? Est-il honnête de tromper l'espérance de quatre mille souscripteurs, et n'avons-nous aucun engagement avec les libraires?[1]

Diderot was conscious of the success which the *Encyclopédie* had secured in France and indeed in Europe: nearly 4,000 subscribers had been attracted by the time the seventh volume appeared.

No doubt the very success of the work drew on it all this hostility. Further attacks were launched on it in 1758, and no Vol.

[1] Roth, ii, 37–8.

VIII appeared in the course of that year. 1759 opened with what must have seemed at the time complete catastrophe, with successive blows from the two warring forces of the Paris Parlement and the government, locked in a long and bitter struggle which was to last down to 1789. On 23 January the *avocat général*, Omer Joly de Fleury, denounced before the Parlement the *Encyclopédie*, along with other reprehensible books. In the section of his *réquisitoire* devoted to the *Encyclopédie* he trotted out criticisms, both of the general tone of the work and of specific articles, which he had culled from the writings of its opponents. The upshot was that the four publishers were forbidden to sell any more copies of the *Encyclopédie* until it had been examined by experts appointed for that purpose by the court. On 6 February the Parlement named nine persons, among them three doctors of theology, to carry out the task.

Undoubtedly the Parlement was here infringing the prerogatives of the Chancellor, who was ultimately responsible for everything relating to the book trade, although in practice he delegated his powers to his son, Malesherbes, who held the post of *Directeur de la librairie*. A month later, on 8 March, the government's retort came in the form of an *arrêt du Conseil* which, at first sight, appeared to put an end to the whole enterprise by simply withdrawing the *privilège* of the *Encyclopédie*. In its legal style the *arrêt du Conseil* offers a severe condemnation of the work:

. . . Les auteurs dudit Dictionnaire en auraient fait paraître les deux premiers volumes, dont Sa Majesté aurait ordonné la suppression par son arrêt du 7 février 1752, pour les causes contenues audit arrêt; mais en considération de l'utilité dont l'ouvrage pouvait être à quelques égards, Sa Majesté n'aurait pas jugé à propos de révoquer pour lors le privilège, et se serait contentée de donner des ordres plus sévères pour l'examen des volumes suivants. Nonobstant ces précautions, Sa Majesté aurait été informée que les auteurs dudit ouvrage, abusant de l'indulgence qu'on avait eue pour eux, ont donné cinq nouveaux volumes qui n'ont pas moins causé de scandale que les premiers et qui ont même déjà excité le zèle du ministère public de son Parlement. Sa Majesté aurait jugé qu' après ces abus réitérés il n'était pas possible de laisser subsister ledit privilège; que l'avantage qu'on peut retirer d'un ouvrage de ce genre pour le progrès des sciences et des arts ne peut jamais balancer le tort irréparable qui en résulte pour les mœurs et la religion; que d'ailleurs, quelques nouvelles mesures qu'on prît pour empêcher qu'il ne se glissât dans les derniers volumes des traits aussi répréhensibles que dans les premiers, il y aurait toujours un inconvénient inévitable à permettre de continuer l'ouvrage, puisque ce serait assurer le débit non seulement des nouveaux volumes, mais aussi de ceux qui ont déjà paru; que ladite *Encyclopédie*, étant devenue un dictionnaire complet et un traité général de toutes les sciences, serait bien plus recherchée du public et bien plus souvent consultée, et que par là on répandrait encore davantage et on accréditerait en quelque sorte les pernicieuses maximes dont les volumes déjà distribués sont remplis.

In addition to revoking the *privilège*, the King 'fait défenses à tous libraires et autres de vendre, débiter ou autrement distribuer les volumes qui ont déjà paru et d'en imprimer de nouveaux, à peine de punition exemplaire'.

As if to ensure that the whole undertaking was now completely wound up, a second *arrêt du Conseil* of 21 July fixed at 72 livres the sum to be repaid by the publishers to subscribers as representing the difference between the amount they had paid and the value of the seven volumes actually received. Yet, for all its public condemnation of the enterprise, it seems clear that the government eventually decided to allow it to continue underground. Malesherbes even kept out of the official press news of the *arrêt du Conseil* of 21 July. In practice, what the publishers did was to count the 72 livres as part payment for their *Recueil de mille planches . . . sur les Sciences, les Arts libéraux et les Arts mécaniques* for which they took out a separate *privilège* on 8 September. Work on these volumes of plates went steadily ahead, the first volume appearing in 1762 and the last two of the eleven volumes which were finally produced, in 1772.[1]

What of the less harmless volumes of text? The official view seems to have been that, if they all appeared together, there would be less of an uproar than when they had appeared one at a time. Although at first there was some suggestion that the volumes of text might be printed abroad—in Holland or Geneva, for instance —the government was most unwilling to see the considerable profits of this large enterprise lost to France. In the end, it would

---

[1] The dates of publication of the volumes were as follows (the figure in brackets indicates the number of plates in the volume—there were 2,885 in all): I, 1762 (269); II (233) and III (201), 1763; IV (298), 1765; V (248), 1767; VI (294), 1768; VII (259), 1769; VIII (254) and IX (253), 1771; X (337) and XI (239), 1772.

seem, the authorities gave permission for the remaining volumes of text to be printed surreptitiously in Paris, although, as we shall see, it intended to keep a close watch on their distribution when they were finally ready for simultaneous publication.

Before the end of April 1759 a dinner brought together the publishers and Diderot, his two indefatigable lieutenants, Baron d'Holbach and the Chevalier de Jaucourt, and the recalcitrant d'Alembert. Although d'Alembert was only asked for the sake of form to resume his functions as joint editor (an offer which he rejected), he was persuaded to undertake to complete his mathematical and scientific articles within two years.[1] As Diderot's correspondence for these years is more abundant than for the earlier period of his editorship, from 1759 onwards we catch frequent glimpses of him at work on the remaining volumes of text. There had been numerous defections, starting with that of Voltaire, in the crisis years 1757–59. There is no question that the last ten volumes which appeared at the end of 1765 were put together with less care than had gone into the first seven; but despite all the obstacles the text was at last both completed and printed.

## Le Breton as censor

Unfortunately Diderot's pride and relief at this achievement were soured by a dreadful discovery which he made in November 1764. The first seven volumes of the text had been submitted to the official censors as they were composed; since the last ten volumes were printed and published surreptitiously, there could be no question of them going through the official machine. The principal publisher, Le Breton, therefore took it upon himself to remove parts of articles or even whole articles which, he feared, might give offence to the authorities when the work appeared in print.

A fascinating discovery of the 1930s[2] threw some light on what occurred, though, as so often happens, it did not completely solve the mystery. A set of the *Encyclopédie* which found its way from the Soviet Union via Germany to the United States had an extra

[1] Roth, ii, 120.
[2] See Gordon and Torrey, *The Censoring of Diderot's Encyclopédie and the Re-established Text.*

volume which, along with other interesting material, contained 318 pages of proofs of various volumes of the work. Thanks to this discovery we now have a clear idea of the nature of the cuts imposed by Le Breton. Phrases, sentences, paragraphs and even whole articles vanished between the proof stage and the final printing. The extent of his intervention, however, is still uncertain. It can be argued that his pruning of the text was limited to what is revealed in the proofs contained in this volume. Yet it is also possible that these are merely specimens of his handiwork and that Diderot's rage at what had been done both to his bolder articles and to those of other contributors was thoroughly justified. It was an action for which he never forgave Le Breton. In an indignant letter of November 1764 he speaks of 'une atrocité dont il n'y a pas d'exemple depuis l'origine de la librairie'. 'En effet', he goes on, 'a-t-on jamais ouï parler de dix volumes in-folio clandestinement mutilés, tronqués, hachés, déshonorés par un imprimeur?'[1] And yet the odd thing is that, despite Le Breton's intervention, the last ten volumes of text contain at least as many bold articles as do the first seven.

At this stage the general public knew nothing of this row behind the scenes. The printing of the ten volumes of text having been completed by the end of 1765 in Le Breton's printing works in the heart of Paris, a stratagem for their distribution had to be produced with the connivance of the government. In January 1766 the following notice appeared in the press:

Samuel Fauche, libraire à Neuchâtel en Suisse, donne avis au public qu'il a achevé d'imprimer la suite de l'*Encyclopédie*, dont il avait acquis les manuscrits après la publication des sept volumes imprimés à Paris. Cette suite commence au tome VIII et contient dix volumes. Ceux qui ont les sept premiers volumes de cet ouvrage et qui désireraient de s'en procurer la suite, sont priés de prendre chez les imprimeurs de Paris un écrit par lequel il soit constaté qu'ils ont souscrit pour cet ouvrage, et les dix nouveaux volumes seront délivrés en feuilles au porteur de cet écrit, moyennant la somme de 200 livres. Cette formalité est absolument essentielle parce qu'on n'a tiré ces nouveaux volumes qu'au même nombre exactement auquel ont été imprimés à Paris les sept premiers, et qu'on s'est engagé, en acquérant les manuscrits, de fournir les souscripteurs préférablement à tous autres.[2]

[1] *Corr. litt.*, ix, 211 (Roth, iv, 302).
[2] *Mémoire à consulter pour les Libraires associés à l'Encyclopédie*, Paris, 1770, p. 16.

Yet even now the distribution of these last ten volumes was carefully regulated by the government. Subscribers abroad or in the provinces had no difficulty in obtaining their copies, but for at least two or three years their distribution in the Paris region was not allowed. Subscribers there had to have their sets sent to an address in the provinces. Indeed in April 1766 Le Breton was sent to the Bastille for a few days for having distributed a certain number of copies at Versailles. As the Assemblée du Clergé which had just condemned the *Encyclopédie* was still in session, the government was most anxious to avoid a scandal.

## Luneau de Boisjermain's lawsuit

Neither Le Breton and his partners nor Diderot were to be left in peace to get on with the publication of the last volumes of plates which continued down to 1772. In 1769 they became involved in a long and complicated lawsuit which dragged on until 1778. However from the historian's point of view it is an advantage that the forty or so documents published by the two parties have preserved for posterity all manner of interesting material about the publication of the *Encyclopédie*, including, for instance, extracts from the missing volume of the accounts of the enterprise, *Journal B*.

Although Diderot was not directly concerned, he must have suffered a great deal of embarrassment from this lawsuit. The publishers' opponent, an eccentric character called Luneau de Boisjermain, had begun by bringing an action against the powerful corporation of the Paris *libraires* in which Diderot, feeling that right was on his side, had offered him his support. Out of this first lawsuit there developed another, directed this time against the four publishers of the *Encyclopédie* on the grounds that, whereas they had promised subscribers ten volumes of text and plates for 280 francs, there were already seventeen volumes of text and six volumes of plates, with still more to come, costing altogether several times the price originally announced. All that Luneau and his supporters demanded was that they should get the work, complete in twenty-eight volumes, for 280 francs!

Crazy as these claims were, Diderot had landed himself in difficulties because, in the beginning, he had apparently furnished Luneau with a good deal of material about the inner history of the

publication of the *Encyclopédie*. Yet when the controversy warmed
up he felt bound to come down on the side of Le Breton and his
partners, as Luneau and his supporters were backing outrageous
demands with outrageous accusations against the publishers. His
letter to Briasson and Le Breton, dated 31 August 1771, which was
printed in one of the publishers' *Mémoires*, aroused Luneau to
furious attacks on him. Diderot was finally persuaded to suppress a
brilliant pamphlet, entitled *Au Public et aux Magistrats*, in which he
wiped the floor with his opponent. The result was that, in the
contemporary press, Diderot showed up rather poorly. The lawsuit lasted until 1772 under the Parlement Maupeou, and was then
revived in the years 1776–8. It ended with the defeat of Luneau.
By this date all the original publishers were dead except for Le
Breton who in any case had disposed of his interest in the
*Encyclopédie*.

## New editions of the ' Encyclopédie' ; the ' Supplément' and ' Table'

It is sometimes assumed that, once some initial difficulties over
their distribution early in 1766 had been overcome, the appearance
of the last ten volumes of text marked the end of the long fight for
the publication of the *Encyclopédie*. Even if we ignore the obstacles
put in the way of the circulation of these volumes in the Paris
region, the struggle was by no means over. The enemies of the
*Encyclopédie* had certainly not thrown up the sponge. In 1768 an
enterprising young publisher, Charles Joseph Panckoucke, conceived the notion of bringing out a new and revised edition.
Diderot offered some very downright criticisms of the first edition
of the work which he himself had directed, but took no further
part in this new project. Although plans for this new edition were
advertised, nothing came of it in the end as the Chancellor refused
to allow a revised edition to be published. All he would permit was
a literal reprint.

The original publishers having sold to Panckoucke their plates
and the right to reproduce the work, the printing of the new
edition was set in hand. By January 1770, 2,000 copies of the first
three volumes of text and of the first volume of plates were ready
for distribution. The enemies of the *Encyclopédie* once again be-
stirred themselves. The Archbishop of Rheims, who presided over

the Assemblée du Clergé which was then again in session, complained to the King, with the result that the 6,000 volumes of text were incarcerated in the Bastille. There they were to remain for six years. Panckoucke was now compelled to transfer the printing of the new edition to Geneva, where he signed an agreement with Gabriel Cramer, Voltaire's publisher, and Samuel de Tournes. When a prospectus for the new edition was published from Geneva, an attempt was made to get the French Foreign Ministry to use its influence to prevent even this foreign reprint from being carried out. In July 1771 both the Archbishop of Paris and Sartines, now the *Directeur de la librairie*, wrote to the Minister for Foreign Affairs to suggest that he should bring pressure to bear on the authorities in Geneva to get them to ban the new edition. A letter was duly dispatched from the Foreign Ministry to the French resident instructing him to inquire into the whole position, but his reply was too discouraging to warrant further steps being taken. It was not, however, for lack of trying that the enemies of the *Encyclopédie* failed to prevent the Geneva reprint from being carried out; and they had certainly succeeded in putting a stop to the publication of a new edition inside France.

The Geneva reprint encountered a great many difficulties, among them the dissensions between Panckoucke and his Genevan partners. However, despite the fact that the three volumes in the Bastille were not released until too late and had consequently to be reprinted, the seventeen volumes of text were produced between 1771 and 1774. The first volume of plates had been ready in Paris by early 1770, along with the three impounded volumes of text; the remaining ten volumes were brought out from Geneva between 1772 and 1776. This raised the number of copies of the *Encyclopédie* to over 6,000.

Publishers outside France had early been attracted by the prospect of making a handsome profit out of reprinting the Paris edition. A group of London publishers appear to have been first in the field. As soon as the first volume appeared they came out with plans for a quarto edition at half the price of the Paris folio edition. An English translation of d'Alembert's *Discours préliminaire*, produced by the same group, contains an 'Advertisement' of *The Plan of the French Encyclopaedia, or Universal Dictionary of Arts, Sciences, Trades and Manufactures, being an Account of the Origin, Design, Conduct and*

*Execution of that Work. Translated from the Preface of the French Editors, Mess. Diderot and Alembert.* This blurb for the pirated edition is a monument to the publishing ethics of bygone days:

The first volume of the French ENCYCLOPAEDIA, herewith published, is printed verbatim from the Paris edition, and was carefully corrected by two ingenious Gentlemen, Natives of France. The Proprietors have engaged in a Design of Reprinting the whole at London, with a view to serve their Country, by encouraging Arts, Manufactures, and Trades; and keeping large sums at Home, that would otherwise be sent Abroad. They offer their Work at Half the Price of the Paris Edition; and hereby promise, in case they meet with no Discouragement, to proceed regularly in printing the subsequent Volumes. But, if they should be obliged to stop short, it is hoped that no Blame will fall upon them, for declining to sacrifice their private Fortunes, upon finding too few to join them in their real Design of promoting the Public good.

The Paris publishers, alarmed by this threat of competition, despatched two of their number to London in November 1751 'pour voir à traiter de manière ou d'autre pour le profit de la Compagnie, soit pour céder un nombre d'exemplaires à très bon prix aux libraires, soit pour les engager à acheter un nombre de nos figures pour leur édition'.[1] Unfortunately the publishers' books do not make altogether clear what was the outcome of this expedition to London. What is absolutely certain is that the first volume of the London quarto edition did appear in the spring of 1752. The Paris publishers' accounts for 1752 contain an item of 20 livres for 'un tome I *Encyclopédie*, 4°, tiré de Londres pour la Société',[2] while the *London Magazine or Gentleman's Monthly Intelligencer* lists in its catalogue of books for March and April 1752 the following item: 'Encyclopaedia, ou, Dictionnaire Raisonné des Sciences, des Arts & des Metiers. Tome Premier, 4to, pr. 18s. in Boards. Innys, &c.'[3] Yet though this first volume undoubtedly came out, no trace of a copy exists today; at least no English library will confess to having one on its shelves. What is in any case certain is that the publishers' appeal to the self-interest and patriotism of potential subscribers fell on deaf ears; there is no evidence that this pirated edition was carried beyond the first volume.

In contrast, Italy proved fertile in new editions. In 1758 the first

[1] May, p. 25.     [2] May, p. 64.     [3] 1752, 194, no. 48.

two volumes of a folio reprint appeared in the small republic of Lucca. The new version, edited by Ottaviano Diodati, contained a considerable number of notes and additions. It was this edition which called forth the Papal condemnation of the whole enterprise in Clement XIII's *Damnatio et prohibitio operis in plures Tomos distributi, cujus est titulus: Encyclopédie* of September 1759. The publisher, Giuntini, who claimed to be producing 3,000 copies at a lower price that that of the Paris edition, took on a task which for various reasons was to be long drawn out. For one thing the gap in the publication of the Paris edition between 1757 and 1765 meant that, although he had brought out the first seven volumes by 1760, he could not make a start on the last ten volumes of text until 1766. In the end he did not manage to publish all the last ten volumes of text until 1771. The publication of the volumes of plates was spread over the years 1765 to 1776.

By this date a second Italian folio reprint was well on the way to completion, even though it did not begin publication until 1770. This edition, published in Leghorn, was dedicated to the Grand Duke of Tuscany, a brother of Marie Antoinette, who in 1790 was to succeed Joseph II as Emperor under the title of Leopold II. During his years in Tuscany he ruled as an enlightened despot, although as Emperor he was to retreat from the policy of reforms inaugurated by his brother and was on the point of becoming embroiled in a war with revolutionary France when he died in 1792. It is somewhat paradoxical that this edition should have appeared with his active encouragement in the very period when Panckoucke and his partners were not allowed to produce a reprint in France.

The seventeen volumes of text contain a substantial number of notes, some of which were taken over from the Lucca edition; their publication was completed by 1775. The eleven volumes of plates appeared between 1771 and 1778. If a complete set of the Lucca edition contains, not twenty-eight, but thirty-three volumes, this is because in 1778 and 1779 the publishers went on to reprint the *Supplément* (four volumes of text and one of plates) which Panckoucke and his partners had brought out in 1776 and 1777.

Plans for this supplement went back to the failure of Panckoucke's original project for a revised edition of the *Encyclopédie*. When he was compelled to abandon this plan, he fell back on a combination of a literal reprint and a supplement. This time Diderot was not to be induced to take on the editorship, though d'Alembert was persuaded to contribute a small number of articles. The editor of the supplement—a much less controversial work than its parent—was Jean Baptiste Robinet (1735–1820), the author of that eccentric, but interesting work, *De la Nature*. The French government granted a *privilège* for the supplement which appeared simultaneously in Paris (under Panckoucke's imprint) and Amsterdam (under that of Marc Michel Rey), the first two volumes of text in 1776, and two more together with one of plates in the following year. Another addition to the *Encyclopédie* in which Diderot had no part was the *Table*, published in two folio volumes by Panckoucke and Rey in 1780. It was the work of Pierre Mouchon (1733–97), a Protestant pastor in Basle and then in his native Geneva. With the twenty-eight volumes of the *Encyclopédie* and the five of the *Supplément* this made a grand total of thirty-five.

At 980 livres, plus the cost of binding twenty-eight folio volumes, the original edition of the *Encyclopédie* was an expensive work, and Panckoucke's reprint was in the end no cheaper. Even if the Italian folio editions were rather less expensive, there was room for a cheaper version to suit more modest purses. It is true that despite their high price the four folio editions must have had a surprising sale; altogether at least 10,000 copies must have been sold. Yet there were obvious economies to be effected by reducing the number of plates—the most expensive part of the work—and by producing the text in a smaller format. This was the aim of the Swiss publishers who appeared on the scene in the latter part of the 1770s.

In 1777 the Genevan publisher, Pellet, began to bring out a quarto edition with thirty-six volumes of text and only three of plates at a cost of a mere 384 livres against the 980 of the original Paris folio edition. What is more, articles from the *Supplément* were also incorporated in the text. This new edition proved very successful; indeed there appear to have been three separate printings, the third of them (labelled 'Troisième Édition') being carried out in Neuchâtel by the Société Typographique. Most library sets of this edition consist of a mixture of volumes bearing Geneva or Neuchâtel or both as place of publication and dates ranging from

1777 to 1779. A *Table* in six quarto volumes was finally published in Lyons between 1780 and 1781.

In 1778 the Sociétés Typographiques of Lausanne and Berne announced yet another edition, this time an octavo one at the very low price of 195 francs. As with the Pellet edition the *Supplément* was incorporated in the text which formed thirty-six double volumes and, in addition, there were three volumes of plates. This edition was also successful enough to go through two printings. Sets available in libraries generally consist of a mixture of volumes bearing Lausanne or Berne or both as place of publication and dates ranging from 1778 to 1782.

In other words, in a period of just over thirty years nine editions of the *Encyclopédie* were published—four folio, three quarto and two octavo. Only the folio editions contained the text edited by Diderot (the two Italian editions with some extra material); the Swiss quarto and octavo editions incorporated articles from the *Supplément* and drastically reduced the number of plates. Only one of these nine editions—the first—could be produced inside France; the attempt to produce a second French edition, whether a revised or a literal version of the original text, was blocked by the authorities.

Yet another Swiss attempt to cash in on the success of the *Encyclopédie* should be noted in passing. Between 1770 and 1780 Barthélemy de Félice produced from Yverdon the fifty-eight quarto volumes (including ten of plates) of his *Encyclopédie ou Dictionnaire universel raisonné des connaissances humaines*. Although, as was freely acknowledged in the preface, this new work owed a considerable debt to the *Encyclopédie*, the Swiss Protestant editor and contributors gave it a tone very different from that of the French work on which it was largely based.

A selection of articles from the *Encyclopédie* which first appeared in 1768 was to enjoy considerable popularity down to the Restoration period. This was the *Esprit de l'Encyclopédie*, originally published in Paris in 1768 in five duodecimo volumes 'avec permission tacite'. Though Geneva is given as the place of publication, the two editions which came out in that year also bear the name of a Paris publisher or publishers; indeed the second has the imprint of two of the original publishers of the *Encyclopédie*, Briasson and Le Breton. This selection, as the preface puts it, is confined 'aux articles de philosophie, de morale, de critique, de galanterie, de politique et de littérature'. Articles which had given offence in high places were also eliminated. At least four more editions of this selection were published by 1772, and enlarged editions—in twelve and fifteen octavo volumes respectively—appeared in 1798–1800 and as late as 1822.

## Attempts at translations

If the rigours of the censorship inside France and the popularity of the French language in eighteenth-century Europe combined to produce a large number of foreign reprints of the original text, the fame of the *Encyclopédie* also led to some attempts to translate it. Here again, English publishers were remarkably quick in getting off the mark by offering a translation of the *Encyclopédie* in ten volumes (eight quarto volumes of text and two of plates) to be published in parts by Christmas 1756 at a total cost of nine guineas. It was the work of Sir Joseph Ayloffe (1709–81), a well-known antiquarian. As early as January 1752 the first part was announced in the *Gentleman's Magazine*:

Encyclopaedia N°. I, or, a rational dictionary of arts, sciences, and trade; by several eminent hands. Methodized, digested, and now published at Paris, by M. Diderot, fellow of the royal academy of sciences and belles-lettres in Prussia; and, as to the mathematical part, by M. d'Alembert, member of the royal academy of sciences at Paris and Berlin, and fellow of the royal society.—Translated from the French, with improvements; in which will be included a great variety of new articles, tending to explain and illustrate the antiquities, history, ecclesiastical, civil and military, laws, customs, manufactures, commerce, curiosities, etc. of Great Britain and Ireland. By Sir Joseph Ayloffe, Bart., fellow of the royal society, and of the society of antiquaries, London, and author of the Universal Librarian (p. 46).

In announcing the work, the review waxes sarcastic on the alleged improvements and additions promised in the translation:

Why these various additions should be made, and how they can be called improvements is a mystery. The room that Abingdon takes up, is well enough in a geographical dictionary, but as they have placed it on the river Ouse instead of the Thames, we have a strange instance of their improvements.

An advertisement for the first weekly part of the *Encyclopaedia* appeared in the *Daily Advertizer* of 11 January, and advertisements for successive parts (as far as the eighth) appeared down to 28 February. That seems to have marked the end of the enterprise. As each sixpenny part was to consist of three sheets, at least twenty-four sheets of the first volume must have been published; yet, like the first volume of the London pirated edition of the *Encyclopédie*, they appear to have left no trace whatever in the libraries of this country.

Little more success attended the attempt, some twenty years later, to publish an English translation of *L'Esprit de l'Encyclopédie*. The first volume appeared in 1772 with the following title-page:

*Select Essays from the Encyclopedy, being the Most Curious, Entertaining, and Instructive Parts of that Very Extensive Work, Written by Mallet, Diderot, D'Alembert and Others, the Most Celebrated Writers of the Age.* London, Printed for Samuel Leacroft, opposite to Spring-Gardens, Charing Cross. M,DCC,LXXII.

No further volumes of this translation appear to have been published.

A small number of articles from the *Encyclopédie* also appeared in German translation. In 1768, for instance, the Hamburg review, *Unterhaltungen*, published a translation of the important article, GÉNIE, often wrongly attributed to Diderot. In 1774 the first volume (no more were to appear) of the *Philosophische Werke des Herrn Diderot,* published in Leipzig, contained the articles *BEAU and *CHINOIS (PHILOSOPHIE DES).[1] Greater interest in the *Encyclopédie* was aroused in the Russia of Catherine the Great. Indeed in 1767 Count Shouvalov wrote an excited letter to Voltaire to announce the preparation of a translation of the work, adding that it was Catherine herself ' qui a désiré de procurer l'*Encyclopédie* à ses peuples et qui même fait les frais de l'impression '.[2] Although there is no trace of any complete or large-scale translation of the *Encyclopédie*, a very considerable number of isolated articles by a wide variety of authors appeared in Russian between 1767 and 1804.[3] Altogether some five hundred articles were translated in these years.

[1] R. Mortier, *Diderot en Allemagne (1750–1850)*, Paris, 1954, pp. 162, 303.        [2] Best. 13378.
[3] See P. N. Berkov, 'Histoire de l'*Encyclopédie* dans la Russie du XVIIIᵉ siècle', *Revue des Études slaves*, 1965, pp. 47–58.

The European success won by the *Encyclopédie* between 1751 and the Revolution is thus beyond question. Of more immediate concern to us here is its diffusion inside France itself as this inevitably conditioned its impact on French opinion in these decades. Undoubtedly a fairly high proportion of the copies of the only edition actually published in France went to subscribers from other European countries. On the other hand it is also clear that the publishers of the editions produced abroad were very much concerned with the French market. Although we have no figures for traffic in either direction, it is a safe guess that of the 20,000 or so copies printed more came into France than were exported. No doubt all sorts of obstacles were put in the way of the import of copies of the work, but the attitude of the government towards it was always hesitant and uncertain and its agents were far from being incorruptible. Persistent as its enemies were, they did not succeed in preventing the original edition being printed in France and in the end circulating freely. Diderot's twenty-five year battle to complete and publish the *Encyclopédie* ended in victory.

One of his cherished hopes was not, however, to be fulfilled. After Catherine the Great had purchased his library in 1765 and then appointed him her librarian, he seems to have conceived the idea of preparing an entirely new edition of the *Encyclopédie* to appear under her auspices. The notion is hinted at in the preface of the sixth volume of plates which appeared in 1768 with fulsome praise of the Empress. When in 1773 he at last made the long journey to St Petersburg to pay his respects, he broached the question with Catherine, and for a while after his return to Paris he was convinced that the necessary funds would be forthcoming. In the end nothing came of all his plans.

*Chapter 3*

# Contributors and subscribers

Consideration of the men who wrote for the *Encyclopédie* and who subscribed for it brings us face to face with the complex society of the last decades of the Ancien Régime. Diderot's struggle to produce these massive volumes between 1747 and 1772 was one small part of an ideological battle which arose out of the disintegration of one society and the first stirrings of the new France which was to emerge from the upheaval of the Revolution. So far as its political and social outlook was concerned the *Encyclopédie* was the mirror of its age—the age of Louis XV and not that of Mirabeau or Robespierre or even that of Louis XVI and Marie Antoinette. It was the product not of revolutionary France, which few of its contributors lived to see, but rather of an earlier age which was a strange blend of economic advance and of political decay.

## The contributors

To generalize about its contributors is no easy task if it is undertaken with due attention to the complicated facts. Large numbers of articles are unsigned, and while occasionally there is evidence which permits us to attribute them to specific authors, often the identity of the writers remains (and will no doubt for ever so remain) a mystery. Various lists of contributors have been drawn up;[1] some 130 names of those who contributed articles to the seventeen volumes of text have so far been identified. Such lists are, however, not only incomplete; they also contain names of

[1] The most recent and the fullest is that provided by J. Proust in the second edition of his *Diderot et l'Encyclopédie*, Paris, 1967, pp. 511–31.

persons who are virtually unknown, and in the nature of things
they fail to distinguish between the very varying contributions
made by individual writers, ranging from a short article or even
merely part of an article to several dozen or several hundred or
even, in one case, several thousand. Montesquieu's name is
associated with the *Encyclopédie* because of a short fragment printed
posthumously as part of the article GOÛT; at the other end of the
scale the Chevalier de Jaucourt was responsible, it has been calculated, for something like a quarter of the text of the whole work.

The two editors were, of course, themselves substantial contributors. Though presumably they took on the job partly because
they needed the money, exactly what they earned it is impossible
to say because of the incomplete state of the publishers' accounts,
but even contemporaries felt that Diderot, who from the start
received higher payments because of his greater responsibilities, was
poorly rewarded for his labours. Yet he himself did not on the
whole complain; his work on the text and plates provided him
with a small but steady income for a quarter of a century.
D'Alembert was more difficult to handle from the publishers'
point of view, but in addition to various presents given him earlier
on he also received, after he had given up the position of joint
editor, what he asked for in return for his limited contribution to
the last ten volumes of text.

In preparing for the publication of the first volumes the two
editors grouped around them a certain number of men who
received modest payments from the publishers for work done.
Even before they took over the editorship, the publishers had made
a payment of 300 livres to Jean Henri Samuel Formey (1711–97),
the descendant of Huguenot refugees who became secretary of
the Berlin academy. According to the *Discours préliminaire* he had
originally intended to produce an encyclopedia of his own and in
1756, much to d'Alembert's indignation, he was to put out from
Berlin a prospectus for an abridged edition of the *Encyclopédie*.
However, this came to nothing as Malesherbes refused to allow it
to be printed in France.

## The original 'Société de gens de lettres'

Paradoxically one finds among the original group of contributors whose names appear in the publishers' accounts a considerable number of *abbés*. The most illustrious of these was Guillaume Raynal (1713–96) who was later to achieve European fame (with considerable assistance from Diderot's pen) for his *Histoire philosophique et politique des établissements et du commerce des Européens dans les deux Indes*. His collaboration presents something of a mystery since, although he received the substantial sum of 1,200 livres in the period 1748–9, nothing is known of his actual contributions. His signature nowhere appears in the seventeen volumes of text. More is known of the contributions of Abbé Edmé Mallet (1713–55) who, after being a *curé* near Melun, was appointed to a chair of theology at the Collège de Navarre and whose articles on a wide variety of topics, literary as well as theological, continued to appear in the volumes published after his death. Another early contributor was Abbé Claude Yvon (*c.* 1714–1791) who was involved in the scandal of his friend, Abbé Jean Martin de Prades (*c.* 1720–82) whose thesis was condemned by the Sorbonne in January 1752 with repercussions on the fate of the *Encyclopédie* to which he too had furnished paid contributions. Like de Prades, Yvon was forced to flee abroad. The third volume of the *Encyclopédie*, in listing the contributors and their symbols, states tactfully: 'M. l'abbé Yvon qui avait la lettre X est absent'. None the less his articles continued to appear in this and later volumes, but they were now unsigned. Another young *abbé* named Pestré, about whom practically nothing is known, was also paid for articles published in the early volumes of the *Encyclopédie*.

Needless to say, the names of laymen were also to be found on the publishers' payroll down to 1751. There was the venerable freethinker, César Chesneau Dumarsais (1676–1756), whose grammatical articles won almost universal praise; and Buffon's collaborator both at the Jardin du Roi and in the *Histoire naturelle,* Louis Jean Marie Daubenton (1716–99), who furnished a large number of articles. Alongside their names one finds those of several minor men of letters: François Vincent Toussaint (1715–72), an *avocat* and the author of *Les Mœurs*, a work which had caused a scandal when it appeared in 1748, who contributed articles on law and was to end his days teaching in Frederick's military academy; the translator, Marc Antoine Eidous (1713?–90?) with whom Diderot had collaborated in producing James's *Dictionnaire de*

*Médecine* and who wrote on heraldry for the *Encyclopédie*; and that somewhat mysterious figure, Paul Landois, known today, if at all, as the author of *Sylvie*, an early example of a *tragédie bourgeoise*, and, above all, as the recipient of a letter of 1756 in which Diderot gave a famous exposition of his determinism (he contributed articles on the fine arts).

A number of medical men were also paid for their articles. Associated with the work from the beginning were the anatomist, Pierre Tarin (1725–61), and another doctor, Urbain de Vandenesse, who was to die before the enterprise had got very far. A larger contribution was made by Gabriel François Venel (1723–75), later professor of medicine at Montpellier, who wrote a large number of articles both on medical matters and on chemistry. Another medical man who was also a professor of chemistry, Paul Jacques Malouin (1701–78), received payment for the scientific articles which he furnished. Among the original contributors whose names appear in the publishers' books were also Jean Baptiste Le Roy (1720–1800), a physicist who was the son and brother of famous watchmakers and contributed articles on astronomical in-struments as well as on their craft; Guillaume Le Blond (1704–81), *professor de mathématiques des pages de la grande écurie du roi*, who taught the subject to Louis XV's children and contributed articles on fortification and tactics; and the well-known architect, Jacques François Blondel (1704–74), who supplied those on his own field.

The publishers' accounts for the period after the appearance of the first volume in 1751 continue to show some payments to contributors as well as to the two editors; but the number of entries gradually diminishes. Nevertheless some new names appear. Thus Daubenton's brother, Pierre (1703–76), described as 'subdélégué de Montbard', drew fairly considerable sums of money over quite a long period. Another newcomer was the *avocat*, Antoine Gaspard Boucher d'Argis (1708–91), who furnished a large number of articles on legal and constitutional questions. Some modest payments were made to the new theo-logian who was recruited after the death of Abbé Mallet—Abbé André Morellet (1727–1819) whose biting tongue earned him the nick-name of 'Abbé Mords-les'. Another fairly late recruit, Nicolas Beauzée (1717–89), who succeeded Dumarsais as the grammarian of the *Encyclopédie*, was also paid for his services.

The total number of contributors who actually received cash from the publishers was very small—not much more than twenty, all told. Even in the first volume the editors inserted a large number of contributions for which no payment had been made. The name of the impecunious Jean Jacques Rousseau, for instance, does not appear in the publishers' accounts, although in addition to his one contribution on political questions—the famous article, ÉCONOMIE POLITIQUE—he also furnished the greater part of the articles on music. These, he later claimed, were composed in three months, since that was all the time the editors allowed him.

In each of the first seven volumes the *Avertissement des Éditeurs* contains long lists of contributors who had furnished or promised articles as well as of those who had produced what are described as *mémoires* or *observations* on particular subjects. Even if we confine ourselves for the most part to persons who contributed actual articles, they will be seen to come from a great variety of occupations and social groups. In addition to the names of the paid contributors already mentioned and that of Rousseau, the list in the first volume also includes the following writers of articles: Louis de Cahusac (1706–59), who wrote *libretti* for Rameau and who furnished articles on such subjects as opera and ballet; the famous surgeon, Antoine Louis (1723–92); the cartographer, Nicolas Bellin (1703–72), who wrote on naval matters; Antoine Joseph Dezallier d'Argenville (1680–1765) who completed articles on gardening and hydraulics; Abbé de la Chapelle (1710?–92?) who wrote on elementary geometry and arithmetic; and another doctor, Louis Guillaume Le Monnier (1717–99), best known as a botanist, who wrote on magnetism and electricity. Finally another important contributor was mentioned—Louis Jacques Goussier (1722–99), who, in addition to writing a number of articles, played a very prominent part in the production of the volumes of plates for which he provided a large number of drawings.

## Other contributors to the first seven volumes

When the first volume of the *Encyclopédie* actually materialized in the summer of 1751, it rapidly drew in a large number of new voluntary contributors. In defending against Luneau de Boisjermain the way in which the publishers had allowed the work to swell from eight volumes of text to seventeen, Diderot in his unpublished pamphlet, *Au Public et aux Magistrats*, stresses the unexpected amount of help which came from a large number of writers outside the original circle of the editors and their contributors:

Lorsqu'on mit sous presse le prospectus de l'*Encyclopédie*, nous annon-çâmes dix[1] volumes de discours et environ six cents planches; c'était en effet tout ce que nous possédions alors. Si j'assure que la nation entière s'intéressa à la perfection de l'ouvrage et qu'il nous vint des secours des contrées les plus éloignées, c'est un fait connu et démontré par les noms des surnuméraires et la multitude de leurs articles. Nous nous trouvâmes en un instant associés à tout ce qu'il y avait de gens habiles en histoire naturelle, en physique, en mathématiques, en théologie, en philosophie, en littérature, en arts libéraux et mécaniques. Que fallait-il faire des matériaux de M. de Voltaire, du président de Montesquieu, de M. Turgot l'intendant, de M. le président de Brosses, de M. de Saint-Lambert, de M. de Marmontel, de M. le chevalier de Jaucourt et d'une infinité d'autres? M. Luneau les aurait peut-être brûlés. Moi, je supprimai souvent mon travail et le remplaçai par celui de ces auxiliaires. C'est ainsi que, pour la première fois peut-être, on a vu un ouvrage souscrit se perfectionner d'un volume à un autre.[2]

If there was some exaggeration in these lines, the flow of new contributors was an impressive one, though occasionally their identity was not revealed.

Thus the *Avertissement des Éditeurs* in the second volume announces the collaboration not only of a fairly obscure figure, Abbé de Sauvages (1709–95), but also of that redoubtable propa-gandist, Baron d'Holbach, the author of the *Système de la Nature*, under the guise of 'une personne dont l'allemand est la langue maternelle'; however, by the time the third volume appeared, this disguise was dropped. Although originally announced as the author of technical and scientific articles on such subjects as mineralogy, metallurgy and physics, d'Holbach was to play an important part in the production of the last ten volumes, contribut-ing, in addition to signed articles on these specialist topics, a large number of unsigned articles on both religion and politics.

An even more substantial contributor is first mentioned in the second volume—the Chevalier de Jaucourt (1704–80), a younger son of an old Huguenot family, who was brought

[1] This should surely read 'huit'.          [2] Roth, xi, 105–6.

up in Geneva, spent some time in Cambridge, studied medicine under Boerhaave at Leyden and then settled down in Paris to a life of scholarly labour. Although he wrote nothing for the first volume of the *Encyclopédie* and only seven articles for the second, so great was his contribution to the remaining volumes, especially to the last ten which appeared in 1765, that he composed altogether, it has been calculated, 28 per cent of the total number of articles contained in the seventeen volumes and 24 per cent of the text.[1] It is in fact difficult to see how without his massive contribution the last ten volumes of the *Encyclopédie* could ever have been completed. There are rather disdainful references to the Chevalier's absorption in the task of churning out articles for the *Encyclopédie* in two letters of Diderot to Sophie Volland, written in 1760 when work on the last ten volumes was going ahead despite the withdrawal of its *privilège*. The first runs: 'Cet homme est depuis six à sept ans au centre de quatre à cinq secrétaires, lisant, dictant, travaillant treize à quatorze heures par jour, et cette position-là ne l'a pas encore ennuyé.' Shortly afterwards Diderot again referred to the Chevalier's remorseless activity:

Le chevalier de Jaucourt?—Ne craignez pas qu'il s'ennuie de moudre des articles; Dieu le fit pour cela. Je voudrais que vous vissiez comme sa physiognomie s'allonge quand on lui annonce la fin de son travail, ou plutôt la nécessité de le finir. Il a vraiment l'air désolé.[2]

However, in the *Avertissement* to Vol. VIII, among all the contributors, new and old, to the last ten volumes of the *Encyclopédie*, Jaucourt alone was singled out for mention by Diderot and awarded a whole paragraph of praise. It begins:

Si nous avons poussé le cri de joie du matelot lorsqu'il aperçoit la terre après une nuit obscure égaré entre le ciel et les eaux, c'est à M. le Chevalier de Jaucourt que nous le devons. Que n'a-t-il pas fait pour nous, surtout dans ces derniers temps? . . .

Yet it is pretty clear that Diderot and his circle looked upon the worthy Chevalier as a pedantic old bore. It is also true that Le Breton and his partners offered Jaucourt singularly little in return

---

[1] R. N. Schwab, 'The extent of the Chevalier de Jaucourt's contribution to Diderot's *Encyclopédie*', *Modern Language Notes*, 1957, pp. 507–8.     [2] Roth, iii, 248, 265.

for writing over 17,000 articles. At various times from 1758 onwards they supplied him with books to the value of some 2,750 livres. They also refunded to him some items of postage and gave his servant a gratuity of 120 livres when the text of the *Encyclopédie* was completed; but that was all. At the height of his labours, in 1761, he sold a house in Paris, inherited from his mother, to, of all people, Le Breton. It is tempting to agree with Grimm's version of the matter:

M. le chevalier de Jaucourt, qui, après M. Diderot, a le plus contribué à mettre fin à cet ouvrage immense, non seulement n'en a jamais tiré aucune récompense, mais s'est trouvé dans le cas de vendre une maison qu'il avait dans Paris afin de pouvoir payer le salaire de trois ou quatre secrétaires, employés sans relâche depuis plus de dix ans. Ce qu'il y a de plaisant, c'est que c'est l'imprimeur Le Breton qui a acheté cette maison avec l'argent que le travail du chevalier de Jaucourt l'a mis à portée de gagner. Aussi ce Le Breton trouve que le chevalier de Jaucourt est un bien honnête homme.[1]

What the Chevalier himself thought about the way the publishers treated him we do not know, but certainly he received little reward for penning thousands of articles on every branch of human knowledge from medicine to the fine arts.

This same preface to the second volume contains an announcement by the editors, made with an appropriate flourish of trumpets, that the illustrious Buffon, whose *Histoire naturelle* had begun its majestic course with the appearance of the first volumes in 1749, had contributed the article NATURE. Even twentieth-century writers on the *Encyclopédie* have found the editors' enthusiasm so infectious that they have enrolled Buffon amongst the contributors to the work. In practice, if one turns to the appropriate point in Vol. XI, all one finds is two articles—NATURE (*Philos.*) and NATURE, *Lois de la*—which, even though the second article is followed by d'Alembert's signature as well as '*Chambers*', are merely a translation of Chambers's article NATURE, NATURA.

The preface to Vol. III could announce fresh recruits to the enterprise. The 'société de gens de lettres' which, according to the title-page of the *Encyclopédie*, was responsible for producing the work, was broadening out to include contributors from all corners of France and from all manner of professions. There was, for instance, the scientist and explorer, La Condamine (1701–74), who furnished articles on the natural history and geography of America. More doctors, all of them from the faculty of Montpellier, were enlisted: Jean Bouillet (1690–1777) of Béziers, and his son, Jean Henri Nicolas (1729–90), Arnulphe d'Aumont (1720–82), professor of medicine at Valence, and Théophile de Bordeu (1722–76) whom Diderot was to immortalize in the *Rêve de d'Alembert*. Another new contributor was the lawyer, Matthieu Antoine Bouchaud (1719–1804), whose articles CONCILE, DÉCRET, DÉCRÉTALES and DÉCRÉTALES (FAUSSES) were to cost him dear since it was not until 1773 that he was able to live them down sufficiently to secure a chair in the Paris Faculty of Law. The *maître de pension*, Joachim Faiguet de Villeneuve (1703–80) (his articles gave considerable offence to the enemies of the *Encyclopédie* who asked whether a man with such beliefs was fit to be entrusted with the instruction of the young) also began to write for the *Encyclopédie*, as did the popular but secondrate author, Jean François Marmontel (1723–99), who furnished a considerable number of literary articles. The aged historian, Abbé Nicolas Lenglet-Dufresnoy (1674–1755), also contributed articles, and so did the economist, François Véron de Forbonnais (1722–1800), though he preferred to remain in the semi-anonymity of the initials 'V.D.F.'.

With Vol. IV fresh names appear, for both articles printed in this volume and for those which were promised for the next. First in the list of these comes a certain Le Romain, described as *ingénieur en chef de l'île de la Grenade*, who produced articles on America. Then there was Charles Pinot Duclos (1704–72), Voltaire's successor as historiographer royal who had recently been appointed secretary of the Académie Française. Claude Henri Watelet (1718–86), a *receveur général des finances* and a prominent art connoisseur, also began his contributions to the *Encyclopédie* with this volume as did the engraver, Jean Baptiste Papillon (1698–1776), and an *avocat au Parlement* named de la Motte-Conflant. Nicolas Antoine Boulanger (1722–59), an *ingénieur des ponts et chaussées*, produced not only the obvious article, CORVÉE, but also DÉLUGE, which contained ideas only to be fully developed in his posthumous works. Among contributors announced as promising articles for future volumes were another doctor, Louis Anne La Virotte (1725–59), a professor in Paris, and Claude Bourgelat of Lyons (1712–79), the founder of French veterinary colleges. An article on the newly founded École Militaire was to be furnished by its *directeur d'études*, Jean Baptiste Paris de Meyzieu (1718–78), son of the second of the famous Paris brothers, the financial wizards of the first half of the reign of Louis XV, one of whom, Paris-Duverney, had been responsible for the setting up of this new establishment.

However, the most important new recruit announced in the preface to Vol. IV was Voltaire, of whom the editors wrote:

Nous ne pouvons trop nous hâter d'annoncer que M. *DE VOLTAIRE* nous a donné les articles ESPRIT, ÉLOQUENCE, ÉLÉGANCE, LITTÉRATURE, etc. et nous en fait espérer d'autres. L'*Encyclopédie*, par la justice qu'elle lui a rendue et qu'elle continuera toujours à lui rendre, méritait l'intérêt qu'il veut bien prendre à elle.

For all sorts of reasons Voltaire's contribution to the *Encyclopédie* proved in practice to be a relatively modest one. It extended merely from Vol. V to Vol. VIII and covered in all forty-three articles, a few of them lengthy and polemical, but most of them short and on purely literary subjects. Although some of his articles, from HABILE to IMAGINATION, did not appear in print in the *Encyclopédie* until 1765, he had already taken leave of the work by the summer of 1758, at the height of the crisis in its fortunes.

More new contributors were announced in the preface to Vol. V. An army officer, Charles Louis d'Authville (1716–?) produced the articles ÉQUITATION and ESCADRON, while Jean Joseph Rallier des Ourmes (1701–71), a judge from Rennes, began to contribute articles on arithmetic. The famous surgeon, Sauveur François Morand (1697–1773), wrote the article DORADE. A certain Dufour produced articles on economic and financial questions such as DROITS DU ROI and EMPRUNT. A better known personage, Charles Georges Leroy (1723–89), *lieutenant des chasses du parc de Versailles*, began his collaboration which was to continue anonymously after 1759 with, for instance, the article INSTINCT (*Métaph. et Hist. nat.*). One of the rare *encyclopédistes* to live long enough to play an active part in the Revolution, Alexander Deleyre (1726–97), furnished the article ÉPINGLE which inspired part of the famous chapter on the advantages of the division of labour in Adam Smith's *Wealth of Nations*. He also contributed to the next volume the outspoken

# ENCYCLOPÉDIE,

## OU

# DICTIONNAIRE RAISONNÉ

# DES SCIENCES,

## DES ARTS ET DES MÉTIERS,

### RECUEILLI

## DES MEILLEURS AUTEURS

#### ET PARTICULIEREMENT

## DES DICTIONNAIRES ANGLOIS

## DE CHAMBERS, D'HARRIS, DE DYCHE, &c.

### *PAR UNE SOCIÉTÉ DE GENS DE LETTRES.*

Mis en ordre & publié par M. *Diderot* : & quant à la Partie Mathématique, par M. *D'Alembert*, de l'Académie Royale des Sciences de Paris & de l'Académie Royale de Berlin.

*Tantum feries juncturaque pollet,*
*Tantum de medio fumptis accedit honoris.* Horat.

## DIX VOLUMES IN-FOLIO,

### DONT DEUX DE PLANCHES EN TAILLE-DOUCE,

## PROPOSÉS PAR SOUSCRIPTION.

PARIS, Chez
{
BRIASSON, *rue Saint Jacques, à la Science.*
DAVID l'aîné, *rue Saint Jacques, à la Plume d'or.*
LE BRETON, Imprimeur ordinaire du Roy, *rue de la Harpe.*
DURAND, *rue Saint Jacques, à Saint Landry, & au Griffon.*

### M. DCC. LI.

### *AVEC APPROBATION ET PRIVILEGE DU ROY.*

*Title-page of the Prospectus*

article, FANATISME, which gave considerable offence in orthodox quarters. Another doctor, Jacques François de Villiers (1727–90?), began to contribute technological and scientific articles, and Ferdinand Berthoud (1727–1807), a native of Neuchâtel who held a post in the French Navy which he supplied with longitude clocks, contributed some articles on watch-making.

The preface to Vol. VI introduces anonymously some interesting new contributors. Among (as the editors put it) the 'quatre personnes que nous regrettons fort de ne pouvoir nommer, mais qui ont exigé de nous cette condition' was the author of ÉTYMOLOGIE, EXISTENCE and EXPANSIBILITÉ, the young Turgot, soon to be an *Intendant* and later, under Louis XVI, *Contrôleur général*. He was also to write FOIRE and FONDATION for the following volume, but after that his collaboration was to cease, presumably because his position did not allow him to continue to write for a work which no longer had an official existence. These are all the articles which Turgot is known to have contributed, but there is the awkward fact that in Diderot's famous letter to Le Breton protesting about the way in which the last ten volumes had been mutilated Turgot is listed among those contributors who would be furious at seeing their articles treated in this way.

Hidden in a similar anonymous fashion was a contribution—the article ÉVIDENCE—from Dr François Quesnay (1694–1774), one of the founders of the Physiocratic movement, whose articles in this field—FERMIERS (*Econ. politiq.*) and GRAINS (*Econom. politiq.*)—were published under the pseudonym of 'Quesnai le fils'. In addition to the new theologian, Abbé Morellet, whose identity was revealed in the preface to Vol. VII, yet another anonymous contributor was mentioned both here and in the preface to the next volume—the author of such articles as FANTAISIE, FRIVOLITÉ and GÉNIE (*Littér.*). This was Jean François, Marquis de Saint-Lambert (1716–1803), who during his lifetime won greatest fame as the author of a poem called *Les Saisons*; he is chiefly remembered today as the lover of Mme du Châtelet and Mme d'Houdetot in which capacity he impinged on the biography of both Voltaire and Rousseau. He contributed articles to some of the later volumes, among them HONNEUR, INTÉRÊT (*Morale*), LÉGISLATEUR and LUXE, which, because they are unsigned, are often wrongly attributed to Diderot.

The preface to Vol. VI also introduces a whole series of new contributors by name. In addition to acknowledging the receipt of a valuable memorandum from Denys Dodart, the *Intendant* of Le Berry, the editors mention such new contributors as the Comte de Tressan (1705–83), a general in Louis XV's armies and the translator of medieval French romances, and Charles de Brosses (1709–1777), a *Président* in the Burgundy Parlement and the author of *Le Culte des dieux fétiches*. The famous civil engineer, Jean Rodolphe Perronet (1708–94), contributed an important article on the steam engine, POMPE À FEU, while the geographer, Jean Baptiste Bourguignon d'Anville (1697–1782), furnished ÉTÉSIENS. FEU D'ARTIFICE and related articles were based on a work sent in by Jean Charles Perrinet d'Orval of Toulouse (1707–80?), a specialist on fireworks. Étienne Hyacinthe de Ratte (1722–1805), secretary of the Société royale des Sciences of Montpellier and later a judge in its Cour des Aides, was responsible for FROID and for articles on associated topics, while Charles Étienne Pesselier (1712–63), whose post in the Fermes Générales left him ample leisure for writing, produced a series of articles on the taxation system, including FERMES DU ROI and FINANCES.

Another young doctor was recruited—Paul Joseph Barthez (1734–1806) of Montpellier, one of the most important figures in the eighteenth-century French medical world, who was to live to be consulting physician to Napoleon. The article GOUTTE was written by a less illustrious physician named Penchenier. Adrien Cuyret de Margency, *gentilhomme ordinaire du roi*, contributed various articles, among them, appropriately enough, GENTILHOMME ORDINAIRE. An anonymous woman (presumably the Marquise de Jaucourt, the Chevalier's sister-in-law) was responsible for such articles as FALBALA and FONTANGE. The poet and playwright, Joseph Desmahis (1722–61), wrote FAT and FEMME (*Morale*); with the latter article he succeeded in infuriating both Voltaire and his arch-enemy, Fréron. Charles Le Roy (1726–79), who was soon to be appointed to a chair of medicine at Montpellier, produced ÉVAPORATION, and Philibert Gueneau de Montbeillard (1720–85), one of Buffon's collaborators in the *Histoire Naturelle*, ÉTENDUE. Louis Necker de Germagny (1730–1804), the elder brother of Louis XVI's minister, who held a chair of mathematics in Geneva and later became a banker in Paris, was responsible for FROTTEMENT, and Baron d'Abbes de Cabrerolles of the Chambre des Comptes in

Montpellier for FIGURE (*Physiologie*). Various articles on military subjects were written by Nicolas Liébault (1723–?), described as *chargé du dépôt de la Guerre*. 'MM. Durival l'aîné et le jeune'— presumably the brothers Nicolas (1723–95) and Claude (1728–1805), high civil servants in Lorraine—were thanked here and in the preface to Vol. VII for contributing 'différentes remarques et quelques morceaux'. Finally M. de Compt, a *curé* from the La Rochelle region, earned the gratitude of the editors by sending in 'pour l'article EAU-DE-VIE la manière de distiller les eaux-de-vie en grand, et d'autres articles'.

Along with a great many names already mentioned, the preface to Vol. VII lists yet more new contributors. Beauzée, one of the writers who received payment from the publishers, is introduced, along with his colleague, Douchet, from the École Militaire, as Dumarsais's successor in the field of grammar, and Montesquieu's fragment, incorporated in the article GOÛT (*Littér.*), is also announced. Antoine Gautier de Montdorge (1707–68), a wealthy *financier* who dabbled in the arts, contributed GRAVURE EN COULEURS and GRAVURE EN MANIÈRE NOIRE, while an *avocat* turned tutor, André Lefèvre (1717–68), was responsible for such articles as FAIBLESSE (*Morale*) and GOUVERNEUR ET GOUVERNANTE. Nicolas Desmarest (1725–1815), an *inspecteur des manufactures* and scientist, contributed FONTAINE and GÉOGRAPHIE PHYSIQUE, and a notable geographer, Didier Robert de Vaugondy (1723–86), was enlisted for GÉOGRAPHIE and GLOBE. Étienne Jean Bouchu (1714–73), like Diderot a native of Langres, who managed the Duc de Penthièvre's forges at Arc-en-Barrois, was responsible for the important article, FORGES, and a well-known Genevan watchmaker who had settled in Paris, Jean Romilly (1714–96), produced for this volume FUSÉE (*Horlogerie*).

## The contributors to the last ten volumes

This broadening out of the 'société de gens de lettres' responsible for the production of the *Encyclopédie* in the volumes published between 1751 and 1757, came to an abrupt halt with the crisis in the history of its publication in the years 1757–9. Some of the earlier contributors—Vandenesse, Dumarsais and Mallet, for instance—had died before 1757; others—Boulanger and Cahusac, for instance

—died shortly afterwards. Some had simply faded out—Abbé
Pestré, Abbé Yvon (though unsigned articles of his continued to
appear to the end), Toussaint and Eidous. The preface to Vol.
VIII, as we have seen, mentions only one contributor to the last ten
volumes—Jaucourt. Diderot glides over the awkward point of the
defections which had taken place among earlier contributors in the
crisis years: Voltaire (a number of his articles were printed in Vol.
VIII, but they were written before he washed his hands of the
whole enterprise in 1758), Duclos, Marmontel, Turgot (though his
defection is not absolutely certain) and so on. Before his eulogy of
Jaucourt Diderot speaks of those persons, vaguely described as 'des
hommes de lettres et des gens du monde', who had come to his aid,
adding: 'Que ne nous est-il permis de désigner à la reconnaissance
publique tous ces habiles et courageux auxiliaires!'

We thus lack the convenient lists of contributors which we find
in the prefaces to the first seven volumes as well as the lists of
symbols used to designate regular contributors—'(A)' for Boucher
d'Argis, '(O)' for d'Alembert, '(S)' for Rousseau and so on. It is
true that in the last ten volumes a certain number of new symbols—
'(m)' and '(q)', for instance—make their appearance at the end of
articles, but as no key to them is provided, this does not help one to
establish the identity of their authors. However, it is known that
'(m)' stands for yet another doctor from Montpellier, Jean Joseph
Ménuret de Chambaud (1733–1815), who also contributed other
articles, some of them bearing his full signature and some of them
unsigned.

On the other hand, a study of the 9,000 or so pages of these last
ten volumes does reveal quite a number of names of new as well as
of earlier contributors, although it is true that there are hundreds of
unsigned articles, the authors of which will probably never be
identified. As in the earlier volumes a certain number of foreign
contributors made their appearance, for obvious reasons French-
speaking Swiss being among the most prominent. These included
Théodore Tronchin (1709–81), the famous Genevan doctor, who
contributed the lengthy article, INOCULATION; the Genevan
mathematician, Georges Louis Le Sage (1724–1803); the Berne
pastor, Élie Bertrand (1713–97), who furnished articles on mineralogy; the Genevan pastor, Jean Edmé Romilly (1739–79), the son
of the watchmaker Jean Romilly, who wrote TOLÉRANCE and

VERTU; and—anonymously with good reason—the *premier pasteur de Lausanne*, Antoine Noé de Polier de Bottens (1713–83). The last named sent in through, of all improbable people, Voltaire, nine articles of a most extraordinary unorthodoxy: KIJUN, LITURGIE, LOGOMACHIE, MAGICIENS, MAGIE, MALACHBELUS, MANES, MAOSIM and MESSIE. Jean Romilly's articles on watchmaking were supplemented by the article MONTRE by another Genevan, Pierre Soubeyran (1709–75). Occasional contributions came from countries further afield: PILE (*Géom. & Phys.*) was sent in by Jan Stefan Ligenza Kurdwanowski (1680–1780), a gentleman of the bedchamber to King Stanislas, who as a physicist was elected a member of the Berlin Academy, while HARPE (*Hist. anc. & Lutherie*) was furnished by Prince Michael Casimir Oginski (1728–1800), a Lithuanian great nobleman, who was to fight on the losing side in the conflict over the first partition of Poland.

The new French contributors whose names are encountered in the pages of these last ten volumes are not on the whole an inspiring lot; nor do their individual contributions appear to have been large. Thus Jacques André Naigeon (1738–1810), the first editor of Diderot's works, put his signature to only two articles, RICHESSE and the extremely unorthodox UNITAIRES which delighted Voltaire, although he also furnished anonymously the first four columns of the article LIBERTÉ (*Morale*). Diderot's bosom friend, Friedrich Melchior Grimm (1723–1807), also wrote two signed articles, MOTIF (*Musique*) and POÈME LYRIQUE. D'Arclais de Montamy (1703–65), *premier maître d'hôtel* of the Duc d'Orléans and an old friend of d'Holbach and also of Diderot, who brought out posthumously his *Traité de la peinture sur émail*, contributed several columns of *Observations* on Jaucourt's article PORCELAINE. Another member of the circle of the *philosophes*—indeed for a while their link with Voltaire at Ferney—the civil servant, Étienne Noël Damilaville (1723–68), signed two articles, MOUTURE (suggesting new methods of milling grain so as to reduce the ever-present risk of famine) and POPULATION, while Diderot and he published under the name of the late Nicolas Antoine Boulanger the important VINGTIÈME. Another friend of Diderot, the sculptor Étienne Maurice Falconet (1716–91), furnished the article SCULPTURE.

A number of doctors were also recruited to write medical and scientific articles, for instance, Henri Fouquet (1727–1806)

of Montpellier who contributed five articles, among them
SENSIBILITÉ and VÉSICATOIRE; Antoine Petit (1722–94), professor of
anatomy in Paris and member of the Academy of Sciences, who
contributed HOMME (*Exposition anatomique du corps de l'*); Augustin
Roux (1726–76), professor of chemistry in Paris, who was responsible for REFROIDISSEMENT (*Physiq. Chim.*) and SUCCIN; the Portu-
guese, Antonio Nunes Ribeiro Sanchez (1699–1783), who furnished the article VÉROLE, *grosse*, and Pierre Jacques Willermoz
(1735–99) who taught chemistry at Montpellier and produced the
article PHOSPHORE.

New contributors on technology were also enlisted. Part of
VERRERIE was contributed by the *avocat*, Antoine Allut (1743–94),
who ended his career on the scaffold as a Girondin, while SUISSES
(*Privilèges des Suisses en France pour leur commerce*), and TOILERIE
were supplied by an *inspecteur des manufactures* from Villefranche-
sur-Saône named Brisson. Following in the footsteps of his master
who, like David, another of the four publishers, had contributed to
the earlier volumes, Brullé, the foreman in Le Breton's printing
shop and his accomplice in the mutilation of the text of the last ten
volumes of the *Encyclopédie*, furnished IMPRIMERIE and PROTE.
SALINE DE SALINS and SALINE DE MONTMOROT bear the signature of
Abbé Fenouillot, to be identified as Charles Georges Fenouillot de
Falbaire (1727–1800), who was later to be the author of some
peculiarly dreary *Drames* as well as an *inspecteur général des salines*. A
certain Lucotte put his signature to a whole series of articles such as
MAÇONNERIE, MARBRIER, MARQUETERIE and MENUISERIE. TARTRE and
TOURNESOL (*Chimie*) were supplied by a well-known chemist from
Montpellier, Jacques Montet (1722–82), while LETTRES (*Gramm.*)
and MAÎTRES ÉCRIVAINS came from the pen of a certain Paillasson,
described as an *expert écrivain juré*. The article PONTS (*Architecture*)
was written by Benti de Voglie (1723?–77), *ingénieur du roi en chef
dans la généralité de Tours*, and hunting was treated at great length
in VÉNERIE by another expert, Vinfrais, 'de la vénerie du roi'.
TROUPEAUX DES BÊTES À LAINE was furnished by Dr Barthez's
father, Guillaume Barthez de Marmorières (1707–99), another
*ingénieur des ponts et chaussées*.

Military matters were handled by a variety of army officers. A
*commissaire des guerres*, Jean François Henri Collot (1716–1804),
contributed to the 'Articles omis' of Vol. XVII an addition to

INVALIDES as well as OUVRIERS ÉTRANGERS. Another of the Durival brothers, Jean Baptiste (1728–1810) described as 'M. Durival, cadet', contributed such articles as HABILLEMENT, ÉQUIPEMENT ET ARMEMENT DES TROUPES, LEVÉE DES TROUPES and LICENCIEMENT. The article PONT MILITAIRE was produced by a certain Guillotte, *officier dans la maréchaussée générale de l'île de France*. Two young noblemen contributed to MARAUDEUR (under VOLEUR)—Claude François Adrien, Marquis de Lezay-Marnesia (1735–1800), a future member of the Constituent Assembly, and Jean Denis de Mont-lovier (1733–1804), described as 'gendarme de la garde du roi'. VALEUR (*Morale*) was the work of the even younger Alexandre Masson, Marquis de Pezay (1741–77), who, as well as being a minor poet, enjoyed considerable favour at court for a short period at the beginning of the reign of Louis XVI.

Two further contributors deserve a brief mention—a Chevalier de Seguiran whose article VÉRITÉ was tacked on to Romilly's VERTU as it had arrived too late to be put in its proper place in the alphabet, and Charles Millot (*c*. 1717–69), described as 'curé de Loisey, diocèse de Toul', whose AFFABILITÉ and ENTÊTEMENT appear among the 'Articles omis' of Vol. XVII.

If we put together these lists of contributors—regular or oc-casional, in at the very beginning or writing only for the last ten volumes—we may draw certain deductions. Perhaps too much has been made in the past of the great names associated with the *Encyclopédie*. If we leave aside the two editors, we find that the contribution of the great names of the age was very small. Buffon never wrote the promised article NATURE; though Montesquieu's death gave rise to a magnificent *éloge* by d'Alembert in Vol. V, he is represented by only a small fragment inserted in the article GOÛT; though music played an important part in Rousseau's life, his in-fluence on his contemporaries and posterity derived from his ideas, and these are represented only by one article, ÉCONOMIE POLITIQUE; Voltaire's contribution was relatively modest, since his forty-three articles extended merely from Vol. V to Vol. VIII and were rarely of any considerable ideological significance. When Turgot became *contrôleur général* in 1774, he had difficulty in living down the bad reputation which he had earned in official quarters as an *encyclo-pédiste*; but his known contribution was limited to five articles, interesting no doubt, but hardly of any great practical significance.

The real mainstay of the work—the man who was more than anyone else responsible for completing the last ten volumes and bringing the *Encyclopédie* to a successful conclusion—was a much more modest figure, that ruthless compiler, the Chevalier de Jaucourt. If Baron d'Holbach played a greater part than is often realized in the composition of these last ten volumes, one could not claim either that he was one of the leading thinkers of his age or that what he contributed to the *Encyclopédie* was as radical in thought as his *Système de la Nature*. And a great deal of the text of the *Encyclopédie* was in fact contributed by fairly obscure figures such as Abbé Mallet, Abbé Yvon (the bulk of his articles unsigned), Boucher d'Argis, Dumarsais, Beauzée, and a large number of doctors the size of whose contribution tended to be in inverse ratio to their fame.

Attempts have been made to treat the contributors on a sociological basis, but these are not always convincing. When one puts together the lists of regular and occasional contributors all one can really say is that they offer a cross-section of the professional and upper classes of France in the period 1745–65. Impecunious men of letters from the same social stratum as Diderot and d'Alembert were inevitably prominent among the paid contributors— whether they were *abbés* like Mallet, Yvon, Raynal and Morellet or laymen like Landois, the Daubenton brothers, Boucher d'Argis or Beauzée. Various unpaid contributors also belonged to the same social group—Rousseau, Cahusac, Dumarsais and Abbé Lenglet-Dufresnoy. A great number of medical men wrote both on medicine and on the various sciences. A fairly considerable number of civil servants, manufacturers and merchants supplied articles on technology. Military and naval matters were handled by officers, many of them drawn from the nobility. The *noblesse d'épée* furnished its contingent of contributors, ranging from the Comte de Tressan, Louis XV's aide de camp at the battle of Fontenoy, to that scion of an old feudal family, Jaucourt, who because of his Protestant origins had been educated in Geneva and who, to the horror of his family and friends, had studied medicine. A future *Intendant* in the person of Turgot also contributed, as did a certain number of members of the judicial caste. If some of the early recruits joined in partly because Le Breton and his partners offered some sort of payment to a limited number of contributors, no doubt the work gradually attracted men who were vaguely progressive in outlook. Even here one notices that some contributors, even when writing before 1757 and the ban on the *Encyclopédie* which was to follow, found it prudent to keep their names a secret, and at times one has the feeling that the success of the early volumes attracted some contributors in the same sort of way as the correspondence columns of modern newspapers draw in those who like to see their name in print. Whether a sociological approach to the contributors really takes one beyond the obvious conclusion that they were drawn from the more intellectually inclined members of the middle and upper classes of society is doubtful.

## The subscribers

What of the 3,931 subscribers whom, according to the publishers' books which had to be produced in the course of their lawsuit with Luneau de Boisjermain, the *Encyclopédie* finally attracted? For a study of its influence both in France and abroad it would be extremely interesting to know how many of the sets stayed in France and how many were exported. Unfortunately it is impossible to produce even approximate figures, though a great many were bandied about by both sides in this lawsuit. For instance Luneau was castigated by one of the publishers' lawyers for his lack of patriotism in urging his fellow subscribers, abroad as well as at home, to ask for most of their money back:

Il n'y a eu qu'environ douze cents souscriptions prises en France; tout le reste a été enlevé par l'étranger. Ce sera donc l'étranger qui profiterait d'environ les trois quarts de cette somme immense. C'est ainsi que le sieur Luneau est citoyen; c'est ainsi qu'il a au cœur les intérêts de sa patrie.[1]

Another document from the publishers' side was no doubt nearer the truth when it stated that 'les trois quarts des souscriptions ont été prises par les libraires de province et des pays étrangers'.[2] Yet this does not tell us what proportion of the subscriptions were taken out by provincial booksellers and by foreign booksellers.

---

[1] *Précis pour les libraires associés à l'Encyclopédie contre le sieur Luneau de Boisjermain et contre sept intervenants*, Paris, 1772, p. 6.
[2] *Précis pour la dame veuve Briasson . . . et le sieur Le Breton . . . contre le sieur Luneau et contre les intervenants*, Paris, 1776, p. 31.

Like ourselves contemporaries were reduced to mere guesses. In 1771, in a letter to his partner Panckoucke about their plans for re-printing the *Encyclopédie*, Cramer estimated the number of French subscribers to the first edition as 2,000, i.e. roughly half, and also spoke of half of their new edition finding a home in France.[1] One must regretfully conclude that we simply do not know what pro-portion of the first edition was sold in France or was sent abroad.

On the other hand the documents of the lawsuit with Luneau do contain a good deal of information about the individuals who sub-scribed to the *Encyclopédie*. They furnish details about a certain number of subscribers, illustrious or otherwise, and their social status or occupation. In 1776, for instance, the publishers produced certificates, signed by a number of great noblemen, declaring that they were quite satisfied with their bargain as subscribers. The names of the signatories are given as 'M. le Maréchal Duc de Noailles, M. le Maréchal de Mouchy, M. le Duc de la Vallière, M. le Marquis de Paulmy, M. le Marquis de Noailles'.[2] Another document from Luneau's side gives the names of his fellow-sub-scribers who had publicly come to his support as 'le marquis de Camille Massimo, le marquis de la Saône, le marquis de Lansègue, Conseiller au Parlement de Toulouse, le sieur de Jossan, résident en France du prince de Hohenlohe, le sieur de Lalande, de l'Académie des Sciences, etc., le sieur Bachelier, directeur des Écoles gratuites de dessin, le sieur Péchin, conseiller au Présidial de Langres, et les sieurs Boitel de Richeville, de La Court, Hillou et autres'.[3]

Of all the forty or so documents put out by the two sides in this protracted lawsuit the most important as a source for names of subscribers is Luneau's last *Mémoire*.[4] This contains letters of support from a dozen fellow-subscribers and, in addition, supplies a long list of names of subscribers who had signed a document to back up his claim. Indeed adding together all the names mentioned in the documents put out by both sides between 1769 and 1778, we have those of something like two per cent of the subscribers. It is inevitably a somewhat random sample in which foreign sub-scribers are definitely underrepresented and in which, since most of them are names of Luneau's supporters, those who wanted

---

[1] *Essays*, p. 87.          [2] *Précis pour la dame veuve Briasson . . .*, Paris, 1776, p. 26.
[3] *Mémoire pour le Marquis de Camille Massimo . . . et autres*, Paris, 1777, p. 1.
[4] *Mémoire pour P. J. Fr. Luneau de Boisjermain, servant de réponse à un mémoire du sieur Le Breton et de ses associés . . .*, Paris, 1778, *Pièces justificatives*, pp. 2–13.

something for nothing (or next to nothing) are overrepresented. Yet this list does give us some idea of what sort of people put their money into this expensive investment.

The first edition could clearly only be purchased by fairly well-to-do people since its price was 980 livres, and as binding involved something like 160 livres extra for the twenty-eight volumes, the total cost came to some 1,140 livres—equivalent to roughly £50 in English currency *of the time*. It cannot be said that, given what we know of the high price of the work and of the society of eighteenth-century France, our list contains any surprises. It merely serves to bring a little more detail into the picture produced by Daniel Mornet when he examined 500 library catalogues of the period 1750–80:

L'*Encyclopédie* se rencontre dans les bibliothèques de 5 avocats, 6 membres de la noblesse, 14 fonctionnaires, 3 parlementaires, 3 ecclésiastiques, 2 abbés, Choiseul archevêque de Cambrai, 2 apothicaires, 2 médecins, 1 académicien (académie des Sciences), La Popelinière, Lamoignon, Hénault.[1]

The names to be found in the list furnished by Luneau's lawsuit are those of *grands seigneurs* of the court and of country gentlemen; representatives of the secular and regular clergy (and their libraries); a great number of lawyers, in particular judges and *avocats*; quite a number of relatively high officials; one or two doctors; some merchants, and so on. We also learn something about the diffusion of the *Encyclopédie* in the provinces of France, although here our sample is too small for us to draw any deductions about its popularity in the different regions of the country.

It is interesting to compare this list with one for subscribers to the much cheaper quarto edition produced by the Genevan publisher, Pellet, from 1777 onwards. At the end of the first volume of the Bibliothèque Nationale set of this edition there is a four-page list of subscribers compiled by a Besançon bookseller. It lists 253 persons (two of them without names attached) and in a high proportion of cases it also gives the profession or social status of the subscriber. A small number of those listed were the customers of a bookseller in the neighbouring town of Dole. Inevitably the names given here were drawn from a small area of France—roughly the four

---

[1] 'Les Enseignements des bibliothèques privées (1750–80)', *Revue d'histoire littéraire de la France*, 1910, p. 169.

departments of Doubs, Jura, Haute-Saône and Côte d'Or—and we have no means of telling how many people in that particular region subscribed to the first edition. It must be remembered that the work they were offered was not the original *Encyclopédie*; the number of plates was drastically reduced in the Pellet edition and articles from the *Supplément* were incorporated in the text. It was also substantially cheaper—384 livres (about £16 in English money *of the time*) as against 980 for the first edition.

In examining this list one comes up against the fact that it is not easy to establish a clear line of demarcation between nobleman and *roturier* in eighteenth-century France. All we can safely say is that it contains the names of thirteen titled persons, some of whom are included among the army officers; these come to over thirty. The legal world is heavily represented: no fewer than forty-two *avocats* are listed with forty-five other lawyers, ranging from high dignitaries of the Besançon Parlement to holders of more modest posts. The list also includes twenty-one holders of a variety of administrative posts, and six *docteurs en médecine* are listed along with fifteen *négociants*. The clergy, regular and secular, is well represented with thirty-eight names, among them those of nine *curés*.

Broadly speaking, although the names of a considerable number of eminent personages of the Besançon-Dole region are to be found in this list, the lower price of the Pellet quarto edition seems to have appealed to a large number of members of the professional classes. That a good third of the subscribers in this corner of France were lawyers is a striking phenomenon. Yet we must not try to read too much into this isolated document or to draw too close comparisons with the list of subscribers to the first edition which we have just examined. Neither list contains any real surprises. It is clear that both editions, even the cheaper one, were bought only by reasonably prosperous people drawn from the middle and upper ranks of pre-revolutionary French society.

## Chapter 4

# *Reference work or 'machine de guerre'?*

Although at the time some of its friends and many of its enemies saw in the *Encyclopédie* merely an agent for the diffusion of the outlook of the Enlightenment, it would be wrong to exaggerate this side of the work and to forget that for publishers and editors alike the first aim of the enterprise was merely to provide what was for its time the largest sum of human knowledge ever published in France or England. Clearly Le Breton and his partners were interested, not in the Enlightenment, but in profits; and while Diderot and d'Alembert had, as we shall see in a moment, certain additional aims, the task with which they were entrusted was to use as a starting point the translation of Chambers's *Cyclopaedia* and to bring out a series of massive volumes which would summarize the existing state of man's knowledge over a very wide field.

## *The aims of the editors*

The professed aims of the two editors can be studied in a number of documents, in particular the *Prospectus*, written by Diderot and published in October 1750; d'Alembert's *Discours Préliminaire*, which was placed at the head of the first volume of the *Encyclopédie* (June 1751) and incorporated the *Prospectus*; the haughty *Avertissement* written by d'Alembert for the third volume, published in October 1753, after the work had been interrupted by the first *arrêt du Conseil*; and the lengthy account of his aims given by the editor-in-chief in the article *ENCYCLOPÉDIE which appeared in the fifth volume in November 1755.

## The ' Prospectus'

Diderot begins the *Prospectus* by stressing the importance of having a work which could be consulted on all the different branches of knowledge and then goes on to speak of the aims of the whole enterprise in the following terms:

En réduisant sous la forme de dictionnaire tout ce qui concerne les sciences et les arts, il s'agissait encore de faire sentir les secours mutuels qu'ils se prêtent; d'user de ces secours pour en rendre les principes plus sûrs et leurs conséquences plus claires; d'indiquer les liaisons éloignées ou prochaines des êtres qui composent la Nature et qui ont occupé les hommes; de montrer, par l'entrelacement des racines et par celui des branches, l'impossibilité de bien connaître quelques parties de ce tout, sans remonter ou descendre à beaucoup d'autres; de former un tableau général des efforts de l'esprit humain dans tous les genres et dans tous les siècles; de présenter ces objets avec clarté; de donner à chacun d'eux l'étendue convenable; et de vérifier, s'il était possible, notre épigraphe par notre succès:

> Tantum series juncturaque pollet,
> Tantum de medio sumptis accedit honoris!
> Horat. Art. poet. [p. 1a][1]

Nothing could appear more objective or more harmless than such a programme.

While Diderot praises Chambers's *Cyclopaedia*, he maintains that, owing to its debt to various French works, a mere translation of it would have aroused indignation in France. Two folio volumes were not in any case, he adds, sufficient to cover such an enormous field: 'La traduction entière du Chambers nous a passé sous les yeux; et nous avons trouvé une multitude prodigieuse de choses à désirer dans les sciences; dans les arts libéraux, un mot où il fallait des pages, et tout à suppléer dans les arts mécaniques' [p. 2a]. Perhaps inevitably Diderot even exaggerates the new project's independence of its English model:

Mais sans nous étendre davantage sur les imperfections de l'encyclopédie anglaise, nous annonçons que l'ouvrage de Chambers n'est point la base sur laquelle nous avons élevé; que nous avons refait un grand nombre de

---

[1] The meaning of these lines of Horace is still the subject of debate among classical scholars (see 'The language of Virgil and Horace', *Classical Quarterly*, 1959, pp. 181–91, by L. P. Wilkinson, who translates them by 'Such is the power of texture and combination, such the dignity that can accrue to words taken from the common stock').

ses articles, et que nous n'avons employé presque aucun des autres sans addition, correction ou retranchement; qu'il rentre simplement dans la classe des auteurs que nous avons particulièrement consultés, et que la disposition générale est la seule chose qui soit commune entre notre ouvrage et le sien.

The genealogical tree of all forms of knowledge, a diagram of which the editors of the *Encyclopédie* affixed to the *Prospectus* and to the preface of their first volume in a folding sheet headed 'Système figuré des connaissances humaines', was much more fully developed than that of Chambers, being adapted from the scheme set out by Francis Bacon over a century earlier. It was based, Diderot explained, on the three faculties—on memory, from which history was derived; on reason, which gave rise to philosophy; and on imagination, from which came poetry and the fine arts.

Such a vast work, as the example of Chambers had shown, could not be the work of one man; the editors had therefore assembled a team of specialists to write articles on the subjects in which they were experts. The field which they and the editors had to cover falls into three parts: 'les sciences, les arts libéraux et les arts mécaniques' [p. 3]. Diderot has most to say about the last of these; here he claimed almost complete originality for the projected work, a claim which, as we shall see, was disputed at the time and has been disputed in our own day. Finally, before embarking on a detailed explanation of the 'Système figuré des connaissances humaines', Diderot sums up the advantages of the projected encyclopedia in the following words:

D'où nous inférons que cet ouvrage pourrait tenir lieu de bibliothèque dans tous les genres à un homme du monde, et dans tous les genres, excepté le sien, à un savant de profession; qu'il suppléera aux livres élémentaires; qu'il développera les vrais principes des choses; qu'il en marquera les rapports; qu'il contribuera à la certitude et au progrès des connaissances humaines, et qu'en multipliant le nombre des vrais savants, des artistes[1] distingués et des amateurs éclairés, il répandra dans la société de nouveaux avantages. [p. 5b]

What is stressed here is obviously the usefulness of such an encyclopedia as a reference work.

---

[1] Cf. the unsigned article ARTISTE: 'nom que l'on donne aux ouvriers qui excellent dans ceux d'entre les arts mécaniques qui supposent l'intelligence. . . .'

## The ' Discours préliminaire'

D'Alembert's *Discours préliminaire*, a much lengthier and more ambitious piece of writing, won praise even from critics of the *Encyclopédie* in France and brought him European fame. 'One of the most capital productions of which the philosophy of the present age can boast' a writer in the *Monthly Review* was later to call it.[1] In forty-five large folio pages, from which must be deducted the seven pages in which he reproduces Diderot's *Prospectus* in a slightly revised form, d'Alembert could spread himself and rise up to philosophical heights. He takes as his starting-point the dual aim of the whole work:

Comme *Encyclopédie*, il doit exposer, autant qu'il est possible, l'ordre et l'enchaînement des connaissances humaines; comme *Dictionnaire raisonné des sciences, des arts et des métiers*, il doit contenir sur chaque science et sur chaque art, soit libéral, soit mécanique, les principes généraux qui en sont la base, et les détails les plus essentiels qui en font le corps et la substance. Ces deux points de vue, d'*Encyclopédie* et de *Dictionnaire raisonné*, formeront donc le plan et la division de notre *Discours préliminaire*. [I.i]

His first aim then is to examine what he calls 'la généalogie et la filiation de nos connaissances'. Starting from the fashionable Lockean theory that all our knowledge derives directly or indirectly from the senses, he proceeds to trace in detail the stages by which its different branches emerged. This leads to the classification of the different forms of human knowledge, already set forth briefly by Diderot in the *Prospectus*, according to the three faculties concerned—memory, reason and imagination:

Ces trois facultés forment d'abord les trois divisions générales de notre système et les trois objects généraux des connaissances humaines: l'Histoire, qui se rapporte à la mémoire; la Philosophie, qui est le fruit de la raison; et les Beaux-Arts, que l'imagination fait naître. [I.xvi]

In the following pages d'Alembert proceeds to show how the different forms of knowledge may be derived from these three faculties and then refers the reader to the more detailed account of this system of classification given by Diderot at the end of the *Prospectus* and in the accompanying diagram, both of which were

[1] 1787, i, 243.

reprinted after his *Discours préliminaire*. Inevitably this system of classification was more than a little arbitrary; at times the results are even mildly comic. 'Raison', we have seen, gives birth to 'Philosophie' (in the older and wider sense of the term which includes what we should call Science); 'Philosophie' includes therefore everything from 'Métaphysique générale' and 'Théologie révélée' to 'Architecture militaire' and 'Jardinage'. That this genealogical tree of knowledge does not take one very far is freely admitted by d'Alembert himself.

In the second half of the *Discours préliminaire* he considers the *Encyclopédie* from a different angle, as a *Dictionnaire raisonné des sciences et des arts*. As a preliminary he offers the reader a sketch of the present state of the arts and sciences along with an account of how they have arrived at this position:

L'exposition métaphysique de l'origine et de la liaison des sciences nous a été d'une grande utilité pour en former l'arbre encyclopédique; l'exposition historique de l'ordre dans lequel nos connaissances se sont succédé, ne sera pas moins avantageuse pour nous éclairer nous-mêmes sur la manière dont nous devons transmettre ces connaissances à nos lecteurs. [I.xix]

These remarks introduce the famous account of how the three branches of knowledge—erudition (memory), literature and the arts (imagination), and sciences and philosophy (reason)—have developed since the Renaissance. Naturally most attention is given to the progress of philosophy and science since the sixteenth century. The historical account of their development is built round a series of great names. In the seventeenth century Bacon, Descartes, Newton, Locke and Leibniz are given detailed treatment, and in the eighteenth Fontenelle, Buffon, Voltaire and Montesquieu. It is noticeable that, despite his pride in the progress achieved by man since the Renaissance, d'Alembert is far from being lost in admiration for the achievements of his own age. He regrets, for instance, the disappearance of Latin as the international language of learning, and holds that the literature of his day is in many ways inferior to that of Louis XIV. Not for him a starry-eyed belief in the indefinite perfectibility of the human species. Reason and good taste alternate in man's history with periods of barbarism: 'La barbarie dure des siècles, il semble que ce soit notre élément; la raison et le bon goût ne font que passer' [I.xxxiii].

At this point in the *Discours préliminaire* the main part of Diderot's *Prospectus* is reprinted with slight modifications. After this d'Alembert offers an account of the principal contributors who had undertaken to supply articles in their own field, giving a special mention to Diderot both for his technological articles and for the enormous number of gaps which he had filled in in the first volume. The preface ends with a mild epigram: 'C'est au public qui lit à nous juger: nous croyons devoir le distinguer de celui qui parle!' [I.xlv].

## The 'Avertissement' to the third volume

A distinct contrast to the predominantly objective tone of the *Discours préliminaire* is furnished by the *Avertissement* which d'Alembert composed for the third volume, the appearance of which was delayed by the *arrêt du Conseil* of February 1752 banning the first two. In his defence of the *Encyclopédie* against hostile criticism he adopts a distinctly polemical tone. After speaking of the way in which the editors had followed the general layout of Chambers, seeking merely to improve the execution of the work, he answers their critics in haughty tones:

C'est dans cette vue que l'on a cru devoir exclure de cet ouvrage une multitude de noms propres qui n'auraient fait que le grossir assez inutilement; que l'on a conservé et complété plusieurs articles d'histoire et de mythologie, qui ont paru nécessaires pour la connaissance des différentes sectes de philosophes, des différentes religions, de quelques usages anciens et modernes; et qui d'ailleurs donnent souvent occasion à des réflexions philosophiques, pour lesquelles le public semble avoir aujourd'hui plus de goût que jamais: aussi est-ce principalement par l'esprit philosophique que nous tâcherons de distinguer ce dictionnaire. C'est par là surtout qu'il obtiendra les suffrages auxquels nous sommes le plus sensibles. [III.iv]

These last lines reveal with sudden clarity the underlying aim of the editors.

A similar sharpness of tone is to be found in the passage which follows, even though d'Alembert is merely explaining why certain subjects are not dealt with in what was, after all, *a dictionnaire des sciences et des arts*. Why certain philosophers, but not the

Fathers, are included in the *Encyclopédie* is put with almost brutal irony:

Les premiers ont été créateurs d'opinions, quelquefois bonnes, quelque-fois mauvaises, mais dont notre plan nous oblige à parler. On n'a rappelé qu'en peu de mots et par occasion quelques circonstances de leur vie; on a fait l'histoire de leurs pensées plus que de leurs personnes. Les Pères de l'Église, au contraire, chargés du dépôt précieux et inviolable de la foi et de la tradition, n'ont pu ni dû rien apprendre de nouveau aux hommes sur les matières importantes dont ils se sont occupés. Ainsi la doctrine de saint Augustin, qui n'est autre que celle de l'Église, se trouvera aux articles PRÉDESTINATION, GRACE, PÉLAGIANISME; mais comme évêque d'Hippone, fils de sainte Monique et saint lui-même, sa place est au *Martyrologe*, et préférable à tous égards à celle qu'on aurait pu lui donner dans l'*Encyclo-pédie*. [III.iv]

A similar polemical tone is adopted in accounting for other gaps in the work:

On ne trouvera dans cet ouvrage, comme un journaliste l'a subtilement observé, ni la *vie des Saints*, que M. Baillet a suffisament écrite,[1] et qui n'est point de notre objet; ni la *généalogie des grandes maisons*, mais la généalogie des sciences, plus précieuse pour qui sait penser; ni les aven-tures peu intéressantes des littérateurs anciens et modernes, mais le fruit de leurs travaux et de leurs découvertes; ni la description détaillée de chaque village, telle que certains érudits prennent la peine de la faire aujourd'hui, mais une notice du commerce des provinces et des villes principales, et des détails curieux sur leur histoire naturelle; ni les *conquérants* qui ont désolé la terre, mais les génies immortels qui l'ont éclairée; ni enfin une foule de *souverains* que l'histoire aurait dû proscrire. Le nom même des princes et des grands n'a droit de se trouver dans l'*Encyclopédie* que par le bien qu'ils ont fait aux sciences; parce que l'*Encyclopédie* doit tout aux talents, rien aux titres, et qu'elle est l'histoire de l'esprit humain, et non de la vanité des hommes. [III.iv]

Here again the *philosophe* lets himself go.

After recalling how the Jesuit *Journal de Trévoux* which had praised the plan of Chambers when it announced the prospectus of Mills's projected translation in 1745, had taken a very different line when Diderot's *Prospectus* appeared five years later, d'Alembert

---

[1] *Les Vies des saints* (1701–03) by Adrien Baillet, the first biographer of Descartes.

goes on to claim that the new work has advantages over its English model:

Il pourra, par exemple, être fort riche en physique générale et en chimie, du moins quant à la partie qui regarde les observations et l'expérience; car, pour ce qui concerne les causes, il ne saurait être au contraire trop réservé et trop sage. . . . On ne se refusera pourtant pas aux conjectures, surtout dans les articles dont l'objet est utile ou nécessaire, comme la médecine, où l'on est obligé de conjecturer, parce que la nature force d'agir en empêchant de voir. La métaphysique des sciences, car il n'en est point qui n'ait la sienne, fondée sur des principes simples et sur des notions communes à tous les hommes, fera, nous l'espérons, un des principaux mérites de cet ouvrage. Celle de la grammaire surtout et celle de la géométrie sublime seront exposées avec une clarté qui ne laissera rien à désirer, et que peut-être elles attendent encore. A l'égard de la métaphysique proprement dite, sur laquelle on croit s'être trop étendu dans les premiers volumes, elle sera réduite dans les suivants à ce qu'elle contient de vrai et d'utile, c'est-à-dire à très peu de chose. Enfin dans la partie des arts, si étendue, si délicate, si importante et si peu connue, l'*Encyclopédie* commencera ce que les générations suivantes finiront ou perfectionneront. Elle fera l'histoire des richesses de notre siècle en ce genre; elle la fera à ce siècle qui l'ignore, et aux siècles à venir, qu'elle mettra sur la voie pour aller plus loin. [III.v]

Here we find d'Alembert in a rather more sober mood.

For the *Encyclopédie* he goes on to claim that, despite its debt—acknowledged or otherwise—to Chambers and to other sources, many of its articles in a great variety of fields show distinct originality:

Combien d'articles de théologie, de belles-lettres, de poétique, d'histoire naturelle, de grammaire, de musique, de chimie, de mathématique élémentaire et transcendante, de physique, d'astronomie, de tactique, d'horlogerie, d'optique, de jardinage, de chirurgerie et de diverses autres sciences, qui certainement ne se trouvent dans aucun dictionnaire, et dont plusieurs même, en plus grand nombre qu'on ne pense, n'ont pu être fournis par aucun livre! Combien surtout d'articles immenses dans la descriptions des arts, pour lesquels on n'a eu d'autres secours que les lumières des amateurs et des artistes et la fréquentation des ateliers! [III.viii–ix]

The very wide spread of the subjects here listed makes this a large claim.

## The article *ENCYCLOPÉDIE

Diderot's article *ENCYCLOPÉDIE (it occupies twenty-seven double-columned pages in the fifth volume[1]) is not nearly as well known as d'Alembert's *Discours préliminaire*. It has never been reprinted on its own with full annotation and therefore has never had the honour of being a prescribed text in universities. Yet in some ways it is a more interesting piece of work, partly because it reflects the experience which by 1755 the editor-in-chief had acquired in seeing several volumes of the work through the press. If the article lacks the lucid and orderly arrangement and the clear and logical style of the *Discours préliminaire*, it is bursting with life and also with indiscretions of a kind which delighted the enemies of the *Encyclopédie*. It meanders from one subject to another and is full of characteristic digressions, the most interesting of which is a long disquisition on language, penned because Diderot had suddenly felt that the subject had so far been neglected in the *Encyclopédie*.

If, as we shall see later, *ENCYCLOPÉDIE contains some rash remarks about the underlying spirit of the work and the methods used to instil it in the reader, none the less it has a more objective side when Diderot is dealing both with the work he was editing and with the problem of producing at some future date the ideal encyclopedia of his dreams. The man who later in his life was to use the words, 'Il faut *sabrer* la théologie', could write here at least with impartiality:

Nous répondrons seulement à ceux qui auraient voulu qu'on supprimât la théologie: que c'est une science; que cette science est très étendue et très curieuse, et qu'on aurait pu la rendre plus intéressante que la mythologie, qu'ils auraient regrettée si nous l'eussions omise. [V.646v/a]

The objectivity of his opening definition of the aims of an encyclopedia[2] is echoed later on in the article when he compares a work of this kind with the periodical press:

Une *encyclopédie* est une exposition rapide et désintéressée des découvertes des hommes dans tous les lieux, dans tous les genres et dans tous les siècles,

---

[1] The article is foliated not paginated, hence the references which follow are to folios (r=recto, v=verso). It is obvious that it was composed in a hurry at the last moment and that the printer had to fit it into the volume as best he could. According to Rousseau Diderot was ill at the time: 'L'article *Encyclopédie* qui est de Diderot fait l'admiration de tout Paris, et ce qui augmentera votre étonnement, c'est qu'il l'a fait étant malade'. (Leigh 337)

[2] Quoted above, p. 2.

sans aucun jugement des personnes; au lieu que les journaux ne sont qu'une histoire momentanée des ouvrages et des auteurs. [V.645v/a]

That at any rate was the ideal.

On the relationship of the *Encyclopédie* to Chambers Diderot speaks with almost embarrassing frankness. He concedes that the English author was more regular in the distribution of his material: 'C'était un laboureur qui traçait son sillon superficiel, mais égal et droit' [V.641v/a]. The *Encyclopédie*, he admits, is very different in this respect:

On se pique. On veut avoir des morceaux d'appareil. C'est même peut-être en ce moment ma vanité. L'exemple de l'un en entraîne un autre. Les éditeurs se plaignent, mais inutilement. On se prévaut de leurs propres fautes contre eux-mêmes, et tout se porte à l'excès. Les articles de Chambers sont assez régulièrement distribués, mais ils sont vides; les nôtres sont pleins, mais irréguliers. [V.641v/a–b]

The failure to relate the length of articles to their importance is freely confessed in a passage which was seized upon by contemporary critics and repeatedly quoted against the whole work:

Ici nous sommes boursouflés et d'un volume exorbitant: là maigres, petits, mesquins, secs et décharnés. Dans un endroit nous ressemblons à des squelettes; dans un autre nous avons un air hydropique. Nous sommes alternativement nains et géants, colosses et pygmées; droits, bien faits et proportionnés, bossus, boiteux et contrefaits. [V.641r/b–641v/a]

He admits again that the style of many articles leaves much to be desired, being 'tantôt abstrait, obscur ou recherché, plus souvent négligé, traînant et lâche' [*ibid.*].

Diderot shows similar frankness in discussing the relationship between articles in the *Encyclopédie* and those in the French translation of Chambers which were apparently distributed to the contributors as a bait to encourage them to produce what was asked of them. If these had not been sent out to contributors, Diderot argues, the *Encyclopédie* would never have been completed:

Mais en présentant â chacun un rouleau de papiers qu'il ne s'agissait que de revoir, corriger, augmenter, le travail de création, qui est toujours celui qu'on redoute, disparaissait, et l'on se laissait engager par la considération la plus chimérique; car ces lambeaux décousus se sont trouvés si incomplets, si mal composés, si mal traduits, si pleins d'omissions, d'erreurs et d'inexactitudes, si contraires aux idées de nos collègues, que la plupart les ont rejetés. Que n'ont-ils eu tous le même courage! [V.644v/b–645r/a]

Diderot might perhaps have carried frankness a little further at this point. A considerable number of articles from Chambers—including some bearing his editorial asterisk or the signature of d'Alembert—passed straight into the pages of the *Encyclopédie*; and some of these continue to reappear in modern editions of extracts from the *Encyclopédie* as if they were their own work. He comes closer to the truth when he goes on to exclaim:

Ce frivole avantage a coûté bien cher. Que de temps perdu à traduire de mauvaises choses! que de dépenses pour se procurer un plagiat continuel! combien de fautes et de reproches qu'on se serait épargnés avec une simple nomenclature! Mais eût-elle suffi à déterminer nos collègues? [V.654r/a]

At this point in \*ENCYCLOPÉDIE he carries objectivity to considerable lengths in judging the work of which he was the editor:

J'examine notre travail sans partialité; je vois qu'il n'y a peut-être aucune sorte de faute que nous n'ayons commise; et je suis forcé d'avouer que d'une *encyclopédie* telle que la nôtre, il en entrerait à peine les deux tiers dans une véritable *encyclopédie*. [V.644v/b]

Frankness could scarcely be taken further.

Yet there is nothing at all apologetic about the tone of this article. Like d'Alembert in the *Avertissement* to the third volume, Diderot makes high claims for the originality of the work. Originality is not what the modern user of encyclopedias seeks in their articles; what he wants is an accurate and up-to-date account of the present state of knowledge on any given subject. Yet, like his fellow editor Diderot proclaims with obvious pride that the *Encyclopédie* contains 'une infinité de choses nouvelles et qu'on chercherait inutilement ailleurs' [V.645r/b]. It is noticeable, however that the part of the *Encyclopédie* the originality of which he particularly stresses at this point is the technological articles and plates for which he himself was largely responsible. 'Il ne s'est point encore fait et il ne se fera de longtemps', he declares, 'une collection aussi considérable et aussi belle de machines.' However, he later offers a more realistic appraisal of the functions of an encyclopedia when, in stressing the importance of good bibliographies in a work of this kind, he writes: 'Observons que, excepté la matière des arts, il n'y a proprement du ressort d'un dictionnaire que ce qui est déjà publié' [V.645r/a].

Although free in his criticisms of what he and his contributors had achieved and lavish in his suggestions for all manner of improvements which would lead in the future to the production of a better encyclopedia, Diderot was not in the least abashed by his consciousness of the shortcomings of his own work. Paraphrasing almost certainly a passage from a eulogistic review of the fourth volume which had recently appeared in the *Journal des Savants*,[1] Diderot declares: 'Il y a des personnes qui ont lu l'*Encyclopédie* d'un bout à l'autre; et si l'on en excepte le dictionnaire de Bayle, qui perd tous les jours un peu de cette prérogative, il n'y guère que le nôtre qui en ait joui, et qui en jouisse' [V.648r/a]. The modern reader who blinks at this statement has to bear in mind that at that moment only four volumes of the *Encyclopédie* were in print; even so, despite what one is told of the greater leisure enjoyed by some sections of the community in the eighteenth century, there does seem a certain element of hyperbole in this claim.

Of the importance of the task on which he was engaged Diderot had no doubt. In a passage which aroused the sarcasm of several contemporary critics he exalts the value of an encyclopedia:

Le moment le plus glorieux pour un ouvrage de cette nature, ce serait celui qui succéderait immédiatement à quelque grande révolution qui aurait suspendu les progrès des sciences, interrompu les travaux des arts, et replongé dans les ténèbres une portion de notre hémisphère. Quelle reconnaissance la génération qui viendrait après ces temps de trouble ne porterait-elle pas aux hommes qui les auraient redoutés de loin, et qui en auraient prévenu le ravage, en mettant à l'abri les connaissances des siècles passés. [V.637r/b]

For all his devotion to the ideas of the Enlightenment Diderot, like d'Alembert, had no vision of humanity, guided by Reason, marching 'on and on and on, and up and up and up'. One day, he held, some mighty cataclysm might suddenly plunge mankind

[1] See below, p. 105.

back into barbarism, and then an encyclopedia like theirs would come into its own.

## Technical deficiencies of the 'Encyclopédie'

If we seek now to examine how justified were the claims made for the *Encyclopédie* by its two editors, we may either look at the work as Diderot's contemporaries did or we may view it from the standpoint of the twentieth-century reader who takes for granted the existence of reference works on this scale or even larger. In considering the reactions, and especially the criticisms of contemporaries, one must bear in mind that for them an encyclopedia was a novelty. This is amusingly brought out by the remarks of the Swiss critic, Meister, when in 1780 the index of the *Encyclopédie* at last appeared in two large folio volumes. Far from finding it useful, he wrote impatiently in his review of the work: 'Le but de cet énorme travail est de rapprocher les articles de l'*Encyclopédie* qui s'éclairent, s'expliquent et se développent mutuellement. Cela était-il donc bien nécessaire?'[1] Some contemporaries went even further and regarded the whole undertaking—particularly as it was the work not of one, but of many hands—as a mistake.

D'Alembert had made it clear that a *dictionnaire des sciences et des arts* did not aim to cover every branch of human knowledge. Philosophers from Aristotle to Descartes, Hobbes and Locke receive detailed treatment, but only under the heading of ARISTOTÉLISME, CARTÉSIANISME, HOBBISME and LOCKE (PHILOSOPHIE DE) and with merely a brief sketch of their lives, attention being concentrated on their ideas. In the first five volumes biographical articles as such, whether of saints or historical figures, of writers or scientists, do not exist. However, from the sixth volume onwards Jaucourt began to work in a great many biographical notices into articles on places. This has the bizarre result that, for instance, Shakespeare has to be sought under STRATFORD, and Newton under WOLSTROPE, while the great eighteenth-century doctor, Boerhaave, under whom Jaucourt studied and to whom he pays a moving tribute, is hidden away under VOORHOUT, the little Dutch village where he happened to be born. In other words these biographical articles can be dug out only with the aid of the *Table*.

[1] *Corr. litt.*, xii, 334.

If one seeks in vain for articles on historical figures such as Louis XIV or Joan of Arc or Richelieu, the *Encyclopédie* contains none the less a considerable number of articles on history, ancient and modern, particularly on institutions and usages. Greece and Rome are fairly well covered from this point of view, and if, as regards modern times, France naturally receives most attention, other countries are by no means neglected. A good deal of information about English institutions was, of course, taken over from Chambers.

The treatment of geography varied considerably. At first towns (many of the articles bear Diderot's editorial asterisk) would be dismissed in laconic articles of the type of ' DURHAM, (*Géog. mod.*) capitale de la province d'Angleterre qui a le même nom; elle est sur la Ware. *Long.* 15.55. *lat.* 54.45.' Whole countries, as in *ANGLE-TERRE, or even whole continents, as in *AMÉRIQUE, would be disposed of in just over half a column. However, Diderot soon abandoned the compilation of geographical articles of this kind, and the task passed to more expert hands, so that such articles gradually became much fuller and more communicative. It will be noticed, however, that in the *Avertissement* to the third volume d'Alembert had refused to make any apology for the scrappiness of this section of the *Encyclopédie*. In the later volumes, as we have seen, Jaucourt was responsible for a great many geographical articles to which he added notes on the famous men and women born in a particular place.

If the modern reader is apt to be taken aback at the absence of biographical articles as such, if he also looks in vain for well-known historical figures and finds some of the geographical articles astonishing in their brevity, he is perhaps even more disconcerted by the extraordinary disparities in length between different articles. He will find column upon column on some insignificant topic followed by next to nothing on an important subject. Dozens of examples of this disparity in the length of articles could be quoted, but one example (it was pointed out by a contemporary critic) must suffice. In EMPIRE (*Hist. anc.*) one single column has to suffice for all the empires of the ancient world while in EMPIRE (*Hist. & Droit politique*) the Holy Roman Empire is dispatched in two columns. In contrast in EMPIRE DE GALILÉE which follows immediately on these two articles no fewer than six columns are given up to an altogether trivial topic—the *confrérie* of the clerks attached to the Chambre des Comptes in Paris! That this disparity existed Diderot, as we have seen, cheerfully admitted.

Perhaps too much has been made, from 1751 down to the present day, of the plagiarisms of the *Encyclopédie*. The work began, after all, as an adaptation of Chambers, and it is not surprising to see whole articles transferred from its pages to those of the *Encyclopédie*, although it is perhaps a little odd to see Diderot's editorial asterisk attached to an article like *AVALER which is merely Chambers's SWALLOWING with the addition of an insignificant reference, or to discover that, although both 'Chambers' and d'Alembert's signature appear at the end of the second article on NATURE, the two articles are merely a translation of Chambers's NATURE, NATURA.

If the two editors and their contributors made use both of reference works and of many other books in writing their articles, this is hardly to be wondered at. By its very nature an encyclopedia is a compilation of existing knowledge, and anyone who takes the trouble to compare nineteenth- and twentieth-century encyclopedias in a variety of languages, will soon find that many of these works merely repeat one another, churning out relentlessly a stream of wrong dates, legends and bogus information. Twentieth-century editors of encyclopedias now find it necessary to draw the attention of what they call 'inexperienced contributors' to the existence of copyright laws.

In the *Avertissement* to the third volume d'Alembert made a somewhat embarrassed reply to the criticisms levelled against the obvious plagiarisms of the first two volumes and the failure of some contributors to indicate what was their own work and what came from other works of reference or from well-known books. He could, of course, point out with justice—quoting four words from the title-page of the *Prospectus*—that an encyclopedia 'n'est et ne doit être absolument dans sa plus grand partie qu'un ouvrage *recueilli des meilleurs auteurs*' [III.vii]. He admits, however, that too much use had been made of existing reference works: 'Nous convenons que l'on aurait dû en faire un plus sobre usage, parce que ces dictionnaires ne sont pas les sources primitives et que l'*Encyclopédie* doit puiser surtout dans celles-ci' [III.viii]. However, he was entitled to point out that other reference works, such as

Chambers or the Jesuits' own *Dictionnaire de Trévoux* drew, without acknowledgment, on earlier works, and that, for instance, the description of a plant or the recipe for some remedy could not be correctly given except in more or less identical terms. He could claim with justice that sources are often duly quoted in the *Encyclopédie*; he was, however, compelled to add: 'Mais on tâchera dans la suite de rendre encore et les emprunts moins fréquents et les citations plus exactes' [III.viii]. It cannot honestly be said that this promise was kept; to the very end of the seventeenth volume of text one finds obvious borrowings from other sources, sometimes duly acknowledged with both inverted commas and indication of source, but sometimes with neither.

In considering the *Encyclopédie* as a work of reference we must bear in mind the varying conditions under which the different volumes were produced. The first seven, apart from the somewhat longer period of time between the second and the third, appeared at more or less regular intervals between 1751 and 1757. If the first volume had a relatively limited number of contributors, its appearance very quickly brought in new specialists who enriched subsequent volumes, and the appearance of these volumes attracted in its turn still further able contributors. At times the influx of fresh names had rather bizarre consequences; the appearance on the scene of Claude Bourgelat, the founder of veterinary colleges in France, led to the production of a large number of lengthy articles in his field, particularly on horses and their ailments. Even given the greater importance of that animal in the whole life of the country two centuries ago, one cannot help feeling as one turns the pages of those volumes (V, VI and VII) to which he contributed on so lavish a scale, that too much space is devoted to this topic. It was, however, generally agreed at the time that the *Encyclopédie* steadily improved, volume by volume, between 1751 and 1757.

The last ten volumes were produced under less favourable circumstances. Many of the contributors who had offered their services before the crisis of 1759 now withdrew, and although some new ones took their place, the loss was considerable. An enormous proportion of the work fell on Jaucourt. When in 1766 Voltaire had had time to study his set of the last ten volumes, he wrote to a Paris correspondent: 'En lisant le *Dictionnaire*, je m'aperçois que le chevalier de Jaucourt en a fait les trois quarts. Votre ami

[Diderot] était donc occupé ailleurs?'[1] This was an exaggeration, of course; yet in the writing of these last ten volumes Jaucourt played a truly staggering part. It has been calculated that to the last ten volumes he never contributed less than 25 per cent of the text and that his quota rose as high as 45 per cent in Vol. XVI.[2] Contemporaries, starting, alas, with Diderot himself, speak in contemptuous terms of Jaucourt as a mere compiler. In the earlier volumes as in the last ten he produced on occasion interesting and original articles; and even when he merely compiled, he did so with an intelligence which revealed a truly encyclopedic spread of knowledge, ranging from medicine to the arts and from political theory to botany. Yet, given the millions of words which he contributed to the last ten volumes, it was simply inevitable that the great bulk of them should be extracted from existing works, without any changes and often without acknowledgment.

Diderot was not without his responsibilities as editor of these ten volumes. It is true that he now had to battle along on his own since d'Alembert was no longer joint editor; it is also true that in these years he was heavily engaged in the task of preparing the volumes of plates which began to appear in 1762 and which had swollen far beyond the original 600 promised to subscribers in 1750. In the end there were to be well over four times that number. Even so, one cannot help feeling that there was something in Voltaire's question as to where Diderot had been all this time. Just because his editorial asterisk no longer appears in most of these ten volumes, it cannot be assumed that he himself contributed very little in the way of articles: in addition to his articles on technology and a considerable number on the history of philosophy which can be confidently attributed to him, he also produced a large number of shorter articles as well as some interesting additions to articles by other contributors.

Even so it seems quite clear that he wrote less for the later volumes than he had done for the first seven or eight; and one cannot help forming the impression that he took his editorial duties rather lightly. Certainly the last ten volumes seem to have been shoved together without much care. We find, for instance, in the

---

[1] Best. 12361.
[2] R. N. Schwab, 'The extent of the Chevalier de Jaucourt's contribution to Diderot's *Encyclopédie*', *Modern Language Notes*, 1957, p. 508.

twelfth volume an article POLITIQUE ARITHMÉTIQUE which is simply a translation of the article POLITICAL ARITHMETIC in Chambers; yet in the first volume there had already been printed an article *ARITHMÉTIQUE POLITIQUE which, while based on Chambers, contains original ideas of Diderot's own. In the ninth volume there are two different articles on maelstrom: Jaucourt's MAELSTROM (p. 843) and d'Holbach's MAHLSTROM (pp. 863–4). In the twelfth volume, in addition to d'Holbach's PIERRE-PONCE (p. 578), there is an unsigned article on the same subject six pages later, and on p. 598 one finds yet a third article, taken this time straight from Chambers. In the same volume there is an article PHANTÔME by Jaucourt which Pierre Rousseau found quite superfluous in view of the presence of *FANTÔME in the sixth volume.[1]

Indeed this critic who was on the whole very favourably disposed towards the *Encyclopédie* has some harsh things to say about the technical shortcomings of the last ten volumes. Though he recognizes that the work was produced under very unfavourable conditions after the official ban on its continuation, he feels compelled to voice his dissatisfaction with the last volumes:

Nous avons dit encore que cet ouvrage serait sans contredit le plus parfait qui eût jamais paru si les six[2] derniers volumes eussent été écrits et composés avec autant de soin qu'en ont pris les savants éditeurs des sept premiers tomes. Mais soit que les circonstances n'aient point permis à ces éditeurs éclairés[3] de se charger de la rédaction des articles insérés dans les dix derniers volumes, soit que ces articles aient été écrits et rédigés avec trop de précipitation, il est constant qu'il s'en faut bien qu'ils remplissent l'idée qu'en avaient donnée par avance les excellents articles qui forment les sept premiers volumes et qu'on y trouve toujours les secours et les lumières qu'on devait se flatter d'y trouver. Nous attribuons ces incorrections, ces fautes, ces inexactitudes qui rendent si désirable une édition nouvelle de cet immense dictionnaire,[4] à la contrainte, au découragement et à la précipitation des gens de lettres, autres que les éditeurs des sept premiers volumes, qui se sont chargés de remplir cette pénible tâche; car il n'est point à présumer que sans ces causes et surtout sans cette précipitation on trouvât dans les derniers volumes tant de renvois et si peu d'éclaircissements dans les articles où l'on est renvoyé;

---

[1] *Journal encyclopédique*, 15 Feb. 1769.          [2] A misprint for 'dix'.
[3] There was, of course, only one editor after d'Alembert's defection.
[4] When reading these lines one must bear in mind that at this moment Rousseau was financially interested in plans for a revised edition of the *Encyclopédie* or for a supplement.

tant de décisions et si peu de preuves, tant d'assertions et si peu de principes. Nous ne présumons pas qu'on retrouverait les mêmes articles sous
divers mots ou sous les mêmes mots différemment orthographiés.[1]

In considering these last ten volumes one has also to remember
that it is still by no means clear what was the extent of Le Breton's
suppressions and consequently what effect they had on their text,
taken as a whole.

It can well be imagined that even the first seven volumes of the
*Encyclopédie* did not escape censure from really hostile critics of the
work writing in periodicals, books and pamphlets. From the
beginning they found all sorts of technical deficiencies in these
volumes as they appeared between 1751 and 1757, and this sniping
was continued by Abbé Saas down to 1764. In dealing with the
first volume the Abbé criticizes the way in which two geographical
articles are sometimes given for the same place and sometimes for
an imaginary place.[2] The articles on mythology are similarly
criticized: 'C'est toujours la même méthode de copier sans
examen, de copier jusqu'aux fautes d'impression, de copier des
dictionnaires, guides plus propres à égarer qu'à éclairer.'[3] He next
subjects to detailed, even microscopic examination all manner of
points of erudition arising out of the first volume, even listing
obvious misprints such as wrong spellings or dates, and argues that
the whole work ought to have been properly revised or, alterna-
tively, that a work by so many hands was bound to be a failure.

In his second attack on the work—*Lettres sur l'Encyclopédie pour
servir de supplément aux sept volumes de ce dictionnaire*—he reprints his
examination of the first volume and extends the same criticisms to
the remaining six. It is true that he concedes that, though still
defective, the geographical articles are rather better from the fourth
volume onwards;[4] but he continues to track down all sorts of
errors of fact and examples of two articles on the same topic. He
quotes, for instance, the example of Mallet's CONVENANT [IV.161]
and Jaucourt's COVENANT [IV.324]: 'Le premier article, qui est le
meilleur, est tiré du *Dictionnaire des Arts* de M. Corneille qu'on ne
cite point, l'autre ne vaut pas l'honneur d'être examiné.'[5] Accusations of plagiarism are continually made. He points out, for

---

[1] 15 Feb. 1769, pp. 9–10.
[2] *Lettre d'un professeur de Douai à un professeur de Louvain sur l'Encyclopédie*, p. 77.
[3] *Ibid.*, p. 99.     [4] *Lettres*, p. 68.     [5] *Ibid.*, p. 76.

instance, that Jaucourt's article ENDYMATIES is derived from the *Mémoires de l'Académie des Inscriptions*, and continues on the following page:

Il y a encore dans cette même page un autre article tiré des mêmes *Mémoires de l'Académie des Inscriptions*. C'est celui d'ENDROMIS, et on cite à la fin *Chambers* et la lettre G, nom de l'Encyclopédiste . . .[1] [*sic*]. Il faut avouer que les auteurs de pareils articles n'ont pas eu beaucoup de peine à les composer.[2]

Towards the end of the work the Abbé suspends for a moment his detailed inquiry into the shortcomings of the *Encyclopédie*, and seeks for their fundamental cause. This he finds precisely in what Diderot claimed to be the great advantage of the *Encyclopédie* over a one-man effort like that of Chambers—the fact that it was the work of a team, 'une société de gens de lettres':

Un ouvrage de plusieurs mains se fait à la hâte et chaque travailleur ne s'y intéresse que médiocrement. Il en résulte un grand défaut, c'est que différents ouvriers qui s'entendent mal composent sous différents titres différents articles qui, reportés à la masse, sont employés par un reviseur peu attentif ou peu éclairé. Il est impossible qu'il y ait un reviseur de l'*Encyclopédie* au fait de toutes les matières qui y sont traitées, et voilà d'où proviennent les répétitions, les contradictions, les bévues qui s'y rencontrent. Il y a du bon, du médiocre, du mauvais, du vieux, du neuf, du régulier, de l'irrégulier.[3]

Though he does not deny that the *Encyclopédie* possesses 'de grandes beautés', he had found a great many faults in the first seven volumes.

There was nothing new in these criticisms except that the Abbé went into minute points of detail and, in his second book, extended his examination to the first seven volumes as a whole. Over a decade earlier, in 1751 and 1752, Father Berthier had subjected the first volume to detailed examination in the *Journal de Trévoux* and from the very start had found much the same technical deficiencies, although he had been prepared to admit that it had some good, indeed excellent articles. He complains of mistakes in the printing of foreign words and proper names and emphasizes how many articles are taken without acknowledgement from works like the *Dictionnaire de Trévoux* and the *Dictionnaire de Commerce*.[4] In the

[1] i.e. Mallet.     [2] *Lettres*, pp. 104–5.     [3] *Ibid.*, pp. 160–1.     [4] Oct. 1751, pp. 2288–90.

next number Berthier finds fresh examples of plagiarism, from, for instance, the *Grand dictionnaire historique* of Moreri,[1] and in later numbers he proceeds to point out that quite a number of Yvon's articles such as AGIR and AMITIÉ had been lifted straight from Father Buffier's writings.[2] Although Berthier praises a considerable number of articles covering a very wide range in this first volume, from those of Dumarsais on grammar to those of Diderot on technology, at the end of his review he stresses once more the amount of borrowed material in the *Encyclopédie*: 'On a trop abusé de la liberté d'employer les richesses contenues dans les autres livres. On a trop multiplié les emprunts: pratiques qui pourraient à la longue obscurcir la gloire de l'entreprise et répandre des ombres sur le mérite des auteurs.'[3] Similar criticisms were, of course, to be repeated by a series of hostile writers in the 1750s and beyond, often with the same examples.

Another technical criticism brought against the *Encyclopédie* by a variety of contemporaries was its use of alphabetical order and the accompanying cross-references. It is true that some later encyclopedias—starting with its immediate successor in France, the *Encyclopédie méthodique*, published in 166½ volumes of text and with over 6,000 plates between 1782 and 1832—abandoned alphabetical order in favour of arrangement under subjects, but the great majority have followed the example of Diderot and d'Alembert (and of Chambers before them), since the disadvantages of their system have been found to be outweighed by its advantages. The criticism offered by contemporaries on this score—it is often couched in the most violent terms—is not one which the modern user of the *Encyclopédie* can take very seriously, even though at moments he may get tired of going off in search of another heavy volume to look up an article to which he has been referred.

## Diderot's criticisms of the 'Encyclopédie'

Paradoxically one of the most biting contemporary criticisms of the shortcomings of the *Encyclopédie* came from Diderot himself. When in 1768 Panckoucke and his partners were planning a revised version of the nearly completed work, they approached the editor of the first edition and, in order to put to the authorities

[1] Nov. 1751, pp.2429–35.   [2] Jan. 1752, pp. 172–3, 186.   [3] March 1752, pp. 467–8.

their case for a new licence (*privilège*), got him to state in which respects he considered the *Encyclopédie* stood in need of revision. Unfortunately for Diderot his confidential remarks, though with the contributors' names suppressed, were made public during his publishers' lawsuit with Luneau de Boisjermain;[1] however, from our point of view this frank assessment of the qualities and defects of the work is of great interest.

In his general observations on the work Diderot freely admits that many of the contributors were mediocre or worse:

On n'eut pas le temps d'être scrupuleux sur le choix des travailleurs. Parmi quelques hommes excellents il y en eut de faibles, de médiocres et de tout à fait mauvais. De là cette bigarrure dans l'ouvrage où l'on trouve une ébauche d'écolier à côté d'un morceau de main de maître; une sottise voisine d'une chose sublime; une page écrite avec force, pureté, chaleur, jugement, raison, élégance au verso d'une page pauvre, mesquine, plate et misérable.[2]

Many of the work's faults he attributes to the parsimony of the publishers:

Les uns travaillant sans honoraires, par pur attachement pour les éditeurs et par goût pour l'ouvrage, perdirent bientôt leur première ferveur; d'autres, mal récompensés, nous en donnèrent, comme on dit, pour notre argent. . . . Il y en eut qui remirent toute leur besogne à des espèces de tartares[3] qui s'en chargèrent pour la moitié du prix qu'ils en avaient reçu.[4]

This far from flattering account of his contributors is continued in the following terms:

Il y eut une race détestable de travailleurs qui, ne sachant rien, et qui, se piquant de savoir tout, cherchèrent à se distinguer par une universalité désespérante, se jetèrent sur tout, brouillèrent tout, gâtèrent tout, mettant leur énorme faucille dans la moisson des autres. L'*Encyclopédie* fut un gouffre où ces espèces de chiffonniers jetèrent pêle-mêle une infinité de choses mal vues, mal digérées, bonnes, mauvaises, détestables, vraies, fausses, incertaines et toujours incohérentes et disparates.[5]

On reading these lines the modern reader is bound to ask himself what the editor or editors were doing in all this: surely an essential part of their task was to sift what contributors sent in.

[1] See *Réponse signifiée de M. Luneau de Boisjermain au Précis des Libraires associés à l'impression de l'Encyclopédie*, Paris, 1772, pp. 10–13 (the text is reproduced in AT, xx, 129–33).
[2] *Réponse*, p. 10 (AT, xx, 130).        [3] 'Hacks, drudges'.        [4] *Réponse*, p. 11 (AT, xx, 130).
[5] *Réponse*, p. 11 (AT, xx, 130).

The same reflection is inspired by Diderot's next complaint—that contributors did not bother to supply the necessary cross-references even in their own field. He goes so far as to confess that there was no close relationship between the technological articles and the plates on the same subject which appeared later, and that his attempt to make up for this by inserting long explanations in the volumes of plates was a failure. To complain that, like the contributors, the editors were poorly paid scarcely justifies these failings. One last general remark is of interest: Diderot insists that in a new edition it would be necessary to have bad handwriting carefully copied before the articles were sent to the printer: 'L'on n'y trouvera pas, comme dans la précédente, des noms estropiés et des phrases tronquées qui manquent de sens.'[1]

So far as the treatment of the different subjects was concerned Diderot felt that a great deal of revision—and sometimes more than revision—would be necessary. There were, of course, exceptions—those parts of the work for which he had been mainly responsible: 'Quant à l'histoire ancienne et moderne de la philosophie dont je me suis chargé, ce n'est pas la partie honteuse de l'*Encyclopédie*; elle est à revoir, à rectifier, petit travail.' With his technological articles rather more needed to be done:

Les arts mécaniques à perfectionner et à compléter, surtout à rapporter le discours[2] aux planches, ce qui n'a presque pas été fait, et à faire rentrer dans le discours les explications qui sont à la tête des planches, et surtout à rendre leur énorme nomenclature exacte par le dépouillement général des planches. C'est moi qui m'en suis chargé; et je sais ce qui reste à y faire, ce qui n'est pas petite besogne.

These were, however, mild criticisms compared with what Diderot had to say about the treatment of other subjects in the *Encyclopédie*.

Though mathematics, he said, could scarcely have been in better hands (those of d'Alembert), 'j'ai souvent entendu accuser sa physique d'être un peu maigre'. On natural history, entrusted to Louis Jean Marie Daubenton, there is this criticism: 'Il y a beaucoup à ajouter au règne végétal; la partie physique de ce règne a été fort négligée.' On mineralogy and metallurgy for which Baron d'Holbach was mainly responsible the verdict is fairly

---

[1] *Réponse*, p. 12 (AT, xx, 131).    [2] i.e. the text.

severe, though Diderot admits extenuating circumstances:

Ces deux branches sont tout à fait défectueuses. . . . Elles demandent d'être soigneusement retouchées. M. ∗∗∗ a fait comme tous les autres auxiliaires, il a travaillé sans plan; d'ailleurs sans cesse occupé à réparer les âneries de notre mauvais chimiste, ∗∗∗,[1] il a été forcé à tout moment de déplacer les matières qui ne se trouvent pas où ils devraient être.

After these rude remarks about Dr Venel it is no surprise to discover that the treatment of chemistry is described as 'détestable'. Considering that he recruited some distinguished doctors from Paris and Montpellier, the verdict on the medical articles appears surprisingly harsh: 'La médecine, la matière médicale et la pharmacie . . . est pauvre. . . . L'anatomie et la physiologie, je ne dis pas à refaire, mais à faire.' The articles on logic, metaphysics and ethics, mainly the work of Abbé Yvon, are justly described as 'un plagiat continuel'; here Diderot was merely echoing what critics of the *Encyclopédie* like Father Berthier had long since pointed out. The articles on literature (by Marmontel down to 1757 and after that mostly by Jaucourt) are dismissed as feeble, while those on painting, sculpture and engraving (a few by Diderot himself, others by Watelet and a great number by Jaucourt) are described as 'à refaire', while the section on architecture (despite the eminence of their author, Jacques François Blondel) is dismissed as 'mauvaise et à refaire en entier'. Of that on geography Diderot says: 'mauvaise dans les deux premiers volumes, d'une étendue effroyable dans tous les volumes suivants, à corriger et à resserrer'. And then at the end comes the unkindest cut of all—for the Chevalier de Jaucourt: 'J'oubliais de dire qu'il y a en tout genre au moins quatre volumes in-folio du ∗∗∗, dont il y a très peu de choses à conserver. Il n'en peut rester que la nomenclature.'[2] Such a curt dismissal of the Chevalier's contributions, without which the last ten volumes of the *Encyclopédie* could never have seen the light of day, seems rather cruel.

Interesting as this document is (and despite its suspect source it does read like authentic Diderot), it can scarcely be said to present a balanced view of the merits and shortcomings of the *Encyclopédie*, if only because these comments were intended to convince the authorities that a new and revised version of the whole work was

---

[1] Dr Venel.          [2] *Réponse*, p. 13 (AT, xx, 133).

needed. No doubt in private, as he had done in public, Diderot was in the habit of making rather higher claims not only for his own contributions to the work, but also for those of his colleagues. In his *Mémoire de d'Alembert par lui-même* the other editor certainly spoke more highly of his own part as a contributor, even though he implicitly acknowledges that he owed a considerable debt to Chambers:

Il a revu toute la partie de mathématique et de physique générale de l'*Encyclopédie*, et il a même refait en entier ou presque en entier plusieurs articles considérables relatifs à ces sciences et qui contiennent, sur des objets élémentaires, des choses nouvelles, tels que *Cas irréductible, Courbe, Équation, Différentiel, Figure de la terre, Géométrie, Infini* etc., et un grand nombre d'autres. D'Alembert a donné en outre à l'*Encyclopédie* un nombre assez considérable d'articles de littérature ou de philosophie; on peut citer les articles *Éléments des sciences, Érudition, Dictionnaire* et plusieurs autres moins considérables, sans compter divers synonymes.[1]

Among these articles those like ÉLÉMENTS DES SCIENCES are masterpieces of scientific popularization.

It is virtually impossible to offer an overall assessment of the merits and weaknesses of the *Encyclopédie* as a work of reference. If the claims made for it in public by the two editors were excessive, the denigrations of contemporary enemies no doubt went too far. To judge of its value two centuries later is simply not possible, given the extraordinary increase in knowledge which has taken place in the intervening years. It has also to be borne in mind that, as Diderot was the first to proclaim in the very honest pages of his article *ENCYCLOPÉDIE, it was a first attempt, at any rate in France (and for that matter England), to produce a work of reference on such a scale. Moreover, before we laugh at the oddities and blunders of the *Encyclopédie*, we have to remember the sad fact that many of the encyclopedias being turned out in the second half of the twentieth century are inferior in size, thoroughness and accuracy to those produced in the previous hundred years.

## The technological articles and plates

One section of the work should, however, be examined more closely from this point of view—the part for which d'Alembert as

[1] *Œuvres philosophiques, historiques et littéraires*, Paris, 1805, 18 vols, i, xlii.

well as Diderot claimed the highest degree of originality: the
articles and plates on technology. From the very beginning down
to our own day controversy has raged around this part of the
*Encyclopédie*. While some contemporaries, including Father
Berthier in the *Journal de Trévoux*, spoke highly of Diderot's
articles in this field, others disapproved of the whole idea of filling
page upon page of an encyclopedia with such sordid details. In
1754 the anonymous author of the *Avis au Public sur le troisième
volume de l'Encyclopédie* objected strongly to the space which was
devoted to such articles. 'Par exemple', he asks, 'qui voudra lire
l'article *Chapeau*? Il contient cependant quatorze pages in-folio.'
Other articles in the same volume he also regarded as superfluous
—for instance, CHANDELLE, CHAISE, CHANVRE, CHARBON and
CHAUDRON (p. 10). In his *Préjugés légitimes* Chaumeix showed
nothing but contempt for articles on such worldly subjects:

Je ne me suis pas mis en peine de m'informer si M. Diderot avait fait une
description exacte du *Métier à faire des bas* et des différentes manières de
tailler une chemise; mais je me suis arrêté à considérer quelle idée
l'*Encyclopédie* me donnait de l'homme, de sa nature, de sa fin, de ses
devoirs et de son bonheur.

He has, he tells us, deliberately set aside consideration of such purely
secular matters and instead has concentrated his attention on discovering 'quel respect les Encyclopédistes avaient pour Jésus-
Christ, pour l'Écriture sainte, pour la religion'. (i.xxvii–xxviii)
   Another line taken by contemporary critics such as Fréron was
to denounce this part of the *Encyclopédie* as worthless. Much more
important, however, was the charge to which Fréron first gave
publicity in his *Année littéraire*—that the famous collection of
plates, announced with a great flourish of trumpets as early as the
*Prospectus* as illuminating the text of the technological articles in
the *Encyclopédie*, were not in the least original. In 1759 the *Année
littéraire* (Vol. vii) published a letter from an architect named Patte,
headed *Dénonciation d'un plagiat à M. Fréron*. Patte purported to
reveal 'le plagiat le plus insigne et le plus adroit peut-être dont il
soit fait mention dans les fastes littéraires' (p. 341). The controversy
about the originality or otherwise of the plates of the *Encyclopédie*
has continued down to the present day.
   The story of these plates takes us back almost a whole century, to

the time of Louis XIV and Colbert. In 1675 Colbert entrusted the recently founded Académie des Sciences with the task of assembling a collection of descriptions of the technological processes current both in France and elsewhere. Progress on this task proved extremely slow: it was not indeed until 1761 that *L'Art du charbonnier*, the first part of the Academy's *Descriptions des Arts et Métiers*, actually saw the light of day. It was followed, down to 1788, by a considerable number of such illustrated descriptions, which form altogether a total of seventy-three parts.[1] For something like half a century before he died in 1757 the great scientist, Réaumur, whose memory is kept alive by the temperature scale bearing his name and whose interests extended from insects to steel technology, had been entrusted with the assembling of the text and plates necessary for these descriptions. Yet after three-quarters of a century nothing had come of Colbert's plans in this field when in 1750 Diderot announced in the *Prospectus* his intention to devote a considerable portion of both the text and the plates of the *Encyclopédie* to 'les arts mécaniques'.

In a letter written in 1756, the year before he died, Réaumur described the work on which he had been engaged for decades in preparing these descriptions and went on:

J'ai fait graver plus de 150 planches in-folio qui sont des tableaux agréables, et j'en ai beaucoup d'autres qui ne sont que dessinées. J'aurais pu faire retentir mes cris dans tout le monde littéraire du vol qui m'a été fait des premières et prendre des voies de m'en faire rendre justice. L'infidélité et la négligence de mes graveurs, dont plusieurs sont morts, ont donné la facilité à gens peu délicats sur les procédés de rassembler des épreuves de ces planches et on les a fait graver de nouveau pour les faire entrer dans le *Dictionnaire encyclopédique*.[2]

Réaumur himself never made public this accusation, but after his death Patte, who was later to play a part in producing the Academy's *Descriptions*, took up the charge and Fréron was naturally only too willing to give it full publicity in the *Année littéraire*.

Patte who in June 1759 had received 600 l. from the publishers of the *Encyclopédie* for his work in checking and putting in order drawings for the plates of the work, alleged five months later that

---

[1] See A. H. Cole and G. B. Watts, *The Handicrafts of France as recorded in the 'Descriptions des Arts et Métiers'*, Boston, 1952.

[2] A facsimile of the relevant part of the letter is to be found in J. Torlais, *Un Esprit encyclopédique en dehors de l'Encyclopédie, Réaumur*, 2nd edn, Paris, 1961, facing p. 256.

Diderot had simply bought up from the engravers employed by Réaumur the plates which he had assembled over the years:

D'après ce plan M. Diderot, ce même M. Diderot qui dans ses discours et dans ses écrits décriait à tout propos M. de Réaumur, alla trouver M. Lucas qui avait gravé la plus grande partie de l'ouvrage de ce laborieux académicien. Moyennant dix louis[1] et de belles promesses pour la nouvelle entreprise des planches de l'*Encyclopédie* il lui tira des épreuves de tout ce qu'il avait fait. On fit la même chose à l'égard de quelques autres graveurs que M. de Réaumur avait employés, de sorte qu'on parvint bientôt à rassembler toutes les planches de notre académicien.[2]

He appended a list of some seventy subjects—from AIGUILLERIE to TIREUR D'OR—for which, he alleged, the publishers of the *Encyclopédie* did not possess original drawings, but merely Réaumur's engravings.

In January of the following year he addressed a second letter to Fréron, which was duly published in the *Année littéraire*.[3] In the meantime the publishers had inserted a brief answer to this charge in the Abbé de la Porte's *Observateur littéraire*; this ended with the counter-accusation that Patte had been sacked from the *Encyclopédie* 'pour deux raisons' which were not specified.[4] The Académie des Sciences had naturally interested itself in the matter and had appointed a committee of six of its members to examine the drawings and engravings which had been put on show by the publishers. On 19 December they submitted a somewhat ambiguous report to the Academy; this was seized upon by Patte in his second letter to Fréron. He pointed out that the articles on technology in the first seven volumes of the *Encyclopédie* were based on Réaumur's plates and constantly referred to them. 'Je pense bien', were his concluding words on the publishers, 'qu'ils seront obligés de faire changer toutes ces gravures. . . . La grande difficulté sera sans doute de faire cadrer ces nouveaus dessins avec les descriptions déjà faites.'[5]

The publishers did not leave the matter there. Shortly afterwards Fréron published (under duress?) a reply from them dated 24 February, in which they were able to produce a fresh certificate signed by four of the members of the academy who had inspected

[1] 240 livres, i.e. about £10 in English money of the time.     [2] *Année littéraire*, 1759, vii, 345–6.
[3] *AL*, 1760, i, 246–57.     [4] *Observateur littéraire*, v, 1759, 216 (see also the *Mercure*, Jan. 1760, i, 176).
[5] *AL*, 1760, i, 257.

their plates and drawings in the previous December. This certificate, which the publishers were careful to print in every one of the eleven volumes of plates, ran as follows:

Messieurs les libraires associés à l'*Encyclopédie* ayant demandé à l'Académie des commissaires pour vérifier le nombre des dessins et gravures concernant les arts et métiers qu'ils se proposent de publier, nous, commissaires soussignés, avons vu, examiné et vérifié toutes les planches et dessins mentionnés au présent état, montant au nombre de six cents planches ou environ sur cent trente arts, dans lesquels nous n'avons rien reconnu qui ait été copié d'après les planches de M. de Réaumur; en foi de quoi nous avons signé le présent certificat, à Paris le 16 janvier 1760, et ont signé Messieurs Nollet, Morand, de Parcieux, de Lalande.[1]

The publishers went on to point out that Patte had accused them of copying plates on subjects which Réaumur had never even dealt with and concluded by quoting the terms of the receipt which Patte had signed for the payment received from them in June 1759. They did not, however, answer Patte's point that they would have to change quite a number of their engravings and that as a result the references in the technological articles of the first seven volumes would be found not to correspond to the plates when these came to be published.

Eleven volumes of plates duly appeared between 1762 and 1772, and if because of their high cost they were only slowly bought up by the public, they were reproduced in the three folio reprints published in Geneva, Lucca and Leghorn. Although Fréron continued to make unflattering comparisons between these volumes and those produced by the Académie des Sciences, the controversy gradually died down and was not revived for nearly two centuries. The whole question came to life again in 1951 when among the multitude of publications inspired by the bicentenary of the launching of the whole enterprise M. Georges Huard published an article on the plates of the *Encyclopédie* and those of the Academy's *Descriptions des Arts et Métiers*.[2] Broadly speaking the author accepted Réaumur's and Patte's accusations of plagiarism and treated Diderot and his publishers as liars for repudiating them.

---

[1] *AL*, 1760, ii, 46–7.

[2] The article was reprinted in *L'Encyclopédie et le progrès des sciences et des techniques*, ed. Suzanne Delorme and René Taton, Paris, 1952, pp. 35–46.

Since then fresh work has been put in on the question both by Professor Jacques Proust[1] and by M. Jean Pierre Seguin.[2] Their conclusions are rather different. While there is no doubt that the accusations of plagiarism were founded (indeed Diderot continued until the end of the enterprise in 1772 to draw on many other collections of plates besides those of the Académie des Sciences), not only did Patte exaggerate these borrowings, but in many cases Diderot saw to it that his plates were a great improvement on earlier ones in their presentation of objects. 'Les volumes de planches de l'*Encyclopédie*', M. Seguin concludes, 'doivent beaucoup aux *Descriptions*, en gros et dans le détail, mais ils ont sur elles deux grandes supériorités: l'unité et la clarté.'[3] There we may leave the question for another and more important point of controversy which, in the nature of things, has given rise to argument only in our own time.

How far do the technological articles and plates of the *Encyclopédie*, produced between about 1747 and 1772, reflect the progress which was taking place in these very years, especially on this side of the Channel? Despite their many merits the answer, according to an economic historian, Professor Bertrand Gille,[4] is not at all. Although articles like FORGES (*Grosses*) and FEU (*Pompe à*) were written, not by Diderot, but by experts, they give no hint of such features of the coming industrial revolution as the use of coke or the potentialities of the steam-engine. That the *Encyclopédie* was not in the van of technological progress in the years when its volumes of text and plates came on the market is asserted even more bluntly by Professor Roland Mousnier.[5] Given what we already know about the origin of some of the plates on technology which appeared in the *Encyclopédie*—many of these were several decades old—it should not in fact surprise us if they did not represent the latest progress in this field or, even less, point towards the developments of the future. As in many other matters concerning the *Encyclopédie* Professor Proust has provided us with a more carefully

[1] See especially 'La Documentation technique de Diderot dans l'*Encyclopédie*', *Revue d'Histoire littéraire*, 1957, pp. 335–52, and *Diderot et l'Encyclopédie*, pp. 189–231.

[2] See his introduction to a selection of 150 plates from the *Encyclopédie* entitled *L'Univers de l'Encyclopédie*, Paris, 1964, pp. 25–34.

[3] *L'Univers de l'Encyclopédie*, p. 33.

[4] 'L'*Encyclopédie*, dictionnaire technique', reprinted in *L'Encyclopédie et le progrès des sciences et des techniques,* Paris, 1952, pp. 187–214.

[5] *Progrès scientifique et technique au XVIIIᵉ siècle*, Paris, 1958, pp. 232–4.

weighed and better documented verdict on this question. In his opinion l'*Encyclopédie* 'reflète dans l'ensemble de façon fidèle les connaissances du temps, sans retard scandaleux mais sans anticipation prophétique. Elle n'est pas à la pointe du progrès, mais comme tout bilan bien fait elle est tout de même un remarquable *instrument de progrès*.'[1] Certainly the text of the technological articles and the plates provide the historian with a splendid collection of documents.

## The 'Encyclopédie' as 'machine de guerre'

So far in this chapter we have stressed that in the eyes of its editors, and even more in those of its publishers, the *Encyclopédie* was primarily a massive work of reference, far larger than any so far undertaken in France or for that matter in England. Yet from the very first, writers of the time, in journals, books and pamphlets, attributed to the work another purpose: the spreading of the ideas of the Enlightenment. These two sides of the *Encyclopédie* were well described by a writer in the *Monthly Review* in discussing in 1787 Condorcet's *Éloge de d'Alembert*. After giving high praise to the *Discours préliminaire*, he continues:

Nor will it be disputed that the master-builders of this new and stupendous temple of science for the worship of Nature had also really in view the advancement of human knowledge and the improvement of the arts and sciences. This no true, no candid philosopher will call in question; but that, in the inner court of this temple there was a confederacy formed against all those who looked higher than Nature for the principal object of their veneration and confidence is a fact too palpable, nay too boldly avowed, to stand in need of any proof.[2]

In 1801 after the upheaval of the Revolution the same point was to be made, not in such tactful and objective terms, but with the most extreme exaggeration in the dedication to George III of the *Supplement* to the third edition of the *Encyclopaedia Britannica*:

The French *Encyclopédie* has been accused, and justly accused, of having disseminated far and wide the seeds of Anarchy and Atheism. If the *Encyclopaedia Britannica* shall in any degree counteract the tendency of that

---

[1] *Diderot et l'Encyclopédie*, p. 163 n.       [2] *Monthly Review*, 1787, i, 243.

pestiferous work, even these two volumes will not be wholly unworthy of Your Majesty's patronage.

How far the *Encyclopédie* was a *machine de guerre* as well as a reference work is a question which will be discussed in detail in later chapters. Yet before attempting to examine the views expressed in the work on the controversies of the second half of the reign of Louis XV it would be well to see what the editors themselves have to say on their aims, both in their published writings and, where they are available, their more private comments.

## Statements by the editors

D'Alembert, it is true, always pursued a cautious line in public; unlike Diderot he never saw the inside of a state prison. As Condorcet put it in his *Éloge*, 'sage sans être timide, alliant la prudence et l'amour de la vérité, d'Alembert semblait pouvoir espérer que son repos ne serait pas troublé'.[1] After Vol. VII he ceased to contribute the polemical articles which he had inserted in the earlier volumes, and his abandonment of the joint editorship in the period of crisis in the work's publication shows that he was not prepared to take more than limited risks in this field. Even so, his spirited reply to critics in the *Encyclopédie* in the *Avertissement* to Vol. III and such polemical articles as ÉCOLE (*Philosophie de l'*) or GENÈVE made his position in the ideological battles of the 1750s perfectly clear to contemporaries who could read between the lines. Indeed, this is also true even of the more guarded *Discours prélimi-naire* with its omission—duly noted by hostile critics—of any but the most perfunctory references to religion and its purely secular attitude to the different branches of human knowledge and their history.

Diderot, in contrast, was far more outspoken in his exposition of the underlying aims of the *Encyclopédie*. Into the pages of *ENCYCLOPÉDIE, alongside his purely objective observations on the aims of such a work of reference, he inserted passages in which he shows his pride in the progress of the Enlightenment and his determination to use the *Encyclopédie* to hasten that progress. The *philosophe* pens characteristic lines on the dawning of the Age of

[1] D'Alembert, *Œuvres philosophiques, historiques et littéraires*, Paris, 1805, 18 vols, i, 101.

Reason: 'Aujourd'hui que la philosophie s'avance à grands pas; qu'elle soumet à son empire tous les objets de son ressort; que son ton est le ton dominant; et qu'on commence à secouer le joug de l'autorité et de l'exemple pour s'en tenir aux lois de la raison . . .' [V.636v/a]. A work like the *Encyclopédie*, he openly declares, could be attempted only in such an enlightened age: 'Nous avons vu que l'*Encyclopédie* ne pouvait être que la tentative d'un siècle philosophe; que ce siècle était arrivé . . .' [V.644r/b]. The essentially secular outlook of the editors and main contributors is brought out in a striking passage which occurs in the the course of Diderot's discussion of the classification of knowledge according to the faculties of memory, imagination and reason:

Une considération surtout qu'il ne faut point perdre de vue, c'est que si l'on bannit l'homme ou l'être pensant et contemplateur de dessus la surface de la terre, ce spectacle pathétique et sublime de la nature n'est plus qu'une scène triste et muette. L'univers se tait; le silence et la nuit s'en emparent. Tout se change en une vaste solitude où les phénomènes inobservés se passent d'une manière obscure et sourde. C'est la présence de l'homme qui rend l'existence des êtres intéressante; et que peut-on se proposer de mieux dans l'histoire de ces êtres que de se soumettre à cette considération? Pourquoi n'introduirons-nous pas l'homme dans notre ouvrage comme il est placé dans l'univers? Pourquoi n'en ferons-nous pas un centre commun? [V.641r/a]

Such an approach was hardly likely to appeal to contemporary orthodoxy.

When he came to deal with such technical details of the work as the use of cross-references Diderot expressed himself with a vigorous frankness which delighted contemporary critics who quoted over and over again his rash observations on this subject in the polemical works of the 1750s and 1760s. Cross-references, he points out, serve to link together the different articles and branches of knowledge. 'Mais', he continues in oft-quoted words, 'quand il le faudra, ils produiront aussi un effet tout contraire; ils opposeront les notions; ils feront contraster les principes; ils attaqueront, ébranleront, renverseront secrètement quelques opinions ridicules qu'on n'oserait insulter ouvertement.' As if this discreet hint were not enough, Diderot goes on to make his meaning even clearer:

Toutes les fois, par exemple, qu'un préjugé national mériterait du respect, il faudrait à son article particulier l'exposer respectueusement et avec tout son cortège de vraisemblance et de séduction; mais renverser l'édifice de fange, dissiper un vain amas de poussière en renvoyant aux articles où des principes solides servent de base aux vérités opposées. Cette manière de détromper les hommes opère très promptement sur les bons esprits, et elle opère infailliblement et sans aucune fâcheuse conséquence, secrète-ment et sans éclat, sur tous les esprits.

This use of cross-references, Diderot declares in a famous phrase, will help to achieve the aim of such a work as the *Encyclopédie*; this is to 'changer la façon commune de penser' [V.642v/a–b].

Another type of cross-reference recommended by Diderot, though he considers that it should be used with discretion, again revealed to contemporaries his propagandist aim. He gives quite cheerfully an example of what he calls 'renvois satiriques ou épigrammatiques'—the apparently eulogistic article CORDELIER with its cross-reference at the end to *CAPUCHON: 'Le mot burlesque *capuchon* et ce qu'on trouve à l'article CAPUCHON pourrait faire soupçonner que l'éloge pompeux n'est qu'une ironie, et qu'il faut lire l'article avec précaution et en peser exacte-ment tous les termes' [V.643r/a]. Contemporary critics (they have been followed by some modern writers on the *Encyclopédie*) took these remarks rather too literally. To begin with, the number of cross-references in the *Encyclopédie* varies enormously from article to article. Where they are thickest is, generally speaking, in articles taken over or adapted from Chambers. Some contributors also made considerable use of them, though quite often the article referred to, as angry readers of the time pointed out, did not exist. Diderot himself made relatively sparing use of cross-references, and examples of polemical or satirical cross-references in the *Encyclopédie* are in practice very hard to find. What is really im-portant about this part of the article *ENCYCLOPÉDIE is the clear revelation of the writer's propagandist aim; he and other like-minded contributors sought more often to attain this aim either by putting their bolder thoughts into short and relatively out-of-the-way articles or quite often simply by working them into longer and more prominent ones.

The contemporary user of the *Encyclopédie* was accustomed to reading between the lines, and we today have to be ready to do the same thing. In a passage the unorthodoxy of which was commented upon by a contemporary critic Diderot warns the reader of this necessity when dealing with the works of philosophers, ancient and modern, and with the *Encyclopédie* itself:

L'intolérance, le manque de la double doctrine, le défaut d'une langue hiéroglyphique et sacrée perpétueront à jamais ces contradictions et continueront de tacher nos plus belles productions. On ne sait souvent ce qu'un homme a pensé sur les matières les plus importantes. Il s'enveloppe dans des ténèbres affectées; ses contemporains même ignorent ses sentiments, et l'on ne doit pas s'attendre que l'*Encyclopédie* soit exempte de ces défauts. [V. 648r/a]

The meaning of this veiled hint did not escape the authors of *La Religion vengée* who translate this seemingly obscure verbiage into plain French:

Sans doute, Monsieur, que vous entendez parfaitement ce langage. Le chef des Encyclopédistes promet d'être impie, mais de manière qu'en se montrant tel qu'il est aux adeptes de l'impiété, il tâchera de dérober sa marche à ceux qu'il regarde comme ses ennemis. Au moyen de quoi tous les endroits de l'*Encyclopédie* où l'on parle bien de la religion ne prouvent rien pour la sienne. Il n'adopte ces endroits que comme un voile nécessaire à sa politique. Stratagème hypocrite et néanmoins peu propre à en imposer, puisque l'on a eu la maladresse ou plutôt l'audace d'en avertir le public. (x.96)

The article *ENCYCLOPÉDIE contains, in short, some quite objective passages on the problems of editing a work of this kind; but, as critics were quick to note at the time, it also clearly reveals Diderot's underlying aim of using the *Encyclopédie* as a vehicle for the ideas of the Enlightenment.

Naturally this propaganda purpose is expressed with greater clarity in his letters for this period. If few of these have been preserved for the period down to 1757 when he was editing the first seven volumes, we are more fortunate with those for the years when he was struggling on his own to complete the work. In September 1762 he wrote to Sophie Volland: 'Cet ouvrage produira sûrement avec le temps une révolution dans les esprits, et j'espère que les tyrans, les oppresseurs, les fanatiques et les intolérants n'y gagneront pas. Nous aurons servi l'humanité.'[1] It will be noticed how it is made plain here that it was against political as well

---

[1] Roth, iv, 172.

as religious tyranny that the *Encyclopédie* was directed. Three days later, in a letter to Voltaire in which he gives his reasons for declining Catherine the Great's proposal that the work be finished on Russian territory, Diderot expresses himself with equal vigour:

Quoi qu'il en soit, ne craignez pas que le péril que je cours en travaillant au milieu des barbares me rende pusillanime. Notre devise est: Sans quartier pour les superstitieux, pour les fanatiques, pour les ignorants, pour les fous, pour les méchants et pour les tyrans: et j'espère que vous le reconnaîtrez en plus d'un endroit. Est-ce qu'on s'appelle philosophe pour rien? Quoi! le mensonge aura ses martyrs, et la vérité ne sera prêchée que par des lâches?[1]

Once again political tyranny is denounced along with other forms of oppression.

Perhaps most striking of all is a passage in the furious letter which Diderot wrote to Le Breton in November 1764 when he had just discovered that the last ten volumes of text had been mutilated. In his rage at what he regarded as the unpardonable behaviour of his publisher Diderot was willing to sacrifice all the purely informative side of his encyclopedia, including his own articles on technology of which he was so proud, to the passages in which he and other contributors had expressed their true thoughts on the struggle of ideas—religious, philosophical and political—which was raging in France in the 1750s and 1760s. Le Breton is threatened with both financial loss and dishonour when the publication of the last ten volumes brings his misdeeds out into the open:

Vous avez oublié que ce n'est pas aux choses courantes, sensées et communes que vous deviez vos premiers succès; qu'il n'y a peut-être pas deux hommes dans le monde qui se soient donné la peine de lire une ligne d'histoire, de géographie, de mathématiques et même d'arts, et que ce qu'on y a recherché et ce qu'on y recherchera, c'est la philosophie ferme et hardie de quelques-uns de vos travailleurs. Vous l'avez châtrée, dépecée, mutilée, mise en lambeaux, sans jugement, sans ménagement et sans goût. Vous nous avez rendus insipides et plats. Vous avez banni de votre livre ce qui en a fait, ce qui en aurait fait encore l'attrait, le piquant, l'intéressant et la nouveauté. Vous en serez châtié par la perte pécuniaire et par le déshonneur.[2]

[1] Roth, iv, 176.     [2] Roth, iv, 303.

# ENCYCLOPÉDIE,

## OU

## DICTIONNAIRE RAISONNÉ

## DES SCIENCES,

## DES ARTS ET DES MÉTIERS,

### *PAR UNE SOCIÉTÉ DE GENS DE LETTRES.*

Mis en ordre & publié par M. *DIDEROT*, de l'Académie Royale des Sciences & des Belles-Lettres de Pruſſe ; & quant à la PARTIE MATHÉMATIQUE, par M. *D'ALEMBERT*, de l'Académie Royale des Sciences de Paris, de celle de Pruſſe, & de la Société Royale de Londres.

*Tantùm ſeries juncturaque pollet,*
*Tantùm de medio ſumptis accedit honoris !* HORAT.

## TOME PREMIER.

### A PARIS,

Chez
{
BRIASSON, *rue Saint Jacques, à la Science.*
DAVID l'aîné, *rue Saint Jacques, à la Plume d'or.*
LE BRETON, Imprimeur ordinaire du Roy, *rue de la Harpe.*
DURAND, *rue Saint Jacques, à Saint Landry, & au Griffon.*

### M. DCC. LI.
### *AVEC APPROBATION ET PRIVILEGE DU ROY.*

*Title-page of the first volume of the Paris edition*

No doubt this passage is full of wild exaggerations. For one thing, whatever the extent of Le Breton's cuts, he certainly did not remove from the last ten volumes all traces of this 'philosophie ferme et hardie'. And clearly Diderot did not attach so little importance to the *Encyclopédie* as a reference work as he makes out here. Yet his stress on the propaganda purpose of the whole enterprise is surely significant.

In April 1766, by which time these volumes had appeared, the young Naigeon who had contributed UNITAIRES, one of the boldest articles to be found in them, and the editor of the first edition of Diderot's collected works, wrote to him:

Si, lorsque vous avez entrepris l'*Encyclopédie*, vous n'aviez pas été soutenu par l'espoir si doux, si flatteur et si consolant de porter dans l'âme de nos contemporains l'amour de la vérité, de l'humanité et de toutes les vertus sociales et, pour tout dire en un mot, d'éclairer et de perfectionner l'espèce humaine, croyez-vous que vous auriez résisté avec tant de courage et de fermeté aux persécutions de tout genre que vous avez éprouvées pendant vingt ans?[1]

For its editors the *Encyclopédie* was not only a new reference work on a massive scale; at the same time, both for them and for like-minded contributors, it was also a means of propounding the ideas of the Enlightenment. How this second aim was achieved and what ideas were put forward in the pages of the *Encyclopédie* will be examined in later chapters.

[1] Roth, vi, 171.

*Chapter 5*

# Critics

## *Difficulties in assessing the reactions of subscribers*

To ascertain what subscribers to the first and later editions thought of their bargain and what opinion other readers of the time formed of the work is by no means an easy task. As the publication of the first edition was spread over such a long period of years, quite a number of subscribers died before it was completed. It would seem that others simply failed to stay the course; the relatively high cost (654 out of 980 livres) of the eleven volumes of plates (eleven against the two advertised in the prospectus of 1750) seems to have discouraged a number of subscribers. Thus we find M. Morel de Villiers, *trésorier de France* at Châtillon-sur-Seine in Burgundy, writing in the 1770s:

Je suis le seul des trois de ma ville qui avaient souscrit pour cet ouvrage, qui ai reçu les 17 volumes de discours et les 11 volumes de planches. L'un des trois est mort, et ce qu'il avait de ce livre a passé à son héritier qui est Président à la Chambre des Comptes de Dijon. L'autre a seulement tiré les 17 volumes de discours et la première livraison des planches qui a été faite, n'ayant pas voulu les suivantes à cause du prix excessif que l'on en a voulu avoir et de l'augmentation.[1]

However, this subscriber was one of Luneau's disgruntled supporters and we should not look to such quarters for an impartial account of the reactions of the purchasers of the work. After all, nine successive editions—in varying formats and at varying prices —were brought out over a period of thirty years, and neither the original publishers who made a very handsome profit nor those

---

[1] *Mémoire pour P. J. Fr. Luneau de Boisjermain . . .* , Paris, 1778, *Pièces justificatives,* pp. 9–10.

who were responsible for successive reprints seem to have had any great difficulty in disposing of their stocks.

## Contemporary periodicals and the 'Encyclopédie'

For contemporary reactions to the *Encyclopédie* one turns hopefully to the periodicals published in France in these years. One embarks on the search in the full realization that comment was limited by various factors. In the 1750s and 1760s Frenchmen and Frenchwomen had other things to think about besides the *Encyclopédie*, and in any case in the absence of a free press the periodicals of these years could not be expected to mirror at all adequately the reactions, favourable or unfavourable, to the work. Even so, comment, whether friendly or hostile, is surprisingly difficult to come by. A great deal of interesting material is, of course, to be found in Grimm's *Correspondance littéraire* between its foundation in 1753 and his abandonment of the editorship twenty years later. This news-sheet which circulated in a small number of manuscript copies in the courts of central and eastern Europe was obviously not subject to censorship in the same way as a periodical appearing in print in the France of Louis XV. Yet interesting as Grimm's comments are to the historian of the *Encyclopédie*, coming as they do from a friend and confidant of Diderot, they do not give us any real idea of the reactions of ordinary readers of the period.

It is obvious that in the 1750s and 1760s no journal could appear inside France which expressed openly the views—even the more moderate views—of men like Diderot and d'Alembert or the more radical of their contributors. The nearest approach to such a periodical was one which borrowed its very title from the *Encyclopédie*—the *Journal encyclopédique*, founded in 1756 outside France at Liège by Pierre Rousseau (1725–85), a native of Toulouse whose efforts to establish himself in the literary world of Paris had been a failure. When clerical influences drove him out of Liège, he moved his journal to the little town of Bouillon, now in the Belgian province of Luxembourg, but then the capital of a semi-independent duchy. Despite local as well as French censors Pierre Rousseau did enjoy a rather greater measure of freedom than if he had tried to produce such a periodical inside France.

In its Liège period (1756–9) the *Journal encyclopédique* dealt with Vols V–VII of the *Encyclopédie*; though it does occasionally offer critical comments, on the whole it presents an apologia for the whole enterprise and defends it vigorously against its opponents. The number for 15 November 1757, for instance, opens with an 'Avis des auteurs de ce journal' which draws a parallel between the *Encyclopédie* and the *Journal encyclopédique* in which lavish praise is bestowed on the former:

Formé sur le même plan et dirigé par les mêmes vues que cet ouvrage célèbre, notre journal, s'il est bien fait, doit le représenter en tout, imiter sa manière, prendre son ton et faire sur les ouvrages que chaque jour fait éclore, ce que ce dictionnaire fait sur tous ceux dont se compose la sphère immense des connaissances humaines. Il doit surtout prendre de l'*Encyclopédie* cet esprit philosophique qui la caractérise et qui, répandu dans toute la masse de l'ouvrage, anime et vivifie toutes les parties. . . .

L'*Encyclopédie* par sa nature conservera toujours un grand avantage sur un journal, fût-il entre les mêmes mains qui élèvent cet édifice majestueux à la gloire de la nation française et pour le bonheur de l'humanité. Les découvertes des hommes dans tous les lieux, dans tous les genres et dans tous les siècles sont les riches matériaux qu'elle peut et doit mettre en œuvre.[1]

Not only were many articles in these three volumes singled out for praise and lengthy extracts from them reproduced, but critics of the work were hotly attacked.

On 1 February 1758 Pierre Rousseau compares the campaign which was being waged against the *Encyclopédie* after the appearance of the seventh volume, with the earlier agitation which had led to the banning of the first two volumes in 1752:

Les mêmes ressorts qu'on fit alors jouer pour perdre un ouvrage qui n'avait été entrepris que pour la gloire de la nation, sont aujourd'hui mis en œuvre pour lui porter des coups encore plus dangereux. Ce sont les mêmes intrigues secrètes, les mêmes manœuvres sourdes, le même manège politique, les mêmes routes obliques. Aujourd'hui comme alors on emploie la main de la religion pour rendre plus profondes les blessures légères que jusqu'ici de petits littérateurs ont faites à l'*Encyclopédie*. Aujourd'hui comme alors on y découvre ce cri, le signal d'une conspiration philosophique contre toute espèce de gouvernement et de religion.[2]

---

[1] 15 Nov. 1757, pp. 4–6.          [2] 1 Feb. 1758, pp. 112–13.

After announcing that, in his disgust with the attacks being launched against the *Encyclopédie*, d'Alembert had decided to sever his connection with it, Pierre Rousseau exclaims: 'Ainsi cette grande entreprise que toutes les autres nations enviaient à la France et que chaque jour voyait s'avancer rapidement vers sa perfection, va donc de nouveau être interrompue!'[1]

As soon as the last ten volumes of text appeared at the end of 1765 Pierre Rousseau, now established at Bouillon, began to publish a long series of extracts from articles from the *Encyclopédie*. This was to last with only one short break from 1 September 1766 to 15 July 1770. No other journal anywhere devoted anything like comparable attention to the appearance of those last ten volumes. What is more, the number for 15 August 1766 contained a long article with the pompous heading: '*Observations historiques, littéraires, critiques et apologétiques des auteurs de ce journal* au sujet des 14 [sic] derniers volumes de l'*encyclopédie*'. It is noticeable that in his treatment of the last ten volumes in the *Journal encyclopédique* the tone of the editor's comments is decidedly less enthusiastic than in the period 1756–9 when his journal was published at Liège. Yet, if Rousseau had to tread warily in view of both the local and the French censorship, the more critical of his remarks can scarcely be attributed to fears for the future of the *Journal encyclopédique*. If as in the past he repeatedly heaps praise on the whole undertaking, he is far from blind to the technical shortcomings of the work and, what is more, there are occasions when he refuses very emphatically to accept the ideas put forward by Diderot and his collaborators.

The long essay published on 15 August 1766 contains, of course, the most fulsome praise of the *Encyclopédie*, from its opening paragraph onwards:

Il a paru enfin, cet ouvrage immortel qui fait tant d'honneur à la France, aux philosophes, aux savants, aux littérateurs, aux artistes qui en sont les auteurs. Monument plus durable que ces fameuses constructions dont l'Égypte se vante, l'*Encyclopédie* francaise n'a plus à redouter l'inquiétante incertitude des événements. A l'abri désormais des passions humaines, des efforts de l'envie, des orages et des révolutions, l'édifice est élevé. ((pp. 3–4)

Yet, alongside praise of this kind which is scattered through the

[1] *Ibid.*, p. 115.

whole article, there are quite strong criticisms—both of the technical weaknesses of the *Encyclopédie* and, more important, of its unorthodox ideas. Far from meeting with approval, they are denounced in no uncertain terms; indeed the Paris Parlement is even applauded for the vigilance which it had shown in 1759. It would be absurd, Rousseau argues, to follow hostile critics of the work in condemning nearly every article in it:

Il ne fallait s'élever que contre ceux qui étaient vraiment répréhensibles; il fallait imiter la prudence élevée de ces sages magistrats qui, indignés de la hardiesse de quelques systèmes ou de quelques propositions que tout bon citoyen doit détester, ont fait entendre leur voix patriotique en faveur des lois outragées et des atteintes portées à nos dogmes; mais le corps auguste qui a sévi contre ce dictionnaire n'a pas certainement étendu sa juste indignation sur les parties les plus intéressantes et les plus lumineuses de cet ouvrage, sur celles qui développent les éléments des arts utiles, les principes et les rapports des connaissances humaines. (p. 10)

If at first one is inclined to wonder whether such criticisms of certain ideas expressed in the *Encyclopédie* were simply a concession to the powers that be, such an interpretation is shaken when one discovers that, a couple of pages later, Rousseau admits that 'ce dictionnaire est rempli de fautes de toutes les espèces, d'erreurs choquantes, de folles opinions, de pernicieuses maximes'. He is even prepared to concede that 'il y a plusieurs articles, dans ces derniers volumes, aussi répréhensibles que ceux qui ont déjà été condamnés avec tant de raison' (p. 12). It is clear that in spite of his admiration for the *Encyclopédie* Rousseau was not blind either to its technical deficiencies or to the ideological gulf which separated him from Diderot and some of his collaborators.

Eulogy and criticism are mingled in the comments on the long series of articles from the last ten volumes from which Rousseau printed extracts over the next four years. Where he differed from Diderot and his colleagues was, above all, in the religious sphere. He refused to accept the liberal doctrine of toleration set forth by Jaucourt in HÉRÉSIE and HÉRÉTIQUE, but praised the very traditionalist view set forth by Abbé Mallet in LIBERTÉ DE PENSER.[1] What is even more striking is his violent attack on *HOBBISME (though the editorial asterisk clearly indicates Diderot's authorship, Rousseau

[1] 1 Oct. 1766, p. 17; 1 Sept. 1767, p. 18.

never mentions him by name).[1] Another article of Diderot, VINDICATIF (it is unsigned, but it may be attributed to him on the authority of Naigeon) is also severely criticized; here too Diderot's materialism peeps through.

No other periodical of the time devoted anything like the same amount of space to the *Encyclopédie*; indeed, no periodical published inside France devoted any space at all to a discussion of the last ten volumes of the work, or for that matter even as much as mentioned their appearance. This is true even of the clandestine Jansenist organ, *Les Nouvelles ecclésiastiques*, which in the 1750s showed the same bitter hostility to the *Encyclopédie* as to the works of Montesquieu and Buffon, and greeted with joy the withdrawal of its *privilège* in 1759. Its attacks were answered in successive volumes of the *Encyclopédie*. Thus in Vol. V under ECCLÉSIASTIQUE d'Alembert worked in a violent onslaught on what he calls 'une feuille ou plutôt . . . un libelle périodique, sans esprit, sans vérité, sans charité et sans aveu'; and *ENCYCLOPÉDIE refers to its editor as 'un scélérat obscur' who has produced one more calumny 'parmi celles dont il remplit depuis si longtemps ses feuilles hebdomadaires' [V.646r/a]. The Jansenist editor greeted with satisfaction the *arrêt du Conseil* which suppressed the first two volumes; his only sorrow was that the government had not gone further and simply revoked the *privilège*. He several times repeats his surprise at the lenient treatment meted out to a work which had been officially denounced in the *arrêt du Conseil* as filled with subversive and irreligious views. 'Cependant l'*Encyclopédie* subsiste toujours' wrote the editor sadly two years later.[2] The crisis years 1758–9 contain a particularly large number of attacks on the *Encyclopédie*. Thus in March 1758 the editor made a general onslaught on the work:

Nos lecteurs doivent aisément se persuader que nous n'avons pas le temps de lire, encore moins d'examiner le dictionnaire immense de l'*Encyclopédie*. Nous ne doutons en aucune sorte qu'il n'y eût beaucoup de choses à relever. Mais nos feuilles y pourraient-elles suffire? D'ailleurs peut-on parler religion avec MM. les encyclopédistes? L'Écriture sainte, les conciles, les pères de l'Église sont nos guides; et ces messieurs (nous parlons des éditeurs et des chefs) n'y croient pas. Les affaires de l'Église sont notre objet, et ces beaux esprits, ces prétendus sages, ne s'y intéressent point.[3]

---

[1] See below, pp. 153–4.        [2] 3 July 1754, p. 107.        [3] 27 March 1758, p. 56.

In the following month the appearance of the publishers' *Mémoire* on the suspension of the work gave rise to another denunciation of 'la liberté effrénée qu'on s'est donnée dans ce dictionnaire de débiter du ton le plus hardi les maximes les plus dangereuses et les plus condamnables'.[1] A delightful prospect now opened up—that the *Encyclopédie* might be cut off after seven volumes, thus bringing to an end 'un scandale qui dure depuis trop longtemps et dont la cessation paraît intéresser également la religion et l'État'. Naturally the proceedings taken by the Parlement in January 1759 and even more the *arrêt du Conseil* which followed caused the liveliest satisfaction. Even so that satisfaction was not absolutely complete: 'On assure que MM. les encyclopédistes font imprimer leur ouvrage en pays étranger; et les sept volumes imprimés et distribués sont une peste et un poison qui subsistent dans le royaume.'[2]

Yet, for all its bitter hostility to the *Encyclopédie*, the *Nouvelles ecclésiastiques* never really gets beyond denouncing it in quite general terms; nowhere in its pages is it explained exactly which articles are pernicious and why. And although the journal continued to appear until 1803, it never made any mention of the publication of the last ten volumes, let alone denounce the appalling views which they contained.

Although published in France, the *Nouvelles ecclésiastiques* evaded the official censorship. If we turn now to the censored periodicals which appeared there in these years, we find surprisingly little information about the *Encyclopédie*. Obviously one must not expect much from an official news-sheet like the *Gazette de France,* which limited itself to an announcement of the work when the prospectus appeared in 1750 and to a mention of the publication of one or two of the early volumes. Even the *Journal des Savants* has not all that much to say about the *Encyclopédie*. It salutes the appearance of the prospectus and offers in the following year a review of the first volume. This mainly consists, however, of extracts from the *Discours préliminaire*, with, tacked on to the end, a surprisingly sharp attack on d'Alembert's unorthodox religious views. Although the writer speaks warmly of the work as a whole, he criticizes the secular spirit underlying it:

On pourrait soupçonner dans cette préface un laconisme affecté sur ce qui

---

[1] 17 April 1758, p. 65.    [2] 15 May 1759, p. 83.

regarde la religion. La science de la religion est de toutes les sciences la plus étendue; ne mérite-t-elle pas qu'on en recherche l'origine et qu'on en développe les progrès? L'auteur examine fort au long et avec beaucoup de sagacité comment les hommes sont devenus géomètres, physiciens, musiciens, etc. N'aurait-il pas dû aussi examiner les efforts que les hommes ont faits pendant quatre mille ans pour acquérir la connaissance de Dieu et d'eux-mêmes, et comment cette connaissance, commencée par la religion naturelle, plus développée par la révélation faite à Moïse, a été enfin perfectionnée par la religion chrétienne?[1]

D'Alembert was furious at this attack and protested strongly to Malesherbes who took up the matter with the editor.

The reviews of Vols II, III and IV were certainly more uniformly favourable. That of the fourth volume (June 1755), for instance, concludes thus:

Nous finirons cet extrait par une observation générale sur la nature de cette encyclopédie: c'est que de tous les dictionnaires français que nous avons, il n'est arrivé qu'à celui-ci, si cependant on excepte celui de Bayle, d'avoir été lu tout de suite. C'est un effet de cet esprit philosophique qui en vivifie, pour ainsi dire, jusqu'aux moindres parties. On se résout à ne rien omettre parce qu'on rencontre des vues dans les articles où l'on en soupçonnerait le moins. (p. 398)

Yet such enthusiasm did not extend to reviewing any further volumes of the work. The appearance of Vols V, VI and VII was duly announced, but although reviews of the last two of these volumes were definitely promised, they were never printed; and the *Journal des Savants*, a periodical under fairly close government control, did not mention the publication of the last ten volumes in 1765, acting no doubt on official instructions.

Another semi-official periodical, the *Mercure de France,* showed a slightly less detached attitude towards the *Encyclopédie*, but it too devoted relatively little space to the work and to the controversy which it aroused in the 1750s, and it also made no mention of the appearance of the last ten volumes. In the year of publication of its first volume the editor, who happened to be Abbé Raynal, gave a great deal of publicity to the *Encyclopédie*. In March 1751 the *Nouvelles littéraires* of the *Mercure* began with the following item:

M. Diderot, un des éditeurs de l'*Encyclopédie*, que les gens du monde et les gens de lettres attendent avec une si grande impatience, et auteur du

[1] *Journal des Savants*, Sept. 1751, pp. 626–7.

*Prospectus* que toute la France a lu avec tant d'empressement et de plaisir, vient de publier séparément un des articles qui doivent entrer dans le premier volume de cette encyclopédie.

This article, ART, is given a very eulogistic mention, accompanied by a hint that readers would be foolish not to join the rush of subscribers to the *Encyclopédie*: 'Cet article a eu un si grand succès que nous connaissons plusieurs personnes qui, après l'avoir lu, ont été souscrire' (pp. 103–4). Further publicity for the forthcoming first volume was given in the April and June numbers which printed the text of two articles of Daubenton, ABEILLE and AGATE. The appearance of the first volume was greeted with enthusiasm in the July number: 'Voilà le commencement d'un des plus grands ouvrages qui aient jamais été entrepris. La préface est un chef-d'œuvre' (p. 112). Most striking of all is the conclusion of the review: 'Ce qui domine dans l'*Encyclopédie* et qui n'est pas commun dans les dictionnaires, c'est l'esprit philosophique' (p. 114).

However, the *Mercure*'s enthusiasm for the *Encyclopédie* did not last. The second volume was not even mentioned, let alone reviewed. The third volume received more attention, though the lengthy review devoted to it consists almost entirely of extracts from the *Avertissement des Éditeurs*. However, two sentences from the conclusion are worth quoting:

Quelque accueil que le public ait fait aux deux premiers volumes, il nous paraît que celui-ci leur est généralement trouvé fort supérieur. . . . Il nous paraît que le gouvernement et le public ne sauraient trop favoriser cette grande entreprise dont l'exécution se perfectionne de jour en jour.[1]

Raynal gave up the editorship shortly afterwards; and after this date the *Mercure* offers singularly little about either the *Encyclopédie* or the controversy which raged around it in the period 1757–60.

Another periodical—the *Affiches de province*, which began publication in May 1752—contains a number of references to the work from the third volume onwards. Occasionally, as with the sixth volume for instance, the editor goes so far as to list interesting articles, not all of which are of unimpeachable orthodoxy.[2] Yet such references gradually fade out, and once again there is no mention of the appearance of the last ten volumes of text.

---

[1] *Mercure*, Dec. 1753, p. 141.      [2] *Affiches de province*, 17 Nov. 1756, p. 181.

At first sight the Jesuit organ, the *Journal de Trévoux*, promises to offer a rich store of comment, mainly, as one might expect, critical. As early as January 1751 the editor, Father Berthier, began his campaign against the work. While declaring that men of letters had found the *Prospectus* 'très bien écrit', he insinuated that the editors had cribbed their classification of human knowledge from Bacon.[1] Diderot and the publishers took this attack seriously. The latter's accounts for 1751 contain the enigmatic item: 'Voitures pour la dispute avec les journalistes de Trévoux 31 [livres] 16 [sous]'. Diderot retorted by printing his article ART along with an ironical letter to Father Berthier. The latter replied in the February number, and Diderot came back with a second letter which Berthier left unanswered, though in the March number he devoted some thirty pages to a further development of his charge of plagiarism in an article entitled 'Parallèle de la branche philosophique du système de l'*Encyclopédie* avec la partie philosophique du livre *De la Dignité et de l'Accroissment des Sciences* du chancelier Bacon'.[2]

This preliminary skirmishing on the purely technical question of the debt of the *Encyclopédie*'s classification of knowledge to Bacon was followed, from October 1751 to March 1752, by a long review of the first volume of the *Encyclopédie*—by far the longest that any single volume of the work was ever to receive.[3] This detailed examination is by no means uniformly hostile to Diderot and d'Alembert. The latter's *Discours préliminaire* comes in for some mild criticism, but the section concludes: 'Son discours nous donne une grande idée de ses talents littéraires'.[4] The second article devoted to the *Encyclopédie* opens with a surprisingly flattering remark: '. . . Ce livre est toujours une entreprise très haute, très forte, telle en un mot qu'après l'édition de tout l'ouvrage les auteurs pourront s'approprier en toute justice les expressions de la belle ode: *Exegi monumentum aeare perennius*, etc.'[5]

However, despite such eulogistic remarks, these articles are filled with criticisms—often penetrating—not only of the technical deficiencies of the *Encyclopédie* but also of its underlying spirit. Several articles are singled out for attack because of their unortho-

[1] *Journal de Trévoux*, 1751, i, 188–9; ii, 302–27.    [2] *JT*, 1 March 1751, pp. 708–37.
[3] *JT*, 2 Oct. 1751, pp. 2250–95; Nov., pp. 2419–57; Dec., pp. 2592–623; Jan., pp. 146–90; Feb., pp. 296–322; March, pp. 424–69.
[4] *JT*, Oct. 1751, p. 2287.    [5] *JT*, Nov. 1751, p. 2423.

dox views, and the last instalment of this long review concludes with an attack on the outlook underlying the whole enterprise:

En plusieurs endroits la religion n'a point été respectée; sur quoi nous prions sincèrement tous ceux qui mettent la main à cet ouvrage, d'être infiniment circonspects sur un point de si grande importance. Le premier et le plus grand de nos soins sera de veiller aussi sur cette partie, d'exercer même une critique grave et soutenue contre tout ce qui donnerait atteinte aux vérités révélées et à la doctrine des mœurs. Heureux si, par l'étendue de ce zèle, nous pouvons remplir tout notre devoir et répondre à tous les désirs des gens de bien![1]

This programme, however, was not destined to be carried out.

All the attention the second volume was to receive was a bare five pages in the *Nouvelles littéraires* for February 1752,[2] while in November 1753 the review of the third volume was devoted entirely to answering d'Alembert's attack on the *Journal de Trévoux* in the *Avertissement des Éditeurs*.[3] Thereafter, down to the end of his editorship in 1762, Berthier remained silent on the subject of the *Encyclopédie* except for a bare mention of the publication of the first volume of plates in that year. Why did the promised examination of the later volumes of text never appear? The answer must be that the censor, behind whom stood Malesherbes, would not allow Berthier to continue his detailed analysis of the work. One of d'Alembert's conditions for resuming work on the *Encyclopédie* in the summer of 1752 had been ' qu'il sera défendu aux Jésuites, nos ennemis déclarés, d'écrire contre cet ouvrage, d'en dire même ni bien ni mal, ou bien qu'il nous sera permis d'user de représailles '.[4] No other explanation except such an intervention by Malesherbes could account for this sudden silence.

That there was an instruction of this kind in the case of Fréron's *Année littéraire* is definitely proved. Fréron's hostility to the *philosophes* in general and to the editors of the *Encyclopédie* in particular is beyond doubt. Yet in the years immediately after the foundation of his journal in 1754 Fréron was remarkably reticent in his comments on the whole work. He did not review a single one of the volumes which appeared between 1753 and 1757, and, to begin with, his incidental references to the *Encyclopédie* are few and far between. The attack which he made on the work in 1756 and

[1] *JT*, March 1752, p. 469.          [2] *JT*, Feb. 1752, pp. 378–82.          [3] *JT*, Nov. 1753, pp. 2659–77.
[4] Letter to Formey, 24 May 1752 (see Formey, *Souvenirs d'un Citoyen*, ii, 47).

which caused d'Alembert to make a furious protest to Malesherbes was a mere pinprick. In reviewing a fairly obscure work, Barral's *Dictionnaire portatif, historique, théologique et moral de la Bible,* Fréron inserted 'l'*Encyclopédie*' after the epithet 'un ouvrage très scandaleux' which the author had applied to the work without actually naming it.[1]

Fréron's addition of this one word led to a considerable row. Urged on by the angry d'Alembert, Malesherbes sent a severe rebuke to the censor of the review, Abbé Trublet, for letting this item pass.[2] The latter's apologetic reply throws a good deal of light on the instructions which Malesherbes had given to the censors of periodicals about attacks on the *Encyclopédie*:

Il est vrai que Fréron a souvent voulu attaque dans ses feuilles l'*Encyclopédie* et ses éditeurs parce que, dit-il, ils l'ont souvent attaqué dans leur ouvrage. Je n'ai jamais voulu passer ces attaques. J'en ai donné un jour la preuve à M. d'Alembert en lui faisant lire dans quelques épreuves des feuilles ce que j'y avais rayé. Il me parut sensible à cette attention. Depuis Fréron est souvent revenu à la charge et moi aux ratures. Jamais je n'ai voulu permettre aucun extrait d'aucun ouvrage fait expressément contre l'*Encyclopédie*.[3]

Such an attitude on the part of the censor explains Fréron's relative moderation as well as the rarity of his attacks on the *Encyclopédie*; it also accounts for the absence of reviews both of its successive volumes and of works hostile to it. Indeed, although in his next letter to this censor Malesherbes holds that this particular attack was indefensible, he hints to him that he has rather gone beyond his instructions in cutting out all criticisms of the *Encyclopédie*. What does seem clear is that, at any rate down to the crisis which began in 1757, not only the *Année littéraire*, but also other periodicals such as the *Journal de Trévoux* were firmly discouraged from making any serious and detailed criticism of the *Encyclopédie* and that similarly attempts to give publicity to works which had taken on this task were simply struck out by the censor.

By 1757, however, Fréron seems to have secured rather greater freedom to comment on the *Encyclopédie*. During the next few

[1] *AL*, 1756, iii, 192–3.     [2] Bibliothèque Nationale, Nouv. acq. fr. 3531, f. 62.
[3] *Ibid.*, f. 64. Malesherbes's reply is to be found, *ibid.*, f. 65 (all three letters are reproduced in *Correspondance de l'abbé Trublet*, ed. J. Jacquart, Paris, 1926, pp. 58–62).

years he made a good few attacks both on the work and its editors, though he never actually published a review of Vol. VII which appeared in that year. His hostility to the whole enterprise stands out most clearly in his publication of the accusations of plagiarism brought by the architect, Patte, against Diderot and the publishers. The much advertised plates of the *Encyclopédie*, he alleged, were simply those assembled by Réaumur.[1] The striking thing about the various criticisms of the *Encyclopédie* which Fréron published for about ten years or so from 1757 onwards is that he lays stress, not, as many critics of the work had done, on the subversive nature of the views expressed in it, but rather on its technical shortcomings. Characteristic of his attitude are the following lines from a review which he published in 1762:

... Les encyclopédistes ... n'avaient qu'à nous donner des notions justes des arts et des sciences exprimées dans un style vif et rapide, qu'à nous faire grâce de leurs réflexions éternelles et déplacées, qu'à nous exposer un précis de tout ce que les autres avaient pensé. Ils devaient surtout nous épargner l'ennui de lire leurs décisions magistrales, avoir plus de connaissance et de pratique des arts dont ils nous tracent des règles d'un air impérieux, ne pas grossir leur ouvrage volumineux de plats articles, comme à l'article *Femme* où l'on examine avec un esprit de ruelle et un ton précieux la *capricieuse*, la *boudeuse*, etc. Voilà les défauts que pouvait relever notre censeur.[2]

The impression which one in fact derives from a close study of the references to the *Encyclopédie* in the *Année littéraire* is far from coinciding with the conventional picture of the gallant Fréron fighting a losing battle in defence of the old order and striving bravely if vainly to uphold the traditional ideas in politics and religion. At least so far as the *Encyclopédie* is concerned, even when he had won the freedom to show his hatred of the work and its editors, ideological factors seem to have played little part in his animosity. This comes out in accusations of plagiarism and in attacks on the technical inadequacies of the work; nowhere does he make any detailed criticism of its unorthodox ideas.

The crisis in the history of the *Encyclopédie* in the period 1757–60 coincided with the appearance of a number of reviews dedicated to

[1] See above, pp. 86–9.
[2] *AL*, 1762, i, 38–9. (The work under review was Abbé Irail's *Querelles littéraires*.)

the struggle against the rising tide of unorthodox religious ideas. There is little of interest to be found in periodicals such as Abbé Joannet's *Journal chrétien* (1758–64) or even in *Le Censeur Hebdomadaire* (1760–61) which had for a time as joint editor Abraham Chaumeix, the author of one of the most bitter and detailed contemporary attacks on the *Encyclopédie*.[1] Much more important was the thoroughgoing attack on the first seven volumes delivered in a periodical dedicated to the Dauphin, *La Religion vengée ou Réfutation des auteurs impies* (1757–63), the principal editor of which appears to have been a Recollect friar named Jean Nicolas Hubert Hayer (1708–80). The greater part of the three volumes published in 1760 is devoted to a detailed examination of the *Encyclopédie*, and this gives us a really clear picture of what remarkably shrewd opponents of the whole work found reprehensible in it. For them the hostility to all religion, and especially to Christianity, of the editors and some of their contributors was only too clear. Despite some exaggerations *La Religion vengée*'s detailed criticisms of individual articles are both shrewd and, at any rate from the standpoint of the author or authors, generally fair. We shall meet them again when we come to deal with the *Encyclopédie*'s attitude to philosophy, religion and, to a slight extent, political questions. A historian of the work can only regret that this periodical did not survive long enough to take in the last ten volumes of text.

## Books and pamphlets on the 'Encyclopédie'

That is also one drawback of the books and pamphlets to which the publication of the *Encyclopédie* gave rise. Here again the controversy was confined almost entirely to the decade 1751–60; the appearance of the last ten volumes in 1765 passed, as we shall see, almost unnoticed and a really detailed criticism of their contents by contemporary writers is nowhere to be found. It need hardly be said that contemporary books and pamphlets on the *Encyclopédie* are, with rare exceptions, the work of hostile critics; given the fairly rigid censorship under which books were published before 1789, that is hardly surprising. On the other hand Malesherbes did occasionally allow a certain freedom to writers attacking or defend-

[1] See below, pp. 119–23.

ing the *Encyclopédie*: some books and pamphlets were published with a *privilège*, others with a *permission tacite* (i.e. with the approval of the authorities, though without any formal permission) and others again were simply published without any sort of authorization being asked for. This greater freedom made for more lively controversy than in the periodical press of the time; and as several of the writers of attacks on the *Encyclopédie* do not confine themselves to vague generalities, but examine in considerable detail quite a number of articles which gave offence to the orthodox, they offer the modern reader a fairly precise notion of what contemporary critics thought of the first seven volumes.

They alleged that, considered as a work of reference, the *Encyclopédie* was marred by a host of errors and imperfections and that, from the point of view of ideas, it was polluted by all manner of subversive doctrines affecting religion and morality as well as the very foundations of the political and social order. Their views throw light on two important problems—the originality of the *Encyclopédie* and its unorthodox opinions. Yet clearly such writings have to be interpreted with considerable caution. In general, they are far from being inspired by a spirit of detached inquiry; they are often marred by stupidity, exaggeration, bad faith (particularly in the manufacture of faked quotations) and occasionally a parrot-like repetition of earlier attacks.

The main part of the controversy took place in the period between 1752 and 1760 or 1761, reaching its height with the publication of Vol. VII in 1757 and the events which followed. As might be expected, the argument was to continue rather longer than in the periodical press of the period. Indeed in the writings of Abbé Barruel, that fanatical defender of the old régime, it was to last down to 1797 with the appearance of his *Mémoires pour servir à l'histoire du Jacobinisme*.

The publication of the prospectus in October 1750 sparked off the controversy. Early in the following year there appeared two satirical pamphlets, the *Lettre de M. ***, l'un des XXIV, à M. Diderot, directeur de la manufacture encyclopédique* and the *Lettre d'un souscripteur pour le Dictionnaire encyclopédique à M. Diderot*. These were followed by another slim pamphlet, the *Lettre à M. *** de la Société royale de Londres*, which at first sight appears hostile to the *Encyclopédie*. In practice, while keeping up an air of impartiality, the author was certainly well disposed towards Diderot. He mentions, for instance, the proposed translation by Ayloffe as a proof of the success of the prospectus in England.

The first polemical work inspired by the actual text of the *Encyclopédie* appeared in the Amsterdam edition of the *Journal des Savants* in November 1751. This *Apologie de la métaphysique à l'occasion du Discours préliminaire de l'Encyclopédie*, which was to be reprinted in 1753 and 1759 with other writings of the same author, was the work of David Renaud Boullier (1699–1759), the son of Huguenot parents who was a pastor in Amsterdam and later in London. Although the *Discours préliminaire* is awarded fulsome praise, d'Alembert is criticized at length for his attitude to Descartes and in particular for his rejection of innate ideas, while his praise of Locke—described as 'l'idole de nos beaux esprits pyrrhoniens'— is challenged.

The first work to be directed against the text of the *Encyclopédie* inside France was the anonymous *Réflexions d'un Franciscain, avec une lettre préliminaire, adressées à M.* ***, *auteur en partie du Dictionnaire encyclopédique*, the appearance of which coincided with the publication of the second volume in January 1752. Inevitably the author does his best to exploit the scandal of the thesis sustained in the previous November at the Paris Faculty of Theology by the Abbé de Prades whom we have already encountered as one of the early contributors to the *Encyclopédie*. The author makes every effort to link the censurable propositions in the Abbé's thesis with similar ideas contained in d'Alembert's *Discours préliminaire*. Thereafter, apart from complaining about the obscurity of the article AGIR (originally announced as being by Abbé Yvon, but in practice culled from the pages of the Jesuit philosopher, Father Buffier) and of Diderot's ART, the author devotes the rest of this longish pamphlet to an attack on the unsigned article ARISTOTÉLISME, or rather on half a paragraph in it which spoke disparagingly of Franciscans in general and in particular of Duns Scotus.

Despite the uproar caused by Abbé de Prades's thesis and the attempts of the enemies of the *Encyclopédie* to link the two works in a common reprobation, little detailed criticism of Diderot and his colleagues emerged from it all. Some hostile references to the work were, however, made in the *Instruction pastorale* directed against the Abbé's thesis by the Jansenist bishop of Auxerre, Charles de

Caylus. In it we find an extremely hostile criticism of Diderot's AUTORITÉ POLITIQUE as well as an attack on Yvon's AME in the course of which he puts the blame for the Abbé's reprehensible notions on 'les encyclopédistes qui lui ont fourni les principes de sa thèse' (p. 171).

The appearance of the third volume in October 1753 stirred up fresh controversy. Before the year was out d'Alembert's article COLLÈGE, with its sharp attack on the existing system of secondary education which was largely under the control of the Jesuits, was challenged in another anonymous pamphlet, printed without official permission: the *Observations de M. \*\*\*, principal du Collège de \*\*\*, sur un des articles du Dictionnaire encyclopédique*. The author defends the existing system, including the teaching of the classical tongues and rhetoric.[1]

Now that the critics had three volumes of the text of the *Encyclopédie* to work on, their attacks increased in number. 1754 saw the publication of two more pamphlets. The shorter of these—an *Avis au public sur le troisième volume de l'Encyclopédie*—mainly concentrates on its deficiencies as a work of reference. The author considers the haughty tone of the *Avertissement des Éditeurs* out of place in view of the notorious defects of the first two volumes:

. . . Le plagiat immense et inexcusable, les propositions hardies et dangereuses, le défaut d'exactitude dans les dates et dans les faits qui ont excité tant d'orages contre les premiers tomes de l'*Encyclopédie*, ne leur sont point imputés faussement; et cet ouvrage, quoique fait en partie par des auteurs estimables, ne mérite certainement point notre estime. Il ne faut pas croire que le public excusera les plagiaires qui ont rempli ces deux volumes de productions étrangères sans y rien ajouter du leur, sans en corriger les fautes, pas même celles d'impression; qu'il pardonnera au géographe d'avoir copié mot pour mot le plus mauvais dictionnaire de géographie que nous ayons, à l'abbé Yvon de s'être donné pour auteur de l'article *Agir*, d'avoir présenté cet article comme une preuve de sa pénétration, de sa précision et de son goût; et quand après avoir essuyé de tels reproches et des reproches plus sanglants encore, on ose se présenter au public avec la même confiance et la même sécurité, le public sait qu'en penser, il sait ce qu'il doit faire (pp. 3–4).

When he comes to the third volume, the author finds plenty in it to criticize. He objects to what he considers the excessive length of

[1] See below, pp. 268–9.

some of the articles, particularly those on technology. If so much space had not been given to articles of this kind, this volume could have covered not only the whole of the letter C, but also D and E. Ideological considerations are not entirely neglected in this pamphlet as we have seen from the reference to 'les propositions hardies et dangereuses' contained in the first two volumes; but the author's obvious hostility to the underlying ideas of the *Encyclopédie* seldom results in references to those articles which particularly offended him.

The second of the two attacks on the *Encyclopédie* to appear in 1754—the *Réflexions d'un Franciscain sur les trois premiers volumes de l'Encyclopédie avec une lettre préliminaire aux éditeurs*—was more substantial as well as more precise in its criticisms. The *Lettre préliminaire* links the work with the earlier *Réflexions d'un Franciscain* of 1752. The name of a Jesuit, François Marie Hervé, is associated with both, but there is no certainty as to its author or authors. Here at last we find a work which goes into considerable detail to make clear and explicit what it objected to in the *Encyclopédie* and why. Once again the link between Abbé de Prades's thesis and the *Encyclopédie* is affirmed, but this time in considerable detail, with parallels between the thesis and specific articles. The Abbé's article CERTITUDE, along with Diderot's introductory and concluding comments on it, is subjected to severe criticism. Other subversive articles from all three volumes are singled out for adverse and generally very pertinent comment—for instance, *AIUS-LOCUTIUS, *ADORER, d'Alembert's AVEUGLE with its praise of the *Lettre sur les Aveugles* which had landed Diderot in Vincennes, Diderot's AUTORITÉ POLITIQUE, the anonymous CHRISTIANISME, Jaucourt's CONSCIENCE (LIBERTÉ DE), *CHRONOLOGIE SACRÉE, Faiguet de Villeneuve's CITATION and, of course, d'Alembert's COLLÈGE. Characteristic of the tone of the work is the answer given to the complaint in the *Avertissement des Éditeurs* of the third volume about the unfairness of the accusation of irreligion:

Votre ouvrage, messieurs, n'est-il pas plein de ces principes qui renversent les fondements du christianisme? Il semble que vous n'avez conçu le projet d'un vaste dictionnaire que pour l'attaquer ouvertement. . . . Il fallait ou ne point parler de la religion, ce n'était pas là en effet votre affaire, ou il fallait en parler avec respect. . . . La rivalité n'a point eu de part aux coups qu'on vous a portés. La seule envie de venger l'honneur de la religion a armé la main qui vous a fait de profondes blessures. (pp. 85–6).

The work ends with a warning that the author or authors intended to continue their criticism as successive volumes of the *Encyclopédie* appeared. This intention was not realized; all that happened was that a revised version of the work appeared in 1759, at the height of the controversy, under the ironical title of *Éloge de l'Encyclopédie et des Encyclopédistes*. However, this new version with minor changes at the beginning and end, which were obviously the work of another hand, really adds nothing to the detailed criticism of the first three volumes contained in the 1754 *Réflexions*.

The years 1755 and 1756 passed without any significant attack on the *Encyclopédie*, but the situation changed radically in the following year, November of which saw the publication of Vol. VII. There was, for instance, the *Petites Lettres sur de grands philosophes* of Charles Palissot (1730–1814); this was described by the enraged d'Alembert in a letter of 1 January 1758 as being 'parmi tous les libelles qu'on publie contre nous le plus infâme, quoiqu'il ne soit pas le plus dangereux'.[1] Yet despite his indignation the work makes only rare and fairly insignificant references to the *Encyclopédie*. The first of its four letters offers only vague criticisms of the work as of the *philosophes* in general except for a satirical reference, by no means new, to the article *CERF: 'Il sera permis de trouver des fautes même dans ce grand dictionnaire qui est leur ouvrage de prédilection et de ne pas croire, par exemple, sur leur parole que les cerfs atteignent au bout d'un certain temps l'âge de raison, etc. etc. etc.' (p. 16).

The second letter is mainly concerned with attacking Diderot's newly published play, *Le Fils naturel*. It contains only one criticism of the *Encyclopédie*—the well-worn one that the contributors contradict one another: 'Enfin . . . l'*Encyclopédie*, au lieu de former un corps de doctrine, n'est qu'un chaos de contradictions où l'on trouve autant de systèmes et de principes différents qu'il y a d'auteurs qui ont fourni des articles' (p. 73). Although despite its exaggeration this was in many ways a valid criticism, it fitted in oddly with the other accusation frequently directed against the *Encyclopédie*, that its editors and contributors were engaged in a

[1] *Revue d'Histoire des Sciences*, 1954, pp. 2–3.

systematic attempt to undermine everything in Church and State. The last letter contains a relatively mild complaint about the obscurity of certain articles, especially Yvon's AME; but, however much the *philosophes* may have resented the *Petites Lettres*, it cannot be said to represent a serious attack on the *Encyclopédie*.

Nor is there really much more in another pamphlet which appeared at the end of 1757, the *Nouveau mémoire pour servir à l'histoire des Cacouacs*, the work of a government propagandist named Jacob Nicolas Moreau (1717–1804). Despite the stir caused by its publication and the anger of the *philosophes* against whom it was directed, it has relatively little to say about the *Encyclopédie*. A footnote (p. 8) contains a reference to the stale joke about the reasoning powers of stags in *CERF. Then there is a passage in which the hero of the work is shown

sept coffres d'un pied de long sur un demi-pied de large et sur un pouce et demi d'épaisseur. Ils étaient revêtus d'un maroquin bleu et ne paraissaient distingués l'un de l'autre que par les sept premières lettres de l'alphabet que l'on y voyait formées par des lignes de petits clous de diamant. Chaque coffre avait sa lettre qui lui paraissait servir d'étiquette. (p. 56)

These mysterious objects are, one is left to gather, the first seven volumes of the *Encyclopédie*, but neither this passage nor the pages which follow on it can be said to contain any worthwhile criticism of the work. Finally there is an attack on the notion of the contract in political theory, its sources being given as Locke's *Civil Government*, Rousseau's *Discours sur l'inégalité* and Diderot's article, AUTORITÉ POLITIQUE. As in Palissot's *Petites lettres* the *Encyclopédie*, as distinct from the writings of the *philosophes* in general, comes off practically unscathed.

A much more dangerous work—indeed a mine of unreliable quotations which the enemies of the *Encyclopédie* were to exploit for years to come—was the *Catéchisme et décisions de cas de conscience à l'usage des Cacouacs, avec un discours du patriarche des Cacouacs pour la réception d'un nouveau disciple*. This was the work of Abbé Giry de Saint-Cyr (1694–1761), *sous-précepteur du Dauphin* and a member of the Académie Française, who is said to have been responsible for the starting-point of Moreau's pamphlet—the anonymous *Avis utile*, published in the *Mercure* of October 1757, which first used the term *cacouacs*. The *Catéchisme* contains a host of quotations from all manner of works of the period, among them a considerable number from the *Encyclopédie*, often torn from their context or even simply inaccurately reproduced. D'Alembert, for instance, was wrongly alleged to have stated in the *Discours préliminaire* that 'l'inégalité des conditions est un droit barbare' (pp. xxi–xxii). The author often puts together snippets from the *Encyclopédie* with those from more outspoken works of the period to give the impression that all of these expressed the ideas of Diderot and his contributors.

He prints, for instance, a considerable number of extracts from La Mettrie's *Discours sur la vie heureuse*, regardless of the fact that Diderot and other materialists of the time disowned such compromising ideas. The way in which the author of this strange catechism takes passages from La Mettrie and also from Helvétius whose *De l'Esprit* had caused a tremendous scandal in the summer of 1758, mixing them in with extracts from the *Encyclopédie* to give the impression that all the writers concerned shared the same outlook, can be seen in his treatment of Quesnay's ÉVIDENCE and Turgot's EXISTENCE:

*D.* Si le sentiment est une propriété de la matière, la pensée n'en sera-t-elle pas aussi un attribut?

*R.* Oui, sans doute; car 'penser est une manière de sentir (*a*). Le discernement s'exécute par les sensations mêmes (*b*). Juger n'est jamais que sentir (*c*). Ce qu'on appelle *conséquence* dans une suite de jugements n'est que l'accord des sensations (*d*). C'est le véritable point où nous devons nous placer pour suivre la génération de toutes nos idées (*e*).'

   (*a*)  *Discours sur la vie heureuse*, p. 77.
   (*b*)  *Encycl.* au mot *Évidence*, t. 6, p. 148.
   (*c*)  *De l'Esprit*, p. 3.
   (*d*)  *Encycl.* au mot *Évidence*, t. 6, p. 148.
   (*e*)  ibid. au mot *Existence*, t. 6, p. 262. (pp. 22–3)

Despite the obvious unfairness of such polemical methods, it must be said that the author does probe some dangerously unorthodox articles in the *Encyclopédie*, for instance *AIUS-LOCUTIUS, *ANIMAL and Deleyre's FANATISME in the field of philosophy and religion and in the political sphere Diderot's AUTORITÉ POLITIQUE and Jaucourt's GOUVERNEMENT. Though the author's criticisms are never in the nature of things detailed, as a polemical work the *Catéchisme* was undoubtedly a great success.

For the critical year 1758 when controversy over the *Encyclopédie* reached a new high point we even have to record for once a work in its defence—an anonymous pamphlet entitled *L'Aléthophile ou l'ami de la vérité* which is generally attributed to the young La Harpe (1739–1803) who, after the Revolution, was to denounce the *Encyclopédie* in quite unmeasured terms. The author makes a spirited defence of the *philosophes* in general and of Diderot in particular, but there is really little of interest in this pamphlet. This same year actually saw a defence of the *Encyclopédie* written in verse; it bore the title, *Poème sur la cabale anti-encyclopédique au sujet du dessein qu'ont eu les encyclopédistes de discontinuer leurs travaux*. This was an early work of Edmé Louis Billardon de Sauvigny (1736–1812), a young lieutenant in the guards of King Stanislas of Lorraine who was soon to embark on a prolific career as a writer. It is a strangely naïve production. Take, for instance, the lines in which, after a fulsome eulogy of d'Alembert, he apostrophizes Diderot, and the footnote to them:

> Et toi* qu'à ce mortel un penchant secret lie,
> Philosophe hardi dont le bouillant génie
> Répand sur ce qu'il touche un souffle créateur
> Et semble à chaque objet vouloir donner un cœur;
> Toi qui, cherchant le vrai dans une source pure,
> Marches d'un pas timide en suivant la nature
> Et voyant son flambeau s'éteindre devant toi,
> Fais courber ta raison sous le joug de la foi,
> A la face du ciel un dévot implacable
> Te peint par charité sous les traits d'un coupable.[1]

\* M. Diderot. On a jugé à propos dans la suite de faire deux syllabes de son nom pour l'harmonie du vers.

Ce philosophe, après les plus grandes réflexions, convient que sans la foi il se serait égaré.

It is doubtful whether either of these youthful effusions brought much comfort to the two editors in the midst of their tribulations at this difficult moment in the history of the *Encyclopédie*.

In November 1758 a massive attack on the whole enterprise was begun by a staunch Jansenist named Abraham Joseph Chaumeix (1725?–90) who according to a police report had come to Paris

---

[1] *La Religion vengée, poème en réponse à celui de la religion naturelle*, Geneva, 1758, p. 52.

from Orleans where he had acted as tutor and had not paid his debts, and as a relaxation from teaching found pleasure in the company of serving maids. In due course he was to enter the service of Catherine the Great and spent many years teaching in Russia, ending his days in Moscow.

Eight volumes in all of his *Préjugés légitimes contre l'Encyclopédie* appeared before the end of 1759, but despite its title only the first two volumes are in fact devoted to this end, the remainder being given up to a sustained attack on Locke and Helvétius and to a defence of religion. Like the only comparable attack on the *Encyclopédie* (the relevant volumes of *La Religion vengée*), this work inevitably confines its attentions to the seven volumes of the *Encyclopédie* which had appeared by the end of 1757. What is more, Chaumeix is very far from being as shrewd a critic as the editor of *La Religion vengée*; he often gives the impression of lashing out blindly at anything which happened to catch his attention without being able to see the wood for the trees in the 7,000 or so folio pages which he was supposed to be refuting. Quite a number of his criticisms are palpably unfounded since he has a tendency to see subversive intentions where none probably existed and to miss both sly digs and more daring unorthodoxies where they certainly were intended.

Yet he did devote some 500 pages to a detailed examination of the *Encyclopédie*, and there is no doubt that Diderot and his supporters were angered by this onslaught, though they affected to despise him utterly (Diderot refers to him in an editorial addition to the article SUBSIDE as 'le plat Ch . . .'). Chaumeix opens his first volume with what is described as an *Avertissement de l'Éditeur* in which he hypocritically maintains that he does not impute to Diderot and his contributors the horrifying ideas which Helvétius had just expounded in that scandalous work, *De l'Esprit*. Almost in the same breath he claims that he will show how 'le livre *De l'Esprit*, partant de la métaphysique et de la morale encyclopédiques, a démontré que toutes ses assertions n'en étaient que des développements' (i.iv–v). This linking of the *Encyclopédie* and *De l'Esprit* was to be taken up by other critics and in particular, as we shall see, by the Paris Parlement.

In his preface Chaumeix claims quite correctly to be the first person to produce a detailed refutation of the *Encyclopédie*, lamenting the fact that so dangerous a work should not have had the trouncing it deserved: 'Combien de personnes se gâtent l'esprit et puisent les principes d'erreur dans ce dictionnaire!' (i.xvii). He goes on to list the defects of the *Encyclopédie* which he proposes to criticize. The first six of these concern technical matters such as the disadvantages of employing a large number of contributors and of using alphabetical order, the superficial treatment of important topics and the presence of too many useless articles. Only the last four criticisms are directed against the ideas set forth by the editors and contributors. Chaumeix maintains:

7°. Qu'ils ont abusé en plusieurs manières des renvois qu'ils ont mis aux divers articles de ce dictionnaire.

8°. Que l'*Encyclopédie* est une collection d'objections contre les vérités les plus importantes et que les auteurs se sont dispensés de répondre à la plupart de ces objections.

9°. Que la manière dont les encyclopédistes écrivent, le choix des auteurs dont ils font l'éloge et de ceux qu'ils prennent pour garants suffisent pour prévenir contre leur ouvrage.

10°. Que la manière dont ils répondent à leurs censeurs et celle avec laquelle ils tâchent de prévenir la critique de leur ouvrage sont contre eux un violent préjugé. (i.5)

Chaumeix has no difficulty in showing up the cunning use made of cross-references to destroy the effect of an orthodox article; after all, to do so he only needed to quote the relevant passage from *ENCYCLOPÉDIE. Again it was easy to give examples of the way in which the editors and contributors paraded objections to orthodox beliefs and somehow forgot to refute them. Chaumeix also gives numerous examples of the suspect authors quoted with admiration in the *Encyclopédie*:

Ce n'est pas seulement Voltaire qui trouve dans l'*Encyclopédie* des témoignages d'admiration de la part de ces écrivains. Tous ceux contre lesquels les auteurs chrétiens se sont élevés avec le plus de force y reçoivent un égal tribut de louanges. Locke, par exemple, leur paraît le créateur de la métaphysique; B***,[1] de Prades, etc. etc. sont loués sur les points même sur lesquels ils ont été repris. (i.99–100)

---

[1] Presumably Buffon.

After dealing with the *Encyclopédie*'s attitude to its critics Chaumeix passes on to his exposition of the basic principles of the work. He accuses the editors and contributors of carrying Locke's ideas to materialist conclusions:

... Pourquoi trouve-t-on dans son livre tant d'atteintes données à la spiritualité de l'âme? N'aurait-il pas aussi démontré qu'elle n'est que matière? Non, il l'aurait bien voulu, mais sa puissance créatrice n'est pas allée jusque là ... Il était réservé à ses disciples, les encyclopédistes, de travailler à cette nouvelle création. (i.178)

It cannot be said that Chaumeix is altogether successful in proving this accusation, since he quotes in support of it not only *ANIMAL, but also articles by such authors as d'Alembert, Abbé Yvon, Quesnay and Turgot, none of whom, apart from Diderot, could be regarded as being in the least inclined towards materialism.

Chaumeix opens his second volume with an attack on the secular attitude to morality in the *Encyclopédie*. In a characteristic passage he upbraids d'Alembert for his pessimistic view that for man the supreme good is simply freedom from pain:

Nos auteurs, ignorent-ils que le bonheur de la vie présente ne peut être un autre que celui de la vie future; que l'homme n'a pas deux fins différentes, quoiqu'il soit fait pour passer dans deux différents états de vie; que dans le premier il doit mériter et être récompensé dans le second; désirer dans la vie présente et jouir dans la vie future; chercher son souverain bonheur pendant sa vie mortelle et le posséder dans la vie éternelle ... ? L'homme sans révélation est un mystère impénétrable à nos lumières. Pourquoi donc chercher dans ses propres imaginations pour traiter du bonheur de l'homme et contredire la révélation?[1] (ii.13)

Naturally he has no difficulty in finding in the body of the work numerous examples of articles reflecting an attitude to moral questions which was anathema to a devout Jansenist.

When he comes to the *Encyclopédie*'s treatment of religion, he inevitably finds plenty to censure, since for him it is only too obvious that 'les auteurs de ce dictionnaire ont contredit de la manière la plus hardie et la plus téméraire les vérités de la religion' (ii.102). It is characteristic of his whole outlook that, after stating that new opinions should not be condemned out of hand without examination, he should go on to make some significant reservations:

Mais la liberté que la religion laisse aux savants à faire des découvertes dans les sciences ne s'étend que sur les objets qui sont abandonnés à leurs disputes et sur lesquels la révélation n'a pas prononcé. A l'égard des points sur lesquels il a plu à Dieu de nous instruire par lui-même, il est clair que les savants, non plus que les ignorants, n'ont d'autre parti à prendre que de les croire quand même ils ne les comprendraient pas. (ii.103–4)

It is obvious that for a writer of such views the spirit of free inquiry for which the *Encyclopédie* stood was bound to lead to deplorable results in the religious sphere. Chaumeix brings out in a striking passage the contrast between the attitude of the *Encyclopédie* and that of orthodox Catholicism:

La vraie philosophie, selon les encyclopédistes, est *la liberté de penser.* Cette philosophie est si fort de leur goût qu'ils ne perdent aucune occasion d'en faire l'éloge. . . . Par une raison contraire l'esprit de soumission que demande le christianisme, est bien éloigné de leur plaire; aussi n'en font-ils pas grand cas. (ii.140–1)

Article after article is analysed and denounced for its anti-Christian ideas.

Such a detailed attack on the *Encyclopédie* was naturally made use of in the *réquisitoire* which the *avocat général*, Omer Joly de Fleury, pronounced before the Paris Parlement at the beginning of 1759, a fateful year in the history of the whole enterprise and one which marked the height of the controversy which it aroused. There was nothing in the least original in Joly de Fleury's oration since it was based on the writings of Chaumeix and other critics. None the less by putting the whole weight of the Parlement behind these criticisms this *réquisitoire* assisted in their diffusion. It is also clear that, like other attacks on the *Encyclopédie*, it must have helped those contemporaries who were not necessarily hostile to the work to become aware of the subversive ideas hidden away in its large and unwieldy folios and thus served a purpose which was far from being that of the author. The *Encyclopédie* was certainly denounced in violent terms:

A l'ombre d'un dictionnaire qui rassemble une infinité de notions utiles et curieuses sur les arts et sur les sciences, on y a fait entrer une compilation alphabétique de toutes les absurdités, de toutes les impiétés répandues dans tous les auteurs; on les a embellies, augmentées, mises dans un jour plus frappant. Ce dictionnaire est composé dans le goût de celui de Bayle. On y développe, selon les articles, le *pour* et le *contre*; mais le *contre*, quand il s'agit de la religion, y est toujours exposé clairement et avec affectation.[1]

The editors and certain contributors were also accused of, being materialists and, for good measure, of holding subversive political views.

Omer Joly de Fleury's *réquisitoire* was soon followed by an anonymous pamphlet, entitled *Lettres sur le VII^e volume de l'Encyclopédie*. The author, who appears to have been a member of a religious order, makes clear his hostility from the very outset: '. . . Ces vérités paraîtront peut-être un peu dures, mais les encyclopédistes ne sauraient s'en plaindre avec justice. Quand on ne respecte ni le trône, ni les autels, ni la vertu, on aurait mauvaise [grâce?] d'exiger des ménagements et des égards' (pp. iii–iv). Although he more than once accuses the editors and contributors of harbouring the most subversive political views, he never attempts to substantiate this accusation by reference to specific articles. His attack on Vol. VII is mainly directed against articles on religious and moral questions, several of which he subjects to detailed criticism. A sample of his approach is provided by the following general observations:

La règle de l'*Encyclopédie* est d'exalter les méchants et à proportion de leur méchanceté. Ainsi, toutes choses étant égales, l'hérétique passe devant le catholique, et le déiste a la préférence sur l'hérétique. . . . S'il est un pays où il leur paraisse que la religion n'est pas un objet qui intéresse et où l'hérétique et le juif soient regardés du même œil que le catholique, c'est un pays enchanté, c'est la patrie des sages au jugement de ces messieurs. . . . Pour les déistes, l'*Encyclopédie* les préconise avec une affectation encore plus marquée, et même son estime s'étend jusqu'à ceux qui ont le plus léger trait de ressemblance avec eux. (pp. 18–19)

Although this is not a particularly significant work, it has a certain interest. The author does not simply repeat parrot-like earlier criticisms of the *Encyclopédie*; it is clear that he had subjected Vol. VII to a close examination.

In condemning Helvétius's scandalous work, *De l'Esprit*, in

[1] *Arrêts de la Cour de Parlement du 23 janvier 1759*, Paris, 1759, p. 13.

April 1759, the Faculty of Theology at the Sorbonne singled out for denunciation two articles from the *Encyclopédie*—AUTORITÉ POLITIQUE and ÉVIDENCE. Moreover, a detailed diatribe against the work is contained in a long pastoral letter published in far away Montpellier in November of the same year by the bishop of Lodève, Jean Félix Henri de Fumel (1717–90). In his *Mandement et instruction pastorale touchant plusieurs livres ou écrits modernes, portant condamnation desdits livres ou écrits* he attacks the political as well as the religious ideas of the *Encyclopédie*:

A des systèmes impies si favorables à l'irréligion, à des systèmes pervers si relatifs au plus désordonné libertinage on ajoute des systèmes séditieux, contraires à l'esprit de dépendance et de subordination. . . . L'autorité des puissances légitimes, leur souveraineté, leur indépendance, le respect, la soumission, l'obéissance qu'on leur doit sont un article fondamental de notre religion trop gênant pour eux pour qu'ils n'aient pas cherché à l'ébranler. (pp. 49–50)

In his best sermon style the bishop reaffirms the principle of the Divine Right of Kings:

Les rois sont donc nos maîtres, nos souverains et nos juges, établis par l'ordre de Dieu pour nous gouverner. Leur autorité ne dépend point de notre consentement *exprès* ou *tacite*. Elle est fondée sur celle de Dieu même, et elle est une suite des dispositions de la Providence Divine sur le sort des humains. (p. 59)

While the bishop is not in the least original in his choice of articles to criticize, he does show an uncompromising vigour in restating the traditional outlook on the relations of the individual with the State as well as the Church.

The year 1760 stands out in the history of the controversy because of the performance, in May, of Palissot's satirical comedy, *Les Philosophes*, at the Comédie Française. However, before dealing with the uproar which it created, we must first give attention to a work actually written in defence of the *Encyclopédie*: the *Justification de plusieurs articles du Dictionnaire encyclopédique ou Préjugés légitimes contre Abraham Joseph de Chaumeix,* published anonymously by Abbé Charles Leclerc de Montlinot (1732–1801), apparently with a *permission tacite* from Malesherbes.

The author claims to have no connection whatever with the

editors of the *Encyclopédie* or its contributors. He has little difficulty in showing up Chaumeix's exaggerations and his bad faith in quoting out of context. He goes into some detail to defend a number of the articles attacked in the *Préjugés légitimes* and concludes his work with the statement: 'J'ose affirmer (et je suis à même de le démontrer) qu'il n'est pas un seul article extrait du *Dictionnaire encyclopédique* où M. Chaumeix n'ait commis les mêmes infidélités que je lui ai déjà reprochées' (p. 184). The trouble with this able work is that it proves too much. For all his bull-in-a-china-shop tactics, his exaggerations and his unfair quotations there is no doubt that Chaumeix was right, from his blinkered point of view, in scenting the basic unorthodoxy of the *Encyclopédie*. He did not let this work go unanswered. He published a short, but extremely irate reply, *Les Philosophes aux abois, ou Lettres de M. de Chaumeix à MM. les Encyclopédistes au sujet d'un libelle anonyme,* but this contributes nothing new to the controversy.

On 2 May the Comédie Française—then as now a state theatre and one which was at that date subject to rigid government control as well as to the stage censorship—put on Palissot's *Les Philosophes.* Down to the end of the month the play was given fourteen performances, and it was published before its first run was over. It contained scurrilous attacks on Diderot (Dortidius) and Helvétius (Valère), while Rousseau (Crispin), still regarded as one of the *philosophes* despite the breach with Diderot and his group, was made fun of by being brought on to the stage on all fours and pulling a lettuce out of his pocket. Yet the play itself can scarcely be said to be an all-out attack on the *Encyclopédie*. References to it are in fact hard to find, and in the end one discovers that there are only two. In Act I, sc. 4 Cydalise, the dupe of the *philosophes*, is made to say to her maid:

> Retirez-vous, Marton.
> Prenez mes clefs, allez renfermer mon Platon.
> De son monde idéal, j'ai la tête engourdie.
> J'attendais à l'instant mon *Encyclopédie*;
> Ce livre ne doit plus quitter mon cabinet.

The other allusion is less direct and even more harmless. In the next scene, in speaking to her daughter of the book she is writing,

Cydalise says:

> J'ai fait exprès pour vous un chapitre profond.
> Je veux l'intituler: *Les devoirs tels qu'ils sont.*
> Enfin, c'est en morale une encyclopédie,
> Et Valère l'appelle un livre de génie.

It was not the play itself, but rather the war of pamphlets which it sparked off, that stirred up again the controversy around the *Encyclopédie* which, for over a year since the withdrawal of its *privilège*, had been officially dead and buried.

Abbé Morellet, its latest theologian, got in the first blow in the controversy with a scathing attack on Palissot which he published under the title of *Préface de la comédie des Philosophes*; this pamphlet earned him six weeks in the Bastille. Palissot was compelled to publish his real preface to the play under the title of *Lettre de l'auteur de la comédie des Philosophes au public, pour servir de préface à la pièce*. Unlike his play, Palissot's preface does contain a large number of references to the *Encyclopédie*. He makes it clear that in writing his satire of the *philosophes* he had this work very much in mind: 'L'*Encyclopédie*, cet ouvrage qui devait être le livre de la nation, en était devenue la honte; mais de ses cendres mêmes il était né des prosélytes qui, sous le nom d'esprits forts, inspiraient à des femmes des idées d'anarchie et de matérialisme' (p. 6).

The pot-pourri of quotations from the *Encyclopédie* and other contemporary works which follows was not the result of long research on Palissot's part; the whole lot were lifted, without acknowledgment, from Abbé Giry de Saint-Cyr's *Catéchisme des Cacouacs*. Palissot seems to have opened the book more or less at random and copied down snippets of snippets, sometimes re-arranging the order of words and even adding to them when he felt like it. If the Abbé could scarcely be said to have given a fair picture of the contents of the *Encyclopédie*, that offered by Palissot was even more unfair.

In his satire he had been careful to spare Voltaire, who aroused considerable indignation among his friends in Paris by entering into correspondence with the author of *Les Philosophes* instead of flaying him in his usual merciless fashion as a public enemy. However, at two centuries' distance it would seem that Voltaire's answers, which Palissot published along with his own letters, offered a skilful defence of the *Encyclopédie* and its contributors. In his three letters he not only works in a eulogy of the whole enterprise and of its principal contributors, but also comments scathingly on the shocking mixture of truncated extracts from the *Encyclopédie* and other works which Palissot had put into his preface:

Vous m'assurez que vous n'avez point accusé le chevalier de Jaucourt. Cependant c'est lui qui est l'auteur de l'article *Gouvernement*; son nom est en grosses lettres à la fin de cet article. Vous en déférez plusieurs traits qui pourraient lui faire grand tort, dépouillés de tout ce qui précède et qui les suit. . . .

Vous voulez rendre odieux un passage de l'excellente préface que M. d'Alembert a mise au-devant de l'*Encyclopédie*, et il n'y pas un mot de ce passage dans sa préface. Vous imputez à M. Diderot ce qui se trouve dans les *Lettres juives*. Il faut que quelque Abraham Chaumeix vous ait fourni des mémoires comme à M. J*****,[1] et qu'il vous ait trompé, comme il a trompé ce magistrat. Vous faites plus; vous joignez à vos accusations contre les plus honnêtes gens du monde des horreurs tirées de je ne sais quelle brochure intitulée *La Vie heureuse* et *L'Homme plante* qu'un fou nommé La Mettrie composa un jour, étant ivre, à Berlin il y a douze ans. Cette satire de La Mettrie, oubliée pour jamais et que vous faites revivre, n'a pas plus de rapport avec la philosophie et l'*Encyclopédie* que *Le Portier des Chartreux* n'en a avec l'histoire de l'Église. Cependant vous joignez toutes ces accusations ensemble.[2]

It is not easy to see why Palissot should have published the letters which he exchanged with Voltaire between May and July 1760; those which he received from Ferney unmasked very skilfully his misquotations and at the same time made an eloquent defence of the *Encyclopédie* at a very difficult moment in its history.

It would be wearisome to enter into a detailed examination of the attacks on the *Encyclopédie* contained in various anonymous pamphlets which appeared in the course of the year 1760 in the train of Palissot's *Philosophes*. By now we have passed the high point of the whole controversy, though, despite the *Encyclopédie*'s disappearance underground since the apparently fatal blow of the withdrawal of its *privilège*, it did not die out immediately. In 1761 a fairly objective account of the battle down to that date appeared in one of the chapters of the *Querelles littéraires* of Abbé Simon Augustin Irail (1719–94). The author was no admirer of Chaumeix

---

[1] Joly de Fleury, the *avocat général* of the Paris Parlement.        [2] Best. 8257.

and his *Préjugés légitimes*. 'Quel style! quel fatras de raisonnements et de paroles!' he exclaims. The fatal blow of the *arrêt du Conseil* he attributes, as did many *philosophes*, to the publication of Helvétius's *De l'Esprit*. He criticizes the disparity in style between the different articles of the *Encyclopédie* and, above all, puts down the failure to complete the work to the attempt to deal with politics and religion in what should have been purely and simply a dictionary of the arts and sciences.

The controversy continued with the appearance, in May 1761, of another satirical work, entitled *La Petite Encyclopédie ou Dictionnaire des philosophes, ouvrage posthume d'un de ces messieurs*. The anonymous author offers the reader a series of articles in alphabetical order, ranging from AGE to VERTU, made up of quotations not only from the *Encyclopédie*, but also from the writings of Diderot, Toussaint, Helvétius and La Mettrie. In the article CATÉCHISME the compiler of this work admits that he owes his quotations, not to a diligent study of the first seven volumes of the *Encyclopédie*, but to the *Catéchisme des Cacouacs* of Giry de Saint-Cyr. All he had done was to arrange under alphabetical headings extracts from this and other works culled from the *Catéchisme*. Such small originality as the work possesses lies in the ironical comments added by the author.

While Diderot, d'Holbach, Jaucourt and the rest of the contributors were toiling over the last ten volumes of the *Encyclopédie*, in Rouen a learned Abbé, Jean Saas (1703–74), was busily engaged in assembling a list of errors contained in the first seven. The first instalment of his work appeared in 1762, attached to a longer essay, under the title of *Lettre d'un professeur de Douai à un professeur de Louvain sur l'Encyclopédie*. This short work which confines itself to the first volume of the *Encyclopédie* was expanded two years later into *Lettres sur l'Encyclopédie pour servir de supplément aux sept volumes de ce dictionnaire*. The first work is relatively moderate in tone; it even offers a modicum of praise for the *Encyclopédie*. Here the author confines himself to what he calls 'la géographie, la mythologie et la bibliographie', leaving out, for instance, politics and religion. He has no difficulty in pointing out quite a number of errors, especially as he lists even obvious misprints which the reader could well have corrected for himself.

The second work has a more definitely polemical purpose; the

Abbé attacks the ideas contained in a number of articles drawn from all the first seven volumes. Although it does not have anything essentially new to say either about the errors of fact or the plagiarisms or the unorthodox ideas to be found in the *Encyclopédie*, its appearance angered the *philosophes*. D'Alembert worked a bitter retort to the Abbé into the fifth volume of his *Mélanges de littérature, d'histoire et de Philosophie*, published in 1767 (pp. 563–5), while shortly after the appearance of Saas's second volume Voltaire wrote a letter to Damilaville[1] containing opprobrious references to him which Diderot promptly inserted in the *Encyclopédie* in his introduction to the article SUBSIDE. After speaking of 'l'hypocrite abbé de S . . .', Diderot goes on:

M. de Voltaire . . . a dit dans une de ses lettres à propos de la brochure de cet abbé de S . . . : 'Quel est celui qui s'est occupé à vider les fosses d'un palais où il n'est jamais entré? . . . Tel misérable petit architecte qui n'est pas en état de tailler un chapiteau, ose critiquer le portail de Saint-Pierre de Rome'. Nous voudrions bien que ces comparaisons flatteuses, plus méritées de notre part, nous honorassent autant qu'elles doivent humilier nos ennemis. [XV.573a–b]

It is possible that the reason why this second work got under the skin of Diderot and other *philosophes* was that it revived the controversy on the *Encyclopédie* at the moment when the publication of the last ten volumes was in sight. In itself it does not seem to merit all this indignation, compared with the attacks of Chaumeix and *La Religion vengée* some years earlier.

The appearance of these last ten volumes at the end of 1765 should have been greeted, one feels, by a renewal of the whole controversy. The surprising thing is that the silence of the periodical press published inside France was echoed by an absence of books and pamphlets of the kind which had greeted the publication of the first seven volumes. The only work of any size directed against the *Encyclopédie* to be published in the period following this notable event was the *Histoire critique de l'Éclectisme ou des nouveaux Platoniciens* of Abbé Guillaume Malleville. The author—a 'docteur de Sorbonne' according to Grimm—devotes most of the first of his two volumes to a critical examination of *ÉCLECTISME and also makes one or two references to other articles such as *ÉPIDELIUS,

[1] Best. 11304 (15 Oct. 1764).

*CHYTHONIES and CHALCÉDOINE (though unsigned, the last may well be by Diderot). The second volume is much less concerned with the *Encyclopédie*, though it does criticize Mallet's DÉMON and DIABLE. Penetrating as the Abbé's comments on these articles are, it will be noticed that they all come from Vols III–V which had appeared a good ten years earlier; there is not a single reference to the last ten volumes.

What is more, this was the last work ever to appear which was mainly devoted to a thorough criticism of the *Encyclopédie*. After this date one finds only scattered references to this nefarious work in books hostile to the *philosophes* in general which attempted to arrest the growing trend towards free thought in religion. Thus the *Dictionnaire antiphilosophique* of the Benedictine, Dom Louis Mayeul Chaudon (1737–1817), which went through several editions after its first publication in 1767, contains hostile articles on both Diderot and the *Encyclopédie*, while the *Dictionnaire philoso-phico-théologique portatif* of an ex-Jesuit, Father Aimé Henri Paulian (1722–1802), published in 1770 and also several times re-printed, does no more than list the *Encyclopédie* among those works which contain propositions which are described as 'exécrables et abominables'.

Palissot, it is true, carried on his guerilla warfare against the *Encyclopédie* well beyond 1760. In his poem, *La Dunciade*, pub-lished in 1764, he made several attacks on Diderot, but only one of these contains a reference (and that insignificant) to the *Encyclopédie*:

> C'est ce héros de la philosophie,
> Cet écrivain dont l'esprit rédacteur
> Depuis dix ans compile avec génie
> Pour élever à sa juste hauteur
> Le monument de l'*Encyclopédie*.[1]

Five years later he produced a vitriolic pamphlet entitled *Dénoncia-tion aux honnêtes gens d'un libelle philosophique contre M. Palissot, inséré dans l'Encyclopédie et faussement attribué à M. le comte de Tressan*. The *libelle* in question was to be found in the article PARADE, printed in Vol. XI over the signature of Tressan; this violent onslaught on Palissot may well have been written by

---

[1] *La Dunciade*, Chelsea, 1764, p. 30.

Diderot himself. However, the pamphlet deals only with a personal grudge and not with any wider questions.

Palissot continued his attacks on the *Encyclopédie* in a work which was later to be enlarged and several times reprinted, his *Mémoires pour servir à l'histoire de notre littérature*—first published in 1771 along with an expanded version of *La Dunciade*. Praise is given to some contributors, in particular to Jaucourt and the Romillys, *père et fils*, but none the less most of the references to the *Encyclopédie* and its editor seek to belittle both.

If d'Alembert is on the whole praised, the opportunity is taken to maintain that the *Encyclopédie* did not fulfil the expectations aroused by the *Discours préliminaire*. It is true that Chaumeix is treated in disparaging fashion, but only in order to work in a sneer at the *Encyclopédie*. When we come to the section on Diderot, we find his writings systematically run down and inevitably another attack on the *Encyclopédie* is brought in. The most detailed criticism of it is, however, in the article on Charles Perrault whom Diderot had singled out for praise in *ENCYCLOPÉDIE as one of the rare men of the age of Louis XIV who would have been capable of contributing a page to a worthwhile encyclopedia. Though Palissot grudgingly concedes that the *Encyclopédie* has some merits, he soon launches out into a series of extremely hostile criticisms:

Pourquoi assujettir au ridicule désordre d'une nomenclature alphabétique toutes les sciences et tous les arts de manière que, par la multitude de renvois qu'entraîne nécessairement cette méthode ou plutôt ce défaut de méthode, il faut parcourir les vingt énormes volumes pour savoir précisément comment se fait une aiguille?

Pourquoi s'être flatté d'avoir donné la description fidèle de tous les arts pour en avoir semé çà et là quelques notices imparfaites et superficielles tandis que l'Académie des Sciences, si respectable à toute l'Europe, s'occupe depuis environ un siècle à donner cette même description dans un ordre bien plus convenable et qu'elle n'a pu remplir encore, à cet égard, qu'une faible partie de ses engagements?

Pourquoi avoir fait tant de larcins déguisés sous le nom d'articles? Pourquoi tant de paradoxes dangereux sous le nom de vérités utiles? pourquoi tant d'erreurs de géographie, d'histoire, de morale, de goût, qui dupent à chaque moment la confiance ou la curiosité du lecteur? Pourquoi tant d'impertinences érigées en préceptes, surtout en matière de littérature?

Pourquoi, comme M. de Voltaire en convient lui-même, tant de déclamations puériles et de lieux communs insipides . . . ? Mais les pourquoi ne finiraient jamais.[1]

To round off this rather spiteful and superficial attack Palissot expresses the hope that the new *Encyclopédie d'Yverdon* will be purged of all the errors in Diderot's compilation.

A rather similar work which was also hostile to the *Encyclopédie* was *Les Trois Siècles de la littérature française,* which was brought out in 1772 by Abbé Antoine Sabatier de Castres (1742–1817). Despite its date the author simply chews over the controversies of the 1750s, attacking articles from the early volumes which had been criticized when they first appeared. He has not one word to say, any more than has Palissot, about the contents of the last ten volumes. His remarks on Diderot's part in the *Encyclopédie* are extremely unflattering:

Enfin M. Diderot est connu par excellence pour avoir été le dessinateur de l'*Encyclopédie*, l'enrôleur des ouvriers et l'ordonnateur des travaux. Nous répéterons d'abord, d'après une foule de critiques, que cet ouvrage n'a été pour lui qu'un enfant adoptif dont Bacon et Chambers ne l'avaient pas fait légataire. Nous ajouterons ensuite que l'excellent prospectus qui l'annonçait avec tant de pompe, n'a produit comme la caverne d'Éole que du vent, du bruit et du désordre, et que la plupart des articles de ce dictionnaire informe auxquels on a mis les nom de M. Diderot ne sont que la compilation de quelques ouvrages médiocres qu'il n'a fait qu'altérer et abréger.[2]

It is pretty clear that none of his references to the *Encyclopédie* shows any direct acquaintance with even the first seven volumes.

It is only when we reach the 1780s that we at last find some discussion, however fragmentary, of the last ten volumes. It occurs in the writings of one of the sworn opponents of the *philosophes*, the ex-Jesuit, Abbé Augustin Barruel (1741–1820). He is best known for his *Mémoires pour servir à l'histoire du Jacobinisme* (1797) which saw in the French Revolution the fruits of a gigantic conspiracy in which the *philosophes* and the *Encyclopédie* had played an important part. An earlier work of his, the *Les Helviennes ou Lettres provinciales philosophiques*, published in five volumes between 1781 and 1788,

---

[1] *La Dunciade*, London, 1771, 2 vols, ii, 206–8 (the Voltaire reference is to his *Siècle de Louis XIV, Œuvres complètes*, ed. L. Moland, Paris, 1877–85, 52 vols, xiv, 153).

[2] *Les Trois Siècles de la littérature*, The Hague-Paris, 1781, 4 vols, ii, 173–4.

contains a large number of scattered quotations from articles from the *Encyclopédie* together with criticisms of them. It is true that a great many of these articles come from the first few volumes and had already been subjected to criticism. However, even here Barruel does occasionally produce original comments, and in addition he does actually quote from and comment on quite a number of articles from the volumes published in 1765—for instance, Yvon's LIBERTÉ (*Morale*), Diderot's LOCKE, PYRRHONIENNE, SOCRATIQUE and his editorial addition to Jaucourt's VICE. In the nature of things *Les Helviennes* is not a straightforward and detailed refutation of the *Encyclopédie* comparable to Chaumeix's *Préjugés légitimes* or the relevant volumes of *La Religion vengée*. It consists of snippets taken from a considerable number of articles, along with a great many more from all manner of works by the *philosophes*, which are woven into the framework provided by the author for his denunciation of the contradictions, impiety, immorality and subversive notions of his opponents.

Barruel continued to denounce the *Encyclopédie* in his later and more famous work, the *Mémoires pour servir à l'histoire de Jacobinisme*. It is characteristic of the author's 'conspiratorial' approach to the Revolution that the chapter in which the *Encyclopédie* is discussed should be headed: 'Premier moyen des conjurés'. He inevitably takes the narrow view that the main aim of Diderot and d'Alembert in producing the whole work was to undermine religion:

Cet objet si secret était de faire de l'*Encyclopédie* un immense dépôt de toutes les erreurs, de tous les sophismes, de toutes les calomnies qui, depuis les premières écoles de l'impiété jusques à cette énorme compilation, pouvaient avoir été inventées contre la religion, mais de cacher si bien le poison qu'il se versât très insensiblement dans l'âme des lecteurs sans qu'ils pussent s'en apercevoir.[1]

He enumerates with some skill the various methods used by the editors and some of their contributors to achieve this end—the insertion of remarks hostile to orthodox religion in out-of-the-way articles, the use of cross-references from articles of perfect orthodoxy to others which destroyed the arguments advanced there (an effect sometimes achieved simply by directing the reader at the end of one article to another with such a title as PRÉJUGÉ, SUPERSTITION

---

[1] *Mémoires pour servir à l'histoire du Jacobinisme*, London, 1797, 4 vols, i, 60.

or FANATISME), and finally the addition of editorial comments which wiped out the effect of an orthodox article written by one of the contributors. Some of Barruel's general observations are, however, less convincing. He considers, for instance, that d'Alembert (that 'sophiste renard' he calls him) played the role of general reviser, moderating the excesses of Diderot himself—a part which he certainly did not play in the last ten volumes and which it is improbable that he played in the first seven. Nor can one accept the view that all along the editors had plans for both a supplement and cheap foreign reprints which would contribute still further to the diffusion of the work and 'mettre le poison à la portée des lecteurs les moins riches'.[1] Clearly both the supplement (in any case a relatively harmless work from the point of view of orthodoxy) and the foreign reprints were brought into being by a variety of publishers whose sole aim was commercial profit.

When he tries to furnish proofs of his conspiratorial theory by producing quotations from individual articles, Barruel has really nothing new to add to the controversy. He does, however, make skilful use of the correspondence of Voltaire and d'Alembert to show what were the secret aims of the editors and how they set about achieving them. On the other hand, his account of the controversy caused by the publication of the *Encyclopédie* and of its principal contributors is far from accurate, and although the chapter contains some observations of interest to a specialist in the history of the work, its value is limited by the fact that it is only one link in the chain of Barruel's theory which attributes the whole of the revolutionary cataclysm to a dark conspiracy.

If on the whole one gleans more from the books and pamphlets brought forth by the controversy which, from the time of the appearance of its prospectus, surrounded the *Encyclopédie*, than from the periodical press of the 1750s and 1760s, it must be said that, taken all in all, the amount of ink devoted by friends and especially enemies to a discussion of the work was not nearly as great as has often been made out. As we have seen, the greatest controversy was during the 1750s; it reached its height between the publication of the seventh volume in 1757 and 1760, the year of the row stirred up by Palissot's *Les Philosophes*. This inevitably meant that what was fought over was the first seven volumes; the

[1] *Ibid.*, i, 63.

last ten passed almost unnoticed except in the relatively friendly but far from uncritical pages of the *Journal encyclopédique* and a few snippets in Barruel's two books. None the less, now that we turn to study the contents of the *Encyclopédie*, we shall continually be meeting again with the writings of its critics. The comments of contemporaries who were fully absorbed in the intellectual climate of their age can serve to illuminate for the modern reader the significance of a great many of the more important articles.

## Chapter 6

# *Philosophy*

*Restrictions on the free expressions of ideas*

In considering how far the *Encyclopédie* served as a vehicle for the ideas of the Enlightenment we must never forget what heavy restrictions lay on its editors and contributors in the 1750s and 1760s when they sought to express their outlook on the world. Scattered through its pages we find again and again their cries of frustration at the obstacles which State, Church and Parlement put in the way of the free expression of their rationalist and secular approach to problems. Thus in GENÈVE d'Alembert praises 'cette noble liberté de penser et d'écrire' which was now to be found in what had once been the city of Calvin, and then turns a sorrowful eye on the very different state of affairs which reigned in countries like France:

Combien de pays où la philosophie n'a pas fait moins de progrès, mais où la vérité est encore captive, où la raison n'ose élever la voix pour foudroyer ce qu'elle condamne en silence, où même trop d'écrivains pusillanimes, qu'on appelle *sages*, respectent les préjugés qu'ils pourraient combattre avec autant de décence que de sûreté! [VII.578a]

In the very first volume we find tucked away in the article *AIUS-LOCUTIUS a plea for a very modest amount of freedom to express their ideas. Diderot begins by speaking of the high degree of liberty enjoyed in matters of religion by writers among the Ancients. 'Ces chrétiens, qu'ils ont tant persécutés, disaient-ils rien de plus fort que ce qu'on lit dans Cicéron?' he asks. Then he goes on to make a suggestion which, if accepted, would, he declares, allow as much freedom as was possible in a properly organized state, adding hypocritically that the English and Dutch carry such matters to the extremes of licence:

... Un moyen d'accorder le respect que l'on doit à la croyance d'une peuple et au culte national avec la liberté de penser qui est si fort à souhaiter pour la découverte de la vérité, et avec la tranquillité publique, sans laquelle il n'y a point de bonheur ni pour le philosophe, ni pour le peuple; ce serait de défendre tout écrit contre le gouvernement et la religion en langue vulgaire; de laisser oublier ceux qui écriraient dans une langue savante, et d'en poursuivre les seuls traducteurs. [I.241a]

Needless to say, this very modest suggestion was not well received; no doubt the enemies of the *Encyclopédie* saw in it merely the thin end of the wedge.

'Nous avons voulu transcrire ce morceau', wrote Father Berthier severely in the *Journal de Trévoux*,[1] 'qui doit surprendre tout lecteur raisonnable, tout citoyen bien instruit et tout chrétien attaché à sa religion'; the article earns several pages of censure. Nearly a decade later *La Religion vengée* is still found thundering against *AIUS-LOCUTIUS. If the author is compelled to agree with Diderot that one cannot prevent men from thinking, he will not accept that they cannot be prevented from making their thoughts public:

Mais pourquoi ne parviendrait-on pas à empêcher que les idées ne soient transmises sur le papier? Que le prince ou les magistrats sévissent contre les auteurs satiriques, blasphémateurs ou séditieux, vous ne verrez plus de livres sortir de leur fabrique, ou du moins n'en verrez-vous que fort peu. (ii.299)

What Diderot meant by 'liberté de penser' is denounced in strong terms:

Vouloir penser librement, c'est résister à toute autorité divine ou humaine; c'est ne reconnaître ni celle de l'Église, ni celle même de Dieu, lorsqu'il s'agit de croire à sa parole. ... Pour que l'impiété ne soit pas à craindre, Monsieur, nul autre moyen que de se soumettre et de s'attacher à l'autorité de l'Église romaine ... (xi.303–4)

[1] Nov. 1751, p. 2442.

The concluding remarks on Diderot's suggestion about making use of learned tongues are very pointed:

Il est aisé, Monsieur, de s'apercevoir que tout ceci n'est de la part de M. Did . . . qu'un jeu impie, quand on fait attention que ce même auteur prend à tâche de glisser partout l'impiété, même en langue vulgaire, et qu'il l'a fait non seulement dans plus d'un article de son *Encyclopédie*, mais encore dans différentes brochures que nous examinerons à leur tour. (xi.306–7)

It can well be imagined that *AIUS-LOCUTIUS did not find favour with Chaumeix in his *Préjugés légitimes*. It gives rise to a string of angry questions:

Que veulent-ils nous dire ici en opposant, comme ils n'ont pas honte de le faire, *la croyance du peuple* français, notre *culte national*, avec cette liberté de penser qu'ils disent être si fort à souhaiter? Est-ce donc un moyen de découvrir la vérité que de travailler à la combattre? Qui ne voit que de tels auteurs ne veulent d'autre règle que leur goût ni d'autre autorité que leur propre raison? (ii.114)

Such comments take us back into the atmosphere of a past age when to follow one's reason wherever it led was a crime in the eyes of the orthodox; but if it is the past for us, it was the present with which Diderot and his colleagues had to do battle.

Indeed one can find in the pages of the *Encyclopédie* itself echoes of the orthodox rejection of the very notion of freedom of thought; there is, for instance, the highly conventional article, LIBERTÉ DE PENSER, by Abbé Mallet, who attacks, for instance, Anthony Collins's *Discourse of Free-thinking* in strong language:

Le traité de *La Liberté de penser* de Collins passe, parmi les inconvaincus, pour le chef-d'œuvre de la raison humaine; et les jeunes inconvaincus se cachent derrière ce redoutable volume comme si c'était l'égide de Minerve. On y abuse de ce que présente de bon ce mot *liberté de penser* pour la réduire à l'irréligion, comme si toute recherche libre de la vérité devait nécessairement y aboutir. C'est supposer ce qu'il s'agissait de prouver, savoir si s'éloigner des opinions généralement reçus est un caractère distinctif d'une raison asservie à la seule évidence. La paresse et le respect aveugle pour l'autorité ne sont pas les seules entraves de l'esprit humain. La corruption du cœur, la vaine gloire, l'ambition de s'ériger en chef de parti n'exercent que trop souvent un pouvoir tyrannique sur notre âme qu'elles détournent avec violence de l'amour pur de la vérité. [IX.473a–b]

However, the true views of the main contributors are clearly voiced in the last ten volumes by Jaucourt. In LIBELLE (*Gouvern. politiq.*), for instance, he lays down the fundamental principle that 'en général tout pays où il n'est pas permis de penser et d'écrire ses pensées doit nécessairement tomber dans la stupidité, la superstition et la barbarie' [IX.459b].

He praises the English attitude towards scurrilous satires:

Ils croient qu'il faut laisser aller, non la licence effrénée de la satire, mais la liberté des discours et des écrits, comme des gages de la liberté civile et politique d'un état, parce qu'il est moins dangereux que quelques gens d'honneur soient mal à propos diffamés que si l'on n'osait éclairer son pays sur la conduite des gens puissants en autorité. [IX.459b]

In such matters, he concludes, it is possible to reconcile justice with 'le plus grand bonheur de la société et la conservation du gouvernement' [IX.460a]. PRESSE (*Droit polit.*) opens with a remarkably clear call for freedom:

On demande si la liberté de la *presse* est avantageuse ou préjudiciable à un état. La réponse n'est pas difficile. Il est de la plus grande importance de conserver cet usage dans tous les états fondés sur la liberté. Je dis plus: les inconvénients de cette liberté sont si peu considérables vis-à-vis de ses avantages que ce devrait être le droit commun de l'univers et qu'il est à propos de l'autoriser dans tous les gouvernements. [XIII.320b]

That, no doubt, was the ideal; but in the France of Louis XV Diderot and his colleagues were far from enjoying such freedom to discuss philosophy, religion or politics. It is also true that a proportion of the articles on philosophical subjects, especially in the earlier volumes, were written by *abbés* (in particular by Yvon) who were distinguished for their very mild unorthodoxy and for a total lack of originality which brought on them well-founded accusations of plagiarism. This is one reason why one can find throughout the pages of the *Encyclopédie* a great deal of the conventional thought of the middle of the eighteenth century.

## The attack on Scholastic philosophy

Yet one does not need to look far to find ideas which one associates with the Enlightenment, starting with a bitter hostility to

Scholasticism. Both editors devoted an article to denouncing it, d'Alembert in ÉCOLE (*Philosophie de l'*) and Diderot in SCOLASTIQUES (*Philosophie des*). D'Alembert begins his article thus:

On désigne par ces mots l'espèce de philosophie qu'on nomme autrement et plus communément *scolastique*, qui a substitué les mots aux choses, et les questions frivoles ou ridicules aux grands objets de la véritable philosophie; qui explique par des termes barbares des choses inintelligibles; qui a fait naître ou mis en honneur les universaux, les catégories, les prédicaments, les degrés métaphysiques, les secondes intentions, l'horreur du vide, etc. Cette philosophie est née de l'esprit et de l'ignorance. [V.303b–304a]

If, he says, this 'lèpre' is gradually disappearing from the University of Paris, thanks to the Inquisition this is not the case in the universities of Spain and Portugal:

Dans un des *Journaux des Savants* de l'année 1752, à l'article des *Nouvelles littéraires*, on ne peut lire sans étonnement et sans affliction le titre de ce livre, nouvellement imprimé à Lisbonne (au milieu du dix-huitième siècle): *Systema aristotelicum de formis substantialibus*, etc. *cum dissertatione de accidentibus absolutis. Ulyssipone*, 1750. On serait tenté de croire que c'est une faute d'impression et qu'il faut lire '1550'. [V.304a]

The article contains only three paragraphs, but, though brief, it is certainly pungent in its comments.

Diderot spread himself more in the article which he devoted to Scholasticism in Vol. XIV and which ends with a magnificent indictment from which we can quote only the last few lines. It follows from his account of Scholastic philosophers, he declares,

Que leur logique n'est qu'une sophisticaillerie puérile.
Leur physique, un tissu d'impertinences.
Leur métaphysique, un galimatias inintelligible.
Leur théologie naturelle ou révélée, leur morale, leur jurisprudence, leur politique, un fatras d'idées bonnes et mauvaises.
En un mot, que cette philosophie a été une des plus grandes plaies de l'esprit humain. [XIV.777a–b]

## Bacon, Descartes and Locke

The name of Francis Bacon is trumpeted forth in the *Prospectus* (p. 2b) ('ce génie extraordinaire') and in the *Discours préliminaire*

[I.xxiv] ('l'immortel chancelier d'Angleterre', 'le plus grand, le plus universel et le plus éloquent des philosophes', 'cet esprit lumineux et profond'). Yet even he, d'Alembert declares, was infected by the disease of Scholasticism:

Quoiqu'il avoue que les scolastiques ont énervé les sciences par leurs questions minutieuses, et que l'esprit doit sacrifier l'étude des êtres généraux à celle des objets particuliers, il semble pourtant par l'emploi fréquent qu'il fait des termes de l'école, quelquefois même par celui des principes scolastiques, et par des divisions et des subdivisions dont l'usage était alors fort à la mode, avoir marqué un peu trop de ménagement ou de déférence pour le goût dominant de son siècle. [I.xxv]

Even so, both here and in the article EXPÉRIMENTAL, d'Alembert follows Voltaire in describing Bacon as the founder of modern science, while Abbé Pestré sings his praises in BACONISME.

Descartes appears even more prominently in the *Encyclopédie*, though certain aspects of his philosophy and scientific theories are decisively rejected. Characteristically d'Alembert wrote in ÉCOLE (*Philosophie de l'*): 'C'est à Descartes que nous avons l'obligation principale d'avoir secoué le joug de cette barbarie; ce grand homme nous a détrompés de la philosophie de l'école (et peut-être même, sans le vouloir, de la sienne . . .)' [V.304a].

In the *Discours préliminaire* d'Alembert had already expounded in more detail his view of both the greatness and the limitations of Descartes. His contribution to mathematics he held to be the most solid and enduring basis of his fame. In science his theory of vortices (*tourbillons*) had been superseded by Newton's theory of gravitation, though d'Alembert pays tribute to the ingenuity of Descartes's hypothesis:

Reconnaissons donc que Descartes, forcé de créer une physique toute nouvelle, n'a pu la créer meilleure; qu'il a fallu, pour ainsi dire, passer par les tourbillons pour arriver au vrai système du monde; et que s'il s'est trompé sur les lois du mouvement, il a du moins deviné le premier qu'il devait y en avoir. [I.xxvi]

If Descartes erred in putting forward the theory of innate ideas, he still has one great achievement to his credit as a philosopher:

Descartes a osé du moins montrer aux bons esprits à secouer le joug de la scolastique, de l'opinion, de l'autorité, en un mot des préjugés et de la barbarie; et par cette révolte dont nous recueillons aujourd'hui les fruits, la philosophie a reçu de lui un service plus difficile peut-être à rendre que tous ceux qu'elle doit à ses illustres successeurs. . . . S'il a fini par croire tout expliquer, il a du moins commencé par douter de tout; et les armes dont nous nous servons pour le combattre ne lui en appartiennent pas moins, parce que nous les tournons contre lui. [I.xxvi]

Not content with this tribute d'Alembert made a long editorial addition to the rather plodding article CARTÉSIANISME, furnished by Abbé Pestré. Here, after speaking of the slowness with which the ideas first of Descartes and then of Newton were accepted in France, he concludes with some ironical observations:

Les persécutions que ce philosophe a essuyées pour avoir déclaré la guerre aux préjugés et à l'ignorance, doivent être la consolation de ceux qui, ayant le même courage, éprouveront les mêmes traverses. Il est honoré aujourd'hui dans cette même patrie où peut-être il eût vecu plus malheureux qu'en Hollande. [II.725b–726a]

It is clear that d'Alembert, and the other *philosophes*, regarded themselves, rightly or wrongly, as the spiritual heirs of Descartes.

It might be expected that the seventeenth-century philosopher who was nearest to the hearts of both Diderot and d'Alembert was Locke, then at the very height of his reputation in France. 'On peut dire', exclaimed d'Alembert in the *Discours préliminaire* [I.xxvii], 'qu'il créa la métaphysique à peu près comme Newton avait créé la physique.' Locke's rejection of innate ideas and his derivation of all our ideas from the senses are celebrated in the most eulogistic terms:

Pour connaître notre âme, ses idées et ses affections, il n'étudia point les livres, parce qu'ils l'auraient mal instruit. Il se contenta de descendre profondément en lui-même; et après s'être, pour ainsi dire, contemplé longtemps, il ne fit dans son traité *De l'entendement humain* que présenter aux hommes le miroir dans lequel il s'était vu. En un mot il réduisit la métaphysique à ce qu'elle doit être en effet, la physique expérimentale de l'âme. [I.xxvii]

In contrast to this praise the article LOCKE (*Philosophie de*) which, over a decade later, Diderot contributed to Vol. IX, seems decidedly on the thin side, so much so that one is rather left wondering whether this was one of that articles to which Le Breton

applied his blue pencil. Roughly half the relatively brief article is
given up to an account of Locke's life and career, and in what
follows we find none of the lavish praise bestowed by d'Alembert
or, before him, by Voltaire in his *Lettres philosophiques*. Diderot
insinuates that Locke might have derived more than merely the
rejection of innate ideas from the axiom that there is nothing in the
intellect which was not previously in the senses, for he goes on:

D'où il aurait pu tirer une autre conséquence très utile: c'est que toute
idée doit se résoudre en dernière décomposition en une représentation
sensible, et que puisque tout ce qui est dans notre entendement est venu
par la voie de la sensation, tout ce qui sort de notre entendement est
chimérique ou doit, en retournant par le même chemin, trouver hors de
nous un objet sensible pour s'y rattacher.

De là une grande règle en philosophie, c'est que toute expression qui ne
trouve pas hors de notre esprit un objet sensible auquel elle puisse se
rattacher est vide de sens.[1] [IX.626b]

A similar suggestion as to how Locke's ideas could be worked out
further is found in the following observations on grammar:

Malgré tout ce que *Locke* et d'autres ont écrit sur les idées et sur les signes
de nos idées, je crois la matière toute nouvelle et la source intacte d'une
infinité de vérités, dont la connaissance simplifiera beaucoup la machine
qu'on appelle *esprit* et compliquera prodigieusement la science qu'on
appelle *grammaire*. La logique vraie peut se réduire à un très petit nombre
de pages; mais plus cette étude sera courte, plus celle des mots sera
longue. [IX.626b]

The article is rounded off by a reference to the chance remark of
Locke which Voltaire had already exploited in the *Lettres philosophiques* several decades earlier: 'We have the ideas of matter and
thinking, but possibly shall never be able to know whether any
material being can think or no.' From this Diderot derives the
usual materialist conclusion that the soul is material and not there-

---

[1] Cf. *INCOMPRÉHENSIBLE . . . Il y a deux grands principes qu'il ne faut point perdre de vue: c'est qu'il n'y a rien dans
l'etendement qui n'y soit venu par la voie des sens, et qui par conséquent ne doive, en sortant de l'entendement,
retrouver des objets sensibles pour se rattacher. Voilà en philosophie le moyen de reconnaître les mots vides
d'idées. Prenez un mot; prenez le plus abstrait; décomposez-le, décomposez-le encore, et il se résoudra en dernier
lieu en une représentation sensible. C'est qu'il n'y a en nous que des représentations sensibles, et des mots
particuliers qui les désignent, ou des mots généraux qui les rassemblent sous une même classe, et qui indiquent
que toutes ces représentation sensibles, quelque diverses qu'elles soient, ont cependant une qualité commune.
[VIII.653b–654a]

*Agriculture: Labourage (Vol. I, Plate I)*

fore immortal, but he covers up his tracks with considerable ingenuity:

*Locke* avait dit, dans son *Essai sur l'entendement humain*, qu'il ne voyait aucune impossibilité à ce que la matière pensât. Des hommes pusillanimes s'effrayeront de cette assertion. Et qu'importe que la matière pense ou non? Qu'est-ce que cela fait à la justice ou à l'injustice, à l'immortalité, et à toutes les vérités du système, soit politique, soit religieux?

Quand la sensibilité serait la germe premier de la pensée; quand elle serait une propriété générale de la matière; quand, inégalement distribuée entre toutes les productions de la nature, elle s'exercerait avec plus ou moins d'énergie, selon la variété de l'organisation, quelle conséquence fâcheuse en pourrait-on tirer? *aucune*. L'homme serait toujours ce qu'il est, jugé par le bon et le mauvais usage de ses facultés. [IX.627a]

The conclusion of the article did not escape the eagle eye of Abbé Barruel;[1] like many passages in the other contributions of this type furnished by Diderot, it betrays clear signs of the materialist philosophy which he was working out in the very years when he was actively engaged on the *Encyclopédie*.

However, it must be said that this article is one of the tamest of the large number which Diderot devoted to the history of philosophy. It is obvious that Locke was not a thinker who thrilled him. In an editorial addition to Saint-Lambert's GÉNIE he produces a parallel between Locke and Shaftesbury which is by no means to the advantage of the former to whom we owe, he says, 'de grandes vérités froidement aperçues, méthodiquement suivies, sèchement annoncées' [VII.583b]. Even clearer is the comparison between Locke and Malebranche in MALEBRANCHISME: 'Une page de Locke contient plus de vérités que tous les volumes de Malebranche; mais une ligne de celui-ci montre plus de subtilité, d'imagination, de finesse et de génie peut-etre que tout le gros livre de Locke' [IX.943b]. In contrast, d'Alembert follows Voltaire in taking a more enthusiastic view of Locke and his philosophy.

## Diderot's articles on the history of philosophy

In the first two volumes of the *Encyclopédie* most of the longer articles devoted to the history of philosophy were left to the *abbés*.

[1] See *Les Helviennes ou Lettres provinciales philosophiques*, Amsterdam, 1781–8, 5 vols, ii, 205.

Thus Yvon was responsible for ACADÉMICIENS, ARISTOTÉLISME and CELTES, while Pestré produced such articles as BACONISME, CAMPANELLA and CARTÉSIANISME. However, though unsigned, three articles by Diderot—ANTÉDILUVIENNE (PHILOSOPHIE), ARABES (PHILOSOPHIE DES) and ASIATIQUES (PHILOSOPHIE DES)—were already to be found in the first volume, and if he wrote none for the second volume, from the third down to the very last he contributed a large number on individual philosophers or schools of philosophy, ancient and modern.

Many of these articles in the first seven volumes gave great offence to orthodox writers of the 1750s and 1760s, and although those of the last ten volumes were never subjected to such detailed scrutiny, his LOCKE (PHILOSOPHIE DE) did not pass altogether unnoticed, while *HOBBISME attracted very hostile attention. In the main the contents of these articles were unoriginal; they were compiled from a variety of sources which are sometimes specified at the end of the article. The most important of these was the work of a contemporary German writer, Jakob Brucker, whose massive *Historia critica philosophiae* in five volumes had conveniently appeared at Leipzig between 1742 and 1744. What angered contemporary critics was Diderot's tolerant attitude towards various philosophers whose views were highly suspect to orthodox Catholic writers. What was even worse was his habit of working into his account of the views of thinkers, ancient and modern, some of his own more daring ideas.

Thus *CYNIQUE (*Secte de philosophes anciens*) gave offence to a variety of writers, from those of the 1750s down to Abbé Barruel, particularly because of the spirited way in which Diderot defended these philosophers and in particular Diogenes:

Voilà ce que nous devons à la vérité et à la mémoire de cet indécent, mais très vertueux philosophe. De petits esprits, animés d'une jalousie basse contre toute vertu qui n'est pas renfermée dans leur secte, ne s'acharneront que trop à déchirer les sages de l'antiquité, sans que nous les secondions. Faisons plutôt ce que l'honneur de la philosophie et même de l'humanité doit attendre de nous; réclamons contre ces voix imbéciles, et tâchons de relever, s'il se peut, dans nos écrits, les monuments que la reconnaissance et la vénération avaient érigés aux philosophes anciens, que le temps a détruits et dont la superstition voudrait encore abolir la mémoire. [IV.597a]

His description of Diogenes as 'cet indécent, mais très vertueux philosophe' continued to exasperate critics down to the 1780s as we see from a passage in *Les Helviennes* of Abbé Barruel (iv.26), while Chaumeix retorts to Diderot's eulogy of these philosophers:

Je sais très bien que saint Paul, les pères de l'Eglise et tous les chrétiens portent de ces anciens philosophes un jugement bien différent de celui-là; mais c'est ce qui fâche beaucoup nos auteurs. Ils se regardent comme les successeurs de ces philosophes. On voit très bien qu'ils comptent soutenir leur propre cause en défendant celle des anciens.

He objects particularly to Diderot's reference to 'la superstition':

Dans l'excès de leur colère rien ne peut plus les arrêter. Ils oublient le respect qu'ils avaient promis de conserver *pour la croyance du peuple et pour le culte national*; et s'ils se ressouviennent que la religion chrétienne regarde tous ces prétendus sages comme des fous et des insensés, ce n'est que pour injurier . . . ceux qui les jugent d'après ces principes. (*PL* ii.142)

The article also earns a whole letter—a very indignant one—in *La Religion vengée* (xii.122–48).

*ÉPICURÉISME encountered equally hostile criticism. Despite Diderot's claim that he is simply going to expound the doctrines of Epicurus—'c'est donc lui qui va parler dans le reste de cet article; et nous espérons de l'équité du lecteur qu'il voudra bien s'en souvenir' [V.779b]—the article was soon heavily attacked. For once it almost made the heavy Chaumeix witty. This is how he introduces the long section which he devotes to it:

Les encyclopédistes vont présentement introduire Épicure pour jouer leur propre rôle. . . . Le comédien qui les représente a été si bien instruit par M. Diderot qu'on ne lui entendra réciter que les sentiments et presque les propres termes de l'auteur de l'*Interprétation de la Nature*, recueil d'extravagances . . . (*PL* ii.208)

Chaumeix sees through Diderot's claim that all he has added to his exposition of the doctrines of Epicurus is 'quelques-unes des conséquences les plus immédiates qu'on en peut déduire':

Il aurait fallu, pour une exactitude entière, mettre quelque marque distinctive par laquelle on pût reconnaître ce qui est de vous d'avec ce qui est d'Épicure. Vous n'avez garde; Épicure n'est ici qu'un prête-nom. (*PL* ii.213)

Among the passages from Diderot's account of the philosophy of Epicurus which Chaumeix selects for comment is the following:

Gardons-nous bien de rapporter à nous les transactions de la nature; les choses se sont faites sans qu'il y eût d'autre cause que l'enchaînement universel des êtres matériels qui travaillât soit à notre bonheur, soit à notre malheur. [V.781b]

To the first part of the sentence Chaumeix appends the sarcastic note: 'Épicure n'a jamais dit ceci; ces expressions sentent bien plus le Diderotisme que l'Épicuréisme, d'autant plus qu'elles ne sont pas fort claires.' The rest earns this comment: 'C'est aussi le système des encyclopédistes. M. d'Alembert a travaillé à le soutenir dans l'article *Fortuit*,[1] et nous y répondrons dans la seconde partie' (*PL* ii.217).

Another striking passage from Diderot's article is quoted by Chaumeix:

Les yeux n'ont point été faits pour voir ni les pieds pour marcher; mais l'animal a eu des pieds et il a marché, des yeux et il a vu. L'âme humaine est corporelle; ceux qui assurent le contraire ne s'entendent pas et parlent sans avoir d'idées. Si elle était incorporelle comme ils le prétendent, elle ne pourrait ni agir ni souffrir; son hétérogénéité rendrait impossible son action sur le corps. Recourir à quelque principe immatériel afin d'expliquer cette action, ce n'est pas résoudre la difficulté, c'est seulement la transporter à un autre objet. [V.782a][2]

On this Chaumeix comments: 'Si quelqu'un veut savoir à qui appartient le reste de ce paragraphe, il n'a qu'à lire l'*Interprétation de la nature*. Tout ce que l'on dit n'est que le résultat des extravagances de l'auteur de ce livre' (*PL* ii.219). In speaking of the conclusion of the article Chaumeix accuses Diderot and his colleagues of being 'plus épicuriens qu'Épicure même' (*PL* ii.223).

Two whole letters of *La Religion vengée* are devoted to a close examination of this one article. The following section in which Diderot summarized the theological views of Epicurus is singled out for criticiism:

Après avoir posé pour principe qu'il n'y a dans la nature que de la matière et du vide, que penserons-nous des dieux? Abandonnerons-nous notre

---

[1] See below, pp. 161–2.          [2] See Diderot's article INCORPOREL (pp. 178–9).

philosophie pour nous asservir à des opinions populaires, ou dirons-nous que les dieux sont des êtres corporels? . . . L'être qui est immortel est inaltérable, et l'être qui est inaltérable est parfaitement heureux, puisqu'il n'agit sur rien, ni rien sur lui. L'existence des dieux a donc été et sera à jamais une existence stérile, et par la raison même qu'elle ne peut être altérée; car il faut que le principe d'activité, qui est la source de toute destruction et de toute reproduction, soit anéanti dans ces êtres. Nous n'en avons donc rien à espérer ni à craindre. Qu'est-ce donc que la divination? qu'est-ce que les prodiges? qu'est-ce que les religions? S'il était dû quelque culte aux dieux, ce serait d'une admiration qu'on ne peut refuser à tout ce qui nous offre l'image séduisante de la perfection et du bonheur. Nous sommes portés à croire les dieux de forme humaine; c'est celle que toutes les nations leur ont attribuée; c'est la seule sous laquelle la raison soit exercée, et la vertu pratiquée. Si leur substance était in-corporelle, ils n'auraient ni sens, ni perception, ni plaisir, ni peine. Leur corps toutefois n'est pas tel que le nôtre; c'est seulement une combinaison semblable d'atomes plus subtils; c'est la même organisation, mais ce sont des organes infiniment plus parfaits; c'est une nature particulière si déliée, si ténue, qu'aucune cause ne peut ni l'atteindre, ni l'altérer, ni s'y unir, ni la diviser, et qu'elle ne peut avoir aucune action. Nous ignorons les lieux que les dieux habitent. Ce monde n'est pas digne d'eux sans doute; ils pourraient bien s'être réfugiés dans les intervalles vides que laissent entre eux les mondes contigus. [V.783a–b]

These lines are severely criticized, and the censure falls on Diderot as well as Epicurus:

Ce long extrait, Monsieur, était nécessaire pour vous faire mieux com-prendre le génie d'Épicure et celui de son apologiste. On voit de part et d'autre une dérision extravagante et impie. . . . C'est une dérision que la formation de ces dieux. Des dieux formés par le hasard! des dieux uniquement composés d'atomes! . . . Pour nous, Monsieur, ce que nous admirons, c'est qu'un tel insensé, un tel fourbe puisse avoir des apologistes dans ce siècle de lumière, et chez des hommes qui se croient nés pour la porter dans tous les esprits. (*RV* x.280–3)

Diderot's description of Gassendi as 'le restaurateur de la *philosophie d'Épicure*' [V.785a] is rejected, except in a very limited sense; their treatment of Epicurus and his philosophy is contrasted in the sharpest terms:

Gassendi et M. Did . . . ont fait parler le philosophe d'Athènes, mais avec cette différence que l'encyclopédiste ne l'a fait parler que pour applaudir à ses impiétés; et le prétendu restaurateur de sa philosophie que pour les combattre et en inspirer de l'horreur; d'où il résulte que les louanges qu'il reçoit dans l'*Encyclopédie* sont l'opprobre de celui qui les donne. (*RV* x.285)

After further extracts from Diderot's account of Epicureanism, ending with an incautious remark about 'la conformité de ses principes avec les sentiments de la nature' [V.784b], we find the following comment:

Ces divers extraits nous font naître quelques réflexions dont il faut vous faire part; et en commençant par ce dernier, vous voyez, Monsieur, que l'auteur de l'article *Épicuréisme*, après avoir fait parler Épicure comme il lui a plu, adopte assez ouvertement toute sa doctrine, sans restriction ni réserve. Les éloges qu'il fait de sa personne sont autant d'actes d'approbation de sa philosophie. (*RV* x.295)

The second letter devoted to ÉPICURÉISME ends with a nasty swipe at its author since *La Religion vengée* declares that 'si Épicure fut un insensé, son interprète et son apologiste ne peut pas être un sage, et qu'il n'est même qu'un impudent imposteur quand il dit: *Je suis chrétien parce qu'il est raisonnable de l'être* (*Pens. Philosoph.* Pensée LVII) (x.301)'. It is clear that the true meaning of Diderots account of Epicurus and his philosophy did not escape his contemporaries.

Even less obscure to hostile critics of his day was the long article, *ÉCLECTISME, which he devoted to the neo-Platonists. Not only did it receive attention from Chaumeix and *La Religion vengée*; but it was subjected to a most detailed examination in the first volume of Abbé Malleville's *Histoire critique de l'éclectisme* which appeared in 1766, more than a decade after its publication. When he reviewed Malleville's work in the *Correspondance littéraire*, Grimm made it clear that the author was justified in his hostility to the article:

Le docteur a raison, ces encyclopédistes sont des gens sans foi ni loi. Ils s'abandonnent à leur imagination et font dire aux anciens philosophes des choses auxquelles ils n'ont jamais pensé. Si l'auteur de cet article, M. Diderot, est obligé de répondre de tout ce qu'il a mis proditoirement[1] dans la bouche des autres, je ne me soucie pas d'être à côté de lui le jour de la grande trompette. (vii.30)

---

[1] 'Ancien terme de palais. En trahison' (Littré).

The very opening of this article shows how Diderot tends throughout to identify eclecticism with the outlook of a man of the
Enlightenment:

L'éclectique est un philosophe qui, foulant aux pieds le préjugé, la tradition, l'ancienneté, le consentement universel, l'autorité, en un mot tout ce
qui subjugue la foule des esprits, ose penser de lui-même, remonter aux
principes généraux les plus clairs, les examiner, les discuter, n'admettre
rien que sur le témoignage de son expérience et de sa raison; et de toutes
les philosophies qu'il a analysées sans égard et sans partialité, s'en faire une
particulière et domestique qui lui appartienne. [V.270a]

Amongst the passages singled out for attack by Malleville is the
account of the ideas of the third-century philosopher, Ammonius
Saccas, of which Diderot writes:

Cette philosophie conciliatrice, paisible et secrète, qui s'imposait un
silence rigoureux et qui était toujours disposée à écouter et à s'instruire,
plut beaucoup aux hommes sensés. Elle fut aussi favorisée par le gouvernement, qui ne demandait pas mieux de voir les esprits se porter de ce côté;
non qu'il se souciât beaucoup que telle secte prévalût sur telle autre, mais
il n'ignorait pas que tous ceux qui entraient dans l'école d'Ammonius
étaient perdus pour celle de Jésus-Christ. [V.274b]

Diderot's true meaning here is brought out by the Abbé in the
comments which follow:

... Ce pourrait bien n'être ici qu'une espèce d'énigme que les amis de
l'encyclopédiste n'auront point de peine à entendre. Il désigne en plus d'un
endroit et même sans ambiguïté la coterie moderne de ces hommes
sensés qui sont les zélés partisans de *cette philosophie conciliatrice paisible et
secrète, toujours disposée à écouter et à s'instruire*. La prudence ne voulait pas
que l'on réunît tous les traits semés par-ci par-là qui caractérisent les
philosophes de nos jours. Un peu d'obscurité est le sel le plus piquant des
allégories. Sous le voile d'un récit historique l'encyclopédiste nous
apprend ce que méritait, suivant sa manière de penser, l'ancienne secte
éclectique rivale du christianisme, et ce que mérite encore mieux la
société des éclectiques modernes qui adoptent les principes de l'*Encyclopédie*. En le prenant ainsi, on a, ou peu s'en faut, trouvé la clef de l'énigme.
... Comme l'encyclopédiste est persuadé que la seule philosophie
raisonnable est cet éclectisme, il ne perd pas l'occasion d'en faire l'éloge.
Ce n'est pas néanmoins pour l'éclectisme ancien qu'il s'intéresse.

L'éclectisme moderne, qu'il nous peint sous le voile et sous le nom de l'ancien, a toute sa prédilection.[1]

The modern reader cannot but accept this explanation of Diderot's enthusiasm for the neo-Platonist philosophers.

Diderot's account of the origins of eclecticism was scarcely likely to please an orthodox writer, especially as it once more betrays the same desire to assimilate neo-Platonist with eighteenth-century *philosophe*:

L'*éclectisme*, qui avait été la philosophie des bons esprits depuis la naissance du monde, ne forma une secte et n'eut un nom que vers la fin du second siècle et le commencement du troisième. La seule raison qu'on en puisse apporter, c'est que jusqu'alors les sectes s'étaient, pour ainsi dire, succédé ou souffertes et que l'*éclectisme* ne pouvait guère sortir que de leur conflit, ce qui arriva lorsque la religion chrétienne commença à les alarmer toutes par la rapidité de ses progrès et à les révolter par une intolérance qui n'avait point encore d'exemple. Jusqu'alors on avait été pyrrhonien, sceptique, cynique, stoïcien, platonicien, épicurien, sans conséquence. Quelle sensation ne dut point produire, au milieu de ces tranquilles philosophes, une nouvelle école qui établissait pour premier principe que hors de son sein il n'y avait ni probité dans ce monde, ni salut dans l'autre, parce que sa morale était la seule véritable morale et que son Dieu était le seul vrai Dieu? Le soulèvement des prêtres, du peuple et des philosophes aurait été général sans un petit nombre d'hommes froids, tels qu'il s'en trouve toujours dans les sociétés, qui demeurent longtemps spectateurs indifférents; qui écoutent, qui pèsent, qui n'appartiennent à aucun parti et qui finissent par se faire un système conciliateur auquel ils se flattent que le grand nombre reviendra. [V.271a–b]

After dismissing this account of matters as quite unhistorical, Malleville continues:

Ces sages qui écoutent, qui pèsent, qui n'appartiennent à aucun parti, qui par conséquent regardent d'un œil indifférent les controverses de religion, qui se flattent que le grand nombre reviendra à leur système conciliateur, ce sont Messieurs les encyclopédistes. C'est ici leur portrait tracé par un de leurs principaux chefs. Que personne ne l'ignore. L'encyclopédiste, parlant selon les désirs de son cœur, se flatte avec ses amis que ce système conciliateur, qui est la destruction de la foi chrétienne, sera adopté par le grand nombre et qu'il prévaudra enfin.[2]

[1] *Histoire de l'éclectisme*, i, 33–5.        [2] *Ibid.*, i, 102.

This interpretation of the passage in question seems sound enough to the modern reader. Another couple of hundred pages are devoted to *ÉCLECTISME in this volume, but as most of what the author has to say against the article concerns its anti-Christian bias, the work need not detain us further.

Another of Diderot's articles on the history of philosophy which was to be attacked when it finally appeared, was *HOBBISME. This article did not, of course, see the light of day until 1765, and oddly enough, it was the *Journal encyclopédique*, normally well disposed towards the *Encyclopédie*, which carried out the attack. In the 1760s Hobbes was still very much of a bogeyman, and Diderot's defence of the man and his ideas angered Pierre Rousseau:

. . . Il n'y a personne qui ne connaisse les erreurs, les principes absurdes et la doctrine, plus insensée encore qu'elle n'est dangereuse, du trop célèbre Hobbes. Mais aucun écrivain ne s'était encore hasardé à le justifier, et nul n'avait songé à publier l'apologie de ses pernicieux ouvrages. Pourquoi donc trouvons-nous dans ce dictionnaire consacré aux vérités utiles un article étendu, tout à l'honneur de Hobbes?[1]

Rousseau disapproves of the eulogistic account which Diderot gives of the man, but he objects even more to the summary of his ideas which he offers. Diderot introduced this summary with the prudent words:

Nous allons en exposer les principes avec la précaution de citer le texte partout où la superstition, l'ignorance et la calomnie, qui semblent s'être réunies pour attaquer cet ouvrage, seraient tentées de nous attribuer des sentiments dont nous ne sommes que les historiens. [VIII.234b–235a]

Rousseau is not to be taken in:

Afin qu'on ne vous attribue pas ces sentiments, exposez-les sans art et combattez les plus dangereux avec cet avantage que vous donne la supériorité de votre génie et de votre raison sur le génie et la raison de Hobbes. Car enfin tout le monde sait quelles furent les opinions et les maximes de cet homme hardi; mais tout le monde ne peut pas se garantir de leur venin.[2]

He picks out for critical comment various sections of Diderot's summary of Hobbes's philosophy, among them the following

[1] *Journal encyclopédique*, 15 Nov. 1766, p. 3.     [2] *JE*, 15 Nov. 1766, p. 18.

lines from the summary of his ideas on human nature:

Il ne faut pas rechercher l'origine des passions ailleurs que dans l'organisation, le sang, les fibres, les esprits, les humeurs, etc. . . .
   Mais tout n'est pas également bon ou mauvais pour tous. Les mœurs
qui sont vertueuses au jugement des uns sont vicieuses au jugement des
autres. [VIII.236b]

The idea of the relativity of moral judgments was not one which
appealed to Rousseau:

Cela est faux dans tous les points, en dépit même des sophismes de
Montaigne, qui s'est inutilement efforcé de prouver par quelques usages
des nations sauvages que ce qui est cruauté et crime parmi nous est ailleurs
bienfaisance et vertu. Mais Montaigne ne faisait que s'exercer sur une
proposition à laquelle il ne tenait pas, au lieu que Hobbes fait de cette
opinion un des principes fondamentaux de sa philosophie.[1]

Rousseau goes on to extract from Diderot's summary of Hobbes's
ideas a whole series of dangerous thoughts and then quotes the
eulogistic lines which Diderot devotes to his character:

Hobbes, plein de confiance dans son jugement, philosopha d'après lui-
même. Il fut honnête homme, sujet attaché à son roi, citoyen zélé, homme
simple, droit, ouvert et bienfaisant. Il eut des amis et des ennemis. Il fut
loué et blâmé sans mesure; la plupart de ceux qui ne peuvent entendre son
nom sans frémir n'ont pas lu et ne sont pas en état de lire une page de ses
ouvrages. [VIII.241a]

These lines annoyed Rousseau:

Ce n'est point là apprécier, c'est prononcer en dictateur une décision
offensante. La plupart de ceux qui ont lu les ouvrages de Hobbes, tous ceux
qui ont été en état de les lire et qui en détestent les principes, appelleront
de cet impérieux et très faux jugement à la raison, au bon sens et à la
vérité. . . . L'auteur de cet article est très certainement en état de lire
Hobbes et même de penser et d'écrire plus fortement que ce philosophe;
ainsi on ne peut pas le soupçonner de n'avoir pas su voir . . . dans les
ouvrages de Hobbes une perpétuelle et révoltante apologie du despotisme,
du spinozisme, de la plus féroce tyrannie.[2]

In the eyes of the editor of the *Journal encyclopédique* Diderot had
gone too far in this article.

[1] *Ibid.*, p. 19.          [2] *Ibid.*, pp. 21–3.

As the last ten volumes of the *Encyclopédie* attracted very little hostile criticism, Diderot's articles on the history of philosophy were seldom attacked. Whereas, in addition to *CYNIQUE, *ÉCLECTISME and *ÉPICURÉISME, several other articles from the first seven volumes—*CHINOIS (PHILOSOPHIE DES), *CYRÉNAÏQUE (SECTE), *ÉGYPTIENS (PHILOSOPHIE DES), *ÉLÉATIQUE (SECTE) and *ÉTHIOPIENS (PHILOSOPHIE DES), for instance—were denounced by contemporary critics, only *HOBBISME and LOCKE (PHILOSOPHIE DE) from those in the last ten volumes were so dealt with. Diderot had none the less continued to use these articles to summarize many philosophical systems, ancient and modern, which were far from being acceptable to orthodox opinion in eighteenth-century France.

In the course of these articles he continued to work in his own ideas as opportunity offered. To the modern reader who knows his Diderot, and no doubt to the reader of the time who was sympathetic to his ideas and was accustomed to reading between the lines, the outlook of the *philosophe* emerges clearly from them. While what Diderot succeeded in insinuating in many of these articles was primarily his anti-Christian attitude, he also reveals fairly clearly his own philosophical standpoint. For instance, the conclusion of the article SYNCRÉTISTES makes his own attitude plain:

Il s'agit bien de concilier un philosophe avec un autre philosophe; et qu'est-ce que cela nous importe? Ce qu'il faut savoir, c'est qui est-ce qui a tort ou raison?

Il s'agit bien de savoir si un système de philosophie s'accorde avec l'Écriture ou non; et qu'est-ce que cela nous importe? Ce qu'il faut savoir, c'est s'il est conforme à l'expérience ou non.

Quelle est l'autorité que le philosophe doit avoir pour soi? Celle de la nature, de la raison, de l'observation et de l'expérience. [XV.750a]

Again in the opening lines of MOSAÏQUE ET CHRÉTIENNE (PHILO-SOPHIE) we can hear Diderot the *philosophe* speaking:

Le scepticisme et la crédulité sont deux vices également indignes d'un homme qui pense. Parce qu'il y a des choses fausses, toutes ne le sont pas; parce qu'il y a des choses vraies, toutes ne le sont pas. Le philosophe ne nie ni n'admet rien sans examen; il a dans sa raison une juste confiance; il sait par expérience que la recherche de la vérité est pénible, mais il ne la croit point impossible. Il ose descendre au fond de son puits, tandis que l'homme méfiant et pusillanime se tient courbé sur les bords et juge de là, se trompant, soit qu'il prononce qu'il l'aperçoit malgré la distance et l'obscurité, soit qu'il prononce qu'il n'y a personne.

He then goes on to distinguish between the realm of philosophy and that of theology:

De là cette multitude incroyable d'opinions diverses; de là le doute; de là le mépris de la raison et de la philosophie; de là la nécessité prétendue de recourir à la révélation comme au seul flambeau qui puisse nous éclairer dans les sciences naturelles et morales; de là le mélange monstrueux de la théologie et des systèmes, mélange qui a achevé de dégrader la religion et la philosophie; la religion, en l'assujettissant à la discussion, la philosophie en l'assujettissant à la foi. On raisonna quand il fallait croire; on crut quand il fallait raisonner; et l'on vit éclore en un moment une foule de mauvais chrétiens et de mauvais philosophes. La nature est le seul livre du philosophe; les saintes Écritures sont le seul livre du théologien. Ils ont chacun leur argumentation particulière: l'autorité de l'Église, de la tradition, des Pères, de la révélation fixe l'un; l'autre ne reconnaît que l'expérience et l'observation pour guides. Tous les deux usent de leur raison, mais d'une manière particulière et diverse qu'on ne confond point sans inconvénient pour les progrès de l'esprit humain, sans péril pour la foi. [X.741a–b]

Which side Diderot was on must have been perfectly clear to any reader of the time.


## Other philosophical articles

It was not only Diderot, however, who got into trouble for the philosophical articles which he contributed to the first seven volumes; other contributors were also attacked by contemporary critics. Abbé Yvon, for instance, was censured not only for his flagrant plagiarisms, but also for the unorthodox ideas expressed in such articles as ÂME DES BÊTES and CELTES (PHILOSOPHIE DES). Another *abbé* who got into trouble was Morellet whose article FATALITÉ appeared in Vol. VI with the signature '(h)' the anonymity of which was to be removed in the preface to the next volume. Over fifty pages of *La Religion vengée* are devoted to a critical examination of this one article and to a defence of the position that free will is an essential part of the Christian doctrine. Morellet is rebuked for his starting-point:

Ce principe, c'est-à-dire l'existence d'une force qui lie tous les faits et qui enchaîne toutes les causes ne saurait être contesté pour ce qui regarde l'ordre physique où nous voyons chaque phénomène naître des phénomènes antérieurs et en amener d'autres à sa suite. Mais en supposant l'existence d'un ordre moral qui entre dans le système de l'univers, la même loi de continuité d'action doit s'y observer que dans le monde physique; dans l'un et dans l'autre toute cause doit être mise en mouvement pour agir, et toute modification en amener une autre. [VI.423a]

This assimilation of the moral and physical worlds is rejected by *La Religion vengée*:

. . . Nous convenons avec l'encyclopédiste que *tout est lié* dans l'ordre purement physique, parce que tout y est soumis aux lois du mécanisme et aux règles du mouvement, lois et règles établies par celui qui a créé cet ordre physique et qui le gouverne; mais nous disons qu'il n'y a en cela aucune *fatalité* et que c'est abuser de la notion de ce terme que de l'y appliquer.

   On ajoute qu'*en supposant l'existence d'un ordre moral* . . . Mais quoi! N'est-ce donc ici qu'une *supposition*? Si vous rapprochez ce langage de bien d'autres endroits où l'auteur, tantôt plus clairement, tantôt en termes plus obscurs, paraît vouloir réduire l'homme au pur mécanisme, vous n'aurez pas de peine à voir que cette *existrnce d'un ordre moral* n'est de sa part qu'une concession gratuite. (x.358–9)

After subjecting the text of this article to a detailed examination, *La Religion vengée* concludes:

Si l'on pense comme les chrétiens, pourquoi ne pas parler comme eux? Mais il n'est que trop aisé de voir, Monsieur, que cet article de l'*Encyclopédie*, malgré le ton philosophique et l'air d'érudition qui y règne, est l'ouvrage d'un séducteur qui ne prend un langage différent de celui de la religion que pour saper sourdement sa doctrine. (xi.42–3)

This was no doubt rather hard on the worthy Abbé who tells us in his memoirs that in writing for the *Encyclopédie* 'je faisais la théologie chrétienne historiquement et point du tout dogmatiquement ni pour mon compte';[1] yet there is no doubt that this article did set before the reader some pretty unorthodox ideas.

---

[1] *Mémoires sur le dix-huitième siècle et sur la Révolution*, Paris, 1821, 2 vols, i, 39.

It is a curious fact that two of the philosophical articles which aroused most criticism at the time came from men who, though they preferred to remain anonymous, could scarcely be described as *philosophes* in the narrow sense of the term—Quesnay, the founder of the Physiocratic movement, and the future *Contrôleur-général*, Turgot. Both the latter's EXISTENCE and even more Quesnay's ÉVIDENCE were frequently criticized for their unorthodox views; it is puzzling that this should have happened. There was obviously much more substance in the attacks on some of the philosophical articles which d'Alembert contributed to the first seven volumes. Take, for instance, the extraordinarily bold, not to say rash, article AVEUGLE which he contributed to the very first volume; in it he offers a summary of the famous *Lettre sur les Aveugles* for which only two years earlier Diderot had spent three months in prison at Vincennes. This work is described as 'un petit ouvrage très philosophique et très bien écrit . . . dont la métaphysique est partout très fine et très vraie, si on en excepte quelques endroits qui n'ont pas un rapport immédiat au sujet et qui peuvent blesser les oreilles pieuses' [I.870b]. In the course of the article d'Alembert goes so far as to admit that the English biography of Nicholas Saunderson on which Diderot claimed to have drawn for his highly unorthodox account of the last moments of this blind mathematician was a complete invention:

Je dois avertir ici que la prétendue histoire des derniers moments de Saunderson, imprimée en anglais selon l'auteur, est absolument supposée. Cette supposition que bien des érudits regardent comme un crime de lèse-érudition, ne serait qu'une plaisanterie si l'objet n'en était aussi sérieux. [I.872a]

The *Réflexions d'un Franciscain sur les trois premiers volumes de l'Encyclopédie* drew attention to this praise of the *Lettre sur les Aveugles* and to this confession; the reader was reminded of the materialist sentiments put into the mouth of the dying Saunderson and in particular of the words: 'Si vous voulez que je croie en Dieu, il faut que vous me le fassiez toucher.' 'Et ce blasphème', the author continues, 'ne peut être attribué qu'à l'auteur de la *Lettre*, puisque l'encyclopédiste nous avertit que "la prétendue histoire des derniers moments de Saunderson est absolument supposée".'[1]

---

[1] *Réflexions d'un Franciscain*, Berlin, 1754, p. 34.

Two of the articles which d'Alembert contributed to Vol. IV, CORRUPTION and DÉMONSTRATION (*Philos.*), also got him into trouble. They are linked by both Chaumeix and *La Religion vengée* with Formey's article, DIEU, which contains cross-references to them. After setting out the ontological proofs of the existence of God, Formey sends the reader to DÉMONSTRATION where d'Alembert shows himself decidedly sceptical as to their value:

Les philosophes et même les théologiens sont partagés sur les *démonstrations a priori*, et quelques-uns même les rejettent. Toutes ces *démonstrations*, disent-ils, supposent l'idée de l'infini qui n'est pas fort claire. Quoi qu'il en soit, peu importe que l'on soit partagé sur quelques preuves de cette vérité, pourvu qu'on l'admette. Au fond les preuves sensibles sont les meilleures. Aux yeux du peuple, et même du philosophe, un insecte prouve plus un Dieu que tous les raisonnements métaphysiques; et aux yeux du même philosophe les lois générales de la nature prouvent encore mieux l'existence de Dieu qu'un insecte, lois simples qui dérivent de la forme même imprimée par l'Etre suprême à la matière, qui ne changent jamais, et en vertu desquelles l'univers est assujetti à un mécanisme uniforme et réglé, résultant du premier mouvement que lui a donné l'intelligence souveraine. [IV.823b]

Chaumeix draws the following consequences from d'Alembert's article: 'Voilà donc d'abord les preuves métaphysiques de l'existence de Dieu renversées, et tout ce qu'on a dit dans l'article *Dieu* d'après ces preuves, regardé comme nul' (*PL* i.59). *La Religion vengée* (x.306–20) takes him up at great length on the same point.

Like Chaumeix, this periodical also follows up Formey's cross-reference to CORRUPTION which precedes his statement that 'ce sont les animaux qui portent, pour ainsi dire, l'inscription la plus nette, et qui nous apprennent le mieux qu'il y a un *Dieu*, auteur de l'univers' [IV.983a]. In his article d'Alembert sets forth quite impartially the arguments on the hotly debated question of spontaneous generation. After stating the case against, he quotes Buffon for the opposite view:

M. de Buffon, dans son *Histoire naturelle*, p. 320, II$^e$ vol., paraît incliner à cette opinion. Après avoir exposé son système des molécules organiques, dont il sera parlé à l'article GÉNÉRATION, il en conclut qu'il y a peut-être autant d'êtres, soit vivants, soit végétants, qui se produisent par l'assemblage fortuit des molécules organiques, qu'il y en a qui se produisent par la voie ordinaire de la génération. [IV.278b]

D'Alembert refuses to take up a dogmatic position on this question:

On ne peut nier que, généralement parlant, les particules qui composent un insecte, ne puissent être rassemblées par une autre voie que par celle de la génération. Du moins nous connaissons trop peu les voies et le méca-nisme de la nature pour avancer là-dessus une assertion trop exclusive. Il est certain, par l'expérience, que dans la plupart des cas où les insectes paraissent engendrés par *corruption*, ils le sont par génération ; mais est-il démontré dans tous les cas que la *corruption* ne puisse jamais engendrer de corps animé ? [IV.278b]

*La Religion vengée* sees in all this the sinister hand of Diderot and the system of cross-references which he had so rashly boasted of in the article \*ENCYCLOPÉDIE:

Mais avec cet *assemblage fortuit* que devient cette *inscription* si *nette* que portent les animaux pour annoncer *un Dieu auteur de l'univers* ? Le dessein de notre compilateur ne peut échapper ici qu'à quiconque voudra se prêter à l'illusion. L'article *Dieu* n'était probablement dans ses idées qu'un *édifice de fange* qu'il s'est proposé sans doute de renverser ailleurs. (x.337–8)

The same point is also made by Chaumeix (*PL* i.61–2).

It was, however, in Vol. VII that d'Alembert produced the largest number of articles which gave offence in orthodox circles. In addition to the notorious GENÈVE there were also the philo-sophical articles FORME SUBSTANTIELLE, FORTUIT (*Métaphys.*) and FUTUR CONTINGENT. There was besides in GÉOMÈTRE a reference to Bayle which attracted much unfavourable comment—'Bayle qui doutait et se moquait de tout' [VII.629a]. FORME SUBSTANTIELLE was hotly attacked by Chaumeix who alleged that in writing it d'Alembert had two aims in view: '1°. De renverser la preuve du péché originel que Saint-Augustin tire des souffrances de l'homme. 2°. De nous faire entendre que l'Église a cru longtemps la maté-rialité de l'âme et de tourner en ridicule le canon d'un concile' (*PL* ii.245). The article in question is concerned with the problem of whether or not animals possess souls, and it must be confessed that the way d'Alembert handles the whole matter bears out the first of Chaumeix's accusations. After expounding the complexities of the problem and pouring ridicule on the expression *forme substantielle*, invented by Scholastic philosophers in a vain effort to dispose of them, d'Alembert goes on:

Les philosophes modernes, plus raisonnables, conviennent de la spiritualité de l'âme des bêtes et se bornent à dire qu'elle n'est pas immortelle, parce que Dieu l'a voulu ainsi.

Mais l'expérience nous prouve que les bêtes souffrent, que leur condition sur ce point est à peu près pareille à la nôtre, et souvent pire. Or pourquoi Dieu, cet être si bon et si juste, a-t-il condamné à tant de peines des êtres qui ne l'ont point offensé et qu'il ne peut même dédommager de ces peines dans une vie future? Croire que les bêtes sentent et par conséquent qu'elles souffrent, n'est-ce pas enlever à la religion le grand argument que saint Augustin tire des souffrances de l'homme pour prouver le péché originel? *Sous un Dieu juste*, dit ce père, *toute créature qui souffre doit avoir péché.* [VII.177a]

The second accusation concerns the last paragraph of d'Alembert's article:

Au reste, la définition que nous avons donnée du mot *forme substantielle*, ne doit pas s'appliquer à l'usage qui est fait de ce même mot dans le premier canon du concile général de Vienne qui décide contre le cordelier Pierre Jean d'Olive que *quiconque osera soutenir que l'âme raisonnable n'est pas essentiellement la forme substantielle du corps humain, doit être tenu pour hérétique.* Ce décret, qu'on aurait peut-être dû énoncer plus clairement, ne prouve pas, comme quelques incrédules l'ont prétendu, que du temps du concile de Vienne on admettait la matérialité de l'âme, ou du moins qu'on n'avait pas d'idée distincte de sa spiritualité; car l'Église ne peut ni se tromper, ni par conséquent varier sur cette matière importante. [VII.177b]

This is an excellent example of d'Alembert's lofty irony; it infuriated his opponents all the more because he manages to insinuate his unorthodox views while keeping up the appearance of complete orthodoxy.

FORTUIT (*Métaphys.*) received detailed attention from *La Religion vengée*. It brings out the contradictions in the article which argues first for determinism and then for free will. First, the case for determinism:

Soit que les lois du mouvement instituées par le Créateur aient leur source dans la nature même de la matière, soit que l'Etre suprême les ait librement établies (*voyez* ÉQUILIBRE), il est constant que notre corps est assujetti à ces lois, qu'il en résulte dans notre machine depuis le premier instant de son existence une suite de mouvements dépendant les uns des autres, dont nous ne sommes nullement les maîtres et auxquels notre âme obéit par les lois de son union avec le corps. [VII.204b–205a]

After stating the case for free will, d'Alembert, in his usual sceptical fashion, proceeds to show the problem created by the necessity of reconciling man's free will with the divine prescience:

A l'égard de la manière dont notre liberté subsiste avec la providence éternelle, avec la justice par laquelle Dieu punit le crime, avec les lois immuables auxquelles tous les êtres sont soumis, c'est un secret incompréhensible pour nous dont il n'a pas plu au Créateur de nous révélet la connaissance; mais ce qui n'est peut-être pas moins incompréhensible, c'est la témérité avec laquelle certains hommes qui se croient ou qui se disent sages, ont entrepris d'expliquer et de concilier de tels mystères. [VII.205a–b]

This mingling of contradictory arguments drew from *La Religion vengée* the comment: 'Qu'est-ce que tout cela, Monsieur, sinon le procédé d'un ennemi qui sent bien que ses assertions sont contradictoires, mais qui se propose un objet fixe et qui avance ou recule selon qu'il le croit à propos pour faire tomber son adversaire dans le piège?' (xi.46). Despite the cautious conclusion which d'Alembert gives to the article (it even earns the approval of *La Religion vengée*) there is no doubt that his aim was to cast doubt on orthodox attitudes.

FUTUR CONTINGENT which also attracted the attention of *La Religion vengée* deals with the same problems from the same sceptical standpoint:

L'existence des *futurs contingents* libres, c'est-à-dire qui dépendent de la volonté humaine, n'est pas moins infaillible que celle des *futurs* non libres. Par exemple, si en vertu du décret éternel de Dieu je dois aller demain à la campagne, il est aussi infaillible que je ferai ce voyage qu'il l'est qu'il pleuvra demain si Dieu l'a résolu ainsi. C'est pourquoi la distinction qu'on a voulu faire dans les écoles des *futurs contingents* libres et de ceux qui ne le sont pas, est en elle-même chimérique, puisque tous les *futurs contingents* sont dans le même cas quant à l'infaillibilité de l'existence. On nous demandera sans doute de faire sentir clairement en quoi l'existence infaillible diffère de l'existence nécessaire; c'est à quoi nous ne nous engageons pas. Il nous suffit que cette différence soit réelle; tant pis même pour qui l'expliquerait, puisqu'elle tient à un des mystères de notre religion, l'accord de la science et de la puissance divine avec la liberté.

Dans le langage commun *infaillible* et *nécessaire* sont la même chose; il n'en est pas ainsi en métaphysique théologique. L'essence de tout mystère consiste dans une chose exprimée par des mots dont la contradiction apparente choque la raison, mais que la foi nous apprend n'être pas contradictoires. [VII.405a].

For *La Religion vengée* d'Alembert's purpose is quite clear:

On voit bien où il tend à travers ce galimatias. C'est une poussière excitée pour nous porter des coups plus sûrs, sans craindre aucun retour fâcheux. On retrouve ici le même esprit qui a fabriquée l'article *Fortuit*. L'auteur en veut à la liberté; le fait est évident. Dès qu'il assure que la différence que nous mettons entre les futurs contingents libres et ceux qui ne le sont pas, *est en elle-même chimérique*, c'est donc, selon lui, une même nécessité qui assujettit tout, et l'homme n'est pas plus libre qu'un moulin ou qu'une pendule. (xi.60)

Whether one would be entitled to draw this conclusion from an article by so sceptical a writer as d'Alembert is by no means certain; but the unorthodoxy of the views contained in it is clear.

If the philosophical articles of the last ten volumes did not encounter the same number of attacks as those in the first seven, that is not to say that there were none which could have given offence to the enemies of the *philosophes*. In the unsigned article LIBERTÉ MORALE which was probably by Abbé Yvon, the opening paragraphs, added by Diderot's young disciple, Naigeon, preach the doctrine of necessity:

. . . Supposons une femme qui soit entraînée par sa passion à se jeter tout à l'heure entre les bras de son amant; si nous imaginons cent mille femmes entièrement semblables à la première, d'âge, de tempérament, d'éducation, d'organisation, d'idées, telles, en un mot, qu'il n'y ait aucune différence assignable entre elles et la première. On les voit toutes également soumises à la passion dominante et précipitées entre les bras de leurs amants, sans qu'on puisse concevoir aucune raison pour laquelle l'une ne ferait pas ce que toutes les autres feront.[1] Nous ne faisons rien qu'on puisse appeler bien ou mal sans motif. Or il n'y a aucun motif qui dépend de nous, soit eu égard à sa production, soit eu égard à son énergie. . . . Ce que nous sommes dans l'instant qui va suivre dépend donc absolument de ce que nous sommes dans l'instant présent; ce que nous sommes dans l'instant présent dépend donc de ce que nous étions dans l'instant pré-

---

[1] See MACHINAL (pp. 182–3).

cédent; et ainsi de suite, en remontant jusqu'au premier instant de notre existence, s'il y en a un. Notre vie n'est donc qu'un enchaînement d'instants d'existence et d'actions nécessaires; notre volonté, un acquiescement à être ce que nous sommes nécessairement dans chacun de ces instants; et notre liberté une chimère. [IX.463a]

All this is, of course, prudently attributed to 'Spinoza et ses sectateurs', but the meaning of the passages and the consequences for our moral ideas, which are dealt with in the rest of the paragraph, are obvious.

Even more striking is Naigeon's signed article, UNITAIRES (*Théol. & Métaph.*). This was one of the articles on which Voltaire commented when he at last received his copy of the last ten volumes. In a letter to Damilaville he wrote ironically: 'L'article *Unitaire* est terrible. J'ai bien peur qu'on ne rende pas justice à l'auteur de cet article, et qu'on ne lui impute d'être trop favorable aux sociniens. Ce serait assurément une extrême injustice: et c'est pour cela que je le crains.'[1] We shall meet this article again in the next chapter;[2] but, as the heading of the article indicates, Naigeon is not content to expound his version of the religious beliefs of Unitarians; he also uses the article as a vehicle for his own philosophical views. Throughout the article his tactic is to keep on repeating that such dreadful religious and philosophical beliefs are the inevitable outcome of a refusal to recognize an infallible judge of one's faith; he then proceeds to set forth views which are the last word in unorthodoxy. The Unitarians, he maintains, reject the conventional proofs of the existence of God. They hold, he declares,

Que mieux on connaît toute la force des objections métaphysiques et physiques, toutes plus insolubles les unes que les autres, que l'homme abandonné à ses propres réflexions peut faire contre l'existence de Dieu considéré en tant que distinct du monde et contre la providence, plus on est convaincu qu'il est absolument impossible que les lumières naturelles de la raison puissent jamais conduire aucun homme à une ferme et entière persuasion de ces deux dogmes. *Voyez* DIEU.

Qu'il semble au contraire qu'elles le conduiraient plutôt à n'admettre d'autre Dieu que la nature universelle, etc.

Qu'il n'est pas moins impossible à quiconque veut raisonner profondément, de s'élever à la connaissance de l'Etre suprême par la contemplation de ses ouvrages.

[1] Best. 12332 (12 March 1766).        [2] See below, pp. 223–8.

Que le spectacle de la nature ne prouve rien, puisqu'il n'est, à parler avec précision, ni beau ni laid.

Qu'il n'y a point dans l'univers un ordre, une harmonie, ni un désordre et une dissonance absolus, mais seulement relatifs, et déterminés par la nature de notre existence pure et simple.

Que s'appliquer à la recherche des causes finales des choses naturelles, c'est le fait d'un homme qui établit sa faible intelligence pour la véritable mesure du beau et du bon, de la perfection et de l'imperfection. *Voyez* CAUSES FINALES.

Que les physiciens qui ont voulu démontrer l'existence et les attributs de Dieu par les œuvres de la création, n'ont jamais fait faire un pas à la science et n'ont fait au fond que préconiser, sans s'en apercevoir, leur propre sagesse et leurs petites vues.

Que ceux qui ont reculé les bornes de l'esprit humain et perfectionné la philosophie rationnelle, sont ceux qui, appliquant sans cesse le raisonnement à l'expérience, n'ont point fait servir à l'explication de quelques phénomènes l'existence d'un être dont ils n'auraient su que faire un moment après.

Qu'une des plus hautes et des plus profondes idées qui soient jamais entrées dans l'esprit humain, c'est celle de Descartes qui ne demandait, pour faire un monde comme le nôtre, que de la matière et du mouvement. *Voyez* CARTÉSIANISME. [XVII.396b]

The same Unitarians are cheerfully credited with a belief in materialism. They hold, Naigeon goes on,

Que la matière est éternelle et nécessaire et renferme nécessairement une infinité d'attributs, tant connus qu'inconnus. *Voyez* MATIÈRE *et* SPINOZISME.

Que l'homogénéité de ses molécules est une supposition absurde et insoutenable par laquelle le système de l'univers devient une énigme inexplicable; ce qui n'arrive pas si, en suivant l'expérience, on considère la matière comme un agrégat d'éléments hétérogènes et par conséquent doués de propriétés différentes.

Que c'est une assertion téméraire de dire avec quelques métaphysiciens que la matière n'a ni ne peut avoir certaines propriétés, comme si on ne lui en découvrait pas tous les jours de nouvelles qu'on ne lui aurait jamais soupçonnées. *Voyez* ÂME, PENSÉE, SENSATION, SENSIBILITÉ etc. [XVII.397a]

The Unitarians, according to Naigeon, also believe in determinism; they hold, he tells us,

Que la liberté considérée comme le pouvoir de faire ou de ne faire pas est une chimère.

Qu'à la vérité on peut ce qu'on veut, mais qu'on est déterminé invinciblement à vouloir. *Voyez* VOLONTÉ.

En un mot, qu'il n'y a point d'actions libres, proprement dites, mais seulement spontanées. *Voyez* LIBERTÉ.

Si on leur objecte que nous sommes libres d'une liberté d'indifférence et que le christianisme enseigne que nous avons cette liberté, ils répondent par ce raisonnement emprunté des Stoïciens: 'La liberté, disent ces philosophes, n'existe pas. Faute de connaître les motifs, de rassembler les circonstances qui nous déterminent à agir d'une certaine manière, nous nous croyons libres. Peut-on penser que l'homme ait véritablement le pouvoir de se déterminer? Ne sont-ce pas plutôt les objets extérieurs, combinés de mille façons différentes, qui le poussent et le déterminent? Sa volonté est-elle une faculté vague et indépendante qui agisse sans choix et par caprice? Elle agit, soit en conséquence d'un jugement, d'un acte de l'entendement, qui lui représente que telle chose est plus avanta-geuse à ses intérêts que toute autre, soit qu'indépendamment de cet acte les circonstances où un homme se trouve, l'inclinent, le forcent, à se tourner d'un certain côté; et il se flatte alors qu'il s'y est tourné librement, quoiqu'il n'ait pu vouloir se tourner d'un autre', etc. [XVII.398a]

In other words man knows that his existence

est le résultat déterminé et infaillible d'un mécanisme secret et universel.

Qu'à l'égard de la liberté et des événements heureux ou malheureux qu'on éprouve pendant la vie, il voit que, tout étant lié dans la nature, il n'y a rien de contingent dans les déterminations de nos volontés; mais que toutes les actions des êtres sensibles, ainsi que tout ce qui arrive dans les deux ordres, a son principe dans un enchaînement immuable et une coordination fatale de causes et d'effets nécessaires. [XVII.398b]

Naigeon has the grace to admit that such ideas cannot be attributed to Socinians as a whole, because, as he insolently puts it, they have varied in their beliefs like all other Christian sects:

Ce n'est donc pas là le système philosophique reçu et adopté unanime-ment par ces hérétiques, mais seulement l'opinion particulière de plusieurs savants *unitaires* anciens et modernes. [XVII.398b]

Why the words '*Article de* M. NAIGEON' should have been placed at the end of this extremely daring contribution when so many of the bolder articles in the last ten volumes remain unsigned, is a mystery.

## Diderot and the fabulous

From the first volume to the very last it was the editor-in-chief of the whole enterprise who furnished most of the articles which, long or short, seek to insinuate a highly orthodox outlook on the world. One of the articles in the first volume to attract the attention of the critics was *AGNUS SCYTHICUS which was summarized by the *Réflexions d'un Franciscain* as 'les règles de certitude données dans un article de botanique' (p. 77). Basing himself on material drawn from Robert James's *Medicinal Dictionary* in the translation of which he had played his part, Diderot takes the example of a mysterious plant which, among other strange properties, was alleged to have exactly the appearance of a lamb, in order to lay down rules for ascertaining the truth in such matters. The existence of this plant is, he points out, attested by a host of authorities, including, of all people, Bacon:

Voilà l'histoire de l'*agnus scythicus* ou de la plante merveilleuse de Scaliger, de Kircher, de Sigismond d'Herberstein, d'Hayton Arménien, de Surius, du chancelier Bacon (*du chancelier Bacon*, notez bien ce témoignage), de Fortunius Licetus, d'André Libavius, d'Eusèbe de Nuremberg, d'Adam Olearius, d'Olaus Vormius et d'une infinité d'autres botanistes.

Serait-il bien possible qu'après tant d'autorités qui attestent l'existence de l'agneau de Scythie, à qui il ne restait plus qu'à savoir comment les pieds se formaient, l'agneau de Scythie fût une fable? Que croire en histoire naturelle, si cela est? [I.179b]

In practice the said plant, when properly described, turns out to have nothing very special about it; from this Diderot proceeds to draw conclusions which, as he bluntly puts it, will be useful 'contre la superstition et le préjugé' [I.180a]. These take us a long way from the fabulous plant which is the starting point of the article and into very dangerous regions:

Il faut distinguer les faits en deux classes: en faits simples et ordinaires, et en faits extraordinaires et prodigieux. Les témoignages de quelques personnes instruites et véridiques suffisent pour les faits simples; les autres demandent, pour l'homme qui pense, des autorités plus fortes.

Then comes a mathematical expression of which Diderot was extremely fond:

Il faut en général que les autorités soient en raison inverse de la vraisemblance des faits, c'est-à-dire d'autant plus nombreuses et plus grands que la vraisemblance est moindre.

He goes on to lay down further rules:

Il faut subdiviser les faits, tant simples qu'extraordinaires, en transitoires et permanents. Les transitoires, ce sont ceux qui n'ont existé que l'instant de leur durée; les permanents, ce sont ceux qui existent toujours et dont on peut s'assurer en tout temps. On voit que ces derniers sont moins difficiles à croire que les premiers, et que la facilité que chacun a de s'assurer de la vérité ou de la fausseté des témoignages, doit rendre les témoins circonspects et disposer les autres hommes à les croire.

Il faut distribuer les faits transitoires en faits qui se sont passés dans un siècle éclairé, et en faits qui se sont passés dans des temps de ténèbres et d'ignorance; et les faits permanents, en faits permanents dans un lieu accessible ou dans un lieu inaccessible.

Il faut considérer les témoignages en eux-mêmes, puis les comparer entre eux: les considérer en eux-mêmes pour voir s'ils n'impliquent aucune contradiction et s'ils sont de gens éclairés et instruits; les comparer entre eux pour découvrir s'ils ne sont point calqués les uns sur les autres, et si toute cette foule d'autorités, de Kircher, de Scaliger, de Bacon, de Libavius, de Licetus, d'Eusèbe, etc. ne se réduirat pas par hasard à rien ou à l'autorité d'un seul homme.

Il faut considérer si les témoins sont oculaires ou non; ce qu'ils ont risqué pour se faire croire; quelle crainte ou quelles espérances ils avaient en annonçant aux autres des faits dont ils se disaient témoins oculaires. S'ils avaient exposé leur vie pour soutenir leur déposition, il faut avouer qu'elle acquerrait une grande force; que serait-ce donc s'ils l'avaient sacrifiée et perdue?

Il ne faut pas non plus confondre les faits qui se sont passés à la face de tout un peuple, avec ceux qui n'ont eu pour spectateurs qu'un petit nombre de personnes. Les faits clandestins, pour peu qu'ils soient merveilleux, ne méritent presque pas d'être crus. Les faits publics, contre lesquels on n'a point réclamé dans le temps ou contre lesquels il n'y a eu de réclamation que de la part de gens peu nombreux et mal intentionnés ou mal instruits, ne peuvent presque pas être contredits.

Voilà une partie des principes d'après lesquels on accordera ou l'on refusera sa croyance, si on ne veut pas donner dans des rêveries et si l'on aime sincèrement la vérité. [I.180a–b]

One of the two cross-references which Diderot gives at the end of this article is to CERTITUDE by Abbé de Prades. This was to appear in the second volume, escorted by an editorial introduction and conclusion from Diderot's pen. Here the question of certainty is pursued into the field of religion and we shall meet it in the next chapter.[1]

The opening volumes of the *Encyclopédie* contain quite a number of short articles by Diderot on a variety of plants which were either fabulous or alleged to possess fabulous properties. In Vol. I we find, for instance:

*ASSAZOÉ, subst. f. (*Hist. nat. bot.*) plante de l'Abyssinie, qui passe pour un préservatif contre les serpents; son ombre seule les engourdit; ils tombent morts s'ils en sont touchés . . .

From this Diderot proceeds to draw certain lessons:

Une observation que nous ferons sur l'*assazoé* et sur beaucoup d'autres substances naturelles, auxquelles on attribue des propriétés merveilleuses, c'est que plus ces propriétés sont merveilleuses et en grand nombre, plus les descriptions qu'on fait des substances sont mauvaises; ce qui doit donner de grands soupçons contre l'existence réelle des substances ou celle des propriétés qu'on leur attribue. [I.766b]

In Vol. V we find another short article of the same type:

*ÉGAGROPILES, s.f.pl. (*Mat. méd.*) Elles n'ont aucune propriété médicinale. Cependant combien ne leur en a-t-on pas attribué? Avant qu'on en connût la nature, elles étaient bonnes pour le flux de sang, pour les hémorragies; elles avaient les vertus de toutes les plantes dont on les croyait composées; elles guérissaient du vertige et des étourdissements. Quand la nature en a été connue, elles n'ont plus été bonnes à rien.

Once again Diderot draws the moral:

Il est donc de la dernière importance de ne rien assurer sur la formation et les éléments des choses qu'après un grand nombre d'expériences. Quand on a obtenu de l'expérience tout ce qu'on pouvait en attendre sur la nature des choses, il en faut faire de nouvelles sur leurs propriétés, si l'on ne veut pas prendre les substances pour ce qu'elles ne sont pas, ordonner des masses de poil et d'herbes pour des spécifiques et tomber dans le ridicule de Velschius qui a composé un livre des propriétés de l'*égagropile*. [V.413b]

The moral of all these articles is summed up in the conclusion of *BESANÇON which is mainly concerned with a cave in that part of

France which was alleged quite erroneously to have the most remarkable properties. It is simply: 'Apprendre à douter' [II.213a].

## Diderot's materialism

From the beginning of the enterprise Diderot worked in passages which revealed his inclination towards materialism. In the very first volume we find a long editorial addition to Abbé Yvon's ÂME which aroused unfavourable comment in works hostile to the *Encyclopédie*. Diderot's scepticism about the nature of the soul comes out in the lines:

Non seulement nous ne connaissons pas notre âme, ni la manière dont elle agit sur les organes matériels; mais dans ces organes mêmes nous ne pouvons apercevoir aucune disposition qui détermine l'un plutôt que l'autre à être le siège de l'*âme*. [I.341a]

After discussing various theories about which part of the body the soul is situated in, Diderot goes on to quote a number of examples of the way in which it is influenced by various conditions of the body. He introduces his remarks with the following passage:

Après avoir employé tant d'espace à établir la spiritualité et l'immortalité de l'*âme*, deux sentiments très capables d'enorgueillir l'homme sur sa condition à venir, qu'il nous soit permis d'employer quelques lignes à l'humilier sur sa condition présente par la contemplation des choses futiles d'où dépendent les qualités dont il fait plus de cas. [I.342b]

*La Religion vengée* saw through the humbug and the hypocritical prudence of these introductory lines:

S'il était vrai, Monsieur, que l'homme, par cela seul qu'il serait persuadé de la spiritualité et de l'immortalité de son âme, pût se permettre un avenir heureux, sans doute que cette persuasion serait *très capable de l'enorgueillir*. Mais comment pourrait-il en concevoir de l'orgueil dès qu'il sait en même temps que cet heureux avenir ne peut être que le prix d'une humilité profonde? Et pourquoi les matérialistes qui s'arrogent le titre de sages et de philosophes à l'exclusion du reste des hommes, sont-ils de si orgueilleux personnages, eux qui n'ont aucun sentiment de leur *condition à venir*? (xii.163)

This was certainly a shrewd thrust.

One of the most frequently attacked articles in the first seven volumes was *ANIMAL, a curious combination of extracts from the second volume of Buffon's *Histoire naturelle* with Diderot's own comments. With this article one must associate both Diderot's addition to Yvon's ÂME and the apparently harmless synonym article, *BÊTE, ANIMAL, BRUTE, which Diderot himself rounded off with the cross-reference '*Voyez les articles* ÂME *et* ANIMAL'. Chaumeix points out a curious contradiction between *ANIMAL and *BÊTE, ANIMAL, BRUTE. In the former Buffon's views on the vexed question of the intelligence of animals are reproduced:

Quand même on voudrait leur accorder quelque chose de semblable à nos premières appréhensions et à nos sensations grossières et les plus machinales, il paraît certain qu'ils sont incapables de former cette association d'idées qui seule peut produire la réflexion, dans laquelle cependant consiste l'essence de la pensée. C'est parce qu'ils ne peuvent joindre ensemble aucune idée qu'ils ne pensent ni ne parlent . . . [I.469b]

Yet in the second article Diderot casts doubt on the validity of this attitude:

On ne sait si les bêtes sont gouvernées par les lois générales du mouvement ou par une motion particulière; l'un et l'autre sentiment a ses difficultés. *V. l'article* ÂME DES BÊTES. Si elles agissent par une motion particulière, si elles pensent, si elles ont une âme, etc., qu'est-ce que cette âme? On ne peut la supposer matérielle: la supposera-t-on spirituelle? Assurer qu'elles n'ont point d'âme et qu'elles ne pensent point, c'est les réduire à la qualité de machines, à quoi l'on ne semble guère plus autorisé qu'à prétendre qu'un homme dont on n'entend pas la langue est un automate. L'argument qu'on tire de la perfection qu'elles mettent dans leurs ouvrages est fort; car il semblerait, à juger de leurs premiers pas, qu'elles devraient aller fort loin; cependant toutes s'arrêtent au même point, ce qui est presque le caractère machinal. Mais celui qu'on tire de l'uniformité de leurs productions ne me paraît pas tout à fait aussi bien fondé. Les nids des hirondelles et les habitations des castors ne se ressemblent pas plus que les maisons des hommes. Si une hirondelle place son nid dans un angle, il n'aura de circonférence que l'arc compris entre les côtés de l'angle; si elle l'applique au contraire contre un mur, il aura pour mesure la demi-circonférence. Si vous délogez les castors de l'endroit où ils sont et qu'ils aillent s'établir ailleurs, comme il n'est pas possible qu'ils rencontrent le même terrain, il y aura nécessairement variété dans les moyens dont ils useront et variété dans les habitations qu'ils se construiront. [II.214b]

As Chaumeix pointed out,[1] there was here a significant contra-diction between one article and the other.

Buffon as well as Diderot comes in for criticism from Chaumeix. For instance, he is accused of confusing man with animals[2] in a passage from the section establishing the difference between animal and vegetable which is quoted by Diderot:

L'*animal* réunit toutes les puissances de la nature; les sources qui l'animent lui sont propres et particulières; il veut, il agit, il se détermine, il opère, il communique par ses sens avec les objets les plus éloignés; son individu est un centre où tout se rapporte; un point où l'univers entier se réfléchit; un monde en raccourci. [I.471a]

Chaumeix also took exception to another passage from Buffon:

Quoique nous ne distinguions pas bien nettement les qualités que nous avons en vertu de notre animalité seule de celles que nous avons en vertu de la spiritualité de notre âme ou plutôt de la supériorité de notre entende-ment sur celui des bêtes, nous ne pouvons guère douter que les animaux . . . n'aient avec les objets extérieurs des rapports du même ordre que les nôtres et que par conséquent nous ne leur ressemblions à bien des égards. [I.471a]

On this Chaumeix comments:

Le lecteur s'aperçoit aisément que quand dans ce passage on parle de la *spiritualité* de notre âme, ce n'est que pour se conformer à l'usage ordi-naire. Mais afin qu'on ne le prenne pas trop à la lettre, on reprend, *ou plutôt la supériorité de notre entendement sur celui des bêtes.* (PL i.207)

However, Chaumeix had his eye mainly on the italicized passages in which Diderot in his comments on the text of the *Histoire naturelle* carried on a kind of dialogue with Buffon.

Thus, after quoting a passage in which Buffon declares that to attribute to inanimate matter feeling, sensation and consciousness of its existence, would be to endow it with the same faculties of thought and feeling as we possess, which would be contrary to both reason and religion, Chaumeix points to Diderot's comment:

Mais une considération qui s'accorde avec l'une et l'autre et qui nous est suggérée par le spectacle de la nature dans les individus, c'est que l'état de

----

[1] *PL*, i, 129.       [2] *PL*, i, 205.

cette faculté de penser, d'agir, de sentir réside dans quelques hommes dans un degré éminent, dans un degré moins éminent en d'autres hommes, va en s'affaiblissant à mesure qu'on suit la chaîne des êtres en descendant et s'éteint dans quelque point de la chaîne très éloigné, placé entre le règne animal et le règne végétal. [I.470b]

'Voilà une considération', Chaumeix exclaims ironically, 'qui, suivant M. Diderot, s'accorde avec la raison et avec la religion. Il n'est pas difficile de s'apercevoir qu'il contredit formellement M. de Buffon et qu'en raisonnant par analogie il prétend qu'il faut décider tout autrement' (*PL* i.213).

In his debate with Buffon Diderot quotes the following passage from the *Histoire naturelle*:

C'est donc l'organisation, la vie, l'âme, qui fait proprement notre existence. La matière, considérée sous ce point de vue, en est moins le sujet que l'accessoire; c'est une enveloppe étrangère dont l'union nous est inconnue et la présence nuisible; et cet ordre de pensées qui constitue notre être en est peut-être tout à fait indépendant.

Diderot's retort needs to be read carefully if one is to see its true implications:

Il me semble que l'historien de la nature accorde ici aux métaphysiciens bien plus qu'ils n'oseraient lui demander. Quelle que soit la manière dont nous penserons quand notre âme sera débarrassée de son enveloppe et sortira de l'état de chrysalide, il est constant que cette coque méprisable dans laquelle elle reste détenue pour un temps, influe prodigieusement sur l'ordre de pensées qui constitue son être; et, malgré les suites quelquefois très fâcheuses de cette influence, elle n'en montre pas moins évidemment la sagesse de la providence qui se sert de cet aiguillon pour nous rappeler sans cesse à la conservation de nous-mêmes et de notre espèce. [I.470b]

Chaumeix's comment on the first sentence of this passage is a shrewd one: 'Pourquoi cela? C'est apparemment parce qu'il semble leur accorder que nous pourrions penser sans corps et qu'ainsi le corps ne sert que d'enveloppe à l'âme.' He goes on: 'D'ailleurs quoi dire à ceux qui pensent avec les chrétiens de tous les temps et de tous les lieux que l'âme pensera après qu'elle sera séparée du corps? Comment y répondre, pour un encyclopédiste? En s'en moquant de cette manière.' As for the rest of what Diderot has to say here, it provokes the angry comment: 'On aperçoit tout d'un coup le cas que les encyclopédistes font de cette doctrine. Ils ne croient pas qu'elle mérite d'autre réponse qu'une raillerie' (*PL* i.219–20). Once again he seems to bring out correctly the true meaning of Diderot's remarks.

Buffon himself again gets into trouble for a passage which attracted a good deal of attention from the enemies of the *Encyclopédie*:

Plus on fera d'observations, plus on se convaincra qu'entre les animaux et les végétaux le créateur n'a pas mis de terme fixe; que ces deux genres d'êtres organisés ont beaucoup plus de propriétés communes que de différences réelles; que la production de l'*animal* ne coûte pas plus et peut-être moins à la nature que celle du végétal; qu'en général la production des êtres organisés ne lui coûte rien; et qu'enfin le vivant et l'animé, au lieu d'être un degré métaphysique des êtres, est une propriété physique de la matière. [I.474a]

This passage is used by Chaumeix to introduce a section of his *Préjugés légitimes* entitled 'La faculté de penser est, selon les encyclopédistes, une propriété de la matière' (i.224–6). 'Voilà', he declares, 'ce dont Locke avait fait . . . un problème qu'il n'avait pas tout à fait osé résoudre. . . . Les encyclopédistes, plus hardis, ont résolu ce problème' (i.225). Next it is Diderot who gets into trouble for what is one of the most striking of his comments on Buffon in \*ANIMAL. This time he is dealing with Buffon's statement that the differences between animals and plants cannot lie in the different manner in which they feed themselves:

Cela peut être d'autant plus que cet air de spontanéité qui nous frappe dans les animaux qui se meuvent soit quand ils cherchent leur proie ou dans d'autres occasions, et que nous ne voyons point dans les végétaux, est peut-être un préjugé, une illusion de nos sens trompés par la variété des mouvements animaux, mouvements qui seraient cent fois encore plus variés qu'ils n'en seraient pas pour cela plus libres. Mais pourquoi, me demandera-t-on, ces mouvements sont-ils si variés dans les animaux et si uniformes dans les végétaux? C'est, ce me semble, parce que les végétaux ne sont mus que par la résistance ou le choc, au lieu que les animaux, ayant des yeux, des oreilles et tous les organes de la sensation comme nous, et ces organes pouvant être affectés ensemble ou séparément, toute cette combinaison de résistance ou de choc, quand il n'y aurait que cela et que l'animal serait purement passif, doit l'agiter d'une infinité de diverses manières; en sorte que nous ne pouvons plus remarquer d'uniformité dans son action. De là il arrive que nous disons que la pierre tombe nécessairement et que le chien appelé vient librement; que nous ne nous plaignons point d'une tuile qui nous casse un bras et que nous nous emportons contre un chien qui nous mord la jambe, quoique toute la différence qu'il y ait peut-être entre la tuile et le chien, c'est que toutes les tuiles tombent de même et qu'un chien ne se meut pas deux fois dans sa vie précisément de la même manière. Nous n'avons d'autre idée de la *nécessité* que celle qui nous vient de la permanence et de l'uniformité de l'événement. [I.472a]

Chaumeix's comments on this passage of Diderot seem pertinent: 'Voilà l'idée que l'*Encyclopédie* nous trace de la liberté qu'elle accorde aux animaux aussi bien qu'à l'homme' followed by 'Les encyclopédistes ne font ici les animaux machines que pour rendre l'homme lui-même une machine, et la faculté de penser, une propriété du corps et de la matière' (*PL* i.237–9).

It would seem as if, after the first two volumes, Diderot rather drew in his horns and, apart from his historical articles, contributed very little of a philosophical nature to those volumes which appeared freely and openly down to 1757. However, in the last ten volumes he let himself go, particularly in bold short articles which Le Breton, the self-appointed censor, somehow omitted to strike out. These contributions are especially interesting as they form a kind of link between his earlier philosophical writings, the last of which, the *Pensées sur l'interprétation de la nature*, appeared in 1753, and such later works as the *Rêve de d'Alembert*, composed in 1769 after his task as editor of the *Encyclopédie* was practically completed.

His materialism finds expression in more than half a dozen articles scattered over the last ten volumes. In MATÉRIALISTES we find added to the text of Chambers's article article a new paragraph:

On donne encore aujourd'hui le nom de *matérialistes* à ceux qui soutiennent ou que l'âme de l'homme est matière, ou que la matière est éternelle et qu'elle est Dieu; ou que Dieu n'est qu'une âme universelle répandue dans la matière, qui la meut et la dispose, soit pour produire les êtres, soit pour former les divers arrangements que nous voyons dans l'univers. *Voyez* SPINOZISTES. [X.188b]

It is a fair assumption that this addition to MATÉRIALISTES came from Diderot's pen, especially as we have the authority of Naigeon for attributing SPINOZISTES to him. If we follow up the cross-references this is what we find:

SPINOZISTE, s.m. (*Gram.*), sectateur de la philosophie de Spinoza. Il ne faut pas confondre les *Spinozistes* anciens avec les *Spinozistes* modernes. Le principe général de ceux-ci, c'est que la matière est sensible, ce qu'ils démontrent par le développement de l'œuf, corps inerte, qui par le seul instrument de la chaleur graduée passe à l'état d'être sentant et vivant, et par l'accroissement de tout animal qui dans son principe n'est qu'un point et qui par l'assimilation nutritive des plantes, en un mot, de toutes les substances qui servent à la nutrition, devient un grand corps sentant et vivant dans un grand espace. De là ils concluent qu'il n'y a que de la matière et qu'elle suffit pour tout expliquer. Du reste ils suivent l'ancien spinozisme dans toutes ses conséquences. [XV.474a]

With this passage we can compare a letter written by Diderot in 1765 in which he develops further his belief that 'la sensibilité est une propriété universelle de la matière'[1] and the later *Rêve de d'Alembert* with its famous passage beginning: 'Voyez-vous cet oeuf? c'est avec cela que l'on renverse toutes les écoles de théologie et tous les temples de la terre.'[2]

The article NATURALISTE also adds a paragraph to what one finds in Chambers:

On donne encore le nom de *naturalistes* à ceux qui n'admettent point de Dieu, mais qui croient qu'il n'y a qu'une substance matérielle, revêtue de diverses qualités qui lui sont aussi essentielles que la longeur, la largeur, la profondeur, et en conséquence desquelles tout s'exécute nécessairement dans la nature comme nous le voyons. *Naturaliste* en ce sens est synonyme à *athée, spinoziste, matérialiste*, etc. [XI.39b]

We hardly need Naigeon's help to recognize here the hand of Diderot. Hidden away in an unusually long grammatical article we find the following views on the origins of life:

NAITRE, v.neut. (*Gram.*), venir au monde. S'il fallait donner une définition bien rigoureuse de ces deux mots *naître* et *mourir*, on y trouverait peut-être de la difficulté. *Ce que nous en allons dire est purement systématique.* A proprement parler, on ne *naît* point, on ne meurt point; on était dès le

[1] Roth, v, 141.        [2] *AT*, ii, 115.

commencement des choses, et on sera jusqu'à leur consommation. Un point qui vivait s'est accru, développé, jusqu'à un certain terme, par la juxtaposition successive d'une infinité de molécules. Passé ce terme, il décroît et se résout en molécules séparées qui vont se répandre dans la masse générale et commune. La vie ne peut être le résultat de l'organisation. Imaginez les trois molécules *A, B, C* : si elles sont sans vie dans la combinaison *A, B, C,* pourquoi commenceraient-elles à vivre dans la combinaison *B, C, A* ou *C, A, B* ? Cela ne se conçoit pas. Il n'en est pas de la vie comme du mouvement ; c'est autre chose. Ce qui a vie a mouvement, mais ce qui se meut ne vit pas pour cela. Si l'air, l'eau, la terre et le feu viennent à se combiner, d'inertes qu'ils étaient auparavant, ils deviendront d'une mobilité incoercible ; mais ils ne produiront pas la vie. La vie est une qualité essentielle et primitive dans l'être vivant ; il ne l'acquiert point ; il ne la perd point. Il faut distinguer une vie inerte et une vie active. Elles sont entre elles comme la force vive et la force morte ; ôtez l'obstacle et la force morte deviendra force vive ; ôtez l'obstacle et la vie inerte deviendra vie active. Il y a encore la vie de l'élément, et la vie de l'agrégat ou de la masse. Rien n'ôte et ne peut ôter à l'élément sa vie. L'agrégat ou la masse est avec le temps privée de la sienne. On vit en un point qui s'étend jusqu'à une certaine limite, sous laquelle la vie est circonscrite en tous sens ; cet espace sous lequel on vit diminue peu à peu ; la vie devient moins active sous chaque point de cet espace ; il y en a même sous lesquels elle a perdu toute son activité avant la dissolution de la masse, et l'on finit par vivre en une infinité d'atomes isolés. Les termes de vie et de mort n'ont rien d'absolu ; ils ne désignent que les états successifs d'un même être . . . [XI.10a–b][1]

To this article corresponds another grammatical one (unsigned, but surely by Diderot) PÉRIR :

Rien ne s'anéantit, mais tout change d'état. En ce sens nous *périssons* sans cesse ou nous ne *périssons* point du tout, puisqu'il n'y a aucun instant dans l'éternité de notre durée où nous différons plus de nous-mêmes que dans aucun autre instant antérieur ou postérieur et que nous sommes dans un flux perpétuel . . . [XII.379b]

Even more pointed is the article *IMPÉRISSABLE, the authorship of which is beyond doubt:

IMPÉRISSABLE, adj. (*Gram. et philosoph.*), qui ne peut périr. Ceux qui

---

[1] Cf. the words put into the mouth of d'Alembert in *Le Rêve* : . . . 'Et la vie ? . . . La vie, une suite d'actions et de réactions. . . . Vivant, j'agis et je réagis en masse . . . mort, j'agis et je réagis en molécules. . . . Je ne meurs donc point ? . . . Non, sans doute, je ne meurs point en ce sens, ni moi, ni quoi que ce soit . . . Naitre, vivre et passer, c'est changer de formes . . . Et qu'importe une forme ou une autre ?' (AT, ii, 139–40)

regardent la matière comme éternelle, la regardent aussi comme *impérissable*. Rien, selon eux, ne se perd de la quantité du mouvement, rien de la quantité de la matière. Les êtres naissants s'accroissent et disparaissent, mais leurs éléments sont éternels. La destruction d'une chose a été, est et sera à jamais la génération d'une autre. Ce sentiment a été celui de presque tous les anciens philosophes, qui n'avaient aucune idée de la création. [VII.593a]

The same idea is put even more directly in the second half of another grammatical article, PRODUCTION, which is attributed to Diderot by Naigeon:

La *production* des êtres est l'état opposé à leur destruction. Cependant, pour un homme qui y regarde de près, il n'y a proprement dans la nature aucune *production*, aucune destruction absolue, aucun commencement, aucune fin; ce qui est a toujours été et sera toujours, passant seulement sous une infinité de formes successives. [XIII.424a]

Finally one may instance the decidedly materialistic twist given by Diderot to an article taken over from Chambers. It opens thus:

INCORPOREL, adj. (*Gram. & Métaphys.*) substance spirituelle qui n'a point de corps. *Voyez* ESPRIT *et* CORPS.

   L'âme de l'homme est *incorporelle* et peut subsister sans le corps. *Voyez* ÂME *et* IMMATÉRIEL.

   Les idées indépendantes du corps ne peuvent ni être corporelles, ni être reçues dans un sujet corporel.

Down to this point the *Encyclopédie* is simply translating Chambers, but now they diverge. Chambers continues:

They discover to us the nature of the soul, which receives within itself what is *incorporeal*, and receives it in a corporeal manner too. Whence it is that we have *incorporeal* ideas even of bodies themselves. Fénelon. See IDEA.

Diderot ends his article very differently:

Elles nous découvrent la nature de notre âme, qui reçoit ce qui est *incorporel* et qui le reçoit au-dedans de soi d'une manière *incorporelle*, excepté le mouvement que mon âme reçoit quand je me meus et qu'elle reçoit tout à fait à la manière des corps. Voilà donc une modification[1] divisible dans un sujet indivisible. [VIII.659b]

---

[1] In the technical sense defined by the *Dictionnaire de l'Académie française* (1762 edition) as 'une manière d'être d'une substance'.

'Diderot', Naigeon commented in reproducing this unsigned
article in his *Philosophie ancienne et moderne*, 'aurait pu écrire au bas
de cet article, *Sapienti sat*'.

## Diderot and determinism

The determinism which formed so basic a part of Diderot's final
philosophy stands out even more clearly in a whole series of
articles scattered through the last ten volumes. Indeed there is one
article on this topic as early as Vol. VII:

\*FORTUIT, adj. (*Gram.*), terme assez commun dans la langue, et tout à fait
vide de sens dans la nature. *Voyez l'article suivant*.[1] Nous disons d'un
événement qu'il est *fortuit* lorsque la cause nous en est inconnue, que sa
liaison avec ceux qui le précédent, l'accompagnent ou le suivent, nous
échappe, en un mot lorsqu'il est au-dessus de nos connaissances et indépendant de notre volonté. L'homme peut être heureux ou malheureux
par des cas *fortuits*; mais ils ne le rendent point dignes d'éloge ou de blâme,
de châtiment ou de récompense. Celui qui réfléchira profondément à
l'enchaînement des événements, verra avec une sorte d'effroi combien la
vie est *fortuite*, et il se familiarisera avec l'idée de la mort, le seul événement qui puisse nous soustraire à la servitude générale des êtres. [VII.204b]

What is only hinted at in this early article is made explicit in the
volumes published in 1765. In Vol. VIII we find the following
passage in the article \*IMPARFAIT:

. . . Il n'y a rien d'imparfait dans la nature, pas même les monstres. Tout y
est enchaîné, et le monstre y est un effet aussi nécessaire que l'animal parfait. Les causes qui ont concouru à sa production tiennent à une infinité
d'autres, et celles-ci à une infinité d'autres, et ainsi de suite en remontant
jusqu'à l'éternité des choses. Il n'y a d'*imperfection* que dans l'art, parce que
l'art a un modèle subsistant dans la nature auquel on peut comparer ses
productions. Nous ne sommes pas dignes de louer ou de blâmer l'ensemble
général des choses dont nous ne connaissons ni l'harmonie ni la fin; et
*bien* et *mal* sont des mots vides de sens, lorsque le tout excède l'étendue de
nos facultés et de nos connaissances. [VIII.584a]

The same point is put more succinctly in the unsigned article
PARFAIT, which must surely be attributed to Diderot:

. . . Il n'y a rien d'imparfait dans la nature; tout ce qui est nécessaire dans
toutes ses parties est *parfait*. [XI.940a]

[1] D'Alembert's FORTUIT (*Métaphys.*) which, as we have seen, got him into trouble with critics at the time (pp. 161–2).

\*IRRÉGULARITÉ also seeks to drive home the same message:

. . . On peut même quelquefois en accuser les ouvrages de la nature; mais alors il y a deux motifs qui doivent nous rendre très circonspects: la nécessité absolue de ses lois et le peu de connaissance de sa variété et de son opération. [VIII.907a]

So does a sentence from PRODUIRE:

La nature ne *produit* des monstres que par la comparaison d'un être à un autre; mais tout naît également de ses lois, et la masse de chair informe et l'être le mieux organisé. [XIII.424a]

In the short article LAIDEUR which corresponds to the long essay, \*BEAU, which Diderot had contributed to Vol. II of the *Encyclopédie*, we find the same idea:

Ce qui est nécessaire n'est en soi ni bon ni mauvais, ni beau ni laid en lui-même. Ce monde n'est donc ni bon, ni mauvais, ni beau, ni laid en lui-même; ce qui n'est pas entièrement connu ne peut être dit ni bon, ni mauvais, ni beau, ni laid. Or on ne connaît ni l'univers entier, ni son but; on ne peut donc rien prononcer ni sur sa perfection ni sur son imperfection. [IX.176b]

Finally, in a short unsigned grammatical article which must have come from Diderot's pen, we find man clearly included in this system of universal necessity:

JAMAIS, adv. de temps (*Gram.*) Il se dit par négation de tous les périodes de la durée, du passé, du présent, de l'avenir. Il est impossible que l'ordre de la nature soit *jamais* suspendu. De quelque phénomène que les temps passés aient été témoins, et quelque phénomène qui frappe les yeux des hommes à venir, il a la raison de son existence, de sa durée et de toutes ses circonstances dans l'enchaînement universel des causes qui comprend l'homme ainsi que tous les autres êtres, sensibles ou non. [VIII.440a]

Putting together such articles, we find clearly set forth a belief in universal necessity.

One of the difficulties produced by such a doctrine was its consequences in the realm of ethics. However, already in the articles which he inserted in the last ten volumes of the *Encyclopédie* we find Diderot's answer to this problem. As early as Vol. VIII we encounter an unsigned article, HABITUDE (*Morale*) which, although

Naigeon does not associate it with Diderot, must be his since one paragraph contains expressions which we find over and over again in his writings of the later period:

Si l'on considère jusqu'où les enfants ressemblent quelquefois à leurs parents, on ne doutera guère qu'il n'y ait des penchants héréditaires. Ces penchants nous portent-ils à des choses honnêtes et louables, on est heureusement né; à des choses déshonnêtes et honteuses, on est malheureusement né. [VIII.17b]

In the same volume we find these very expressions—'heureusement né' and 'malheureusement né'—in another unsigned article which is definitely attributed to Diderot by Naigeon:

INVOLONTAIRE, adj. (*Gram.*), ce à quoi la volonté n'a point eu de part; ce qui n'a point été ou n'est pas voulu, consenti. Il paraît à celui qui examinera les actions humaines de près que toute la différence des *volontaires* et des *involontaires* consiste à avoir été ou n'avoir pas été réfléchies. Je marche, et sous mes pieds il se rencontre des insectes que j'écrase *involontairement*. Je marche, et je vois un serpent endormi, je lui appuie mon talon sur la tête, et je l'écrase *volontairement*. Ma réflexion est la seule chose qui distingue ces deux mouvements, et ma réflexion, considérée relativement à tous les instants de ma durée, et à ce que je suis dans le moment où j'agis, est absolument indépendante de moi. J'écrase le serpent de réflexion; de réflexion Cléopâtre le prend et s'en pique le sein. C'est l'amour de la vie qui m'entraîne; c'est la haine de la vie qui entraîne Cléopâtre. Ce sont deux poids qui agissent en sens contraires sur les bras de la balance, qui oscillent et se fixent nécessairement. Selon le côté ou le point où ils s'arrêtent, l'homme est bienfaisant ou malfaisant, heureusement ou malheureusement né, exterminable ou digne de récompense selon les lois. [VIII.865b]

The same theory is set forth in a later volume, in an article which is also attributed to Diderot by Naigeon:

VOLONTÉ, s.f. (*Gram. & Philosophie morale*). C'est l'effet de l'impression d'un objet présent à nos sens ou à notre réflexion, en conséquence de laquelle nous sommes portés tout entiers vers cet objet comme vers un bien dont nous avons la connaissance et qui excite notre appétit, ou nous en sommes éloignés comme d'un mal que nous connaissons aussi et qui excite notre crainte et notre aversion. Aussi il y a toujours un objet dans l'action de la *volonté*, car quand on veut, on veut quelque chose; de l'attention à cet objet, une crainte ou un désir excité. De là vient que nous prenons à tout moment la *volonté* pour la liberté. Si l'on pouvait supposer cent mille hommes tous absolument conditionnés de même et qu'on leur présentât un même objet de désir ou d'aversion, ils le désireraient tous et tous de la même manière, ou le rejetteraient tous et tous de la même manière. Il n'y a nulle différence entre la *volonté* des fous et des hommes dans leur bon sens, de l'homme qui veille et de l'homme qui rêve, du malade qui a la fièvre chaude et de l'homme qui jouit de la plus parfaite santé, de l'homme tranquille et de l'homme passionné, de celui qu'on traîne au supplice ou de celui qui y marche intrépidement. Ils sont tous également emportés tout entiers par l'impression d'un objet qui les attire ou qui les repousse. S'ils veulent subitement le contraire de ce qu'ils voulaient, c'est qu'il est tombé un atome sur le bras de la balance qui l'a fait pencher du côté opposé. On ne sait ce qu'on veut lorsque les deux bras sont a peu près également chargés. Si l'on pèse bien ces considérations, on sentira combien il est difficile de se faire une notion quelconque de la liberté, surtout dans un enchaînement des causes et des effets tel que celui dont nous faisons partie. [XVII.454b]

This idea is developed further in MACHINAL (unsigned, but almost certainly by Diderot). Here Diderot distinguishes between a purely mechanical movement, such as the action one takes to avoid a fall, and 'un mouvement qu'on appelle *libre* ou *volontaire*' of which he gives the following example:

Il y a sans doute actuellement quelque femme dans la société déterminée à s'aller jeter ce soir entre les bras de son amant et qui n'y manquera pas. Si je suppose cent mille femmes tout à fait semblables à cette première femme, de même âge, de même état, ayant des amants tous semblables, le même tempérament, la même vie antérieure, dans un espace conditionné de la même manière, il est certain qu'un être élevé au-dessus de ces cent mille femmes les verrait toutes agir de la même manière, toutes se porter entre les bras de leurs amants, à la même heure, au même moment, de la même manière. Une armée qui fait l'exercice et qui est commandée dans ses mouvements, des capucins de carte qui tombent tous les uns à la file des autres, ne se ressembleraient pas davantage, le moment où nous agissons paraissant si parfaitement dépendre du moment qui l'a précédé, et celui-ci du précédent encore. Cependant toutes ces femmes sont libres, et il ne faut pas confondre leurs actions quand elles se rendent à leurs amants, avec leur action quand elles se secourent *machinalement* dans une chute. Si l'on ne faisait aucune distinction réelle entre ces deux cas, il s'ensuivrait que notre vie n'est qu'une suite d'instants nécessairement tels et nécessairement enchaînés les uns aux autres, que notre volonté n'est qu'un acquiescement nécessaire à être ce que nous sommes nécessairement dans chacun de ces instants, et que notre liberté est un mot vide de sens ; mais en examinant les choses en nous-mêmes, quand nous parlons de nos actions et de celles des autres, quand nous les louons ou que nous les blâmons, nous ne sommes certainement pas de cet avis. [IX.794a]

The 'précautions oratoires' of this article should not hide its real meaning from the reader. In an unsigned addition to Jaucourt's article VICE (it is again attributed to him by Naigeon) Diderot makes his position perfectly clear:

L'usage a mis de la différence entre un *défaut* et un *vice*; tout *vice* est *défaut*, mais tout *défaut* n'est pas *vice*. On suppose à l'homme qui a un *vice*, une liberté qui le rend coupable à nos yeux; le défaut tombe communément sur le compte de la nature; on excuse l'homme, on accuse la nature. Lorsque la philosophie discute ces distinctions avec une attention bien scrupuleuse, elle les trouve souvent vides de sens. Un homme est-il plus maître d'être pusillanime, voluptueux, colère en un mot, que louche, bossu ou boiteux? Plus on accorde à l'organisation, à l'éducation, aux mœurs nationales, au climat, aux circonstances qui ont disposé de notre vie depuis l'instant où nous sommes tombés du sein de la nature jusqu'à celui où nous existons, moins on est vain des bonnes qualités qu'on possède et qu'on se doit si peu à soi-même, plus on est indulgent pour les défauts et les *vices* des autres, plus on est circonspect dans l'emploi des mots 'vicieux' et 'vertueux' qu'on ne prononce jamais sans amour ou sans haine, plus on a de penchant à leur substituer ceux de 'malheureusement' et d' 'heureusement nés' qu'un sentiment de commisération accompagne toujours. Vous avez pitié d'un aveugle; et qu'est-ce qu'un méchant sinon un homme qui a la vue courte et qui ne voit pas au delà du moment où il agit? [XVII.235b]

MALFAISANT (also attributed to Diderot by Naigeon) carries the argument a stage further:

MALFAISANT, adj. (*Gram. et Morale*), qui nuit, qui fait du mal. Si l'homme est libre, c'est-à-dire, si l'âme a une activité qui lui soit propre et en vertu de laquelle elle puisse se déterminer à faire ou ne pas faire une action, quelles que soient ses habitudes ou celles du corps, ses idées, ses passions, le tempérament, l'âge, les préjugés etc., il y a certainement des hommes vertueux et des hommes vicieux. S'il n'y a point de liberté, il n'y a plus que des hommes bienfaisants et des hommes *malfaisants*, mais les hommes n'en sont pas moins modifiables en bien et en mal; les bons exemples, les bons discours, les châtiments, les récompenses, le blâme, la louange, les lois ont toujours leur effet. L'homme *malfaisant* est toujours malheureusement né. [IX.945a–b]

The possibility of modifying the conduct of individuals in a system of rigid determinism is developed further in the course of another grammatical article—MODIFICATION, MODIFIER, MODIFICATIF, MODIFIABLE—which is again attributed to Diderot by Naigeon:

... L'homme, libre ou non, est un être qu'on *modifie* ... Moins un être est libre, plus on est sûr de le *modifier*, et plus la *modification* lui est nécessairement attachée. Les *modifications* qui nous ont été imprimées nous changent sans ressource, et pour le moment et pour toute la suite de la vie, parce qu'il ne se peut jamais faire que ce qui a été une fois tel, n'ait pas été tel. [X.602a]

As almost all these articles which insinuate or openly preach determinism appeared in the last ten volumes of the *Encyclopédie*, they passed almost unnoticed at the time, although Abbé Barruel did pick out for unfavourable comment the editorial addition to VICE which he quite correctly attributes to Diderot.[1]

## Ethical problems

This was not, however, the case with the articles on ethics in the first seven volumes, even with the only mildly unorthodox ones of the *abbés* among the contributors. Yvon's BIEN, for instance, came in for quite a lot of criticism. It opens thus:

BIEN, s.m. (*en Morale*) est équivoque: il signifie, ou le *plaisir* qui nous rend heureux, ou *la cause du plaisir*.

　　Dieu seul, à proprement parler, mérite le nom de *bien* parce qu'il n'y a que lui seul qui produise dans notre âme des sensations agréables. On peut néanmoins donner ce nom à toutes les choses qui, dans l'ordre établi par l'auteur de la nature, sont les canaux par lesquels il fait, pour ainsi dire, couler le plaisir jusqu'à l'âme. Plus les plaisirs qu'elles nous procurent sont vifs, solides et durables, plus elles participent à la qualité de *bien*. [II.243a]

If a Jansenist writer like Chaumeix can approve of the opening

[1] *Les Helviennes*, iv, 136.

sentence of the second paragraph, he denounces what follows for its pagan attitude to morality:

Il est aisé de voir que . . . le chrétien qui veut connaître en quoi consiste son souverain bien, ne doit pas l'aller chercher dans cet article, puisqu'il n'y trouverait qu'un alliage bizarre d'Épicure et d'Épictète au lieu d'y trouver l'Évangile. M. l'abbé Yvon l'a mis à part dans cet article ainsi que dans tous les autres de sa façon. (*PL* ii.6)

The second and third sentences of this second paragraph aroused unfavourable comment in several quarters.

Abbé Pestré's BONHEUR did not fare any better. It can well be imagined that sentiments such as the following did not appeal to the orthodox:

Tous les hommes se réunissent dans le désir d'être heureux. La nature nous a fait à tous une loi de notre propre *bonheur*. Tout ce qui n'est point *bonheur* nous est étranger; lui seul a un pouvoir marqué sur notre cœur. Nous y sommes tous entraînés par une pente rapide, par un charme puissant, par un attrait vainqueur; c'est une impression ineffaçable de la nature qui l'a gravé dans nos cœurs, il en est le charme et la perfection. [II.322a]

Worse still was to follow later in the article when, after declaring that philosophers agree with Epicurus 'qui faisait consister essentiellement la félicité dans le plaisir', he goes on:

Il ne faut point opposer à cette maxime qui est certaine, la morale et la religion de J.C., notre législateur et en même temps notre Dieu, lequel n'est point venu pour anéantir la nature, mais pour la perfectionner. Il ne nous fait point renoncer à l'amour du plaisir et ne condamne point la vertu à être malheureuse ici-bas. Sa loi est pleine de charmes et d'attraits; elle est toute comprise dans l'amour de Dieu et du prochain. La source des plaisirs légitimes ne coule pas moins pour le chrétien que pour l'homme profane, mais dans l'ordre de la grâce il est infiniment plus heureux par ce qu'il espère que par ce qu'il possède. Le *bonheur* qu'il goûte ici-bas devient pour lui le germe d'un *bonheur* éternel. Ses plaisirs sont ceux de la modération, de la bienfaisance, de la tempérance, de la conscience, plaisirs purs, nobles, spirituels et fort supérieurs aux plaisirs des sens. [II.322b]

Such sentiments were roundly condemned by several hostile critics. Chaumeix was roused to fury by them:

Vous nous dites donc que le sentiment d'Épicure est le vôtre, et vous avez l'audace impie de prétendre que c'est aussi celle [*sic*] de Jésus-Christ.

Avez-vous lu l'Évangile? Il n'est point de chrétien qui ne frémisse à ce blasphème. (*PL* ii.25–6)

It can well be imagined that some of Diderot's articles on moral questions in the early volumes of the *Encyclopédie* were ill-received by enemies of the work. *DÉLICIEUX, which was much admired by his friend Grimm, contains the famous passage:

. . . Le repos a aussi son *délice*; mais qu'est-ce qu'un repos *délicieux*? Celui-là seul en a connu le charme inexprimable dont les organes étaient sensibles et délicats; qui avait reçu de la nature une âme tendre et un tempérament voluptueux; qui jouissait d'une santé parfaite; qui se trouvait à la fleur de son âge; qui n'avait l'esprit troublé d'aucun nuage, l'âme agitée d'aucune émotion trop vive; qui sortait d'une fatigue douce et légère et qui éprouvait dans toutes les parties de son corps un plaisir si également répandu qu'il ne se faisait distinguer dans aucun. Il ne lui restait dans ce moment d'enchantement et de faiblesse, ni mémoire du passé, ni désir de l'avenir, ni inquiétude sur le présent. Le temps avait cessé de couler pour lui parce qu'il existait tout en lui-même; le sentiment de son bonheur ne s'affaiblissait qu'avec celui de son existence. Il passait par un mouvement imperceptible de la veille au sommeil; mais sur ce passage imperceptible, au milieu de la défaillance de toutes ses facultés, il veillait encore assez, sinon pour penser à quelque chose de distinct, du moins pour sentir toute la douceur de son existence; mais il en jouissait d'une jouissance tout à fait passive, sans y être attaché, sans y réfléchir, sans s'en réjouir, sans s'en féliciter. Si l'on pouvait fixer par la pensée cette situation de pur sentiment, où toutes les facultés du corps et de l'âme sont vivantes sans être agissantes, et attacher à ce quiétisme *délicieux* l'idée d'immutabilité, on se formerait la notion du bonheur le plus grand et le plus pur que l'homme puisse imaginer. [IV.784a]

This passage, which a modern critic can compare with parts of the famous *Cinquième Promenade* of Rousseau's *Rêveries du promeneur solitaire*,[1] obviously gave less pleasure to Chaumeix who links Diderot with Abbés Yvon and Pestré and makes all three of them proclaim the same outrageous views on the subject of happiness:

Qu'est-ce donc qu'être heureux? C'est avoir du plaisir, c'est éprouver des sensations agréables; et celui qui ne possédera pas Dieu, mais qui sera dans l'état que nous avons tracé dans l'article *Délicieux*, sera parvenu au plus

---

[1] R. Mortier, 'A propos du sentiment de l'existence chez Diderot et Rousseau' (*Diderot Studies vi*, Geneva, 1964, pp. 183–95).

parfait bonheur. C'est pourquoi nous ne disons pas que, pour être souverainement heureux, il faut travailler à connaître Dieu, lui demander qu'il nous remplisse de son esprit et de son amour; mais nous disons 'qu'il faut faire couler la joie jusqu'au plus intime de notre cœur, l'animer par des sensations agréables, l'agiter par de douces secousses, lui imprimer des mouvement délicieux'. (PL ii.28–9)

This final quotation comes from Pestré's BONHEUR [II.322a].

A short article, *FIN (Morale), also displeased Chaumeix because of its last sentence: 'Pressez un homme de motifs en motifs, et vous trouverez que son bonheur particulier est toujours la fin dernière de toutes ses actions réfléchies' [VI.810a]. He was dissatisfied with this purely secular approach to the question: 'Ces auteurs ne nous en disent pas davantage. Ils ne se sont pas souvenus apparemment que c'était ici le lieu de s'étendre sur la fin que tout chrétien doit se proposer dans ses actions; ils ont oublié de parler de la fin dernière' (PL ii.3). However, other contributors to the first seven volumes besides Diderot got into trouble for their ethical ideas. Saint-Lambert's FRAGILITÉ (Morale) contains a paragraph which was to displease La Religion vengée:

Quoique nous connaissions une secrète disposition à nous dérober fréquemment à toute espèce de joug; quoique très sûrs que le regret de nous être écartés de ce que nous appelons nos devoirs nous poursuivra longtemps, nous nous laissons surcharger de lois inutiles qu'on ajoute aux lois nécessaires à la société: nous nous forgeons des chaînes qu'il est presque impossible de porter. On sème parmi nous les occasions des petites fautes et des grands remords. [VII.273b]

The meaning of this somewhat veiled language is clearly brought out by La Religion vengée:

Quelles sont, Monsieur, ces lois inutiles qu'on ajoute aux lois nécessaires à la société? Ce sont les lois de la religion; cela est clair pour quiconque est au fait des principes encyclopédiques. N'en concluez pas que, selon nous, les lois de la religion ne sont pas nécessaires à la société en tant que telles; nous disons seulement que, selon l'Encyclopédie, la société a par elle-même et indépendamment de la religion toutes les lois nécessaires pour être tout ce qu'elle doit être, langage du déiste et de l'athée. On prétend encore, comme vous le voyez, que la transgression de ces lois ajoutées aux lois nécessaires de la société ne fait que de petites fautes, lesquelles néanmoins, par notre illusion, nous causent de grands remords. C'est dire en termes équivalents que toutes les religions, et la religion chrétienne comme toutes les autres, ne sont que de pures chimères. (xii.22–3)

With his usual shrewdness the editor brings out the purely secular approach to morality which underlies this whole article.

In the same chapter he quotes with approval d'Alembert's condemnation of the profession dealt with in COURTISANE:

Nous ne nous étendrons pas beaucoup sur cet article dans un ouvrage aussi grave que celui-ci. Nous croyons devoir dire seulement, indépendamment des lumières de la religion et en nous bornant au pur moral, que la passion pour les *courtisanes* énerve également l'âme et le corps, et qu'elle porte les plus funestes atteintes à la fortune, à la santé, au repos et au bonheur. On peut se rappeler à cette occasion le mot de Démosthène: 'Je n'achète pas si cher un repentir' . . . [IV.401a]

But this is only to condemn d'Alembert (and Buffon whose ideas he is reproducing) for other sentiments expressed in this same article:

Un célèbre philosophe de nos jours examine dans son *Histoire naturelle* pourquoi l'amour fait le bonheur de tous les êtres et le malheur de l'homme. Il répond que c'est qu'il n'y a dans cette passion que le physique de bon et que le moral, c'est-à-dire le sentiment qui l'accompagne, n'en vaut rien. Ce philosophe n'a pas prétendu que ce moral n'ajoute pas au plaisir physique, l'expérience serait contre lui; ni que le moral de l'amour ne soit qu'une illusion, ce qui est vrai, mais ne détruit pas la vivacité du plaisir (et combien peu de plaisirs ont un objet réel!). Il a voulu dire sans doute que ce moral est ce qui cause tous les maux de l'amour, et en cela on ne saurait trop être de son avis. [IV.401a]

Such an attitude does not at all fit in with the ideas of *La Religion vengée*:

Voilà certainement, Monsieur, une idée bien singulière du *moral de l'amour*. On fait consister ce *moral*, non dans la conformité ou l'opposition de cette passion avec la droite raison, avec la loi, avec l'Évangile, mais dans le *sentiment*, et ce sentiment, on le traite d'illusion. Quel entassement de notions absurdes! (xii.28–9)

Once again the clash between secular morality and orthodoxy comes out clearly.

Not content with getting Voltaire to produce an article on FORNICATION (*Morale*), d'Alembert added one of his own on the same subject which did not give pleasure to *La Religion vengée*. His opening definition: 'La *fornication* . . . est proprement un commerce charnel dont le prêtre n'a point donné la permission' [VII.188b], is denounced as being 'd'un ton trop manifestement dérisoire' (*RV* xii.44). But d'Alembert goes much further than this mere pinprick; he argues that civil laws take a different view on this as on many other questions from that taken by the Church. In the eyes of the Gospel adultery is a worse sin than fornication:

Cependant, abstraction faite de la religion, de la probité même, et considérant uniquement l'économie de la société, il n'est pas difficile de sentir que *la fornication* lui est, en un sens, plus nuisible que l'adultère; car elle tend, ou à multiplier dans la société la misère et le trouble en y introduisant des citoyens sans état et sans ressource, ou, ce qui est peut-être encore plus funeste, à faciliter la dépopulation par la ruine de la fécondité. Cette observation n'a point pour objet de diminuer la juste horreur qu'on doit avoir de l'adultère, mais seulement de faire sentir les différents aspects sous lesquels on peut envisager la morale, soit par rapport à la religion, soit par rapport à l'État. [VII.189a]

After making this contrast between secular and religious morality d'Alembert proceeds to widen the argument still further, to take in the difference (theoretical rather than real in eighteenth-century France) between the attitude of Church and State to free-thought:

Les législateurs ont principalement décerné des peines contre les forfaits qui portent le trouble parmi les hommes; il est d'autres crimes que la religion ne condamne pas moins, mais dont l'Etre suprême se réserve la punition. L'incrédulité, par exemple, est pour un chrétien un aussi grand crime, et peut-être un plus grand crime, que le vol; cependant il y a des lois contre le vol, et il n'y en a pas contre les incrédules qui n'attaquent point ouvertement la religion dominante; c'est que des opinions (même absurdes) qu'on ne cherche point à répandre, n'apportent aux citoyens aucun dommage. Aussi y a-t-il plus d'incrédules que de voleurs. [VII.189a]

It can be imagined that such ideas were hardly likely to go down well in 1757.

Diderot had, of course, his word to say on many aspects of the relations between the sexes. In *CHASTETÉ he rounds off the article with a clear attack on religious morality:

Voilà tout ce que la philosophie semble nous dicter sur la *chasteté*. Mais les
lois de la religion chrétienne sont beaucoup plus étroites; un mot, un
regard, une parole, un geste mal intentionnés flétrissent la *chasteté*
chrétienne. Le chrétien n'est parvenu à la vraie *chasteté* que quand il a su se
conserver dans un état de pureté évangélique malgré les suggestions
perpétuelles du démon de la chair. Tout ce qui peut favoriser les efforts de
cet ennemi de notre innocence passe dans son esprit pour autant d'obstacles à la *chasteté*, tels que les excès dans le boire et le manger, la fréquentation de personnes déréglées ou même d'un autre sexe, la vue d'un objet
indécent, un discours équivoque, une lecture déshonnête, une pensée
libre, etc. [III.234a]

The famous unsigned article, JOUISSANCE (the word is here used in
its technical sense of 'plaisir, orgasme vénérien'), which Diderot
contributed to Vol. VIII, leads us on to one of his last articles in the
*Encyclopédie*, VOLUPTUEUX, which, though unsigned too, is also
attributed to him by Naigeon. A *philosophe*'s revolt against the
ascetic morality of the Church is brought out clearly in this article,
too clearly for Le Breton who toned it down slightly:

VOLUPTUEUX, adj. (*Gram.*) qui aime les plaisirs sensuels; en ce sens tout
homme est plus ou moins voluptueux. Ceux qui enseignent[1] je ne sais
quelle doctrine austère qui nous affligerait sur la sensibilité d'organes que
nous avons reçue de la nature qui voulait que la conservation de l'espèce
et la nôtre fussent encore un objet de plaisirs, et sur cette foule d'objets qui
nous entourent et qui sont destinés à émouvoir cette sensibilité en cent
manières agréables, sont des atrabilaires à enfermer aux petites maisons.
Ils remercieraient volontiers l'Être tout-puissant d'avoir fait des ronces,
des épines, des venins, des tigres, des serpents, en un mot tout ce qu'il y a
de nuisible et de malfaisant; et ils sont tout prêts à lui reprocher l'ombre,
les eaux fraîches, les fruits exquis, les vins délicieux, en un mot les marques
de bonté et de bienfaisance qu'il a semées entre les choses que nous appelons *mauvaises* et *nuisibles*. A leur gré la peine, la douleur ne se rencontrent pas assez souvent sur notre route. Ils voudraient que la souffrance
précédât, accompagnât et suivît toujours le besoin; ils croient honorer
Dieu par la privation des choses qu'il a créées. Ils ne s'aperçoivent pas que
s'ils font bien de s'en priver, il a mal fait de les créer, qu'ils sont plus sages
que lui, et qu'ils ont reconnu et évité le piège qu'il leur a tendu.[2] [XVII.
460b]

[1] Le Breton replaced 'nous prêchent' by 'enseignent' (Gordon and Torrey, p. 107).
[2] Before being censored by Le Breton, the last words read: 'leur a aussi bêtement que méchamment tendu'.

Here, of course, Diderot, like other *philosophes* who rejected religion in any form, assumes the disguise of a deist; but his hatred of a narrow religious morality comes through none the less strongly.

The indissolubility of marriages was another point at which the new secular morality clashed with the orthodox Catholic position. In the short article *INDISSOLUBLE Diderot comes out clearly against it:

*INDISSOLUBLE, adj. (*Gram.*), qui ne peut être dissous, rompu. Le mariage est un engagement *indissoluble*. L'homme sage frémit à l'idée seule d'un engagement *indissoluble*. Les législateurs qui ont préparé aux hommes des liens *indissolubles*, n'ont guère connu son inconstance naturelle. Combien ils ont fait de criminels et de malheureux! [VIII.684a]

It is true that in the legal article DIVORCE the lawyer, Boucher d'Argis, had simply stated the official doctrine: 'Le *divorce* est certainement contraire à la première institution du mariage, qui de sa nature est indissoluble' [IV.1083a]; but, as usual, there were other voices to put the opposite view. Jaucourt, for instance, in MARIAGE (*Droit naturel*), argues that, while because of the children, such unions must be of considerable duration, there is no reason why they should last for life:

... Il n'y a rien, ce me semble, dans la nature et dans le but de cette union qui demande que le mari et la femme soient obligés de demeurer ensemble toute leur vie, après avoir élevé leurs enfants et leur avoir laissé de quoi s'entretenir. Il n'y a rien, dis-je, qui empêche alors qu'on n'ait à l'égard du *mariage* la même liberté qu'on a en matière de toute sorte de société et de convention. De sorte que, moyennant qu'on pourvoie d'une manière ou d'autre à cette éducation, on peut régler d'un commun accord, comme on le juge à propos, la durée de l'union conjugale, soit dans l'indépendance de l'état de nature, ou lorsque les lois civiles sous lesquelles on vit n'ont rien déterminé là-dessus. [X.106a–b]

This is, of course, prudently expressed, but the meaning is none the less clear.

In POPULATION Damilaville is much more direct, not to say brutal, in his approach to the question. Not only does he denounce the Catholic attitude to celibacy in the clergy, both secular and regular, but he attacks the whole Christian approach to sex and particularly to divorce:

Le christianisme n'a pas proprement pour objet de peupler la terre; son vrai but est de peupler le ciel. Ses dogmes sont divins, et il faut convenir que cette religion sainte y réussirait si sa croyance était universelle et si l'impulsion de la nature n'était malheureusement plus forte que toutes les opinions dogmatiques.

Ce culte proscrit le divorce que permettaient les anciens, et en cela il devient un obstacle aux fins du mariage. Ajoutez que la pureté de sa morale réduit l'acte de la génération à l'insipidité du besoin physique et condamne rigoureusement les attraits du sentiment qui peuvent y inviter, et vous conclurez que des êtres enchaînés dans de semblable fers ne se porteront guère à en procréer d'autres. D'ailleurs si l'un des deux n'est pas propre à la génération, la vertu prolifique de l'autre reste nulle et en pure perte pour la société. [XIII.92a]

Once more the attitude of the *Encyclopédie* is a purely secular one.

An interesting attempt to trace the relativity of manners and morals to such causes as different forms of government and society is made in the unsigned article, MŒURS, which one may tentatively attribute to Diderot:

MŒURS, s.f. (*Morale*), actions libres des hommes, naturelles ou acquises, bonnes ou mauvaises, susceptibles de règles et de direction.

Leur variété chez les divers peuples du monde dépend du climat, de la religion, des lois, du gouvernement, des besoins, de l'éducation, des manières et des exemples. A mesure que dans chaque nation une de ces causes agit avec plus de force, les autres lui cèdent d'autant.

Pour justifier toutes ces vérités, il faudrait entrer dans des détails que les bornes de cet ouvrage ne sauraient nous permettre; mais en jetant seulement les yeux sur les différentes formes du gouvernement de nos climats tempérés, on devinerait assez juste par cette unique considération les *mœurs* des citoyens. Ainsi dans une république, qui ne peut subsister que du commerce d'économie, la simplicité des *mœurs*, la tolérance en matière de religion, l'amour de la frugalité, l'épargne, l'esprit d'intérêt et d'avarice devront nécessairement dominer. Dans une monarchie limitée, où chaque citoyen prend part à l'administration de l'État, la liberté y sera regardée comme un si grand bien que toute guerre entreprise pour la soutenir y passera pour un mal peu considérable; les peuples de cette monarchie seront fiers, généreux, profonds dans les sciences et dans la politique, ne perdant jamais de vue leurs privilèges, pas même au milieu du loisir et de la débauche. Dans une riche monarchie absolue, où les femmes

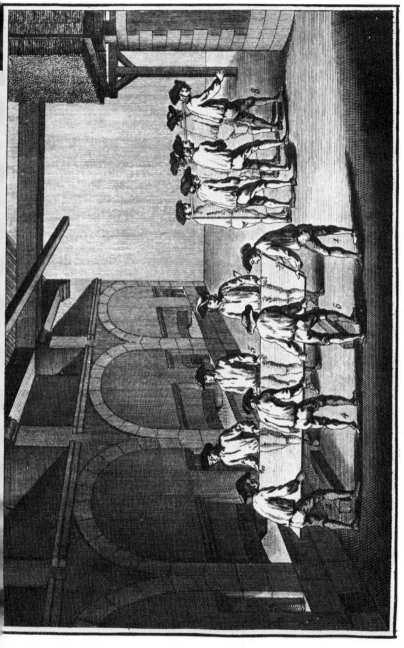

Glaces:: *L'Opération de sortir les Glaces des Carcaises* (*Vol. IV*, Glaces, Plate XXVI)

donnent le ton, l'honneur, l'ambition, la galantérie, le goût des plaisirs, la vanité, la mollesse seront le caractère distinctif des sujets; et comme ce gouvernement produit encore l'oisiveté, cette oisiveté, corrompant les *mœurs*, fera naître à leur place la politesse des manières. *Voyez* MANIÈRES.[1] [X.611b]

In addition to the very interesting comparison between the national character of the eighteenth-century Englishman and Frenchman we have here once more a purely secular approach to moral questions.

One of the articles in this field which is most characteristic of the outlook of the *philosophes* is Saint-Lambert's INTÉRÊT (*Morale*). He begins by defining 'intérêt' as 'ce v̄ic̄e qui nous fait chercher nos avantages au mépris de la justice et de la vertu, et c'est une vile ambition, c'est l'avarice, la passion de l'argent' [VIII.818a]. He goes on to distinguish it carefully from 'amour-propre' in its primary sense of 'self-love' which, as a typical *philosophe*, he considers a necessary and on the whole a good feature of human nature:

L'amour-propre ou le désir continu du bien-être, l'attachement à notre être, est un effet nécessaire de notre constitution, de notre instinct, de nos sensations, de nos réflexions, un principe qui, tendant à notre conservation et répondant aux vues de la nature, serait plutôt vertueux que vicieux dans l'état de nature.

Mais l'homme né en société tire de cette société des avantages qu'il doit payer par des services; l'homme a des devoirs à remplir, des lois à suivre, l'amour-propre des autres à ménager.

Son amour-propre est alors juste ou injuste, vertueux ou vicieux, et selon les différentes qualités, il prend différentes dénominations; on a vu celle d'*intérêt*, d'*intérêt personnel*, et dans quel sens.

Lorsque l'amour-propre est trop l'estime de nous-mêmes et le mépris des autres, il s'appelle *orgueil*; lorsqu'il veut se répandre au dehors et sans mérite occuper les autres de lui, on l'appelle *vanité*.

Dans ces différents cas l'amour-propre est désordonné, c'est-à-dire hors de l'ordre.

Mais cet amour-propre peut inspirer des passions, chercher des plaisirs utiles à l'ordre, à la société; alors il est bien éloigné d'être un principe vicieux.

L'amour d'un père pour ses enfants est une vertu, quoiqu'il s'aime en

---

[1] MANIÈRES is by Saint-Lambert; MŒURS might therefore also be by him though he did not lay claim to it in his *Œuvres philosophiques*, vol. vi.

eux, quoique le souvenir de ce qu'il a été et la prévoyance de ce qu'il sera soient les principaux motifs des secours qu'il leur donne.

Les services rendus à la patrie seront toujours des actions vertueuses, quoiqu'elles soient inspirées par le désir de conserver notre bien-être ou par l'amour de la gloire.

L'amitié sera toujours une vertu, quoiqu'elle ne soit fondée que sur le besoin qu'une âme a d'une autre âme.

La passion de l'ordre, de la justice, sera la première vertu, le véritable héroïsme, quoiqu'elle ait sa source dans l'amour de nous-mêmes. [VIII.818b]

These characteristically utilitarian views lead Saint-Lambert to attack seventeenth-century moralists like Nicole, Pascal and La Rochefoucauld who denounce what he calls 'ce sentiment de l'amour de nous-mêmes que Dieu nous a donné et qui est le mobile éternel de notre être' [VIII. 818b]. He has some interesting remarks to make on the subject of Helvétius's *De l'Esprit*, the publication of which, in 1758, had caused a famous scandal:

L'auteur du livre *De l'Esprit* a été fort accusé, en dernier lieu, d'établir qu'il n'y a aucune vertu; et on ne lui a pas fait ce reproche pour avoir dit que la vertu est purement l'effet des conventions humaines, mais pour s'être presque toujours servi du mot d'*intérêt* à la place de celui d'*amour-propre*. [VIII.819a]

These views did not meet with the approval of Pierre Rousseau when he gave extracts from the article in the *Journal encyclopédique*:

L'auteur de cet article est dans l'erreur, ou c'est nous qui nous trompons; car il nous semble que ce n'est point du tout le terme d'*intérêt*, bien ou mal entendu, qui a rendu répréhensible le livre *De l'Esprit*, mais les funestes conséquences que l'auteur a tirées d'un principe très vrai. On peut dire, et il est démontré, que l'amour-propre ou l'intérêt personnel est le mobile unique et sans cesse agissant de toutes les actions humaines: mais il est faux que ce mobile justifie les vices; il est faux qu'on ne puisse résister au cri de l'intérêt ou de l'amour-propre quand il conseille le crime ou le débordement. Il est faux que la vertu soit purement l'effet des conventions humaines; elle existe par elle-même et indépendamment des hommes qui sont convenus de son existence. Il est faux que les excès les plus scandaleux et les plus effrénés de l'amour-propre, quand il n'a pour objet que la licence et la perversité, tournent au profit de la société et même des mœurs. Avec de telles conséquences il n'est rien qu'on ne puisse justifier;

mais ces conséquences sont fausses, quoique, par des détours ingénieux et des sophismes éblouissants, on les fasse découler du principe très vrai de l'amour-propre.[1]

This defence of Helvétius was still unacceptable nearly a decade after the appearance of his scandalous work.

The views of Diderot, d'Alembert and other contributors which we have examined in this chapter cannot be fully understood until they have been combined with those which they expressed on the subject of religion. The clash of views in this field between *philosophes* and orthodox writers in the France of the 1750s and 1760s is, as we shall now see, clearly reflected in the pages of the *Encyclopédie*.

[1] *Journal Encyclopédique*, 1 June 1767, pp. 16–17.

## Chapter 7

# *Religion*

## *The call for toleration*

In the field of religion what stands out most clearly in the *Encyclopédie* as in the writings of the *philosophes* in general is the demand for toleration. The message is driven home in a series of long articles by a variety of hands, in CONSCIENCE (LIBERTÉ DE) (Jaucourt), FANATISME (Deleyre), INTOLÉRANCE (Diderot) and TOLÉRANCE (Jean Edmé Romilly). Indeed for once one can almost sympathize with Le Breton when he deleted yet another long article on the same subject—a second TOLÉRANCE by Jaucourt—on the grounds that it merely duplicated Romilly's article.[1] In addition, a whole series of short articles attack all forms of religious fanaticism and plead the cause of toleration.

Of the longer articles the least liberal is that of Jean Edmé Romilly, a young pastor from Geneva, who, basing himself on a quotation from the notorious chapter on civil religion in the *Contrat social*, refuses to extend toleration to atheists:

On peut tirer de ces paroles ces conséquences légitimes. La première, c'est que les souverains ne doivent point tolérer les dogmes qui sont opposés à la société civile; ils n'ont point, il est vrai, d'inspection sur les consciences, mais ils doivent réprimer ces discours téméraires qui pourraient porter dans les cœurs la licence et le dégoût des devoirs. Les athées en particulier, qui enlèvent aux puissants le seul frein qui les retienne et aux faibles leur unique espoir, qui énervent toutes les lois humaines en leur ôtant la force qu'ils tirent d'une sanction divine, qui ne laissent entre le juste et l'injuste qu'une distinction politique et frivole, qui ne voient l'opprobre du crime que dans la peine du criminel: les athées, dis-je, ne doivent pas réclamer la

---

[1] Gordon and Torrey, pp. 95–106.

tolérance en leur faveur; qu'on les instruise d'abord, qu'on les exhorte
avec bonté; s'ils persistent, qu'on les réprime; enfin rompez avec eux,
bannissez-les de la société; eux-mêmes en ont brisé les liens. [XVI.394a]

The mildest statement of the case for freedom of conscience is to
be found in one of the earlier articles contributed to the *Encyclopédie*
by the Chevalier de Jaucourt, in his CONSCIENCE (LIBERTÉ DE):

La dernière question est si, en conséquence du jugement que l'on fait de
l'ignorance ou des erreurs d'autrui en matière de *conscience*, on peut se
porter à quelque action contre ceux que l'on croit être dans cette ignorance
ou dans ces erreurs? Ici nous répondons que lorsque l'erreur ne va point à
faire ou à enseigner des choses manifestement contraires aux lois de la
société humaine en général et à celles de la société civile en particulier,
l'action la plus convenable par rapport aux errants est le soin charitable de
les ramener à la vérité par des instructions paisibles et solides.

   Persécuter quelqu'un par un motif de *conscience* deviendrait une espèce
de contradiction. Ce serait renfermer dans l'étendue d'un droit une chose
qui par elle-même détruit le fondement de ce droit. En effet, dans cette
supposition on serait autorisé à forcer les *consciences* en vertu du droit
qu'on a d'agir selon sa *conscience*. [III.903b]

Yet, as we shall see, even such extremely moderate views, expressed in the gentlest and most abstract terms, were to be attacked
by orthodox critics of the *Encyclopédie*.

   In contrast one finds in Deleyre's FANATISME a violent onslaught
on what he defines as

un zèle aveugle et passionné qui naît des opinions superstitieuses et fait
commettre des actions ridicules, injustes et cruelles, non seulement sans
honte et sans remords, mais encore avec une sorte de joie et de consolation.
Le *fanatisme* n'est donc que la superstition mise en action. [VI.393a]

This long and wide-ranging article covers a multitude of different
forms of religious fanaticism:

Comptez maintenant les milliers d'esclaves que le *fanatisme* a faits, soit en
Asie, où l'incirconcision était une tache d'infamie; soit en Afrique, où le
nom de chrétien était un crime; soit en Amérique, où le prétexte
du baptême étouffa l'humanité. Comptez les milliers d'hommes
que le monde a vu périr, ou sur les échafauds dans les siècles de persécution, ou dans les guerres civiles par la main de leurs concitoyens, ou de
leurs propres mains par des macérations excessives. La terre devient un

lieu d'exil, de périls et de larmes. Ses habitants, ennemis d'eux-mêmes et de leurs semblables, vont partager la couche et la nourriture des ours. Tremblant entre l'enfer et le ciel qu'ils n'osent regarder, les cavernes retentissent des gémissements des criminels et du bruit des supplices. [VI.397a]

Toleration is among the virtues preached by the writer:

Un peu de tolérance et de modération! Surtout ne confondez jamais un malheur tel que l'incrédulité avec un crime qui est toujours volontaire. Toute l'amertume du zèle devrait se tourner contre ceux qui croient et n'agissent pas; les incrédules resteraient dans l'oubli qu'ils méritent et qu'ils doivent souhaiter. Punissez à la bonne heure ces libertins qui ne secouent la religion que parce qu'ils sont révoltés contre toute espèce de joug, qui attaquent les mœurs et les lois en secret et en public. Punissez-les parce qu'ils déshonorent et la religion où ils sont nés, et la philosophie dont ils font profession. Poursuivez-les comme les ennemis de l'ordre et de la société; mais plaignez ceux qui regrettent de n'être pas persuadés. Eh, n'est-ce pas une assez grande perte pour eux que celle de la foi, sans qu'on y ajoute la calomnie et les tribulations? Qu'il ne soit donc pas permis à la canaille d'insulter la maison d'un honnête homme à coups de pierre parce qu'il est excommunié. Qu'il jouisse encore de l'eau et du feu, quand on lui a interdit le pain des fidèles. Qu'on ne prive pas son corps de la sépulture, sous prétexte qu'il n'est point mort dans le sein des élus; en un mot, que les tribunaux de la justice puissent servir d'asile au défaut des autels. [VI.400a]

Even this relatively mild conclusion to the onslaught on fanaticism was bitterly attacked by contemporary critics.

Diderot's INTOLÉRANCE which almost certainly grew out of a letter written at the end of 1760 to his own brother, a priest, with whom he was on bad terms,[1] offers an eloquent plea for toleration. It opens quietly, with a series of definitions:

Le mot *intolérance* s'entend communément de cette passion féroce qui porte à haïr et à persécuter ceux qui sont dans l'erreur. Mais pour ne pas confondre des choses fort diverses, il faut distinguer deux sortes d'*intolérance*, l'ecclésiastique et la civile.

L'*intolérance* ecclésiastique consiste à regarder comme fausse toute autre religion que celle que l'on professe et à le démontrer sur les toits, sans être arrêté par aucune terreur, par aucun respect humain, au hasard

[1] Roth, iii, 283–8.

même de perdre la vie. Il ne s'agira point dans cet article de cet héroïsme qui a fait tant de martyrs dans tous les siècles de l'Église.

L'*intolérance* civile consiste à rompre tout commerce et à poursuivre, par toutes sortes de moyens violents, ceux qui ont une façon de penser sur Dieu et sur son culte autre que le nôtre.

Quelques lignes détachées de l'Écriture sainte, des pères, des conciles suffiront pour montrer que l'*intolérant*, pris en ce dernier sens, est un méchant homme, un mauvais chrétien, un sujet dangereux, un mauvais politique et un mauvais citoyen. [VIII.843a]

Diderot next proceeds to lay down certain general principles:

Il est impie d'exposer la religion aux imputations odieuses de tyrannie, de dureté, d'injustice, d'insociabilité, même dans le dessein d'y ramener ceux qui s'en seraient malheureusement écartés.

L'esprit ne peut acquiescer qu'à ce qui lui paraît vrai; le cœur ne peut aimer que ce qui lui semble bon. La violence fera de l'homme un hypocrite, s'il est faible; un martyr, s'il est courageux. Faible ou courageux, il sentira l'injustice de la persécution et s'en indignera.

L'instruction, la persuasion et la prière, voilà les seuls moyens légitimes d'étendre la religion.

Tout moyen qui excite la haine, l'indignation et le mépris, est impie.

Tout moyen qui réveille les passions et qui tient à des vues intéressées, est impie.

Tout moyen qui relâche les liens naturels et éloigne les pères des enfants, les frères des frères, les sœurs des sœurs, est impie.

Tout moyen qui tendrait à soulever les hommes, à armer les nations et tremper la terre de sang, est impie.

Il est impie de vouloir imposer des lois à la conscience, règle universelle des actions. Il faut l'éclairer et non la contraindre.

Les hommes qui se trompent de bonne foi sont à plaindre, jamais à punir.

Il ne faut tourmenter ni les hommes de bonne foi, ni les hommes de mauvaise foi, mais en abandonner le jugement à Dieu.

Si l'on rompt le lien avec celui qu'on appelle impie, on rompra le lien avec celui qu'on appellera avare, impudique, ambitieux, colère, vicieux. On conseillera cette rupture aux autres, et trois ou quatre *intolérants* suffiront pour déchirer toute la société.

Si l'on peut arracher un cheveu à celui qui pense autrement que nous, on pourra disposer de sa tête, parce qu'il n'y a point de limites à l'injustice. Ce sera ou l'intérêt, ou le fanatisme, ou le moment, ou la circonstance qui décidera du plus ou du moins de mal qu'on se permettra.

Si un prince infidèle demandait aux missionnaires d'une religion *intolérante* comment elle en use avec ceux qui n'y croient point, il faudrait ou qu'ils avouassent une chose odieuse, ou qu'ils mentissent, ou qu'ils gardassent un honteux silence. [VIII.843b]

Interlarded with quotations from the Bible and the Fathers come fresh general principles:

Dans un état *intolérant* le prince ne serait qu'un bourreau aux gages du prêtre. Le prince est le père commun de ses sujets; et son apostolat est de les rendre tous heureux.

S'il suffisait de publier une loi pour être en droit de sévir, il n'y aurait point de tyran.

Il y a des circonstances où l'on est aussi fortement persuadé de l'erreur que de la vérité. Cela ne peut être contesté que par celui qui n'a jamais été sincèrement dans l'erreur.

Si votre vérité me proscrit, mon erreur que je prends pour la vérité, vous proscrira.

Cessez d'être violents, ou cessez de reprocher la violence aux païens et aux musulmans. [VIII.844a]

After more quotations comes the eloquent and highly unencyclopedia-like conclusion:

Quelle est la voie de l'humanité? est-ce celle du persécuteur qui frappe ou celle du persécuté qui se plaint?

Si un prince incrédule a un droit incontestable à l'obéissance de son sujet, un sujet mécroyant a un droit incontestable à la protection de son prince. C'est une obligation réciproque.

Si le prince dit que le sujet mécroyant est indigne de vivre, n'est-il pas à craindre que le sujet ne dise que le prince infidèle est indigne de régner? *Intolérants*, hommes de sang, voyez les suites de vos principes et frémissez-en. Hommes que j'aime, quels que soient vos sentiments, c'est pour vous que j'ai recueilli ces pensées que je vous conjure de méditer. Méditez-les et vous abdiquerez un système atroce qui ne convient ni à la droiture de l'esprit ni à la bonté du cœur.

Opérez votre salut. Priez pour le mien, et croyez que tout ce que vous vous permettrez au delà est d'une injustice abominable aux yeux de Dieu et des hommes. [VIII.844b]

With minor changes such was the new year's gift for 1761 which Abbé Diderot received from his infidel brother.

In an earlier volume, in the article *CROISADES, Diderot had penned an indignant attack on the crusades of medieval times. Of the expeditions to the Holy Land he writes scathingly, referring to the pilgrims who on their return endeavoured by their lamentations to stir up the feelings of their fellow-Christians:

On traita longtemps les déclamations de ces bonnes gens avec l'indifférence qu'elles méritaient, et l'on était bien éloigné de croire qu'il viendrait jamais des temps de ténèbres assez profondes, et d'un étourdissement assez grand dans les peuples et dans les souverains sur leurs vrais intérêts, pour entraîner une partie du monde dans une malheureuse petite contrée, afin d'en égorger les habitants et de s'emparer d'une pointe de rocher qui ne valait pas une goutte de sang, qu'ils pouvaient vénérer en esprit de loin comme de près, et dont la possession était si étrangère à l'honneur de la religion. [IV.502b]

Contributors to the *Encyclopédie* were two hundred years nearer than we are to the horrors of the Wars of Religion; and these were still the subject of violent controversy in the years when the work was being compiled. In 1758 a certain Abbé de Caveirac published a *Dissertation sur la journée de la Saint-Barthélemy* along with an *Apologie de Louis XIV et de son conseil sur la révocation de l'édit de Nantes*. These works aroused Diderot's fury in several of his articles which appeared in the last ten volumes, for instance:

*JOURNÉE *de la Saint-Barthélemy* (*Hist. mod.*) C'est cette *journée* à jamais exécrable dont le crime inouï dans le reste des annales du monde, tramé, médité, préparé pendant deux années entières, se consomma dans la capitale de ce royaume, dans la plupart de nos grandes villes, dans le palais même de nos rois, le 24 août 1572, par le massacre de plusieurs milliers d'hommes. . . . Je n'ai pas la force d'en dire davantage. Lorsque Agamemnon vit entrer sa fille dans la forêt où elle devait être immolée, il se couvrit le visage du pan de sa robe. . . . Un homme a osé de nos jours entreprendre l'apologie de cette *journée*. Lecteur, devine quel fut l'état de cet homme de sang; et si son ouvrage te tombe jamais sous la main, dis à Dieu avec moi: O Dieu, garantis-moi d'habiter avec ses pareils sous un même toit. [VIII.898b]

The anonymous author of OBÉISSANCE (*Droit naturel et politique*) in arguing that obedience to a legitimate power must not be blind and must not lead to the violation of the laws of nature, quotes the example of the Vicomte d'Orte's disobedience to the commands of Charles IX on this occasion:

Charles IX, dont la politique inhumaine le détermina à immoler à sa religion ceux de ses sujets qui avaient embrassé les opinions de la Réforme, non content de l'affreux massacre qu'il en fit sous ses yeux et dans sa capitale, envoya des ordres aux gouverneurs des autres villes du royaume pour qu'on exerçât les mêmes cruautés sur ces sectaires infortunés. Le brave d'Orte, commandant à Bayonne, ne crut point que son devoir pût l'engager à obéir à ces ordres sanguinaires. 'J'ai communiqué, dit-il au Roi, le commandement de V.M. à ses fidèles habitants et gens de guerre de la garnison. Je n'y ai trouvé que bons citoyens et braves soldats, mais pas un bourreau. C'est pourquoi eux et moi supplions très humblement V.M. de vouloir employer nos bras et nos vies en choses possibles; quelque hasardeuses qu'elles soient, nous y mettrons jusqu'à la dernière goutte de notre sang.' Le comte de Tende et Charny répondirent à ceux qui leur apportaient les mêmes ordres, qu'ils respectaient trop le roi pour croire que ces ordres inhumains pussent venir de lui. Quel est l'homme vertueux, quel est le chrétien qui puisse blâmer ces sujets généreux d'avoir désobéi? [XI.298a–b]

Diderot and his contributors lived in a France in which the legislation against Protestants which followed the revocation of the Edict of Nantes still obtained, in which pastors were still being hanged and their lay followers sent to the galleys. The *Encyclopédie* condemns the treatment of the Huguenots in the strongest terms. In one of the early volumes one finds, for instance, the following brief, but pungent article by Jaucourt:

DRAGONNADE, s.f. (*Hist. mod.*), nom donné par les calvinistes à l'exécution faite contre eux en France en 1684. Vous trouverez dans l'histoire du *Siècle de Louis XIV* l'origine du mot *dragonnade* et des détails sur cette exécution que la nation condamne unanimement aujourd'hui. En effet toute persécution est contre le but de la bonne politique et, ce qui n'est pas moins important, contre la doctrine, contre la morale de la religion qui ne respire que douceur, que charité, que miséricorde. [V.104b–105a]

The unsigned article, PACIFICATION (*Hist. mod.*), combines a denunciation of the persecution which the Huguenots had suffered with praise of the Enlightenment's attitude to toleration:

Les protestants se sont plaints avec amertume de la révocation de l'édit de Nantes, et leurs plaintes ont été fortifiées de celles de tous les gens de bien catholiques, qui tolèrent d'autant plus volontiers l'attachement d'un protestant à ses opinions qu'ils auraient plus de peine à supporter qu'on les troublât dans la profession des leurs; de celles de tous les philosophes qui savent combien notre façon de penser religieuse dépend peu de nous et qui prêchent sans cesse aux souverains la tolérance générale et aux peuples l'amour et la concorde; de celles de tous les bons politiques qui savent les pertes immenses que l'État a faites par cet édit de révocation qui exila du royaume une infinité de familles et envoya nos ouvriers et nos manufactures chez l'étranger.

Il est certain qu'on viola, à l'égard des protestants, la foi des traités et édits donnés et confirmés par tant de rois; et c'est ce que Bayle démontre sans réplique dans ses *Lettres critiques sur l'Histoire du Calvinisme*. Sans entrer ici dans la question si le prince a droit ou non de ne point tolérer les sectes opposées à la religion dominante dans son état, je dis que celui qui penserait aujourd'hui qu'un prince doit ramener par la force tous ses sujets à la même croyance passerait pour un homme de sang; que, grâce à une infinité de sages écrivains, on a compris que rien n'est plus contraire à la saine religion, à la justice, à la bonne politique et à l'intérêt public que la tyrannie sur les âmes. [XI.736b–737a]

In an unsigned article attributed to Diderot by Naigeon, we find the same point put with equal frankness:

RÉFUGIÉS (*Hist. mod. politiq.*) C'est ainsi que l'on nomme les protestants français que la révocation de l'édit de Nantes a forcés de sortir de France et de chercher un asile dans les pays étrangers afin de se soustraire aux persécutions qu'un zèle aveugle et inconsidéré leur faisait éprouver dans leur patrie. Depuis ce temps la France s'est vue privée d'un grand nombre de citoyens qui ont porté à ses ennemis des arts, des talents et des ressources dont ils ont souvent usé contre elle. Il n'est point de bon Français qui ne gémisse depuis longtemps de la plaie profonde causée au royaume par la perte de tant de sujets utiles. Cependant, à la honte de notre siècle il s'est trouvé de nos jours des hommes assez aveugles ou assez impudents pour justifier aux yeux de la politique et de la raison la plus funeste démarche qu'ait jamais pu entreprendre le conseil d'un souverain.[1] Louis XIV, en persécutant les protestants, a privé son royame de près d'un million d'hommes industrieux qu'il a sacrifiés aux vues intéressées et ambitieuses de quelques mauvais citoyens qui sont les ennemis de toute liberté de penser parce qu'ils ne peuvent régner qu'à l'ombre de l'ignorance. L'esprit persécuteur devrait être réprimé par tout gouvernement éclairé. Si l'on punissait les perturbateurs qui veulent sans cesse

---

[1] Here Diderot was no doubt thinking in particular of Abbé de Caveirac.

troubler les consciences de leurs concitoyens lorsqu'ils diffèrent dans leurs opinions, on verrait toutes les sectes vivre dans une parfaite harmonie et fournir à l'envi des citoyens utiles à la patrie et fidèles à leur prince.

Quelle idée prendre de l'humanité et de la religion des partisans de l'intolérance? Ceux qui croient que la violence peut ébranler la foi des autres, donnent une opinion bien méprisable de leurs sentiments et de leur propre constance. *Voyez* PERSÉCUTION et TOLÉRANCE [XIV.907a]

By the 1760s the notion that it was the affair of the individual to choose what religion (if any) he cared to hold was gaining ground, although it was not until the eve of the Revolution, in 1787, that a very limited degree of toleration was accorded to the Huguenots.

## This attitude to toleration sharply attacked

When the first seven volumes of the *Encyclopédie* appeared in the 1750s its advocacy of religious toleration was very ill received in orthodox Catholic circles. Its plea for toleration was dismissed by its critics as mere *tolérantisme* in the worst sense of the word. 'Vous flétrissez l'indulgence, la tolérance du nom *tolérantisme*, comme si c'était une hérésie', wrote Voltaire in a letter of 1768.[1] The unknown author of the article CHRISTIANISME is castigated in the *Réflexions d'un Franciscain* for declaring that 'l'intolérance du *christianisme* se borne à ne pas admettre dans sa communion ceux qui voudraient lui associer d'autres religions, et non à les persécuter' [III.384b]. Bossuet is brought in to introduce a diatribe against such views with his declaration that all they amount to is to 'cacher l'indifférence des religions sous l'apparence miséricordieuse de la tolérance civile'. The *Réflexions* goes on:

N'est-il pas évident que c'est là le but qu'on se propose lorsqu'on réduit l'intolérance du christianisme à l'excommunication ecclésiastique et qu'on se récrie tant contre la persécution qu'il est si facile d'éviter en n'écrivant ni contre la religion ni contre l'État? Mais n'est-il pas évident aussi que c'est là le grand principe de tous les indifférents, qu'il n'est point d'athée, de matérialiste, de déiste qui ne se contente de la tolérance civile puisque, si elle était accordée, elle procurerait cette liberté tant désirée de tout faire, de tout enseigner. Et qu'importe si l'Église lance ses foudres pourvu que l'État laisse tranquille et ne persécute point!

[1] Best. 13855.

L'Église n'a en main que des armes spirituelles; tout ce qu'elle peut faire, c'est de ne point admettre dans sa communion l'infidèle qui ne la connaît pas ou qui refuse de l'écouter, en retrancher l'opiniâtre qui persévère dans l'erreur qu'elle a proscrite, prononcer des anathèmes, condamner à des peines canoniques. C'est une juridiction à laquelle on peut facilement se soustraire et que l'indifférent ne reconnaît ni ne redoute.

Mais le souverain est le maître de ses états; il a le pouvoir de porter des lois pour faire observer celles de l'Église et de les faire exécuter. Il peut exclure *des arts, des charges, des emplois les plus importants* et condamner à des peines temporelles. C'est ce que l'homme sans religion appelle persécuter, c'est cette autorité réunie avec la force qui l'intimide et qu'il voudrait qu'on ne déployât point contre lui. (pp. 111–13)

This was the attitude against which the *Encyclopédie* was struggling, and not only on the ideological plane; in the France of Louis XV the State *did* tend to back up the Church, to impose religious uniformity by persecuting both the Huguenot minority and all those who manifested any signs of free thought in the matter of religion.

The same work goes on to attack Jaucourt's very mild article, CONSCIENCE (LIBERTÉ DE), for its suggestion that persecution being ruled out, all that can be done with persons who are in error is to 'les ramener à la vérité par des instructions paisibles et solides'. This gives rise to a furious diatribe:

Mais si l'impie continue, n'est-il pas évident que si on le tolère sous le prétexte de ne point faire violence à sa conscience, ce sera autoriser l'impiété, qui, n'étant pas *réprimée*, deviendra elle-même *réprimante*. Mille exemples prouvent qu'alors *la voie de l'instruction* n'est pas l'unique moyen qu'il faille employer; tandis qu'on travaille à convertir un impie ou un hérétique décidé, le mal va toujours en croissant, il force ensuite d'employer les remèdes les plus violents, souvent même il devient incurable. La religion protestante ne doit son établissement, le déisme ses progrès, qu'à la tolérance civile. L'erreur protégée cherche toujours à anéantir la vérité.[1]

Since the article deals with the state of affairs in a country where Christianity (i.e. Roman Catholicism) is the dominant religion, the authors of this attack are scandalized by Jaucourt's suggestion that the rights of conscience should prevent the civil authority from proceeding against unbelievers. They will have none of this

---

[1] Berlin, 1754, pp. 111–13.

pernicious doctrine:

Il sera permis de n'être point chrétien dans le sein même du christianisme et de s'élever contre ses plus saints mystères. Qu'on montre le masque d'une probité païenne, et l'on sera tranquillement tout ce qu'on voudra être—protestant, socinien, déiste, matérialiste, athée. Là conduit la morale de l'*Encyclopédie*.[1]

And that, of course, was sufficient to damn the work completely. This article even had the honour of being denounced in Joly de Fleury's *réquisitoire* before the Paris Parlement in 1759:

Parlent-ils de la conscience? ils en sollicitent la liberté et, par une suite nécessaire, la tolérance universelle. Quelle liberté funeste si on l'accordait à tant de consciences erronées et fanatiques! Parler ainsi, n'est-ce pas du même coup renverser les lois et ouvrir les portes à tous les désordres?[2]

Here we see the union of the secular and the ecclesiastical powers under the *Ancien régime*.

The same passage from CONSCIENCE (LIBERTÉ DE) is also criticized in *La Religion vengée*. The attack is introduced by a characteristic *cri de cœur*:

Liberté, liberté de conscience! voilà, Monsieur, le cri général des consciences erronées. On donne à cette liberté la plus grande étendue; on voudrait que nul homme ne s'intéressât à ce que pense un autre homme, et cela non seulement sur les affaires civiles et politiques, mais encore sur ce qui concerne la religion, la Divinité même. (xii.30)

It is clear that to the writer, even in 1760, this was a revolutionary, indeed an intolerable notion.

Deleyre's long and outspoken article, FANATISME—'un des beaux et des bons articles de l'*Encyclopédie*' Jaucourt was later to declare in giving a cross-reference to it at the end of his SUPERSTI-TION [XV.669b]—received a good deal of hostile attention from contemporary critics of the *Encyclopédie*. Chaumeix, for instance, devotes a dozen pages to denouncing it. He quotes the passage:

Mais quel dut être l'étonnement des païens, continuent les historiens ecclésiastiques, quand ils virent les chrétiens, devenus plus nombreux par la persécution, se déclarer une guerre plus implacable que celle des

---

[1] *Ibid.*, 121.        [2] *Arrêts de la cour de Parlement*, p. 15.

Nérons et des Domitiens, et continuer entre eux les hostilités de ces deux monstres? Au défaut d'autres armes ils s'attaquent d'abord par la calomnie, sans songer qu'on ne se fait point des amis de tous ceux qu'on suscite contre ses ennemis. On accuse les uns d'adorer Caïn et Judas pour s'encourager à la méchanceté : les autres de pétrir des azymes avec le sang des enfants immolés. On reproche à ceux-là des impudicités infâmes, à ceux-ci des commerces diaboliques. Nicolaïtes, Carpocratiens, Montanistes, Adamites, Donatistes, Ariens, tout cela confondu sous le nom de *chrétiens*, donne aux idolâtres la plus mauvaise idée de la religion des saints. [VI.395a]

The meaning of all this, Chaumeix declares, is perfectly plain : 'En vérité, vous ne faites guère d'honneur à la capacité de vos lecteurs. Il n'en est aucun qui ne voie que le vrai sens de vos paroles est qu'il vaut mieux suivre votre façon de penser que la doctrine de la religion chrétienne' (*PL* ii.274).

Another of Deleyre's observations—that one of the sources of fanaticism was the intolerant attitude of one religion to another—produced a nasty outburst from Chaumeix: 'Les encyclopédistes n'aiment pas cette intolérance, ils aiment bien mieux la disposition des pasteurs de Genève.[1] Quand on ne croit rien, on n'est guère intolérant' (*PL* ii.276).

*La Religion vengée* devoted no fewer than thirty pages to a detailed refutation of FANATISME, seeing in it a particularly dangerous article :

... L'impie ... confond malignement le chrétien avec le fanatique. Ceux des encyclopédistes qui ont conspiré contre la religion n'ont pas manqué de saisir ce procédé tortueux; et il paraît que l'auteur de l'article *Fanatisme* n'est pas le moins zélé de toute cette funeste cabale. (xi.237)

However, the most interesting remarks on this article are to be found later in a letter with the revealing title, 'Étranges principes de l'*Encyclopédie* sur la tolérance'. The position of the Roman Catholic church in these matters is made plain :

L'Église romaine est essentiellement intolérante, et nous avons déjà dit plus d'une fois dans quel sens. Elle anathémise tout chrétien qui ne pense pas comme elle ... La communion romaine est un vaste corps qui ne se soutient que par son intolérance. Si elle était tolérante, elle laisserait donc

---

[1] See d'Alembert's account of their beliefs, below, pp. 221–3.

à chacun de ses membres son opinion particulière; et ne serait-ce pas là le vrai moyen de multiplier dans son sein les divisions à l'infini? (xi.314)

This letter is followed by one headed, 'L'intolérance chrétienne est-elle nuisible aux états?' which rebukes d'Alembert for what it calls his 'éloge du tolérantisme' in GENÈVE and then returns to the attack on CHRISTIANISME. Here we find yet another forthright denunciation of the principle of toleration:

Une tolérance universelle ne serait qu'une irréligion universelle, qu'une indifférence absolue sur toutes les religions, couverte du beau prétexte de la charité et du bien de la société. (xi.328)

The twentieth-century reader who ploughs his way through the innumerable articles on toleration in the *Encyclopédie* feels at moments a certain lassitude; all this seems pretty obvious stuff now that the principle is accepted that every man is free to have any or no religious views, according to his individual taste. It is clear, however, from the views of the critics of the *Encyclopédie* set forth here that this was very far from being the case in France in the middle of the eighteenth century, and that the struggle between the *philosophes* and the orthodox was no sham fight.

## The contradictions in the 'Encyclopédie's' attitude to Christianity

If we turn now to examine the attitude of the *Encyclopédie* to Christianity and in particular to the Roman Catholicism in which almost all its contributors had been brought up, we find, as did their contemporaries, a strange medley of articles, some completely orthodox, some outwardly so, and some—often hidden away in obscure corners—the very opposite of orthodox. When in 1757 Voltaire complained to d'Alembert about the excessive orthodoxy of some of the articles on theology and metaphysics, the latter wrote back:

Sans doute nous avons de mauvais articles de théologie et de métaphysique, mais, avec des censeurs théologiens et un privilège, je vous défie de les faire meilleurs. Il y a d'autres articles, moins au jour, où tout est réparé. Le temps fera distinguer ce que nous avons pensé de ce que nous avons dit.[1]

[1] Best. 6624 (21 July 1757).

A contributor like Abbé Mallet produced quite a number of articles which earned praise from Abbé Bergier when he took on the task of dealing with the volumes on theology in the *Encyclopédie méthodique*. In the 1760s and 1770s Bergier was officially entrusted with the refutation of various anti-religious works of the *philosophes*, including the notorious *Système de la Nature*. In the prospectus of the *Encyclopédie méthodique* he lists seven defects in the treatment of theology in the *Encyclopédie*. Two of these are extremely interesting:

6°. Un défaut beaucoup plus répréhensible est l'affectation de prendre dans des auteurs hétérodoxes la notion des dogmes, des lois, des usages de l'Église catholique; de copier leurs déclamations contre les théologiens et contre les pères de l'Église; de disculper les hérésiarques et les incrédules; d'aggraver les torts, vrais ou prétendus, des pasteurs et des écrivains ecclésiastiques. Les articles *Jésus-Christ, Immatérialisme, Pères de l'Église*, etc. sont dans ce cas. Dans plusieurs autres on étale les objections des hérétiques et l'on supprime les réponses des théologiens catholiques.

7°. De ces divers défauts il en est résulté un plus grand: c'est que la doctrine de l'*Encyclopédie* est un tissu de contradictions. Les articles faits par les théologiens, surtout par M. Mallet, sont en général assez bien; les autres, composés par des littérateurs mal instruits ou infidèles, ont été servilement copiés d'après les controversistes protestants ou sociniens.[1]

This section of the *Encyclopédie* was not then entirely worthless in the eyes of a man who was regarded by his contemporaries as a pillar of orthodoxy. At the end of his section of the prospectus Bergier tells the reader:

On se fera une loi de conserver en entier tous les articles qui paraissent bien faits, et ils sont en grand nombre, surtout ceux qui sont de M. Mallet, théologien très instruit, judicieux et modéré. C'est un acte de justice de conserver à un auteur estimable tout l'honneur de son travail.[2]

In a kind of progress report which appeared in 1789 on the publication of this vast new enterprise (it was a very slow business), Bergier even attempted to quantify the work which had to be done to complete the volumes on theology:

D'environ deux mille cinq cents articles dont cet ouvrage est composé, il y en a au moins une moitié qui manquait dans l'ancienne *Encyclopédie* et

[1] *Encyclopédie méthodique ou par ordre de matières* . . . *proposée par souscription*, n.p., 1782, pp. 49–50.
[2] *Ibid.*, p. 51.

qu'il a fallu faire. Un nombre presque égal contenait une doctrine fausse ou suspecte; il fallut les corriger.[1]

Even though Bergier inevitably tends to stress the additions and corrections which had to be made to the theological articles of the *Encyclopédie*, he was very far from rejecting with horror everything which had appeared in its pages on that subject.

Diderot's orthodox contemporaries were not in the least grateful for his insistence that a dictionary of arts and sciences must not leave out theology. Clearly they would much have preferred it to have done so, unless, as was unthinkable with such an obvious reprobate, he had been willing to insert only orthodox Catholic doctrine. The result, as *La Religion vengée* pointed out, was completely chaotic:

... Deux chefs d'encyclopédie qui eussent eu à cœur les intérêts du christianisme, ou se seraient contentés de nous donner un dictionnaire raisonné des sciences et des arts sans parler de religion, ou n'auraient rien admis dans ce dictionnaire qui n'eût été conforme aux principes de la religion. Quand on n'est pas théologien, on ne doit pas se mettre à la tête d'un ouvrage qui traite de théologie. Mais ces messieurs n'ont pas cru que cette loi fût faite pour eux. L'esprit d'erreur et l'esprit de vérité parlent tour à tour dans leur encyclopédie, ce qui en a fait une rapsodie monstrueuse en fait de religion. (xii.117)

The author confesses that he is baffled by the contradictions in the articles on religion:

S'ils n'ont été employés que pour faire illusion, le piège est grossier. Aussi, Monsieur, n'en a-t-il imposé à aucun des lecteurs instruits qui ont eu assez de constance pour suivre cette multitude d'articles et d'y chercher l'*enchaînement* nécessaire dans une encyclopédie. Que n'a-t-on borné celle-ci, sur le fait de la religion, aux excellentes choses qu'elle renferme? (xii.118)

To the very end this problem continued to bother the author. In the last letter devoted to the *Encyclopédie* he asks once again:

Mais pourquoi s'est-on avisé d'en faire un ouvrage théologique? Et si on voulait y traiter ces matières, que ne l'a-t-on fait d'une manière conforme

---

[1] *Encyclopédie méthodique, Mathématiques*, vol. iii, Paris, 1789: *Tableau et aperçu du nombre de volumes de discours et de planches que doit avoir l'Encyclopédie par ordre de matières*, p. 15.

à la doctrine catholique? Ou si le dessein était pris de soutenir les intérêts de l'incrédulité, à quoi bon ces alternatives d'erreur et de vérité, d'irréligion et de christianisme?

To this he returns the obvious answer:

Il est trop évident, Monsieur, que le but des encyclopédistes, je parle des chefs et de quelques-uns de leurs associés ou plutôt de leurs complices, il est, dis-je, trop évident que leur but a moins été de répandre de nouvelles lumières sur les sciences et sur les arts que de saper les fondements de toute religion, surtout de la religion chrétienne. (xii.197–8)

The orthodox articles to be found in the pages of the *Encyclopédie* are too numerous to be examined here; we shall have sufficient to cope with in the large number of articles which reflect the outlook of the Enlightenment.

## The origins of religion

The view of the origins of religion which is generally associated with the *philosophes*—namely, that it was the invention of crafty priests who imposed their ideas on the ignorant and superstitious masses—is to be found in the *Encyclopédie*, particularly in the last ten volumes. We find there, for instance, the article PRÊTRES, long attributed to Diderot, but now restored to its true author, Baron d'Holbach. Here we find a black picture of cunning and cruel priests lording it over the ignorant and terrified masses:

La superstition ayant multiplié les cérémonies des différents cultes, les personnes destinées à les remplir ne tardèrent point à former un ordre séparé qui fut uniquement destiné au service des autels. On crut que ceux qui étaient chargés de soins si importants, se devaient tout entiers à la divinité. Dès lors ils partagèrent avec elle le respect des humains; les occupations du vulgaire parurent au-dessous d'eux, et les peuples se crurent obligés de pourvoir à la subsistance de ceux qui étaient revêtus du plus saint et du plus important des ministères. Ces derniers, renfermés dans l'enceinte de leurs temples, se communiquèrent peu; cela dut augmenter encore le respect qu'on avait pour ces hommes isolés. On s'accoutuma à les regarder comme des favoris des dieux, comme les dépositaires et les interprètes de leurs volontés, comme des médiateurs entre eux et les mortels.

Il est doux de dominer sur ses semblables. Les *prêtres* surent mettre à profit la haute opinion qu'ils avaient fait naître dans l'esprit de leurs concitoyens; ils prétendirent que les dieux se manifestaient à eux; ils annoncèrent leurs décrets; ils enseignèrent des dogmes; ils prescrivirent ce qu'il fallait croire et ce qu'il fallait rejeter; ils fixèrent ce qui plaisait ou déplaisait à la divinité; ils rendirent des oracles; ils prédirent l'avenir à l'homme inquiet et curieux, ils le firent trembler par la crainte des châtiments dont les dieux irrités menaçaient les téméraires qui oseraient douter de leur mission ou discuter leur doctrine.

Pour établir plus sûrement leur empire ils peignirent les dieux comme cruels, vindicatifs, implacables. Ils introduisirent des cérémonies, des initiations, des mystères dont l'atrocité pût nourrir dans les hommes cette sombre mélancolie, si favorable à l'empire du fanatisme. Alors le sang humain coula à grands flots sur les autels; les peuples, subjugués par la crainte et enivrés de superstition, ne crurent jamais payer trop chèrement la bienveillance céleste. [XIII.340b–341a]

These, d'Holbach is careful to point out, were 'les prêtres du paganisme', and he rounds off the article with praise of those enlightened Christian countries which do not know the Inquisition and all its horrors, 'des contrées éclairées par les lumières de la raison et de la philosophie; le *prêtre* n'y oublie jamais qu'il est homme, sujet et citoyen' [XIII,341b]. But earlier in this final paragraph he gives a terrifying picture of the Catholic priesthood, leading up to the Inquisition with its human sacrifices which are the equivalent of those made by pagan priests:

Les peuples eussent été trop heureux si les *prêtres* de l'imposture eussent seuls abusé du pouvoir que leur ministère leur donnait sur les hommes. Malgré la soumission et la douceur si recommandées par l'Évangile, dans des siècles de ténèbres on a vu des *prêtres* du Dieu de paix arborer l'étendard de la révolte, armer les mains des sujets contre leurs souverains, ordonner insolemment aux rois de descendre du trône, s'arroger le droit de rompre les liens sacrés qui unissent les peuples à leurs maîtres, traiter de tyrans les princes qui s'opposaient à leurs entreprises audacieuses, prétendre pour eux-mêmes une indépendance chimérique des lois, faites pour obliger également tous les citoyens. Ces vaines prétentions ont été cimentées quelquefois par des flots de sang; elles se sont établies en raison de l'ignorance des peuples, de la faiblesse des souverains et de l'adresse des *prêtres*. [XIII.341b]

In THÉOCRATIE, another of his articles, to which he gives a cross-reference at the end of PRÊTRES, d'Holbach offers once more a terrifying picture of the power usurped by priests, and again includes an account of the medieval struggle between the spiritual and the temporal powers.

In a series of unsigned articles dealing with religions in various parts of the world which it is reasonable to think were contributed by d'Holbach to the last ten volumes of the *Encyclopédie* we find numerous examples given of the usurpation of political power by priests. Thus in NÉGUS we learn of strange happenings in ancient Ethiopia:

Les anciens rois d'Éthiopie fournissent un exemple frappant de l'abus du pouvoir sacerdotal. Diodore de Sicile nous apprend que les prêtres de Meroe, les plus révérés de toute l'Éthiopie, ordonnaient quelquefois à leurs rois de se tuer eux-mêmes et que ces princes dociles ne manquaient point de se conformer à cet ordre qui leur était signifié de la part des dieux. Le même auteur dit que ce pouvoir exorbitant des prêtres dura jusqu'au règne d'Ergamenes qui, étant un prince guerrier, marcha à la tête d'une armée pour réduire les pontifes impérieux qui avaient fait la loi à ses prédécesseurs. [XI.85a]

The crafty and cruel priests of the Congo are depicted in another unsigned article (this one is certainly by d'Holbach):

NGOMBOS (*Hist. mod. Superstition*), prêtres imposteurs des peuples idolâtres du royaume de Congo en Afrique. On nous les dépeint comme des fripons avides qui ont une infinité de moyens pour tirer des libéralités des peuples superstitieux et crédules. Toutes les calamités publiques et particulières tournent à leur profit, parce qu'ils persuadent aux peuples que ce sont des effets de la colère des dieux que l'on ne peut apaiser que par des sacrifices et surtout par des présents à leurs ministres. Comme ils prétendent être sorciers et devins, on s'adresse à eux pour connaître l'avenir et les choses cachées. Mais une source intarissable de richesses pour les *Ngombos*, c'est qu'ils persuadent aux nègres qu'aucun d'eux ne meurt d'une mort naturelle et qu'elle est due à quelque empoisonnement ou maléfice dont ils veulent bien découvrir les auteurs moyennant une rétribution; et toujours ils font tomber la vengeance sur ceux qui leur ont déplu, quelque innocents qu'ils puissent être. Sur la déclaration du prêtre on saisit le prétendu coupable à qui l'on fait boire un breuvage préparé par le *ngombos* et dans lequel il a eu soin de mêler un poison très vif, qui empêche les innocents de pouvoir se justifier en se tirant de l'épreuve. Les *ngombos* ont au-dessous d'eux des prêtres ordinaires appelés *gangas* qui ne sont que des fripons subalternes. [XI.129a]

The *shamans* of Siberia are depicted in similar dark colours:

CHAMANS, s.m.pl. (*Hist. mod.*) C'est le nom que les habitants de Sibérie donnent à des imposteurs qui chez eux font les fonctions de prêtres, de jongleurs, de sorciers et de médecins. Ces chamans prétendent avoir du crédit sur le diable qu'ils consultent pour savoir l'avenir, pour la guérison des maladies et pour faire des tours qui paraissent surnaturels à un peuple ignorant et superstitieux. Ils se servent pour cela de tambours qu'ils frappent avec force en dansant et tournant avec une rapidité surprenante ; lorsqu'ils se sont aliénés à force de contorsions et de fatigue, ils prétendent que le diable se manifeste à eux quand il est de bonne humeur. Quelque-fois la cérémonie finit par feindre de se percer d'un coup de couteau, ce qui redouble l'étonnement et le respect des spectateurs imbéciles. Ces contorsions sont ordinairement précédées du sacrifice d'un chien ou d'un cheval que l'on mange en buvant force eau-de-vie, et la comédie finit par donner de l'argent au *chaman* qui ne se pique pas plus de désintéressement que les autres imposteurs de la même espèce. [XIV.759b]

A most frightening picture of priestly power and cruelty is given in TOPILZIN, an unsigned article which we definitely know to have been written by d'Holbach:

TOPILZIN, s.m. (*Hist. mod. superstition*). C'est le nom que les Mexicains donnaient à leur grand prêtre ou chef des sacrificateurs. Cette éminente dignité était héréditaire et passait toujours au fils aîné. Sa robe était une tunique rouge, bordée de franges ou de flocons de coton ; il portait sur sa tête une couronne de plumes vertes ou jaunes ; il avait des anneaux d'or enrichis de pierres vertes aux oreilles, et sur ses lèvres il portait un tuyau de pierre d'un bleu d'azur. Son visage était peint d'un noir très épais.

Le *topilzin* avait le privilège d'égorger les victimes humaines que les barbares mexicains immolaient à leurs dieux ; il s'acquittait de cette horrible cérémonie avec un couteau de caillou fort tranchant. Il était assisté dans cette odieuse fonction par cinq autres prêtres subalternes qui tenaient les malheureux que l'on sacrifiait. Ces derniers étaient vêtus de tuniques blanches et noires : ils avaient une chevelure artificielle qui était retenue par des bandes de cuir.

Lorsque le *topilzin* avait arraché le cœur de la victime, il l'offrait au soleil et en frottait le visage de l'idole avec des prières mystérieuses, et l'on précipitait le corps du sacrifié le long des dégrés de l'escalier ; il était mangé par ceux qui l'avaient fait prisonnier à la guerre et qui l'avaient livré à la cruauté des prêtres. Dans de certaines solennités on immolait jusqu'à vingt mille de ces victimes à Mexico.

Lorsque la paix durait trop longtemps au gré des prêtres, le *topilzin* allait trouver l'empereur et lui disait, *Le dieu a faim.* Aussitôt toute la nation prenait les armes et l'on allait faire des captifs pour assouvir la prétendue faim du dieu et la barbarie réelle de ses ministres. [XVI.417b]

It can be imagined that it was not the purpose of such articles to increase respect and affection for the Catholic priesthood of the France of d'Holbach's day, but to show how, in their exploitation of the ignorance and credulity of the masses, they were tarred with the same brush as what d'Holbach prudently called 'les prêtres de l'imposture'.

## The rationalist approach to religion

The rationalist approach to religion of Diderot and many of the principal contributors is clearly marked from the very beginning of the *Encyclopédie*, even though this is often cautiously covered over with a mask of deism by writers who rejected religion in all its forms. One of the articles in the very first volume which gave most offence to the orthodox was on the apparently harmless subject of synonyms in *ADORER, honorer, révérer.* Into it Diderot inserted the following paragraph:

La manière d'*adorer* le vrai Dieu ne doit jamais s'écarter de la raison parce que Dieu est l'auteur de la raison et qu'il a voulu qu'on s'en servît même dans les jugements de ce qu'il convient de faire ou de ne pas faire à son égard. On n'*honorait* peut-être pas les saints, ni on ne *révérait* peut-être pas leurs images et leurs reliques dans les premiers siècles de l'Église comme on a fait depuis, par l'aversion qu'on portait à l'idolâtrie, et la circonspection qu'on avait sur un culte dont le précepte n'était pas assez formel. [I.144b]

This article was attacked in due course by both Chaumeix and *La Religion vengée*, and earlier still by the *Réflexions d'un Franciscain*. The first of the two sentences quoted above gave rise to the obvious comment: 'Le déiste, s'exprimerait-il autrement? Partisan de la seule raison, il croit que la révélation s'en *écarte* et rejette tout culte surnaturel.'[1] As for the second sentence it provoked a series of questions, followed by a general comment which brings out the ideological gulf between the leading *encyclopédistes* and their opponents:

Dans quel siècle n'a-t-on donc pas honoré les saints, révéré leurs images et leurs reliques? Dans quel siècle a-t-on confondu ce culte avec l'idolâtrie? Veut-on donc ici excuser les iconoclastes ou renouveler leur erreur?

. . . Il serait à souhaiter que l'auteur de cet article eût pris autant de soins pour se mettre au fait de la tradition que M. Did . . . a pris pour s'instruire dans les arts mécaniques; il n'ébranlerait pas par un *peut-être* le fondement de notre croyance, qui est celle des premiers siècles de l'Église. Mais telle est la frivolité de quelques savants de notre siècle; ils négligent la science de la Foi et se donnent tout entiers à l'étude de la Nature. Ce serait faire un bon usage de la philosophie de se taire sur ce qu'on ne sait pas.[2]

Jaucourt who, with his Protestant background, probably remained a deist, takes the same rationalist line in SUPERSTITION:

SUPERSTITION (*Métaphys. et Philos.*), tout excès de la religion en général; suivant l'ancien mot du paganisme: 'il faut être pieux et se bien garder de tomber dans la *superstition*'.

En effet, la *superstition* est un culte de religion faux, mal dirigé, plein de vaines terreurs, contraire à la raison et aux saines idées qu'on doit avoir de l'Être suprême. . . . Enfin, c'est le plus terrible fléau de l'humanité. L'athéisme même (c'est tout dire) ne détruit point cependant les sentiments naturels, ne porte aucune atteinte aux lois, ni aux mœurs du peuple; mais la *superstition* est un tyran despotique qui fait tout céder à ses chimères. Ses préjugés sont supérieurs à tous les autres préjugés. Un athée est intéressé à la tranquillité publique par l'amour de son propre repos; mais la *superstition* fanatique, née du trouble de l'imagination, renverse les empires. . . . [XV.669b–670a]

The unsigned article MAGIE, contributed by Polier de Bottens, *premier pasteur de Lausanne*, is full of pride in the scientific achievements of the age which are gradually dispelling ignorance and hence the belief in magic of past centuries:

Mais nous reprenons insensiblement le dessus, et l'on peut dire qu'aux yeux mêmes de la multitude les bornes de cette prétendue *magie* naturelle se rétrécissent tous les jours, parce que, éclairés du flambeau de la philo-

---

[1] *Réflexions d'un Franciscain*, p. 30.     [2] *Ibid.*, pp. 31–3.

sophie, nous faisons tous les jours d'heureuses découvertes dans les secrets de la nature, et que de bons systèmes soutenus par une multitude de belles expériences annoncent à l'humanité de quoi elle peut être capable par elle-même et sans *magie*. Ainsi la boussole, les télescopes, les microscopes, etc. et de nos jours les polypes,[1] l'électricité; dans la chimie, dans la mécanique et la statique les découvertes les plus belles et les plus utiles vont immortaliser notre siècle: et si l'Europe retombait jamais dans la barbarie dont elle est enfin sortie, nous passerons chez de barbares successeurs pour autant de magiciens. [IX.852a]

After showing how in past ages the most absurd remedies relied for their effect on the faith of the patient, the writer brings religion into the picture:

C'est à cette foi qu'on peut et qu'on doit rapporter ces guérisons, si extra-ordinaires dans le récit qu'elles semblent tenir de la *magie*, mais qui, appro-fondies, sont presque toujours des fraudes pieuses ou les suites de cette superstition qui n'a que trop souvent triomphé du bon sens, de la raison et même de la philosophie. Nos préjugés, nos erreurs et nos folies se tiennent toutes par la main. La crainte est fille de l'ignorance; celle-ci a produit la superstition, qui est à son tour la mère du fanatisme, source féconde d'erreurs, d'illusions, de fantômes, d'une imagnination échauffée qui change en lutins, en loups-garous, en revenants, en démons mêmes tout ce qui le heurte. Comment dans cette disposition d'esprit ne pas croire à tous les rêves de la *magie*? Si le fanatisme est pieux et dévot (et c'est presque toujours ce ton sur lequel il est monté), il se croira magicien pour la gloire de Dieu; du moins s'attribuera-t-il l'important privilège de sauver et de damner sans appel. Il n'est pire *magie* que celle des faux dévots. [IX.854a]

This somewhat rambling article certainly throws out some very far-reaching ideas.

In \*IRRÉLIGIEUX Diderot once more puts on the deist mask:

\*IRRÉLIGIEUX, adj. (*Gram.*), qui n'a point de religion, qui manque de respect pour les choses saintes et qui, n'admettant point de Dieu, regarde la piété et les autres vertus qui tiennent à leur existence et à leur culte comme des mots vides de sens.

On n'est *irréligieux* que dans la société dont on est membre; il est certain qu'on ne fera à Paris aucun crime à un mahométan de son mépris pour la loi de Mahomet, ni à Constantinople aucun crime à un chrétien de l'oubli de son culte.

---

[1] Polyps were discovered in 1740 by the naturalist, Abraham Trembley (1700–84).

Il n'en est pas ainsi des principes moraux; ils sont les mêmes partout. L'inobservance en est et en sera répréhensible dans tous les lieux et dans tous les temps. Les peuples sont partagés en différents cultes, religieux ou irréligieux, selon l'endroit de la surface de la terre où ils se transportent ou qu'ils habitent; la morale est la même partout.

C'est la loi universelle que le doigt de Dieu a gravée dans tous les cœurs.

C'est le précepte éternel de la sensibilité et des besoins communs. [VIII.909a]

'Religions vary from country to country, morality is everywhere the same' is an argument used by all the *philosophes*, from deists like Voltaire to more radical thinkers. 'Morality is independent of religion' is another typical *philosophe* doctrine which Diderot sets forth in the second part of the same article:

Il ne faut donc pas confondre l'immoralité et l'irréligion. La moralité peut être sans la religion; et la religion peut être, est même souvent, avec l'immoralité.

Sans étendre ses vues au delà de cette vie, il y a une foule de raisons qui peuvent démontrer à un homme que, pour être heureux dans ce monde, tout bien pesé, il n'y a rien de mieux à faire que d'être vertueux.

Il ne faut que du sens et de l'expérience pour sentir qu'il n'y a aucun vice qui n'entraîne avec lui quelque portion de malheur, et aucune vertu qui ne soit accompagnée de quelque portion de bonheur; qu'il est impossible que le méchant soit tout à fait heureux, et l'homme de bien tout à fait malheureux; et que, malgré l'intérêt et l'attrait du moment, il n'a pourtant qu'une conduite à tenir. [VIII.909a–b]

The same volume of the *Encyclopédie* contains a cheekily ironical article (unsigned, but attributed to Diderot by Naigeon) in which it is suggested that the Sorbonne, the Faculty of Theology, instead of merely censuring the works which it held to be unorthodox or leaving them to be burned by the hangman, might care for a change to republish them with a refutation:

IMPIE, adj. (*Gram.*) . . . Un homme a ses doutes; il les propose au public. Il me semble qu'au lieu de brûler son livre il vaudrait beaucoup mieux l'envoyer en Sorbonne pour qu'on en préparât une édition où l'on verrait, d'un côté les objections de l'auteur, de l'autre les réponses des docteurs. Que nous apprennent une censure qui proscrit, un arrêt qui condamne au feu? rien. Ne serait-ce pas le comble de la témérité que de douter que nos habiles théologiens dispersassent comme la poussière toutes les misérables subtilités du mécréant? Il en serait ramené dans le sein de l'Église, et tous les fidèles édifiés s'en fortifieraient encore dans leur foi. Un homme de goût avait proposé à l'Académie française une occupation bien digne d'elle; c'était de publier, de nos meilleurs auteurs, des éditions où ils remarqueraient toutes les fautes de langue qui leur auraient échappé. J'oserais proposer à la Sorbonne un projet bien digne d'elle et d'une tout autre importance; ce serait de nous donner des éditions de nos hétérodoxes les plus célèbres avec une réfutation, page à page. [VIII.597b]

Besides bringing up once again the denial to the *philosophes* of freedom of the press, the article also insinuates that their criticisms of religion are, because grounded on reason, irrefutable.

## Favourable treatment of unorthodox Christian sects

One thing which particularly annoyed contemporary critics of the *Encyclopédie* was the way in which its editors and several of its contributors gave an impartial or even favourable account of all manner of persons and groups whose religious ideas were unorthodox. For instance, in *CHERCHEURS, despite some ironical concessions to orthodoxy, Diderot aroused criticism with his account of the sect of the Seekers:

*CHERCHEURS, s.m.pl. (*Théolog.*) Hérétiques dont M. Stoup a fait mention dans son traité de *La religion des Hollandais*. Il dit que les *chercheurs* conviennent de la vérité de la religion de Jésus-Christ, mais qu'ils prétendent que cette religion n'est professée dans sa pureté dans aucune église du christianisme; qu'en conséquence ils n'ont pris aucun parti, mais qu'ils lisent sans cesse les Écritures et prient Dieu de les aider à démêler ce que les hommes ont ajouté ou retranché de sa véritable doctrine. Ces *chercheurs* infortunés, selon cette description, seraient précisément dans la religion chrétienne ce que les sceptiques sont en philosophie. L'auteur que nous venons de citer dit que les *chercheurs* ne sont pas rares en Angleterre et qu'ils sont communs en Hollande, deux points sur lesquels il est contredit par Moreri, sans aucun fondement à ce qu'il me semble. L'état de *chercheurs* est une malédiction de Dieu plus ou moins commune à tous les pays, mais très fréquente dans ceux où l'incrédulité n'a pas encore fait les derniers progrès; plus l'incrédulité sera grande, plus le nombre des *chercheurs* sera petit. Ainsi il y aura infiniment moins de ces hérétiques en Angleterre qu'en Hollande. [III.297b]

Fortunately *La Religion vengée* is there to interpret these last lines for us. Combining them with a quotation from Voltaire's FRANÇAIS—'Il y a plus de philosophie dans Paris que dans aucune ville de la terre excepté Londres'—the review declares:

On vient d'assurer, Monsieur, que Londres est de toute la terre la ville où *il y a le plus de philosophie*. On nous dit assez clairement que l'*incrédulité* est *grande* en Angleterre. La conséquence est toute simple: donc, selon l'*Encyclopédie*, l'esprit philosophique est l'*incrédulité*. (*RV* xi.351–2)

It could hardly be said that this was an unfair deduction.

Jaucourt got into trouble with contemporary critics for several of the biographical notices which he inserted under place-names. In FRANCONIE, for instance, he wrote: 'Entre les personnes illustres qu'a produites la Franconie, je ne nommerai que le sage et habile Œcolampade' [VII.287b]. This praise of one of the German reformers annoyed Abbé Saas who retorts:

Pourquoi lui donnent-ils ici l'épithète de *sage*? Est-ce parce qu'il quitta son couvent et apostasia pour se marier?... C'est l'exemple que donna 'le sage et habile Œcolampade' des *encyclopédistes*. Il n'est pas étonnant qu'ils aient loué cet apostat, ils en ont loué plusieurs autres. Ils disent dans l'article FRANÇAIS que 'L'empereur Julien est le premier des princes et des hommes après Marc-Aurèle.'

Messieurs les encyclopédistes règlent les rangs en ce monde. Marc-Aurèle est le premier des princes et des hommes, et Julien le second. Remarquez, Monsieur, qu'il faut que ce soit deux païens qui aient les deux premiers rangs.[1]

Another article of Jaucourt—GALLES (*Pays de*)—is also censured by the Abbé for its praise of Lord Herbert of Cherbury, the seventeenth-century deist, who is described as 'un écrivain très distingué par ses ouvrages' [VII.449b]. After quoting an orthodox attack on Lord Herbert, Saas comments: 'Il faut se défier des écrivains qu'on exalte dans l'*Encyclopédie*.'[2] What aroused most criticism was the eulogy of Pierre Bayle which Jaucourt inserted into his article, FOIX:

Ce comté peut se glorifier d'avoir donné le jour à Bayle. Il naquit à Carla le 8 novembre 1647, et mourut à Rotterdam, la plume à la main, le 28

---

[1] *Lettres sur l'Encyclopédie*, Amsterdam, 1764, pp. 164–5.          [2] *Ibid.*, p. 176.

décembre 1706. Son *Dictionnaire historique* est le premier ouvrage de raisonnement en ce genre où l'on peut apprendre à penser. [VII.42a]

This quotation is given in the anonymous *Lettres sur le VII<sup>e</sup> volume de l'Encyclopédie*, preceded and followed by these sentences:

. . . Lisez surtout à l'article *Foix* l'éloge qu'on y fait d'un des plus déterminés déistes que nous connaissions, car il en existe aujourd'hui de plus méchants encore; et il a des disciples qui font voir qu'il ne leur manque plus que du savoir pour marcher au moins d'un pas égal à côté de ce fameux imposteur . . . Apprendre à penser dans Bayle! chez un homme qui ne pensait rien! car c'est sur ce pied que Bayle est connu, et la chose n'est que trop démontrée pour son honneur et pour celui de ses admirateurs.[1]

The sympathies of a writer like Jaucourt come out only too clearly in these biographical articles.

However, the article on heretics which caused the greatest scandal among those appearing in the first seven volumes was undoubtedly d'Alembert's GENÈVE. If it is chiefly remembered today because it gave rise to Rousseau's *Lettre à M. d'Alembert sur les spectacles* in which he refuted the suggestion that Calvinist Geneva should now be broadminded enough to have a theatre, the section of the letter dealing with religion also led to much controversy at the time. D'Alembert's account of the state of Calvinism in Geneva not only offended the 'Vénérable compagnie des pasteurs'; what is more important from our point of view is the anger which it caused in Catholic France. In denouncing the article *La Religion vengée* rightly stresses its bearing on conditions at home:

Qui ne voit que l'intention de l'auteur est d'opposer à l'unité de la foi catholique cette *noble liberté de penser et d'écrire* qu'il prétend être si glorieuse à M. de Voltaire et aux Genevois? que c'est la France qu'il a principalement en vue lorsqu'il parle de ces pays *où la philosophie n'a pas fait moins de progrès qu'à* Genève, *mais où la verité est encore captive?* (xi. 354–5)

Like the picture of England given in Voltaire's *Lettres philosophiques*, d'Alembert's account of conditions in Geneva was calculated to make the thinking reader institute comparisons with conditions in

---

[1] *Lettres sur le VII<sup>e</sup> volume de l'Encyclopédie*, n.p., 1759, p. 20.

9

France. Nowhere is this more obvious than in his praise of the pastors of Geneva and their doctrines. First, his picture of the clergy:

Les ministres sont ou *pasteurs*, comme nos curés, ou *postulants*, comme nos prêtres sans bénéfice. Le revenu des pasteurs ne va pas au delà de 1200 livres sans aucun casuel; c'est l'État qui le donne, car l'Église n'a rien. Les ministres ne sont reçus qu'à vingt-quatre ans, après des examens qui sont très rigides quant à la science et quant aux mœurs, et dont il serait à souhaiter que la plupart de nos églises catholiques suivissent l'exemple. . . .

Le clergé de *Genève* a des mœurs exemplaires. Les ministres vivent dans une grande union; on ne les voit point, comme dans d'autres pays, disputer entre eux avec aigreur sur des matières inintelligibles, se persécuter mutuellement, s'accuser indécemment auprès des magistrats. [VII.577b]

This leads to a discussion of the doctrines of the pastors:

Il s'en faut cependant beaucoup qu'ils pensent tous de même sur les articles qu'on regarde ailleurs comme les plus importants à la religion. Plusieurs ne croient plus à la divinité de Jésus-Christ, dont Calvin, leur chef, était si zélé défenseur et pour laquelle il fit brûler Servet. [VII.577b–578a]

However, the pastors of today condemn such fanaticism. D'Alembert goes on:

L'enfer, un des points principaux de notre croyance,[1] n'en est pas un aujourd'hui pour plusieurs ministres de *Genève*. Ce serait, selon eux, faire injure à la Divinité d'imaginer que cet Etre plein de bonté et de justice fût capable de punir nos fautes par une éternité de tourments. Ils expliquent le moins mal qu'ils peuvent les passages formels de l'Écriture qui sont contraires à leur opinion, prétendant qu'il ne faut jamais prendre à la lettre dans des Livres saints tout ce qui paraît blesser l'humanité et la raison. . . .

Pour tout dire en un mot, plusieurs pasteurs de *Genève* n'ont d'autre religion qu'un socinianisme parfait, rejetant tout ce qu'on appelle *mystères* et s'imaginant que le premier principe d'une religion véritable est de ne rien proposer à croire qui heurte la raison. Aussi quand on les presse sur la *nécessité* de la révélation, ce dogme si essentiel du christianisme, plusieurs y substituent le terme d'*utilité* qui leur paraît plus doux. . . .

Un clergé qui pense ainsi, doit être tolérant, et l'est assez en effet pour

[1] See the ironical article, *DAMNATION, quoted below, p. 241, and Jaucourt's attack on the doctrine in PEINES, ÉTERNITÉ DES (p. 250).

n'être pas regardé de bon œil par les ministres des autres églises réformées. On peut dire encore, sans prétendre approuver d'ailleurs la religion de *Genève*, qu'il y a peu de pays où les théologiens et les ecclésiastiques soient plus ennemis de la superstition. Mais en récompense, comme l'intolérance et la superstition ne servent qu'à multiplier les incrédules, on se plaint moins à *Genève* qu'ailleurs des progrès de l'incrédulité, ce qui ne doit pas surprendre. La religion y est presque réduite à l'adoration d'un seul Dieu, du moins chez presque tout ce qui n'est pas peuple; le respect pour Jésus-Christ et pour les Écritures sont peut-être la seule chose qui distingue d'un pur déisme le christianisme de *Genève*. [VII. 578a–b]

It will be seen how, like Diderot, the sceptical agnostic d'Alembert writes for public consumption from the standpoint of a deist.

From among the many outraged comments which this article aroused in 1757 we need quote only one, Chaumeix's conclusion to his detailed examination of it: 'Vous ne faites ici un éloge si pompeux de Genève qu'afin de nous tracer l'état de religion que vous pensez être conforme à cette raison dont vous nous vantez partout les avantages; un 'socinianisme parfait': telle est votre croyance' (*PL* ii.182). Though a natural deduction from what d'Alembert wrote in the article, that is, of course, a false conclusion; d'Alembert was merely using his account of the beliefs of the Genevan pastors to cast doubt on orthodox Christian beliefs.

Probably the boldest article on the subject of religion in the last ten volumes is one which we have already encountered in a previous chapter—Naigeon's UNITAIRES which, as we have seen,[1] immediately attracted Voltaire's attention. This long article defines Socinianism as 'un pur déisme assez artificieusement déguisé [XVII.389a]. In expounding its doctrines Naigeon repeatedly makes ironical use of a kind of refrain: 'This is what happens once you cease to accept the infallibility of the Church of Rome.' Thus, after expounding the shocking views of Socinians on the subject of the Church, he continues, tongue in cheek:

C'est par ces arguments et d'autres semblables que les *Sociniens* anéantissent la visibilité, l'indéfectibilité, l'infaillibilité et les autres caractères ou prérogatives de l'Église, la primauté du pape, etc. Tel est le premier pas qu'ils font dans l'erreur; mais ce qui est plus triste pour eux, c'est que ce

---

[1] Chap. 6, p. 164.

premier pas a décidé dans la suite de leur foi. Aussi nous ne croirons pas rendre un service peu important à la religion chrétienne en général et au catholicisme en particulier en faisant voir au lecteur attentif et surtout à ceux qui sont faibles et chancelants dans leur foi, où l'on va se perdre insensiblement lorsqu'on s'écarte une fois de la créance pure et inaltérable de l'Église et qu'on refuse de reconnaître un juge souverain et infaillible des controverses et du vrai sens de l'Écriture. *Voyez* ÉGLISE, PAPE et INFAILLIBILITÉ. [XVII.389b–390a]

Under cover of this specious pretext Naigeon goes on to set out the heretical views of Unitarians. On Original Sin, for instance, they maintain, he declares,

Que la doctrine du péché originel imputé et inhérent est évidemment impie.

Que Moïse n'a jamais enseigné ce dogme, qui fait Dieu injuste et cruel, et qu'on le cherche vainement dans ses écrits.

Que c'est à saint Augustin que l'on doit cette doctrine qu'ils traitent de désolante et de préjudiciable à la religion.

Que c'est lui qui l'a introduite dans le monde où elle avait été inconnue pendant l'espace de 4400 ans; mais que son autorité ne doit pas être préférée à celle de l'Écriture, qui ne dit pas un mot de cette prétendue corruption originelle, ni de ses suites. [XVII.390a]

As for the doctrine of grace, Naigeon continues,

ils demandent pourquoi les chrétiens auraient besoin de ce secours surnaturel pour ordonner leur conduite selon la droite raison, puisque les païens, par leurs propres forces et sans autre règle que la voix de la nature qui se fait entendre à tous les hommes, ont pu être justes, honnêtes, vertueux, et s'avancer dans le chemin du ciel. [XVII.390a]

Predestination is treated with similar scorn by Socinians who hold, says Naigeon,

Qu'il n'y a point en Dieu de décret par lequel il ait prédestiné de toute éternité ceux qui seront sauvés et ceux qui ne le seront pas.

Qu'un tel décret, s'il existait, serait digne du mauvais principe des manichéens.

Ils ne peuvent concevoir qu'un dogme, selon eux, si barbare, si injurieux à la divinité, si révoltant pour la raison, de quelque manière qu'on l'explique, soit admis dans presque toutes les communions chrétiennes, et qu'on y traite hardiment d'impies ceux qui le rejettent et

qui s'en tiennent fermement à ce que la raison et l'Écriture sainement
interprétée leur enseignent à cet égard. [XVII.390b]

Their views on the doctrine of the eternity of hell are introduced
with the usual smug, pseudo-orthodox corrective:

Pour montrer à quel point cette secte hétérodoxe pousse la liberté de penser
et la fureur d'innover en matière de religion, je vais traduire ici trois ou
quatre morceaux de leurs ouvrages sur le sujet en question. Ce sera une
nouvelle confirmation de ce que j'ai dit ci-dessus de la nécessité d'un juge
infaillible de la foi, et en même temps une terrible leçon pour ceux qui ne
voudront pas captiver leur entendement sous l'obéissance de la foi,
*captivantes intellectum ad obsequium fidei,* pour me servir des propres
termes de saint Paul. Mais écoutons nos hérétiques réfractaires.

'Il est certain, disent-ils, que de toutes les idées creuses, de tous les
dogmes absurdes et souvent impies que les théologiens catholiques et
protestants ont avancés comme autant d'oracles célestes, il n'y en a peut-
être point, excepté la Trinité et l'Incarnation, contre lesquels la raison
fournisse de plus fortes et de plus solides objections que contre ceux de la
*résurrection des corps* et l'*éternité des peines.* La première de ces opinions n'est
à la vérité qu'une rêverie extravagante qui ne séduira jamais un bon esprit
quand il n'aurait d'ailleurs aucune teinture de physique expérimentale;
mais la seconde est un blasphème dont tout bon chrétien doit avoir
horreur. Juste ciel! quelle idée faudrait-il avoir de Dieu si cette hypothèse
était seulement vraisemblable? Comment ces âmes de pierre, qui osent
déterminer le degré et la durée des tourments que l'Être suprême infligera,
selon eux, aux pécheurs impénitents, peuvent-ils, sans trembler, annoncer
ce terrible arrêt? De quel droit et à quel titre se donnent-ils ainsi l'exclusion
et s'exemptent-ils des peines dont ils menacent si inhumainement leurs
frères?...' [XVII.391a–b]

From the same source Naigeon claims to derive a purely secular
attitude to morality:

'... Mais comme les termes de *juste* et d'*injuste,* de *vertu* et de *vice* sont des
mots abstraits et métaphysiques absolument inintelligibles si on ne les
applique à des êtres physiques, sensibles, unis ensemble par un acte exprès
ou tacite d'association, il s'ensuit que tout ce qui est utile ou nuisible au
bien général et particulier d'une société, tout ce qui est ordonné ou
défendu par les lois positives de cette société, est pour elle la vraie et
unique mesure du *juste* et de l'*injuste,* de la *vertu* et du *vice,* et par conséquent qu'il n'y a réellement de *bons* et de *méchants,* de *vertueux* et de

*vicieux*, que ceux qui font le bien ou le mal des corps politiques dont ils sont membres et qui en enfreignent ou qui en observent les lois. Il n'y a donc, à parler exactement, aucune *moralité* dans les actions humaines ; ce n'est donc point à Dieu à punir, ni à récompenser, mais aux lois civiles....' [XVII.392a]

Naigeon goes on to summarize with obvious relish the Socinians' objections to the doctrine of the Trinity :

Pour faire connaître leurs sentiments sur ce dogme, il suffit de dire qu'ils soutiennent que rien n'est plus contraire à la droite raison que ce que l'on enseigne parmi les chrétiens touchant la *Trinité* des personnes dans une seule essence divine, dont la seconde est engendrée par la première, et la troisième procède des deux autres.

Que cette doctrine inintelligible ne se trouve dans aucun endroit de l'Écriture.

Qu'on ne peut produire un seul passage qui l'autorise et auquel on ne puisse, sans s'écarter en aucune façon de l'esprit du texte, donner un sens plus clair, plus naturel, plus conforme aux notions communes et aux vérités primitives et immuables.

Que soutenir, comme font leurs adversaires, qu'il y a plusieurs *personnes* distinctes dans l'essence divine et que ce n'est pas l'Éternel qui est le seul vrai Dieu, mais qu'il y faut joindre le Fils et le Saint-Esprit, c'est introduire dans l'église de Jésus-Christ l'erreur la plus grossière et la plus dangereuse, puisque c'est favoriser ouvertement le polythéisme. [XVII.393a]

By their refusal to bow to authority Socinians were committed, Naigeon declares, to rejecting equally the doctrine of the Incarnation :

Non contents d'accommoder l'Écriture à leurs hypothèses, ils soutiennent

Que l'*incarnation* était inutile et qu'avec la foi la plus vive il est impossible d'en voir le *cui bono*.

Ils appliquent à l'envoi que Dieu a fait de son fils pour le salut des hommes, le fameux passage d'Horace :

*Ne Deus intersit, nisi dignus vindice nodus*
*Inciderit.*[1]

Si on leur répond qu'il ne fallait pas moins que le sang d'un Dieu-homme pour expier nos péchés et pour nous racheter, ils demandent pourquoi Dieu a eu besoin de cette *incarnation* et pourquoi, au lieu d'abandonner aux douleurs, à l'ignominie et à la mort son fils Dieu, égal et

---

[1] 'A God must not be introduced unless a difficulty arises worthy of such a deliverer' (*Ars Poetica*, 191–2).

consubstantiel à lui, il n'a pas au contraire changé le cœur de tous les hommes, ou plutôt pourquoi il n'a pas opéré de toute éternité leur sanctification par une seule volition. [XVII.394a]

After the doctrines of the Catholic Church, its clergy next comes under attack. This section of the article is introduced by the usual hypocritical reference to the dreadful consequences which flow from a rejection of authority in the matter of religion, but this time we find an important addition:

... En partant comme eux de la réjection d'une autorité infaillible en matière de foi, et en soumettant toutes les doctrines religieuses au tribunal de la raison, on marche dès ce moment à grands pas vers le déisme; mais, ce qui est plus triste encore, c'est que le déisme n'est lui-même, quoi qu'en puissent dire ses apologistes, qu'une religion inconséquente, et que vouloir s'y arrêter, c'est errer inconséquemment et jeter l'ancre dans les sables mouvants. C'est ce qu'il me serait très facile de démontrer, mais il vaut mieux suivre nos sectaires et achever le tableau de leurs erreurs théologiques. [XVII.394b]

There is a vice, the Socinians allege, from which all Christian states suffer:

Que ce vice est le pouvoir usurpé et par conséquent injuste des ecclésiastiques qui, faisant dans chaque état un corps à part qui a ses lois, ses privilèges, sa police et quelquefois son chef particulier, rompent par cela même cette union de toutes les forces et de toutes les volontés qui doit être le caractère de toute société politique bien constituée, et introduisent réellement deux maîtres au lieu d'un.

The remedy for this state of affairs suggested, according to Naigeon, by the Socinians, is a drastic one:

Que pour ôter aux prêtres l'autorité qu'ils ont usurpée et arracher pour jamais de leurs mains le glaive encore sanglant de la superstition et du fanatisme, le moyen le plus efficace est de bien persuader au peuple,
    Qu'il n'y a aucune religion bonne exclusivement.
    Que le culte le plus agréable à Dieu, si toutefois Dieu en peut exiger des hommes, est l'obéissance aux lois de l'État.
    Que les véritables saints sont les bons citoyens et que les gens sensés n'en reconnaîtront jamais d'autres.

Qu'il n'y a d'impies envers les dieux que les infracteurs du contrat social.[1]

En un mot, qu'il ne doit regarder, respecter et aimer la religion, quelle qu'elle soit, que comme une pure institution de police relative, que le souverain peut modifier, changer et même abolir d'un instant à l'autre, sans que le prétendu salut spirituel des sujets soit pour cela en danger. [XVIII.395b]

It goes without saying that the Socinians are also alleged to demand the abolition of all the privileges and immunities of the clergy as well as of their celibacy.

After producing a long list of the doubts of the Socinians as to the text of the Bible, Naigeon goes on once more to make his usual obeisance to orthodoxy:

Rien n'est plus capable, ce me semble, que cette lecture d'intimider désormais ceux qui se sont éloignés de la communion romaine et qui refusent de reconnaître un juge infaillible de la foi, je ne dis pas dans le pape, car ce serait se déclarer contre les libertés de l'église gallicane, mais dans les conciles généraux présidés par le pape. [XVII.396a]

Yet this did not prevent him, as we have seen, from using the remaining pages of the article to preach materialism in the pages of the *Encyclopédie*.

## Non-Christian religions

Throughout its seventeen volumes large numbers of articles are devoted to a great variety of religions other than Christianity. A great many of these articles had a purpose which went beyond the provision of objective information on religious beliefs, ancient and modern; as critics of the first seven volumes were quick to point out, they were vehicles for more or less veiled attacks on Christian doctrines, rites and ceremonies. One of the underlying ideas of Diderot and like-minded contributors is expressed with brutal frankness in one sentence hidden away in a brief grammatical article in Vol. XI:

ORIGINE, s.f. (*Gram.*) commencement, naissance, germe, principe de quelque chose. L'*origine* des plus grandes maisons a d'abord été fort obscure. Les pratiques religieuses de nos jours ont presque toutes leur *origine* dans le paganisme. . . . [XI.648b]

[1] For a discussion of the political ideas hidden away in this article see Chap. 8, pp. 309–10.

This was, of course, only one of the approaches employed in their articles on these religions; the method of attack on the one orthodox religion of their day was extremely varied. For instance, in his editorial addition to the article AIGLE Diderot passes on from an account of the place of this bird in ancient religion to certain general considerations which, despite their smugly orthodox conclusion, were calculated to stimulate comparisons in the reader's mind:

Il n'y avait qu'à mettre les païens en train quand il fallait honorer leurs dieux; la superstition imagine plutôt les visions les plus extravagantes et les plus grossières que de rester en repos. Ces visions sont ensuite con-sacrées par le temps et la crédulité des peuples; et malheur à celui qui, sans être appelé par Dieu au grand et périlleux état de missionnaire, aimera assez peu son repos et connaîtra assez peu les hommes pour se charger de les instruire. Si vous introduisez un rayon de lumière dans un nid de hiboux, vous ne ferez que blesser leurs yeux et exciter leurs cris. Heureux cent fois le peuple à qui la religion ne propose à croire que des choses vraies, sublimes et saintes, et à imiter que des actions vertueuses; telle est la nôtre, où le philosophe n'a qu'à suivre sa raison pour arriver aux pieds de nos autels. [I.196a–b]

It is quite obvious that in the last sentence Diderot has his tongue in his cheek and that what he is trying to insinuate is that Christian beliefs, which it is dangerous to challenge, are just as irrational and superstitious as those of pagan religions.

In this first volume Diderot also inserted an article, *ASCHA-RIOUNS, which treats of the divided views of various Mohammedan sects on the subject of free will and predestination. The conclusion of the article is highly sceptical in tone:

Au reste, j'observerai que le concours de Dieu, sa providence, sa pres-cience, la prédestination, la liberté occasionnent des disputes et des hérésies partout où il en est question, et que les chrétiens feraient bien, dit M. d'Herbelot dans sa *Bibliothèque orientale*, dans ces questions difficiles de chercher paisiblement à s'instruire, s'il est possible, et de se supporter charitablement dans les occasions où ils sont de sentiments différents. En effet, que savons-nous là-dessus? *Quis consiliarus ejus fuit.*[1] [I.751a]

In this passage, Chaumeix declares, Diderot's aim is to

nous faire douter que nous puissions nous instruire des vérités que la religion nous enseigne. *S'il est possible:* cette expression ne lui est pas

---

[1] 'For who hath known the mind of the Lord? or who hath been his counsellor?' (Romans, 12:34).

échappée, il ajoute cette réflexion: *En effet, que savons-nous là-dessus? Ce que nous savons? Etudiez votre catéchisme et vous l'y verrez!* (*PL* i.81)

In *BELBUCH et ZEOMBUCH (*Myth*.) he touches on Manicheism, a topic which fascinated many eighteenth-century *philosophes*, since the notion that the universe was created and governed by two principles, a good and a bad, deriving as it did from the spectacle of the amount of evil in the world, threw doubt on orthodox Christian beliefs. This doctrine, Diderot argues, is older than the third century A.D. in which Manes lived:

Le manichéisme est un système dont on trouve des traces dans les siècles les plus reculés et chez les nations les plus sauvages; il a la même origine que la métempsycose, les désordres réels ou apparents qui règnent dans l'ordre moral et dans l'ordre physique, que les uns ont attribués à un mauvais génie, et que ceux qui n'admettaient qu'un seul génie ont regardés comme la preuve d'un état à venir, où, selon eux, les choses morales seraient dans une position renversée de celle qu'elles ont. Mais ces deux opinions ont leurs difficultés.

Admettre deux dieux, c'est proprement n'en admettre aucun. *Voyez* MANICHÉISME. Dire que l'ordre des choses subsistant est mauvais en lui-même, c'est donner des soupçons sur l'ordre des choses à venir; car celui qui a pu permettre le désordre une fois, pourrait bien le permettre deux. Il n'y a que la révélation qui puisse nous rassurer, et il n'y a que le christianisme qui jouisse de cette grande prérogative. [II.193b]

The effect of the article taken as a whole is not cancelled out by the last sentence.

In contrast to this article *BRAMINES, after giving an account of the beliefs of this sect, concludes, after an obeisance to orthodox beliefs, with a triumphant affirmation of the progress of the Enlightenment:

Nous pourrions pousser plus loin l'exposition des extravagances de la philosophie et de la religion des *Bramines*, mais leur absurdité, leur nombre et leur durée ne doivent rien avoir d'étonnant; un chrétien y voit l'effet de la colère céleste. Tout se tient dans l'entendement humain; l'obscurité d'une idée se répand sur celles qui l'environnent. Une erreur jette des ténèbres sur des vérités contiguës, et s'il arrive qu'il y ait dans une société des gens intéressés à former, pour ainsi dire, des centres de ténèbres, bientôt le peuple se trouve plongé dans une nuit profonde. Nous n'avons point ce malheur à craindre. Jamais les centres de ténèbres n'ont été plus rares et plus resserrés qu'aujourd'hui; la philosophie s'avance à pas de géant, et la lumière l'accompagne et la suit. [II.394a]

In several articles in these opening volumes Diderot uses an account of pagan miracles to cast discredit on all miracles. *EPIDÉLIUS, for instance, recounts one such miracle only to reject it for obviously insincere reasons:

Quoiqu'il n'y ait guère de faits merveilleux accompagnés d'un plus grand nombre de circonstances difficiles à rejeter en doute; que le miracle dont il s'agit ait un caractère d'authenticité qui n'est pas commun, et qu'il soit confirmé par le témoignage et le monument de tout un peuple, il ne faut pas le croire. Il n'est pas nécessaire d'en exposer les raisons. Il suffit, pour le rejeter, de savoir que le vrai Dieu eût engagé les hommes dans l'idolâtrie s'il eût permis de pareils prodiges. [V.787b–788a]

In dealing with another article on pagan miracles, *CHYTHONIES, a contemporary critic writes: 'L'encyclopédiste veut trouver des prodiges ridicules et indignes de créance, attestés cependant dans les livres des anciens, pour pouvoir se moquer de tous ceux dont ils nous parlent.'[1] More bluntly still, in attacking the unsigned article CHALCÉDOINE (it is almost certainly by Diderot), the same critic declares:

Les événements qui déposent pour la vérité du christianisme, sont odieux à l'encyclopédiste. S'il ne peut les réfuter par des raisons solides, il les tourne en ridicule, il en élude les conséquences; il insinue que les païens avaient aussi des miracles pour établir le culte de leurs idoles; il voudrait faire croire que les miracles du paganisme n'avaient guère moins d'authenticité que les nôtres.[2]

This sums up the point of such articles very accurately.

The same tactics of using accounts of other religions to throw doubt on Christian beliefs and institutions is pursued in a whole series of articles in the last ten volumes, nearly all of them unsigned. One of these—MANES (*Mythologie*), by the Lausanne pastor, Polier de Bottens—has a somewhat unorthodox conclusion:

Au reste il paraît clairement par une multitude d'auteurs que les païens attribuaient aux âmes des défunts des espèces de corps très subtils, de la

[1] Abbé Malleville, *Histoire critique de l'Éclectisme*, vol. i, pp. xxxii–xxxiii.          [2] *Ibid.*, vol. i, p. xxxviii.

nature de l'air, mais cependant organisés et capables des diverses fonctions de la vie humaine, comme voir, parler, entendre, se communiquer, passer d'un lieu à un autre, etc. Il semble même que sans cette supposition nous ayons de la peine à nous tirer des grandes difficultés que l'on fait tous les jours contre les dogmes fondamentaux et consolants de l'immortalité de l'âme et de la résurrection des corps.

Chacun sait que l'idée de corps ou du moins de figures particulières unies aux intelligences célestes, à la divinité même, a été adoptée par ceux des chrétiens qu'on appelle *Anthropomorphites*, parce qu'ils représentaient Dieu sous la figure humaine.

Nous sommes redevables à cette erreur de je ne sais combien de belles peintures du Père Éternel, qui ont immortalisé le pinceau qui les a faites, décorent aujourd'hui plusieurs autels, et servent à soutenir la foi et la piété des fidèles, qui souvent ont besoin de ce secours. [X.17b–18a]

If these last are sentiments which one might expect from a Calvinist (though they were scarcely likely to be popular in Catholic France), the scepticism about the immortality of the soul is not a little surprising.

Another of these articles—IDOLE, IDOLÂTRE, IDOLÂTRIE—came from the pen of the man who transmitted the pastor's articles to the editors of the *Encyclopédie*, Voltaire himself. This article is, of course, an example of Voltaire on his best behaviour, insinuating his point rather than driving it home with hammer-blows. The point of this contribution is to deny that pagan peoples are or were idolatrous and thus to insinuate that if they must be described as such, then so must Roman Catholics. He denies that the pagans worshipped their idols:

De quel œil voyaient-ils donc les statues de leurs fausses divinités dans les temples? Du même œil, s'il était permis de s'exprimer ainsi, que nous voyons les images des vrais objets de notre vénération. L'erreur n'était pas d'adorer un morceau de bois ou de marbre, mais d'adorer une fausse divinité représentée par ce bois et par ce marbre. La différence entre eux et nous n'est pas qu'ils eussent des images et que nous n'en ayons point; qu'ils aient fait des prières devant des images et que nous n'en faisons point. La différence est que leurs images figuraient des êtres fantastiques dans une religion fausse et que les nôtres figurent des êtres réels dans une religion véritable.

. . . Les Romains et les Grecs se mettaient à genoux devant des statues, leur donnaient des couronnes, de l'encens, des fleurs, les promenaient en triomphe dans les places publiques. Nous avons sanctifié ces coutumes, et nous ne sommes point *idolâtres*.

Les femmes en temps de sécheresse portaient les statues des faux dieux après avoir jeûné. Elles marchaient pieds nus, les cheveux épars, et aussitôt il pleuvait à seaux, comme dit ironiquement Pétrone: *et statim urceatim pluebat*. Nous avons consacré cet usage, illégitime chez les gentils et légitime parmi nous. Dans combien de villes ne porte-t-on pas nu-pieds les châsses des saints pour obtenir les bontés de l'Etre suprême? [VIII. 500b–501a]

This is certainly an example of Voltaire at his most tactful, though actually, owing to the enforced delay in the publication of the last ten volumes of the *Encyclopédie*, this article first appeared in print, in 1764, in that scandalous work, the *Dictionnaire philosophique*.

Among the unsigned articles on non-Christian religions in these ten volumes are a number which can be attributed to that bold controversialist, Baron d'Holbach. He too was, of course, on his best behaviour when writing for the *Encyclopédie*. None the less he manages to work into his contributions a considerable number of attacks on the religion he so passionately hated, varying from minor pinpricks to the insinuation of his own atheistic views. Hidden away in two little articles on Japanese religion we find an ironical attack on the warring factions of Jesuits and Jansenists:

XENXUS, s.m. (*Hist. mod. superstit.*) Ce sont des moines du Japon qui professent la religion de Budsdo. Le P. Charlevoix, jésuite, nous apprend que, pour se rendre agréables aux grands, ils ont cherché à rendre la morale facile et à débarrasser la religion de tout ce qu'elle peut avoir de gênant. Ce sont des casuistes relâchés qui décident toujours en faveur des passions . . . [XVII.654b]

XODOXINS, s.m.plur. (*Hist. mod. superstit.*) Ce sont des bonzes ou moines japonais de la secte de Budsdo ou de Siaka, qui suivent littéralement les préceptes de Siaka et qui ont en horreur la morale relâchée des Xenxus. . . . [XVII.656b–657a]

The use of an ancient tongue in the Roman Catholic Church is paralleled by the use of an ancient form of Ethiopian:

LECHONA-GEEZ (*Hist. mod.*) Ce mot signifie *langue savante*. Les Éthiopiens et les Abyssins s'en servent pour désigner la langue dans laquelle sont écrits leurs livres sacrés; elle n'est point entendue par le peuple, étant réservée aux seuls prêtres, qui souvent ne l'entendent pas mieux que les autres. . . . [IX.332b]

A similar ignorance amongst priests in eighteenth-century France is here insinuated. This use by priests of an ancient tongue, incomprehensible to the masses, is referred to in other articles:

PALLI *ou* BALLI (*Hist. mod.*) C'est le nom que les Siamois donnent à une langue savante dans laquelle sont écrits les livres de leur théologie et qui n'est connue que des talapoins ou prêtres siamois. . . . [XI.791a]

The same point is referred to yet again in VÉDA, the article dealing with the ancient Hindu scriptures written in an old form of Sanskrit:

. . . La lecture du *véda* n'est permise qu'aux bramines ou prêtres et aux rajahs ou nobles. Le peuple ne peut pas même le nommer ni faire usage des prières qui y sont contenues, non seulement parce que ce livre contient des mystères incompréhensibles pour le vulgaire, mais encore parce qu'il est écrit dans une langue qui n'est entendue que des prêtres. On prétend même que tous ne l'entendent point, et que c'est tout ce que peuvent faire les plus habiles docteurs d'entre eux. [XVI.868a]

Yet another article institutes an interesting parallel between the powers of the Pope and those of his Japanese counterpart:

SIAKO *ou* XACO (*Hist. mod.*) C'est le nom que l'on donne au Japon au souverain pontife du Budsdoïsme ou de la religion de Siaka. Il est regardé par ceux de la secte comme le vicaire du grand Budsdo ou Siaka. *Voyez l'article qui précède.* Le *siako* a un pouvoir absolu sur tous les ministres de sa religion; c'est lui qui consacre les tundes, dont la dignité répond à celle de nos évêques, mais ils sont nommés par le cubo ou empereur séculier. Il est le chef suprême de tous les ordres monastiques du Budsdoïsme; il décide toutes les questions qui s'élèvent au sujet des livres sacrés, et ses jugements sont regardés comme infaillibles. Le *siako* a, suivant le P. Charlevoix, le droit de canoniser les saints et de leur décerner un culte religieux. On lui attribue le pouvoir d'abréger les peines du purgatoire et même celui de tirer les âmes de l'enfer pour les placer en paradis. [XV. 148a–b]

Most daring of all from this point of view is the article, YPAINA, devoted to a Mexican religious festival in honour of the god,

Vitziliputzli. The full meaning of the relevant part of the article is brought out by a passage in *Le Christianisme dévoilé* in which, in attacking the doctrine of transubstantiation, d'Holbach wrote: 'Les Brames de l'Indostan distribuent du riz dans leurs pagodes; cette distribution se nomme *Prajadam* ou Eucharistie. Les Mexicains croyaient une sorte de transubstantiation. . . . Ainsi les catholiques romains ne sont pas les seuls qui aient donné dans cette extravagance.'[1] YPAINA begins by describing how 'deux jeunes filles, consacrées au service du temple, formaient une pâte composée de miel et de farine de maïs dont on faisait une grande idole que l'on parait d'ornements très riches'. After being taken to a mountain outside Mexico City where a sacrifice was carried out, the idol was brought back to the temple. The article concludes:

Pendant ce temps de jeunes filles formaient avec la même pâte dont l'idole était faite, des masses semblables à des os qu'elles nommaient les *os du dieu Vitzilipuztli*. Les prêtres offraient des victimes sans nombre et bénissaient les morceaux de pâte que l'on distribuait au peuple; chacun les mangeait avec une dévotion merveilleuse, croyant se nourrir réellement de la chair du dieu. On en portrait aux malades, et il n'était point permis de rien boire ou manger avant que de l'avoir consommée. [XVII.676b]

This was one of the numerous passages in the last ten volumes which, disconcertingly, Le Breton failed to strike out.

Another topic on which these unsigned articles several times touched was the atheistic beliefs of various Oriental sects, an indirect form of propaganda for the rejection of religion in all its forms which d'Holbach was soon to advocate so passionately in works like *Le Christianisme dévoilé* and *Le Système de la Nature*. In his account of Indian religions we find the following passage which stresses that rejection of all religion can be combined with high moral standards:

SHARVAKKA (*Hist. mod.*), nom d'une secte de bramines ou de prêtres indiens qui ont des sentiments très peu orthodoxes et conformes à ceux des Épicuriens. Ils ne croient point l'immortalité de l'âme, ni la vie à venir, et ils exigent de leurs adversaires des preuves sensibles et positives que l'on ne peut point trouver dans une fausse religion. Malgré cela on dit que les *sharvakkas* mènent une vie très exemplaire. [XV.140a–b]

---

[1] *Le Christianisme dévoilé*, London, 1767, p. 108n.

Similarly another article deals with a Japanese sect which, despite a vague belief in a Supreme Being, concentrates all its attention on the things of this world:

SIUTO, s.m. (*Hist. mod. relig. et philos.*) C'est le nom sous lequel on désigne au Japon une secte de philosophes qui font profession de ne suivre aucune des religions admises dans cet empire. Ces philosophes font consister la perfection et le souverain bien dans une vie sage et vertueuse. Ils ne reconnaissent point un état futur et prétendent que les bonnes actions et les crimes n'ont point hors de ce monde de récompenses ou de punitions à attendre. L'homme, selon eux, étant doué de la raison, doit vivre conformément aux lumières qu'il a reçues, et par conséquent il est obligé de vivre sagement. Les *siutoïstes* rejettent les chimères de la métempsycose et toutes les divinités ridicules des religions du sintos et de siaka. *Voyez* SINTOS *et* SIAKA. Ils croient que nos âmes, issues d'un esprit universel qui anime toute la nature, après avoir été séparées du corps, retournent dans le sein de ce même esprit, de même que les fleuves, après avoir terminé leur cours, rentrent dans la mer d'où ils tiraient leur origine. [XV.233b]

The aim of such articles as these is clear: to insinuate into the mind of the reader that in the different religions of the world there are men who reject all established beliefs and substitute for faith adherence to a secular moral code which ignores the possibility of any future life.

## Attacks on Christian doctrines

Such indirect methods of propaganda, however, are not by any means the only ones employed by Diderot and his colleagues in dealing with religion. Scattered through the work is a series of straightforward attacks on Christian doctrines, more or less carefully veiled for the most part, but at times brutally frank, a fact which added to the indignation of critics who subjected the first seven volumes to a detailed examination as they appeared. In *CHRONOLOGIE SACRÉE Diderot deals boldly with a question which greatly agitated eighteenth-century thinkers, orthodox and otherwise—the age of the world. After giving a summary of all the conflicting views on this subject, Diderot goes on to state the principles on which his article will be based:

Notre dictionnaire étant particulièrement philosophique, il est également de notre devoir d'indiquer les vérités découvertes et les voies qui pourraient conduire à celles qui sont inconnues. C'est la méthode que nous avons suivie à l'article CANON DES SAINTES ÉCRITURES (*Voyez cet article*),[1] et c'est encore celle que nous allons suivre ici. [III.393a]

In face of the contradictions between the different versions of the Old Testament on the question of the age of the world, Diderot refuses to be disheartened:

. . . Le chrétien n'imite point dans son respect pour les livres qui contiennent les fondements de sa foi la pusillanimité du Juif ou le scrupule du Musulman. Il ose leur appliquer les règles de la critique, soumettre leur *chronologie* aux discussions de la raison, et chercher dans ces occasions la vérité avec toute la liberté possible, sans craindre d'encourir le reproche d'impiété. [III.395a]

It can well be imagined that an article inspired by such principles did not escape the attentions of Chaumeix who very conveniently summarizes it for us:

Dans l'article *Chronologie* les encyclopédistes se sont signalés par les soins qu'ils se sont donnés et les peines qu'ils ont prises pour y entasser toutes les objections et toutes les difficultés qu'ils ont pu trouver dans les autres auteurs, et y en ajouter de leur propre fonds. Il faudrait presque rapporter l'article entier si l'on voulait citer tout ce qu'il y a de répréhensible. Ils commencent d'abord par rapporter ce que les divers peuples ont cru sur la durée du monde et se plaisent à confondre la révélation avec les idées fabuleuses des peuples idolâtres. Ils exagèrent les différences qui se trouvent entre les chronologistes et les différents textes de l'Écriture. Ils passent ensuite au système de l'abbé de Prades en faveur duquel ils rapportent tout ce que l'on peut dire de plus séduisant. Ils proposent ensuite un nouveau système dans lequel ils nous disent qu'ils respectent tous les textes; et ce respect consiste à n'en suivre aucun et à nous insinuer qu'ils sont tous faux. (*PL* ii.134–5)

This is a perfectly fair summary of the contents and purpose of Diderot's article.

There is an important editorial addition to Abbé Mallet's BIBLE. In it Diderot sets forth a detailed plan for a treatise containing what he calls 'tout ce qu'on peut désirer sur les questions préliminaires de la *Bible*' [II.226b]. Though outwardly respectful (indeed it contains an astonishing eulogy of theologians in general and those

[1] This cross-reference will be followed up in due course (see below, pp. 238–9).

of the Sorbonne in particular!), the article sets out a programme which implies a purely secular approach to the study of the Bible and the whole world to which it, historically speaking, belongs. More important still is *CANON, *en Théologie,* which is entirely Diderot's own work; in this he sets out the principles of biblical criticism. The starting-point of the article is described in a few lines:

Le *canon* de la Bible n'a pas été le même en tout temps; il n'a pas été uniforme dans toutes les sociétés qui reconnaissent ce recueil pour un livre divin. Les catholiques romains sont en contestation sur ce point avec les protestants. L'Église chrétienne, outre les livres du Nouveau Testament qu'elle a admis dans son *canon,* en a encore ajouté, dans le *canon* de l'Ancien Testament qu'elle a reçu de l'Église juive, quelques-uns qui n'étaient point dans le *canon* de celle-ci et qu'elle ne reconnaissait point pour des livres divins. [II.601a]

After discussing at length the problems raised in establishing what was the Jewish canon of the Old Testament, Diderot goes on to make another highly significant remark:

Il ne nous reste plus qu'une observation à faire, c'est que le *canon* qui fixe au nombre de vingt-deux les livres divins de l'Ancien Testament a été suivi dans la première Église jusqu'au concile de Carthage; que ce concile augmenta beaucoup ce *canon,* comme il en avait le droit, et que le concile de Trente a encore été au delà du concile de Carthage, prononçant anathème contre ceux qui refuseront de se soumettre à ses décisions. [II.604a]

After this bold thrust comes an unctuous passage which obviously means the exact opposite of what it appears to mean:

D'où il s'ensuit que dans toutes discussions critiques sur ces matières délicates le jugement de l'Église doit toujours aller avant le nôtre, et que dans les occasions où il arriverait que le résultat de nos recherches ne serait pas conforme à ses décrets, nous devons croire que l'erreur est de notre côté. L'autorité que nous avons alors contre nous est d'un si grand poids qu'elle ne nous laisse pas seulement le mérite de la modestie quand nous nous y soumettons, et que nous montrons une vanité impardonnable quand nous balançons à nous soumettre. Tels sont les sentiments dans lesquels j'ai commencé, continué et fini cet article, pour lequel je demande au lecteur un peu d'indulgence; il la doit à la difficulté de la matière et aux soins que j'ai pris pour la discuter comme elle le mérite. [II.604a–b]

Oddly enough, neither this article nor the editorial addition to BIBLE were severely attacked by contemporary critics.

In the last ten volumes there is one striking example of biblical criticism, MAGES (*Théologie*). The authorship of this extremely bold article is a mystery; it has even been suggested that it might be by Voltaire himself, though this seems unlikely as he is not known to have contributed anything to the *Encyclopédie* after the letter I. The article begins thus:

Des quatre évangélistes saint Matthieu est le seul qui fasse mention de l'adoration des *mages* qui vinrent exprès d'Orient, de la fuite de Joseph en Égypte avec sa famille, et du massacre des Innocents qui se fit dans Beth-léem et ses environs par les ordres cruels d'Hérode l'ancien, roi de Judée. Quoique cette autorité suffise pour établir la croyance de ce fait dans l'esprit d'un chrétien. . . ., cependant il y a des difficultés qu'on ne saurait se dissimuler. Tel est le silence des trois autres évangélistes, celui de l'historien Josèphe, sur un événement aussi extraordinaire, et la peine qu'on a d'accorder le récit de saint Luc avec celui de saint Matthieu. [IX.847b]

The author of the article goes into considerable detail to bring out all these 'difficulties'. The effect of this demonstration is not wiped out by the concluding paragraphs of the article which form an extraordinary contrast with the deadly analysis which precedes them. They begin with the unexpected turnabout:

Voilà les difficultés qu'ont fait naître, de la part des anti-chrétiens, la diversité des évangiles sur l'adoration des *mages*, l'apparition de l'étoile, la fuite de Joseph en Égypte et le massacre des Innocents. Que s'ensuit-il? Rien; rien ni sur la vérité de la religion, ni sur la sincérité des historiens sacrés.
Il y a bien de la différence entre la vérité de la religion et la vérité de l'histoire, entre la certitude d'un fait et la sincérité de celui qui le raconte. [IX.849a–b]

And so the article goes on for another half column, filled with unctuous sentiments which are in flat contradiction with the detailed demonstration which has gone before.

Critics of the time were not in fact all that discriminating in their choice of offending articles. One of those most criticized (it was denounced by the *Journal de Trévoux*, the *Réflexions d'un Franciscain*,

and *La Religion vengée* among others) was Abbé Yvon's AMOUR DES
SCIENCES ET DES LETTRES. And all for one sentence: 'La plupart des
hommes honorent les lettres comme la religion et la vertu, c'est-à-
dire, comme une chose qu'ils ne peuvent ni connaître, ni pratiquer,
ni aimer' [I.368b]. Father Berthier set the ball rolling with a long
denunciation of this proposition as 'très irréligieuse'. It was in vain
that the editors pointed out in the *Errata* to Vol. III (pp. xv–xvi)
that the sentence in question came literally and word for word
from Vauvenargues's *Introduction à la connaissance de l'esprit
humain*, published in Paris in 1746 'avec approbation et privilège du
Roi' and favourably reviewed the following January by the said
Father Berthier; critics of the work continued to hammer away at
this particular sentence.

There were after all plenty of more dangerous articles, long and
short, in the first seven volumes for them to get their teeth into.
Diderot furnished his usual quota in short articles or even just in a
passing remark, hidden away in the text. Thus in the dozen or so
lines of *BÉATITUDE, BONHEUR, FÉLICITÉ, which is based on the
*Synonymes français* of Abbé Girard, we find a definition which is
definitely not in the source he was using: 'la *béatitude*, l'état d'une
âme que la présence immédiate de son Dieu remplit dans ce
monde-ci ou dans l'autre; état qui serait au-dessus de toute expression sans doute, si nous le connaissions' [II.169b]. On this *La
Religion vengée* offers the following comment:

Ce n'est pas toujours, Monsieur, par des blasphèmes bien articulés qu'on
attaque la foi. C'est le plus souvent en couvrant le blasphème du voile de
la piété qu'on parvient à séduire la multitude. M. Did... a senti l'effica-
cité de ce moyen et l'a mis en usage dans son article *Béatitude*. (xii.103)

On the other hand a short article of Diderot which strikes at the
very root of Christian doctrine while preserving the appearance of
a most smug orthodoxy, seems to have passed unnoticed by
contemporary critics:

*CAUCASE, s.m. (*Myth. et Géog.*), chaîne de montagnes qui commence au-
dessus de la Colchide et finit à la Mer Caspienne. C'est là que Prométhée
enchaîné eut le foie déchiré par un vautour ou par un aigle. Les habitants
de cette contrée, prenant, si l'on en croit Philostrate, cette fable à la lettre,
faisaient la guerre aux aigles, dénichaient leurs petits et les perçaient avec
des flèches ardentes; ou, l'interprétant, selon Strabon, de la condition

*Forges: Fourneau à fer, Charger (Vol. IV*, Forges, *2e section, Plate VII)*

malheureuse des humains, ils se mettaient en deuil à la naissance des enfants et se réjouissaient à leurs funérailles. Il n'y a point de chrétien vraiment pénétré des vérités de sa religion qui ne dût imiter l'habitant du *Caucase* et se féliciter de la mort de ses enfants. La mort assure à l'enfant qui vient de naître une félicité éternelle, et le sort de l'homme qui paraît avoir vécu le plus saintement est encore incertain. Que notre religion est tout à la fois terrible et consolante! [II.783a]

In another article we even find Diderot defending, though with obvious irony, a doctrine which was meeting with increasing criticism at that moment inside the various Christian churches, that of eternal punishment:

*DAMNATION, s.f. (*Théol.*) peine éternelle de l'enfer. Le dogme de la *damnation* ou des peines éternelles est clairement révélé dans l'Écriture. Il ne s'agit donc plus de chercher par la raison s'il est possible ou non qu'un être fini fasse à Dieu une injure infinie; si l'éternité des peines est ou n'est pas plus contraire à sa bonté que conforme à sa justice; si parce qu'il lui a plu d'attacher une récompense infinie au bien, il a pu ou non attacher un châtiment infini au mal. Au lieu de s'embarrasser dans une suite de raisonnements captieux et propres à ébranler une foi peu affermie, il faut se soumettre à l'autorité des livres saints et aux décisions de l'Église et opérer son salut en tremblant, considérant sans cesse que la grandeur de l'offense est en raison directe de la dignité de l'offensé, et inverse de l'offenseur, et quelle est l'énormité de notre désobéissance puisque celle du premier homme n'a pu être effacée que par le sang du Fils de Dieu. [IV.619b–620a]

This article was left alone by critics of the *Encyclopédie*; yet it is difficult to imagine irony and smug orthodoxy being combined more perfectly to demolish a doctrine.

Even briefer and certainly more direct is a Diderot article from a later volume:

*FUTURITION, s.f. *terme de théologie*. Il se dit d'un effet dont on considère l'événement à venir, relativement à la prescience de Dieu qui voyait en lui-même ou dans les choses cet événement avant qu'il fût. Cette *futurition* a fait dire bien des sottises. Les uns ont prétendu que Dieu voyait les actions libres des hommes avant que d'avoir formé aucun décret sur leur *futurition*. D'autres ont prétendu le contraire; et voilà les questions importantes qui ont allumé entre les chrétiens la fureur de la haine et toutes les suites sanglantes de cette fureur. *Voyez* FORTUIT *et l'article précédent.*[1] [VII.405b]

La *Religion vengée* took offence at this passage; considering that he could only be referring to the clash between Catholics and Calvinists over the question of predestination, the editor asks indignantly: 'Mais quoi? une pareille question n'était-elle donc pas une *question importante*? Que signifie donc ici l'ironie de M. Did . . . ?' Clearly Diderot and he were not on the same wavelength.

Another article which attracted some attention at the time, largely because it appeared in the second volume at the very moment when Abbé de Prades's thesis was condemned and its author compelled to seek refuge in Prussia, was his CERTITUDE for which Diderot furnished both an editorial introduction and an epilogue. It is in practice difficult to share Diderot's enthusiasm for the Abbé's long and rambling contribution in the course of which he seeks to refute the famous sentence in the *Pensées philosophiques* (xlvi): 'Je croirais sans peine un seul honnête homme qui m'annoncerait *que Sa Majesté vient de remporter une victoire complète sur les alliés*; mais tout Paris m'assurerait qu'un mort vient de ressusciter à Passy, que je n'en croirais rien.' Nor is it easy at first sight to see why Diderot in his final note to the article should admit that he had been vanquished in argument by the Abbé. However, a hostile critic of the time—the author of the *Réflexions d'un Franciscain sur les trois premiers volumes de l'Encyclopédie*—throws some light on the problem. After declaring that de Prades's aim was to 'rendre tout incertain et accréditer le scepticisme en feignant de le combattre', he goes on to account for Diderot's modesty:

L'auteur des *Pensées philosophiques* ne persuadera donc point qu'il fait un sacrifice gratuit. L'aveu de la défaite paraît simulé, et on le voit triompher dans le temps même qu'il abandonne la victoire. Ce *sceptique* révoquait en doute la résurrection de Jésus-Christ et portait le *pyrrhonisme* jusqu'à refuser de croire tout Paris qui attesterait qu'un mort reparaît au nombre des vivants. On prouve à la vérité dans l'article *Certitude* que le témoignage d'une ville aussi peuplée que la capitale de la France ne peut être suspect. Mais était-ce là le point réel de la difficulté, et pour croire le miracle faut-il un nombre si prodigieux de témoins oculaires? Le témoignage de douze

---

[1] i.e. FUTUR CONTINGENT which, like FORTUIT, is by d'Alembert (see above, pp. 162–3).

hommes d'une probité reconnue, qui n'ont d'autre intérêt à publier le miracle que celui de la vérité, qui risquent tout en le publiant, qui *se laissent égorger pour le soutenir,* ne suffirait donc pour le rendre certain? Non, dit l'athlète qui se présente pour combattre le *scepticisme, dès qu'il m'est impossible de lire dans leur cœur, je ne suis point assuré de leur probité.* Dès lors les apôtres attestent inutilement qu'ils ont vu plusieurs fois leur divin Maître, qu'ils ont touché sa chair et reconnu sur ses pieds et sur ses mains les cicatrices de ses plaies. Pour établir la foi de sa résurrection il devait se montrer en public, et la réunion de la multitude à publier son triomphe pouvait seule en établir la vérité. C'est tout ce que demandait le *sceptique.* A ce prix il reconnaît son vainqueur, et pour abandonner son doute il attend qu'on lui produise le témoignage exprès de tous les habitants de Jérusalem lorsque Jésus-Christ sortit des liens de la mort. (pp.13–14)

If one has some doubts as to whether this is altogether a fair interpretation of the performance put up by Diderot and the Abbé in this article, it does none the less come from a contemporary writer who was accustomed to reading between the lines.

D'Alembert was not to be left out of this attempt to use the *Encyclopédie* as a vehicle for the Enlightenment's attitude to religion. In addition to GENÈVE, Vol. VII also contains an outspoken article on the century-old controversy between Jansenists and Jesuits, FORMULAIRE. Here he is dealing with what he describes as the 'fameux *formulaire* dont le clergé de France a ordonné la signature en 1661 et par lequel l'on condamne les cinq propositions dites de Jansénius' [VII.183b]. As a *philosophe* he naturally regards this whole controversy as completely futile:

... Que l'Église et l'État aient été bouleversés pour savoir si cinq propositions inintelligibles sont dans un livre que personne ne lit; que des hommes, tels qu'Arnauld, qui auraient pu éclairer le genre humain par leurs écrits, aient consacré leur vie et sacrifié leur repos à ces querelles frivoles; que l'on ait porté la démence jusqu'à s'imaginer que l'Etre suprême ait décidé par des miracles[1] une controverse si digne des temps barbares; c'est, il faut l'avouer, le comble de l'humiliation pour notre siècle. [VII.183b]

The article ends with some advice to governments on their handling of religious controversies. D'Alembert argues that Mazarin blundered in not stifling the dispute at the very beginning:

La faute que ce grand ministre fit en cette occasion, apprend à ceux qui ont l'autorité en main, que les querelles de religion, même les plus futiles, ne

---

[1] The Jansenist miracles performed on the tomb of the *diacre* Pâris in the Cimetière Saint-Médard in 1732.

sont jamais à mépriser; qu'il faut bien se garder de les aigrir par la persécution; que le ridicule dont on peut les couvrir dès leur origine, est le
moyen le plus sûr de les anéantir de bonne heure; qu'on ne saurait surtout
trop favoriser les progrès de l'esprit philosophique qui, en inspirant aux
hommes l'indifférence pour ces frivoles disputes, est le plus ferme appui
de la paix dans la religion et dans l'état et le fondement le plus sûr du
bonheur des hommes. [VII.183b]

It can well be imagined what was the reaction of a rabid Jansenist
like Chaumeix to such an outspoken statement of a *philosophe*'s
attitude of contemptuous indifference to such controversies. It is
true that he was inhibited in the expression of his true feelings by the
so-called 'déclaration de silence', the ban on further discussion of
the controversy over Jansenism imposed by the government of
Louis XV in 1754. Even so, his rage at the haughty manner in
which d'Alembert dismisses the whole theological dispute is plain
enough in these indignant lines:

Quel est le chrétien qui sera satisfait de la manière dont les encyclopédistes traitent ici de ce qu'ils appellent les fanatiques des deux partis et
qu'ils opposent à *ces sages qui rient de ces vaines contestations?* Il n'y a que les
prétendus philosophes qui rient des contestations qui partagent les théologiens, lors surtout qu'elles ont des suites funestes. Le vrai chrétien s'en
afflige. Il désire la paix, il la demande, mais il ne prétend pas l'établir sur
l'indifférence pour les objets de la religion. (*PL* ii.264)

The clash of viewpoints stands out strikingly.

The two editors were not the only contributors to the first seven
volumes to get into trouble with the orthodox. One who was very
severely handled was Faiguet de Villeneuve, 'maître de pension à
Paris'. In the journal, *Le Censeur hebdomadaire*, of which he was for
a short time joint-editor, Chaumeix launched a bitter attack on
Faiguet's CITATION (*Gram.*) in which, in speaking of the abuse of
quotations, this contributor declares that several biblical texts are
given a sinister meaning which nothing in their context justifies:

Je conclus de ces réflexions si simples que le *multi vocati, pauci vero electi*
dont il s'agit, est cité mal à propos dans un sens sinistre et qu'on a tort d'en
tirer des inductions désespérantes, puisqu'enfin ce passage, bien entendu
et déterminé comme il convient par les circonstances de notre parabole,
inspirera toujours moins d'effroi que de confiance en la divine bonté et

qu'il indique tout au plus les divers degrés de béatitude que Dieu prépare dans le ciel à ses *serviteurs*: *erunt novissimi primi, et primi novissimi.* . . .

J'ai aussi un mot à dire sur le fameux *o altitudo* de saint Paul, et je montrerai sans peine que l'on abuse encore de ce passage dans les applications qu'on en fait. On le cite presque toujours en parlant du jugement de Dieu, et il semble que ce soit pour couvrir ce qui paraît trop dur dans le mystère de la prédestination, ou pour calmer les fidèles effrayés des célestes vengeances. Mais ce passage au sens qu'il est cité, loin d'éclairer ou de calmer les esprits, inspire au contraire une frayeur ténébreuse et nous montre un Dieu plus terrible qu'aimable.

. . . Saint Paul . . . , loin de nous annoncer ici la rigueur des jugements de Dieu, nous rappelle au contraire les effets ineffables de sa bonté: *O altitudo divitiarum sapientiae et scientiae Dei!* Le dogme de la prédestination n'a donc rien d'effrayant dans ce passage de saint Paul.

Quoi qu'il en soit, certain prédicateurs, abusant de ces expressions et outrant les vérités évangéliques, n'ont que trop souvent alarmé les consciences et jeté la terreur, le désespoir où ils devaient inspirer au contraire les plus tendres sentiments de la reconnaissance pour le Dieu des miséricordes. Mais, hélas, que ce prétendu zèle, que ce zèle outré a causé de maux! (III.483a)

A dyed-in-the-wool Jansenist like Chaumeix was profoundly shocked at the thought of what deplorable effects such teachings could have on the young:

Que l'on mette en opposition ces principes singuliers de M. *Faiguet* avec ceux des Saints Pères, . . . et que tout le monde ensuite prononce sur l'extravagance inouïe de l'*Encyclopédie*.

Une doctrine telle que la sienne, prêchée à la jeunesse, n'est-elle pas capable de porter dans leur cœur la plus grande dépravation? Quoi donc! ceux même qui se chargent d'instruire cette partie si chère de l'état, osent soutenir de tels dogmes![1]

However, much more ink was spilt in these years of controversy over what was obviously one of the key articles on religion in the early volume—the unsigned CHRISTIANISME. This long contribution, often in the past attributed to Diderot, but certainly not his work, can probably be attributed to one of the *abbés* associated with the *Encyclopédie* in its early stages. It is strangely ambiguous in its standpoint: full at moments of orthodox sentiments, at others giving expression to ideas and comparisons which angered the

[1] *Le Censeur hebdomadaire*, i, 1760, 60.

orthodox. For instance, after producing an enormous list of law-givers from Amasis to Gengis-Khan who are said to have given themselves out to be the mouthpieces of God so as to instil in their people respect for their laws, the article goes on:

Cette conduite des législateurs que nous voyons si constamment soutenue et que nul d'entre eux n'a jamais démentie, nous fait voir évidemment qu'on a cru dans tous les temps que le dogme d'une providence qui se mêle des affaires humaines est le plus puissant frein qu'on puisse donner aux hommes, et que ceux qui regardent la religion comme un ressort inutile dans les états connaissent bien peu la force de son influence sur les esprits. Mais, en faisant descendre du ciel en terre comme d'une machine tous ces dieux pour leur inspirer les lois qu'ils devaient dicter aux hommes, les législateurs nous montrent dans leurs personnes des fourbes et des imposteurs qui pour se rendre utiles au genre humain dans cette vie, ne pensaient guère à le rendre heureux dans une autre. [III.382a]

On this the *Réflexions d'un Franciscain* offers the pointed comment:

Quelques précautions que l'on prenne pour éviter le soupçon d'avoir voulu confondre Jésus-Christ avec ces 'imposteurs qui, pour se rendre utiles au genre humain dans cette vie, ne pensaient guère à le rendre heureux dans l'autre', qu'il nous soit permis d'observer qu'il aurait été plus à propos de ne point entrer à ce sujet dans un si grand détail, surtout dans un siècle où l'impiété conteste la divinité de Jésus-Christ. (p. 95)

One of the most striking passages in the whole article is a spirited defence of Christian ethics:

Ici l'impiété se confond et, ne voyant aucune ressource à attaquer la morale du *christianisme* du côté de sa perfection, elle se retranche à dire que c'est cette perfection même qui le rend nuisible aux états. Elle distille son fiel contre le célibat qu'il conseille à un certain ordre de personnes pour une plus grande perfection; elle ne peut pardonner au juste courroux qu'il témoigne contre le luxe; elle ose même condamner en lui cet esprit de douceur et de modération qui le porte à pardonner, à aimer même ses ennemis; elle ne rougit pas d'avancer que de véritables chrétiens ne formeraient pas un état qui pût subsister; elle ne craint pas de le flétrir en opposant à cet esprit d'intolérance qui le caractérise et qui n'est propre, selon elle, qu'à former des monstres, cet esprit de tolérance qui dominait dans l'ancien paganisme et qui faisait des frères de tous ceux qu'il portait dans son sein. Étrange excès de l'aveuglement de l'esprit humain qui tourne contre la religion même ce qui devrait à jamais la lui rendre respectable! Qui l'eût cru que le *christianisme*, en proposant aux hommes sa sublime morale, aurait un jour à se défendre du reproche de rendre les hommes malheureux dans cette vie pour vouloir les rendre heureux dans l'autre? [II.382b–383a]

While it is true that the author goes on to refute these criticisms of the Christian ethic, he does it in the oddest of fashions, by appealing to the authority of Montesquieu who, after his condemnation by both the Sorbonne and the Holy See, could scarcely be regarded as orthodox. These constant references to 'l'illustre auteur de l'*Esprit des lois*' thoroughly annoyed the critics of the *Encyclopédie*. 'Est-ce sérieusement ou pour se jouer du christianisme', asks the *Réflexions d'un Franciscain* (p. 102), 'qu'on renvoie à de pareilles sources pour y en puiser les principes?' The whole article is decidedly odd in tone and it is certainly not what an orthodox writer of the time would have produced.

Another key article in the first seven volumes was FOI, contributed by Abbé Morellet who had succeeded Mallet as the principal theologian of the *Encyclopédie*. In his *Préjugés légitimes* Chaumeix introduces the new contributor in far from flattering terms:

Si les encyclopédistes, dans les articles que nous venons d'examiner, ont attaqué si ouvertement les mystères de notre religion, ils ont été bien secondés dans cette entreprise par leurs théologiens. Nous les allons voir achever de persuader à leurs lecteurs que la foi n'est pas nécessaire pour être sauvé, selon même les théologiens catholiques. C'est ce que soutient ici et ce qu'entreprend de prouver le nouveau théologien encyclopédique, qui a trouvé le moyen de nous faire regretter l'ancien, quelque mauvais qu'il fût d'ailleurs. (ii.237)

In discussing the problem of the fate of pagans and others to whom the Gospel had never been preached, Morellet had written:

Le dogme de la nécessité de la *foi* ne reçoit donc aucune atteinte de l'opinion de ceux qui disent que des païens et des sauvages se sont sauvés par la *foi*.

Mais, dit-on, ces gens-là ne peuvent pas croire selon ce passage de saint Paul: *Quomodo credent, si non audierunt; quomodo audient, sine predicante?*[1] Ils sont donc sauvés sans la *foi*.

---

[1] 'How shall they believe in him of whom they have not heard? and how shall they hear without a preacher?' (Romans, 10: 14).

Ces théologiens répondent que les païens et les sauvages en question ne peuvent pas croire par les voies ordinaires, mais que rien n'empêche que Dieu n'éclaire leur esprit extraordinairement; que personne ne peut borner la puissance et la bonté de Dieu jusqu'à décider qu'il n'accorde jamais ces secours extraordinaires, et qu'il est bien plus raisonnable de le penser que de s'obstiner à croire que tous ceux à qui l'Évangile n'a pas été prêché et qui sont la plus grande partie du genre humain, périssent éternellement, sans qu'un seul arrive au salut que Dieu veut pourtant accorder à tous. [VII.22b]

This is no problem at all for a fanatical Jansenist like Chaumeix who calmly retorts: 'Quelle difficulté trouvez-vous à ce que la plus grande partie du genre humain périsse éternellement? Le nombre des élus doit-il être celui de la plus grande partie des hommes?' (*PL* ii.239–40). Chaumeix takes exception to several other passages in this article, for instance:

En admettant une fois la doctrine du péché originel et de la nécessité du baptême, et en regardant, comme on le fait, les enfants morts sans le baptême comme déchus du salut éternel, on ne doit pas avoir tant de scrupule pour porter le même jugement des adultes qui auraient observé la loi naturelle, car ces adultes ont toujours cette tache. Ils sont enfants de colère; ils sont dans la masse de perdition; ainsi la difficulté n'est pas plus grande que pour les enfants. Il est vrai que, comme elle n'est pas petite pour les enfants, il serait à souhaiter qu'on n'eût pas encore à la résoudre pour les adultes. [VII.23b]

These last lines were scarcely likely to please Chaumeix who concludes his discussions of FOI with this sweeping condemnation:

Tous les lecteurs sentiront aisément combien est impie cette manière de parler sur les dogmes les plus importants de la religion. M. Morellet fait tous ses efforts pour les combattre et finit par insinuer que le péché originel et la nécessité du baptême sont dans l'Église une doctrine que l'on peut admettre ou nier à son choix. (*PL* ii.244–5)

Morellet's attempt to treat Christian theology 'historiquement et point du tout dogmatiquement' was certainly far from giving satisfaction to this critic.

GRACE (*Théologie*) was another article which displeased Chaumeix; although it is unsigned, he insisted on attributing it to d'Alembert. *La Religion vengée* devotes even more space to its refutation; its section on the subject is entitled 'Indécents propos d'un encyclopédiste sur la grâce'. After setting forth in some detail the conflicting views of theologians, both Catholic and Protestant, the article concludes on a sceptical note which enraged orthodox critics:

D'ailleurs on a tant écrit sur cette matière sans rien éclaircir que nous craindrions de travailler tout aussi inutilement. On peut lire sur ces matières les principaux ouvrages des théologiens des divers partis; les discussions auxquelles ils se sont livrés ne méritent pas de trouver leur place dans un ouvrage philosophique, quelque encyclopédique qu'il soit. [VII.802b]

Chaumeix comments ironically: 'Il est vrai que l'éloge des comédiens, par exemple, figure mieux dans votre encyclopédie que les matières théologiques' (*PL* ii.256). And he goes on: 'L'encyclopédiste en serait resté là s'il n'avait aperçu une occasion d'insulter le docteur de la grâce', a reference to the following tailpiece to the article:

On a donné à saint Augustin le nom de *docteur de la grâce* à cause des ouvrages qu'il a composés sur cette matière. Il paraît qu'effectivement on lui est redevable de beaucoup de lumières sur cet article important, car il assure que Dieu lui avait révélé la doctrine qu'il développe. *Dixi hoc apostolico praecipue testimonio me ipsum fuisse convictum, cum in hac questione solvendi* (comment la foi vient de Dieu)[1] *cum ad episcopum Simplicianum scriberem, revelavit*. S. Augustin, *lib. de praed. sanct. c. iv*. [VII.802b–803a]

*La Religion vengée* comments severely on various passages in the article and then attacks the conclusion:

Vous croiriez d'abord, Monsieur, que l'encyclopédiste se contredit puisque, après avoir avancé qu'on a beaucoup écrit sur la grâce *sans rien éclaircir*, il ne laisse pas d'ajouter qu'on est redevable à saint Augustin de *beaucoup de lumières* sur cet important objet. Mais ce qui suit fait disparaître la contradiction pour ne laisser voir que l'insolence. Cet écrivain tâche d'insinuer que le *docteur de la grâce* n'était qu'un visionnaire. On n'est redevable à saint Augustin d'aucunes lumières sur la grâce puisqu'on n'a jamais rien éclairci sur cette matière: voilà, Monsieur, en dernière analyse le vrai sentiment de l'auteur. (XI.113)

---

[1] 'Cette parenthèse est une ironie impie qu'il a placée là pour faire entendre le cas que l'on doit faire de ce que dit ici saint Augustin' (Chaumeix's footnote).

The offhand way in which this important theological doctrine was dealt with in the *Encyclopédie* was scarcely likely to be pleasing to the orthodox.

Despite Le Breton's efforts at censorship in the last ten volumes of the *Encyclopédie*, some pretty unorthodox views of Christian theology are to be found there. In PEINES, ÉTERNITÉ DES, Jaucourt, fortified by quotations from Tillotson and Samuel Clarke, takes up an unambiguous attitude on this hotly debated question:

Tout homme qui ne consulte que la lumière naturelle et cette idée aussi vraie que brillante d'une bonté infinie qui constitue le principal caractère de la nature divine, ne peut adopter la croyance de l'*éternité des peines*. . . . Cette idée naturelle du souverain Être trouve sa confirmation dans l'Évangile, qui ne cesse de relever la bonté de Dieu sur ses autres attributs. Faire du bien, user de miséricorde, c'est l'occupation favorite de Dieu; châtier, punir, user de rigueur, c'est son œuvre non accoutumée et mal plaisante, dit l'Écriture. Or cette peinture de la bonté de Dieu paraît incompatible avec les *peines* éternelles de l'enfer; c'est pourquoi, dès les premiers siècles de l'Église, plusieurs savants hommes ont cru qu'il ne fallait pas prendre à la lettre les textes de l'Évangile qui parlent de tourments et de supplices sans bornes dans leur durée. Tel a été le sentiment d'Origène, de saint Jérôme et d'autres pères cités dans les *Origeniana* de M. Huet, I.II, *quaest. 11.* [XII.249a]

Jaucourt's SERMON DE JÉSUS-CHRIST attempts to deal with the awkward problem of reconciling the precepts of the Sermon on the Mount with the demands of everyday life in society:

Il importe de nous étendre plus que de coutume sur ce discours de Notre Seigneur parce qu'il renferme plusieurs préceptes qui paraissent impraticables à cause des conséquences qui en résultent nécessairement. . . . Comme on convient que si les chrétiens voulaient observer plusieurs de ces commandements de J.-C., la société serait bientôt renversée, les gens de bien en proie à la violence des méchants, le fidèle exposé à mourir de faim parce qu'il n'aurait rien épargné dans sa prospérité pour se nourrir et se vêtir dans l'adversité. En un mot, tout le monde avoue que les préceptes de N.-S. ne sont pas compatibles[1] avec la sûreté et la tranquillité publiques. [XV.105a–b]

---

[1] The *Encyclopédie* has 'incompatibles'.

The solution which Jaucourt puts forward to this problem is simply that many of these precepts were intended not for all Christians, but only for the Apostles:

Dès qu'on a posé ce principe, que le *sermon de Notre Seigneur* s'adresse à ses apôtres, il n'y a plus aucune difficulté. Tous les préceptes qui semblent choquer la prudence, la justice, ruiner la sûreté publique et jeter le trouble dans la société, tous ces préceptes, dis-je, sont très justes et n'ont plus besoin de limitation ni de restriction. [XV.106a]

It is doubtful whether such a solution would have been acceptable to theologians of that or any other time.

However, in these ten volumes it is once again Diderot who, mainly in unsigned articles, gave bold expression to his attitude on theological questions. Two of these articles—*JUIFS (PHILOSOPHIE DES) and JÉSUS-CHRIST (unsigned)—are long and prominent contributions, and one feels that in them Diderot is weighing his words very carefully so as to insinuate his true ideas without giving himself away entirely. In *JUIFS he naturally takes up an attitude towards the Jews which was current among the *philosophes* and which, quite irrelevantly because the context is wholly different, brings down on them nowadays the charge of antisemitism. Like Voltaire and other *philosophes* Diderot stresses the crudity of the ancient Jews simply for ideological reasons—because their religion was the foundation of the Christianity which he rejected, and to show what a barbarous and uncivilised cradle Christianity had was one method of attacking it:

Personne n'ignore que les *Juifs* n'ont jamais passé pour un peuple savant. Il est certain qu'ils n'avaient aucune teinture des sciences exactes et qu'ils se trompaient grossièrement sur tous les articles qui en dépendent. Pour ce qui regarde la physique et le détail immense qui lui appartient, il n'est pas moins constant qu'ils n'en avaient aucune connaissance, non plus que des diverses parties de l'histoire naturelle. Il faut donc donner ici au mot *philosophie* une signification plus étendue que celle qu'il a ordinairement. [IX.25a]

Scattered through this long article there are typical Diderot touches, for instance:

Quelques chrétiens se sont imaginé que comme les Saducéens niaient les peines et les récompenses de l'autre vie et l'immortalité des âmes, leur doctrine les conduisait à un affreux libertinage. Mais il ne faut pas tirer des conséquences de cette nature, car elles sont souvent fausses. Il y a deux barrières à la corruption humaine, les châtiments de la vie présente et les peines de l'enfer. Les Saducéens avaient abattu la dernière barrière, mais ils laissaient subsister l'autre. Ils ne croyaient ni peine ni récompense pour l'avenir; mais ils admettaient une providence qui punissait le vice et qui récompensait la vertu pendant cette vie. Le désir d'être heureux sur la terre suffisait pour les retenir dans le devoir. Il y a bien des gens qui se mettraient peu en peine de l'éternité s'ils pouvaient être heureux dans cette vie. C'est là le but de leurs travaux et de leurs soins. [IX.31b]

Here we see Diderot's secular attitude to morality peeping through. JÉSUS-CHRIST (*Histoire & Philosophie*)—although unsigned, it is attributed to Diderot by Naigeon—is an extraordinary piece of work. Obviously Diderot had to be very much on his guard in such a prominent article. It opens with the following statement of its aim:

Cette religion, qu'on peut appeler la *Philosophie par excellence*, si l'on veut s'en tenir à la chose sans disputer sur les mots, a beaucoup influé sur la morale et la métaphysique des Anciens pour l'épurer, et la métaphysique et la morale des Anciens sur la religion chrétienne pour la corrompre. C'est sous ce point de vue que nous nous proposons de la considérer. [VIII.516a]

In carrying out this programme Diderot works in a great many reflections of his own which can scarcely be considered orthodox. For instance, like many another *philosophe*, he quotes with satisfaction Tertullian's belief in the corporeal nature of God and the soul:

Nous voici arrivés au temps de Tertullien, ce bouillant Africain qui a plus d'idées que de mots et qui serait peut-être à la tête de tous les docteurs du christianisme s'il eût pu concevoir la distinction des deux substances et ne pas se faire un Dieu et une âme corporels. Ses expressions ne sont point équivoques. *Quis negabit*, dit-il, *Deum corpus esse, et si spiritus sit?* [VIII. 518a]

The letter of Synesius to his brother is quoted from with obvious approval:

Il est difficile, il est impossible de chasser de son esprit des opinions qui y sont entrées par la voie de la raison, et que la force de la démonstration y retient; et vous n'ignorez pas qu'en plusieurs points la philosophie ne s'accorde ni avec nos dogmes, ni avec nos décrets. Jamais, mon frère, je ne me persuaderai que l'origine de l'âme soit postérieure au corps; je ne prendrai jamais sur moi de dire que ce monde et ses autres parties puissent passer en même temps. J'ai une façon de penser qui n'est point celle du vulgaire, et il y a, dans cette doctrine usée et rebattue de la résurrection, je ne sais quoi de ténébreux et de sacré que je ne saurais digérer. [VIII.519a]

The article takes the reader down to the Middle Ages and the cult of Aristotle. Its last sentences are filled with sentiments, boldly expressed, which are typical of a *philosophe*:

L'aristotélisme s'étendit peu à peu, et ce fut la philosophie régnante pendant le XIII$^e$ et le XIV$^e$ siècles entiers. Elle prit alors le nom de scolastique. *Voyez* SCOLASTIQUE, *Philosophie*. C'est à ce moment qu'il faut aussi rapporter l'origine du droit canonique, dont les premiers fondements avaient été jetés dans le cours du XII$^e$ siècle. Du droit canonique, de la théologie scolastique et de la philosophie, mêlés ensemble, il naquit une espèce de monstre qui subsiste encore et qui n'expirera pas sitôt. [VIII.521a]

Once again we may ask: where was Le Breton's blue pencil?

In these last ten volumes it is, however, mainly in more out-of-the-way articles that Christian doctrines and beliefs are challenged. Asceticism is violently attacked in this unsigned article:

MACÉRATION (*Morale. Gram.*) C'est une douleur corporelle qu'on se procure dans l'intention de plaire à la Divinité. Les hommes ont partout des peines, et ils ont très naturellement conclu que les douleurs des êtres sensibles donnaient un spectacle agréable à Dieu. Cette triste superstition a été répandue et l'est encore dans beaucoup de pays du monde.

Si l'esprit de *macération* est presque toujours un effet de la crainte et de l'ignorance des vrais attributs de la Divinité, il a d'autres causes, surtout dans ceux qui cherchent à le répandre. La plupart sont des charlatans qui veulent en imposer au people par de l'extraordinaire.

Le bonze, le talapoin, le marabout, le derviche, le fakir, pour la plupart, se livrent à différentes sortes de supplices par vanité et par ambition. Ils ont encore d'autres motifs. Le jeune fakir se tient debout, les bras en croix, se poudre de fiente de vache et va tout nu; mais les femmes vont lui faire dévotement des caresses indécentes. Plus d'une femme à Rome, en voyant la procession du jubilé monter à genoux la *scala santa*, a remarqué que certain flagellant était bien fait et avait la peau belle.

Les moyens de se macérer les plus ordinaires dans quelques religions sont le jeûne, les étrivières et la malpropreté.

Le caractère de la *macération* est partout cruel, petit, pusillanime.

La mortification consiste plus dans la privation des plaisirs ; la *macération* s'impose des peines. On mortifie ses sens parce qu'on leur refuse ; on macère son corps parce qu'on le déchire ; on mortifie son esprit, on macère son corps ; il y a cependant la *macération* de l'âme ; elle consiste à se détacher des affections qu'inspirent la nature et l'état de l'homme dans la société. [IX.790b–791a]

In another unsigned article the doctrine of the small number of the Elect is attacked:

PROMISSION, s.f. (*Gram.*) Il ne se dit guère que du pays que Dieu promit à Abraham et à sa postérité. De tous les Hébreux qui sortirent d'Égypte, il n'y eut que Josué et Caleb qui entrèrent dans la terre de *promission*.

Il y a des chrétiens d'une doctrine affreuse qui ont comparé ce monde à l'Égypte, les Hébreux partant pour la terre *promise* à la multitude de ceux qui vont à la vie[1] éternelle, et Josué et Caleb au petit nombre de ceux à qui elle est accordée. Ou il n'y a point de doctrine impie, ou celle-là l'est ; ce n'est pas sous l'aspect d'un bon père, mais sous celui d'un tyran inhumain, qu'elle nous montre Dieu. Elle anéantit le mérite de l'incarnation et de la passion de Jésus-Christ. Ce sera donc pour deux hommes que son sang aura été versé sur la terre, tandis que cent mille se seront perdus, en unissant leurs voix et en criant, *Tolle, tolle, crucifige.* [XIII.446b]

This attack on Jansenism is to be compared with an article in which Diderot deals sceptically with the clash between Jansenists and Jesuits:

RIGORISME, s.m. (*Gram.*), profession de la morale chrétienne ou de la morale en général dans toute sa rigueur. La plupart des fondateurs de religions, de sociétés, de sectes, de monastères, ont destiné leurs institutions à un grand nombre d'hommes, quelquefois à toute la terre, tandis qu'elles ne pouvaient convenir qu'au petit nombre de ceux qui leur ressemblaient. D'où il est arrivé à la longue qu'elles sont devenues impraticables pour ceux-ci, et il s'en est suivi la division en deux bandes, l'une de rigoristes et l'autre de relâchés. Il n'y a guère qu'une morale ordinaire et commune qui puisse être pratiquée et suivie constamment par la multitude. Il y a et il y aura dans tout établissement, dans toute profession théologique, monastique, philosophique et morale, du jansénisme et du molinisme ; cela est nécessaire. [XIV.290b]

[1] The *Encyclopédie* has 'ville'.

To Chambers's article SOCIETY FOR PROPAGATING THE GOSPEL IN
FOREIGN PARTS Diderot adds the following paragraph in his
PROPAGATION DE L'ÉVANGILE in which he combines an implicit condemnation of missionary activity with yet another plea for religious
toleration:

Nous avons dans notre royaume plusieurs établissements de cette nature,
des missionnaires en titre et d'autres qui font la même fonction par un
beau et louable zèle d'étendre une religion hors du sein de laquelle ils sont
persuadés qu'il n'y a point de salut. Mais un point important que ces
dignes imitateurs des Apôtres devraient bien concevoir, c'est que leur
profession suppose dans les peuples qu'ils vont prêcher, un esprit de
tolérance qui leur permette d'annoncer des dogmes contraires au culte
national, sans qu'on se croie en droit de les regarder comme perturbateurs
de la tranquillité publique et autorisé à les punir de mort ou de prison.
Sans quoi ils seraient forcés de convenir de la folie de leur état et de la
sagesse de leurs persécuteurs. Pourquoi donc ont-ils si rarement eux-
mêmes une vertu dont ils ont si grand besoin dans les autres? [XIII.459b]

If there is no definite proof that unsigned articles like MACÉRA-
TION, PROMISSION and PROPAGATION DE L'ÉVANGILE came from
Diderot's pen, we can attribute RIGORISME to him on Naigeon's
authority along with a brief, but very significant article the irony
of which is obvious:

RESSUSCITER, v.act. (*Gram.*), revenir à la vie. Jésus-Christ a *ressuscité* le
Lazare. Lui-même est *ressuscité*. Il y a des *résurrections* dans toutes les
religions du monde, mais il n'y a que celles du christianisme qui soient
vraies; toutes les autres, sans exception, sont fausses . . . *Voyez* RÉSURREC-
TION. [XIV.193a]

The unctuous conclusion does not wipe out the force of 'Il y a des
*résurrections* dans toutes les religions du monde'.

It can well be imagined that casuistry was a subject which
Diderot did not fail to deal with in the *Encyclopédie*. There is, first,
the short article, *CAS DE CONSCIENCE (*Morale*) with its ironical
definition:

Qu'est-ce qu'un *cas de conscience*? C'est une question relative aux devoirs
de l'homme et du chrétien dont il appartient au théologien appelé
*casuiste* de peser la nature et les circonstances et de décider selon la

lumière de la raison, les lois de la société, les canons de l'Église et les maximes de l'Évangile, quatre grandes autorités qui ne peuvent jamais être en contradiction. *Voyez* CASUISTE. [II.738b]

Following up the cross-reference, we find in *CASUISTE a defence of his suggestion in *AIUS-LOCUTIUS that unorthodox works should be permitted provided they are published in learned tongues. This gives him an opportunity to point to the unfortunate consequences of Pascal's exposure of Jesuit laxity in the *Lettres provinciales*:

. . . Je ne sais s'il faut approuver la plaisanterie éloquente et redoutable de Pascal et le zèle peut-être indiscret avec lequel d'autres auteurs, d'ailleurs très habiles et très respectables, poursuivirent vers le milieu du siècle dernier la morale relâchée de quelques *casuistes* obscurs. Ils ne s'aperçurent pas sans doute que les principes de ces *casuistes* recueillis en un corps et exposés *en langue vulgaire* ne manqueraient pas d'enhardir les passions, toujours disposées à s'appuyer de l'autorité la plus frêle. Le monde ignorait qu'on eût osé enseigner *qu'il est quelquefois permis de mentir, de voler, de calomnier, d'assassiner pour une pomme, etc.* Quelle nécessité de l'en instruire? Le scandale que la délation de ces maximes occasionna dans l'Église fut un mal plus grand que celui qu'auraient jamais fait des volumes poudreux relégués dans les ténèbres de quelques bibliothèques monastiques.

En effet, qui connaissait Villalobos, Connink, Llamas, Achokier, Dealkoser, Squilanti, Bizozeri, Iribarne, de Grassalis, de Pitigianis, Strevesdorf et tant d'autres, qu'on prendrait à leurs noms et à leurs opinions pour des Algériens? [II.757a]

This article was far from commending itself to the orthodox.

One of the boldest articles in the opening volumes of the *Encyclopédie* is *CHAOS. Here Diderot touches on the ticklish question of the creation. The last paragraph opens with the hypocritical statement: 'Il ne faut, dans aucun système de physique, contredire les vérités primordiales de la religion que la *Genèse* nous enseigne' [III.159a]. He continues, however, in terms which end by flatly contradicting this principle:

2° qu'il ne doit être permis aux philosophes de faire des hypothèses que dans les choses sur lesquelles la *Genèse* ne s'explique pas clairement; 3° que par conséquent on aurait tort d'accuser d'impiété, comme l'ont fait quelques zélés de nos jours, un physicien qui soutiendrait que la terre a été couverte autrefois par des eaux différentes de celles du déluge. Il ne faut

lire que le premier chapitre de la *Genèse* pour voir combien cette hypothèse est soutenable. . . . 4° que les saintes Écritures, ayant été faites, non
pour nous instruire des sciences profanes et de la physique, mais des
vérités de foi que nous devons croire et des vertus que nous devons
pratiquer, il n'y a aucun danger à se montrer indulgent sur le reste,
surtout lorsqu'on ne contredit point la révélation. . . . 5° que si quelques
savants ont cru et croient encore qu'au lieu de *creavit* dans le premier
verset de la *Genèse* il faut lire, suivant l'hébreu, *formavit, disposuit*, cette
idée n'a rien d'hétérodoxe quand même on ferait exister le *chaos* longtemps avant la formation de l'univers; bien entendu qu'on le regardera
toujours comme créé et qu'on ne s'avisera pas de conclure du *formavit,
disposuit* de l'hébreu que Moïse a cru la matière nécessaire. Ce serait lui
faire dire une absurdité dont il était bien éloigne, lui qui ne cesse de nous
répéter que Dieu a fait de rien toutes choses; ce serait supposer que l'Écriture, inspirée tout entière par l'Esprit Saint, quoique écrite par différentes
mains, a contredit grossièrement, dès le premier verset, ce qu'elle nous
enseigne en mille autres endroits avec autant d'élévation que de vérité,
*qu'il n'y a que Dieu qui soit;* 6° qu'en prenant les précautions précédentes,
on peut dire du *chaos* tout ce qu'on voudra. [III.159a–b]

Though the *Journal des Savants* singled out this article for special
praise,[1] it was attacked, one feels not unfairly, by Chaumeix.
After quoting the passage at the beginning of the fifth section
printed above, he goes on: 'C'est-à-dire en deux mots que, selon
l'hébreu, le premier verset de la Genèse ne dit pas que Dieu a créé le
monde et que tout le récit de Moïse n'est pas différent de ce
qu'Ovide nous débite au premier livre de ses *Métamorphoses*' (*PL*
ii.120). He refuses to accept the view of the Bible and science taken
up by Diderot who in the fourth section of the passage quoted
above had put forward a hypothesis which, he declared, 'concilie
les Écritures avec la bonne physique'. This rouses Chaumeix to one
of his furious outbursts:

Vous croyez donc qu'il est difficile de concilier les Écritures avec la bonne
physique; et moi, je vous dis que la bonne physique est celle qui s'accorde
avec les Écritures, puisqu'elles ne peuvent être fausses et qu'ainsi elles
doivent servir à distinguer la physique qui est bonne d'avec celle qui ne l'est
pas. (*PL* ii.121)

The gulf which separated the attitude to science of a *philosophe* and
that of the orthodox could scarcely be more clearly revealed.

[1] August 1754, p. 558.

## *Attacks on the Catholic Church and its clergy*

The attack on the institutions of the Church and its clergy is obviously much more direct than that on its doctrines. One contributor whose articles in this field in the early volumes aroused a considerable amount of criticism was Faiguet de Villeneuve. DIMANCHE, ÉPARGNE and FÊTES DES CHRÉTIENS were all blacklisted by the orthodox for their secular spirit. In the first of these articles the author argues that the poorer classes of society ought to be allowed to devote part of Sunday to work in order to augment their meagre earnings:

. . . L'artisan, le manouvrier qui, en travaillant, ne vit d'ordinaire qu'à demi, peut employer partie du *dimanche* à des opérations utiles, tant pour éviter le désordre et les folles dépenses que pour être en état de fournir aux besoins d'une famille languissante et d'éloigner de lui, s'il le peut, la disette et la misère, maladies trop communes en Europe, surtout parmi nous. [IV.1008b]

He also suggests that part of Sunday might be used for such minor public works as improving local roads:

Je crois donc qu'un curé intelligent, un gentilhomme et toute autre personne de poids et de mérite en chaque village pourraient, sans s'éloigner des vues de la religion, se mettre en quelque sorte à la tête de ces petits travaux, et qu'ainsi l'on pourrait engager tous les habitants de la campagne à se procurer par un travail mutuel et légitime la facilité des voyages et des charrois et tant d'autres commodités publiques dont ils sont communément dépourvus. [IV.1009b]

Abbé Saas was unfavourably impressed by this secular attitude to the sabbath: 'Voilà les curés', he exclaimed, 'bien dispensés de dire vêpres les fêtes et les dimanches, et les paroissiens d'y assister.'[1]

FÊTES DES CHRÉTIENS attacks, like a well-known fable of La Fontaine, the excessive number of Church festivals. Here the author is not only echoing a widely held feeling, but was even close to government policy. Colbert had reduced their number in the diocese of Paris, and a royal decree of 1778 was to cut out even

[1] *Lettres sur l'Encyclopédie*, p. 81.

more. Their excessive number, Faiguet argues, is contrary to the national interest:

Il est visible que si nous travaillons davantage, nous augmenterons par cela même la quantité de nos biens; et cette augmentation sera plus sensible encore si nous faisons beaucoup moins de dépense. Or je trouve qu'en diminuant le nombre des *fêtes*, on remplirait tout à la fois ces deux objets, puisque multipliant par là les jours ouvrables et par conséquent les produits ordinaires du travail, on multiplierait à proportion toutes les espèces de biens, et de plus on sauverait des dépenses considérables qui sont une suite naturelle de nos *fêtes*. [VI.565a]

He suggests that the number should be reduced to five—Easter Monday, Ascension Day, the Assumption, All Saints Day and Christmas Day—and that the rest should be celebrated on Sundays. Once again these proposals were displeasing to Abbé Saas who exclaims ironically: 'Quel dommage que ce prétendu législateur n'ait aucune autorité ni dans l'Église ni dans l'État.'[1]

Amongst the economies suggested by Faiguet in ÉPARGNE were some which concerned religion. In addition to demanding the suppression of most Church festivals, he suggests for instance, the abolition of the hiring of seats in church and of the custom of distributing blessed bread on the occasion of a solemn mass. This again annoyed Abbé Saas. 'Je prie ces messieurs', he wrote, 'de considérer que sans en avoir le dessein ils s'approchent un peu trop des protestants par l'épargne qu'ils proposent.'[2] PAIN BÉNIT (*Hist. ecclés.*), an unsigned article in the last ten volumes which can be attributed to Diderot with a fair degree of certainty, takes up one of Faiguet's points. After entering into large-scale calculations of the amount wasted on blessed bread and on church candles, the article concludes eloquently:

Que de biens plus importants à faire, plus dignes des imitateurs de Jésus-Christ! Combien de malheureux estropiés, infirmes, sans secours et sans consolation! Combien de pauvres honteux sans fortune et sans emploi! Combien de pauvres ménages accablés d'enfants! Combien enfin de misérables de toute espèce et dont le soulagement devrait être le grand objet de la commisération chrétienne! objet par conséquent auquel nous devrions consacrer tant de sommes que nous prodiguons ailleurs sans fruit et sans nécessité. [XV.751b]

[1] *Ibid.*, p. 135.          [2] *Ibid.*, p. 106.

Here the *philosophe*'s ideal of *bienfaisance* (the word occurs in the article) is opposed to the extravagance of Church ceremonies.

It can well be imagined that religious orders receive unfavourable treatment in the *Encyclopédie*. Not that the contributors, including Diderot himself, do not on occasion speak well of certain orders which are praised for their learning. Take, for instance, this editorial addition to BLANCS-MANTEAUX:

Cette maison est aujourd'hui remplie de religieux très savants et d'un grand mérite, auteurs d'ouvrages fort estimables et fort utiles, comme l'*Art de vérifier les dates*, qui a été si bien reçu du public, *La nouvelle Diplomatique*, la collection des *Historiens de France* etc. Nous saisissons avec plaisir cette occasion de célébrer leurs talents et leurs travaux. [II.271b–272a]

However the general climate of opinion in the world outside was unfavourable to such institutions, and here the contributors could let themselves go and express freely their hatred of this way of life. In such articles as MONASTÈRE, ORDRE RELIGIEUX, RELIGIEUX and RELIGIEUSE, for instance, Jaucourt brings together all the usual arguments advanced by the *philosophes*. In MONASTÈRE (*Hist. ecclésiastiq.*), after conceding the usefulness of such institutions in earlier ages, he goes on:

Cependant, comme les choses ont entièrement changé de face en Europe depuis la renaissance des lettres et l'établissement de la réformation, le nombre prodigieux de *monastères* qui a continué de subsister dans l'église catholique, est devenu à charge au public, oppressif, et procurant manifestement la dépopulation; il suffit pour s'en convaincre de jeter un coup d'œil sur les pays protestants et catholiques. Le commerce ranime tout chez les uns, et les *monastères* portent partout la mort chez les autres. [X.638a]

The economic argument is pressed further in a reference to the dissolution of the monasteries in England (most of what follows is taken from the *Esprit des lois*):

Henri VIII, voulant réformer l'église d'Angleterre, détruisit tous les *monastères* parce que, les moines y pratiquant l'hospitalité, une infinité de gens oisifs, gentilshommes et bourgeois, y trouvaient leur subsistance, et passaient leur vie à courir de couvent en couvent. Depuis ce changement l'esprit de commerce et d'industrie s'est établi dans la Grande-Bretagne et les revenus de l'État en ont singulièrement profité. En général, toute nation qui a converti les *monastères* à l'usage public, y a beaucoup gagné, humainement parlant, sans que personne y ait perdu. [X.638b]

Diderot's contribution in this field was very varied. He was undoubtedly responsible for the short grammatical article:

*HUÉE, s.f. (*Gram.*), cri d'improbation de la multitude. Un mauvais poète se fait huer au théâtre. On hue un mauvais acteur, une mauvaise actrice. On hue dans les rues un prêtre ou un moine qui sort d'un mauvais lieu. [VIII.332b]

Into the same category falls another unsigned article which finds an echo in two of his letters to Sophie Volland and in a famous passage in *Jacques le fataliste*:

PASSAGER, adj. (*Gram.*), qui passe vite, qui ne dure qu'un instant. Les joies de ce monde sont *passagères*. C'est une ferveur *passagère* qui tient quelque-fois à l'ennui d'un tempérament qui fait effort pour se développer dans l'un et dans l'autre sexe, ou qui, s'étant développé, porte à de nouveaux besoins dont on ignore l'objet ou qu'on ne saurait satisfaire, qui entraîne tant de jeunes et malheureuses victimes de leur inexpérience au fond des cloîtres où elles se croient appelées par la grâce et où elles ne rencontrent que la douleur et le désespoir. [XII.122a]

Among the articles which first saw the light of day in 1765 was the long and fierce indictment of the order to which, like many other *philosophes*, Diderot owed his schooling. JÉSUITE is full of passages of great rhetorical power, such as:

Soumis au despotisme le plus excessif dans leurs maisons, les *Jésuites* en sont les fauteurs les plus abjects dans l'état. Ils prêchent aux sujets une obéissance sans réserve pour leurs souverains; aux rois, l'indépendance des lois et l'obéissance au pape; ils accordent au pape l'infaillibilité et la domination universelle afin que, maîtres d'un seul, ils soient maîtres de tous. [VIII.513a]

Or again, explaining why the Society has managed to survive so long:

C'est qu'on a vu en même temps dans le même corps la raison assise à côté du fanatisme, la vertu à côté du vice, la religion à côté de l'impiété, le rigorisme à côté du relâchement, la science à côté de l'ignorance, l'esprit de retraite à côté de l'esprit de cabale et d'intrigue, tous les contrastes réunis. Il n'y a que l'humilité qui n'a jamais pu trouver un asile parmi ces hommes. [VIII.515a]

Obviously none of the passionate eloquence which we find in this article could have been poured forth anywhere in the first seven volumes of the *Encyclopédie*; it was written after the fall of the Jesuits, after their suppression by the Paris Parlement in August 1762. This is brought out in the mild ending with its prophecy of their return:

Ce n'est ni par haine, ni par ressentiment contre les *Jésuites* que j'ai écrit ces choses. Mon but a été de justifier le gouvernement qui les a abandonnés, les magistrats qui en ont fait justice, et d'apprendre aux religieux de cet ordre qui tenteront un jour de se rétablir dans ce royaume, s'ils y réussissent, comme je le crois, à quelles conditions ils peuvent espérer de s'y maintenir. [VIII.516a]

Clearly so outspoken an article was altogether exceptional.

Much more characteristic of the approach which Diderot and other contributors to the *Encyclopédie* were compelled to adopt in these matters was that to be found in *CÉLIBAT which appeared in the second volume. Here Diderot begins by giving a history of celibacy, following a work by a contemporary scholar. At the end of his summary we find the following passage:

Tout ce qui précède n'est absolument que l'analyse de ce mémoire; nous en avons retranché quelques endroits longs, mais à peine nous sommes-nous accordé la liberté de changer une seule expression dans ce que nous en avons employé. Il en sera de même dans la suite de cet article; nous ne prenons rien sur nous, nous nous contenterons seulement de rapporter fidèlement, non seulement les opinions, mais les discours mêmes des auteurs et de ne puiser ici que dans les sources approuvées de tous les honnêtes gens. [II.803b]

In handling such a ticklish subject it was necessary to hide behind other writers; for the section of the article which discusses whether priests should be allowed freedom to marry he relies above all on one of the innumerable writings of Abbé de Saint-Pierre. Diderot ends with a listing of the sources used in the article and with this sentence:

Malgré ces autorités je ne serais pas étonné qu'il trouvât des critiques et des contradicteurs; mais il pourrait arriver aussi que, de même qu'au concile de Trente ce furent, à ce qu'on dit, les jeunes ecclésiastiques qui rejetèrent le plus opiniâtrément la proposition du mariage des prêtres, ce soient ceux d'entre les *célibataires* qui ont le plus besoin de femmes et qui ont le moins lu les auteurs que je viens de citer, qui en blâmeront le plus hautement les principes. [II.806b]

Diderot was right to anticipate criticism. The *Réflexions d'un Franciscain* devoted a long chapter (pp. 40–76) to an attack on this article, and in due course *La Religion vengée* followed suit.

Damilaville's article POPULATION denounces the celibacy of the Catholic clergy as contrary to the increase in population in extremely brutal terms, despite the rather cautious use of the term 'Les cultes européens' in the opening sentence:

Les cultes européens lui sont encore plus contraires. Leur doctrine porte les hommes à s'isoler, elle les éloigne des devoirs de la vie civile. Chez eux l'état le plus parfait est le plus opposé à la nature et le plus préjudiciable au bien public; c'est le célibat. Une multitude d'êtres des deux sexes vont ensevelir avec eux dans des retraites des postérités perdues, sans compter les ministres de la religion et les rigoristes qui font vœu d'être inutiles à la propagation; et cette abstinence est dans ces religions la vertu par excellence. Comme si le plus grand des vices n'était pas de tromper la nature et de subsister aux dépens de l'espèce envers laquelle on ne remplit aucune de ses obligations! Un homme dont personne ne contestera la vertu, les bonnes mœurs et les lumières, l'abbé de ∗∗∗∗, fortement touché des obligations de la nature, avait consacré un des jours de la semaine à la propagation. [XIII.93a]

The tone of this paragraph is certainly in marked contrast to that of ∗CELIBAT.

Amongst the outspoken articles which d'Alembert produced for Vol. VII was a series of attacks on religious orders, in FRATRI-CELLES, FRÈRES LAIS and especially FRÈRES DE LA CHARITÉ. This last article in particular provoked several angry retorts because of its brutally secular attitude, summed up in the concluding declaration that the best way to honour God, 'c'est de nous rendre le plus utiles

qu'il est possible à la société dans laquelle il nous a placés' [VII. 301b].
After praising this particular order for its services in nursing the
poor, d'Alembert goes on to ask whether this is not after all the
only useful task which members of religious orders are qualified to
carry out:

En effet, à quel autre travail pourrait-on les appliquer? A remplir les
fonctions du ministère évangelique? Mais les prêtres séculiers, destinés
par état à ce ministère, ne sont déjà que trop nombreux, et par bien des
raisons doivent être plus propres à cette fonction que les moines. Ils sont
plus à portée de connaître les vices et les besoins des hommes; ils ont
moins de maîtres, moins de préjugés de corps, moins d'intérêt de communauté et d'esprit de parti. Appliquera-t-on les religieux à l'instruction
de la jeunesse? Mais ces mêmes préjugés de corps, ces mêmes intérêts de
communauté ou parti, ne doivent-ils pas faire craindre que l'éducation
qu'ils donneront ne soit ou dangereuse, ou tout au moins puérile; qu'elle
ne serve même quelquefois à ces religieux de moyen de gouverner, ou
d'instrument d'ambition, auquel cas ils seraient plus nuisibles que nécessaires? Les moines s'occuperont-ils à écrire? Mais dans quel genre?
L'histoire? L'âme de l'histoire est la vérité; et des hommes si chargés
d'entraves doivent être presque toujours mal à leur aise pour la dire,
souvent réduits à la taire, et quelquefois forcés de la déguiser. L'éloquence
et la poésie latine? Le latin est une langue morte qu'aucun moderne n'est en
état d'écrire, et nous avons assez en ce genre de Cicéron, de Virgile,
d'Horace, de Tacite et des autres. Les matières de goût? Ces matières,
pour être traitées avec succès, demandent le commerce du monde,
commerce interdit aux religieux. La philosophie? Elle veut de la liberté,
et les religieux n'en ont point. Les hautes sciences, comme la géométrie,
la physique, etc.? Elles exigent un esprit tout entier et par conséquent ne
peuvent être cultivées que faiblement par des personnes vouées à la
prière. Aussi les hommes *du premier ordre* en ce genre, les Boyle, les Descartes, les Viète, les Newton etc., ne sont point sortis des cloîtres. Reste
les matières d'érudition. Ce sont celles auxquelles la vie sédentaire des
religieux les rend plus propres, qui demandent d'ailleurs le moins d'application et souffrent les distractions plus aisément. Ce sont aussi celles où les
religieux peuvent le mieux réussir et où ils ont en effet réussi le mieux.
Cette occupation, quoique fort inférieure pour des religieux au soulagement des malades et au travail des mains, est au moins plus utile que la vie
de ces reclus obscurs absolument perdus pour la société. Il est vrai que ces
derniers religieux paraissent suivre le grand précepte de l'Évangile, qui
nous ordonne d'abandonner pour Dieu notre père, notre mère, notre
famille, nos amis et nos biens. Mais s'il fallait prendre ces mots à la lettre,

soit comme précepte, soit même comme conseil, chaque homme serait obligé, ou au moins ferait bien, de s'y conformer; et que deviendrait alors le genre humain? [VII.301a–b]

The angriest reply to this pungent attack came from Abbé Saas. He takes up, for instance, d'Alembert's assertion that monks are unfitted to write about philosophy by their lack of freedom, and retorts: 'Mais qu'appelle-t-on la liberté? Ne serait-ce point ce funeste pouvoir d'écrire contre la religion, les mœurs et le gouvernement, source des maux qui inondent les empires?'[1]

Certain practices of the Catholic Church are severely condemned in outspoken articles in the last ten volumes. Jaucourt, for instance, speaks with some scorn of the reverence shown to relics in a short, but pointed article:

RELIQUE, s.f. (*Hist. ecclés. & prof.*) Ce mot, tiré du latin *reliquiae*, indique que c'est ce qui nous reste d'un saint: os, cendres, vêtements, et qu'on garde respectueusement pour honorer sa mémoire. Cependant, si on faisait la revision des *reliques* avec une exactitude un peu rigoureuse, dit un savant bénédictin, il se trouverait qu'on a proposé à la piété des fidèles un grand nombre de fausses *reliques* à révérer et qu'on a consacré des ossements qui, loin d'être d'un bienheureux, n'étaient peut-être même d'un chrétien. [XIV.88a]

Before 1789 the French clergy, at any rate the higher clergy, enjoyed scandalous wealth and successfully fought off every attempt by the government to compel it to make a larger contribution in the way of taxation. The unsigned article, SÉCULARISATION, which can be attributed with reasonable certainty to Baron d'Holbach, describes how certain Protestant princes of Germany had secularized the property of the Catholic Church and then proceeds to apply the moral to France:

Les immenses revenus que possèdent un grand nombre d'évêchés et abbayes d'Allemagne fournissaient une manière facile de terminer les disputes sanglantes qui déchirent souvent les princes et les états séculiers dont le corps germanique est composé. Il serait à désirer que l'on eût recours à la *sécularisation* pour tirer des mains des ecclésiastiques des biens que l'ignorance et la superstition ont fait autrefois prodiguer à des hommes que la puissance et la grandeur temporelles détournent des fonctions du ministère sacré auxquelles ils se doivent tout entiers. [XIV.883b]

---

[1] *Lettres sur l'Encyclopédie*, p. 172.

A much more direct attack on the wealth of the French clergy is found in Damilaville's articles, POPULATION and especially VINGTIÈME. Here he argues that if the clergy is unwilling to assume its fair share of the burden of taxation, then it should hand back most of its land to the poor:

... Qu'il n'en réserve que ce qu'il faut pour vivre dans la modestie et dans la frugalité; qu'il restitue tout le reste aux pauvres et qu'il leur soit distribué, non pas pour subsister dans la paresse et dans les vices qu'elle engendre toujours, mais pour en obtenir leur subsistance par le travail. Que de familles à charge à l'état lui deviendraient utiles et lui rendraient le tribut que les autres lui refusent! Combien j'en établirais sur ces vastes possessions! Que d'hommes produiraient ces terres ainsi cultivées par un plus grand nombre de mains! [XVII.88ob]

Not without decided exaggeration Damilaville claims elsewhere in this article [XVII.865b] that in one form or another (including tithes) the French clergy had in its hands nearly half the national wealth. It was to emerge from the Revolution very much poorer.

Scattered through the pages of the *Encyclopédie*, as we have already seen, one finds stated in a dozen different forms and contexts the theme that morality is independent of religion, that it is possible to be an unbeliever and yet to lead a moral life. It is characteristic of the attitude of the *Encyclopédie* that Diderot should work into the article *CEPENDANT, POURTANT, NÉANMOINS, TOUTEFOIS, the sentence:

Quelques écrivains ont répandu dans leurs ouvrages les maximes les plus opposées à la morale chrétienne; d'autres ont publié les systèmes les plus contraires à ses dogmes; *cependant* les uns et les autres ont été bons parents, bons amis, bons citoyens même, si on leur pardonne la faute qu'ils ont commise en qualité d'auteurs. [II.831a]

The last words of the sentence can have deceived no one; and the message is repeated in every volume.

## The Church's attitude to actors

One topic in which the *Encyclopédie* challenged the clerical outlook on the world was the Church's attitude to actors. Even its first theologian, Abbé Mallet, follows in Voltaire's footsteps in

COMÉDIEN by comparing the enlightened English with the backward French in this field:

La profession de *comédien* est honorée en Angleterre; on n'y a fait point difficulté d'accorder à mademoiselle Oldfield un tombeau à Westminster à côté de Newton et des rois. En France elle est moins honorée. L'Église romaine les excommunie et leur refuse la sépulture chrétienne s'ils n'ont pas renoncé au théâtre avant leur mort. [III.671b]

Diderot followed this up with an editorial addition in which he stresses the moral aim of the contemporary theatre: 'Il s'agit maintenant, sur notre théâtre français particulièrement, d'exciter à la vertu, d'inspirer l'horreur du vice et d'exposer les ridicules.' Respect is therefore due to the profession. Chaumeix found such an attitude wholly unacceptable, and Diderot's praise of actors arouses the sarcastic comment: 'Ce livre, au reste, est digne de pareils éloges et je les y trouve fort bien placés' (*PL* i.19). D'Alembert's suggestion that the Republic of Geneva should allow the introduction of a company of actors was not only made to please Voltaire; it also provided him with an opportunity to attack the attitude of the Catholic Church in France in this matter:

Une autre considération, digne d'une république si sage et si éclairée, devrait peut-être l'engager à permettre les spectacles. Le préjugé barbare contre la profession de comédien, l'espèce d'avilissement où nous avons mis ces hommes si nécessaires au progrès et au soutien des arts, est certainement une des principales causes qui contribue au dérèglement que nous leur reprochons; ils cherchent à se dédommager par les plaisirs de l'estime que leur état ne peut obtenir. Parmi nous un comédien qui a des mœurs est doublement respectable, mais à peine lui en sait-on quelque gré. Le traitant qui insulte à l'indigence publique et qui s'en nourrit, le courtisan qui rampe et qui ne paie point ses dettes, voilà l'espèce d'hommes que nous honorons le plus. [VII.577a]

If Geneva had a company of actors, this would set an example to other countries:

On ne les verrait pas d'un côté pensionnés par le gouvernement, et de l'autre un objet d'anathème; nos prêtres perdraient l'habitude de les excommunier, et nos bourgeois de les regarder avec mépris; et une petite république aurait la gloire d'avoir réformé l'Europe sur ce point, plus important peut-être qu'on ne pense. [VII.577a]

In the controversy aroused by the article GENÈVE, this was one of the many points which gave offence to d'Alembert's critics.

## The Church and education

Down to the Revolution secondary education in France was almost exclusively in the hands of the clergy. Until the suppression of the Jesuits in 1762, members of this order had, of course, been the leading educators. Most of the *philosophes* were their pupils, although d'Alembert, whose attack on the existing system of secondary education in the article COLLÈGE aroused great controversy when it was published in 1753, had been to a Jansenist school in Paris. This article naturally deals in considerable detail with the more technical problems of education. D'Alembert prefers a private education to a public one in schools and colleges; he attacks the teaching offered in existing schools with its concentration on the traditional humanities, rhetoric and philosophy. He argues in favour of sweeping changes in the curriculum: less time spent on Latin (a reading knowledge would suffice) and more on French and modern languages, history, geography and the arts (particularly music). One paragraph in his article gave particular offence:

Dans la philosophie on bornerait la logique à quelques lignes; la métaphysique, à un abrégé de Locke; la morale purement philosophique, aux ouvrages de Sénèque et d'Épictète; la morale chrétienne, au sermon de Jésus-Christ sur la montagne; la physique, aux expériences et à la géométrie, qui est de toutes les logiques et physiques la meilleure. [III.637a]

D'Alembert's secular outlook came out too clearly in this article for it not to arouse an outcry when Vol. III of the *Encyclopédie* appeared in print.

Shortly after its publication came an indignant refutation in the shape of the *Observations de M. ***, principal du Collège de ***, sur un des articles du Dictionnaire encyclopédique*. This fifty-three page pamphlet offers a defence of the existing educational system, including the teaching of the classical tongues and of rhetoric; the author naturally favours public as against private education. When he comes to deal with d'Alembert's ideas on the teaching of philosophy, he sees grave dangers in allowing the subject to fall into the hands of 'des maîtres particuliers qui ne rendent compte à personne de leur doctrine et de leurs sentiments'. If the government were to let them loose in this field, it would have no control over what the young were taught:

Si l'on adopte le sentiment de M. d'Al....., chacun ayant chez soi des maîtres particuliers pourra impunément faire enseigner dans sa famille les opinions les plus dangereuses. Celui-ci, prévenu en faveur de Locke, voudra que son fils embrasse sa doctrine, toute dangereuse qu'elle est pour la religion; celui-là, admirateur aveugle de Machiavel, le fera admirer à ses enfants, le leur fera aimer; d'autres enfin qui ne voient rien de mieux pensé et de plus judicieux que l'*Esprit des lois*, préviendront leurs enfants en faveur de ce pernicieux ouvrage, leur feront boire jusqu'à la lie le poison qu'il renferme, et, au lieu de laisser à la religion des enfants chrétiens et à la couronne des sujets soumis, ils ne laisseront après eux que des rebelles de cœur et d'esprit, des athées de conduite et de croyance. (p. 24)

To set forth an alternative to the existing system of education which aimed at producing Christian pupils who would also prove submissive subjects was obviously a criminal enterprise on d'Alembert's part.

The author of another pamphlet of the time—*Avis au public sur le troisième volume de l'Encyclopédie*—denounces COLLÈGE in more violent terms:

L'article *Collège* est encore un champ de bataille où leur fureur s'est satis-faite. Les collèges sont, selon eux, des écoles de libertinage, l'éducation qu'on y donne est la cause de l'impiété et des vices qui règnent dans le monde, la méthode qu'on y observe la ressource de l'ignorance. Ici une colonne ne suffit pas pour leurs reproches, leur haine vomit des torrents, des pages entières en sont infectées. Voici l'*esprit philosophique* qui règne dans le dictionnaire. (pp. 16–17)

The article is also criticized at length in the *Réflexions d'un Franciscain*. Once again, d'Alembert's observations on the teaching of philosophy are attacked:

Ce qu'il y a surtout à réformer dans votre plan, c'est ce qui regarde la philosophie. Aucun professeur ne bornera la logique à quelques lignes. L'art de penser doit être plus étendu que vous ne croyez, et, si vous en doutez, on vous conseille de l'apprendre. Aucun professeur chrétien ne réduira la métaphysique à *un abrégé de Locke*; la morale que vous appelez *purement philosophique*, aux ouvrages *de Sénèque et d'Épictète*; la morale chrétienne *aux discours de Jésus-Christ sur la montagne*.

To d'Alembert's complaint that to mix up the proofs of the existence of God with the verbiage of Scholastic philosophy is to 'outrager et blasphémer en quelque sorte la plus grande des vérités' [III.635b] comes this furious retort:

Si ce sont là des blasphèmes, quel nom donnerons-nous à l'assemblage que vous proposez des questions de l'existence de Dieu, de ses perfections infinies et des délires de Locke sur le pouvoir de penser qu'il croit être dans la matière; de la morale des païens, et surtout d'Épictète, et de celle de Jésus-Christ? (pp. 157–8)

D'Alembert's clerical critics had thus no difficulty in seeing through to the fundamentally secular approach to education in this famous article, and their anger comes out clearly in their attacks on it.

Despite the somewhat confused approach of the *Encyclopédie* to a subject which it was utterly impossible to discuss freely in print in the France of Louis XV, there can be no doubt that Diderot, d'Alembert and a number of their contributors must have succeeded in getting across to the observant reader many of their unorthodox views. Those views naturally varied, and even men like Diderot and d'Holbach, who utterly rejected religion in any shape or form, were compelled to tone down their ideas and now to simulate orthodoxy, now to write from a vaguely deistic standpoint. Yet, like contemporary critics of the work, those readers who were either neutral or inclined towards the outlook of the *philosophes* must have been clearly conscious of the general unorthodoxy both of the articles devoted to purely religious matters and of those which dealt nominally with other topics, from philosophy to almost anything under the sun.

## Chapter 8

# *Politics*

### *The Age of Madame de Pompadour*

In considering the political ideas of the *Encyclopédie* it has to be remembered that the views of the *philosophes* on both political and social questions were much less radical than in the sphere of philosophy and religion. It would be idle to seek in the pages of the seventeen volumes of text the equivalent of the highly unorthodox attitude to religion of men like Diderot or d'Holbach. What is more, the *Encyclopédie* was produced in a country in which absolutism had reigned for over a century, and in which neither political theorizing nor comment on existing institutions was exactly encouraged. Again, the *Encyclopédie* did not appear in the 1770s and 1780s when political discontent was becoming more and more vocal in France; the articles which we are about to study were produced in the period between about 1750 and the early 1760s. They reflect up to a point the growing dissatisfaction with absolute monarchy and in particular the form which that dissatisfaction took in these years: the struggle for power between Crown and Parlements. Yet even in the boldest articles which show a clear hostility to absolutism and a hankering after a constitutional monarchy, there is never a demand for an immediate and radical recasting of political institutions in France, let alone a revolution like the one which was to begin in 1789.

### *Rousseau's article* ÉCONOMIE *(Morale et Politique)*

There is one political article which for the last two hundred years has been subjected to minute analysis: Rousseau's ÉCONOMIE

(*Morale et Politique*) which appeared in Vol. V in 1755. His views
were, of course, to be developed further and placed in a wider context in his *Contrat social*, published seven years later. Yet students of
Rousseau have traced back to this article some of his main political
ideas. First, the distinction between civil power and paternal power
and the consequent rejection of the attempt of men like Filmer and
Bossuet to justify absolute monarchy by tracing it back to the
family:

De tout ce que je viens d'exposer, il s'ensuit que c'est avec raison qu'on a
distingué l'*économie publique* de l'*économie particulière*, et que l'État n'ayant
rien de commun avec la famille que l'obligation qu'ont les chefs de
rendre heureux l'un et l'autre, les mêmes règles de conduite ne sauraient
convenir à tous les deux. J'ai cru qu'il suffirait de ce peu de lignes pour
renverser l'odieux système que le chevalier Filmer a tâché d'établir dans
un ouvrage intitulé *Patriarcha*, auquel deux hommes illustres ont fait trop
d'honneur en écrivant des livres pour le réfuter. [V.338a]

More important still is the distinction, fundamental in his eyes,
between the sovereign body which makes the laws and the government which, being subordinate to it, is concerned merely with
their execution:

Je prie mes lecteurs de bien distinguer encore l'*économie publique* dont j'ai
à parler et que j'appelle *gouvernement,* de l'autorité suprême que j'appelle
*souveraineté*, distinction qui consiste en ce que l'une a le droit législatif et
oblige en certains cas le corps même de la nation, tandis que l'autre n'a
que la puissance exécutrice et ne peut obliger que les particuliers. [V.338a]

It will be noticed that while he makes clear the subordinate position
of the government, Rousseau does not yet argue, as he was later to
do in the *Contrat social*, that sovereignty belongs to the people and
can only belong to it. One finds here also one of his leading principles—the notion of the General Will:

Le corps politique est donc aussi un être moral qui a une volonté; et cette
volonté générale qui tend toujours à la conservation et au bien-être du
tout et de chaque partie et qui est la source des lois, est pour tous les
membres de l'état par rapport à eux et à lui la règle du juste et de l'injuste.
[V.338b]

The article covers, of course, much else besides these fundamental
principles. The subject of the second part is love of one's country
which can be fostered, Rousseau argues, if the authority of the

State is directed towards securing the liberty and security of its citizens and if a public system of education is established. The third, the longest and least interesting part of the article, is concerned with public finance and in particular taxation.

If for several generations scholars have examined minutely every sentence of ÉCONOMIE POLITIQUE, the article—like the *Contrat social* seven years later—created singularly little stir on its appearance. Not that, any more than the *Contrat social*, it passed entirely unnoticed; but it attracted much less attention than Diderot's AUTORITÉ POLITIQUE or *DROIT NATUREL, to mention only two other political articles from the first seven volumes. In his *Lettres sur l'Encyclopédie* Abbé Saas writes somewhat laconically: 'ÉCONOMIE. Cet article a été proscrit avec raison. On y combat la loi naturelle et les idées du juste et de l'injuste. Voyez la brochure qui a pour titre *Les Philosophes aux abois*' (pp. 101–2). This pamphlet of Chaumeix is so obscure that I have been unable to trace a copy of any but the first letter of the work and this does not refer to Rousseau's article. Shortly after its publication this article was reviewed in some detail by Pierre Rousseau in his newly founded *Journal encyclopédique*; most of the passage devoted to it consists merely of a summary, interspersed with frequent praise combined with some criticism. Pierre Rousseau completely fails to understand the importance of the opening section of the article and even speaks of 'un premier mouvement d'ennui' being caused by the first two columns;[1] he does not even grasp the importance of the distinction drawn by Jean Jacques between civil power and paternal power when he writes: 'On ne voit pas à quel propos il s'attache si fort, en commençant, à distinguer le gouvernement politique du gouvernement paternel. Y a-t-il de plus beau modèle à offrir aux princes que la nature?'[2] In general, like the *Contrat social*, ÉCONOMIE POLITIQUE tended to be treated purely as a piece of theoretical writing; the radical implications of the introduction to the article were certainly not seized on by contemporaries.

## Other political articles and their debt to earlier writers

Not all the political articles in the *Encyclopédie* are signed. Jaucourt supplied a large number which bear his signature though they are

---

[1] *Journal encyclopédique*, 15 Feb. 1756, p. 25.    [2] *Ibid.*, p. 30.

merely compiled from a variety of sources. Some bear Diderot's editorial asterisk, and others may be attributed to him with varying degrees of certainty. In recent years some of those in the last ten volumes have been restored to their rightful authors—LÉGISLATEUR, for instance, is by Saint-Lambert while the very important REPRÉSENTANTS came from the pen of Baron d'Holbach. In these volumes there are a large number of unsigned articles; some of these might be by Diderot, but most (so far as one can judge by internal evidence alone) would seem to be by another hand or hands.

Apart from Jean Jacques, none of the authors of political articles whose identity is known to us could really be classed as a political thinker. A good many of the political ideas to be found in the *Encyclopédie* are decidedly secondhand. The *Esprit des lois* was chopped up into appropriate articles. To take an extreme example: an editorial addition by Diderot to Mallet's ARISTOCRATIE opens with the sentence: 'Quant aux lois relatives à l'*aristocratie* on peut consulter l'excellent ouvrage de M. de Montesquieu.' This introduces twenty-three paragraphs taken from the *Esprit des lois* [I. 652a–b]. Jaucourt transcribes Montesquieu right and left, with or without acknowledgements. Another favourite source, particularly with Jaucourt, but also at times with Diderot, was the works of the Natural Law writers, Grotius and Pufendorf. Their writings were studied in the heavily annotated Barbeyrac translations: in PREMIER OCCUPANT Jaucourt goes out of his way to praise Barbeyrac's notes to Pufendorf. The more recent writings of the Genevan Burlamaqui—*Principes du droit naturel* (1747) and his posthumous *Principes du droit politique* (1751)—were also brought under contribution. Yet although such borrowings will frequently be brought to light in this chapter, that does not mean that even a compiler like Jaucourt was altogether lacking in originality. Even if contributors to the *Encyclopédie* had simply pillaged Montesquieu, the Natural Law writers and, of course, Locke, they would still have helped to diffuse their ideas in absolutist France; but this was far from being the case. The political articles are more original than that, as the hubbub stirred up by some of those which appeared in the first seven volumes very clearly shows.

Natural Law is the subject of a large number of articles, many of them derived *via* Barbeyrac from Grotius and especially Pufendorf.

In writing *CITOYEN, for instance, Diderot, it is clear, must simply have turned up the index to the Barbeyrac translation of Pufendorf's *Droit de la nature et des gens* and then looked up the first reference under *Citoyen*—'Ce que c'est proprement' [VII.2.20]— and used the text and the translator's notes as the starting point for his article. No doubt it has other sources too; they include the inevitable *Esprit des lois*. This article produced very little comment from contemporary critics, unlike the famous *DROIT NATUREL which Rousseau was to attack so hotly in the first version of his *Contrat social*.

Among the articles on this subject there is in Vol. V, in addition to *DROIT NATUREL (*Morale*), an article by the lawyer, Boucher d'Argis, entitled DROIT DE LA NATURE *ou* DROIT NATUREL; this includes an account of the writings of Grotius, Pufendorf, Barbeyrac and Burlamaqui. In Vol. IX there is an article LOI NATURELLE (*Morale*) which has on occasion been attributed to Diderot, but without any evidence to support the attribution. Not to be outdone, Jaucourt produced yet another article in Vol. XI, NATURELLE, *loi*.

## The article *DROIT NATUREL

Of all these articles *DROIT NATUREL is by far the most original. After rejecting in somewhat tortuous language the notion of free will, Diderot eliminates from the concept of Natural Law the divine origin attributed to it by writers in the past. For him it is the product of human reason. To expound his ideas on the whole subject he raises the question as to what answer one can give to the man of violent passions who claims the right to murder anyone who gets in his way, but admits the right of his fellowmen to do the same to him. Paragraph V begins with the question: 'Que répondrons-nous donc à notre raisonneur violent avant que de l'étouffer?' It is not for the individual to settle such questions, he argues; the General Will alone can decide. Although in discussing the notion of the General Will in his article ÉCONOMIE POLITIQUE Rousseau expressly refers the reader to *DROIT NATUREL,[1] this does not mean either that he had derived it from Diderot or that their ideas on the subject were identical. For Diderot the General Will is

---

[1] 'Voy. au mot DROIT la source de ce grand et lumineux principe, dont cet article est le développement' [V.338b].

that of humanity as a species; for Rousseau, at any rate in his fully developed thought, that of a given political society. What he vehemently denounced in Diderot's article in the first version of the *Contrat social* was the latter's belief in the natural sociability of man; in a famous sentence he declared: 'Nous ne commençons à devenir hommes qu'après avoir été citoyens.'[1]

In the following passage Diderot expounds his conception of the General Will:

VI. Mais si nous ôtons à l'individu le droit de décider de la nature du juste et de l'injuste, où porterons-nous cette grande question? Ou? Devant le genre humain; c'est à lui seul qu'il appartient de la décider, parce que le bien de tous est la seule passion qu'il ait. Les volontés particulières sont suspectes; elles peuvent être bonnes ou méchantes; mais la volonté générale est toujours bonne; elle n'a jamais trompé, elle ne trompera jamais. . . .

VII. C'est à la volonté générale que l'individu doit s'adresser pour savoir jusqu'où il doit être homme, citoyen, sujet, père, enfant, et quand il lui convient de vivre ou de mourir. C'est à elle à fixer les limites de tous les devoirs. Vous avez le *droit naturel* le plus sacré à tout ce qui ne vous est point contesté par l'espèce entière. C'est elle qui vous éclairera sur la nature de vos pensées et de vos désirs. Tout ce que vous concevrez, tout ce que vous méditerez, sera bon, grand, élevé, sublime, s'il est de l'intérêt général et commun. Il n'y a de qualité essentielle à votre espèce que celle que vous exigez dans tous vos semblables, pour votre bonheur et pour le leur. C'est cette conformité de vous à eux tous et d'eux tous à vous qui vous marquera quand vous sortirez de votre espèce et quand vous y resterez. Ne la perdez donc jamais de vue; sans quoi vous verrez les notions de la bonté, de la justice, de l'humanité, de la vertu chanceler dans votre entendement. Dites-vous souvent: Je suis homme, et je n'ai d'autres *droits naturels* véritablement inaliénables que ceux de l'humanité.

VIII. Mais, me direz-vous, où est la dépôt de cette volonté générale? Où pourrai-je la consulter? . . . Dans les principes du droit écrit de toutes les nations policées; dans les actions sociales des peuples sauvages et barbares; dans les conventions tacites des ennemis du genre humain entre eux; et même dans l'indignation et le ressentiment, ces deux passions que la nature semble avoir placées jusque dans les animaux pour suppléer au défaut des lois sociales et de la vengeance publique.

---

[1] *Œuvres complètes*, ed. B. Gagnebin and M. Raymond, iii, 287.

IX. Si vous méditez donc attentivement tout ce qui précède, vous resterez convaincu: 1° que l'homme qui n'écoute que sa volonté particulière est l'ennemi du genre humain; 2° que la volonté générale est dans chaque individu un acte pur de l'entendement qui raisonne dans le silence des passions sur ce que l'homme peut exiger de son semblable et sur ce que son semblable est en droit d'exiger de lui; 3° que cette considération de la volonté générale de l'espèce et du désir commun est la règle de la conduite relative d'un particulier à un particulier dans la même société, d'un particulier envers la société dont il est membre, et de la société dont il est membre, envers les autres sociétés; 4° que la soumission à la volonté générale est le lien de toutes les sociétés, sans en excepter celles qui sont formées par le crime. Hélas, la vertu est si belle que les voleurs en respectent l'image dans le fond même de leurs cavernes![1] 5° que les lois doivent être faites pour tous, et non pour un; autrement cet être solitaire ressemblerait au raisonneur violent que nous avons étouffé dans le paragraphe V; 6° que, puisque des deux volontés, l'une générale et l'autre particulière, la volonté générale n'erre jamais, il n'est pas difficile de voir à laquelle il faudrait, pour le bonheur du genre humain, que la puissance législative appartînt et quelle vénération on doit aux mortels augustes dont la volonté particulière réunit et l'autorité et l'infaillibilité de la volonté générale; 7° que, quand on supposerait la notion des espèces dans un flux perpétuel, la nature du *droit naturel* ne changerait pas, puisqu'elle serait toujours relative à la volonté générale et au désir commun de l'espece entière; 8° que l'équité est à la justice comme la cause est à son effet, ou la justice ne peut être autre chose que l'équité déclarée; 9° enfin que toutes ces conséquences sont évidentes pour celui qui raisonne et que celui qui ne veut pas raisonner, renonçant à la qualité d'homme, doit être traité comme un être dénaturé. [V.116a–b]

This article earned pages of highly critical analysis from *La Religion vengée*. In this detailed examination we find, for instance, a sharp criticism of Diderot's formulation of the notion of the General Will:

On nous dit au même endroit que 'les volontés particulières sont suspectes'. Mais les volontés qui naissent d'" un acte pur de l'entendement qui raisonne dans le silence des passions' sont toutes des 'volontés particulières'; elles doivent donc toutes être 'suspectes'. Or de cet assemblage de volontés particulières toutes 'suspectes', comment peut-il en résulter une volonté générale qui nous conduise à la sagesse et à la

---

[1] Rousseau refers to this sentence in ÉCONOMIE POLITIQUE when he writes: 'C'est ainsi (comme on l'a remarqué à l'article DROIT) que les brigands mêmes, qui sont les ennemis de la vertu dans la grande société, en adorent le simulacre dans leurs cavernes' [V.339a].

vérité? Certes, si ma volonté particulière m'est suspecte, celle de tout autre homme me le sera également. Et si je ne puis pas me répondre d'un acte pur de mon entendement, comment discernerai-je ce qui est un acte pur de l'entendement des autres? Comment les autres le discerneront-ils en moi? (x.191–2)

In its summing up on the *Encyclopédie* as a whole the review returns again to *DROIT NATUREL and argues that Diderot's intention was in fact to destroy the whole notion of such a law:

Quelle confusion, quel désordre, quelle fausseté d'idées dans ce qu'ils disent du droit naturel, ce premier principe de nos mœurs! L'auteur de cet article s'est imaginé que le ton d'orgueil et de présomption qu'il affecte éternellement suffirait pour détruire des maximes gravées par la nature même dans l'esprit et dans le cœur de tous les hommes. (xii.198–9)

Chaumeix too devotes a great deal of space to a refutation of this article. It is typical of his hostile interpretation of it that he should offer these furious comments on paragraph VII:

Comme plusieurs lecteurs seraient dans le cas de ne pas voir tout d'un coup où les conduisent ces affreux principes, il est bon de les leur dévoiler afin qu'ils en aperçoivent toute la laideur. Cette vie est la seule à laquelle vous deviez vous attacher et dont vous puissiez jouir. Vous êtes un individu de l'espèce humaine; vous êtes citoyen du monde et patriote de nulle part. Vous ne devez rien faire, rien concevoir, rien méditer que pour l'intérêt temporel de vous et des autres hommes. Vous n'avez pas d'autre supérieur que la volonté de l'humanité; c'est à elle seule de vous prescrire tous vos devoirs, toutes vos obligations . . . Si quelqu'un s'avisait de vouloir vous faire entendre que vous êtes soumis à un Dieu comme sa créature ou que vous avez des devoirs que vous impose votre qualité de chrétien ou même celle de Français, dites: Je suis homme et je n'ai d'autres droits naturels à remplir que ceux qui me sont dictés par la volonté générale. (*PL* ii.78–9)

There can be no doubt that in his blundering way Chaumeix had somehow hit upon some of the underlying ideas of the article.

## Jaucourt's early political articles

Jaucourt's articles on natural law are far from original, but they do occasionally serve as a vehicle for criticisms of the France of his day. In ÉGALITÉ NATURELLE, for instance, while he argues that in society natural equality must vanish and give way simply to equality before the law, he considers the principle none the less essential:

... C'est la violation de ce principe qui a établi l'esclavage politique et civil. Il est arrivé de là que, dans les pays soumis au pouvoir arbitraire, les princes, les courtisans, les premiers ministres, ceux qui manient les finances, possèdent toutes les richesses de la nation, pendant que le reste des citoyens n'a que le nécessaire et que la plus grande partie du peuple gémit dans la pauvreté. [V.415a]

If we turn now to articles which have a more direct bearing on conditions in France under the Ancien Régime, we find that these are less numerous in the first seven volumes than in those which appeared all together in 1765. Nor is it always easy to interpret contemporary reactions to those in the first seven volumes since these seem at times bizarre. For instance, Jaucourt was soundly rebuked for the following passage in CONQUÊTE:

Il est effectivement du devoir des peuples de résister dans les commence-ments à l'usurpateur de toutes leurs forces et de demeurer fidèles à leur souverain; mais si malgré tous leurs efforts leur souverain a du dessous et qu'il ne soit plus en état de faire valoir son droit, ils ne sont obligés à rien de plus et ils peuvent pourvoir a leur conservation.
Les peuples ne sauraient se passer de gouvernement, et comme ils ne sont pas tenus à s'exposer à des guerres perpétuelles pour soutenir les intérêts de leur premier souverain, ils peuvent rendre légitime par leur consentement le droit de l'usurpateur; et dans ces circonstances le souverain dépouillé doit se consoler de la perte de ses états comme d'un malheur sans remède. [III.901a]

This drew cries of rage from the *Réflexions d'un Franciscain*. 'Reconnaît-on un chevalier à ce langage?' the authors indignantly ask. 'N'attribue-t-on point par erreur cet article à M. de Jaucourt?' (p. 176). All Jaucourt had in fact done was to copy out a couple of paragraphs from the chapter entitled 'Des différentes manières d'acquérir la souveraineté' from Burlamaqui's *Principes du droit politique* (p. 101). Yet the whole article is denounced as being 'contre l'autorité des princes légitimes'.

Like virtually all political writers in France before the Revolu-tion Jaucourt regarded a monarchy as indispensable in a country of any size and particularly in one as large and as populous as

France. Yet he had a great admiration for the republics of the ancient world. His article DÉMOCRATIE is typical in this respect:

DÉMOCRATIE, s.f. (*Droit polit.*) est une des formes simples de gouvernement dans lequel le peuple en corps a la souveraineté. Toute république où la souveraineté réside entre les mains du peuple, est une *démocratie*; et si la souveraine puissance se trouve entre les mains d'une partie du peuple seulement, c'est une aristocratie. *Voy.* ARISTOCRATIE.

Quoique je ne pense pas que la *démocratie* soit la plus commode et la plus stable forme du gouvernement; quoique je sois persuadé qu'elle est désavantageuse aux grands états, je la crois néanmoins une des plus anciennes parmi les nations qui ont suivi comme équitable cette maxime: 'Que ce à quoi les membres de la société ont intérêt doit être administré par tous en commun.' [IV.816a]

However, living in an absolute monarchy, Jaucourt was much more concerned with the dangers of despotism, a system of government which is roundly condemned in DESPOTISME:

Concluons que le *despotisme* est également nuisible aux princes et aux peuples dans tous les temps et dans tous les lieux, parce qu'il est partout le même dans son principe et dans ses effets. Ce sont des circonstances particulières, une opinion de religion, des préjugés, des exemples reçus, des coutumes établies, des manières, des mœurs, qui y mettent les différences qu'on y rencontre dans le monde. Mais quelles que soient ces différences, la nature humaine se soulève toujours contre un gouvernement de cette espèce, qui fait le malheur du prince et des sujets. [IV.888b]

Louis XIV, the most absolute king that France had ever known, is dragged in to contribute to this condemnation of despotism. Like Rousseau, Jaucourt had found some useful ammunition in one of the copious notes appended by Barbeyrac to his translation of Pufendorf's *Droit de la nature et des gens.*[1] In 1667 the French government had published a *Traité des droits de la reine sur différents états de la monarchie d'Espagne* as part of its preparations for the war against Spain which began in that year. Jaucourt was no doubt delighted to be able to make use of such an official source in his attack on despotism:

. . . Louis XIV a toujours reconnu qu'il ne pouvait rien de contraire aux droits de la nature, aux droits des gens et aux lois fondamentales de l'État.

[1] Book VII, Chap. vi, §10, n. 2.

Dans le *Traité des droites de la Reine de France*, imprimé en 1667 par ordre de cet auguste monarque pour justifier ses prétentions sur une partie des Pays-Bas catholiques, on y trouve ces belles paroles: 'QUE LES ROIS ONT CETTE BIENHEUREUSE IMPUISSANCE DE NE POUVOIR RIEN FAIRE CONTRE LES LOIS DE LEUR PAYS . . . Ce n'est (ajoute l'auteur) ni imperfection ni faiblesse dans une autorité suprême que de se soumettre à la loi de ses promesses ou à la justice de ses lois. La nécessité de bien faire et l'impuissance de faillir sont les plus hauts degrés de la perfection. Dieu même, selon la pensée de Philon, Juif, ne peut aller plus avant; et c'est dans cette divine impuissance que les souverains, qui sont ses images sur la terre, le doivent particulièrement imiter dans leurs états.' *Page 279, édition faite suivant la copie de l'Imprimerie royale.*

Jaucourt then goes on to reproduce the very same passage that Rousseau was to make use of in the following year in his *Discours sur l'inégalité*:

'Qu'on ne dise donc point (continue le même auteur qui parle au nom et avec l'aveu de Louis XIV) qu'on ne dise donc point que le souverain ne soit pas sujet aux lois de son état puisque la proposition contraire est une vérité du droit des gens que la flatterie a quelquefois attaquée, mais que les bons princes ont toujours défendue, comme divinité tutélaire de leurs états. Combien est-il plus légitime de dire avec le sage Platon que la parfaite félicité d'un royaume est qu'un prince soit obéi de ses sujets, que le prince obéisse à la loi et que la loi soit droite et toujours dirigée au bien public?' Le monarque qui pense et qui agit ainsi, est bien digne du nom de GRAND; et celui qui ne peut augmenter sa gloire qu'en continuant une domination pleine de clémence, mérite sans doute le titre de BIEN-AIMÉ. [IV.889a]

Thus both Louis XIV ('Louis le Grand') and his successor ('Louis le Bien-Aimé') are enlisted, thanks to the *Traité des droits de la Reine* (a work which we shall meet again in the course of this chapter) on the side of those who set limits to the power of the monarchy.

The most notable political article contributed by Jaucourt to the first seven volumes was GOUVERNEMENT. Although this was far from original—it is largely a hotchpotch of Locke's *Two Treatises* and Burlamaqui's *Principes du droit politique* with a piece of the *Esprit des lois* thrown in—it was sharply attacked for its subversive ideas when it appeared in print in 1757. Following Locke, Jaucourt begins by tracing the origins of government to paternal authority. When governments in the modern sense were formed, it could only be by free agreement:

Tous les *gouvernements* publics semblent évidemment avoir été formés par délibération, par consultation et par accord. Qui doute, par exemple, que Rome et Venise n'aient commencé par des hommes libres et indépendants les uns à l'égard des autres, entre lesquels il n'y avait ni supériorité, ni sujétion naturelle, et qui sont convenus de former une société de *gouvernement*? . . . En un mot, toutes les sociétés politiques ont commencé par une union volontaire de particuliers qui ont fait le libre choix d'une sorte de *gouvernement*. [VII.788b]

Like Locke, Jaucourt denies that conquest can be the origin of government:

. . . Il y a des auteurs qui regardent les conquêtes comme l'origine et le fondement des *gouvernements*; mais les conquêtes sont aussi éloignées d'être l'origine et le fondement des *gouvernements* que la démolition d'une maison est éloignée d'être la vraie cause de la construction d'une autre maison dans la même place. A la vérité la destruction d'un état prépare un nouvel état, mais la conquête qui l'établit par la force n'est qu'une injustice de plus. Toute puissance souveraine légitime doit émaner du consentement libre des peuples. [VII.789a]

After defining the different forms of government—democracy, aristocracy, monarchy and mixed forms—in terms borrowed from Burlamaqui, Jaucourt returns to Locke:

Quelques écrivains politiques prétendent que tous les hommes, étant nés sous un *gouvernement*, n'ont point la liberté d'en instituer un nouveau; chacun, disent-ils, naît sujet de son père ou de son prince, et par conséquent chacun est dans une perpétuelle obligation de sujétion ou de fidélité. Ce raisonnement est plus spécieux que solide. Jamais les hommes n'ont regardé aucune sujétion naturelle dans laquelle ils soient nés à l'égard de leur père ou de leur prince, comme un lien qui les oblige sans leur propre consentement à se soumettre à eux. L'histoire sacrée et profane nous fournissent de fréquents exemples d'une multitude de gens qui se sont retirés de l'obéissance et de la juridiction sous laquelle ils étaient nés, de la famille et de la communauté dans laquelle ils avaient été nourris, pour établir ailleurs de nouvelles sociétés et de nouveaux *gouvernements*.

Ce sont ces émigrations, également libres et légitimes, qui ont produit un si grand nombre de petites sociétés, lesquelles se répandirent en différents pays, se multiplièrunt et y séjournèrent autant qu'elles trouvèrent de quoi subsister ou jusqu'à ce que les plus forts, engloutissant les plus faibles, établirent de leurs débris de grands empires, qui à leur tour ont été brisés et dissous en diverses petites dominations. Au lieu de quantité de royaumes, il ne se serait trouvé qu'une seule monarchie dans les premiers siècles s'il était vrai que les hommes n'aient pas eu la liberté naturelle de se séparer de leurs familles et de leur *gouvernement*, quel qu'il ait été, pour en ériger d'autres à leur fantaisie.

Il est clair, par la pratique des *gouvernements* eux-mêmes aussi bien que par les lois de la droite raison, qu'un enfant ne naît sujet d'aucun pays ni d'aucun *gouvernement*; il demeure sous la tutelle et l'autorité de son père jusqu'à ce qu'il soit parvenu à l'âge de raison. A cet âge de raison il est maître de choisir le *gouvernement* sous lequel il trouve bon de vivre et de s'unir au corps politique qui lui plaît davantage; rien n'est capable de le soumettre à la sujétion d'aucun pouvoir sur la terre que son seul consentement. Le consentement qui le soumet à quelque *gouvernement*, est exprès ou tacite. Le consentement exprès le rend sans contredit membre de la société qu'il adopte; le consentement tacite le lie aux lois du *gouvernement* dans lequel il jouit de quelque possession; mais si son obligation commence avec ses possessions, elle finit aussi avec leur jouissance. Alors des propriétaires de cette nature sont maîtres de s'incorporer à une autre communauté et d'en ériger une nouvelle, *in vacuis locis*, comme on dit en termes de droit, dans un désert ou dans quelque endroit du monde qui soit sans possesseurs et sans habitations. [VII.789b]

Such liberal principles with their stress on consent were, we shall see, to be severely criticized. Jaucourt goes on to drive home the point:

Les *gouvernements*, de quelque espèce qu'ils soient, qui ont pour fondement un acquiescement libre des peuples, ou exprès ou justifié par une longue et paisible possession, sont également légitimes, aussi longtemps du moins que par l'intention du souverain ils tendent au bonheur des peuples. [VII.789b–790a]

The question as to which is the best form of government is answered in a series of not particularly helpful passages from Burlamaqui; but Montesquieu's praise of the English constitution is not forgotten (Jaucourt had spent some time on this side of the Channel in his youth):

Il y a dans l'Europe un état extrêmement florissant où les trois pouvoirs sont encore mieux fondus que dans la république des Spartiates. La liberté politique est l'objet direct de la constitution de cet état, qui, selon toute apparence, ne peut périr par les désordres du dedans que lorsque la puissance législative sera plus corrompue que l'exécutrice. Personne n'a mieux développé le beau système du *gouvernement* de l'état dont je parle que l'auteur de l'*Esprit des lois*. [VII.790a]

The discussion of this question is concluded with more passages adapted from Locke:

Quelque forme que l'on préfère, il y a toujours une première fin dans tout *gouvernement* qui doit être prise du bien général de la nation; et sur ce principe le meilleur des *gouvernements* est celui qui fait le plus grand nombre d'heureux. Quelle que soit la forme du *gouvernement* politique, le devoir de quiconque en est chargé, de quelque manière que ce soit, est de travailler à rendre heureux les sujets en leur procurant, d'un côté, les commodités de la vie, la sûreté et la tranquillité, et, de l'autre, tous les moyens qui peuvent contribuer à leurs vertus. La loi souveraine de tout bon *gouvernement* est le bien public, *salus populi suprema lex esto*. [VII.790a]

The search for the perfect form of government is not, Jaucourt declares, a waste of time, since in due course it might be possible to bring existing governments closer to this ideal. 'La succession des siècles', he points out, 'a servi à perfectionner plusieurs arts et plusieurs sciences; pourquoi ne servirait-elle pas à perfectionner les différentes sortes de *gouvernements* et à leur donner la meilleure forme?' [VII.790b].

   Jaucourt proceeds to define further what he means by the good of the people:

Le plus grand bien du peuple, c'est sa liberté. La liberté est au corps de l'état ce que la santé est à chaque individu. Sans la santé l'homme ne peut goûter de plaisir; sans la liberté le bonheur est banni des états. Un gouverneur patriote verra donc que le droit de défendre et de maintenir la liberté est le plus sacré de ses devoirs. [VII.790b–791a]

The article concludes with an account, again largely derived from Locke, of the different causes of the dissolution of governments.

   Mild as this article seems to us today, it was at once bitterly attacked. Abbé Giry de Saint-Cyr tries to make out in his *Caté-chisme des Cacouacs* that Jaucourt's rejection of the theory that since all men are born under a government, they are not free to set up a government in another place, is almost treasonable. He also attacks the principle of government by consent and Jaucourt's definition of the circumstances under which governments cease to be legitimate. This attack was copied by several contemporaries. GOUVERNEMENT was also fiercely criticized by the Bishop of Lodève. Once again, censure falls on the passage in which it is argued that a child is not born a subject of any country or government and that on attaining the age of reason he is free to choose the government under which he wishes to live:

Funeste liberté que celle qui prive la patrie de ses citoyens naturels. Où a-t-on appris qu'une puissance légitime n'a aucune autorité dans son territoire sur cette multitude d'hommes vivant de leur travail ou de leur industrie sans rien posséder? Quel est le code où soit établie la nécessité d'un consentement exprès ou tacite sans lequel le souverain et la patrie n'ont aucun droit à nos services?[1]

The bishop then proceeds to reaffirm the principle of the divine right of kings in face of the subversive doctrines set forth in GOUVERNEMENT.

## Diderot's article AUTORITÉ POLITIQUE

The political article in these seven volumes which created the greatest storm was undoubtedly AUTORITÉ POLITIQUE which appeared towards the end of the very first volume. Although unsigned, this article can definitely be attributed to Diderot himself.[2] After this row he tended to lie low in the next three volumes. There is, however, an exception in a short article which, while its starting point is to be found in Abbé Girard's *Synonymes français*, contains some bold and striking sentences of Diderot's own devising:

*BOURGEOIS, CITOYEN, HABITANT (*Gramm.*), termes relatifs à la résidence que l'on fait dans un lieu. Le *bourgeois* est celui dont la résidence ordinaire est dans une ville; le *citoyen* est un *bourgeois* considéré relativement à la société dont il est membre; l'*habitant* est un particulier considéré relativement à la résidence pure et simple. On est *habitant* de la ville, de la province ou de la campagne; on est *bourgeois* de Paris. Le *bourgeois* de Paris, qui

[1] J. F. H. de Fumel, *Mandement et instruction pastorale de Monseigneur l'évêque de Lodève*, Montpellier, 1759, p. 56.
[2] For a detailed discussion of the authorship, sources and contemporary impact of this article see *Essays*, pp. 424–62.

prend à cœur les intérêts de sa ville contre les attentats qui la menacent, en devient *citoyen*. Les hommes sont *habitants* de la terre. Les villes sont pleines de *bourgeois*; il y a peu de *citoyens* parmi ces *bourgeois*. L'*habitation* suppose un lieu; la *bourgeoisie* suppose une ville; la qualité de *citoyen*, une société dont chaque particulier connaît les affaires et aime le bien, et peut se promettre de parvenir aux premières dignités. [II.370a]

Slipped into this grammatical article, particularly into the second half, are some ideas which could hardly have been considered orthodox in an absolute monarchy.

This is, however, small beer compared with such a prominent article as AUTORITÉ POLITIQUE, in which Diderot sets forth clearly the principle of government by consent:

AUTORITÉ POLITIQUE. Aucun homme n'a reçu de la nature le droit de commander aux autres. La liberté est un présent du ciel, et chaque individu de la même espèce a le droit d'en jouir aussitôt qu'il jouit de la raison. Si la nature a établi quelque *autorité*, c'est la puissance paternelle; mais la puissance paternelle a ses bornes, et dans l'état de nature elle finirait aussitôt que les enfants seraient en état de se conduire. Toute autre *autorité* vient d'une autre origine que de la nature. Qu'on examine bien et on la fera toujours remonter à l'une de ces deux sources: ou la force et la violence de celui qui s'en est emparé, ou le consentement de ceux qui s'y sont soumis par un contrat fait ou supposé entre eux et celui à qui ils ont déféré l'*autorité*.

La puissance qui s'acquiert par la violence, n'est qu'une usurpation et ne dure qu'autant que la force de celui qui commande l'emporte sur celle de ceux qui obéissent; en sorte que si ces derniers deviennent à leur tour les plus forts et qu'ils secouent le joug, ils le font avec autant de droit et de justice que l'autre qui le leur avait imposé. La même loi qui a fait l'*autorité*, la défait alors; c'est la loi du plus fort.

Quelquefois l'*autorité* qui s'établit par la violence change de nature; c'est lorsqu'elle continue et se maintient du consentement exprès de ceux qu'on a soumis; mais elle rentre par là dans la seconde espèce dont je vais parler, et celui qui se l'était arrogée, devenant alors prince, cesse d'être tyran.

La puissance qui vient du consentement des peuples, suppose nécessairement des conditions qui en rendent l'usage légitime, utile à la société, avantageux à la république, et qui la fixent et la restreignent entre des limites. . . . [I.898a]

Taking a hint from articles on synonyms derived from Abbé Girard, Diderot proceeds to back up the principle that political

authority must be limited by putting forward a somewhat unorthodox interpretation of two texts of St Paul—a phrase from
Romans 12:1 'rationabile obsequium vestrum' ('which is your
reasonable service') and a sentence from Romans 13:1, 'Non est
enim potestas nisi a Deo; quae autem sunt, a Deo ordinatae sunt'
('For there is no power but of God; the powers that be are ordained
of God'):

La vraie et légitime puissance a donc nécessairement des bornes. Aussi
l'Écriture nous dit-elle 'que votre soumission soit raisonnable': *sit
rationabile obsequium vestrum.*' 'Toute puissance qui vient de Dieu est une
puissance réglée': *omnis potestas a Deo ordinata est.* Car c'est ainsi qu'il faut
entendre ces paroles, conformément à la droite raison et au sens littéral, et
non conformément à l'interprétation de la bassesse et de la flatterie, qui
prétendent que toute puissance, quelle qu'elle soit, vient de Dieu. . . .
[I.898b]

This interpretation was to be severely criticized.

Diderot then goes on to define his notion of the contract. It is, as
he himself calls it, a 'contrat de soumission', i.e. a contract between
ruler and ruled. This was the typical conception of the contract
among liberal thinkers of the eighteenth century who were concerned to limit the power of the monarchy. It is very different from
the notion of the contract which Rousseau was finally to arrive at
in the *Contrat social*; for him there is no contract between government and subjects since the government is merely an emanation of
the sovereign power which is in the hands of the whole people. His
contract is a 'contrat d'association', an agreement among a
number of individuals to form a society. Diderot's contract serves
to limit the power of the monarch:

Le prince tient de ses sujets mêmes l'*autorité* qu'il a sur eux, et cette
*autorité* est bornée par les lois de la nature et de l'état. Les lois de la nature et
de l'état sont les conditions sous lesquelles ils se sont soumis, ou sont censés
s'être soumis, à son gouvernement. L'une de ces conditions est que,
n'ayant de pouvoir et d'*autorité* sur eux que par leur choix et de leur
consentement, il ne peut jamais employer cette *autorité* pour casser l'acte
ou le contrat par lequel elle lui a été déférée; il agirait dès lors contre lui-
même, puisque son *autorité* ne peut subsister que par le titre qui l'a établie.
Qui annule l'un détruit l'autre. Le prince ne peut donc pas disposer de son
pouvoir et de ses sujets sans le consentement de la nation et indépendamment du choix marqué dans le contrat de soumission. [I.898b–899a]

The conditions of this contract, Diderot continues, vary from country to country:

Mais partout la nation est en droit de maintenir envers et contre tous le contrat qu'elle a fait; aucune puissance ne peut le changer, et quand il n'a plus lieu, elle rentre dans le droit et dans la pleine liberté d'en passer un nouveau avec qui, et comme il lui plaît. C'est ce qui arriverait en France, si par le plus grand des malheurs la famille entière régnante venait à s'éteindre jusque dans ses moindre rejetons; alors le sceptre et la couronne retourneraient à la nation. [I.899a]

After these ten paragraphs full of bold principles the rest of the article comes as a decided anticlimax. The last sentences with their recommendation of blind obedience to the monarch seem to remove all the sting from the article:

Quant aux sujets, la première loi que la religion, la raison et la nature leur imposent, est de respecter eux-mêmes les conditions du contrat qu'ils ont fait, de ne jamais perdre de vue la nature de leur gouvernement; en France, de ne point oublier que tant que la famille régnante subsistera par les mâles, rien ne les dispensera jamais de l'obéissance, d'honorer et de craindre leur maître comme celui par lequel ils ont voulu que l'image de Dieu leur fût présente et visible sur la terre; d'être encore attachés à ces sentiments par un motif de reconnaissance de la tranquillité et des biens dont ils jouissent à l'abri du nom royal; si jamais il leur arrivait d'avoir un roi injuste, ambitieux et violent, de n'opposer au malheur qu'un seul remède, celui de l'apaiser par leur soumission et de fléchir Dieu par leurs prières; parce que ce remède est le seul qui soit légitime, en conséquence du contrat de soumission juré au prince régnant anciennement et à ses descendants par les mâles, quels qu'ils puissent être; et de considérer que tous ces motifs qu'on croit avoir de résister, ne sont, à les bien examiner, qu'autant de prétextes d'infidélités subtilement colorées; qu'avec cette conduite on n'a jamais corrigé les princes, ni aboli les impôts, et qu'on a seulement ajouté aux malheurs dont on se plaignait déjà, un nouveau degré de misère. Voilà les fondements sur lesquels les peuples et ceux qui les gouvernent pourraient établir leur bonheur réciproque. [I.900a–b]

How is one to interpret this strange mixture of attitudes? For some modern writers the last part of the article simply cancels out the bold principles advanced in the opening paragraphs. This was also the view of a contemporary who was closely associated with both Diderot and Rousseau—Deleyre, the author of the bold

*Coupe et vue générale d'une mine (Vol. VI, Minéralogie, 7e collection, Plate VI)*

article, FANATISME. 'Je veux un grand mal à M. Diderot', he wrote indignantly to Jean Jacques in 1756,

de ce qu'il a dit dans l'article *Autorité* que je lisais hier, qu'on n'a, contre les rois ambitieux, injustes et violents que le parti de la soumission et de la prière. La fin de cet article ne correspond pas au commencement. Il ne faut pas toucher à ce qu'on ne peut manier à son gré. Pour peu qu'une âme forte montre de faiblesse, elle détruit son propre ouvrage. Si je suis flatteur dans un endroit, je passerai pour satirique dans un autre, et jamais pour ami de la vérité.[1]

That was not, however, the opinion of such contemporary critics as Father Berthier in the *Journal de Trévoux* (March 1752). He was not to be taken in by the obsequious tone of the conclusion:

Si cette conclusion regardait tous les principes qu'on a posés plus haut sur l'origine, sur les bornes, sur la possession, sur l'exercice de l'autorité, nous ne l'admettrions pas; et nous croirions bien plutôt que tout sujet fidèle, que tout bon Français doit *penser autrement*. Car quelles conséquences ne pourrait-on pas tirer d'une doctrine qui met toute l'autorité essentielle entre les mains du peuple; qui réduit celle des rois a un seul *dépôt*; qui fait dépendre la puissance du consentement des peuples, et l'usage de cette puissance des conditions passées entre le souverain et ses sujets? Il y a, nous l'avouons, dans cet article de l'*Encyclopédie* quelques bons endroits, surtout au milieu et vers la fin; on s'y rapproche un peu des idées communes; on s'y déclare pour la fidélité, pour la subordination constante et inaltérable. Mais la difficulté sera toujours de concilier ces bons endroits avec les principes posés au commencement de l'article, et ces principes (osons le dire avec zèle) nous paraissent très contraires à l'autorité suprême, à la constitution de l'empire français, à la tranquillité publique. (p. 463)

Father Berthier was not the only contemporary to read the article in this way. When Vol. I of the *Encyclopédie* appeared at the end of June 1751, AUTORITÉ POLITIQUE at once made a strong impression. In a verse satire entitled *Dialogue entre un colporteur et Diderot dans la boutique d'un libraire sur le dictionnaire de l'Encyclopédie*, which the *inspecteur de la librairie*, Joseph d'Hémery, copied into his journal on 16 August, the *colporteur* is made to say that, despite its bulk, the work is saleable:

> Dans lui l'*autorité* publique
> N'est pas l'article respecté.

[1] Leigh 415.

and here we find the marginal note: 'L'art. *Autorité* a pensé faire supprimer le dictionnaire'. Later the Jansenist *Nouvelles ecclésiastiques* (1 July 1754) was to claim that it was the cause of the suppression of the first two volumes in 1752: 'C'est cet article qui a donné lieu à l'arrêt du Conseil d'État de supprimer ce dictionnaire comme contenant des maximes *tendant à détruire l'autorité royale et à établir l'esprit d'indépendance et de révolte*' (p. 108). However that may be, no article was more frequently attacked by contemporary critics; Jansenists and Jesuits, laymen and clerics united to denounce such subversive views.

One may also quote, for instance, the *Instruction pastorale* in which the Bishop of Auxerre censured Abbé de Prades's thesis. AUTORITÉ POLITIQUE is included in its censure in passages such as this:

Il est très étonnant que des maximes si manifestement séditieuses et qui sapent par le fondement l'autorité souveraine, aient osé se montrer si hardiment. Elle suppose que l'autorité souveraine réside dans le peuple; qu'il en conserve toujours la propriété et qu'il n'en donne aux rois que l'exercice et l'usage; mais il peut la leur ôter comme il la leur a donnée parce que le violement des conditions annule le contrat de part et d'autre, fait perdre au roi le droit de régner et décharge les sujets de l'obligation de lui obéir.[1]

It is significant that in replying to this attack in his *Suite de l'Apologie de M. l'abbé de Prades* Diderot should have leant for support on the Paris Parlement, that bulwark of resistance to absolutism. He defends his article by seeking to embroil the bishop with the Parlement:

D'ailleurs, il est très douteux que le parlement soit content qu'on ait traité les maximes suivantes de séditieuses, savoir: 'Que les lois de la nature et de l'État sont les conditions sous lesquelles les sujets se sont soumis, ou sont censés s'être soumis, au gouvernement de leur prince. . . . Qu'un prince ne peut jamais employer l'autorité qu'il tient d'eux pour casser le contrat par lequel elle lui a été déférée . . .' Car qu'est-ce qu'un *parlement* sinon un corps chargé du dépôt sacré du *contrat* réel ou supposé par lequel les peuples se sont soumis ou sont censés s'être soumis au gouvernement de leur prince? Si M. d'Auxerre regarde ce *contrat* comme une chimère, je le défie de l'écrire publiquement. Je ne crois pas que le

[1] Charles de Caylus, *Instruction pastorale*, n.p., 1752, p. 81.

parlement de Paris se vît dépouiller tranquillement de sa prérogative la plus auguste, de cette prérogative sans laquelle il perdrait le nom de *Parlement* pour être réduit au nom ordinaire de *corps de judicature*.[1]

The way the Parlement is brought into the argument is at first sight rather puzzling; but we have to remember that its conflict with the Crown was warming up again at the very moment when the first volumes of the *Encyclopédie* appeared.

The *Errata* to Vol. III attempts to answer some of the attacks made on AUTORITÉ POLITIQUE:

Au reste il est bon d'expliquer notre pensée. Nous n'avons jamais prétendu que l'autorité des princes légitimes ne vînt point de Dieu; nous avons seulement voulu la distinguer de celle des usurpateurs qui enlèvent la couronne aux princes légitimes à qui les peuples sont toujours obligés d'obéir, même dans leur disgrâce, parce que l'autorité des princes légitimes vient de Dieu et que celle des usurpateurs est un mal qu'il permet. Le signe que l'autorité vient de Dieu est le consentement des peuples; c'est ce consentement irrévocable qui a assuré la couronne à Hugues Capet et à sa postérité. En un mot, nous n'avons prétendu dans notre article AUTORITÉ que commenter et développer ce passage, tiré d'un ouvrage imprimé par ordre de Louis XIV et qui a pour titre, *Traité des droits de la Reine sur différents endroits de la monarchie d'Espagne, part. I, p. 169, édit. de 1667 in-12.* 'Que la loi fondamentale de l'état forme une liaison réciproque et éternelle entre le prince et ses descendants, d'une part, et les sujets et leurs descendants, de l'autre, par une espèce de contrat qui destine le souverain à régner et les peuples à obéir ... engagement solennel dans lequel ils se sont donnés les uns aux autres pour s'entr'aider mutuellement.' [III.xvi]

Leaving aside for a moment the question of the sincerity of this apparent half-retraction of the bold ideas contained in the original article, we might investigate the source from which the editors derived this quotation from a work which we have already encountered in Jaucourt's DESPOTISME. This particular quotation came not from Barbeyrac, but from the outspoken remonstrances which the Paris Parlement had drawn up six months earlier, remonstrances so bold that Louis XV refused to receive them. In the following month the Parlement went on strike and was exiled from Paris; not until September of the following year were the exiled judges recalled and the conflict temporarily resolved. It was thus in the middle of this acute phase in the struggle between king and Parlement that Vol. III of the *Encyclopédie* made its appearance.

Not only is the passage from the *Traité des droits de la Reine* to be found word for word and dot for dot in the Parlement's remonstrances;[1] six years later d'Alembert admitted where it had been taken from when he wrote ironically that the contributors to the *Encyclopédie* had been accused of maintaining, among other monstrous things, 'avec le plus puissant de nos rois et avec le premier parlement du royaume, que l'autorité légitime est fondée sur le *contrat* fait entre le souverain et ses sujets'.[2] The attitude of the editors of the *Encyclopédie* towards the Parlements was always ambiguous. They hated them for their intolerance, all the more so when in 1759 the Paris Parlement condemned the whole enterprise; yet if the Parlements were mainly concerned to defend the privileges of the aristocracy and their own claims to a share of political power, both they and the principal contributors were united in their hostility to absolutism and the fact remained that in these years the Parlements were the only body in the state in a position to offer resistance to absolutism. No doubt Diderot and d'Alembert were delighted to be able to hide behind this quotation which had been trumpeted forth into the world by the Paris Parlement, the leading *cour souveraine* of France.

The editors' reply to criticisms of AUTORITÉ POLITIQUE was far from satisfying the authors of the *Réflexions d'un Franciscain* who retorted:

Une réponse moins recherchée aurait été plus *satisfaisante*. Si on n'a jamais prétendu que l'autorité des princes légitimes ne vînt pas de Dieu, n'était-il pas plus à propos de rendre aux passages de saint Paul leur sens naturel si contraire aux usurpateurs? N'était-il pas plus à propos de convenir de bonne foi qu'on avait eu tort de compter au nombre de ces prétendus usurpateurs tous les princes qui abusent de leur autorité? (p. 36)

This work's criticisms were relatively mild compared, for instance, with the violent attack delivered on the article in 1759 by Joly de Fleury, the *avocat-général* of the Paris Parlement. After

---

[1] *Remontrances du Parlement de Paris au XVIIIᵉ siècle*, ed. J. Flammermont, 1888–98, 3 vols, i, 522.
[2] *Mélanges de littérature, d'histoire et de philosophie*, Amsterdam, 1763–7, 5 vols, i, p. xvn.

quoting the opening paragraph, he decided that what followed was too subversive to be read out in public:

Les conséquences se présentent ici d'elles-mêmes. Il est de la prudence de notre ministère de ne pas employer les termes dans lesquels sont conçues les maximes séditieuses du rédacteur, maximes bien différentes de celles de l'apôtre qui nous apprend qu'*il n'y a point de puissance qui ne vienne de Dieu et que c'est lui qui a établi celles qui sont sur la terre; qu'il est donc nécessaire de s'y soumettre non seulement par la crainte du châtiment, mais aussi par un* devoir *de conscience,* doctrine seule véritable et qui affermit le bonheur des rois et des peuples.[1]

To this attack Grimm retorted in his privately circulated news-sheet:

Ce morceau ne tend pas moins qu'à déshonorer le Parlement à la face de l'Europe entière, en proscrivant les principes contenus dans l'article *Autorité,* principes avoués et enseignés chez tous les peuples policés et que personne n'a autant d'intérêt à soutenir que ce Parlement même auquel on a osé les déférer comme pernicieux.[2]

Once again we see a *philosophe* stressing the identity of interests between his party and the Parlements in their common hostility to absolutism.

And so the attack continues into the 1760s in *La Religion vengée* and *La Petite Encyclopédie,* and even into the 1770s in Abbé Sabatier de Castres's *Trois siècles de la littérature française.* The number and persistence of the attacks on this article would seem to show that, when it appeared in 1751, contemporaries did not regard it as containing little but a string of harmless platitudes.

## Diderot's later political articles

The last ten volumes of the *Encyclopédie* are relatively much richer in general political articles than those which appeared down to 1757. A good many of these articles are unsigned, and although some of them appear in nineteenth-century editions of Diderot's collected works, there is no evidence on which they can be attributed to him. So far as is yet known, Diderot did not write for these last ten volumes a single political article comparable in

---

1 *Arrêts de la cour de Parlement,* Paris, 1759, p. 15.          2 *Corr. litt.,* iv, 82.

importance to his AUTORITÉ POLITIQUE. His articles on the history
of philosophy include one on MACHIAVÉLISME where he puts
forward the theory, for which he claims the support of Bacon, that
the author's object in writing *Il Principe* was to warn his fellowmen against tyrants:

Comment expliquer qu'un des plus ardents défenseurs de la monarchie
soit devenu tout à coup un infâme apologiste de la tyrannie? le voici. Au
reste, je n'expose ici mon sentiment que comme une idée qui n'est pas
tout à fait destituée de vraisemblance. Lorsque Machiavel écrivit son
traité *Du Prince*, c'est comme s'il eût dit à ses contemporains: *Lisez bien cet
ouvrage. Si vous acceptez jamais un maître, il sera tel que je vous le peins: voilà
la bête féroce à laquelle vous vous abandonnerez.* Ainsi ce fut la faute de ses
contemporains s'ils méconnurent son but; ils prirent une satire pour un
éloge. [IX.793b]

Into the notes of the article SUBSIDE Diderot also inserted some
interesting reflections on absolute monarchy and its ministers in
France in the sixteenth and seventeenth centuries. He has a poor
opinion of Louis XII's minister, Cardinal d'Amboise, as of
Richelieu and Mazarin:

On peut faire de grandes choses sans être un *bon ministre*. Celui qui aurait
vendu le royaume pour acheter la tiare, celui qui sacrifiait tout à son
orgueil et à sa vengeance, celui qui faisait servir son pouvoir à son in-
satiable avarice, ne méritent point le titre de *bon ministre*. [XV.579 note (f)]

In contrast, Diderot speaks in typically enthusiastic fashion of
'l'adorable Henri IV' and his minister, 'le vertueux Sully'
[XV.579 note (g)], and he continues:

Je ne trouve dans l'histoire de France que *Sully* qui ait constamment
voulu le bien; mais il était parvenu dans ces temps orageux qui forment
les âmes vigoureuses et sublimes. Il avait partagé les malheurs de son
maître; il était son ami, et il travaillait sous les yeux et pour la gloire de cet
ami. [XV.579 note (i)]

After contrasting the hatred inspired by Colbert and the rejoicings
at his death with his enhanced reputation in the 1760s, Diderot goes
on to put the blame for his failures on Louis XIV:

Si le maître ne s'était point trompé dans son objet, c'est-à-dire s'il n'eût
pas pris pour la gloire ce qui n'en était que le fantôme, *Colbert* aurait
préféré l'utilité à la splendeur. [XV.579 notes (h) and (k)]

Hidden away in short grammatical articles which may almost certainly be attributed to Diderot are a considerable number of observations on political matters. ILLIMITÉ, for instance, repeats the message of AUTORITÉ POLITIQUE in one short sentence: 'Il n'y a point de puissance légitime et *illimitée* sur la terre' [VIII.556a]. Under ODIEUX, again, we find: 'De tous les méchants les tyrans sont les plus *odieux*, puisqu'ils enlèvent aux hommes des biens in-aliénables, la liberté, la vie, la fortune, etc.' [XI.349b]. A similar attitude is to be found in yet another grammatical article:

OPPRESSEUR, s.m., OPPRIMER, v.act. (*Gram.*), terme relatif au mauvais usage de la puissance. On *opprime*, on mérite le nom d'*oppresseur*, on fait gémir sous l'oppression, lorsque le poids de notre autorité passe sur nos sujets d'une manière qui les écrase et qui leur rend l'existence odieuse. On rend l'existence odieuse en envahissant la liberté, en épuisant la fortune, en gênant les opinions, etc. Un peuple peut être *opprimé* par son souverain, un peuple par un autre peuple. Fléchier dit qu'il y a peu de sûreté pour les oppresseurs de la liberté des peuples; mais c'est seulement dans les premiers instants de l'oppression. A la longue on perd tout sentiment, on s'abrutit, et l'on en vient jusqu'à adorer la tyrannie et à diviniser ses actions les plus atroces. Alors il n'y a plus de ressource pour une nation que dans une grande révolution qui la régénère. Il lui faut une crise. [XI.515b]

A second article drives the point home:

OPPRESSION (s.f. (*Morales et Politiq.*) Par un malheur attaché à la condition humaine les sujets sont quelquefois soumis à des souverains qui, abusant du pouvoir qui leur a été confié, leur font éprouver des rigueurs que la violence seule autorise. L'*oppression* est toujours le fruit d'une mauvaise administration. Lorsque le souverain est injuste, ou lorsque ses repré-sentants se prévalent de son autorité, ils regardent les peuples comme des animaux vils qui ne sont faits que pour ramper et pour satisfaire aux dépens de leur sang, de leur travail et de leurs trésors leurs projets ambitieux ou leurs caprices ridicules. En vain l'innocence gémit, en vain elle implore la protection des lois, la force triomphe et insulte à ses pleurs. Domitien disait: *Omnia tibi in homines licere*, maxime digne d'un monstre et qui pourtant n'a été que trop suivie par quelques souverains. [XI.516a]

In contrast to this obvious hatred of all forms of political oppres-sion we find under MUTUEL a couple of sentences which seem to conflict with what we would expect Diderot to feel on these questions:

Toute obligation est *mutuelle* sans excepter celle des rois envers leurs sujets. Les rois sont obligés de rendre heureux leurs sujets, les sujets d'obéir à leurs rois; mais si l'un manque à son devoir, les autres n'en sont pas moins obligés de persévérer dans le leur. [X.910b]

One even wonders whether this passage was not tampered with by Le Breton, especially when we consider the article MENACE which is certainly by Diderot and into which he inserted among other things a retort to Palissot's satirical comedy, *Les Philosophes*:

Les termes *menace* et *menacer* ont été employés métaphoriquement en cent manières diverses. On dira très bien, par exemple, lorsque le gouvernement d'un peuple se déclare contre la philosophie, c'est qu'il est mauvais; il *menace* le peuple d'une stupidité prochaine. [X.331b]

This was a pretty bold attack on the government of Louis XV which had allowed Palissot's play to be performed at the Comédie Française; that Diderot was very anxious for this article not to be tampered with by Le Breton we know from the stiff note to the printer which he inserted in the margin of his proofs, warning him not to interfere with the text.[1]

## Jaucourt's later political articles

Jaucourt, who furnished an enormously high proportion of the text of these ten volumes, also contributed a large number of political articles, many of them, as before, compiled from the Natural Law writers and from Montesquieu. Yet even so the message, though secondhand, was often made sharper by being compressed into a short article and stripped of its cautious wrappings. LIBERTÉ CIVILE (*Droit des nations*) is a compound of Burlamaqui's *Principes du droit politique* from which Jaucourt takes his definition and of the *Esprit des lois*, Book xi, chaps 1–6. After reproducing Montesquieu's account of the differing notions of what constitutes liberty, he goes on:

Enfin chacun a appelé *liberté* le gouvernement qui était conforme à ses coutumes et à ses inclinations; mais la *liberté* est le droit de faire tout ce que

[1] Gordon and Torrey, pp. 37 and 70.

les lois permettent, et si un citoyen pouvait faire ce qu'elles défendent, il n'aurait plus de liberté, parce que les autres auraient tous de même ce pouvoir. Il est vrai que cette *liberté* ne se trouve que dans les gouvernements modérés, c'est-à-dire dans les gouvernements dont la constitution est telle que personne n'est contraint de faire les choses auxquelles la loi ne l'oblige pas et à ne point faire celles que la loi lui permet.

La *liberté civile* est donc fondée sur les meilleures lois possibles, et dans un état qui les aurait en partage, un homme à qui on ferait son procès selon les lois et qui devrait être pendu le lendemain, serait plus libre qu'un bacha ne l'est en Turquie. Par conséquent il n'y a point de *liberté* dans les états où la puissance législative et la puissance exécutrice sont dans la même main. Il n'y a point à plus forte raison dans ceux où la puissance de juger est réunie à la législatrice et à l'exécutrice. [IX.472a]

The stress here is on the merits of 'gouvernements modérés'; and in the second last sentence which denies that liberty can exist in a country where legislative and executive power are in the same hands there is a clear challenge to the position of the absolute monarch in France, a position which Louis XV was to reaffirm before the Paris Parlement within months of the appearance of these last ten volumes when he declared: 'C'est à moi seul qu'appartient le pouvoir législatif sans dépendance et sans partage.'

LIBERTÉ POLITIQUE is similarly based on Book xi of the *Esprit des lois*, down to the prudent reservations made by Montesquieu as to both the actual existence of English liberties and the desirability of imitating our constitution:

Il y a dans le monde une nation qui a pour objet direct de sa constitution la *liberté politique*; et si les principes sur lesquels elle la fonde sont solides, il faut en reconnaître les avantages. . . .

Je ne prétends point décider que les Anglais jouissent actuellement de la prérogative dont je parle; il me suffit de dire avec M. de Montesquieu qu'elle est établie par leurs lois, et qu'après tout cette *liberté politique* extrême ne doit point mortifier ceux qui n'en ont qu'une modérée, parce que l'excès même de la raison n'est pas toujours désirable et que les hommes en général s'accommodent presque toujours mieux des milieux que des extrémités. [IX.472a–b]

MONARCHIE is little more than a summary of Montesquieu, though that summary does bring out clearly the author's stress on the ideal of a limited monarchy:

La nature de la *monarchie* consiste en ce que le monarque est la source de

tout pouvoir politique et civil, et qu'il régit seul l'état par des lois fondamentales; car s'il n'y avait dans l'état que la volonté momentanée et
capricieuse d'un seul sans lois fondamentales, ce serait un gouvernement
despotique où un seul homme entraîne tout par sa volonté; mais la
*monarchie* commande par des lois dont le dépôt est entre les mains de corps
politiques qui annoncent les lois lorsqu'elles sont faites et les rappellent
lorsqu'on les oublie. [X.636a]

Here we have a clear allusion to the political role which the
Parlements claimed for themselves in eighteenth-century France.

In MONARCHIE ABSOLUE Burlamaqui and Montesquieu are again
blended so as to distinguish clearly between despotism and absolutism, a form of monarchy in which the royal power knows some
limits:

MONARCHIE ABSOLUE (*Gouvernement*), forme de monarchie dans laquelle
le corps entier des citoyens a cru devoir conférer la souveraineté au prince,
avec l'étendue et le pouvoir absolu qui résidait en lui originairement, et
sans y ajouter de restriction particulière que celle des lois établies. Il ne
faut pas confondre le pouvoir absolu d'un tel monarque avec le pouvoir
arbitraire et despotique, car l'origine et la nature de la *monarchie* absolue
est limitée par sa nature même, par l'intention de ceux de qui le monarque
la tient et par les lois fondamentales de son état. Comme les peuples qui
vivent sous une bonne police, sont plus heureux que ceux qui, sans règles
et sans chefs, errent dans les forêts, aussi les monarques qui vivent sous les
lois fondamentales de leur état, sont-ils plus heureux que les princes
despotiques qui n'ont rien qui puisse régler le cœur de leurs peuples, ni le
leur. [X.636b–637a]

MONARCHIE ÉLECTIVE starts off with further borrowings from
Burlamaqui, but it also contains a long harangue addressed to the
newly elected ruler in which he is reminded of his duties towards
his people; and the article ends: 'Que l'on juge sur cet exposé de la
forme ordinaire des gouvernements!' [X.637b]

Finally in MONARCHIE LIMITÉE, which again follows closely the
analysis of the English constitution given in the *Esprit des lois*,
Jaucourt, although without ever actually mentioning France,
makes clear his preference for this form of government:

MONARCHIE LIMITÉE (*Gouvernement*), sorte de *monarchie* où les trois
pouvoirs sont tellement fondus ensemble qu'ils se servent l'un à l'autre de

balance et de contrepoids. La *monarchie limitée* héréditaire paraît être la meilleure forme de *monarchie*, parce que, indépendamment de sa stabilité, le corps législatif y est composé de deux parties, dont l'une enchaîne l'autre par leur faculté mutuelle d'empêcher, et toutes les deux sont liées par la puissance exécutrice, qui l'est elle-même par la législative. Tel est le gouvernement d'Angleterre dont les racines, toujours coupées, toujours sanglantes, ont enfin produit après des siècles, à l'étonnement des nations, le mélange égal de la liberté et de la royauté. Dans les autres *monarchies* européennes que nous connaissons les trois pouvoirs n'y sont point fondus de cette manière; ils ont chacun une distribution particulière suivant laquelle ils approchent plus ou moins de la liberté politique. Il paraît qu'on jouit en Suède de ce précieux avantage, autant qu'on en est éloigné en Danemark; mais la *monarchie* de Russie est un pur despotisme. [X.637b]

In SÉDITIEUX, SÉDITION Jaucourt refuses to condemn outright all forms of rebellion since he holds that some may be justified:

Pour me recueillir en deux mots, je remarquerai qu'en général la tyrannie, les innovations en matière de religion, la pesanteur des impôts, le changement des lois ou des coutumes, le mépris des privilèges de la nation, le mauvais choix des ministres, la cherté des vivres, etc. sont autant de causes de tristes *séditions*.

Les remèdes sont de rétablir les principes du gouvernement, de rendre justice au peuple, d'écarter la disette par la facilité du commerce et l'oisiveté par l'établissement des manufactures, de réprimer le luxe, de faire valoir les terres en donnant du crédit à l'agriculture, de ne point laisser une autorité arbitraire aux chefs, de maintenir les lois et de modérer les subsides. [XIV.887a]

Economic conditions—including the food shortages so frequent in eighteenth-century France—as well as political causes are blamed for such unhappy occurrences.

In other articles in these last ten volumes Jaucourt continually works in praise of the political system on this side of the Channel. He devotes, for instance, a fairly substantial article to PARLEMENT D'ANGLETERRE (*Hist. d'Angl.*) in which he traces its origins back to the Witenagemot. Such general observations as the article contains are taken, however, from Voltaire's *Henriade* and the *Lettres philosophiques*. In TYRANNIE Jaucourt quotes the example of England as a country in which men do not have to 'souffrir les inconvénients des gouvernements comme ceux des climats et supporter ce qu'ils ne peuvent pas ehanger':

Mais si on me parlait en particulier d'un peuple qui a été assez sage et assez heureux pour fonder et pour conserver une libre constitution de gouvernement, comme ont fait par exemple les peuples de la Grande-Bretagne; c'est à eux que je dirais librement que leurs rois sont obligés par les devoirs les plus sacrés que les lois humaines puissent créer et que les lois divines puissent autoriser, de défendre et de maintenir préférablement à toute considération la liberté de la constitution, à la tête de laquelle ils sont placés. [XVI.785b]

Jaucourt then goes on to discuss the right of a people to resist tyranny (here he quotes in support of his views Bacon, Sidney, Grotius, Pufendorf, Locke and Barbeyrac); but he make it clear that by *peuple* he understands 'non pas la canaille, mais la plus saine partie de tous les ordres d'un état'.

## Some anonymous political articles

In these last ten volumes one finds a group of political articles, unsigned but linked together by cross-references—POUVOIR, PROPRIÉTÉ, PROTECTION and SOUVERAINS—all of which are directed against absolute monarchy and are in favour of limiting the royal power. SOUVERAINS (*Droit naturel & politique*) begins by tracing the origins of political society which, it is argued, must be based on consent:

On sentit qu'il fallait que chaque homme renonçât à une partie de son indépendance naturelle pour se soumettre à une volonté qui représentât celle de toute la société et qui fût, pour ainsi dire, le centre commun et le point de réunion de toutes ses volontés et de toutes ses forces. Telle est l'origine des *souverains*. L'on voit que leur pouvoir et leurs droits ne sont fondés que sur le consentement des peuples; ceux qui s'établissent par la violence ne sont que des usurpateurs; ils ne deviennent légitimes que lorsque le consentement des peuples a confirmé aux *souverains* les droits dont ils s'étaient emparés.

   Les hommes ne se sont mis en société que pour être plus heureux: la société ne s'est choisi des *souverains* que pour veiller plus efficacement à son bonheur et à sa conservation. [XV.423b–424a]

Some nations—England is prominent amongst them—have limited the power of their sovereign:

Les peuples n'ont point toujours donné la même étendue de pouvoir aux *souverains* qu'ils ont choisis. L'expérience de tous les temps apprend que plus le pouvoir des hommes est grand, plus leurs passions les portent à en abuser. Cette considération a déterminé quelques nations à mettre des limites à la puissance de ceux qu'elles chargeaient de les gouverner. Ces limitations de la souveraineté ont varié suivant les circonstances, suivant le plus ou moins d'amour des peuples pour la liberté, suivant la grandeur des inconvénients auxquels ils s'étaient trouvés entièrement exposés sous des *souverains* trop arbitraires. C'est là ce qui a donné naissance aux différentes divisions qui ont été faites de la souveraineté et aux différentes formes des gouvernements. En Angleterre la puissance législative réside dans le roi et dans le parlement. Ce dernier corps représente la nation qui, par la constitution britannique, s'est réservé de cette manière une portion de la *puissance souveraine*, tandis qu'elle a abandonné au roi seul le pouvoir de faire exécuter les lois. Dans l'empire d'Allemagne l'empereur ne peut faire des lois qu'avec le concours des états de l'empire. [XV.424a]

After giving a warning that the limitation of sovereign power must not be carried as far as in contemporary Poland and Sweden, the writer then goes on to argue that even in an absolute monarchy (like France, understood) the royal authority could not be unlimited:

D'autres peuples n'ont point stipulé par des actes exprès et authentiques les limites qu'ils fixaient à leurs *souverains*; ils se sont contentés de leur imposer la nécessité de suivre les lois fondamentales de l'état, leur confiant d'ailleurs la puissance législative ainsi que celle d'exécuter. C'est là ce qu'on appelle *souveraineté absolue*. Cependant la droite raison fait voir qu'elle a toujours des limites naturelles; un *souverain*, quelque absolu qu'il soit, n'est point en droit de toucher aux lois constitutives de l'État, non plus qu'à sa religion; il ne peut point altérer la forme du gouvernement, ni changer l'ordre de la succession, à moins d'une autorisation formelle de sa nation. D'ailleurs il est toujours soumis aux lois de la justice et à celles de la raison dont aucune force humaine ne peut le dispenser.

Lorsqu'un *souverain* absolu s'arroge le droit de changer à sa volonté les lois fondamentales de son pays, lorsqu'il prétend un pouvoir arbitraire sur la personne et les possessions de son peuple, il devient un despote. Nul peuple n'a pu ni voulu accorder un pouvoir de cette nature à ses *souverains*; s'il l'avait fait, la nature et la raison le mettent toujours en droit de réclamer contre la violence. *Voyez* l'article POUVOIR. La tyrannie n'est autre chose que l'exercice du despotisme. [XV.424a–b]

The article then goes on to define the duties of the sovereign, both in internal affairs (here there is a cross-reference to PROTECTION) and in external.

The conclusion once again stresses the limits on sovereign power:

Tels sont les principaux droits de la souveraineté, tels sont les droits des *souverains*. L'histoire nous fournit des exemples sans nombre de princes oppresseurs, de lois violées, de sujets révoltés. Si la raison gouvernait les *souverains*, les peuples n'auraient pas besoin de leur lier les mains ou de vivre avec eux dans une défiance continuelle; les chefs des nations, contents de travailler au bonheur de leurs sujets, ne chercheraient point à envahir leurs droits. Par une fatalité attachée à la nature humaine les hommes font des efforts continuels pour étendre leur pouvoir; quelques digues que la prudence des peuples ait voulu leur opposer, il n'en est point que l'ambition et la force ne viennent à bout de rompre ou d'éluder. Les *souverains* ont un trop grand avantage sur les peuples: la dépravation d'une seule volonté suffit dans le *souverain* pour mettre en danger ou pour détruire la félicité de ses sujets; au lieu que ces derniers ne peuvent guère lui opposer l'unanimité ou le concours de volontés et de forces nécessaires pour réprimer ces entreprises injustes.

Il est une erreur funeste au bonheur des peuples, dans laquelle les *souverains* ne tombent que trop communément: ils croient que la souveraineté est avilie dès lors que ses droits sont resserrés dans des bornes. Les chefs de nations qui travailleront à la félicité de leurs peuples s'assureront leur amour, trouveront en eux une obéissance prompte et seront toujours redoutables à leurs ennemis. Le chevalier Temple disait à Charles II *qu'un roi d'Angleterre qui est l'homme de son peuple, est le plus grand roi du monde; mais s'il veut être davantage, il n'est plus rien. Je veux être l'homme de mon peuple*, répondit le monarque. [XV.424b–425a]

And on this moral note this somewhat pessimistic, if at times bold, article ends.

POUVOIR (*Droit nat. & politiq.*), which refers back again to SOUVERAINS, begins with a strong affirmation of the principle of government by consent:

Le consentement des hommes réunis en société est le fondement du *pouvoir*. Celui qui ne s'est établi que par la force ne peut subsister que par la force: jamais elle ne peut conférer de titre, et les peuples conservent toujours le droit de réclamer contre elle. En établissant les sociétés, les hommes n'ont renoncé à une portion de l'indépendance dans laquelle la nature les a fait naître que pour s'assurer les avantages qui résultent de leur soumission à une autorité légitime et raisonnable; ils n'ont jamais prétendu se livrer sans réserve à des maîtres arbitraires, ni donner les mains à la tyrannie et à l'oppression, ni conférer à d'autres le droit de les rendre malheureux. [XIII.255a]

Once again the author insists that sovereign power must be limited, though this limitation should not be carried too far:

Dans quelques états monarchiques le *pouvoir* du souverain est limité par les lois de l'état qui lui fixent des bornes qu'il n'est pas permis d'enfreindre; c'est ainsi qu'en Angleterre le *pouvoir* législatif réside dans le roi et dans les deux chambres du parlement. Dans d'autres pays les monarques exercent, du consentement des peuples, un *pouvoir* absolu, mais il est toujours subordonné aux lois fondamentales de l'état qui font la sûreté réciproque du souverain et des sujets. (XIII.255a)

PROTECTION (*Droit naturel & politique*) explains that men enter into society with a view to their own advantage:

Les hommes ne se sont soumis à des souverains que pour être plus heureux; ils ont senti que tant que chaque individu demeurerait isolé, il serait exposé à devenir la proie d'un homme plus fort que lui, que ses possessions seraient sujettes à la violence et à l'usurpation. La vue de ces inconvénients détermina les hommes à former des sociétés afin que toutes les forces et les volontés des particuliers fussent réunies par des liens communs. Ces sociétés se sont choisi des chefs qui devinrent les dépositaires des forces de tous, et on leur donna le droit de les employer pour l'avantage et la *protection* de tous et de chacun en particulier. On voit donc que les souverains ne peuvent se dispenser de protéger leurs sujets, c'est une des principales conditions sous laquelle ils se sont soumis à eux.

Moreover, the article adds,

ce n'est point seulement contre les ennemis du dehors que les souverains sont tenus de protéger leurs sujets, ils doivent encore réprimer les entreprises de leurs ministres et des hommes puissants qui peuvent les opprimer. [XIII.504b]

The point is made more explicitly in PROPRIÉTÉ (*Droit naturel & politique*) which argues that security for their property was one of the main motives of men when they entered into society:

Une des principales vues des hommes en formant des sociétés civiles a été de s'assurer la possession tranquille des avantages qu'ils avaient acquis ou qu'ils pouvaient acquérir; ils ont voulu que personne ne pût les troubler dans la jouissance de leurs biens. C'est pour cela que chacun a consenti à en sacrifier une portion qu'on appelle *impôts* à la conservation et au maintien de la société entière; on a voulu par là fournir aux chefs qu'on avait choisis les moyens de maintenir chaque particulier dans la jouissance de la portion qu'il s'était réservée. Quelque fort qu'ait pu être l'enthousiasme des hommes pour les souverains auxquels ils se soumettaient, ils n'ont jamais prétendu leur donner un pouvoir absolu et illimité sur tous leurs biens; ils n'ont jamais compté se mettre dans la nécessité de ne travailler que pour eux. La flatterie des courtisans à qui les principes les plus absurdes ne coûtent rien, a quelquefois voulu persuader à des princes qu'ils avaient un droit absolu sur les biens de leurs sujets; il n'y a que les despotes et les tyrans qui aient adopté des maximes si déraisonnables. Le roi de Siam prétend être propriétaire de tous les biens de ses sujets; le fruit d'un droit si barbare est que le premier rebelle heureux se rend propriétaire des biens du roi de Siam. Tout pouvoir qui n'est fondé que sur la force se détruit par la même voie. Dans les états où on suit les règles de la raison, les *propriétés* des particuliers sont sous la protection des lois; le père de famille est assuré de jouir lui-même et de transmettre à sa postérité les biens qu'il a amassés par son travail. Les bons rois ont toujours respecté les possessions de leurs sujets; ils n'ont regardé les deniers publics qui leur ont été confiés que comme un dépôt qu'il ne leur était point permis de détourner pour satisfaire ni leurs passions frivoles, ni l'avidité de leurs favoris, ni la rapacité de leurs courtisans. [XIII.491b]

Whether if judged by this criterion Louis XV would have been counted among 'les bons rois' is somewhat doubtful.

## Saint-Lambert's article LÉGISLATEUR

One of the most important unsigned articles on political matters in the last ten volumes is LÉGISLATEUR. This was long attributed to Diderot, but must now be restored to Saint-Lambert. All that

Diderot contributed at this point was the following brief article which Naigeon guarantees to be his:

LÉGISLATION, s.f. (*Gram. & Politique*), l'art de donner des lois aux peuples. La meilleure législation est celle qui est la plus simple et la plus conforme à la nature; il ne s'agit pas de s'opposer aux passions des hommes, mais au contraire de les encourager en les appliquant à l'intérêt public et particulier. Par ce moyen on diminuera le nombre des crimes et des criminels, et l'on réduira les lois à un très petit nombre. *Voyez les articles* LÉGISLATEUR et LOIS. [IX.363a]

Saint-Lambert's article is obviously much meatier. It opens with a series of definitions and a clear statement of the aims of the lawgiver:

LÉGISLATEUR, s.m. (*Politiq.*) Le *législateur* est celui qui a le pouvoir de donner ou d'abroger les lois. En France le roi est le *législateur*; à Genève c'est le peuple; à Venise, à Gênes c'est la noblesse; en Angleterre ce sont les deux chambres et le roi.

Tout *législateur* doit se proposer la sécurité de l'état et le bonheur des citoyens.

Les hommes, en se réunissant en société, cherchent une situation plus heureuse que l'état de nature, qui avait deux avantages, l'égalité et la liberté, et deux inconvénients, la crainte de la violence et la privation des secours, soit dans les besoins nécessaires, soit dans les dangers. Les hommes, pour se mettre à l'abri de ces inconvénients, ont consenti donc à perdre un peu de leur égalité et liberté; et le *législateur* a rempli son objet lorsqu'en ôtant aux hommes le moins qu'il est possible d'égalité et de liberté, il leur procure le plus qu'il est possible de sécurité et de bonheur. [IX.357a]

If a republic is suited to a small state, a large country (like France, understood) needs a monarchy:

Le *législateur* donnera le gouvernement d'un seul aux états d'une certaine étendue. Leurs différentes parties ont trop de peine à se réunir tout à coup pour y rendre les révolutions faciles. La promptitude des résolutions et de l'exécution, qui est le grand avantage du gouvernement monarchique, fait passer, quand il le faut et dans un moment, d'une province à l'autre les ordres, les châtiments, les secours. Les différentes parties d'un grand état sont unies sous le gouvernement d'un seul; et dans une grande république il se formerait nécessairement des factions qui pourraient la déchirer et la détruire. D'ailleurs les grands états ont beaucoup de voisins, donnent de l'ombrage, sont exposés à des guerres fréquentes; et c'est ici le triomphe du gouvernement monarchique; c'est dans la guerre surtout qu'il a l'avantage sur le gouvernement républicain; il a pour lui le secret, l'union, la célérité, point d'opposition, point de lenteur. [IX.357b]

It was unthinkable at the time this was written that within some thirty years France would be a republic, fighting successfully against the monarchies of Europe.

The civil laws of a country must be related to its constitutional laws: 'Elles ne seront pas sur beaucoup de cas les mêmes dans une monarchie que dans une république, chez un peuple cultivateur et chez un peuple commerçant; elles changeront selon les temps, les mœurs et les climats' [IX.357b]. The debt to Montesquieu is obvious and duly acknowledged, as is that to Hume.

One essential task of the lawgiver, Saint-Lambert continues, is to inspire in a people a patriotic spirit which will make them put the community before their private interest:

Pour que les hommes sentent le moins qu'il est possible qu'ils ont perdu les deux avantages de l'état de nature, l'égalité et l'indépendance, le *législateur*, dans tous les climats, dans toutes les circonstances, dans tous les gouvernements, doit se proposer de changer l'esprit de propriété en esprit de communauté. Les législations sont plus ou moins parfaites selon qu'elles tendent plus ou moins à ce but; et c'est à mesure qu'elles y parviennent le plus qu'elles procurent le plus de sécurité et de bonheur possibles. Chez un peuple où règne l'esprit de communauté, l'ordre du prince ou du magistrat ne paraît que[1] l'ordre de la patrie. Chaque homme y devient, comme dit Métastase, *compagno delle legge e non seguace: l'ami et non l'esclave des lois*. L'amour de la patrie est le seul objet de passion qui unisse les rivaux; il éteint les divisions; chaque citoyen ne voit dans un citoyen qu'un membre utile à l'État; tous marchent ensemble et contents vers le bien commun; l'amour de la patrie donne le plus noble de tous les courages: on se sacrifie à ce qu'on aime. [IX.358b]

The model here is the Swiss people, 'ce peuple citoyen' as Saint-Lambert calls them. He also points to the example of ancient Peru where the laws, he declares,

tendaient à unir les citoyens par les chaînes de l'humanité; et comme dans les autres législations elles défendent aux hommes de se faire du mal, au

---

[1] The *Encyclopédie* has *pas* which does not make sense; *que* is the reading given by Saint-Lambert in his *Œuvres philosophiques*, Paris, 1797, vi, 42.

Pérou elles leur ordonnaient sans cesse de se faire du bien. Ces lois, en établissant (autant qu'il est possible hors de l'état de nature) la communauté des biens, affaiblissaient l'esprit de propriété, source de tous les vices. [IX.359a]

It is interesting that when Saint-Lambert published this article in his *Œuvres philosophiques* in 1797, 'l'esprit de propriété' was watered down to 'l'esprit d'égoïsme'.[1]

Returning nearer home, Saint-Lambert argues that this 'esprit de communauté' can be fostered if the lawgiver establishes what he calls 'un rapport de bienveillance' between himself and his people. 'Sans la superstition qui abrutissait son siècle et rendait ses peuples féroces', he exclaims, 'que n'aurait pas fait en France un prince comme Henri IV!' [IX.359a]. Apparently, though he gives no precise instances, he saw other examples of this 'esprit de bienveillance' in the past history of France:

J'ai du plaisir à dire qu'en France on en a vu des exemples plus d'une fois; la bienveillance est le seul remède aux abus inévitables dans ces gouvernements qui par leurs constitutions laissent le moins de liberté aux citoyens, et le moins d'égalité entre eux. [IX.359a]

An important question in the eyes of a *philosophe* arises next: 'Le *législateur* doit-il faire usage de la religion comme d'un ressort principal dans la machine du gouvernement?' The answer is obviously: No. Religious fanaticism, as is shown by the example of the Anabaptists and of the Puritans who put Charles I to death, is a danger to the state. There is another danger:

Si le *législateur* fait de la religion un ressort principal de l'état, il donne nécessairement trop de crédit aux prêtres, qui prendront bientôt de l'ambition. Dans les pays où le *législateur* a, pour ainsi dire, amalgamé la religion avec le gouvernement, on a vu les prêtres, devenus importants, favoriser le despotisme pour augmenter leur propre autorité, et, cette autorité une fois établie, menacer le despotisme et lui disputer la servitude des peuples. [IX.359b]

Despite the polite genuflexions to religious orthodoxy which follow, it is clear that here Saint-Lambert is following the usual tactic of the *philosophes* in trying to drive a wedge between Church and State.

---

[1] *Œuvres philosophiques*, vi, 45.

Inevitably Saint-Lambert attaches great importance to the role of education in fostering this 'esprit de communauté'. He also stresses the importance of keeping the people informed (this was somewhat remote from the actual practice of the French monarchy in the 1760s):

Comme il faut que les lois ôtent au citoyen le moins de liberté qu'il est possible et laissent le plus qu'il est possible d'égalité entre eux, dans les gouvernements où les hommes sont le moins libres et le moins égaux, il faut que par l'administration le *législateur* leur fasse oublier ce qu'ils ont perdu des deux grands avantages de l'état de nature; il faut qu'il consulte sans cesse les désirs de la nation; il faut qu'il expose aux yeux du public les détails de l'administration; il faut qu'il lui rende compte de ses grâces; il doit même engager les peuples à s'occuper du gouvernement, à le discuter, à en suivre les opérations, et c'est un moyen de les attacher à la patrie. [IX.360b]

Saint-Lambert also maintains that the lawgiver must see that honours and rewards are given only for service to the State:

Si les rangs, les prééminences, les honneurs sont toujours le prix des services et s'ils imposent le devoir d'en rendre de nouveaux, ils n'exciteront point l'envie de la multitude; elle ne sentira point l'humiliation de l'inégalité des rangs. Le *législateur* lui donnera d'autres consolations sur cette inégalité des richesses, qui est un effet inévitable de la grandeur des états. Il faut qu'on ne puisse parvenir à l'extrême opulence que par une industrie qui enrichisse l'État, et jamais aux dépens du peuple; il faut faire tomber les charges de la société sur les hommes riches qui jouissent des avantages de la société. Les impôts entre les mains d'un *législateur* qui administre bien sont un moyen d'abolir certains abus, une industrie funeste ou des vices; ils peuvent être un moyen d'encourager le genre d'industrie le plus utile, d'exciter certains talents, certaines vertus. [IX.361b]

Such was hardly the state of affairs in France before 1789, particularly in the matter of taxation.

The effect of the Enlightenment on men's outlook is discussed in the closing paragraphs of the article. Saint-Lambert is proud of the progress achieved in the course of a generation or two:

Quelques *législateurs* ont profité du progrès des lumières qui, depuis cinquante années, se sont répandues rapidement d'un bout de l'Europe à l'autre; elles ont éclairé sur les détails de l'administration, sur les moyens de favoriser la population, d'exciter l'industrie, de conserver les avantages de sa situation et de s'en procurer de nouveaux. On peut croire que les lumières, conservées par l'imprimerie, ne peuvent s'éteindre et peuvent encore augmenter. Si quelque despote voulait replonger sa nation dans les ténèbres, il se trouvera des nations libres qui lui rendront le jour. [IX.362b]

An exaggerated patriotism is disappearing; trade is bringing all countries closer together. Yet Europe, Saint-Lambert concludes, will always see wars because it is divided into monarchies and republics:

Cette situation de l'Europe entretiendra l'émulation des vertus fortes et guerrières; cette diversité de sentiments et de mœurs qui naissent de différents gouvernements s'opposera au progrès de cette mollesse, de cette douceur excessive des mœurs, effet du commerce, du luxe et des longues paix. [IX.363a]

Saint-Lambert was a professional soldier as well as a *philosophe*.

## *Naigeon's article* UNITAIRES

Naigeon even managed to work certain political ideas into that extraordinary article, UNITAIRES. If he trots out in the name of the Unitarians the hoary tag, *Salus populi suprema lex est*, he also works in some notions which might conceivably have been derived from a reading of the recently published *Contrat social*. They hold the view, he alleges, 'que ce qu'on appelle dans certains états la *parole de Dieu*, ne doit jamais être que *la parole de la loi* ou, si l'on veut, l'expression formelle de la volonté générale statuant sur un objet quelconque' [XVII.395a]. Or again he attributes to them a belief that 'qu'il n'y a d'impies envers les dieux que les infracteurs du contrat social' [XVII.395b].

More specific and more audacious are the political rights which, he declares, the Unitarians claim for all subjects, in addition to 'la liberté de servir Dieu selon les lumières de leur conscience':

De croire et d'écrire ce qu'ils voudront sur la religion, la politique et la morale.

D'attaquer même les opinions les plus anciennes.

De proposer au souverain l'abrogation d'une loi qui leur paraîtra injuste ou préjudiciable en quelque sorte au bien de la communauté.

De l'éclairer sur les moyens de perfectionner la législation et de prévenir les usurpations du gouvernement.

De déterminer exactement la nature et les limites des droits et des devoirs réciproques du prince et des sujets.

De se plaindre hautement des malversations et de la tyrannie des magistrats et d'en demander la déposition ou la punition, selon l'exigence des cas.

En un mot, qu'il est de l'équité du souverain de ne gêner en rien la liberté des citoyens qui ne doivent être soumis qu'aux lois, et non au caprice aveugle d'une puissance exécutrice et tyrannique. [XVII.395a–b]

Even if they are far from precise, such political views were certainly bold in the 1760s.

## The article VINGTIÈME

Some striking political ideas are also to be found hidden away in the long article on taxation, VINGTIÈME, which was inserted at the end of the very last volume of text. Although we are told that 'cet article est tiré des papiers de défunt M. Boulanger, ingénieur des ponts et chaussées', Grimm attributes it to Damilaville, Voltaire's Paris correspondent, who held an official post connected with this tax. He adds however: 'Ce qu'il y a de bon . . . y a été fourré par M. Diderot.'[1] What truth there is in this last statement we have no means of knowing.

Here again we seem to find an echo of the *Contrat social* in a passage which declares that legislative power belongs to the people alone and that while executive power must be entrusted to the government, it is merely a 'pouvoir intermédiaire' between the body politic and the mass of the citizens:

La société ne peut veiller elle-même sur sa conservation et sur celle de ses membres. Il faudrait qu'elle fût incessamment assemblée, ce qui serait non seulement impraticable, mais même contraire à son but. Les hommes ne se sont réunis et n'ont associé leur puissance que pour jouir individuellement d'une plus grande liberté morale et civile, et puis une société qui veillerait sans cesse sur tous ses membres, ne serait plus une société; ce serait un état sans peuple, un souverain sans sujets, une cité sans citoyens. Le surveillant et le surveillé ne peuvent être le même; si tous les citoyens veillaient, sur qui veilleraient-ils? Voilà pourquoi tous ceux qui ont écrit avec quelques principes sur la politique ont établi que le peuple avait seul la puissance

---

[1] *Corr. litt.*, viii, 224.

législative, mais qu'il ne pouvait avoir en même temps la puissance exécutrice. Le pouvoir de faire exécuter par chacun les conventions de l'association civile et de maintenir le corps politique dans les rapports où il doit être avec ses voisins, doit être dans un continuel exercice. Il faut donc introduire une puissance correspondante où toutes les forces de l'état se réunissent, qui soit un point central où elles se rassemblent, et qui les fasse agir selon le bien commun, qui soit enfin le gardien de la liberté civile et politique du corps entier et de chacun de ses membres.

Le pouvoir intermédiaire est ce qu'on appelle *gouvernement*, de quelque espèce ou forme qu'il puisse etre; d'où l'on peut conclure évidemment que le gouvernement n'est point l'état, mais un corps particulier constitué pour le régir suivant ses lois. [XVII.861a]

Earlier [XVII.856b] the author actually used the term *Contrat social*; and perhaps even more striking are the terms in which he sets forth the aim of the whole article:

Trouver une forme d'imposition qui, sans altérer la liberté des citoyens et celle du commerce, sans vexations et sans troubles, assure à l'état des fonds suffisants pour tous les temps et tous les besoins, dans laquelle chacun contribue dans la juste proportion de ses facultés particulières et des avantages dont il bénéficie dans la société. [XVII.866b]

This immediately recalls the famous paragraph in the chapter 'Du pacte social', beginning 'Trouver une forme d'association . . .' in which Rousseau sets forth the problem to which his social contract offers a solution.

The same article contains a curious section on Hobbes. After reaffirming the principle that the person or persons to whom the government of a country has been entrusted must govern in accordance with its laws since their power is limited to seeing that these are carried out, the author goes on:

Je sais bien que Grotius n'a pas été le seul qui ait pensé d'une façon contraire à ces principes. Hobbes ne leur paraît pas plus favorable; mais il ne faut attribuer ce qu'il semble dire d'analogue aux maximes du premier qu'à ses malheurs personnels et à la nécessité des circonstances dans lesquelles il s'est trouvé. Ce philosophe s'est enveloppé; il en est de ses ouvrages comme du *Prince* de Machiavel[1]; ceux qui n'ont vu que le sens apparent qu'ils présentent, n'ont point compris le véritable.

Hobbes avait un autre but; en y regardant de près, on voit qu'il n'a fait

[1] See the quotation from Diderot's MACHIAVÉLISME (p. 294).

l'apologie du souverain que pour avoir un prétexte de faire la satire de la divinité à laquelle il le compare et à qui il n'y a pas un honnête homme qui voulût ressembler.

Cette idée lumineuse et juste ne se trouverait pas ici si elle se fût présentée plus tôt à l'un des plus beaux génies de ce siècle, qui est l'auteur de l'article HOBBES de ce dictionnaire.[1] Elle explique toutes les contradictions apparentes de l'un des plus forts logiciens et des plus hommes de bien de son temps. [XVII.863a]

More than a column is then devoted to an attempt to show that even Hobbes recognized that sovereigns have duties towards their peoples:

Voilà donc les droits des peuples reconnus, ainsi que les obligations des souverains envers eux, par celui même qui les leur refusait et qui niait ces obligations. Les hommes, en mettant tout ce qu'ils avaient en commun, se sont mis sous la puissance de la société pour la maintenir et en être protégés. La société, en confiant son droit à un ou plusieurs, ne l'a fait qu'à la condition de remplir à sa décharge les obligations auxquelles elle est tenue envers les citoyens. Il n'est donc pas vrai que le souverain à qui le peuple a confié le pouvoir de le gouverner, ne soit plus tenu à rien envers ce même peuple ; car il lui doit tout ce que la société lui devrait elle-même ; et ce qu'elle lui devrait serait de le gouverner selon les conditions énoncées ou tacites auxquelles chacun a souscrit en la formant ; mais c'est trop discuter une vérité trop évidente pour avoir besoin d'être démontrée. [XVII.863b]

If this interpretation of Hobbes is scarcely convincing, there can be no doubt about the author's own political standpoint.

## D'Holbach's article REPRÉSENTANTS

The most interesting political article in the last ten volumes is undoubtedly REPRÉSENTANTS, for long attributed to Diderot, but now restored to its rightful owner, Baron d'Holbach. The future author of *La Politique naturelle*, *Le Système social* and *Éthocratie*, all of which appeared in the 1770s, can be seen at work ten years earlier in this essay. It is also interesting to see how in a series of unsigned articles on the religion and institutions of all manner of remote countries which may with reasonable probability be attributed to him, the baron uses the opportunity to work in certain political ideas.

[1] Diderot in *HOBBISME.

In the opening part of the following article, for instance, his remarks have a wider validity than would appear at first sight:

SIRATICK, s.m. (*Hist. mod.*) C'est le nom sous lequel on désigne le souverain d'une nation de nègres d'Afrique, appelée les *foulis*. Contre l'ordinaire des rois de ces climats, il gouverne avec la plus grande modération, ses lois paraissent dictées par l'amour du bien public, et il n'est, pour ainsi dire, que l'organe de sa nation. Cela n'empêche point que son autorité ne soit très respectée et très étendue; les peuples se soumettent avec joie à des volontés qui tendent à leur bonheur . . . [XV.225a]

The lesson is even more pointed in the conclusion of KRAALS (*Hist. mod.*):

Chaque *kraal* est sous l'autorité d'un capitaine dont le pouvoir est limité. Cette dignité est héréditaire; lorsque le capitaine en prend possession, il promet de ne rien changer aux lois et coutumes du *kraal*. Il reçoit les plaintes du peuple, et juge avec les anciens les procès et les disputes qui surviennent. Les capitaines, qui sont les nobles du pays, sont subordonnés au *konquer*. *Voyez cet article*. Ils sont aussi soumis au tribunal du *kraal* qui les juge et les punit lorsqu'ils ont commis quelque faute. D'où l'on voit que les Hottentots vivent sous un gouvernement très prudent et très sage, tandis que des peuples qui se croient beaucoup plus éclairés qu'eux, gémissent sous l'oppression et la tyrannie. [IX.138a]

However, these are mere trifles compared with the long and important article, REPRÉSENTANTS, the most positive attempt in the whole of the *Encyclopédie* to set forth in detail an alternative to the absolute monarchy under which Frenchmen of that age lived.

Not, of course, that the author is very explicit as to the precise part to be played by his elected representatives in the political life of the country, as we see from the opening sentence of the article:

REPRÉSENTANTS (*Droit politiq. Hist. mod.*) Les *représentants* d'une nation sont des citoyens choisis, qui dans un gouvernement tempéré sont chargés par la société de parler en son nom, de stipuler ses intérêts, d'empêcher qu'on ne l'opprime, de concourir à l'administration. [XIV.143a]

The functions of the assembly are certainly left extremely vague. What is striking in the article is its strong historical sense. In contrast to Asia where despotism has always flourished, in Europe, d'Holbach argues, the different nations insisted on putting some sort of a brake on the power of their monarchs by means of representative assemblies:

Telle est l'origine de ces assemblées connues sous le nom de *diètes*, d'*états généraux*, de *parlements*, de *sénats*, qui presque dans tous les pays de l'Europe participèrent à l'administration publique, approuvèrent ou rejetèrent les propositions des souverains, et furent admis à concerter avec eux les mesures nécessaires au maintien de l'état. [XIV.143a]

Whereas in an absolute monarchy 'le souverain ou jouit, du consentement de son peuple, du droit d'être l'unique *représentant* de sa nation, ou bien, contre son gré, il s'arroge ce droit',

dans les monarchies tempérées le souverain n'est dépositaire que de la puissance exécutrice; il ne représente sa nation qu'en cette partie, elle choisit d'autres *représentants* pour les autres branches de l'administration. C'est ainsi qu'en Angleterre la puissance exécutrice réside dans la personne du monarque, tandis que la puissance législative est partagée entre lui et le parlement, c'est-à-dire l'assemblée générale des différents ordres de la nation britannique, composée du clergé, de la noblesse et des communes. Ces dernières sont représentées par un certain nombre de députés choisis par les villes, les bourgs et les provinces de la Grande-Bretagne. Par la constitution de ce pays le parlement concourt avec le monarque à l'administration publique; dès que ces deux puissances sont d'accord, la nation entière est réputée avoir parlé, et leurs décisions deviennent des lois. [XIV.143a–b]

D'Holbach's admiration for the English constitution was, as we shall see, far from complete. He instances other examples of such representative bodies—in Sweden and in Germany (here he could refer to his own signed article, DIÈTE DE L'EMPIRE). He then recalls the existence of the States General in France (it had not met for nearly a century and a half—since 1614, to give the correct date):

La nation française fut autrefois représentée par l'assemblée des états généraux du royaume, composée du clergé et de la noblesse, auxquels par la suite des temps on associa le tiers état, destiné à représenter le peuple. Ces assemblées nationales ont été discontinuées depuis l'année 1628. [XIV.143b]

D'Holbach then proceeds to trace back to the barbarian invaders who took over from the Roman Empire the origin of these assemblies. This origin explains the power given to the nobility as against the common people:

Voilà pourquoi dans toutes les monarchies modernes nous voyons partout les nobles, les grands, c'est-à-dire des guerriers, posséder les terres des anciens habitants et se mettre en possession du droit exclusif de représenter les nations; celles-ci, avilies, écrasées, opprimées, n'eurent point la liberté de joindre leurs voix à celles de leurs superbes vainqueurs. Telle est sans doute la source de cette prétention de la noblesse, qui s'arrogea long-temps le droit de parler exclusivement à tous les autres au nom des nations. [XIV.143b]

To the nobility was soon joined the clergy:

Les rois, fatigués sans doute eux-mêmes des entreprises continuelles d'une noblesse trop puissante pour être soumise, sentirent qu'il était de leur intérêt propre de contrebalancer le pouvoir de leurs vassaux indomptés par celui des interprètes d'une religion respectée par les peuples. D'ailleurs le clergé, devenu possesseur de grands biens, fut intéressé à l'administration publique, et dut à ce titre avoir part aux délibérations. [XIV.144a]

At this stage in history the nobility and clergy excluded the great mass of the nation from any share in political power:

Sous le gouvernement féodal la noblesse et le clergé eurent longtemps le droit exclusif de parler au nom de toute la nation ou d'en être les uniques *représentants*. Le peuple, composé des cultivateurs, des habitants des villes et des campagnes, des manufacturiers, en un mot de la partie la plus nombreuse, la plus laborieuse, la plus utile de la société, ne fut point en droit de parler pour lui-même; il fut forcé de recevoir sans murmurer les lois que quelques grands concertèrent avec le souverain. Ainsi le peuple ne fut point écouté, il ne fut regardé que comme un vil amas de citoyens méprisables, indignes de joindre leurs voix à celles d'un petit nombre de seigneurs orgueilleux et ingrats, qui jouirent de leurs travaux sans s'imaginer leur rien devoir. [XIV.144a]

Feudalism at its height was marked by 'des souverains sans forces et des peuples écrasés et avilis par une aristocratie, armée également contre le monarque et la nation'. Finally, as a counterweight to the power of the nobility and clergy the monarchy summoned to the estates representatives of the mass of the people:

Ainsi la voix du peuple fut enfin entendue, les lois prirent de la vigueur, les excès des grands furent réprimés, ils furent forcés d'être justes envers des citoyens jusque là méprisés; le corps de la nation fut ainsi opposé à une noblesse mutine et intraitable. [XIV.144a]

Power, d'Holbach goes on to declare, must always be limited:

Dans quelques mains que le pouvoir soit placé, il devient funeste s'il n'est contenu dans des bornes; ni le souverain, ni aucun ordre de l'état ne peuvent exercer une autorité nuisible à la nation, s'il est vrai que tout gouvernement n'ait pour objet que le bien du peuple gouverné. [XIV. 144b]

It is impossible for one man to govern a country unaided or for one section of the community to speak for all:

Nul homme, quelles que soient ses lumières, n'est capable sans conseils, sans secours, de gouverner une nation entière; nul ordre dans l'état ne peut avoir la capacité ou la volonté de connaître les besoins des autres. Alors le souverain impartial doit écouter les voix de tous ses sujets, il est également intéressé à les entendre et à remédier à leurs maux; mais, pour que les sujets s'expliquent sans tumulte, il convient qu'ils aient des *représentants*, c'est-à-dire des citoyens plus éclairés que les autres, plus intéressés à la chose, que leurs possessions attachent à la patrie, que leur position mette à portée de sentir les besoins de l'état, les abus qui s'introduisent, et les remèdes qu'il convient d'y porter. [XIV.144b]

Thus we arrive at the obvious conclusion that

rien ne serait plus avantageux qu'une constitution qui permettrait à chaque ordre de citoyens de se faire représenter, de parler dans les assemblées qui ont le bien général pour objet. [XIV.145a]

Who is to be represented in such assemblies, and who are to be the representatives, are the next questions to which d'Holbach addresses himself. The members of these assemblies must be property-owners—'ceux que leurs possessions rendent citoyens, et que leur état et leurs lumières mettent à portée de connaître les intérêts de la nation et les besoins des peuples'. D'Holbach is as convinced of this truth and of the accompanying truth that those who are allowed to choose these representatives must be property-owners as were to be the framers of the constitution of 1791 or of the electoral laws of the *Monarchie censitaire* of the period 1815–48.

En un mot [he writes], c'est la propriété qui fait le citoyen; tout homme qui possède dans l'état est intéressé au bien de l'état et, quel que soit le rang que des conventions particulières lui assignent, c'est toujours comme propriétaire, c'est en raison de ses possessions qu'il doit parler ou qu'il acquiert le droit de se faire représenter. [XIV.145a]

In addition to the clergy and nobility who had formed the kernel of such assemblies in feudal times d'Holbach would also wish to see judges and merchants represented because of their importance to the community:

Le magistrat est citoyen en vertu de ses possessions; mais ses fonctions en font un citoyen plus éclairé à qui l'expérience fait connaître les avantages et les désavantages de la législation, les abus de la jurisprudence, les moyens d'y remédier. C'est la loi qui décide du bonheur des états.

    Le commerce est aujourd'hui pour les états une source de force et de richesse. Le négociant s'enrichit en même temps que l'état qui favorise ses entreprises; il partage sans cesse ses prospérités et ses revers; il ne peut donc sans injustice être réduit au silence; il est un citoyen utile et capable de donner ses avis dans les conseils d'une nation dont il augmente l'aisance et le pouvoir.

Finally, because of the supreme importance of agriculture, the peasant must be represented—but only, it will be noticed, the peasant who owns some land:

Enfin, le cultivateur, c'est-à-dire tout citoyen qui possède des terres, dont les travaux contribuent aux besoins de la société, qui fournit à sa subsistance, sur qui tombent les impôts, doit être représenté. Personne n'est plus que lui intéressé au bien public. La terre est la base physique et politique d'un état; c'est sur le possesseur de la terre que retombent directement ou indirectement tous les avantages et tous les maux des nations. C'est en proportion de ses possessions que la voix du citoyen doit avoir du poids dans les assemblées nationales. [XIV.145a–b]

The importance here attached to agriculture reflects not only its preponderance in the economic life of France before the Industrial Revolution, but also the theories of the new school of economists, the Physiocrats.[1]

    When d'Holbach comes to sum up his views on representation, it will be noticed that a new figure, that of the factory-owner,

[1] See below, pp. 339–50.

appears in his list: 'Le noble ou le guerrier, le prêtre ou le magistrat, le commerçant, le manufacturier et le cultivateur sont des hommes également nécessaires' [XIV.145b]. In the proposed assembly the Third Estate would certainly be strongly represented.

These representatives, d'Holbach declares, would not be free to speak and vote according to their own judgement or whim; they would simply be the mouthpiece of their constituents, being invested merely with what the French call a *mandat impératif*:

Les *représentants* supposent des constituants de qui leur pouvoir est émané, auxquels ils sont par conséquent subordonnés et dont ils ne sont que les organes. Quels que soient les usages ou les abus que le temps a pu introduire dans les gouvernements libres et tempérés, un *représentant* ne peut s'arroger le droit de faire parler à ses constituants un langage opposé à leurs intérêts. Les droits des constituants sont les droits de la nation, ils sont imprescriptibles et inaliénables. Pour peu qu'on consulte la raison, elle prouvera que les constituants peuvent en tout temps démentir, désavouer et révoquer les *représentants* qui les trahissent, qui abusent de leurs pleins pouvoirs contre eux-mêmes, ou qui renoncent pour eux à des droits inhérents à leur essence. En un mot, les *représentants* d'un peuple libre ne peuvent point lui imposer un joug qui détruirait sa félicité; nul homme n'acquiert le droit d'en représenter un autre malgré lui. [XIV.146a]

D'Holbach was not a blind admirer of the English constitution, as we know from such later works as *La Politique naturelle* and *Le Système social*. Like many of his contemporaries he was shocked by the spectacle of political corruption which this country presented in the eighteenth century:

L'expérience nous montre que dans les pays qui se flattent de jouir de la plus grande liberté, ceux qui sont chargés de représenter les peuples ne trahissent que trop souvent leurs intérêts et livrent leurs constituants à l'avidité de ceux qui veulent les dépouiller. Une nation a raison de se défier de semblables *représentants* et de limiter leurs pouvoirs. Un ambitieux, un homme avide de richesses, un prodigue, un débauché ne sont point faits pour représenter leurs concitoyens. Ils les vendront pour des titres, des honneurs, des emplois et de l'argent; ils se croiront intéressés à leurs maux. Que sera-ce si ce commerce infâme semble s'autoriser par la conduite des constituants qui seront eux-mêmes vénaux? Que sera-ce si ces constituants choisissent leurs *représentants* dans le tumulte et dans l'ivresse, ou si, négligeant la vertu, les lumières, les talents, ils ne donnent qu'au plus offrant le droit de stipuler leurs intérêts? De pareils constituants invitent à les trahir: ils perdent le droit de s'en plaindre, et leurs *représentants* leur fermeront la bouche en leur disant: *Je vous ai achetés bien chèrement, et je vous vendrai le plus chèrement que je pourrai.* [XIV.146a]

In condemning the venality of both M.P.s and their constituents d'Holbach shows only moderate enthusiasm for what was at the time the outstanding example of representative government; it is clear that it was far from approaching his ideal of this form of government. To round off the article he insists that elections must be held with fair frequency so that the representatives are reminded that it is from the nation that they derive their powers.

If this substantial article remains decidedly vague as to what should be the exact functions and powers of an assembly of this kind, it does none the less put forward a definite alternative to absolutism. The historical sketch which it contains gives a clear outline of the development of the different social classes in France; it stresses the growing importance of the Third Estate and consequently its right to representation. The kind of monarchy which the article presupposes looks forward to the constitution of 1791 and the constitutional settlement of 1814–15 which was to be further modified by the July Revolution. If d'Holbach speaks up for the claims of the Third Estate to due representation in a national assembly, it is also clear that for him the ownership of property and in particular property in land is essential if one is to have the right to choose one's representative, let alone be elected to a national assembly. Here d'Holbach's championing of the political claims of the Third Estate is matched by a mistrust of the masses which is characteristic of an eighteenth-century *philosophe*.

## Comments on the France of Louis XV

Given the strict censorship under which the first seven volumes appeared, it is not surprising that comment on political conditions in the France of the 1750s should be extremely difficult to find. At most one finds a few hints of dissatisfaction in an article like Jaucourt's FRANCE (*Géog.*) where he gives a gloomy account of the present state of the country:

... Les richesses immenses de la *France*, qui montent peut-être, en matières d'or et d'argent, à un milliard du titre de ce jour (le marc d'or à

680 livres, et celui d'argent à 50 livres), se trouvent malheureusement réparties, comme l'étaient les richesses de Rome lors de la chute de la république. On sait encore que la capitale forme, pour ainsi dire, l'état même; que tout aborde à ce gouffre, à ce centre de puissance; que les provinces se dépeuplent excessivement; et que le labourer, accablé de sa pauvreté, craint de mettre au jour des malheureux. Il est vrai que Louis XIV, s'apercevant, il y a près d'un siècle (en 1666), de ce mal invétéré, crut encourager la propagation de l'espèce en promettant de récompenser ceux qui auraient dix enfants, c'est-à-dire, de récompenser des prodiges; il eût mieux valu remonter aux causes du mal et y porter les véritables remèdes. Or ces causes et ces remèdes ne sont pas difficiles à trouver. *Voyez les articles* IMPOT, TOLÉRANCE etc. [VII.282b]

What these remedies were is not indicated; but in an absolute monarchy all the troubles facing France were obviously to be blamed on the government, and if it was unthinkable to attack Louis le Bien Aimé, it was at least possible to make sarcastic remarks about Louis le Grand. The article FASTE, probably by Saint-Lambert, contains some pointed remarks about the useless display of the court:

On demande si dans ce siècle éclairé il est encore utile que les hommes qui commandent aux nations, annoncent la grandeur et la puissance des nations par des dépenses excessives et par le luxe le plus fastueux. Les peuples de l'Europe sont assez instruits de leurs forces mutuelles pour distinguer chez leurs voisins un vain luxe d'une véritable opulence. Une nation aurait plus de respect pour des chefs qui l'enrichiraient que pour des chefs qui voudraient la faire passer pour riche. Des provinces peuplées, des armées disciplinées, des finances en bon ordre imposeraient plus aux étrangers et aux citoyens que la magnificence de la cour. Le seul *faste* qui convienne à de grands peuples, ce sont les monuments, les grands ouvrages et ces prodiges de l'art qui font admirer le génie autant qu'ils ajoutent à l'idée de la puissance. [VI.419a]

Such views could scarcely have been well received at the court of Louis XV and Mme de Pompadour.

In GALANTERIE (*Morale*) the author (probably Diderot) makes an interesting connection between absolutism and manners which has a bearing on both social life and the arts under the Ancien Régime:

Dans un gouvernement où un seul est chargé des affaires de tous, le citoyen oisif, placé dans une situation qu'il ne saurait changer, pensera du moins à la rendre supportable; et de cette nécessité commune naîtra une société plus étendue. Les femmes y auront plus de liberté; les hommes se feront une habitude de leur plaire; et l'on verra se former peu à peu un art qui sera l'art de la *galanterie*. Alors la *galanterie* répandra une teinte générale sur les mœurs de la nation et sur ses productions en tout genre; elles y perdront de la grandeur et de la force, mais elles y gagneront de la douceur et je ne sais quel agrément original que les autres peuples tâcheront d'imiter et qui leur donnera un air gauche et ridicule. [VII.428a]

In these last lines we see reflected the cultural domination which France exercised in Europe in the eighteenth century.

Even in the last ten volumes we do not find much in the way of direct comment on political conditions and institutions, yet what little there is to be found there has some interest. There is, for instance, a long unsigned addition to the purely factual article, INTENDANTS ET COMMISSAIRES *départis pour S.M. dans les provinces et généralités du royaume,* one of the hundreds of this kind which the indefatigable lawyer, Boucher d'Argis, contributed to the *Encyclopédie.* Who wrote this addition we do not know; what we do know from the furious letter which Diderot wrote to Le Breton on discovering the mutilation of the last ten volumes is that it had been heavily censored by him.

The addition to the article makes fairly severe criticisms of the system, finally established under Louis XIV, by which an agent of the central government, the *intendant* (the ancestor of the modern *préfet*) was established in every province to carry out its orders and to keep an eye on what was going on there. As the article points out, the powers of the *intendant* were greater in the so-called *pays d'élection* (those which did not have provincial estates to assist in local government and in the assessment and collection of taxes) than in the *pays d'états*, i.e. those few provinces (Brittany and Languedoc were the most important) which had retained their estates. After enumerating in considerable detail all the powers enjoyed by an *intendant* in one of the *pays d'états*, the writer proceeds to advocate the setting up of provincial estates in every part of France: 'Les états provinciaux sont le meilleur remède aux inconvénients d'une grande monarchie: ils sont même de l'essence de la monarchie, qui veut non des *pouvoirs*, mais des corps *intermédiaires* entre le prince et le peuple' [VIII.809a]. The expression, *corps intermédiaires*, is, of course, taken from the *Esprit des lois*:

according to Montesquieu, what he calls 'une monarchie modérée' requires such bodies as the nobility, clergy, parlements and provincial estates to act as intermediaries between king and people. Such a system of provincial estates would not, the writer continues, offer any danger to the king; they would certainly be less dangerous than the States General:

Les états provinciaux font pour le prince une partie de ce que feraient les préposés du prince, et s'ils sont à la place du préposé, ils ne veulent ni ne peuvent se mettre à celle du prince; c'est tout au plus ce que l'on pourrait craindre des États généraux. [VIII.809a]

It must be said that some of the arguments set forth here in favour of making universal the system of provincial estates are not very convincing. 'En France', we are told, 'l'autorité du roi n'est nulle part plus respectée que dans les pays d'états.' Events in Brittany in the 1760s were scarcely to bear out this contention, as there the aristocratic forces of Estates and Parlement were soon to unite in opposition to the Crown. Even less convincing is the claim that these provinces which had estates made a greater tax contribution than those which had not. Yet comparisons between the two types of province do reveal some unpleasant features of conditions in those which lacked estates:

Dans les pays éclairés par la continuelle discussion des affaires la taille sur les biens s'est établie sans difficulté; on n'y connaît plus les barbaries et les injustices de la taille personnelle. On n'y voit point un collecteur, suivi d'huissiers ou de soldats, épier s'il pourra découvrir et faire vendre quelques lambeaux qui restent au misérable pour couvrir ses enfants, et qui sont à peine échappés aux exécutions de l'année précédente. On n'y voit point cette multitude d'hommes de finance qui absorbe une partie des impôts et tyrannise le peuple.

   ... On ne voit point dans les pays d'états trois cents collecteurs, baillis ou maires d'une seule province, gémir une année entière et plusieurs mourir dans les prisons, pour n'avoir point apporté la taille de leurs villages qu'on a rendus insolvables. On n'y voit point charger de 7,000 livres d'impôts un village dont le territoire produit 4,000 livres. Le laboureur ne craint point de jouir de son travail et de paraître augmenter son aisance; il sait que ce qu'il payera de plus sera exactement proportionné à ce qu'il aura acquis. Il n'a point à corrompre ou à fléchir un collecteur; il n'a point à plaider à une élection de l'élection,[1] devant l'*intendant* de l'*intendant* au conseil. [VIII.809b]

The rest of this addition to the original article INTENDANTS goes on to make comparisons between provinces like Brittany and Languedoc which had estates and those like Normandy which had lost theirs, arguing, not very convincingly, that these *pays d'états* contribute more in taxes than a rich and fertile province like Normandy. Much of the idyllic picture painted here of the *pays d'états* must appear wide of the mark to a modern historian; what is interesting in this article is the strong criticism of the role of the *intendant* in the great majority of the provinces and particularly of the taxation system in force there down to 1789.

## The struggle between Crown and Parlements

Scattered through the last ten volumes we find a whole series of brief but highly significant comments on the great political struggle between Crown and Parlements which raged in France between the 1750s and Maupeou's *coup d'état* in 1771. That Diderot had not forgiven the Paris Parlement for instituting the proceedings which led, in 1759, to the government withdrawing the *privilège* of the *Encyclopédie* is made clear from a remark which Le Breton prudently removed from the article RÉQUISITOIRE: 'Cet ouvrage a donné lieu à un réquisitoire tendant à ce que ceux qui ont le sens commun fussent chassés du royaume.'[2] On the other hand it is a fact that in quite a number of articles in these last ten volumes the Parlement is presented in a very favourable political light. While most of these references are hidden away in grammatical articles which may be attributed with fair certainty to Diderot himself, two quite prominent articles—MAGISTRAT and MAGISTRATURE— are devoted to praise of the Parlements and support for their political claims. These two unsigned articles may also well be by Diderot himself.

MAGISTRAT (*Politique*) begins by discussing the broader meaning of the term (the equivalent, roughly, of 'ruler') and then continues:

Mais ce nom ne signifie proprement dans notre langue que ceux sur qui le souverain se repose pour rendre la justice en son nom, conserver le dépôt

---

[1] *Élection* is used here in the sense of a law court which tried cases arising out of the assessment and collection of taxes.
[2] Gordon and Torrey, p. 78.

sacré des lois, leur donner par l'enregistrement la notoriété nécessaire, et les faire exécuter, fonctions augustes et saintes qui exigent de celui qui en est chargé les plus grandes qualités. [IX.855b]

On this definition the role of the Parlements is not limited to the administration of justice, but, as they themselves claimed, extends over a much wider field. The same point is made in MAGISTRATURE (*Politiq.*):

On peut aussi entendre par ce mot *magistrature* le corps des magistrats d'un état; il signifiera en France cette partie des citoyens qui, divisée en différents tribunaux, veille au dépôt des lois et à leur exécution, semblables à ces mages dont les fonctions étaient de garder et d'entretenir le feu sacré dans la Perse.

Si l'on peut dire avec assurance qu'un état n'est heureux qu'autant que par sa constitution toutes les parties qui le composent tendent au bien général comme à un centre commun, il s'ensuit que le bonheur de celui dans lequel différents tribunaux sont dépositaires de la volonté du prince dépend de l'harmonie et du parfait accord de tous ces tribunaux sans lequel l'ordre politique ne pourrait subsister. [IX.857b]

In these two articles the wider, political role of the Parlements is discreetly hinted at rather than openly proclaimed; but woven into some short grammatical articles we find more specific reference to these broader functions.

It is true that a mixture of admiration and of a realistic appraisal of the judges of the Parlements is to be found in the following article:

MORGUE, s.f. (*Gram.*) Si vous joignez la dureté et la fierté à la gravité et à la sottise, vous aurez la *morgue*. Elle est de tous les états, mais on en accuse particulièrement la robe, et la raison en est simple. Il y a dans la robe tout autant de gens sots et fiers que dans l'église et le militaire, ni plus ni moins; mais la gravité est particulièrement attachée à la magistrature; dépositaire des lois qu'elle fait parler ou taire à son gré, c'est une tentation bien naturelle que d'en promener partout avec soi la menace. Les gens de lettres ont aussi leur *morgue*, mais elle ne se montrera dans aucun plus fortement que dans le poète satirique. [X.712b]

The conflict between King and Parlement is touched on with appropriate caution in the short article which follows:

PARLEMENTAIRE, s.m. (*Gram. & Hist.*) C'est dans les troubles de l'état celui qui est attaché au parti du parlement contre celui de la cour. Alors il s'agit des intérêts de la nation que le parlement et le roi veulent, mais qu'ils entendent mal l'un ou l'autre. Pour l'ordinaire, lorsqu'il y a deux factions, la faction des *parlementaires* et la faction des royalistes, les premiers pourraient prendre pour devise *pour le roi contre le roi*. [XII.69a]

More definitely on the side of the Parlement is a sentence in RÉVÉRENCE: 'Portez aux magistrats la *révérence* qu'on doit à ceux qui sont chargés du dépôt des lois et du soin de rendre la justice' [XIV.229a]. Again one finds two very precise references to the Parlements' important function of registering royal edicts before they had force of law. Into a grammatical article is worked an allusion to the barrier to despotism presented by this right of the Parlements:

OBVIER, v.n. (*Gram.*) C'est prévenir, empêcher, aller au-devant. On crie sans cesse contre les formalités, et on ne sait pas à combien de maux elles *obvient*. Les enregistrements, par exemple, *obvient* presque à borner les actes du despotisme, que les ministres ne seraient que trop souvent tentés d'exercer sur les peuples au nom du souverain. [XI.330b]

*IMPROBATION, IMPROUVER (this is certainly by Diderot) contains a clear reference to the way in which new edicts were forced through the Parlements by a *lit de justice* held in the presence of the King himself:

M. Duguet[1] dit de certains édits qu'on apporte quelquefois aux parlements pour être enregistrés, que les juges n'opinent alors que par un morne et triste silence, et que la manière dont ils enregistrent est le sceau de leur *improbation*. [VIII.630a]

Finally, hidden away in the article SÉANCE (*Gram.*), there is an apparently harmless sentence which, in the context of the struggle between Crown and Parlements, has a definitely seditious meaning:

Les ducs et pairs ont droit de *séance* à la grand'chambre, et ils entendent mal leur intérêt et celui de la nation de n'en pas user plus souvent. [XIV.851a]

To appreciate the meaning of this sentence one has to remember that in 1756, in one of the crises of the struggle, the Paris Parlement had invited the princes of the blood and *ducs et pairs* to assist in its

---

[1] Abbé Jacques Joseph Duguet (1649–1733) whose posthumous *Institution d'un prince* was banned by Cardinal Fleury when it appeared in 1739.

deliberations to defend the honour of the 'cour des pairs'. In other words, it appealed to the highest members of the aristocracy to come to its aid in its struggle with the Crown. If on this occasion the King's order forbidding them to appear in the Parlement was obeyed, later in the century their part in events, particularly those leading up to the upheaval of 1789, was to add to the discomfiture of the monarchy.

If one were to seek in the pages of the *Encyclopédie* the text of the *Déclaration des droits de l'homme* or a blueprint of the limited monarchy set up by the constitution of 1791, one would certainly be disappointed. Equally one fails to find in its pages a detailed analysis of the shortcomings of absolute monarchy as seen by its critics in the 1750s and 1760s. As we have seen, not only is a great deal of the political theorizing merely secondhand; it is also very cautious in its criticism of the theory of absolutism. Yet the true meaning of an article like AUTORITÉ POLITIQUE is as clear today as it was to hostile contemporaries; and an article like REPRÉSENTANTS, for all its vagueness on essential points, looks forward to a new political framework in which the monarchy would share legislative power with elected representatives of the people—or at least the property-owning sections of the community. If detailed criticism of the workings of absolute monarchy are to be found only in an article like INTENDANTS (or rather the unsigned addition to it), there is no question that the political claims of the Parlements are discreetly supported. That men like Diderot had no illusions about the selfish nature of these claims is quite clear; and yet, in the struggle raging at the time between Crown and Parlements, they saw in the *cours souveraines* of France a bulwark against the governmental despotism which they feared and detested.

# Chapter 9

## Society

### 'Political Arithmetic'

That the editors of a dictionary of arts and sciences, and many of their contributors, were interested in the society around them goes without saying. In the very first volume, in \*ARITHMÉTIQUE POLITIQUE, we find Diderot adapting an article of Chambers along with most of its statistical data. He reproduces summaries of material derived from Sir William Petty's *Political Arithmetic* (1691), Gregory King and Major Graunt, all this interspersed with a certain amount of critical comment. The definition which opens the article is Diderot's own:

C'est celle dont les opérations ont pour but des recherches utiles à l'art de gouverner les peuples, telles que celles du nombre des hommes qui habitent un pays; de la quantité de nourriture qu'ils doivent consommer; du travail qu'ils peuvent faire; du temps qu'ils ont à vivre; de la fertilité des terres; de la fréquence des naufrages, etc. [I.678b]

He is also concerned with the practical application of these statistical data by governments:

On conçoit aisément que ces découvertes et beaucoup d'autres de la même nature, étant acquises par des calculs fondés sur quelques expériences bien constatées, un ministre habile en tirerait une foule de conséquences pour la perfection de l'agriculture, pour le commerce tant intérieur qu'extérieur, pour les colonies, pour le cours et l'emploi de l'argent, etc. Mais souvent les ministres (je n'ai garde de parler sans exception) croient n'avoir pas besoin de passer par des combinaisons et des suites d'opérations arithmétiques. Plusieurs s'imaginent être doués d'un grand génie naturel qui les dispense d'une marche si lente et si pénible, sans compter

que la nature des affaires ne permet ni ne demande presque jamais la précision géométrique. Cependant si la nature des affaires la demandait et la
permettait, je ne doute point qu'on ne parvînt à se convaincre que le
monde politique, aussi bien que le monde physique, peut se régler à
beaucoup d'égards par poids, nombre et mesure. [I.678b]

## The population problem

It is notorious that, although they argued a great deal about these
questions, neither the *philosophes* nor other writers of the eighteenth
century had a clear grasp of the movements of world population;
they thus had no inkling of the 'population explosion' which was
then on the point of beginning. We find a writer like Montesquieu
seriously worried by the problem of depopulation since he was
convinced that the total number of inhabitants of the world had
declined steeply since ancient times. If this view is rejected by
Damilaville in the article POPULATION, he replaces it by one which
is in its way equally at variance with the facts—the notion that the
world's population remains constant:

De ces principes il résulte que la *population* en général a dû être constante
et qu'elle le sera jusqu'à la fin; que la somme de tous les hommes pris
ensemble est égale aujourd'hui à celle de toutes les époques que l'on
voudra choisir dans l'antiquité et à ce qu'elle sera dans les siècles à venir;
qu'enfin à l'exception de ces événements terribles où des fléaux ont
quelquefois dévasté des nations, s'il a été des temps où l'on a remarqué
plus ou moins de rareté dans l'espèce humaine, ce n'est pas que sa totalité
se diminuait, mais parce que la *population* changeait de place, ce qui
rendait les diminutions locales. [XIII.91a]

Yet even this theory is not consistently applied in the course of the
article, since Damilaville holds that 'l'esprit des grandes monarchies
est contraire à la grande *population*', and (here he quotes the
example of Holland and Switzerland) 'c'est dans les gouvernements doux et bornés où les droits de l'humanité seront respectés
que les hommes seront nombreux' [XIII.95a]. As far as France is
concerned, he argues that the provinces acquired since 1600 are
now depopulated:

Depuis le commencement du siècle dernier cette monarchie s'est accrue
de plusieurs grandes provinces très peuplées. Cependant ses habitants sont

moins nombreux d'un cinquième qu'ils ne l'étaient avant ces réunions, et ces belles provinces que la nature semble avoir destinées à fournir des subsistances à toute l'Europe, sont incultes. [XIII.100b]

Such sweeping statements, especially when one thinks of prosperous agricultural regions like Flanders or Alsace, seem so much at variance with the facts that one is not tempted to follow Damilaville any further.

## Usury

The other editor, d'Alembert, got himself into hot water for his article ARRÉRAGES, in which he defended compound interest. His enemy Fréron was delighted to be able both to show two contributors contradicting one another and to have a smack at d'Alembet, by quoting an extract from the Genevan review, Le Choix littéraire, which had commented scathingly on such contradictions:

Par exemple, un des coopérateurs encyclopédiques, à l'article *Anatocisme,*[1] dit que *c'est un contrat usuraire où l'on stipule l'intérêt de l'intérêt même uni au principal*; il ajoute que *c'est la plus criminelle espèce d'usure* etc.; et, à l'article *Arrérages.* M. d'Alembert prouve géométriquement que l'intérêt de l'intérêt est aussi bien et légitimement exigé que l'intérêt même.[2]

D'Alembert answered what he called 'une imputation très injuste' in a letter to the *Mercure.*[3] Both Jaucourt in PRET À INTÉRÊT and Faiguet de Villeneuve in USURE openly criticize the traditional hostility shown to loans at interest by the Church and the law. Faiguet argues that times have changed since the original condemnation of usury:

Revenons donc enfin à la diversité des temps, à la diversité des usages et des lois. Autrefois l'*usure* était exorbitante, on l'exigeait des plus pauvres, et avec une dureté capable de troubler la paix des états, ce qui la rendait justement odieuse. Les choses ont bien changé; les intérêts sont devenus modiques et nullement ruineux. D'ailleurs, grâce à notre heureuse législation, comme on n'a guère de prise aujourd'hui sur la personne, les barbaries qui accompagnaient jadis l'*usure*, sont inconnues de nos jours. [XVII.553a]

[1] By Toussaint.      [2] *AL*, 1757, vi, 305.      [3] Dec. 1757.

For the benefit of the whole economy he calls for a clear legal recognition of the legitimacy of loans at interest:

On reconnaîtra même que ces prêts sont très utiles au corps politique, en ce que les riches fuyant presque toujours le travail et la peine, et par malheur les hommes entreprenants étant rarement pécunieux, les talents de ces derniers sont le plus souvent perdus pour la société, si le prêt de lucre ne les met en œuvre. Conséquemment on sentira que si la législation prenait là-dessus un parti conséquent et qu'elle approuvât nettement le prêt de lucre au taux légal, elle ferait, comme on l'a dit, le vrai bien, le bien général de la société, elle nous épargnerait des formalités obliques et ruineuses et nous déliverait tout d'un coup de ces vaines perplexités qui ralentissent nécessairement le commerce national. [XVII.553a–b]

This writer, as we have already seen, had clashed with the clerical critics of the *Encyclopédie* over such matters as his views on Sunday observance and the suppression of feast days.[1] In ÉPARGNE he makes a vigorous attack on the waste of public money involved in all manner of celebrations—

feux d'artifice et autres feux de joie, bals et festins publics, entrées d'ambassadeurs, etc. Que de momeries, que d'amusements puérils, que de millions prodigués en Europe pour payer tribut à la coutume! tandis qu'on est pressé de besoins réels, auxquels on ne saurait satisfaire, parce qu'on n'est pas fidèle à l'*économie* nationale. [V.747a]

He can, however, applaud a change in official policy in the celebrations for the birth of the future Louis XVI which had taken place in the previous year:

On commence à sentir la futilité de ces dépenses, et notre ministère l'a déjà bien reconnue, lorsque, le ciel ayant comblé nos vœux par la naissance du duc de Bourgogne, ce jeune prince si cher à la France et à l'Europe entière, on a mieux aimé, pour exprimer la joie commune dans cet heureux événement, on a mieux aimé, dis-je, allumer de toutes parts le flambeau de l'hyménée et présenter aux peuples ses ris et ses jeux pour favoriser la population par de nouveaux mariages que de faire, suivant la coutume, des prodigalités mal entendues, que d'allumer des feux inutiles et dispendieux qu'un instant voit briller et s'éteindre. [V.747a]

---

[1] See Chap. 6, pp. 258–9.

In the economic field Faiguet has all sorts of savings to recommend. For instance, many practices among artisans are condemned because in the last resort they have to be paid for by the public:

... Il y a parmi les ouvriers mille usages abusifs et ruineux qu'il faudrait abolir impitoyablement. Tels sont, par exemple, tous droits de compagnonnage, toutes fêtes de communauté, tous frais d'assemblée, jetons, bougies, repas et buvettes, occasions perpétuelles de fainéantise, d'excès et de pertes, qui retombent nécessairement sur le public et qui ne s'accordent point avec l'*économie* nationale. [V.747b]

He is strongly opposed to the superabundance of taverns—these 'cabarets si multipliés, si nuisibles parmi nous, que c'est pour le peuple la cause la plus commune de sa misère et de ses désordres'. He would gradually reduce their number and restrict their hours of opening:

Les cabarets, à le bien prendre, sont une occasion perpétuelle d'excès et de pertes, et il serait très utile, dans les vues de la religion et de la politique, d'en supprimer la meilleure partie à mesure qu'ils viendraient à vaquer. Il ne serait pas moins important de les interdire pendant les jours ouvrables à tous les gens établis et connus en chaque paroisse; de les fermer sévèrement à neuf heures du soir dans toutes les saisons, et de mettre enfin les contrevenants à une bonne amende, dont moitié aux dénonciateurs, moitié aux inspecteurs de police. [V.748b]

Such measures, he argues, would not reduce the yield of taxes on alcohol as more would be consumed in private houses,

mais pour l'ordinaire sans excès et sans perte de temps; au lieu que les cabarets, toujours ouverts, dérangent si bien nos ouvriers qu'on ne peut d'ordinaire compter sur eux, ni voir la fin d'un ouvrage commencé. Nous nous plaignons sans cesse de la dureté des temps; que ne nous plaignons-nous plutôt de notre imprudence qui nous porte à faire et à tolérer des dépenses et des pertes sans nombre?

There is a decidedly puritanical and utilitarian side to the articles of Faiguet de Villeneuve which offer a foretaste of the economic liberalism of Victorian days.

## Economic liberalism

Two of the best-known economic articles in the *Encyclopédie* came from the pen of one of the most distinguished exponents of *laissez-faire*, the future *intendant* and *contrôleur général*, Turgot.

FOIRE and FONDATION, which both appeared unsigned in Vol. VII, are inspired by the new outlook on economic matters. In the first he attacks the privileges and exemptions given to fairs such as those held at Lyons, Bordeaux and Beaucaire. He distinguishes between markets, which arise naturally out of economic causes, and fairs, which are created by government intervention in the mistaken notion that they assist trade:

Une *foire* et un marché sont donc l'un et l'autre un concours de marchands et d'acheteurs dans des lieux et des temps marqués, mais dans les marchés c'est l'intérêt réciproque que les vendeurs et les acheteurs ont de se chercher; dans les foires c'est le désir de jouir de certains privilèges, qui forme ce concours, d'où il suit qu'il doit être bien plus nombreux et bien plus solennel dans les *foires*. Quoique le cours naturel du commerce suffise pour établir des marchés, il est arrivé, par une suite de ce malheureux principe qui dans presque tous les gouvernements a si longtemps infecté l'administration du commerce, je veux dire, la manie de tout conduire, de tout régler et de ne jamais s'en rapporter aux hommes sur leur propre intérêt, il est arrivé, dis-je, que pour établir des marchés on a fait intervenir la police; qu'on en a borné le nombre sous prétexte d'empêcher qu'ils ne se nuisent les uns aux autres; qu'on a défendu de vendre certaines marchandises ailleurs que dans certains lieux désignés, soit pour la commodité des commis chargés de recevoir les droits dont elles sont chargées, soit parce qu'on a voulu les assujettir à des formalités de visite et de marque et qu'on ne peut pas mettre partout des bureaux. On ne peut trop saisir toutes les occasions de combattre ce système fatal à l'industrie. [VII.40b]

Turgot argues that the prosperity of certain fairs is not a proof of the prosperity of the country as a whole, since they merely hinder the development of trade and industry in other parts:

Eh! qu'importe que ce soit Pierre ou Jacques, le Maine ou la Bretagne, qui fabriquent telle ou telle marchandise, pourvu que l'état s'enrichisse et que des Français vivent? Qu'importe qu'une étoffe soit vendue à Beaucaire ou dans le lieu de sa fabrication, pourvu que l'ouvrier reçoive le prix de son travail?... Qu'importe qu'il se fasse un grand commerce dans une certaine ville et dans un certain moment, si ce commerce momentané n'est grand que par les causes mêmes qui gênent le commerce et qui tendent à le diminuer dans tout autre temps et dans toute l'étendue de l'état? [VII.41a]

The principles of *laissez-faire* stand out clearly in this article.

SOCIETY33

The expression is in fact used a few pages later by Turgot in FONDATION (*Politique & Droit naturel*) which seeks to show the disadvantages of foundations:

On dit *fonder une académie, un collège, un hôpital, un couvent, des messes, des prix à distribuer, et des jeux publics, etc.* Fonder dans ce sens, c'est assigner un fonds ou une somme d'argent pour être employée à perpétuité à remplir l'objet que le fondateur s'est proposé, soit que cet objet regarde le culte divin ou l'utilité publique, soit qu'il se borne à satisfaire la vanité du fondateur, motif souvent l'unique véritable, lors même que les deux autres lui servent de voile. [VII.72b]

The aim of the article, we are told, is to

examiner l'utilité des fondations en général par rapport au bien public ou plutôt d'en montrer les inconvénients. Puissent les considérations suivantes concourir avec l'esprit philosophique du siècle à dégoûter des *fondations* nouvelles et à détruire un reste de respect superstitieux pour les anciennes! [VII.72b]

Turgot's hostility to foundations flows from the principles of economic liberalism. This is made clear when he argues that foundations established for the relief of the poor simply have the effect of increasing poverty:

Le pauvre a des droits incontestables sur l'abondance du riche; l'humanité, la religion nous font également un devoir de soulager nos semblables dans le malheur. C'est pour accomplir ces devoirs indispensables que tant d'établissements de charité ont été élevés dans le monde chrétien pour soulager des besoins de toute espèce; que des pauvres sans nombre sont rassemblés dans des hôpitaux, nourris à la porte des couvents par des distributions journalières. Qu'est-il arrivé? c'est que précisément dans les pays où ces ressources gratuites sont les plus abondantes, comme en Espagne et dans quelques parties de l'Italie, la misère est plus commune et plus générale qu'ailleurs. La raison en est bien simple, et mille voyageurs l'ont remarquée. Faire vivre gratuitement un grand nombre d'hommes, c'est soudoyer l'oisiveté et tous les désordres qui en sont la suite; c'est rendre la condition du fainéant préférable à celle de l'homme qui travaille; c'est par conséquent diminuer pour l'État la somme du travail et des productions de la terre, dont une partie devient nécessairement inculte. De là les disettes fréquentes, l'augmentation de la misère et la dépopulation qui en est la suite; la race des citoyens industrieux est remplacée par une populace vile composée de mendiants vagabonds et livrés à toutes sortes de crimes. [VII.73a]

The problem of poverty can be solved, he maintains, if the State removes the obstacles in the way of men earning their own living by the sweat of their brow:

Tout homme sain doit se procurer sa subsistance par son travail, parce que, s'il était nourri sans travailler, il le serait aux dépens de ceux qui travaillent. Ce que l'État doit à chacun de ses membres, c'est la destruction des obstacles qui les gêneraient dans leur industrie ou qui les troubleraient dans la jouissance des produits qui en sont la récompense. [VII.74b]

The principles of *laissez-faire* can similarly be applied to education. Turgot anticipates the familiar criticism brought against the welfare state:

Et puis faut-il accoutumer les hommes à tout demander, à tout recevoir, à ne rien devoir à eux-mêmes? Cette espèce de mendicité qui s'étend dans toutes les conditions, dégrade un peuple et substitue à toutes les passions hautes un caractère de bassesse et d'intrigue. Les hommes sont-ils puissamment intéressés au bien que vous voulez leur procurer? laissez-les faire: voilà le grand, l'unique principe. Vous paraissent-ils s'y porter avec moins d'ardeur que vous ne désireriez? augmentez leur intérêt. [VII.74b]

As applied to education the principle would work out as follows:

. . . Toutes les familles doivent l'éducation aux enfants qui y naissent. Elles y sont toutes intéressées immédiatement; et ce n'est que des efforts de chacune en particulier que peut naître la perfection générale de l'éducation. Si vous vous amusez à fonder des maîtres et des bourses dans des collèges, l'utilité ne s'en fera sentir qu'à un petit nombre d'hommes favorisés au hasard et qui peut-être n'auront point les talents nécessaires pour en profiter. Ce ne sera, pour toute la nation, qu'une goutte d'eau répandue sur une vaste mer; et vous aurez fait à très grands frais de très petites choses. . . . Vous voulez perfectionner l'éducation. Proposez des prix à l'émulation des pères et des enfants; mais que ces prix soient offerts à quiconque peut les mériter, du moins dans chaque ordre de citoyens; que les emplois et les places en tout genre deviennent la récompense du mérite et la perspective assurée du travail; et vous verrez l'émulation s'allumer à la fois dans le sein de toutes les familles. Bientôt votre nation s'élèvera au-dessus d'elle-même, vous aurez éclairé son esprit; vous lui aurez donné des mœurs, vous aurez fait de grandes choses; et il ne vous en aura pas tant coûté que pour fonder un collège. [VII.74b–75a]

That careers should be open to all the talents and not, as under the

Ancien Régime, only to those of the right rank or degree of wealth was certainly a new principle in 1757; but to leave education entirely to private enterprise was scarcely to aim at equality of opportunity.

For other needs Turgot recommends the setting up of societies financed by public subscription on the model of those which existed on this side of the Channel. The economic advantages would be considerable:

Cette méthode ne retire aucun fonds de la circulation générale; les terres ne sont point irrévocablement possédées par des mains paresseuses; et leurs productions, sous les mains d'un propriétaire actif, n'ont de bornes que celles de leur propre fécondité. [VII.75a]

Turgot ends his article by mentioning with approval a recent government edict restricting new foundations and by affirming the principle that, since 'l'utilité publique est la loi suprême' [VII. 75b], the State is free to modify or even abolish existing foundations.

One of the reforms which Turgot tried vainly to carry through in 1776 during his short period of power was the abolition of the guilds, a change which was only finally effected by the Revolution. It is striking how from the beginning various contributors to the *Encyclopédie*, including Diderot himself, are hostile to the guilds. In *BOUCHER Diderot declares that butchers and bakers should not be organized in guilds, 'et il devrait être libre à tout particulier de vendre en étal de la viande et du pain' [II.351a]. In *CHEF-D'ŒUVRE he maintains that the test of the masterpiece before admission to a guild is completely useless:

Si celui qui se présente à la maîtrise sait très bien son métier, il est inutile de l'examiner; s'il ne le sait pas, cela ne doit pas l'empêcher d'être reçu, il ne fera tort qu'à lui-même; bientôt il sera connu pour mauvais ouvrier et forcé de cesser un travail où, ne réussissant pas, il est nécessaire qu'il se ruine. [III.273a]

There follows an amusing, if no doubt somewhat caricatural account of what happened in practice with this test:

Un homme ne se présente point à la maîtrise qu'il n'ait passé par les préliminaires; il est impossible qu'il n'ait appris quelque chose de son métier

pendant les quatre à cinq ans que durent ces préliminaires. S'il est fils de
maître, assez ordinairement il est dispensé du *chef-d'œuvre*; s'il ne l'est pas,
fût-il le plus habile ouvrier d'une ville, il a bien de la peine à faire un *chef-
d'œuvre* qui soit agréé de la communauté, quand il est odieux à cette communauté. S'il est agréable au contraire, ou qu'il ait de l'argent, fût-il le
plus ignorant de tous les ouvriers, il corrompra ceux qui doivent veiller
sur lui tandis qu'il fait son *chef-d'œuvre*; ou il exécutera un mauvais
ouvrage qu'on recevra comme un *chef-d'œuvre*; ou il en présentera un
excellent qu'il n'aura pas fait. On voit que toutes ces manœuvres
anéantissent absolument les avantages qu'on prétend retirer des *chefs-
d'œuvre* et des communautés et que les corps de communauté et de manufacture n'en subsistent pas moins. [III.273a–b]

Whatever the rights and wrongs of the matter, the last sentence
makes clear Diderot's hostility to the guild system as a whole.

Among the measures which Faiguet de Villeneuve proposed in
the article ÉPARGNE was the suppression of the guilds. His attack on
this institution is developed in greater detail in the long article
MAITRISES. He begins by pointing out that there are few guilds in
England, Holland, Portugal and Spain, and, what is more,

Il n'y en a point du tout dans nos colonies, non plus que dans quelques-
unes de nos villes modernes, telles que Lorient, Saint-Germain, Versailles
et autres. Nous avons même des lieux privilégiés à Paris où bien des gens
travaillent et trafiquent sans qualité légale, le tout à la satisfaction du
public. D'ailleurs, combien de professions qui sont encore tout à fait
libres et que l'on voit subsister néanmoins à l'avantage de tous les sujets!
D'où je conclus que les maîtrises ne sont point nécessaires, puisqu'on s'en
est passé longtemps et qu'on s'en passe tous les jours sans inconvénient.
[IX.911b]

The evil consequences of the establishment of guilds are summed up
in the sentence: 'Les plus riches ou les plus forts viennent communément à bout d'exclure les plus faibles et d'attirer ainsi tout à
eux, abus constants que l'on ne pourra jamais déraciner qu'en
introduisant la concurrence et la liberté dans chaque profession'
[IX.911b].

Faiguet goes into considerable detail about the abuses of the
system and his proposals for its gradual suppression. Among the
many vices of the guilds which he describes the worst, he declares,

*Métallurgie: Fer blanc (Vol. VI, Fer blanc, Plate I)*

is the way in which they drive the poor into crime. The remedy is clear:

Qu'on favorise le commerce, l'agriculture et tous les arts nécessaires, qu'on permette à tous les sujets de faire valoir leurs biens et leurs talents, qu'on apprenne des métiers à tous les soldats, qu'on occupe et qu'on instruise les enfants des pauvres, qu'on fasse régner dans les hôpitaux l'ordre, le travail et l'aisance, qu'on reçoive tous ceux qui s'y présenteront, enfin qu'on renferme et qu'on corrige tous les mendiants valides; bientôt, au lieu de vagabonds et de voleurs si communs de nos jours, on ne verra plus que des hommes laborieux, parce que les peuples, trouvant à gagner leur vie et pouvant éviter la misère par le travail, ne seront jamais réduits à des extrémités fâcheuses ou funestes. [IX.915b]

The same theme is taken up in the unsigned article PRIVILÈGE (*Gouv. Comm. Polit.*) which, in a section headed *privilège exclusif,* also includes privileges granted to trading companies and manufacturers of certain products under the Ancien Régime. All these privileges are roundly condemned in the name of economic liberalism. 'La concurrence', exclaims the author, 'fera mieux faire et diminuera le prix de la main-d'œuvre' [XIII.391a]. He too denounces the evil effects of the monopoly enjoyed by the guilds. Not only does it drive men into enlisting in the armed forces or joining the hordes of lackeys who are 'la partie des citoyens la plus inutile et la plus à charge à l'état'; it is also onerous to the general body of citizens:

Le public de sa part y perdit par le renchérissement des marchandies et de la main-d'œuvre. On fut obligé d'acheter 3 livres 10 sols une paire de souliers faits par un maître, qu'on aurait payée bien moins en la prenant d'un ouvrier qui n'y aurait mis que du cuir et sa façon. [XIII.390b]

The writer points out that in recent times the government has restricted the granting of monopolies to large overseas trading companies or to specially important industries, and suggests that this more liberal policy should be extended to the small man:

Il serait fort à souhaiter que des vues aussi sages pussent s'étendre aux objets subalternes; que tout homme qui a de l'industrie, du génie ou du talent, pût en faire librement usage et ne fût pas assujetti à des formalités et des frais qui ne concourent pour rien au bien public. Si un ouvrier essaie, sans être assez instruit, à faire une pièce de toile ou de drap et qu'il la fasse mal, outre que le maître en ferait tout autant, il la vendra moins, mais enfin il la vendra, et il n'aura pas perdu entièrement sa matière et son temps; il apprendra par de premières épreuves qui ne lui auront pas réussi, à faire mieux. Plus de gens travailleront, l'émulation ou plutôt l'envie du succès fera sortir le génie et le talent. [XIII.390b–391b]

If such free competition were established,

de ce goût de travail et de petites manufactures dispersées naîtrait une circulation d'argent et d'industrie et un emploi constant des talents, des forces et du temps. Les *privilèges exclusifs* de toute espèce seraient réduits aux seuls établissements qui, par la nature de leur objet et par la grandeur nécessaire à ces établissements, seraient au-dessus de la force des simples particuliers et auraient surtout pour objet des choses de luxe et non d'absolue nécessité. [XIII.391b]

In certain of his technological articles Diderot himself argues against monopolies and in favour of economic freedom. Of particular interest is the article \*LAITON in which he discusses this question in relation to new inventions:

Il n'y a pas deux partis à prendre avec les inventeurs de machines utiles; il faut, ou les récompenser par le privilège exclusif, ou leur accorder une somme proportionnée à leur travail, aux frais de leurs expériences et à l'utilité de leur invention; sans quoi il faut que l'esprit d'industrie s'éteigne et que les arts demeurent dans un état d'engourdissement. Le privilège exclusif est une mauvaise chose en ce qu'il restreint, du moins pour un temps, les avantages d'une machine à un seul particulier, lorsqu'ils pourraient être étendus à un grand nombre de citoyens qui tous en profiteraient.
    Un autre inconvénient, c'est de ruiner ceux qui s'occupaient, avant l'invention, du même genre de travail qu'ils sont forcés de quitter, parce que leurs frais sont les mêmes et que l'ouvrage baisse nécessairement de prix. Donc il faut que le gouvernement acquière à ses dépens toutes les machines nouvelles et d'une utilité reconnue et qu'il les rende publiques; et s'il arrive qu'il ne puisse pas faire cette dépense, c'est qu'il y a eu et qu'il y a encore quelque vice dans l'administration, un défaut d'économie qu'il faut corriger. [IX.222a]

In other words, Diderot is arguing, the State should intervene in such cases to prevent the formation of a monopoly.

## The economic theories of Dr Quesnay

The most famous articles on economic questions in the *Encyclopédie* are the two, FERMIERS (*Économie politique*) and GRAINS (*Économie politique*), which were contributed to Vols VI and VII under his son's name by Dr François Quesnay, the founder of the Physiocratic school which, to use Adam Smith's words, 'represents the produce of land as the sole source of the revenue and wealth of every country'.[1]

The first of these articles is shorter and the author's ideas are less developed than in GRAINS which appeared a year later. It contains none the less some of his fundamental principles, for instance the contrast between the prosperous *fermier* who ploughs with horses and the much more numerous class of poverty-stricken *métayers* who are reduced to using oxen:

Il n'y a que des *fermiers* riches qui puissent se servir de chevaux pour labourer les terres. Il faut qu'un *fermier* qui s'établit avec une charrue de quatre chevaux, fasse des dépenses considérables avant que d'obtenir une première récolte. Il cultive pendant un an les terres qu'il doit ensemencer en blé; et après qu'il a ensemencé, il ne recueille qu'au mois d'août de l'année suivante. Ainsi il attend près de deux ans les fruits de ses travaux et de ses dépenses. Il a fait les frais des chevaux et des autres bestiaux qui lui sont nécessaires; il fournit les grains pour ensemencer les terres, il nourrit les chevaux, il paie les gages et la nourriture des domestiques. Toutes ces dépenses qu'il est obligé d'avancer pour les deux premières années de culture d'un domaine d'une charrue de quatre chevaux, sont estimés à 10 ou 12 mille livres, et pour deux ou trois charrues, 20 ou 30 mille livres.

Dans les provinces où il n'y a pas de *fermier* en état de se procurer de tels établissements, les propriétaires des terres n'ont d'autres ressources pour retirer quelques produits de leur biens que de les faire cultiver avec des bœufs par des paysans qui leur rendent la moitié de la récolte. Cette sorte de culture exige très peu de frais de la part du métayer; le propriétaire lui fournit les bœufs et la semence. Les bœufs vont après leur travail prendre leur nourriture dans les pâturages; tous les frais du métayer se réduisent aux instruments du labourage et aux dépenses pour sa nourriture jusqu'au temps de la première récolte, souvent même le propriétaire est obligé de lui faire les avances de ces frais. [VI.529a]

After going into some detail to show the economic superiority of the *fermier* over the *métayer*, Quesnay proceeds to try to account for

---

[1] *An Inquiry into the Nature and Causes of the Wealth of Nations*, Book IV, chap. ix.

the sad state of French agriculture with its relatively small number of prosperous tenant farmers:

Ce désastre peut être attribué à trois causes: 1° à la désertion des enfants des laboureurs qui sont forcés à se réfugier dans les grandes villes, où ils portent les richesses que leurs pères emploient à la culture des terres; 2° aux impositions arbitraires qui ne laissent aucune sûreté dans l'emploi des fonds nécessaires pour les dépenses de l'agriculture; 3° à la gêne à laquelle on s'est trouvé assujetti dans le commerce des grains. [VI.532b]

Quesnay casts envious eyes at the flourishing state of English agriculture and draws the moral for France:

La vente des grains forme le quart du commerce intérieur de l'Angleterre, et le produit des bestiaux est bien supérieur à celui des grains. Cette abondance est due aux richesses du cultivateur. En Angleterre l'état de *fermier* est un état fort riche et fort estimé, un état singulièrement protégé par le gouvernement. Le cultivateur y fait valoir ses richesses à découvert, sans craindre que son grain attire sa ruine par des impositions arbitraires et indéterminées.

Plus les laboureurs sont riches, plus ils augmentent par leurs facultés le produit des terres et la puissance de la nation. Un *fermier* pauvre ne peut cultiver qu'au désavantage de l'état, parce qu'il ne peut obtenir par son travail les productions que la terre n'accorde qu'à une culture opulente. [VI.533b]

The chief obstacle to this desirable state of affairs is, in Quesnay's eyes, the low price of grain. How this view of the situation can be reconciled with the modern historian's view that rising agricultural prices in the period from, roughly, 1730 to 1780 were bringing increased prosperity to agriculture is not our present concern. The remedy proposed by Quesnay is that the government should cease to impose restrictions on the grain trade in order to avoid the ever-present risk of famine, and instead should encourage agriculture, as was done in England, by allowing the free export of grain.

Ce ne sont pas seulement les bonnes ou mauvaises récoltes qui règlent le prix du blé; c'est principalement la liberté ou la contrainte dans le commerce de cette denrée qui décide de sa valeur. Si on veut en restreindre ou en gêner le commerce dans les temps des bonnes récoltes, on dérange les produits de l'agriculture, on affaiblit l'état, on diminue le revenu des

propriétaires des terres, on fomente la paresse et l'arrogance du domestique et du manouvrier qui doivent aider à l'agriculture; on ruine les
laboureurs, on dépeuple les campagnes. Ce ne serait pas connaître les
avantages de la France que d'empêcher l'exportation du blé sur la crainte
d'en manquer, dans un royaume qui peut en produire beaucoup plus que
l'on n'en pourrait vendre à l'étranger.

La conduite de l'Angleterre à cet égard prouve, au contraire, qu'il n'y a
point de moyen plus sûr pour soutenir l'agriculture, entretenir l'abondance et obvier aux famines que la vente d'une partie des récoltes à
l'étranger. Cette nation n'a point essuyé de cherté extraordinaire ni de
non-valeur du blé depuis qu'elle a favorisé et excité l'exportation.
[VI.536a–b]

The superiority of the rich *fermiers* over the poor *métayers* is
restated in a striking passage:

Ces pauvres cultivateurs, si peu utiles à l'état, ne représentent point le vrai
laboureur, le riche *fermier* qui cultive en grand, qui gouverne, qui commande, qui multiplie les dépenses pour augmenter les profits; qui, ne
négligeant aucun moyen, aucun avantage particulier, fait le bien général;
qui emploie utilement les habitants de la campagne, qui peut choisir et
attendre les temps favorables pour le débit de ses grains, pour l'achat et
pour la vente de ses bestiaux. [VI.538b]

At this point in the article we also find the rudiments of the
Physiocratic theory that agriculture is the only real source of
wealth, and that other occupations such as trade and industry are
essentially sterile:

Les manufactures et le commerce, entretenus par les désordres du luxe,
accumulent les hommes et les richesses dans les grandes villes, s'opposent
à l'amélioration des biens, dévastent les campagnes, inspirent du mépris
pour l'agriculture, augmentent excessivement les dépenses des particuliers, nuisent au soutien des familles, s'opposent à la propagation des
hommes et affaiblissent l'état.

La décadence des empires a souvent suivi de près un commerce florissant. Quand une nation dépense par le luxe ce qu'elle gagne par le commerce, il n'en résulte qu'un mouvement d'argent sans augmentation
réelle de richesses. [VI.538b]

At present all wealthy people are drawn to Paris or other large towns, and the flourishing state of trade gives the country a false air of prosperity:

Le commerce paraît florissant dans les villes parce qu'elles sont remplies de riches marchands. Mais qu'en résulte-t-il sinon que presque tout l'argent du royaume est employé à un commerce qui n'augmente point les richesses de la nation? . . . L'agriculture est le patrimoine du souverain. Toutes ses productions sont visibles; on peut les assujettir convenablement aux impositions; les richesses pécuniaires échappent à la répartition des subsides, le gouvernement n'y peut prendre que par des moyens onéreux à l'état. [VI.539a]

If the principal direct tax, the *taille*, were assessed on a less arbitrary basis, Quesnay concludes, the inhabitants of the country

vivraient dans la même sécurité que les habitants des grandes villes. Beaucoup de propriétaires iraient faire valoir eux-mêmes leurs biens; on n'abandonnerait plus les campagnes; les richesses et la population s'y rétabliraient. Ainsi, en éloignant d'ailleurs toutes les autres causes préjudiciables aux progrès de l'agriculture, les forces du royaume se répareraient peu à peu par l'augmentation des hommes et par l'accroissement des revenus de l'état. [VI.539b–540a]

It was on this foundation that Quesnay was to develop his ideas further in his second economic article, GRAINS.

Here the stress on the importance of agriculture and on the necessity of offering farmers a good price for their grain is even stronger:

On a fait baisser le prix de nos blés afin que la fabrication et la main-d'œuvre fussent moins chères que chez l'étranger. Les hommes et les richesses se sont accumulés dans les villes; l'agriculture, la plus féconde et la plus noble partie de notre commerce, la source des revenus du royaume, n'a pas été envisagée comme le fond primitif de nos richesses; elle n'a paru intéresser que le fermier et le paysan. On a borné leurs travaux à la subsistance de la nation qui, par l'achat des denrées, paie les dépenses de la culture; et on a cru que c'était un commerce ou un trafic établi sur l'industrie qui devait apporter l'or et l'argent dans le royaume. On a défendu de planter des vignes; on a recommandé la culture des mûriers; on a arrêté le débit des productions de l'agriculture et diminué le revenu des terres pour favoriser des manufactures préjudiciables à notre propre commerce. [VII.812a]

The policy of encouraging industry, pursued by Colbert and his successors, has had disastrous results which Quesnay sums up in a striking sentence: 'Pour gagner quelques millions à fabriquer et à vendre de belles étoffes nous avons perdu des milliards sur le produit de nos terres; ét la nation, parée de tissus d'or et d'argent, a cru jouir d'un commerce florissant' [VII.812b]. It is not cloth, but grain, that France should be exporting. The free export of grain is an essential condition for the prosperity of agriculture and for the avoidance of the food shortages so common under the Ancien Régime:

... Sans cette condition nos récoltes, qui ne sont destinées qu'à la consommation du royaume, ne peuvent pas augmenter, parce que, si elles étaient plus abondantes, elles feraient tomber le blé en non-valeur; les cultivateurs ne pourraient pas en soutenir la culture, les terres ne produiraient rien au roi ni aux propriétaires. Il faudrait donc éviter l'abondance du blé dans un royaume où l'on n'en devrait recueillir que pour la subsistance de la nation. Mais dans ce cas les disettes sont inévitables parce que, quand la récolte donne du blé pour trois ou quatre mois de plus que la consommation de l'année, il est à si bas prix que ce superflu ruine le laboureur, et néanmoins il ne suffit pas pour la consommation de l'année suivante, s'il survient une mauvaise récolte. Ainsi il n'y a que la facilité du débit à bon prix qui puisse maintenir l'abondance et le profit. [VII813a]

As in FERMIERS, Quesnay stresses—this time with elaborate calculations—the superiority of the *fermier* over the *métayer*. The low total production of French agriculture he attributes to a variety of causes:

La gêne dans le commerce des grains, le défaut d'exportation, la dépopulation, le manque de richesses dans les campagnes, l'imposition indéterminée des subsides, la levée des milices, l'excès des corvées ont réduit nos récoltes à ce petit produit. [VII.816a]

But for Quesnay the first remedy is to allow the free export of grain since from this measure will flow all manner of consequences:

La vente à l'étranger facilite le débit, ranime la culture et augmente le revenu des terres; l'accroissement des revenus procure de plus grandes dépenses qui favorisent la population parce que l'augmentation des dépenses procure des gains à un plus grand nombre d'hommes. L'accroissement de la population étend la consommation; la consommation soutient le prix des denrées qui se multiplient par la culture à proportion des besoins des hommes, c'est-à-dire à proportion que la population augmente. Le principe de tous ces progrès est donc l'exportation des denrées du cru; parce que la vente à l'étranger augmente les revenus; que l'accroissement des revenus augmente la population; que l'accroissement de la population augmente la consommation; qu'une plus grande consommation augmente de plus en plus la culture, les revenus des terres et la population; car l'augmentation des revenus augmente la population, et la population augmente les revenus. [VII.817a]

It follows that the first essential is to 'établir invariablement la liberté du commerce des *grains*'.

The prime importance of agriculture in the national economy is underlined in a vivid passage in which he speaks of

l'agriculture qui fournit les matières de premier besoin, qui donne des revenus au roi et aux propriétaires, des dîmes au clergé, des profits aux cultivateurs. Ce sont ces premières richesses, toujours renouvelées, qui soutiennent tous les autres états du royaume, qui donnent de l'activité à toutes les autres professions, qui font fleurir le commerce, qui favorisent la population, qui animent l'industrie, qui entretiennent la prospérité de la nation. [VII.820a]

It goes almost without saying that Sully is Quesnay's hero. And once again he stresses the importance of big farmers for the prosperity of agriculture:

Les avantages de l'agriculture dépendent donc beaucoup de la réunion des terres en grosses fermes, mises dans la meilleure valeur par de riches fermiers. . . .

Nous n'envisageons pas ici le riche fermier comme un ouvrier qui laboure lui-même la terre; c'est un entrepreneur qui gouverne et qui fait valoir son entreprise par son intelligence et par ses richesses. L'agriculture conduite par de riches cultivateurs est une profession très honnête et très lucrative, réservée à des hommes libres en état de faire les avances des frais considérables qu'exige la culture de la terre, et qui occupe les paysans et leur procure toujours un gain convenable et assuré. [VII.821b]

But there is a second condition for their prosperity—a reform of the arbitrary system of direct taxation which can mean, for instance, that a tenant farmer is ruined by increases in his *taille* during the duration of his lease. A better and fairer system,

Quesnay suggests, would be to fix the *taille* at half the rent paid by
the farmer; and some similar arrangement might also be made for
the large class of *métayers*.

Returning to his panacea of free trade in grain Quesnay does
concede to those who are afraid of the dangers of famine that its
export cannot in practice be completely freed from all controls.
Here again he cites the example of England:

L'exportation ne doit pas cependant être illimitée; il faut qu'elle soit,
comme en Angleterre, interdite, lorsque le blé passe un prix marqué par
la loi. . . . En France les famines sont fréquentes parce que l'exportation
du blé y était souvent défendue et que l'abondance est aussi défavorable
aux fermiers que les disettes sont funestes aux peuples. Le prétexte de
remédier aux famines dans un royaume en interceptant le commerce des
*grains* entre les provinces donne encore lieu à des abus qui augmentent la
misère, qui détruisent l'agriculture et qui anéantissent les revenus du
royaume. [VII.825b, note]

From the point of view of theory the most important part of the
article is the section entitled *Maximes de gouvernement économique*.
In these fourteen maxims Quesnay offers a first attempt at a
systematic exposition of the doctrines of the new school of
economists. Here we find some of their main ideas set forth. First,
by its very nature industry is sterile in the sense that 'il n'y a pas
d'accroissement de richesses' [VII.826b]. Agriculture on the other
hand 'produit deux sortes de richesses: savoir, le produit annuel des
revenus des propriétaires et la restitution des frais de la culture'
[VII.827b]. To sacrifice agriculture to industry is a sure way to ruin
a country:

Car si le cultivateur n'est pas dédommagé des grands frais que la culture
exige, et s'il ne gagne pas, l'agriculture périt; la nation perd les revenus de
ses biens-fonds; les travaux des ouvrages de main-d'œuvre diminuent
parce que ces travaux ne peuvent plus être payés par les propriétaires des
biens-fonds; le pays se dépeuple par la misère et la désertion des fabricants,
artisans, manouvriers et paysans qui ne peuvent subsister qu'à proportion
des gains que leur procurent les revenus de la nation. [VII.827b]

The countries which sell abroad articles of first necessity, Quesnay
maintains, are better off than those who export luxury goods:

Une nation qui est assurée par ses biens-fonds d'un commerce de denrées
de son cru et par conséquent aussi d'un commerce de marchandises de

main-d'œuvre est indépendante des autres nations. Elle ne commerce avec celles-ci que pour entretenir, faciliter et étendre son commerce extérieur; et elle doit, autant qu'il est possible, pour conserver son indé-pendance et son avantage dans le commerce réciproque, ne tirer d'elles que des marchandises de luxe et leur vendre des marchandises nécessaires aux besoins de la vie. [VII.828b]

It follows from this that trade, and in particular the grain trade, must be freed from all restrictions, both inside the country and on export. On the importance of agricultural prices Quesnay ex-presses himself in lapidary style:

La non-valeur avec l'abondance n'est point richesse. La cherté avec pénurie est misère. L'abondance avec cherté est opulence. J'entends une cherté et une abondance permanentes; car une cherté passagère ne procurerait pas une distribution générale de richesses à toute la nation, elle n'augmenterait pas les revenus des propriétaires ni les revenus du roi; elle ne serait avanta-geuse qu'à quelques particuliers qui auraient alors des denrées à vendre à haut prix. [VII.830b]

Finally Quesnay deals with the criticism which was frequently to be made by the opponents of the Physiocrats: that a rise in grain prices would mean hardship for the poorer classes of society. He argues that while the increase in the price of bread would be small and compensated for by higher wages, low prices have a bad effect on the masses:

C'est d'ailleurs un grand inconvénient que d'accoutumer le même peuple à acheter le blé à trop bas prix; il en devient moins laborieux, il se nourrit de pain à peu de frais et devient paresseux et arrogant; les laboureurs trouvent difficilement des ouvriers et des domestiques; aussi sont-ils fort mal servis dans les années abondantes. Il est important que le petit peuple gagne davantage et qu'il soit pressé par le besoin de gagner. [VII.831a]

In any case, he maintains, the price of grain would be kept within reasonable limits by the operation of that well-known liberal principle, competition, since, given the free export of grain, French prices would have to be in line with those of the neighbour-ing countries.

## *Physiocratic theory in the 'Encyclopédie'*

Despite his background as a cutler's son and despite his interest in the high proportion of the text and plates of the *Encyclopédie* which aimed at presenting an up-to-date picture of the industrial processes in use when it appeared, Diderot also concerned himself with agriculture. It was he, for instance, who contributed the long, unsigned article AGRICULTURE in the first volume. And—at any rate for a time—he was very much influenced by Physiocratic theory, in particular by its stress on the importance of agriculture. This comes out very clearly in various of his contributions to the last ten volumes. Into the grammatical article *INSIGNE he works praise of Sully for understanding the importance of agriculture:

Sully rendit à la nation un service *insigne* par le bon ordre qu'il introduisit dans les finances. Ce fut en lui une marque *insigne* d'un grand jugement que d'avoir tout rapporté à la population et à l'agriculture ; et ceux qui s'écartèrent dans la suite de ces principes et tournèrent leurs vues du côté des traitants et des manufacturiers, prirent l'accessoire pour le principal. [VIII.788b]

Despite its title *HOMME (*Politique*) is really concerned with economic questions and that in a spirit which is remarkably close to that of the Physiocrats, starting with the opening sentences: 'Il n'y a de véritables richesses que l'*homme* et la terre. L'*homme* ne vaut rien sans la terre, et la terre ne vaut rien sans l'*homme*' [VIII.278b]. After stressing the importance of a large population, Diderot goes on to proclaim:

On aura des *hommes* industrieux s'ils sont libres.
   L'administration est la plus mauvaise qu'il soit possible d'imaginer si, faute de liberté de commerce, l'abondance devient quelquefois pour une province un fléau aussi redoutable que la disette. *Voyez les articles* GOUVERNEMENT, LOIS, IMPÔTS, POPULATION, LIBERTÉ, etc.

He would like to see a reduction in the number of workmen engaged in luxury trades and in the number of servants:

Il faudrait asseoir sur les domestiques un impôt à la décharge des agriculteurs.
   Si les agriculteurs qui sont les *hommes* de l'état qui fatiguent le plus, sont les moins bien nourris, il faut qu'ils se dégoûtent de leur état ou qu'ils y

périssent. Dire que l'aisance les en ferait sortir, c'est être un ignorant et un homme atroce.

In one of the following paragraphs Diderot appears to modify slightly pure Physiocratic principles since these favoured the large farmers well equipped with capital:

Plus le produit net est grand et également partagé, plus l'administration est bonne. Un produit net également partagé peut être préférable à un plus grand produit net dont le partage serait très inégal et qui diviserait le peuple en deux classes dont l'une regorgerait de richesses et l'autre expirerait dans la misère.

If this egalitarian trend is foreign to the Physiocrats, the sentence which follows reflects very clearly the dominant position which they assigned to agriculture: 'Tant qu'il y a des friches dans un état, un *homme* ne peut être employé en manufacture sans perte.'

It is impossible to say who was responsible for the unsigned article LABOUREUR, but it certainly drives home in a short space the arguments advanced by Quesnay in FERMIERS and GRAINS, to which it refers the reader. It begins by making clear that the *laboureur* in question is a man of substance having at his disposal a considerable amount of capital: 'Ce n'est point cet homme de peine, ce mercenaire qui panse les chevaux ou les bœufs et qui conduit la charrue' [IX.148a]. What the writer has in mind is the wealthy *fermier* whose interests the Physiocrats represented:

La culture des terres est une entreprise qui exige beaucoup d'avances, sans lesquelles elle est stérile et ruineuse. Ce n'est point au travail des hommes qu'on doit les grandes récoltes. Ce sont les chevaux et les bœufs qui labourent; ce sont les bestiaux qui engraissent les terres. Une riche récolte suppose nécessairement une richesse précédente à laquelle les travaux, quelque multipliés qu'ils soient, ne peuvent pas suppléer. Il faut donc que le *laboureur* soit propriétaire d'un fonds considérable, soit pour monter la ferme en bestiaux et en instruments, soit pour fournir aux dépenses journalières, dont il ne commence à recueillir le fruit que près de deux ans après ses premières avances. *Voyez* FERME *et* FERMIER (*Économie politique*). [IX.148a]

The land is the only real source of wealth:

De toutes les classes de richesses il n'y a que les dons de la terre qui se reproduisent constamment, parce que les premiers besoins sont toujours les mêmes. Les manufactures ne produisent que très peu au delà du salaire des hommes qu'elles occupent. Le commerce de l'argent ne produit que le mouvement dans un signe qui par lui-même n'a point de valeur réelle. C'est la terre, la terre seule qui donne les vraies richesses, dont la renaissance annuelle assure à un état des revenus fixes, indépendants de l'opinion, visibles, et qu'on ne peut point soustraire à ses besoins. Or les dons de la terre sont toujours proportionnés aux avances du *laboureur* et dépendent des dépenses par lesquelles on les prépare. Ainsi la richesse plus ou moins grande des *laboureurs* peut être un thermomètre fort exact de la prospérité d'une nation qui a un grand territoire. [IX.148a]

To encourage this class of wealthy *laboureurs* the government must see that taxation is not excessive and must give them complete freedom to grow what crops they wish; and above all, whereas the government normally banned the export of corn to avoid the danger of famine, it must allow the free export of their produce:

S'il est vrai qu'on ne puisse pas établir une culture avantageuse sans de grandes avances, l'entière liberté d'exportation des denrées est une condition nécessaire sans laquelle ces avances ne se feront point. Comment, avec l'incertitude du débit qu'entraîne la gêne sur l'exportation, voudrait-on exposer ses fonds? Les grains ont un prix fondamental nécessaire. *Voyez* GRAINS (*Économ. politiq.*) Où l'exportation n'est pas libre, les *laboureurs* sont réduits à craindre l'abondance et une surcharge de denrées dont la valeur vénale est au-dessous des frais auxquels ils ont été obligés. La liberté d'exportation assure, par l'égalité du prix, la rentrée certaine des avances et un produit net, qui est le seul motif qui puisse exciter à de nouvelles. La liberté dans la culture n'est pas une condition moins nécessaire à sa prospérité, et la gêne à cet égard est inutile autant que dure et ridicule. Vous pouvez forcer un *laboureur* à semer du blé, mais vous ne le forcerez pas à donner à sa terre toutes les préparations et les engrais sans lesquels la culture du blé est infructueuse. Ainsi vous anéantissez en pure perte un produit qui eût été avantageux; par une précaution aveugle et imprudente vous préparez de loin la famine que vous vouliez prévenir. [IX.148a–b]

The article follows the Physiocratic attitude to direct taxation, that it should fall, not on the farmer himself, but on the landlord, since, if the farmer's capital is diminished less will be produced and that way lies economic ruin.

Si l'impôt a porté sur les avances nécessaires au *laboureur*, il est devenu spoliatif. La reproduction, diminuée par ce qui a manqué du côté des avances, entraîne assez rapidement à la décadence. [IX.148b]

The article ends by stressing once more that it is a totally false idea that 'le laboureur n'a besoin que de ses bras pour exercer sa profession':

Cette idée destructive n'est vraie qu'à l'égard de quelques pays dans lesquels la culture est dégradée. La pauvreté des *laboureurs* n'y laisse presque point de prise à l'impôt, ni de ressources à l'état. *Voyez* MÉTAYER. [IX.148b]

Here we have the usual Physiocratic stress on the importance of the relatively small but powerful class of wealthy capitalist farmers who are contrasted with the often poverty-stricken *métayers* who eked out a miserable existence over a great part of France.

## The debate on luxury

As on many subjects one finds in the *Encyclopédie* conflicting views on a question which was hotly debated in the eighteenth century— that of the good or bad effects of luxury. In *HOMME (*Politique*) Diderot, as we have seen, had argued in favour of a reduction of the number of workmen engaged in luxury trades. The case against luxury is put at length by his friend Damilaville in POPULATION where it is blamed for the decline of agriculture and for the sorry state of the countryside:

Le commerce de luxe et les arts de la même espèce joignent à tous ces in-convénients la dangereuse séduction d'offrir aux hommes plus de bénéfice et moins de fatigues qu'ils n'en trouvent dans les travaux de la campagne. Qui est-ce qui tracera de pénibles sillons? qui, le corps courbé depuis le lever du soleil jusqu'à son coucher, cultivera les vignes, moissonnera les champs, supportera enfin dans des travaux si durs les ardeurs de l'été et la rigueur des hivers, quand, à l'abri des saisons, on pourra gagner davantage en filant de la soie ou en préparant d'autres matières dans les manufactures de luxe? Aussi ces manufactures et ce commerce ont-ils attiré les hommes dans les villes et leur donnent l'apparence d'une abondante *population*; mais pénétrez dans les campagnes, vous les trouverez désertes et des-séchées. [XIII.101a]

And so the attack continues for several columns.

The unsigned article LUXE, long attributed to Diderot, but now restored to Saint-Lambert, attempts to give a balanced view of the whole question. It opens with a summary of the arguments brought for and against luxury and refutes all of them in turn. Saint-Lambert himself avoids both these extreme views and endeavours to steer a middle course. He begins by asking whether there is any necessary connection between the growth of luxury and the decline and corruption of governments:

Comme il est dans la nature des hommes et des choses que les gouvernements se corrompent avec le temps, et aussi dans la nature des hommes et des choses qu'avec le temps les états s'enrichissent, les arts se perfectionnent et la *luxe* augmente, n'a-t-on pas vu comme cause et comme effet l'un de l'autre ce qui, sans être ni l'effet ni la cause l'un de l'autre, se rencontre ensemble et marche à peu près d'un pas égal? [IX.764b]

He suggests that luxury might well have nothing to do with either the prosperity or the decline of states, and that it must be related to the situation and products of a country and of its neighbours:

De ces observations et de ces réflexions je conclurais que le *luxe* est contraire ou favorable à la richesse des nations selon qu'il consomme plus ou moins le produit de leur sol et de leur industrie, ou qu'il consomme le produit du sol et de l'industrie de l'étranger; qu'il doit avoir un plus grand ou un plus petit nombre d'objets selon que ces nations ont plus ou moins de richesses. Le *luxe* est à cet égard pour les peuples ce qu'il est pour les particuliers; il faut que la multitude des jouissances soit proportionnée aux moyens de jouir. [IX.765b]

Saint-Lambert now reverts to an idea which he had expounded at length in LÉGISLATEUR: that it is essential for governments to encourage what he calls 'l'esprit de communauté'. If that is lacking, then luxury will have evil consequences:

Je porte mes yeux sur des royaumes où règne le plus grand *luxe* et où les campagnes deviennent des déserts; mais avant d'attribuer ce malheur au *luxe* des villes, je me demande quelle a été la conduite des administrateurs de ces royaumes; et je vois de cette conduite naître la dépopulation attribuée au *luxe*, j'en vois naître les abus du *luxe* même. [IX.766a]

What follows is clearly a direct criticism of conditions in the France of Louis XV:

Si dans ces pays on a surchargé d'impôts et de corvées les habitants de la campagne; si l'abus d'une autorité légitime les a tenus souvent dans l'inquiétude et dans l'avilissement; si des monopoles ont arrêté le débit de leurs denrées; si on a fait ces fautes et d'autres dont je ne veux point parler, une partie des habitants des campagnes a dû les abandonner pour chercher la subsistance dans les villes; ces malheureux y ont trouvé le *luxe* et, en se consacrant à son service, ils ont pu vivre dans leur patrie. Le *luxe*, en occupant dans les villes les habitants de la campagne, n'a fait que retarder la dépopulation de l'état; je dis retarder et non empêcher, parce que les mariages sont rares dans des campagnes misérables, et plus rares encore parmi l'espèce d'hommes qui se réfugient de la campagne dans les villes....

L'oppression des campagnes suffit pour avoir établi l'extrême inégalité des richesses dont on attribue l'origine au *luxe*, quoique lui seul au contraire puisse établir une sorte d'équilibre entre les fortunes. Le paysan opprimé cesse d'être propriétaire, il vend le champ de ses pères au maître qu'il s'est donné, et tous les biens de l'état passent insensiblement dans un plus petit nombre de mains. [IX.766b]

Further mistakes made by governments—and despite his cautious wording Saint-Lambert is obviously here referring to France—are then listed:

Il y a des pays où le gouvernement a pris encore d'autres moyens pour augmenter l'inégalité des richesses et dans lesquels on a donné, on a continué des privilèges exclusifs aux entrepreneurs de plusieurs manufactures, à quelques citoyens pour faire valoir des colonies, et à quelques compagnies pour faire seules un riche commerce. Dans d'autres pays, à ces fautes on a ajouté celle de rendre lucratives à l'excès les charges de finance qu'il fallait honorer. [IX.767a]

In a very interesting passage Saint-Lambert traces the change from feudal times when the land, the only form of wealth, was in the hands of the nobility, to modern times when the development of trade, industry and luxury has created a new form of wealth for the *roturier*. He then goes on to describe the ill effects of an excessive inequality of wealth, avoiding all specific reference to the France of his day, but having it very clearly in mind:

Il est moralement nécessaire que l'usage des richesses soit contraire au bon ordre et aux mœurs. Quand les richesses sont acquises sans travail ou par des abus, les nouveaux riches se donnent promptement la jouissance d'une fortune rapide et d'abord s'accoutument à l'inaction et au besoin des dissipations frivoles. Odieux à la plupart de leurs concitoyens, auxquels ils ont été injustement préférés, aux fortunes desquels ils ont été des obstacles, ils ne cherchent point à obtenir d'eux ce qu'ils ne pourraient en espérer, l'estime et la bienveillance. Ce sont surtout les fortunes des monopoleurs, des administrateurs et receveurs des fonds publics qui sont les plus odieuses, et par conséquent celles dont on est le plus tenté d'abuser. Après avoir sacrifié la vertu et la réputation de probité au désir de s'enrichir, on ne s'avise guère de faire de ses richesses un usage vertueux, on cherche à couvrir sous le faste et les décorations du *luxe* l'origine de sa famille et celle de sa fortune, on cherche à perdre dans les plaisirs le souvenir de ce qu'on fait et de ce qu'on a été. [IX.767b]

With the same caution Saint-Lambert continues his picture of the France of his day:

S'il y avait des gouvernements où le législateur aurait trop fixé les grands dans la capitale; s'ils avaient des charges, des commandements, etc. qui ne leur donneraient rien à faire; s'ils n'étaient pas obligés de mériter par de grands services leurs places et leurs honneurs; si on n'excitait pas en eux l'émulation du travail et des vertus; si enfin on leur laissait oublier ce qu'ils doivent à la patrie, contents des avantages de leurs richesses et de leur rang, ils en abuseraient dans l'oisiveté.

Dans plusieurs pays de l'Europe il y a une sorte de propriété qui ne demande au propriétaire ni soins économiques, ni entretien, je veux parler des dettes nationales, et cette sorte de biens est encore très propre à augmenter, dans les grandes villes, les désordres qui sont les effets nécessaires d'une extrême opulence unie à l'oisiveté. [IX.768a]

The effect of this excessive inequality of wealth is to debase morally and physically both peasants and artisans.

Saint-Lambert now turns to a discussion of the remedies for this state of affairs which has been brought about, he insists, less by luxury than through the fault of the government:

Après avoir vu quel est le caractère d'une nation où règnent certains abus dans le gouvernement; après avoir vu que les vices de cette nation sont moins les effets du *luxe* que de ces abus, voyons ce que doit être l'esprit national d'un peuple qui rassemble chez lui tous les objets possibles du plus grand *luxe*, mais que sait maintenir dans l'ordre un gouvernement sage et vigoureux, également attentif à conserver les véritables richesses de l'État et les mœurs. [IX.768b]

The first and most important remedy, since it concerns the greatest part of the population, is to improve the economic position and the morale of the peasants. There should be no *privilèges exclusifs*, no more vast fortunes through a defective taxation system, no more fat sinecures for great noblemen. If things are properly organized, 'il y aura peu de grandes fortunes, et aucune de rapide. Les moyens de s'enrichir, partagés entre un plus grand nombre de citoyens, auront naturellement divisé les richesses; l'extrême pauvreté et l'extrême richesse seront également rares' [IX.769a]. This long article concludes with a summary of the author's views:

... Je ne propose point des lois agraires, un nouveau partage des biens, des moyens violents; qu'il n'y ait plus de privilèges exclusifs pour certaines manufactures et certains genres de commerce; que la finance soit moins lucrative; que les charges, les bénéfices soient moins entassés sur les mêmes têtes; que l'oisiveté soit punie par la honte ou par la privation des emplois; et sans attaquer le *luxe* en lui-même, sans même trop gêner les riches, vous verrez insensiblement les richesses se diviser et augmenter, le *luxe* augmenter et se diviser comme elles, et tout rentrera dans l'ordre. [IX.771a]

LUXE is undoubtedly one of the most interesting articles on economic and social questions, less perhaps for its analysis of this particular problem, than for its acute examination of the society of Saint-Lambert's day.

## Véron de Forbonnais and his economic theories

The early volumes of the *Encyclopédie* contain a certain number of articles on economic subjects by Véron de Forbonnais, an eclectic writer who at times stood close to the Physiocrats, but who in the 1760s was to prove one of their sharpest critics. In COMMERCE, for instance, he rejects in advance their exclusive predilection for agriculture when he maintains that industry is just as essential for the prosperity of trade: 'Leur union est telle que si l'une l'emporte sur l'autre elle vient à se détruire elle-même. Sans l'industrie les fruits de la terre n'auront point de valeur; si l'agriculture est négligée, les sources du *commerce* sont taries' [III.695a]. Here, as in CONCURRENCE *en fait de commerce*, where he declares that 'la *concurrence* est l'âme et l'aiguillon de l'industrie et le principe le plus actif du commerce' [III.832b], he is a strong advocate of the typically liberal principles of competition and of freedom of trade:

La concurrence est une des plus importants principes du *commerce* et une partie considérable de sa liberté. Tout ce qui la gêne ou l'altère . . . est ruineux pour l'état, diamétricalement opposé à son objet, qui est le bonheur et la subsistance aisée du plus grand nombre d'hommes possible. [III.697a]

He is, of course, hostile to such obstacles to foreign trade as internal customs barriers and duties on exports; but he does not go so far as to recommend their abolition:

Les droits des douanes, soit à la sortie, soit dans l'intérieur, sur les productions d'une nation sont les frais auxquels les étrangers se soumettent avec le plus de peine. Le négociant les regarde comme un excédent de la valeur réelle, et la politique les envisage comme une augmentation de richesse relative.

Les peuples intelligents, ou suppriment ces droits à la sortie de leurs productions, ou les proportionnent au besoin que les autres peuples en ont. Surtout ils comparent le prix de leurs productions rendues dans le lieu de la consommation avec le prix des mêmes productions fournies en concurrence par les nations rivales. Cette comparaison est très importante; quoique entre deux peuples manufacturiers la qualité et le prix d'achat des étoffes soient semblables, les droits de sortie ne doivent pas être les mêmes si le prix du transport n'est pas égal; la plus petite différence décide le consommateur. [III.697b]

Véron de Forbonnais is not even opposed to export subsidies:

Quelquefois le législateur, au lieu de prendre des droits sur l'exportation, l'encourage par des récompenses. L'objet de ces récompenses est d'augmenter le profit de l'ouvrier lorsqu'il n'est pas assez considérable pour soutenir un genre de travail utile en concurrence. Si la gratification va jusqu'à diminuer le prix, la préférence de l'étranger pendant quelques années suffit pour établir cette nouvelle branche du *commerce*, qui n'aura bientôt plus besoin de soutien. L'effet est certain, et la pratique n'en peut être que salutaire au corps politique, comme l'est dans le corps humain la communication qu'un membre fait à l'autre de sa chaleur, lorsqu'il en a besoin. [III.697b]

In a more forward-looking passage the writer stresses the importance of using machines and animals to do the work of human beings, rejecting the notion that this leads to depopulation:

L'économie du travail des hommes consiste à le suppléer par celui des machines et des animaux lorsqu'on le peut à moins de frais ou que cela les conserve; c'est multiplier la population bien loin de la détruire. Ce dernier préjugé s'est soutenu plus longtemps dans les pays qui ne s'occupaient que du *commerce* intérieur. En effet, si le *commerce* extérieur est médiocre, l'objet général ne serait pas rempli si l'intérieur n'occupait le plus d'hommes qu'il est possible. Mais si le *commerce* extérieur, c'est-à-dire la navigation, les colonies et les besoins des autres peuples peuvent occuper encore plus de citoyens qu'il ne s'en trouve, il est nécessaire d'économiser leur travail pour remplir de son mieux tous ces objets. [III.697a]

The article COLONIE was also furnished by Véron de Forbonnais. Here his economic liberalism is submerged by the belief that colonies exist solely for the benefit of the mother country. The consequences of this belief are stated with brutal frankness:

De ce calcul on peut tirer plusieurs conséquences:
   La première est que les *colonies* ne seraient plus utiles si elles pouvaient se passer de la métropole. Ainsi c'est une loi prise dans la nature de la chose que l'on doit restreindre les arts et la culture dans une *colonie* à tels et tels objets, suivant les convenances du pays de la domination.
   La seconde conséquence est que si la *colonie* entretient un commerce avec les étrangers ou que si l'on y consomme les marchandises étrangères, le montant de ce commerce et de ces marchandises est un vol fait à la métropole; vol trop commun, mais punissable par les lois, et par lequel la force réelle et relative d'un état est diminuée de tout ce que gagnent les étrangers. [III.650a]

That such an attitude to colonies is in flat contradiction with his general principle of giving the maximum amount of freedom to trade the author coolly denies:

Ce n'est donc point attenter à la liberté de ce commerce que de le re-streindre dans ce cas. Toute police qui le tolère par son indifférence ou qui laisse à certains ports la facilité de contrevenir au premier principe de l'institution des *colonies*, est une police destructive du commerce ou de la richesse d'une nation. [III.650a]

That colonies could bring economic benefits to the mother country was not a view shared by all contributors to the *Encyclopédie*. In POPULATION, for instance, Damilaville argues hotly the case against colonies, denouncing them on political and humanitarian as well as economic grounds. He concludes:

Voilà l'effet que produisent les colonies. Loin d'augmenter la puissance, elles l'affaiblissent en la partageant; il faut diviser ses forces pour les conserver, et encore comment défendre des conquêtes d'un continent à l'autre? Si elles fructifient, il vient tôt ou tard un temps où elles secouent le joug et se soustraient à la puissance qui les a fondées. [XIII.99b]

This prediction was very soon to be fulfilled in North America.

Although Véron de Forbonnais did not contribute to the later volumes of the *Encyclopédie*, he is present in its pages to the very end of the enterprise; Jaucourt in particular made great use of his *Recherches et considérations sur les finances* which conveniently appeared in 1758, particularly for its detailed criticism of the taxation system. In his article, NÉGOCE, for instance, Jaucourt attacks the obstacles put in the way of trade by the tax-farmers and their arbitrary methods:

Le moyen le plus sûr de ruiner le *négoce* dans un royaume est d'autoriser la finance à son préjudice. L'embarras des formalités, les droits des fermiers, des commis, les charges, les visites, les procès-verbaux, le retard des expéditions, les saisies, les discussions qui en résultent, etc. détruisent en peu d'années dans les provinces le *négoce* le plus lucratif et le mieux accrédité. Aussi la pernicieuse liberté accordée au fermier de la douane de Lyon d'établir des bureaux où bon lui semblerait, fut si bien employée dans le dernier siècle qu'en moins de cinquante ans il s'en trouva cent soixante-sept dans le Lyonnais, le Dauphiné, la Provence et le Languedoc; et par là tout le *négoce* des denrées à l'étranger se trouva culbuté. C'est au grand crédit des favoris et des financiers sous le règne d'Henri III que l'on doit rapporter la plupart des établissements funestes au *négoce* du royaume. [XI.75a]

All this comes straight from the *Recherches* of Véron de Forbonnais (i.70–2).

## Praise of the merchant

More interesting in many ways is the opening part of Jaucourt's article. At first sight the status of trade in the East seems remote from eighteenth-century France. The point of the passage is, of course, to contrast conditions in countries like Persia with those in the France of Louis XV where trade and the merchant still tended to be looked down on in aristocratic circles:

Le *négoce* est une profession très honorable en Orient, et elle est exercée non seulement par les roturiers, mais encore par les plus grand seigneurs, et même par les rois, quelquefois en personne, mais toujours par leurs commis.

    C'est surtout en Perse que la qualité de marchand a des honneurs et des prérogatives extraordinaires. Aussi ce nom ne se donne-t-il point aux gens qui tiennent boutique ou qui trafiquent de menues denrées, mais seulement à ceux qui entretiennent des commis et des facteurs dans les pays les plus éloignés. Ces personnes sont souvent élevées aux plus grandes charges, et c'est parmi elles que le roi de Perse choisit ses ambassadeurs. [XI.75a]

This is part and parcel of the campaign waged by the *philosophes* to raise the status of the merchant, a campaign brilliantly inaugurated by Voltaire in a famous passage in the *Lettres philosophiques* in which he contrasts his usefulness to society with the empty existence led by the courtier.

    Both editors join in this campaign. First Diderot in *COMMISSIONNAIRE, the starting-point of which is Chambers's FACTORY:

On donne encore le nom de *commissionnaires* et de *compagnie de commissionnaires* à des facteurs anglais établis dans le Levant. Ce sont des personnes alliées aux familles de la première distinction qui, après un apprentissage, passent principalement à Smyrne. Le préjugé de la noblesse, qui contraint ailleurs, sous peine de déroger, de vivre dans l'ignorance, l'inutilité et la pauvreté, permet là de trafiquer pour son compte, de servir l'état et de faire des fortunes considérables sans manquer à ce qu'on doit à sa naissance. [III.712a]

D'Alembert is even more direct in his outspoken article FORTUNE:

Les moyens honnêtes de faire *fortune* sont ceux qui viennent du talent et de l'industrie; à la tête de ces moyens on doit placer le commerce. Quelle différence pour le sage entre la *fortune* d'un courtisan faite à force de bassesses et d'intrigues, et celle d'un négociant qui ne doit son opulence qu'à lui-même et qui par cette opulence procure le bien de l'état! C'est une étrange barbarie dans nos mœurs et en même temps une contradiction bien ridicule que le commerce, c'est-à-dire la manière la plus noble de s'enrichir, soit regardé par les nobles avec mépris et qu'il serve néanmoins à acheter la noblesse. Mais ce qui met le comble à la contradiction et à la barbarie est qu'on puisse procurer la noblesse avec des richesses acquises par toutes sortes de voies. [VII.206a]

The importance which the *Encyclopédie* attached to trade and to the role of the merchant is too self-evident to need further illustration.

Another interesting article by Jaucourt is MESURE (*Gouvernement*). Here he anticipates one of the practical achievements of the Revolution by his demand for a uniform system of weights and measures to replace the present chaos. After pointing out once again how England had shown the way in this field as in others, he goes on:

Ne nous objectez pas que cette idée n'est qu'un projet spécieux, rempli d'inconvénients dans son exécution et qui dans l'examen n'est qu'une peine inutile, une dispute de mots, parce que le prix des choses suit bientôt leur poids et leur *mesure*. Mais ne serait-il pas encore plus naturel d'éviter cette marche, de la prévenir, de simplifier et de faciliter le cours du commerce intérieur qui se fait toujours difficilement lorsqu'il faut sans cesse avoir présent à son esprit ou devant les yeux le tarif des poids et des *mesures* des diverses provinces d'un royaume pour y ajuster ses opérations? [X.423a]

## Industry

Jaucourt is also the author of the article INDUSTRIE (*Droit politiq. et Commerce*), a word which he employs in the wide sense which was common in the eighteenth century, as is made clear in the opening words of the article:

Ce mot signifie deux choses: ou le simple travail des mains, ou les inventions de l'esprit en machines utiles, relativement aux arts et métiers; l'*industrie* renferme tantôt l'une, tantôt l'autre de ces deux choses, et souvent les réunit toutes les deux.

Elle se porte à la culture des terres, aux manufactures et aux arts. [VIII. 694b]

As regards industry in the narrower, modern sense of the term Jaucourt stresses the importance of machines in reducing the amount of labour required for a given task. He quotes various recent examples of technological advances:

On en peut citer pour exemple les machines inventées par M. de Vaucanson, celle à mouliner les soies connue en Angleterre depuis vingt ans, les moulins à scier les planches, par lesquels, sous l'inspection d'un seul homme et le moyen d'un seul axe, on travaille dans une heure de vent favorable jusqu'à quatre-vingts planches de trois toises de long; les métiers de rubans à plusieurs navettes ont encore mille avantages. [VIII.694b–695a]

The economist, Jean François Melon, is cited as claiming that 'faire avec un homme, par le secours des machines de l'*industrie* ce qu'on ferait sans elles avec deux ou trois hommes, c'est doubler ou tripler le nombre des citoyens' [VIII.695a].

Jaucourt goes on to refute at some length the objection that the introduction of machines will simply throw men out of work and that, since foreign countries will quickly obtain similar machines, there is no advantage for the country which invents them:

Le caractère de pareilles objections est d'être dénuées de bon sens et de lumières; elles ressemblent à celles que les bateliers de la Tamise alléguaient contre la construction du pont de Westminster. N'ont-ils pas trouvé, ces bateliers, de quoi s'occuper, tandis que la construction du pont dont il s'agit, répandait de nouvelles commodités dans la ville de Londres? Vaut-il pas mieux prévenir l'*industrie* des autres peuples à se servir de machines que d'attendre qu'ils nous forcent à en adopter l'usage pour nous conserver la concurrence dans les mêmes marchés? [VIII.695a]

Characteristic of the new doctrine of economic liberalism is the dictum which follows: 'Toutes choses égales, la nation dont l'*industrie* sera la plus libre, sera la plus industrieuse' [VIII.695a]. Even more typical is the unawareness of the great changes in the economic field which were pending and indeed by 1760 had already begun. While Jaucourt recognizes the danger that the sudden introduction of machines might throw large numbers of men out of work, he does not see much prospect of this happening in the existing economic climate: 'D'ailleurs, soit découragement d'invention, soit progrès dans les arts, l'*industrie* semble être parvenue au point que ses gradations sont aujourd'hui très douces, et ses secousses violentes fort peu à craindre' [VIII.695a]. This is not the only article which reveals an unawareness of the great economic changes which were beginning.

The anonymous MANUFACTURES begins by distinguishing between factories ('manufactures réunies') and domestic industry ('manufactures dispersées'):

Celles du premier genre sont établies de toute nécessité pour les ouvrages qui ne peuvent s'exécuter que par un grand nombre de mains rassemblées, qui exigent, soit pour le premier établissement, soit pour la suite des opérations qui s'y font, des avances considérables, dans lesquelles les ouvrages reçoivent successivement différentes préparations et telles qu'il est nécessaire qu'elles se suivent promptement; et enfin celles qui, par leur nature, sont assujetties à être placées dans un certain terrain. Telles sont les forges, les fonderies, les tréfileries, les verreries, les *manufactures* de porcelaine, de tapisseries et autres pareilles. [X.60b]

Among other conditions for the success of factories the author of the article lists the protection of the government:

Cette protection doit avoir pour objet de faciliter la fabrication des ouvrages en modérant les droits sur les matières premières qui s'y consomment et en accordant quelques privilèges et quelques exemptions aux ouvriers les plus nécessaires et dont l'occupation exige des connaissances et des talents; mais aussi, en les réduisant aux ouvriers de cette espèce. Une plus grande extension serait inutile à la *manufacture* et onéreuse au reste du public. . . . Un autre moyen de protéger les *manufactures* est de diminuer les droits de sortie pour l'étranger et ceux de traite et de détail dans l'intérieur de l'état. [X.60b]

It will be noticed that he approves, in moderation, of the granting of certain privileges to manufacturers though, as we have seen, these were hotly attacked by other contributors to the *Encyclopédie*.

Domestic industry is described in familiar terms:

Tous les ouvrages qui peuvent s'exécuter par chacun dans sa maison, dont chaque ouvrier peut se procurer par lui-même ou par d'autres les matières premières qu'il peut fabriquer dans l'intérieur de sa famille, avec le secours de ses enfants, de ses domestiques ou de ses compagnons, peut et doit faire l'objet de ces fabriques dispersées. Telles sont les fabriques de draps, de serges, de toiles, de velours, petites étoffes de laine et de soie ou autres pareilles. [X.61a]

What is surprising, in the light of the industrial development of the last two hundred years, is that the writer should have very gloomy views on the subject of factories. The high costs of buildings, maintenance and labour, he argues, make it difficult for the factory to face the competition of smaller producers:

De là il arrive presque toujours que les grands établissements de cette espèce sont ruineux à ceux qui les entreprennent les premiers, et ne deviennent utiles qu'à ceux qui profitent à bon marché de la déroute des premiers et, réformant les abus, s'y conduisent avec simplicité et économie; plusieurs exemples qu'on pourrait citer ne prouvent que trop cette vérité. [X.61a]

Domestic industry, he holds, has every advantage over the factory system:

Les fabriques dispersées ne sont point exposées à ces inconvénients. Un tisserand en draps, par exemple, ou emploie la laine qu'il a récoltée ou en achète à un prix médiocre, et quand il en trouve l'occasion, a un métier dans sa maison où il fait son drap tout aussi bien que dans un atelier bâti à grands frais; il est à lui-même son directeur, son contre-maître, son teneur de livres, son caissier etc., se fait aider par sa femme et ses enfants, ou par un ou plusieurs compagnons avec lesquels il vit: il peut, par conséquent, vendre son drap à beaucoup meilleur compte que l'entrepreneur d'une *manufacture*. [X.61a]

Labour relations, the writer continues, are more difficult in a factory than in a small workshop:

A la grande *manufacture* tout se fait au coup de cloche; les ouvriers sont plus contraints et plus gourmandés. Les commis accoutumés avec eux à un air de supériorité et de commandement qui véritablement est nécessaire avec la multitude, les traitent durement et avec mépris; de là il arrive que ces ouvriers ou sont plus chers, ou ne font que passer dans la *manufacture*, et jusqu'à ce qu'ils aient trouvé à se placer ailleurs.

Chez le petit fabricant le compagnon est le camarade du maître, vit avec lui comme avec son égal, a place au feu et à la chandelle, a plus de liberté et préfère enfin de travailler chez lui. Cela se voit tous les jours dans les lieux où il y a des *manufactures* réunies et des fabricants particuliers. Les manufacturiers n'y ont d'ouvriers que ceux qui ne peuvent pas se placer chez les petits fabricants, ou des coureurs qui s'engagent et quittent journellement, et le reste du temps battent la campagne tant qu'ils ont de quoi dépenser. [X.61a–b]

In addition, the writer claims that domestic industry is more bene-
ficial from the point of view of the community than the factory
system as it can employ a lot of labour and produce cheaply:

Un laboureur, un journalier de campagne ou autre homme de cette
espèce a dans le cours de l'année un assez grand nombre de jours et
d'heures où il ne peut s'occuper de la culture de la terre ou de son travail
ordinaire. Si cet homme a chez lui un métier à drap, à toile ou à petites
étoffes, il y emploie un temps qui autrement serait perdu pour lui et pour
l'État. Comme ce travail n'est pas sa principale occupation, il ne le regarde
pas comme l'objet d'un profit aussi fort que celui qui en fait son unique
ressource. Ce travail même lui est une espèce de délassement des travaux
plus rudes de la terre; et, par ce moyen, il est en état et en habitude de se
contenter d'un moindre profit. [X.61b]

One of the advantages of domestic industry in the eyes of this
writer is that it keeps large numbers of people on the land, for, he
argues, 'il faut que la culture de la terre soit l'occupation du plus
grand nombre' [X.62a]. Once again we find the *Encyclopédie*
blind to the economic developments which lay in the future.

This limited outlook is not, of course, all-pervading. FORGES, for
instance—the article was written by a *maître de forges* named Bouchu
—stresses the importance of this industry and urges technical improvements in what was in the 1750s a very small-scale and backward, though widely distributed form of activity:

FORGES (GROSSES). C'est ainsi qu'on appelle les usines où l'on travaille la
mine du fer.
    La manufacture du fer, le plus nécessaire de tous les métaux, a été
jusqu'ici négligée. On n'a point encore cherché à connaître et à suivre une
veine de mine, à lui donner ou ôter les adjoints nécessaires ou contraires à
la fusion, et la façon de la convertir en fers utiles au public. Les fourneaux
et les *forges* sont pour la plupart à la disposition d'ouvriers ignorants. Le
point utile serait donc d'apprendre à chercher la mine, la fondre, la
conduire au point de solidité et de dimension qui constituent les différentes espèces de fer; à le travailler en grand au sortir des *forges*, dans les
fonderies, batteries et fileries; d'où il se distribuerait aux différents
besoins de la société. Le fer remue la terre; il ferme nos habitations; il nous
défend; il nous orne. Il est cependant assez commun de trouver des gens
qui regardent d'un air dédaigneux le fer et le manufacturier. La distinction que méritent des manufactures de cette espèce devrait être particulière.
Elles mettent dans la société des matières nouvelles et nécessaires; il en

revient au roi un produit considérable, et à la nation un accroissement de richesses égal à ce qui excède la consommation du royaume et passe chez l'étranger. [VII.135a]

## Hostility to the courtier

If we turn now to social conditions in the France of the 1750s and 1760s, we find at once a large number of articles which express the *philosophes'* hostility to the courtier. In *COUR Diderot devotes nearly half his article to weaving together two quotations from Montesquieu:

L'auteur de l'*Esprit des lois* définit l'air de *cour*: l'échange de sa grandeur naturelle contre une grandeur empruntée. Quoi qu'il en soit de cette définition, cet air, selon lui, est le vernis séduisant sous lequel se dérobent l'ambition dans l'oisiveté, la bassesse dans l'orgueil, le désir de s'enrichir sans travail, l'aversion pour la vérité, la flatterie, la trahison, la perfidie, l'abandon de tout engagement, le mépris des devoirs du citoyen, la crainte de la vertu du prince, l'espérance sur ses faiblesses, etc., en un mot la malhonnêteté avec tout son cortège, sous le dehors de l'honnêteté la plus vraie; la réalité du vice toujours derrière le fantôme de la vertu. Le défaut de succès fait seul dans ce pays donner aux actions le nom qu'elles méritent: aussi n'y a-t-il que la maladresse qui ait des remords. [IV.355a]

Following up the cross-reference '*Voyez l'article* COURTISAN', we find an article by d'Alembert which is milder in tone, but none the less critical:

COURTISAN (*Morale*) que nous prenons ici adjectivement et qu'il ne faut pas toujours confondre avec *homme de la cour*, est l'épithète que l'on donne à cette espèce de gens que le malheur des rois et des peuples a placés entre les rois et la vérité pour l'empêcher de parvenir jusqu'à eux, même lorsqu'ils sont expressément chargés de la leur faire connaître. [IV.400b]

In a later volume Diderot worked into one of his grammatical articles, *INSINUANT, a nasty crack at the expense of courtiers:

. . . L'homme *insinuant* a une éloquence qui lui est propre. Elle a exactement le caractère que les théologiens attribuent à la grâce, *pertingens omnia suaviter et fortiter*. C'est l'art de saisir nos faiblesses, d'user de nos intérêts, de nous en créer; il est possédé par les gens de cour et les autres malheureux. Accoutumés ou contraints à ramper, ils ont appris à subir toutes sortes de formes. [VIII.788b]

Baron d'Holbach, the author of a posthumous 'Essai sur l'art de ramper à l'usage des courtisans', put into his unsigned articles on Oriental and African peoples several thrusts at courtiers, as for instance:

METHER, s.m. (*Hist. mod.*) C'est ainsi que l'on nomme en Perse un des grands officiers de la cour du roi, dont la fonction l'oblige à être toujours auprès de sa personne pour lui présenter des mouchoirs lorsqu'il en a besoin. Ce sublime emploi est rempli par un eunuque, qui a communément le plus grand crédit. [X.445b]

A more interesting, if less satirical account of the men at the apex of French society under the Ancien Régime is to be found in Marmontel's article GRAND (*Philos. Mor. Politiq.*) which deals with 'ceux qui occupent les premières places de l'État, soit dans le gouvernement, soit auprès du prince' [VII.848b]. In a passage on the monarchy Marmontel brings out the role of Richelieu in the destruction of the power of the great nobles:

Le désordre le plus effroyable de la monarchie, c'est que les *grands* parviennent à usurper l'autorité qui leur est confiée et qu'ils tournent contre le prince et contre l'État lui-même les forces de l'État déchiré par les factions. Telle était la situation de la France, lorsque le cardinal de Richelieu, ce génie hardi et vaste, ramena les grands sous l'obéissance du prince et les peuples sous la protection de la loi. On lui reproche d'avoir été trop loin, mais peut-être n'avait-il pas d'autre moyen d'affermir la monarchie, de rétablir dans sa direction naturelle ce grand arbre courbé par l'orage que de le plier dans le sens opposé. [VII.849b]

Marmontel stresses the part played by the royal court in the subjugation of the once turbulent feudal lords:

La France formait autrefois un gouvernement fédératif, très mal combiné et sans cesse en guerre avec lui-même. Depuis Louis XI tous ces co-états avaient été réunis en un; mais les grands vassaux conservaient encore dans leurs domaines l'autorité qu'ils avaient eue sous leurs premiers souverains; et les gouverneurs, qui avaient pris la place de ces souverains, s'en attribuaient la puissance. Ces deux partis opposaient à l'autorité du monarque des obstacles qu'il fallait vaincre. Le moyen le plus doux et par conséquent le plus sage était d'attirer à la cour ceux qui, dans l'éloignement et au milieu des peuples accoutumés à leur obéir, s'étaient rendus si redoutables. Le prince fit briller les distinctions et les grâces; les *grands* accoururent en foule; les gouverneurs furent captivés; leur autorité personnelle s'évanouit en leur absence; leurs gouvernements héréditaires devinrent amovibles, et l'on s'assura de leurs successeurs; les seigneurs oublièrent leurs vassaux; ils en furent oubliés; leurs domaines furent divisés, aliénés, dégradés insensiblement; et il ne resta plus du gouvernement féodal que des blasons et des ruines. [VII.849b]

It goes without saying that Marmontel considers the decline in the power of these lords a good thing:

Cette réduction du gouvernement féodal à une grandeur qui n'en est plus que l'ombre, a dû coûter cher à l'État; mais, à quelque prix qu'on achète l'unité du pouvoir et de l'obéissance, l'avantage de n'être plus en butte au caprice aveugle et tyrannique de l'autorité fiduciaire, le bonheur de vivre sous la tutelle inviolable des lois, toujours prêtes à s'armer contre les usurpations, les vexations et les violences, il est certain que de tels biens ne seront jamais trop payés. [VII.849a]

Marmontel ends this section of the article by declaring that the present position of this privileged minority is about right; in other words he at least among the contributors does not take up a radical attitude on this question.

## Attitude to the nobility

The attitude of the *Encyclopédie* towards the nobility in general is also very varied, though hostility to this class and its privileges is frequently expressed. Hidden away in the articles on remote peoples which may be attributed with reasonable certainty to Baron d'Holbach we find remarks like those in HONDREOUS: 'C'est le nom que l'on donne dans l'île de Ceylan aux nobles qui, ainsi que partout ailleurs, se distinguent du peuple par beaucoup de hauteur et d'arrogance' [VIII.284a]. In *CHASSE Diderot penned a biting attack on the hated monopoly of hunting enjoyed by the nobility down to the Revolution:

Ce droit a été la source d'une infinité de jalousies et de dissensions, même entre les nobles, et d'une infinité de lésions envers leurs vassaux dont les champs ont été abandonnés au ravage des animaux réservés pour la *chasse*. L'agriculteur a vu ses moissons consommées par des cerfs, des sangliers, des daims, des oiseaux de toute espèce, le fruit de ses travaux perdu, sans qu'il fût permis d'y obvier et sans qu'on lui accordât de dédommagement. L'injustice a été portée dans certains pays au point de forcer le paysan à chasser et à acheter ensuite de son argent le gibier qu'il avait pris. C'est dans la même contrée qu'un homme fut condamné à être attaché vif sur un cerf pour avoir chassé un de ces animaux. Si c'est quelque chose de si précieux que d'un cerf, pourquoi en tuer? si ce n'est rien, si la vie d'un homme vaut mieux que celle de tous les cerfs, pourquoi punir un homme de mort pour avoir attenté à la vie d'un cerf? [III.225b]

In PRIVILÈGE (*Gram.*), which is almost certainly by Diderot, we find a sweeping condemnation: 'Les seuls *privilèges* légitimes, ce sont ceux que la nature accorde. Tous les autres peuvent être regardés comme injustices faites à tous les hommes en faveur d'un seul' [XIII.389a]. However, a much more cautious line is taken in the unsigned article PRIVILÈGE (*Gouv. Comm. Polit.*) which we have already examined for its views on industrial questions.

The anonymous author of this article does not dispute that privileges may legitimately be conferred on such members of society as noblemen, members of the royal household and judges; but there privilege should stop:

Il semble qu'il faudrait encore distinguer dans tous les cas les personnes dont les services sont réels et utiles, soit au prince, soit au public, et ne pas avilir les faveurs dont ceux-ci jouissent légitimement en les confondant avec un grand nombre de gens inutiles à tous égards et qui n'ont pour titres qu'un morceau de parchemin acquis presque toujours à très bas prix. Un bourgeois aisé et qui, à lui seul, pourrait payer la moitié de la taille de toute une paroisse s'il était imposé à sa due proportion, pour le montant d'une année ou deux de ses impositions et souvent pour moins, sans naissance, sans éducation et sans talents, achète une charge dans un bureau d'élection ou de grenier à sel, ou une charge inutile et de nul service chez le roi ou chez un prince qui a une maison, charge dont le titre même est souvent ignoré du maître et dont il ne fait jamais aucun usage; ou se fait donner dans les fermes du roi un petit emploi souvent inutile et dont les produits ne sont autres que les exemptions mêmes attachées à la commission, vient jouir à la vue du public de toutes les exemptions dont jouissent la noblesse et la grande magistrature. [XIII.389b]

This section of the article concludes on a cautious note; while it is the duty of the government, the writer argues, to strive to reduce such privileges to those which are genuinely useful, financial stringency has often had the opposite effect of compelling it to grant more and more of such privileges to people who had done nothing to deserve them:

De là aussi est arrivé que la noblesse qui, par elle-même, est ou devrait être la récompense la plus honorable dont le souverain pourrait reconnaître des services importants ou des talents supérieurs, a été prodiguée à des milliers de familles dont les auteurs n'ont eu pour se la procurer que la peine d'employer des sommes, même souvent assez modiques, à acquérir des charges qui la leur donnaient, et dont l'utilité pour le public était nulle, soit par défaut d'objet, soit par défaut de talents. Cet article deviendrait un volume si l'on y recherchait le nombre et la qualité de ces titres, et les abus de tous ces *privilèges*; mais on a été forcé à se restreindre à ce qu'il y a sur cette matière de plus général, de plus connu et de moins contesté. [XIII.390a]

On paper then the writer does not challenge the privileges of the nobility in such matters as taxation; all he does is to suggest that the number of persons enjoying these privileges should be reduced. The Revolution was shortly to produce a more radical solution to this problem.

The Chevalier de Jaucourt takes up a rather ambiguous attitude. In GÉNÉALOGIE he pours scorn on the exaggerated pride of rank among the nobility of his day:

Supposé qu'un homme de la première qualité, plein de sa haute naissance, vît passer en revue sous ses yeux toute la suite de ses ancêtres, à peu près de la même manière que Virgile fait contempler à Énée tous ses descendants, de quelles différentes passions ne serait-il pas agité lorsqu'il verrait des capitaines et des pâtres, des ministres d'État et des artisans, des princes et des goujats, se suivre les uns les autres, peut-être d'assez près, dans l'espace de quatre mille ans! De quelle tristesse ou de quelle joie son cœur ne serait-il pas saisi à la vue de tous les jeux de la fortune, dans une décoration si bigarrée de haillons et de poupre, d'outils et de sceptres, de marques d'honneur et d'opprobre! [VII.549a]

In HÉRALDIQUE he speaks with scorn of what he calls 'la science vaine et ridicule des armoiries', quoting the well-known lines from La Fontaine:

> Le noble poursuivit:
> Moi, je sais le blason; j'en veux tenir école.'
> Comme si, devers l'Inde, on eût eu dans l'esprit
> La sotte vanité de ce jargon frivole![1] [VIII.143a]

[1] *Fables*, x.16.

So vigorous was his onslaught on heraldry that Diderot felt compelled to add an editorial note:

Cependant, comme le temps n'est pas encore venu parmi nous où l'*art héraldique* sera réduit à sa juste valeur, *voyez, volume II de nos planches et de leurs explications,* les principes généraux du blason, avec des figures relatives à chacun des termes qui lui sont propres.

Yet in NAISSANCE (*Société civile*) Jaucourt takes up a position which is not altogether unexpected in the scion of an old noble family. Although in the second half of the article he stresses the obligations which the privileges conferred by birth impose on those who enjoy them, he makes it quite clear that he regards such privileges as thoroughly justified:

C'est un heureux présent de la fortune, qu'on doit considérer et respecter dans les personnes qui en jouissent, non seulement par un principe de reconnaissance envers ceux qui ont rendu de grands services à l'État, mais aussi pour encourager leurs descendants à suivre leurs exemples. On doit prendre les intérêts des gens de *naissance,* parce qu'il est utile à la république qu'il y ait des hommes dignes de leurs ancêtres. Les droits de la *naissance* doivent encore être révérés parce qu'elle est le soutien du trône. Si l'on abat les colonnes, que deviendra l'édifice qu'elles appuyaient? De plus, la *naissance* paraît être un rempart qui les défend contre les entreprises mutuelles de l'un sur l'autre. Enfin la *naissance* donne avec raison des privilèges distinctifs et un grand ascendant sur les membres d'un état qui sont d'une extraction moins élevée. [XI.8b–9a]

Pierre Rousseau took exception to this attitude in the *Journal encyclopédique.* 'L'auteur de cet article', he writes, 'pense sur toute autre matière en philosophe, et cependant sur cet objet il parle le langage du préjugé.'[1]

The sale of official posts is discussed by Jaucourt in VÉNALITÉ DES CHARGES in quite an objective fashion. His conclusion is relatively mild:

Nous nous contenterons d'ajouter ici qu'en regardent la *vénalité* et l'hérédité des charges de finance et de judicature comme utiles, ainsi que le prétend le *Testament politique* du cardinal de Richelieu, on conviendra sans peine qu'il serait encore plus avantageux d'en restreindre le nombre effréné. Quand aux charges militaires, comme elles sont le prix destiné à

---

[1] I July 1768, p. 12.

la noblesse, au courage, aux belles actions, la suppression de toute *vénalité* en ce genre ne saurait trop tôt avoir lieu. [XVI.911a]

Damilaville (or Diderot) takes up a much more hostile attitude in VINGTIÈME, at least so far as the sale of judicial posts is concerned, since in a furious diatribe he links their holders with rapacious courtiers:

Comme il faut acheter, et ce n'est pas le moins cher, jusqu'à la bassesse des courtisans, qui croient effacer la honte de leur avilissement par celle de leur opulence, il faut aussi vendre avec une partie de l'autorité jusqu'au droit d'en trafiquer et de négocier de la justice: droit monstrueux qui soumet la vérité, la raison et le savoir à l'erreur, à l'ignorance et à la sottise, qui livre la vie, la liberté, l'honneur et la fortune des citoyens au fanatisme, à la cruauté, à l'orgueil et à toutes les passions de quiconque a le moyen de payer ce droit effrayant qui fait l'opprobre et la terreur de l'humanité. [XVII.864a]

As we have already seen, the attitude of the *philosophes* towards the judges of the Parlements was a somewhat ambiguous one.

The relationship between nobleman and *roturier* entered into the burning question of taxation which occupies many pages of the *Encyclopédie*. In one of the early volumes the anonymous author of the article EXEMPTIONS (*Finances*) accepts the validity of certain exemptions from taxation, including that of the nobility from the *taille* on the grounds that 'la noblesse a prodigué son sang pour la patrie' [VI.338a]. However, he does insist that such exemptions must be based on real service to the State:

S'il arrivait que la naissance, le crédit, l'opulence ou d'autres considéra-tions étrangères au bien public détruisissent ou même altérassent des maximes si précieuses au gouvernement, il en résulterait, contre la raison, la justice et l'humanité, que certains citoyens jouiraient des plus utiles *exemptions* par la raison même qu'ils sont plus en état de partager le poids des contributions, et que la portion infortunée serait punie de sa pauvreté même par la surcharge dont elle serait accablée. [VI.238b]

It is clear that at heart the writer disapproved of the existing system of taxation where the individual's contribution depended on rank rather than ability to pay; only, like the author of PRIVILÈGE, he did not dare to express himself clearly on such a delicate subject.

No such inhibitions prevented Damilaville (or Diderot) from speaking their mind on this question in the article VINGTIÈME. The privileges of the nobility (and of the clergy and certain provinces) in the matter of taxation are repeatedly condemned in this long article. To take only one example:

L'équité était dans la république romaine, le contraire est dans les gouvernements modernes où les charges sont supportées en raison inverse[1] de la part qu'on y a, du crédit et des richesses qu'on y possède. . . .

Cette exemption . . . n'avait lieu que parce que les nobles étaient chargés de tout le service de l'état; ils le défendaient, le gouvernaient, et administraient la justice à leurs frais. Il était juste alors qu'ils fussent dispensés des tributs que supportaient en échange ceux qui l'étaient de toutes ces charges.

Il ne le serait plus aujourd'hui que la noblesse n'est tenue à aucune de ces obligations; qu'au lieu de mener des troupes à la guerre, de les nourrir, de les entretenir à ses dépens, elle est payée fort chèrement pour y aller seule; que même les récompenses excessives qu'elle exige du gouvernement pour les choses les moins utiles, souvent les plus contraires au bien public, causent la surcharge des peuples. Ce serait non seulement vouloir jouir de tous les avantages d'un traité sans en remplir les conditions, mais encore faire tourner à son profit toutes les charges qu'il nous imposait. [XVII.879b]

The point of view of the *roturier* in this controversial question is put clearly enough.

## Criticism of the system of taxation

The *Encyclopédie* contains a large number of articles on the subject of taxation. Many of these are purely factual; they are the work of the lawyer, Boucher d'Argis, and simply give an objective account of a particular tax. There are on the other hand a number of articles, particularly in the last ten volumes, which deal critically with the whole taxation system or with individual taxes and even on occasion hint at reforms.

The most general article, IMPÔT (*Droit politiq. et Finances*), by Jaucourt, begins with a definition of taxation and its purpose which comes straight from Burlamaqui's *Principes du droit politique*. The general principles on which the article is based are derived from

[1] An expression which occurs over and over again in Diderot's writings.

such obvious sources as Montesquieu and Véron de Forbonnais, as Jaucourt takes care to indicate: 'Tirons-les, ces principes, des écrits lumineux d'excellents citoyens, et faisons-les passer dans un ouvrage où l'on respire les progrès des connaissances, l'amour de l'humanité, la gloire des souverains et le bonheur des sujets' [VIII.601b]. Stated in their broadest terms, these principles imply an attitude to taxation which could scarcely be said to have been that of French governments under the Ancien Régime:

La gloire du souverain est de ne demander que des subsides justes, absolument nécessaires, et le bonheur des sujets est de n'en payer que de pareils. Si le droit du prince pour la perception des *impôts* est fondé sur les besoins de l'État, il ne doit exiger de tributs que conformément à ces besoins, les remettre d'abord après qu'ils sont satisfaits, n'en employer le produit que dans les mêmes vues et ne pas le détourner à ses usages particuliers ou en profusions pour des personnes qui ne contribuent point au bien public. [VIII.601b]

These lines were no doubt penned during the lifetime of Mme de Pompadour.

Another principle which notoriously was not applied under the Ancien Régime is set forth in a discussion of a poll-tax:

Cette taxe est encore admissible, pourvu qu'elle soit proportionnelle et qu'elle charge dans une proportion plus forte les gens aisés, en ne portant point du tout sur la dernière classe du peuple. Quoique tous les sujets jouissent également de la protection du gouvernement et de la sûreté qu'il leur procure, l'inégalité de leurs fortunes et des avantages qu'ils en retirent, veut des impositions conformes à cette inégalité et veut que ces impositions soient, pour ainsi parler, en progression géométrique, deux, quatre, huit, seize, sur les aisés, car cet *impôt* ne doit point s'étendre sur le nécessaire. [VIII.601b]

Jaucourt goes on to apply this principle to a country like the France of his day:

Tant que les *impôts* dans un royaume de luxe ne seront pas assis de manière qu'on perçoive des particuliers en raison de leur aisance, la condition de ce royaume ne saurait s'améliorer; une partie des sujets vivra dans l'opulence et mangera dans un repas la nourriture de cent familles, tandis que l'autre n'aura que du pain et dépérira journellement. Tel *impôt* qui retrancherait par an cinq, dix, trente, cinquante louis sur les dépenses frivoles dans chaque famille aisée, et ce retranchement fait à proportion de l'aisance de cette famille, suffirait avec les revenus courants pour rembourser les charges de l'État ou pour les frais d'une juste guerre, sans que le laboureur en entendît parler que dans les prières publiques. [VIII.602a]

Jaucourt sees much merit in a tax on such luxuries as mirrors, silver-plate, carriages, coachmen, lackeys and sedan chairs, since, he argues, 'c'est une vérité incontestable que le poids des tributs se fait surtout sentir dans ce royaume par l'inégalité de son assiette, et que la force totale du corps politique est prodigieuse' [VIII.602a].

On the subject of a land tax Jaucourt follows in Voltaire's footsteps and makes the same comparison as in the *Lettres philosophiques* between the English and French systems in this matter. In France inequality in assessment leads to all manner of injustices, which in the long run are against the general interest:

Il ne faut donc point que la portion des taxes qu'on met sur le fermier d'une terre, à raison de son industrie, soit forte ou tellement décourageante de sa nature qu'il craigne de défricher un nouveau champ, d'augmenter le nombre de ses bestiaux ou de monter une nouvelle industrie de peur de voir augmenter cette taxe arbitraire qu'il ne pourrait payer. Alors il n'aurait plus d'émulation d'acquérir, et en perdant l'espoir de devenir riche, son intérêt serait de se montrer plus pauvre qu'il n'est réellement. Les gens qui prétendent que le paysan ne doit pas être dans l'aisance, débitent une maxime aussi fausse que contraire à l'humanité. [VIII. 602a–b]

Jaucourt goes on to argue that taxes on consumption are least onerous to the mass of the people provided that they are moderate and proportional and are not imposed on top of heavy direct taxes. Imported luxury goods should be heavily taxed. As far as home produced goods are concerned, it is important that it should be the seller who pays the tax and not the purchaser. Here Jaucourt obviously has in mind the hated system of collecting excise duties in France, whereby the agents of the tax-farmers (the notorious *rats de cave* as they were derisively known) would search private houses to ensure that duty had been paid on wines and other taxable objects. In denouncing this system Jaucourt has recourse to a well-known passage in the *Esprit des lois*:

... Quand c'est le citoyen qui paie, il en résulte toutes sortes de gênes, jusqu'à des recherches qu'on permet dans sa maison. Rien n'est plus contraire à la liberté. Ceux qui établissent ces sortes d'*impôts* n'ont pas le bonheur d'avoir rencontré la meilleure sorte d'administration. [VIII.602b]

The salt tax (*gabelle*) is severely criticized because of the disproportion between the value of the object and the amount of tax levied on it, a disproportion which was enormous in some provinces of France:

Il y a des pays où le droit excède de quinze à vingt fois la valeur de la denrée et d'une denrée essentielle à la vie. Alors le prince qui met de pareilles taxes sur cette denrée, ôte l'illusion à ses sujets; ils voient qu'ils sont imposés à des droits tellement déraisonnables qu'ils ne sentent plus que leur misère et leur servitude. [VIII.602b–603a]

An inevitable consequence of the varying rates of tax levied in different provinces was smuggling from those where salt was relatively cheap to those where it was very heavily taxed; and those caught in the act of smuggling were punished with great severity, a practice denounced by Jaucourt in terms which are once again borrowed from the *Esprit des lois*:

La fraude étant dans ce cas très lucrative, la peine naturelle, celle que la raison demande, qui est la confiscation de la marchandise, devient incapable de l'arrêter; il faut donc avoir recours à des peines japonaises et pareilles à celles qu'on inflige aux plus grands crimes. Des hommes qu'on ne saurait regarder comme des gens méchants, sont punis comme des scélérats; toute la proportion des peines est ôtée. [VIII.603a]

Jaucourt concludes this substantial article with some practical proposals for reforms, economic as well as fiscal. These are introduced by the following considerations:

Il y a cent projets pour rendre l'état riche contre un seul dont l'objet soit de faire jouir chaque citoyen particulier de la richesse de l'état. Gloire, grandeur, puissance d'un royaume! Que ces mots sont vains et vides de sens auprès de ceux de liberté, aisance et bonheur des sujets! [VIII.603b]

His ten-point programme of reforms is as follows:

1°. Il s'agit de favoriser puissamment l'agriculture, la population et le commerce, sources des richesses du sujet et du souverain. 2°. Proportionner le bénéfice des affaires de finance à celui que donne le négoce et le défrichement des terres en général; car alors les entreprises de finances seront encore les meilleures, puisqu'elles sont sans risque, outre qu'il ne faut jamais oublier que le profit des financiers est encore une diminution des revenus du peuple et du roi. 3°. Restreindre l'usage immodéré des richesses et des charges inutiles. 4°. Abolir les monopoles, les péages, les privilèges exclusifs, les lettres de maîtrise, le droit d'aubaine, les droits de franc-fief, le nombre et les vexations des fermiers. 5°. Retrancher la plus grande partie des fêtes. 6°. Corriger les abus et les gênes de la taille, de la milice et de l'imposition du sel. 7°. Ne point faire de traités extraordinaires, ni d'affaiblissement dans les monnaies. 8°. Souffrir le transport des espèces parce que c'est chose juste et avantageuse. 9°. Tenir l'intérêt de l'argent aussi bas que le permet le nombre combiné des prêteurs et des emprunteurs dans l'état. 10°. Enfin alléger les *impôts* et les répartir suivant les principes de la justice distributive, cette justice par laquelle les rois sont les représentants de Dieu sur la terre. [VIII.604a]

Jaucourt rounds off the whole article with the significant sentences:

La France serait trop puissante et les Français seraient trop heureux, si ces moyens étaient mis en usage. Mais l'aurore d'un si beau jour est-elle prête à paraître?

That even such a modest programme of reforms should actually be carried out seems to him almost too much to ask.

The other major article on taxation, VINGTIÈME, is extremely hostile to taxes on consumption. Rousseau is rebuked for suggesting in his article ÉCONOMIE POLITIQUE, contrary to what Montesquieu had argued, that such taxes should be paid by the purchaser and not the seller. 'J'avoue', writes Damilaville (or Diderot), 'que je ne vois dans cette différence que des chaînes ajoutées à la liberté des citoyens, et une contradiction de plus dans celui qui s'en dit le plus grand défenseur' [XVII.868a]. Taxes on consumption are denounced in the most violent terms with a vivid, if somewhat declamatory passage on the *rats de cave* who searched people's houses:

Là où sont ces droits, la guerre civile est perpétuellement avec eux. Cent mille citoyens, armés pour leur conservation et pour en empêcher la fraude, menacent sans cesse la liberté, la sûreté, l'honneur et la fortune des autres.
Un gentilhomme vivant en province est retiré chez lui, il s'y croit paisible au sein de sa famille; trente hommes, la baïonnette au bout du

fusil, investissent sa maison, en violent l'asile, la parcourent du haut en bas, pénètrent forcément dans l'intérieur le plus secret; les enfants éplorés demandent à leur père de quel crime il est coupable; il n'en a point commis. Cet attentat aux droits respectés parmi les nations les plus barbares est commis par ces perturbateurs du repos public pour s'assurer qu'il n'y a point chez ce citoyen de marchandises de l'espèce de celle dont le traitant s'est réservé le débit exclusif pour les survendre à son profit dix-sept ou dix-huit fois leur valeur.

   Ceci n'est point une déclamation, c'est un fait; si c'est là jouir de la liberté civile, je voudrais qu'on me dise ce que c'est que la servitude. Si c'est ainsi que les personnes et les biens sont en sûreté, qu'est-ce donc que de n'y être pas? [XVII.874b]

After an onslaught on the *gabelle* comes a gloomy account of the tribulations undergone by goods in transit:

Depuis l'entrée d'une marchandise étrangère, depuis la sortie de la terre, et même avant, pour celles que le sol produit, jusqu'à leur entière consommation, elles sont entourées de gardes et d'exacteurs qui ne les quittent plus. A chaque pas ce sont des douanes, des barrières, des péages, des bureaux, des déclarations à faire, des visites à souffrir, des mesures, des pesées, des tarifs inintelligibles, des appréciations arbitraires, des discussions à avoir, des droits à supporter et des vexations à éprouver. [XVII. 875b]

The wiles of tax-farmers, bent on wringing the last penny out of the public, are denounced in trenchant terms:

L'intérêt du fermier étant de grossir le droit au lieu de l'assimiler à toutes les vicissitudes du commerce qui pourraient en causer la diminution, il ne cherche qu'à l'étendre en tordant le sens de la loi; il tâche par des interprétations captieuses d'assujettir ce qui ne l'était pas. J'en ai connu qui pâlissaient des mois entiers sur un édit pour trouver dans quelques expressions équivoques, qui n'y manquent jamais, de quoi favoriser une exaction plus forte.

   Un nouveau droit est-il établi, pour lui donner plus d'extension et avoir plus de contraventions à punir, on en suppose. Le fermier se fait à lui-même un procès sous un nom emprunté, surprend un jugement qu'il obtient d'autant plus aisément, qu'il n'y a point de contradicteur réel qui s'y oppose, s'en prévaut ensuite. C'est d'avance la condamnation de ceux que l'ignorance de ces prétendues fraudes en rendra coupable. Jamais l'esprit de ruse et de cupidité n'a rien inventé de plus subtil; aussi ceux qui

imaginent ces sublimes moyens sont-ils appelés les *grands travailleurs* et les
*bons ouvriers.* [XVII.876a]

The remedy which Damilaville (or Diderot) proposes to cure all
these ills is to sweep away all existing taxes and to replace them by a
single tax on land, since, he argues, all taxes fall in the last resort on
the land:

Il est donc vrai . . . que, quelque détournée qu'en paraisse la perception,
les droits remontent toujours à la source de toutes les matières de consommation qui est la terre. Il l'est aussi que ceux sur la terre sont à la charge de
tous les citoyens; mais la répartition et la perception s'en forment d'une
manière simple et naturelle, au lieu que celles des autres se font avec des
incommodités, des dépenses, des embarras et une foule de répétitions
étonnantes. [XVII.873b–874a]

The institution of this land tax would transform the state of France:

Les monuments, l'appareil et tous les instruments de la servitude anéantis;
les règlements qui ne sont que des déclarations de guerre contre les
peuples, abolis, les douanes abattues, les bureaux démolis, les péages
fermés, les barrières renversées, une multitude de citoyens, aujourd'hui la
terreur et le fléau des autres, rendus à la culture des terres qu'ils ont
abandonnée, à l'art militaire et aux arts mécaniques qu'ils auraient dû
suivre; enfin, devenant utiles à la société en cessant de la persécuter.
[XVII.876b]

The article then proceeds to enter into a great deal of detail about
the projected land tax; this is, however, less to our purpose than
the criticisms of the injustices of the existing system of taxation.

Jaucourt developed his ideas further in a number of shorter
articles. In most of these he is heavily indebted to Véron de
Forbonnais. In TAXE, for instance, he takes over from this source a
suggestion for a tax on servants and carriages. TAILLE À VOLONTÉ,
which offers both a history of the tax and some critical comments
on it, is also mostly derived from Véron de Forbonnais. The article
stresses the advantages of the *taille réelle* (based on the value of the
land held) over the more arbitrary *taille personnelle* (based on
estimated income) and points out how shortsighted the Assemblée
des Notables of 1626 was in turning down a proposal to make the
first form of the tax universal. The article concludes: '. . . Il suffit
d'avoir des entrailles pour désirer que son établissement fût général,

ou du moins qu'on mît en pratique quelque expédient d'une exécution plus simple et plus courte, pour le soulagement des peuples' [XV.846b]. Once again, the article contains no really radical proposal.

Jaucourt shares the popular dislike of the tax-farmers in his articles MALTÔTE, PARTISAN and TRAITANT. In MALTÔTE, for instance, he stresses the lowly origins as well as the avidity of many of these men:

Quoiqu'il faille distinguer les maltôtiers qui perçoivent des tributs qui ne sont pas dus, de ceux qui ont pris en parti des contributions imposées par une autorité légitime, cependant on est encore dans le préjugé que ces sortes de gens ont par état le cœur dur, parce qu'ils augmentent leur fortune aux dépens du peuple, dont la misère devient la source de leur abondance. D'abord ce furent des hommes qui s'assemblèrent sans se connaître, qui se lièrent étroitement par le même intérêt, qui, la plupart sans éducation, se distinguèrent par leur faste et qui apportèrent dans l'administration de leur emploi une honteuse et sordide avidité, avec la bassesse des vues que donne ordinairement une extraction vile, lorsque la vertu, l'étude, la philosophie, l'amour du bien public n'a point anobli la naissance. [IX.953b]

TRAITANT is equally severe, though Jaucourt disclaims any personal interest or satirical intent:

On appelle *traitants* des gens d'affaires qui se chargent du recouvrement des impôts, qui traitent avec le souverain de toutes sortes de taxes, revenus, projets de finances, etc. moyennant des avances en deniers qu'ils fournissent sur-le-champ. Ils reçoivent dix à quinze pour cent de leurs traités. Ces hommes avides et en petit nombre ne sont distingués du peuple que par leurs richesses. C'est chez eux que la France vit pour la première fois en argent ces sortes d'ustensiles domestiques que les princes du sang royal n'avaient qu'en fer, en cuivre et en étain : spectacle insultant à la nation. Les richesses qu'ils possèdent, dit l'*édit de 1716*, sont les dépouilles de nos provinces, la subsistance de nos peuples et le patrimoine de l'État.

Je répète ces choses d'après plusieurs citoyens sans aucune passion, sans aucun intérêt particulier, et surtout sans l'esprit d'humeur et de satire qui fait perdre à la vérité même le crédit qu'elle mérite. [XVI.531b]

PARTISAN (*Finances*) is equally bitter, calling on La Bruyère to aid in the denunciation of the greed of such men.

In SEL, *impôt sur le*, Jaucourt—assisted, as usual, by Véron de Forbonnais—duplicates the purely factual article GABELLE, with a detailed attack on the injustice of this tax. The article is outspoken in its condemnation:

La douleur s'empare de notre cœur à la lecture de l'ordonnance des gabelles. Une denrée que les faveurs de la providence entretiennent à vil prix pour une petite partie des citoyens, est vendue chèrement à tous les autres. Des hommes pauvres sont forcés d'acheter au poids de l'or une quantité marquée de cette denrée, et il leur est défendu, sous peine de la ruine totale de leur famille, d'en recevoir d'autre, même en pur don. Celui qui recueille cette denrée, n'a point la permission de la vendre hors de certaines limites, car les mêmes peines le menacent. Des supplices effrayants sont décernés contre des hommes, criminels à la vérité envers le corps politique, mais qui n'ont point violé cependant la loi naturelle. [XIV.927b]

The article concludes:

Enfin, si la taille arbitraire n'existait pas, l'*impôt de sel* serait peut-être le plus funeste qu'il fût possible d'imaginer. Aussi tous les auteurs économiques et les ministres les plus intelligents dans les finances ont regardé le remplacement de ces deux impositions comme l'opération la plus utile au soulagement des peuples et à l'accroissement des revenus publics. Divers expédients ont été proposés, et aucun jusqu'à présent n'a paru assez sûr. [XIV.928a]

Once again we do not find Jaucourt very optimistic about the prospect of reforms, however desirable, actually being carried out.

Jaucourt turned once again to Véron de Forbonnais for his article on an institution, which bore most heavily on the peasantry, the *milice*, the conscript second-line troops. In MILICE (*Gouvern. politiq.*) he defines the institution and its baleful effects in the following terms:

Ce nom se donne aux paysans, aux laboureurs, aux cultivateurs qu'on enrôle de force dans les troupes. Les lois du royaume, dans les temps de guerre, recrutent les armées des habitants de la campagne, qui sont obligés sans distinction de tirer à la *milice*. La crainte qu'inspire cette ordonnance porte également sur le pauvre, le médiocre et le laboureur aisé. Le fils unique d'un cultivateur médiocre, forcé de quitter la maison paternelle au moment où son travail pourrait soutenir et dédommager ses pauvres parents de la dépense de l'avoir élevé, est une perte irréparable; et le fermier un peu aisé préfère à son état toute profession qui peut éloigner de lui un pareil sacrifice. [X.505a]

Needless to say, the article does not propose the abolition of the institution; what it does suggest is that, instead of making all the youths of a parish draw lots, it should be allowed to pay a man or men to do the service in their place, each taxpayer contributing to the maintenance of these replacements according to his taxable capacity. 'Après tout', the article concludes,

les avantages de la *milice* même doivent être mûrement combinés avec les maux qui en résultent, car il faut peser si le bien des campagnes, la culture des terres et la population ne sont pas préférables à la gloire de mettre sur pied de nombreuses armées, à l'exemple de Xerxès. [X.505a]

The grievance of the peasant is clearly brought out in this article, but the solution offered—the use of a hired replacement—is scarcely one which would nowadays be regarded as democratic.

Even less egalitarian was the suggestion propounded by Quesnay both in FERMIERS [VI.536b] and GRAINS [VII.824a]; in his anxiety to increase the number of prosperous tenant-farmers he suggests that their sons be exempted from service in the *milice* since the fear of it drives many of them into the towns, to the detriment of agricultural progress. For once Diderot and d'Alembert produced a joint 'Note des Éditeurs' to back up this argument, stressing the loss to agriculture caused by fear of this enforced military service:

La petite quantité d'enfants de *fermiers* que la milice enlève, est un fort petit objet; mais ceux qu'elle détermine à abandonner la profession de leurs pères méritent une plus grande attention par rapport à l'agriculture qui fait la vraie force de l'état. Il y a actuellement, selon M. Dupré de Saint-Maur, environ les 7/8 du royaume cultivés avec des bœufs. Ainsi il n'y a qu'un huitième des terres cultivées par des fermiers, dont le nombre ne vas pas à 30,000, ce qui ne peut pas fournir 1,000 miliciens fils de *fermiers*. Cette petite quantité est zéro dans nos armées; mais 4,000 qui sont effrayés et qui abandonnent les campagnes chaque fois qu'on tire la milice sont un grand objet pour la culture des terres. [VI.536b–537a]

This editorial intervention in support of Quesnay's proposal is significant.

The *corvée royale*—the obligation to put in several days' unpaid labour on building or repairing roads—was another burden which fell on the peasantry. One of the reforms which Turgot attempted to carry out—indeed it contributed as much as anything to his dismissal in 1776—was to replace this hated custom by a tax payable by all landowners, irrespective of their rank. The article CORVÉE (*Ponts & Chaussées*) in Vol. IV was contributed by Nicolas Antoine Boulanger who at this period in his career was 'sous-ingénieur des ponts et chaussées dans la généralité de Tours'. It is scarcely surprising if, given the nature of his employment, he does not propose the abolition of the *corvée*. What he suggests is merely that better use might be made of this forced labour:

La *corvée* est un ouvrage public que l'on fait faire aux communautés, aux particuliers desquelles on demande dans les saisons mortes quelques journées de leur temps sans salaire. Une telle condition est dure sans doute pour chacun de ces particuliers; elle indique par conséquent toute l'importance dont il est de les bien conduire, pour tirer des jours précieux qu'on leur demande sans salaire le plus d'utilité qu'on peut, afin de ne point perdre à la fois et le temps du particulier et le fruit que l'état en peut retirer. [IV.283a–b]

It is noticeable throughout the article that Boulanger will stand no nonsense from the *corvoyeurs*; if his aim is to reduce the demands made on them, he insists that all must do their share punctually and obediently in what he himself calls 'un service . . . exact et . . . militaire' [IV.288b]. In the later volumes the *corvée* is much more severely criticized, and its replacement by a small tax is proposed. In a footnote to GRAINS Quesnay is quite outspoken on the subject:

Les corvées dont on charge les paysans sont très désavantageuses à l'état et au roi parce qu'en réduisant les paysans à la misère, on les met dans l'impuissance de soutenir leurs petits établissements; d'où résulte un grand dommage sur les produits, sur la consommation et sur les revenus. Ainsi, loin que ce soit une épargne pour l'état de ménager de cette manière les frais des travaux publics, il les paie très cher, tandis qu'ils coûteraient fort peu s'il les faisait faire à ses frais, c'est-à-dire par de petites taxes générales dans chaque province pour le paiement des ouvriers. Toutes les provinces reconnaissent tellement les avantages des travaux qui facilitent le commerce qu'elles se prêtent volontiers à ces sortes de contributions, pourvu qu'elles soient employées sûrement et fidèlement à leurs destinations. [VII.824a]

In POPULATION [XIII.99a] Damilaville proposes a similar tax in place of the *corvée*, though he suggests that work on the roads should be taken over by the army.

## Social inequality and the problem of poverty

A considerable number of articles in the *Encyclopédie* reveal a consciousness on the part of their authors of the gross inequalities of wealth which existed in the society of the day. One of the most outspoken of these articles is d'Alembert's FORTUNE (*Morale*) (the excessively rich men whom he has in mind are, of course, the hated *financiers*):

Les moyens de s'enrichir peuvent etre *criminels* en morale, quoique permis par les lois; il est contre le droit naturel et contre l'humanité que des millions d'hommes soient privés du nécessaire, comme ils le sont dans certains pays, pour nourrir le luxe scandaleux d'un petit nombre de citoyens oisifs. Une injustice si criante et si cruelle ne peut être autorisée par le motif de fournir des ressources à l'État dans des temps difficiles. Multiplier les malheureux pour augmenter les ressources, c'est se couper un bras pour donner plus de nourriture à l'autre. Cette inégalité monstrueuse entre la *fortune* des hommes, qui fait que les uns périssent d'indigence, tandis que les autres regorgent de superflu, était un des principaux arguments des épicuriens contre la providence, et devait paraître sans réplique à des philosophes privés des lumières de l'Évangile. [VII. 206a]

It need hardly be pointed out that the last observation is ironical, coming as it does from such a determined sceptic as d'Alembert.

Similar outbursts come from Diderot's pen, for instance in:

*INDIGENT, adj. (*Gram.*), homme qui manque des choses nécessaires à la vie, au milieu de ses semblables qui jouissent, avec un faste qui l'insulte, de toutes les superfluités possibles. Une des suites les plus fâcheuses de la mauvaise administration, c'est de diviser la société en deux classes d'hommes, dont les uns sont dans l'opulence et les autres dans la misère. L'*indigence* n'est pas un vice, c'est pis. On accueille le vicieux, on fuit l'*indigent*. On ne le voit jamais que la main ouverte et tendue. Il n'y a point d'*indigent* parmi les sauvages. [VIII.676a]

The last sentence reminds us of the theme of the *Supplément au Voyage de Bougainville* which Diderot was to write a decade or so later.

In *INSOLENT he delivers a violent attack on the insolence of the rich:

Quel est donc l'homme *insolent*? c'est celui qui dans la société a des meubles et des équipages, et qui raisonne à peu près ainsi: J'ai cent mille écus de rente; les dix-neuf vingtièmes des hommes n'ont pas mille écus, les autres n'ont rien. Les premiers sont donc à mille degrés au-dessous de moi; le reste en est à une distance infinie. D'après ce calcul, il manque d'égards à tout le monde, de peur d'en accorder à quelqu'un. Il se fait mépriser et haïr; mais qu'est-ce que cela lui fait? *sacram metiente viam cum bis ter ulnarum toga*, la queue de sa robe n'en est pas moins ample. Voilà l'*insolence* financière ou magistrale. [VIII.791a]

*JOURNALIER shows great solicitude for this section of the community:

*JOURNALIER, s.m. (*Gram.*), ouvrier qui travaille de ses mains et qu'on paye au jour la journée. Cette espèce d'hommes forment la plus grande partie d'une nation; c'est son sort qu'un bon gouvernement doit avoir principalement en vue. Si le *journalier* est misérable, la nation est misérable. [VIII.898a–b]

MISÈRE, although unsigned, obviously comes from the same pen (the last words are surely typical):

Il y a peu d'âmes assez fermes que la *misère* n'abatte et n'avilisse à la longue. Le petit peuple est d'une stupidité incroyable. Je ne sais quel prestige lui ferme les yeux sur sa *misère* presente, et sur une *misère* plus grande encore qui attend sa vieillesse. La *misère* est la mère des grands crimes; ce sont les souverains qui font lès misérables, qui répondront dans ce monde et dans l'autre des crimes que la *misère* aura commis. On dit, sans un sens bien opposé: c'est une *misère*, pour dire une chose de rien; dans le premier sens, c'est une *misère* que d'avoir affaire aux gens de loi et aux prêtres. [X.575a]

The editor's interest in the fate of the mass of his contemporaries stands out clearly in such short articles.

A striking article in the last ten volumes is PEUPLE, LE, by Jaucourt. Even though on close inspection it turns out to be merely a rearranged version of Abbé Coyer's *Dissertation sur la nature du peuple*, it is interesting from more than one point of view. Jaucourt begins by pointing out that the expression *peuple* has different

meanings in different times and places. At one time in France it
included all those who were not members of the aristocracy:

Autrefois en France le *peuple* était regardé comme la partie la plus utile, la
plus précieuse et, par conséquent, la plus respectable de la nation. Alors on
croyait que le *peuple* pouvait occuper une place dans les États généraux, et
les parlements du royaume ne faisaient qu'une raison de celle du *peuple* et
de la leur. Les idées ont changé, et même la classe des hommes faits pour
composer le *peuple* se rétrécit tous les jours davantage. Autrefois le *peuple*
était l'état général de la nation, simplement opposé à celui des grands et
des nobles. Il renfermait les laboureurs, les ouvriers, les artisans, les
négociants, les financiers, les gens de lettres et les gens de loi. [XII.476a]

Nowadays—and here as in the rest of the article he is simply
following Coyer's essay, as he himself tells us—things have
changed so much that 'ce corps de la nation se borne actuellement
aux ouvriers et aux laboureurs'.

After describing the present affluent state of the *financiers* and of
the lawyers and merchants who have risen (or hope to rise) into the
nobility, the article continues with a picture of the two classes who
now form *le peuple*:

Je trouve que cet ouvrier habite sous le chaume, ou dans quelque réduit
que nos villes lui abandonnent, parce qu'on a besoin de sa force. Il se lève
avec le soleil et, sans regarder la fortune qui rit au-dessus de lui, il prend
son habit de toutes les saisons, il fouille nos mines et nos carrières, il
dessèche nos marais, il nettoie nos rues, il bâtit nos maisons, il fabrique nos
meubles; la faim arrive, tout lui est bon; le jour finit, il se couche durement dans les bras de la fatigue. [XII.476a–b]

The picture of the peasant is even more in line with the *sensiblerie*
which one associates with so much French writing of the second
half of the eighteenth century:

Le laboureur, autre homme du *peuple*, est avant l'aurore tout occupé à
ensemencer nos terres, à cultiver nos champs, à arroser nos jardins. Il
souffre le chaud, le froid, la hauteur des grands, l'insolence des riches, le
brigandage des traitants, le pillage des commis, le ravage même des bêtes
fauves qu'il n'ose écarter de ses moissons par respect pour les plaisirs des
puissants. Il est sobre, juste, fidèle, religieux, sans considérer ce qui lui en
reviendra. Lucas épouse Colette parce qu'il l'aime; Colette donne son lait
à ses enfants sans connaître le prix de la fraîcheur et du repos. Ils grandis-

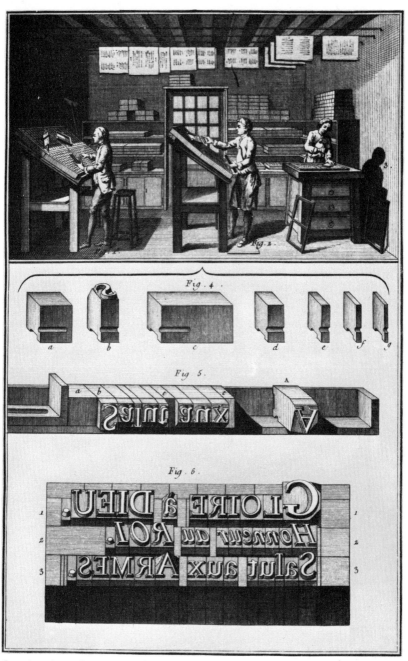

*Imprimerie en Lettres, L'Opération de la Casse (Vol. VII, Plate I)*

sent, ces enfants, et Lucas, ouvrant la terre devant eux, leur apprend à la cultiver. Il meurt et leur laisse son champ à partager également; si Lucas n'était pas un homme du *peuple*, il le laisserait tout entier à l'aîné. [XII. 476b]

Like other articles in the *Encyclopédie*, this refutes the notion that the poorer classes will only work and be docile subjects if they are kept poor:

Qui croirait qu'on a osé avancer de nos jours cette maxime d'une politique infâme que de tels hommes ne doivent point être à leur aise si l'on veut qu'ils soient industrieux et obéissants?... Au contraire, on n'a jamais vu et on ne verra jamais des hommes employer toute leur force et toute leur industrie, s'ils sont accoutumés à voir les taxes engloutir le produit des nouveaux efforts qu'ils pourraient faire, et ils se borneront au soutien d'une vie toujours abandonnée sans aucune espèce de regret.

A l'égard de l'obéissance, c'est une injustice de calomnier ainsi une multitude infinie d'innocents, car les lois n'ont point de sujets plus fidèles et, si j'ose le dire, de meilleurs amis. [XII.476b]

Coyer-Jaucourt's sympathy for the masses is undoubted.

None the less there is another side to the *Encyclopédie*'s attitude which must not be ignored. The *philosophes* as a whole looked down on the ignorant masses whom they regarded as only too easy victims of deceiving priests and fanatical rabble-rousers. The attitude expressed in Diderot's grammatical article MULTITUDE is typical:

Méfiez-vous du jugement de la *multitude* dans les matières de raisonne-ment et de philosophie; sa voix alors est celle de la méchanceté, de la sottise, de l'inhumanité, de la déraison et du préjugé. Méfiez-vous-en encore dans les choses qui supposent ou beaucoup de connaissances, ou un goût exquis. La *multitude* est ignorante et hébétée. [X.860a]

Here, it is true, the writer is not primarily concerned with a social judgement; his *multitude* could well include in this context men and women of quite exalted status. Yet the tone of the article LAQUAIS (again unsigned, but again surely by Diderot himself) could scarcely be described as sympathetic to this large class:

Le luxe les a multipliés sans nombre. Nos antichambres se remplissent, et nos campagnes se dépeuplent; les fils de nos laboureurs quittent la maison de leurs pères et viennent prendre dans la capitale un habit de livrée. Ils y sont conduits par l'indigence et la crainte de la milice, et retenus par la débauche et la fainéantise. Ils se marient; ils font des enfants qui soutiennent la race des *laquais*; les pères meurent dans la misère, à moins qu'ils n'aient été attachés à quelques maîtres bienfaisants qui leur aient laissé en mourant un morceau de pain coupé bien court. [IX.289b]

The article then refers to the proposal to put a tax on the number of lackeys; this would have had at least two advantages—the dismissal of a great number of them and the discouragement of others from leaving the provinces. 'Mais', the article concludes, 'cet impôt était trop sage pour avoir lieu' [IX.289b].

In *HÔPITAL Diderot sets forth his views on the problem of poverty. His first general principle is that 'il serait beaucoup plus important de travailler à prévenir la misère qu'à multiplier les asiles aux misérables' [VIII.294a]. After stating that in a well governed country there should be no poor except for those men who are born in poverty or fall into that state by accident, he makes a vigorous onslaught on sturdy beggars:

Je ne puis mettre au nombre des pauvres ces paresseux jeunes et vigoureux qui, trouvant dans notre charité mal entendue des secours plus faciles et plus considérables que ceux qu'ils se procuraient par le travail, remplissent nos rues, nos temples, nos grands chemins, nos bourgs, nos villes et nos campagnes. Il ne peut y avoir de cette vermine que dans un état où la valeur des hommes est inconnue.

   Rendre la condition des mendiants de profession et des vrais pauvres égale, en les confondant dans les mêmes maisons, c'est oublier qu'il y a des terres incultes à défricher, des colonies à peupler, des manufactures à soutenir, des travaux publics à continuer. [VIII.294a]

The attitude shown here is very much that of Turgot in FONDATION. In MENDIANT Jaucourt takes an even tougher line, as seen from the very definition given at the beginning of the article: 'gueux ou vagabond de profession, qui demande l'aumône par oisiveté et par fainéantise, au lieu de gagner sa vie par le travail' [X.331a]. Jaucourt would reserve hospitals for the sick and for those who were prevented by age from working. As a physician and a humanitarian he is horrified by the inadequacy of the provision made for the sick in view of the money wasted on the undeserving poor:

Ces hôpitaux sont précisément les moins rentés, le nécessaire y manque quelquefois; et tandis que des milliers d'hommes sont richement vêtus et nourris dans l'oisiveté, un ouvrier se voit forcé de consommer dans une maladie tout ce qu'il possède, ou de se faire transporter dans un lit commun avec d'autres malades, dont les maux se compliquent au sien. Que l'on calcule le nombre des malades qui entrent dans le cours d'une année dans les hôtels-Dieu du royaume, et le nombre des morts, on verra si, dans une ville composée du même nombre d'habitants, la peste ferait plus de ravage. [X.332a]

Jaucourt would like to see most of the income from these foundations spent on hospitals for the sick. As for the able-bodied poor, they should be put to work:

Et serait-il impossible, pour la subsistance de ceux-ci, d'affermer leur travail à un entrepreneur dans chaque lieu ? Les bâtiments sont construits, et la dépense d'en convertir une partie en atelier serait assez médiocre. Il ne s'agirait que d'encourager les premiers établissements. Dans un hôpital bien gouverné la nourriture d'un homme ne doit pas coûter plus de cinq sous par jour. Depuis l'âge de dix ans les personnes de tout sexe peuvent les gagner ; et si l'on a l'attention de leur laisser bien exactement le sixième de leur travail lorsqu'il excédera les cinq sous, on en verra monter le produit beaucoup plus haut. [X.332a]

These workhouses, in which even the children would be set to honest toil, would not be available to all poor people: 'Quant aux vagabonds de profession, on a des travaux utiles dans les colonies où l'on peut employer leurs bras à bon marché.' The whole article has a remarkably Victorian flavour.

## Humanitarianism

'Raison, tolérance, humanité', according to Condorcet, was the war-cry of the *philosophes*. Humanitarian sentiments are inevitably a striking feature of the *Encyclopédie*. HUMANITÉ (unsigned, but surely by Diderot) offers a characteristic definition:

HUMANITÉ, s.f. (*Morale*). C'est un sentiment de bienveillance pour tous les hommes, qui ne s'enflamme guère que dans une âme grande et sensible. Ce noble et sublime enthousiasme se tourmente des peines des autres et du besoin de les soulager; il voudrait parcourir l'univers pour abolir l'esclavage, la superstition, le vice et le malheur . . . [VIII.348a]

In CRUAUTÉ (*Morale*) Jaucourt denounces what he calls a 'passion féroce, qui renferme en elle la rigueur, la dureté pour les autres,

l'*incommisération*, la vengeance, le plaisir de faire du mal par in-
sensibilité de cœur ou par le plaisir de voir souffrir' [IV.517b]. He
lists various forms of cruelty and concludes sadly that even in
civilized countries humanity is a rare virtue:

Il faut même avouer ingénument que, dans tous les pays, l'humanité,
prise dans un sens étendu, est une qualité plus rare qu'on ne pense. Quand
on lit l'histoire des peuples les plus policés, on y voit tant d'exemples de
barbarie qu'on est également affligé et confondu. Je suis toujours surpris
d'entendre des personnes d'un certain ordre porter dans la conversation
des jugements contraires à cette humanité générale dont on devrait être
pénétré. [IV.518b]

## War

War being one of the chief sources of inhumanity, it is repeatedly
denounced in the *Encyclopédie*. In Jaucourt's GUERRE (*Droit naturel
& Politique*) authors as diverse as Grotius, La Bruyère and Montesquieu are enlisted to denounce all forms of armed conflict except
the just war undertaken in self-defence. Unfortunately, he has to
admit, in real life the principles of justice are not observed:

Le sang du peuple ne veut être versé que pour sauver ce même peuple
dans les besoins extrêmes. Malheureusement les conseils flatteurs, les
fausses idées de gloire, les vaines jalousies, l'avidité qui se couvre de vains
prétextes, le faux honneur de prouver sa puissance, les alliances, les
engagements insensibles qu'on a contractés par les suggestions des
courtisans et des ministres entraînent presque toujours les rois dans des
*guerres* où ils hasardent tout sans nécessité, épuisent leurs provinces et font
autant de mal à leurs pays et à leurs sujets qu'à leurs propres ennemis.
[VII.997a]

The article concludes with some melancholy reflections on the
Seven Years War which had recently broken out:

La *guerre* étouffe la voix de la nature, de la justice, de la religion et de
l'humanité. Elle n'enfante que des brigandages et des crimes; avec elle
marche l'effroi, la famine et la désolation; elle déchire l'âme des mères,
des épouses et des enfants; elle ravage les campagnes, dépeuple les provinces et réduit les villes en poudre. Elle épuise les états florissants au
milieu des plus grands succès; elle expose les vainqueurs aux tragiques
revers de la fortune. Elle déprave les mœurs de toutes les nations et fait
encore plus de misérables qu'elle n'en emporte. Voilà les fruits de la
*guerre*. Les gazettes ne retentissent actuellement (1757) que des maux

qu'elle cause sur terre et sur mer, dans l'ancien et le nouveau monde, à des peuples qui devraient resserrer les liens d'une bienveillance qui n'est déjà que trop faible, et non pas les couper. [VII.998a]

In the same volume we find Marmontel's article GLOIRE (*Philosoph. Morale*) which contains a fierce attack, not on war in general, but on unjust wars and those who distinguish themselves in them. He denounces in particular the way in which writers prostitute themselves by penning eulogies of conquerors and making them into heroes: 'La patrie d'un sage est la terre, son héros est le genre humain' [VII.717b]. He continues:

Qu'un courtisan soit un flatteur, son état l'excuse en quelque sorte et le rend moins dangereux. On doit se défier de son témoignage, il n'est pas libre; mais qui oblige l'homme de lettres à se trahir lui-même et ses semblables, la nature et la vérité?

Ce n'est pas tant la crainte, l'intérêt, la bassesse, que l'éblouissement, l'illusion, l'enthousiasme, qui ont porté les gens de lettres à décerner la gloire aux forfaits éclatants. [VII.717b]

Marmontel calls on men of letters to do their duty:

Que la force et l'élévation d'une âme bienfaisante et généreuse, que l'activité d'un esprit supérieur, appliquée au bonheur du monde, soient les objets de vos hommages; et de la même main qui élèvera des autels au désintéressement, à la bonté, à l'humanité, à la clémence, que l'orgueil, l'ambition, la vengeance, la cupidité, la fureur, soient traînés au tribunal redoutable de l'incorruptible postérité. C'est alors que vous serez les Némésis de votre siècle, les Rhadamantes des vivants. [VII.718a]

The unsigned article PAIX (*Droit nat., polit. & moral.*) contains another attack on war. The unknown author rebukes Hobbes for holding that in the state of nature men lived in a perpetual state of war one with another. 'Le sentiment de ce philosophe atrabilaire', he declares, 'ne paraît pas mieux fondé que s'il eût dit que l'état de la douleur et de la maladie est naturel à l'homme' [XI.768b]. War is not the natural state of man:

La guerre est un fruit de la dépravation des hommes; c'est une maladie convulsive et violente du corps politique; il n'est en santé, c'est-à-dire dans son état naturel que lorsqu'il jouit de la *paix*; c'est elle qui donne de la vigueur aux empires; elle maintient l'ordre parmi les citoyens; elle laisse aux lois la force qui leur est nécessaire; elle favorise la population, l'agriculture et le commerce; en un mot, elle procure aux peuples le bonheur qui est le but de toute société. [XI.768b]

War, on the other hand, is an unmitigated catastrophe:

La guerre, au contraire, dépeuple les états; elle y fait régner le désordre; les lois sont forcées de se taire à la vue de la licence qu'elle introduit; elle rend incertaines la liberté et la propriété des citoyens; elle trouble et fait négliger le commerce; les terres deviennent incultes et abandonnées. Jamais les triomphes les plus éclatants ne peuvent dédommager une nation de la perte d'une multitude de ses membres que la guerre sacrifie; ses victoires mêmes lui font des plaies profondes que la paix seule peut guérir. [XI.768b]

If only men were governed by reason . . . The rest of the article merely restates views too familiar to need repeating here.

## Negro slavery

Another humanitarian topic which is prominent in the *Encyclopédie* as in other works of the *philosophes* is Negro slavery. The specialist on this question was once again Jaucourt. His ESCLAVAGE (*Droit nat. Religion, Morale*) deals, of course, with various forms of slavery, ancient and modern, including serfdom which, the Chevalier points out, still persists in countries like Poland, Hungary, Bohemia and parts of Germany. Here he rejects utterly the religious pretext used to justify Negro slavery:

C'est donc aller directement contre le droit des gens et contre la nature que de croire que la religion chrétienne donne à ceux qui la professent, un droit de réduire en servitude ceux qui ne la professent pas, pour travailler plus aisément à sa propagation. Ce fut pourtant cette manière de penser qui encouragea les destructeurs de l'Amérique dans leurs crimes; et ce n'est pas la seule fois que l'on se soit servi de la religion contre ses propres maximes qui nous apprennent que la qualité de prochain s'étend sur tout l'univers. [V.938b]

Again, in LIBERTÉ NATURELLE, which is mainly derived from Burlamaqui, he attacks Negro slavery. Christianity has abolished slavery in Europe, but, he asks,

comment les puissances chrétiennes n'ont-elles pas jugé que cette même religion, indépendamment du droit naturel, réclamait contre l'esclavage

des nègres? C'est qu'elles en ont besoin pour leurs colonies, leurs planta-
tions et leurs mines. *Auri sacra fames!* [IX.471b–472a]

The attack is continued in the unsigned article NÈGRES (*Commerce*):

Les Européens font depuis quelques siècles commerce de ces *nègres*, qu'ils
tirent de Guinée et des autres côtes de l'Afrique pour soutenir les colonies
qu'ils ont établies dans plusieurs endroits de l'Amérique et dans les îles
Antilles. On tâche de justifier ce que ce commerce a d'odieux et de
contraire au droit naturel, en disant que ces esclaves trouvent ordinairement le salut de leur âme dans la perte de leur liberté; que l'instruction
chrétienne qu'on leur donne, jointe au besoin indispensable que l'on a
d'eux pour la culture des sucres, des tabacs, des indigos etc., adoucissent
ce qui paraît d'inhumain dans un commerce où des hommes en achètent
et en vendent d'autres comme on ferait des bestiaux pour la culture des
terres. [XI.79b]

Jaucourt contributed another attack on Negro slavery in MARONS:
'On appelle *marons* dans les îles françaises les nègres fugitifs qui se
sauvent de la maison de leurs maîtres . . .' [X.134b]. Pierre Rousseau reproduced this article in his *Journal encyclopédique*, accompanying it with a strong attack on the whole institution of slavery.[1]

Jaucourt's most outspoken contribution on this subject was
reserved for the article TRAITE DES NÈGRES (*Commerce d'Afrique*).
Here he enlists the support of 'un Anglais moderne plein de
lumières et d'humanité' in denouncing this trade, and then
continues:

Si un commerce de ce genre peut être justifié par un principe de morale,
il n'y a point de crime, quelque atroce qu'il soit, qu'on ne puisse légitimer.
Les rois, les princes, les magistrats ne sont point les propriétaires de leurs
sujets; ils ne sont donc pas en droit de disposer de leur liberté et de les
vendre pour esclaves.

   D'un autre côté, aucun homme n'a droit de les acheter ou de s'en rendre
le maître. Les hommes et leur liberté ne sont point un objet de commerce;
ils ne peuvent être ni vendus, ni achetés, ni payés à aucun prix. Il faut
conclure de là qu'un homme dont l'esclave prend la fuite, ne doit s'en
prendre qu'à lui-même, puisqu'il avait acquis à prix d'argent une marchandise illicite et dont l'acquisition lui était interdite par toutes les lois de
l'humanité et de l'équité. [XVI.532b]

---

[1] *Journal encyclopédique*, 15 December 1767, pp. 3–10.

Jaucourt then deals with a question which gave rise to much controversy and to famous law cases in both France and England in the eighteenth century—whether a slave should be declared free when he entered one or other of these countries. It goes without saying that Jaucourt maintains that it is the duty of judges to order a slave to be freed 'puisque c'est leur semblable, ayant une âme comme eux' [XVI.532b].

The argument that the colonies would be ruined if Negro slavery were abolished does not trouble Jaucourt. Even if it were true, he asks: 'Faut-il conclure de là que le genre humain doit être horriblement lésé pour nous enrichir ou fournir à notre luxe?' [XVI.533a]. 'Que les colonies européennes', he exclaims, 'soient donc plutôt détruites que de faire tant de malheureux.' Some temporary inconvenience would no doubt result, he concedes, if slavery were to be abolished; but in the long run it would be to the advantage of the whole American continent: 'C'est la liberté, c'est l'industrie qui sont les sources réelles de l'abondance', he declares. Yet the conclusion is far from optimistic: 'Les âmes sensibles et généreuses applaudiront sans doute à ces raisons en faveur de l'humanité; mais l'avarice et la cupidité qui dominent la terre, ne voudront jamais les entendre' [XVI.533a]. Jaucourt did not see the slave-traders of Bordeaux and Nantes giving up so lucrative an occupation in a hurry.

## Crime and punishment

The administration of justice and in particular of the criminal law is also treated at some length (by Jaucourt among others) in a variety of articles. Two of these—HABEAS CORPUS and PAIRS (*Hist. d'Anglet.*)—show a considerable interest in English institutions. In Chambers HABEAS CORPUS is quite a short article; in the *Encyclopédie* it was considerably expanded by Jaucourt. The last paragraph of this article is taken, with acknowledgements, from Book xi, chap. 6 of the *Esprit des lois*. After a lengthy definition of the workings of the Act comes the following comment:

C'est un des plus beaux privilèges dont une nation libre puisse jouir; car, en conséquence de cet acte, les prisonniers d'État ont le droit de choisir le tribunal où ils veulent être jugés et d'être élargis sous caution si on n'allègue point la cause de leur détention ou qu'on diffère de les juger. [VIII.5b]

Considerable space is then devoted to the occasional suspension of
the Act together with a summary of the debates in the House of
Lords when it was suspended in 1732. Then comes the quotation
from Montesquieu:

Il est vrai, dit à ce sujet l'auteur de l'*Esprit des lois,* que si la puissance
législative laisse à l'exécutrice le droit d'emprisonner des citoyens qui
pourraient donner caution de leur conduite, il n'y a plus de liberté; mais
s'ils ne sont arrêtés que pour répondre sans délai à une accusation que la
loi a rendue capitale, alors ils sont réellement libres, puisqu'ils ne sont
soumis qu'à la puissance de la loi. Enfin, si la puissance législative se croit
en danger par quelque conspiration secrète contre l'État ou quelque
intelligence avec les ennemis du dehors, elle peut, pour un temps court et
limité, permettre à la puissance exécutrice de faire arrêter les citoyens
suspects, qui ne perdront leur liberté pour un temps que pour la conserver pour toujours. [VIII.6b]

Not a word is breathed in this article in the way of a comparison
of English and French laws and institutions; but in the land of
*lettres de cachet* the reader was surely capable of drawing his own
conclusions.

Jaucourt's article, PAIRS (*Hist. d'Anglet.*), praises the English jury
system. He begins by explaining that in England, in contrast to
France, 'le moindre artisan est *pair* de tout gentilhomme qui est
au-dessous du rang de baron' [XI.765b], and that consequently the
right of being tried by one's peers means that holders of peerages
are tried by their equals, and that any other person is tried by
commoners, 'qui sont ses *pairs* à cet égard, quelque distance qu'il y
ait entre eux par rapport aux biens ou à la naissance' [XI.766a].
After tracing back the history of this institution, Jaucourt concludes:

Ce droit des sujets anglais, dont ils jouissent encore aujourd'hui, est sans
doute un des plus beaux et des plus estimables qu'une nation puisse avoir.
Un Anglais accusé de quelque crime ne peut être jugé que par ses *pairs,*
c'est-à-dire par des personnes de son rang. Par cet auguste privilège il se
met hors de danger d'être opprimé, quelque grand que soit le crédit de
ses ennemis. Ces douze hommes ou *pairs,* choisis avec l'approbation de
l'accusé entre un grand nombre d'autres, sont appelés du nom collectif de
*jury.* [XI.766a]

The word had not yet become established in French since the
institution was not created until the Revolution.

One of the most striking articles contributed by Jaucourt on these matters is QUESTION (*Procédure criminelle*), a sharp attack on the use of torture to extract confessions. It follows on the purely factual article, QUESTION *ou* TORTURE (*Jurisprudence*), by the lawyer, Boucher d'Argis. Jaucourt begins his article with a reference to the one which precedes it: 'On vient de lire des détails instructifs pour des juges criminels' [XIII.704a]. He claims his right as a citizen to examine this matter:

La soumission des sujets demande bien qu'on obéisse aux magistrats, mais non pas qu'on les croie infaillibles, et qu'entre deux usages ils n'aient pu embrasser le pire. C'est pour cela qu'il est permis de représenter avec respect les abus afin d'éclairer le souverain et de le porter par sa religion et sa justice à les réformer. [XIII.704a]

Lawyers, the Fathers, theologians, Quintilian, Montaigne and La Bruyère are all called in to condemn the practice. Jaucourt's final argument is the abolition of the use of torture in England:

Enfin la *question* contre les criminels n'est point dans un cas forcé. Nous voyons aujourd'hui une nation très polie et aussi éclairée que respectueuse envers l'humanité, qui a rejeté ce supplice sans inconvénient, même dans le cas de haute trahison. Il n'est donc pas nécessaire par sa nature. [XIII.704b]

Here reform had to wait until the very eve of the Revolution.

The articles in the *Encyclopédie* which deal with economic and social questions are inevitably deeply rooted, especially on the purely factual side, in the realities of life under the Ancien Régime. Many of them could scarcely be described as forward-looking; and yet in all sorts of ways the views put forward in those which have been analysed in this chapter prefigure the new society which was to emerge from the vast upheaval of the Revolutionary and Napoleonic period.

# Conclusion

To set before the reader, as has been done in these last four chapters, a series of extracts from articles in the *Encyclopédie* is inevitably to give him a somewhat misleading impression of the work as a whole. In so limited a space it is impossible to give an altogether accurate idea of a work in seventeen large folio volumes containing something like twenty million words; and even if the reader were prepared to swallow two or three volumes on the subject, he would not necessarily obtain a much more complete picture of the *Encyclopédie*. If inevitably a somewhat one-sided picture of the work has been offered, it still remains that the reader has had some opportunity in the course of these last chapters of making direct contact with the contributors to the *Encyclopédie*—famous or obscure, definitely known, anonymous or uncertain—and with their views on a wide variety of controversial topics. At least he will be somewhat better off than if he had never read a line of the articles entombed in these seventeen folio volumes.

There is no question that in the period between 1751 and 1765, when the volumes of text appeared, and even in the years immediately preceding the appearance of the *Encyclopédie* much more radical and outspoken works appeared in France. To grasp this obvious point one need only think of Diderot's own *Pensées philosophiques* and *Lettre sur les aveugles* or of Voltaire's *Dictionnaire philosophique*. Even the boldest articles—those, for instance, of Diderot, d'Alembert and d'Holbach—are with rare exceptions a very mild reflection of what, but for the whole repressive machinery of State, Parlement and Church, they could have been expected to write on the controversial subjects of their age. And, of course, the *Encyclopédie* does contain, as even its fiercest critics were compelled to admit, a great deal of the conventional ideas of the time.

None the less the *Encyclopédie* is in one respect unique among works of reference of this type. Old encyclopedias litter the shelves of the stacks of our larger libraries; worse still—and this is a tremendous crime in the eyes of historians for whom they will always remain essential works of reference—they have often been pulped or burnt as useless. Even where they have been preserved, they are obviously only infrequently consulted. Even the *Encyclopédie*'s German contemporary, Zedler's *Universal-Lexicon*, invaluable as it is for its biographies and for other detailed historical points, is not read, as distinct from being consulted, in the way that Diderot's volumes still are.

If the *Encyclopédie* is still read today, either directly in one of various eighteenth-century editions or more commonly in the collected works of its contributors or in volumes of selections, it is not only because it enlisted the services of some of the most brilliant writers of the day. Indeed, if one looks with cool detachment at the facts of the situation, one soon sees that the role of men like Montesquieu, Voltaire, Buffon and Rousseau has often been greatly exaggerated. Voltaire was late in starting to contribute and dropped out after Vol. VIII; Rousseau, apart from his musical articles, contributed only ÉCONOMIE POLITIQUE; although Montesquieu and Buffon are to be encountered everywhere in the *Encyclopédie*, one contributed merely a posthumous fragment and the other nothing at all.

If the *Encyclopédie* is still read and argued over today, it is because it reflects very clearly the outlook of the Enlightenment at a given period of its history in the country which took a leading part in the whole movement in the decades before it plunged into revolution. That the last volumes of text appeared nearly a quarter of a century before the fall of the Bastille is a fact which requires constantly to be borne in mind. The *Encyclopédie* belongs to the reign of Louis XV and not to that of his successor; to speak more precisely, it might be said to belong to the age of Madame de Pompadour, of Machault's vain attempts at fiscal reforms, of the growing struggle between Crown and Parlements.

In these years the publication of this mighty work of reference offered a rallying point for men of progressive ideas. They could offer their contributions to its pages, often anonymously, or, if they were well enough off to do so, they could support the enterprise by subscribing to the work. This is not to suggest that either all the contributors or all the subscribers (the latter would appear to have included quite a number of the regular clergy, either for themselves or for the libraries of their religious houses) were imbued with a passionate devotion to reason, toleration and humanitarian feeling. Yet if the *Encyclopédie* was not, as Abbé Barruel was later to claim, the first stage in the mighty conspiracy which brought the established order crashing down in the Revolution, from the start its enemies recognized clearly that this large enterprise was a menace. And the memory of this menace did not entirely fade even after the last volumes of text and plates had appeared.

It is interesting, for instance, to see the bad reputation which Turgot enjoyed at court when he became a minister in 1774 because of his former and entirely anonymous connection with the *Encyclopédie*. One contemporary noted: 'On a beaucoup manœuvré contre le Turgot. . . . On dit qu'il est encyclopédiste, c'est une hérésie abominable à la cour.'[1] The Duc de Croÿ put into his diary a conversation with the *contrôleur-général* and added the comment: 'On sait que tous ces encyclopédistes absolus voulaient le tolérantisme et la liberté entière sur tout.'[2] Moreau, the author of the *Nouveau Mémoire pour servir à l'histoire des Cacouacs,* records in his memoirs for the same date a conversation with one of Louis XVI's aunts: 'Madame Victoire, à qui je contai la manière fraîche dont j'avais été reçu par M. Turgot, s'écria: "Je le crois bien, il est encyclopédiste!" et me promit de me protéger s'il essayait de me toucher.' Moreau goes on: 'Non seulement il était encyclopédiste en diable, mais il était encore partisan de la liberté indéfinie, et économiste.'[3] More significant still is the case of Malesherbes. Although he was in the end to join Turgot in the government for a short period, according to Abbé Véri Louis XVI at first refused even to discuss his claims to appointment. And Malesherbes, although he undoubtedly aided the publication of the *Encyclopédie*

---

[1] Abbé Baudeau, quoted in Turgot, *Œuvres complètes*, ed. G. Schelle, Paris, 1913–23, 5 vols, iv, 77.
[2] *Journal inédit*, ed. Vicomte de Grouchy and P. Cottin, Paris, 1906–7, 4 vols, iii, 142.
[3] *Mes Souvenirs*, ed. C. Hernelin, Paris, 1898, 2 vols, ii, 37.

during his tenure of the post of *Directeur de la Librairie*, had never written a line for it. Louis XVI's hostility is explained thus by Véri: 'La prévention du Roi contre sa personne comme encyclopédiste et antiroyaliste en est le vrai motif. Il est presque le seul sur lequel le Roi ait dit sans souffrir d'examen: "Ne parlons de lui pour rien; c'est un encyclopédiste trop dangereux."'[1]

A 'tour de Babel' was how Voltaire himself described the *Encyclopédie* in private. Its enemies had an easy task in pointing out its innumerable contradictions. Radical and conventional ideas are to be found not only in different articles, but even inside the same one. Yet, as its enemies recognized from the start, here was a work which breathed a new spirit, one which was hostile to tradition and authority, which sought to subject all beliefs and institutions to a searching examination. In a word the *Encyclopédie* stood for the new attitude to the world which was beginning to be more and more openly expressed in the second half of the reign of Louis XV and which in the long run was to triumph not only in France itself, but in an even wider sphere.

[1] *Journal*, ed. J. de Witte, Paris, 1929, 2 vols, i, 128.

## Appendix A

# The different editions of the 'Encyclopédie'

## I. The Paris Folio Edition

*Text*

| Vol. I | A = AZYMITES | June 1751 |
|---|---|---|
| II | B = CEZIMBRA | January 1752[1] |
| III | CHA = CONSÉCRATION | October 1753 |
| IV | CONSEIL = DIZIER, SAINT | October 1754 |
| V | DO = ESMYNETE | November 1755 |
| VI | ET = FNÉ | October 1756 |
| VII | FOANG = GYTHIUM | November 1757 |
| VIII | H = ITZEHOA | |
| IX | JU = MAMIRA | |
| X | MAMELLE = MYVA | |
| XI | N = PARKINSONE | |
| XII | PARLEMENT = POLYTRIC | |
| XIII | POMACIES = REGGIO | December 1765 |
| XIV | REGGIO = SEMYDA | |
| XV | SEN = TCHUPRIKI | |
| XVI | TEANUM = VÉNERIE | |
| XVII | VÉNÉRIEN = ZZUÉNÉ: | |
| | Articles omis | |

*Plates*

| Vol. I | Première livraison | 1762 |
|---|---|---|
| II | Seconde livraison, première partie | 1763 |
| III | Seconde livraison, deuxième partie | |
| IV | Troisième livraison | 1765 |

[1] Despite the date '1751' on the title-page.

| V | Quatrième livraison | 1767 |
|---|---|---|
| VI | Cinquième livraison ou sixième volume | 1768 |
| VII | Sixième livraison ou septième volume | 1769 |
| VIII | Septième livraison ou huitième volume | |
| IX | Huitième livraison ou neuvième volume | } 1771 |
| X | Neuvième livraison ou dixième volume | |
| XI | Dixième livraison ou onzième volume | } 1772 |

*Supplément*

| Vol. I | A = BLOME-KRABBE | |
|---|---|---|
| II | BOATIUM-CIVITAS = EZZAB | } 1776 |
| III | F = MYXINE | |
| IV | NAALOL = ZYGIE | } 1777 |
| V | PLATES | |

*Table*

Vol. I  }
   II   } 1780

## II. *The Geneva Folio Reprint*

*Text:* 17 volumes, 1771–74.
*Plates:* 11 volumes, 1770–76.
The title-pages of most sets of this edition bear the original place and date of publication and the names of the original publishers; in some sets Vols I, II, III and IX have on their title-pages the words: 'À GENÈVE, / Chez CRAMER L'ainé & Compagnie. [double rule] M.DCC.LXXII.'

## III. *The Lucca Folio Edition*

*Text:* 17 volumes, 1758–71.
*Plates:* 11 volumes, 1765–76.

## IV. *The Leghorn Folio Edition*

*Text:* 17 volumes, 1770–75.
*Plates:* 11 volumes, 1771–78.
*Supplément:* 5 volumes, 1778–79.

## V. The Swiss Quarto Editions

*Text:* 36 volumes.

*Plates:* 3 volumes

There would appear to have been three printings of this version published by Pellet of Geneva, as some volumes bear on the title-page the words 'Nouvelle Édition' and some 'Troisième Édition'. Those with the words 'Nouvelle Édition' bear dates ranging from 1777 to 1779, while those with 'Troisième Édition' (many of these would appear to have been printed at Neuchâtel) bear dates ranging from 1778 to 1779. A *Table* in six volumes was published in Lyons in 1780 and 1781.

## VI. The Swiss Octavo Editions

*Text:* 36 volumes.

*Plates:* 3 volumes.

Two editions were produced by the Sociétés Typographiques of Lausanne and Berne between 1778 and 1782.

## Appendix B

# Symbols used to designate contributors to the 'Encyclopédie'

The following list has been compiled for reference purposes by putting together information supplied in various of the first seven volumes:

(A)  Boucher d'Argis

(B)  Cahusac

(C)  Abbé Pestré

(D)  Goussier

(E)  Abbé de la Chapelle

(F)  Dumarsais

(G)  Abbé Mallet

(H)  Toussaint

(I)  Louis Jean Marie Daubenton

(K)  D'Argenville

(L)  Tarin

(M) Malouin

(N)  Vandenesse

(O)  D'Alembert

(P)  Blondel

(Q)  Le Blond

(R)  Landois

(S)  J. J. Rousseau

(T)  Le Roy

(V)  Eidous

(X)  Abbé Yvon

(Y)  Louis

(Z)  Bellin

(a)  Lenglet du Fresnoy

(b)  Venel

(c)  Daubenton (Subdélégué)

(d)  D'Aumont

(e)  Bourgelat

(f)  De Villiers

(g)  Barthès

(h)  Abbé Morellet

(–)  Baron d'Holbach

(E.R.M.) Douchet and Beauzée

There are no corresponding lists in the last ten volumes, though new symbols to which we are given no key occasionally appear— e.g. (*m*) and (*q*). It is, however, possible to identify '(*m*)' as Dr Ménuret de Chambaud.

# Bibliography

It is only in the last fifty years or so that the *Encyclopédie* has been seriously studied. Of the books and articles published before 1939 the following remain of importance:

HUBERT, R., *Les Sciences sociales dans l'Encyclopédie*, Paris, 1923.
——, *Rousseau et l'Encyclopédie*, Paris, n.d.
MAY, L. P., 'Documents nouveaux sur l'*Encyclopédie*. L'histoire et les sources de l'*Encyclopédie*, d'après le registre de délibérations et de comptes des éditeurs, et un mémoire inédit', *Revue de Synthèse*, 1938.
NAVES, R., *Voltaire et l'Encyclopédie*, Paris, 1938.

Since 1945 there has been a great upsurge of interest. This is reflected in the highly selective list of books and articles which follows:

BERKOV, P. N., 'Histoire de l'*Encyclopédie* dans la Russie du XVIII$^e$ siècle', *Revue des Études slaves*, 1965.
DIECKMANN, H., 'L'*Encyclopédie* et le Fonds Vandeul', *Revue d'histoire littéraire*, 1951.
——, 'The sixth volume of Saint-Lambert's works', *Romanic Review*, 1951.
*L'Encyclopédie et le progrès des sciences et des techniques,* ed. Suzanne Delorme and R. Tatou, Paris, 1952.
*L'Encyclopédie française, Annales de l'Université de Paris* (special number), October 1952.
GILLE, B., 'L'*Encyclopédie*, dictionnaire technique', in *L'Encyclopédie et le progrès des sciences et des techniques* (q.v.)

GORDON, D. H. and TORREY, N. L., *The Censoring of Diderot's Encyclopédie and the Re-established Text,* New York, 1947.

GRIMSLEY, R., *Jean d'Alembert,* Oxford, 1963.

GUYOT, C., *Le Rayonnement de l'Encyclopédie en Suisse française,* Neuchâtel, 1955.

GROSCLAUDE, P., *Un audacieux message. L'Encyclopédie,* Paris, 1951.

HUARD, G., 'Les planches de l'*Encyclopédie* et celles de la *Description des Arts et Métiers* de l'Académie des Sciences', in *L'Encyclopédie et le progrès des sciences et des techniques* (q.v.)

KAFKER, F., 'A List of Contributors to Diderot's *Encyclopédie*', *French Historical Studies,* 1963.

LOUGH, J. (ed.), *The Encyclopédie of Diderot and d'Alembert: selected articles,* Cambridge University Press, 1954 (revised edition, 1969).

——, *Essays on the Encyclopédie of Diderot and d'Alembert,* Oxford University Press, 1968.

——, 'Le Breton, Mills et Sellius', *Dix-huitième Siècle,* 1969.

——, *The Encyclopédie in Eighteenth-Century England and Other Studies,* Newcastle upon Tyne, 1970.

LUCQUET, G. H., 'L'*Encyclopédie* fut-elle une entreprise maçonnique?', *Revue d'histoire littéraire,* 1954.

MORTIER, R., *Diderot en Allemagne (1750–1850),* Paris, 1954.

——, 'A propos du sentiment de l'existence chez Diderot et Rousseau', *Diderot Studies VI.*

PONS, A. (ed.), *Encyclopédie ou Dictionnaire raisonné des Sciences, des Arts et des Métiers, 1751–1772,* Paris, 1963.

PROUST, J., 'La Documentation technique de Diderot dans l'*Encyclopédie*', *Revue d'histoire littéraire,* 1957.

——, *Diderot et l'Encyclopédie,* Paris, 1962 (second edition, 1967).

——, 'La contribution de Diderot à l'*Encyclopédie* et les théories du droit naturel', *Annales historiques de la Révolution Française,* 1963.

——, *L'Encyclopédie,* Paris (Collection Armand Colin), 1965 (an excellent introduction with a very full bibliography).

——, *L'Encyclopédisme dans le Bas-Languedoc au XVIII^e siècle,* Montpellier, 1968.

——, 'Diderot, l'Académie de Pétersbourg et le projet d'une *Encyclopédie* russe', *Diderot Studies XII.*

SCHWAB, R. N., 'The Extent of the Chevalier de Jaucourt's Contribution to Diderot's *Encyclopédie*', *Modern Language Notes,* 1957.

SCHWAB, R. N., 'Un encyclopédiste huguenot: le chevalier de Jaucourt', *Bulletin de la Société de l'Histoire du Protestantisme français*, 1962.

——, 'The Diderot Problem, the Starred Articles and the Question of Attribution in the *Encyclopédie*', *Eighteenth Century Studies*, 1969.

SEGUIN, J. P., 'Courte histoire des planches de l'*Encyclopédie*' in *L'Univers de l'Encyclopédie*, Paris, 1964.

SHACKLETON, R., 'The *Encyclopédie* and Freemasonry' in *The Age of Enlightenment. Studies presented to Theodore Besterman*, Edinburgh, 1967.

SOBOUL, A. (ed.), *Textes choisis de l'Encyclopédie*, Paris, 1952 (second edition, 1962).

VENTURI, F., *Le Origini dell'Enciclopedia*, Florence, 1946 (second edition, Turin, 1963).

——, 'Le Origini dell'Enciclopedia in Inghilterra', *Itinerari*, 1954.

VERNIÈRE, P., 'La critique biblique dans l'*Encyclopédie* et ses sources spinozistes', *Revue de Synthèse*, 1951.

WATTS, G. B., see under COLE, p. 408.

——, 'Forgotten folio editions of the *Encyclopédie*', *French Review*, 1953–54.

——, 'The *Supplément* and the *Table analytique et raisonnée* of the *Encyclopédie*', *French Review*, 1954–55.

——, 'The Swiss editions of the *Encyclopédie*', *Harvard Library Bulletin*, 1955.

——, 'The Geneva folio reprinting of the *Encyclopédie*', *Proceedings of the American Philosophical Society*, 1961.

WILSON, A. M., *Diderot. The Testing Years, 1713–1759*, New York, 1957.

The following is a list of the manuscripts referred to in this work and of those books and articles not listed above:

*Manuscripts*

Archives Nationales. U 1051 (The publishers' accounts for the *Encyclopédie*).

Bibliothèque de l'Arsenal. Archives de la Bastille 11671 (Diderot at Vincennes).

Bibliothèque Nationale. Manuscrits français 21958 (Registre des Privilèges).

——, Nouvelles acquisitions françaises 3347, 3531 (Malesherbes papers).

*Books and articles*

ALEMBERT, D', *Mélanges de littérature, d'histoire et de philosophie*, Amsterdam, 1763–67, 5 vols.

——, *Œuvres philosophiques, historiques et littéraires*, Paris, 1805, 18 vols.

*Année littéraire*, Paris, 1754–90.

*Annonces, affiches et avis divers* [=*Affiches de province*], Paris, 1752–84.

*Arrêts de la Cour de Parlement, portant condamnation de plusieurs livres et autres ouvrages imprimés. Extrait des Registres du Parlement du 23 janvier 1759*, Paris, 1759.

*Arrêts du Conseil du Roi,* 7 February 1752; 8 March 1759; 21 July 1759.

*Avis au Public sur le troisième volume de l'Encyclopédie,* n.p.n.d.

BACHAUMONT, L. P. DE, *Mémoires, secrets pour servir à l'histoire de la République des Lettres en France de 1762 jusqu'à nos jours*, London, 1777–89, 36 vols.

BARRUEL, ABBÉ, *Les Helviennes ou Lettres provinciales philosophiques*, Amsterdam, 1781–88, 5 vols.

——, *Mémoires pour servir à l'histoire du Jacobinisme*, London, 1797, 4 vols.

BOULLIER, D. R., *Apologie de la Métaphysique à l'occasion du Discours préliminaire de l'Encyclopédie*, Amsterdam, 1753.

BÜSCHING, A. F., *Beiträge zu der Lebensgeschichte denkwürdiger Personen*, Halle, 1783–86, 6 vols.

BURLAMAQUI, *Principes du droit politique*, Amsterdam, 1751.

CAYLUS, CHARLES DE, *Instruction pastorale de Monseigneur l'évêque d'Auxerre sur la vérité et la sainteté de la religion chrétienne méconnue et attaquée en plusieurs points par la thèse soutenue en Sorbonne le 18 novembre 1751*, n.p., 1752.

*Censeur hebdomadaire, Le*, Paris, 1760–61.

CHAUDON, L. M., *Dictionnaire antiphilosophique*, Avignon, 1769.

CHAUMEIX, A. J., *Préjugés légitimes contre l'Encyclopédie, et Essai de réfutation de cet ouvrage*, Brussels-Paris, 1758–59, 8 vols.

——, *Les Philosophes aux abois, ou Lettres de M. de Chaumeix à MM. les Encyclopédistes au sujet d'un libelle anonyme*, Brussels-Paris, 1760.

CLEMENT XIII, *Damnatio et prohibitio operis in plures Tomos distributi, cujus est titulus: Encyclopédie*, n.p., 1759.

COLE, A. H. and WATTS, G. B., *The Handicrafts of France as recorded in the 'Descriptions des Arts et Métiers'*, Boston, 1952.

COLLISON, R., *Encyclopaedias: Their History throughout the Ages*, London, 1964.

CONDORCET, *Œuvres*, ed. A. C. O'Connor and F. Arago, Paris, 1847–49, 12 vols.

CROŸ, DUC DE, *Journal inédit*, ed. Vicomte de Grouchy and P. Cottin, Paris, 1906–7, 4 vols.

*Determinatio Sacrae Facultatis Parisiensis super Libro cui titulus, De l'Esprit*, Paris, 1759.

DIDEROT, *Correspondence*, ed. G. Roth, Paris, 1955– (in course of publication)

——, *Œuvres complètes*, ed. J. Assézat and M. Tourneux, Paris, 1875–77, 20 vols.

*Encyclopédie méthodique ou par ordre de matières . . . proposée par souscription*, n.p., 1782.

——, *Mathématiques*, ed. d'Alembert and Bossut, Paris, 1784–89, 3 vols.

FORMEY, J. H. S., *Souvenirs d'un Citoyen*, Berlin, 1789, 2 vols.

FUMEL, J. F. H. DE, *Mandement et instruction pastorale de Monseigneur l'évêque de Lodève touchant plusieurs livres ou écrits modernes, portant condamnation desdits livres ou écrits*, Montpellier, 1759.

FUSSELL, G. E., *More Old English Farming Books from Tull to the Board of Agriculture*, London, 1950.

GIRY DE SAINT-CYR, ABBÉ, 'Avis utile', *Mercure de France*, October 1758, Vol. i.

——, *Catéchisme et décisions de cas de conscience à l'usage des Cacouacs, avec un discours du patriarche des Cacouacs pour la réception d'un nouveau disciple*, 'Cacopolis', 1758.

GRIMM, F. M. (ed.), *Correspondance littéraire, philosophique et critique*, ed. M. Tourneux, Paris, 1877–82, 16 vols.

*Gentleman's Magazine*, London, 1735–1807.

HERVÉ, FATHER F. M., *Réflexions d'un Franciscain, avec une lettre préliminaire, adressées à M. ***, auteur en partie du Dictionnaire encyclopédique*, n.p., 1752.

—— and FRUCHET, FATHER, *Réflexions d'un Franciscain sur les trois premiers volumes de l'Encyclopédie, avec une lettre préliminaire aux éditeurs*, Berlin, 1754.

HOLBACH, BARON, D', *Le Christianisme dévoilé*, London, 1767.

IRAIL, ABBÉ, *Querelles littéraires, ou Mémoires pour servir à l'histoire des révolutions de la république des lettres depuis Homère jusqu'à nos jours*, Paris, 1761, 4 vols.

*Journal des Savants*, Paris, 1665–1792.

*Journal de Trévoux*, Trévoux-Paris, 1701–67.

*Journal encyclopédique*, Liège, 1756–59; Bouillon, 1760–93.

LA HARPE, *L'Aléthophile ou l'ami de la vérité*, Amsterdam, 1758.

LAISSUS, Y., 'Une lettre inédite de d'Alembert', *Revue de l'Histoire des Sciences et de leurs applications*, 1954.

LECLERC DE MONTLINOT, ABBÉ, *Justification de plusieurs articles du Dictionnaire encyclopédique, ou Préjugés légitimes contre Abraham-Joseph de Chaumeix*, Brussels-Paris, 1759.

*Lettre à M. ***, de la Société royale de Londres*, n.p.n.d.

*Lettre de M. ***, l'un des XXIV, à M. Diderot, Directeur de la Manufacture encyclopédique*, n.p., 1751.

*Lettre d'un souscripteur pour le Dictionnaire encyclopédique, à M. Diderot*, n.p., 1751.

*Lettres sur le VII^e volume de l'Encyclopédie*, n.p., 1759.

*London Magazine or Gentleman's Monthly Intelligencer*, London, 1732–85.

LÜTHY, H., *La Banque protestante en France de la Révocation de l'Édit de Nantes à la Révolution*, Paris, 1959–61, 2 vols.

MALLEVILLE, ABBÉ, *Histoire critique de l'Éclectisme ou des nouveaux Platoniciens*, n.p., 1766, 2 vols.

*Mémoire pour André-François Le Breton, Libraire et imprimeur ordinaire du Roi . . . contre le sieur Mills, se disant gentilhomme anglais*, Paris, 1745.

*Mémoire des Libraires associés à l'Encyclopédie sur les motifs de la suspension actuelle de cet ouvrage*, Paris, 1758.

*Mémoire à consulter pour les libraires associés à l'Encyclopédie*, Paris, 1770.

*Mémoire pour Pierre-Joseph-François Luneau de Boisjermain, Sou-scripteur de l'Encyclopédie*, Paris, 1771.

*Mémoire pour le Marquis de Camille Massimo . . . et autres*, Paris, 1777.

*Mémoire pour P. J. Fr. Luneau de Boisjermain, servant de réponse à un mémoire du sieur Le Breton et de ses associés*, Paris, 1778.

*Mercure de France*, Paris, 1724–91.

MICHAUD, J. F. and MICHAUD, L. G., *Biographie universelle*, Nouvelle édition, Paris, 1843–65.

*Monthly Review*, London, 1749–89.

MOREAU, J. N., *Nouveau mémoire pour servir à l'histoire des Cacouacs*, Amsterdam, 1757.

——, *Mes Souvenirs*, ed. C. Hernelin, Paris, 1898, 2 vols.

MORELLET, ABBÉ, *Préface de la Comédie des Philosophes, ou la Vision de Charles Palissot*, Paris, 1760.

——, *Mémoires sur le dix-huitième siècle et sur la Révolution*, Paris, 1821, 2 vols.

MORNET, D., 'Les Enseignements des bibliothèques privées (1750–1780)', *Revue d'histoire littéraire*, 1910.

MOUSNIER, R., *Progrès scientifique et technique au XVIII$^e$ siècle*, Paris, 1958.

*Nouvelles ecclésiastiques, Les*, Paris, 1728–1803.

*Observations de M. ***, principal du Collège de ***, sur un des articles du Dictionnaire encyclopédique*, n.p.n.d.

PALISSOT, *Petites lettres sur de grands philosophes*, Paris, 1757.

——, *Les Philosophes, comédie en trois actes en vers*, Paris, 1760.

——, *Lettre de l'auteur de la comédie des Philosophes au public pour servir de préface à la pièce*, n.p., 1760.

——, *Lettres et réponses de M. Palissot à M. de Voltaire*, n.p.n.d.

——, *La Dunciade*, Chelsea, 1764.

——, *Dénonciation aux honnêtes gens d'un nouveau libelle*, n.p., 1769.

——, *Mémoires pour servir à l'histoire de notre littérature depuis François Premier jusqu'à nos jours* in vol. ii of *La Dunciade*, London, 1771, 2 vols.

PAULIAN, FATHER A. H., *Dictionnaire philosophico-théologique portatif*, Nîmes, 1778.

*Petite Encyclopédie ou Dictionnaire des Philosophes, ouvrage posthume d'un de ces messieurs, La*, Antwerp, n.d.

*Précis pour la dame veuve Briasson . . . et le sieur Le Breton . . . contre le sieur Luneau et contre les intervenants*, Paris, 1776.

*Précis pour les Libraires associés à l'Encyclopédie contre le sieur Luneau de Boisjermain et contre sept intervenants*, Paris, 1772.

PUFENDORF, *Du Droit de la nature et des gens*, transl. J. Barbeyrac, Basle, 1771, 2 vols.

*Religion vengée ou réfutation des auteurs impies, La*, Paris, 1757–63.

*Remontrances du Parlement de Paris au XVIII<sup>e</sup> siècle*, ed. J. Flammermont, Paris, 1888–98, 3 vols.

*Réponse signifiée de M. Luneau de Boisjermain au Précis des Libraires associés à l'impression de l'Encyclopédie*, Paris, 1772.

ROUSSEAU, J. J., *Œuvres complètes*, ed. B. Gagnebin and M. Raymond, Paris, 1959– (in course of publication).

——, *Correspondance complète*, ed. R. A. Leigh, Geneva, 1965– (in course of publication).

SAAS, ABBÉ J., *Lettre d'un professeur de Douai à un professeur de Louvain sur le Dictionnaire historique portatif de M. l'abbé Ladvocat. Lettre d'un professeur de Douai à un professeur de Louvain sur l'Encyclopédie*, Douai, 1762.

——, *Lettres sur l'Encyclopédie pour servir de Supplément aux sept volumes de ce dictionnaire*, Amsterdam, 1764.

SABATIER DE CASTRES, ABBÉ, *Les Trois Siècles de la littérature française*, The Hague-Paris, 1781, 4 vols.

SAINT-LAMBERT, *Œuvres philosophiques*, Paris, 1797, 6 vols.

SAUVIGNY, *La Religion révélée, poème en réponse à celui de la Religion naturelle, avec un poème sur la cabale anti-encyclopédique*, Geneva, 1758.

TORLAIS, J., *Un Esprit encyclopédique en dehors de l'Encyclopédie, Réaumur*, second edition, Paris, 1961.

*Traité des droits de la Reine sur différents états de la monarchie d'Espagne*, Paris, 1667.

TRUBLET, ABBÉ, *Correspondence*, ed. J. Jacquart, Paris, 1926.

TURGOT, *Œuvres complètes*, ed. G. Schelle, Paris, 1913–23, 5 vols.

VÉRI, ABBÉ DE, *Journal*, ed. J. de Witte, Paris, 1929, 2 vols.

VÉRON DE FORBONNAIS, *Recherches et considérations sur les finances de France*, Basle, 1758, 2 vols.

VOLTAIRE, *Correspondence*, ed. Theodore Besterman, Geneva, 1953–66, 107 vols.

VOLTAIRE, *Lettres de M. de Voltaire, avec plusieurs pièces de différents auteurs*, The Hague, 1738.

——, *Œuvres complètes*, ed. L. Moland, Paris, 1877–85, 52 vols.

WILKINSON, L. P., 'The language of Virgil and Horace', *Classical Quarterly*, 1959.

# Index

Note Articles from the *Encyclopédie*, which are printed in small capitals, are listed in alphabetical order. Where it is known, the name of the author or authors is given in parentheses; where the attribution is not absolutely certain, the name is followed by a question mark.

Articles are also listed under the name of their author or authors; a name in brackets after an article indicates that it was the work of more than one contributor. A question mark precedes those articles whose attribution is not absolutely certain.

\* in front of an article stands for Diderot's editorial asterisk, whether he was responsible for the whole or only for a small addition.

Diderot, Denis—*cont.*
 *INCOMPRÉHENSIBLE, 144n.
 INCORPOREL, 178–9
 *INDIGENT, 382
 *INDISSOLUBLE, 191
 *INSIGNE, 347
 *INSINUANT, 364
 *INSOLENT, 383
 INTOLÉRANCE, 196, 198–200
 INVOLONTAIRE, 181
 *IRRÉGULARITÉ, 180
 *IRRÉLIGIEUX, 217–18
 ?JAMAIS, 180
 JÉSUITE, 261–2
 JÉSUS-CHRIST, 209, 251, 252–3
 JOUISSANCE, 190
 *JOURNALIER, 383
 *JOURNÉE *de la Saint-Barthélemy*, 201
 JUIFS (PHILOSOPHIE DES), 251–2
 LAIDEUR, 180
 *LAITON, 338
 ?LAQUAIS, 385–6
 LÉGISLATION, 305
 LOCKE (PHILOSOPHIE DE), 73, 134, 143–5,
   146, 155
 ?MACÉRATION, 253–4
 MACHIAVÉLISME, 294, 311n.
 ?MACHINAL, 182–3
 ?MAGISTRAT, 323–4
 ?MAGISTRATURE, 323, 324
 MALEBRANCHISME, 145
 MALFAISANT, 183–4
 ?MATÉRIALISTES, 175–6
 MENACE, 296
 ?MISÈRE, 383
 MODIFICATION, 184
 ?MŒURS, 192–3
 ?MORGUE, 324
 MOSAÏQUE ET CHRÉTIENNE (PHILOSOPHIE),
   155–6
 MULTITUDE, 385
 ?MUTUEL, 295–6
 NAITRE, 176–7
 NATURALISTE, 176
 ?OBVIER, 325
 ?ODIEUX, 295
 ?OPPRESSEUR, OPPRIMER, 295
 ?OPPRESSION, 295
 ?ORIGINE, 228
 ?PAIN BÉNIT, 259–60
 ?PARFAIT, 179

?PARLEMENTAIRE, 324–5
?PASSAGER, 261
?PÉRIR, 177
?PRIVILÈGE (*Gram.*), 367
PRODUCTION, 178
PRODUIRE, 180
?PROMISSION, 254
?PROPAGATION DE L'ÉVANGILE, 255
PYRRHONIENNE (PHILOSOPHIE), 134
RÉFUGIÉS, 203–4
?RÉQUISITOIRE, 323
RESSUSCITER, 255
?RÉVÉRENCE, 325
RIGORISME, 254
SCOLASTIQUES (*Philosophie des*), 141, 253
?SÉANCE, 325–6
SOCRATIQUE (PHILOSOPHIE), 134
SPINOZISTE, 176
SUBSIDE (with another), 120, 130, 294
SYNCRÉTISTES, 155
VICE (Jaucourt), 134, 183, 184
VINDICATIF, 103
VINGTIÈME (Damilaville), 53, 266, 310–
   312, 370, 371, 375–7
VOLONTÉ, 181–2
VOLUPTUEUX, 190–1
Diderot, Abbé Didier Pierre, 198–200
DIÈTE DE L'EMPIRE (d'Holbach), 314
DIFFÉRENTIEL (d'Alembert), 85
DIMANCHE (Faiguet de Villeneuve), 258,
   330
Diodati, Ottaviano, 33
Diogenes, 146–7
Divorce, 191–2
DIVORCE (Boucher d'Argis), 191
Dodart, Denys, 49
Domestic industry, 361–3
DORADE (Morand), 48
Douchet, Jacques Philippe Auguste, 51
DRAGONNADE (Jaucourt), 202
DROIT DE LA NATURE *ou* DROIT NATUREL
   (Boucher d'Argis), 275
*DROIT NATUREL, 273, 275–8
DROITS DU ROI (Dufour), 48
Du Châtelet, Gabrielle Émilie, Marquise,
   49
Duclos, Charles Pinot, 47, 52
Dufour, 48
 DROITS DU ROI, 48
 EMPRUNT, 48
Duguet, Abbé Jacques Jospeh, 325